Book 2: Workbooks

Student Centered Learning.
Freedom to Learn...Your Way!
Get the Score you Need!

These materials will teach you How to Learn Your Way and get the score you need to get into the college of your choice. These books are designed to be used in conjunction with the PowerPrep DVD or they can be used stand alone. Either way, you have the most complete and thorough SAT and ACT exam prep materials available.

The software and books were in development for over three years and cost over $1.5 million. The books contain 800+ pages, 2500+ Questions, quizzes, practice questions, and samples, with intensely detailed explanations containing, diagrams, images, drawings, photos, and all manner of visual aids to assist our students so they thoroughly understand every concept taught in these materials.

Workbook questions: 487   **Drill Questions:** 276   **Dictionary:** 550+ words   **Grammar Questions:** 1800+

To the Student:

We reviewed years of SAT and ACT tests and developed our materials to teach you every single testable point and concept ever presented on either exam. Each concept is taught on the DVD and in the print materials and then followed with practice questions keyed to the concept being taught. Each practice question (PQ) also has incredibly detailed explanations. The explanations do not just give you a "right" answer, our materials take the time to explain the step-by-step process behind the "right" answer, and then we also explain why each wrong answer is flawed. In many instances, the materials also provide several alternative methods for arriving at the correct answer. This level of detail is at the heart of *the Student Center Learning Process* giving you all the resources necessary so you have the *Freedom to Learn... Your Way* and achieve the score you need to get into the school of your choice.

<u>Book 1: Getting Started</u> (130 pages)-- **EVERYTHING you want to know a**bout the exam. 122 pages explaining everything about both exams and how to use the PowerPrep[tm] DVD, including: What's tested, Sample Schedule, and Tracking. This book answers every question about the exam: When to take the test, How often can students take the test? Should I test again? How often is the test administered? What is the difference between the SAT and ACT? College Requirements. Comparing SAT and ACT Scores. Calculator Policy. How to score your exam. And much, much more.

<u>Book 2: Workbooks</u> (480 pages)-- **The heart of the course takes place here. The c**lassroom instruction is keyed to the DVD, but intuitive even without the DVD. This is where the bulk of your learning takes place. Every concept and testable point ever presented on either exam is carefully taught in this workbook. The concepts are taught one at a time followed by detailed practice questions keyed to each concept with painstakingly detailed explanations so you can learn what the right answer is and WHY it's right and why the other answer choices are wrong. You will also learn custom approaches and special tips for every section on the exam.

<u>Book 3: Drills</u> (192 pages)-- **more practice on each concept**. use these questions and their detailed explanations to hone your skills and work on your timing and comprehension.

Bonus Materials:

The Big Book of Grammar: Many students feel weak in their grammar skills. That's why we created the ultimate Big Book of Grammar prep. No other course offers this level of organization and detail. We analyzed and categorized every grammar question ever asked for the past 10 years and these materials focus on what we discovered. The book contains a major section on **Subject Verb Agreement** (see Book 2: Workbook: page 292) and also includes an exclusive **90 page section that covers every tricky and confusing word and grammar rule** tested over the past 10 years (see Book 2: Workbook: page 328)--but we did not stop there. We also included over **1800 quiz questions with detailed answers** to give you TONS of practice to make sure you understand every single grammar rule.

Vocabulary: We also analyzed the past 10 years of exams and found the top 500 SAT and ACT words with definitions. **See Workbook page 426 for a list of these words and their definitions.**

eKnowledge a division of INTERNATIONAL TECHNOLOGY DEVELOPMENT & CONSULTING LTD.
support@eknowledge.com   51 256-4076

ISBN 978-0-9828493-0-9

Printed and bound in China

Workbooks

Book 2
Table of Contents

Keyed to Virtual Classroom on DVD/Internet/iApp
Pages 1-472

Workbook Math Index

Big Book of Grammar Index

Arithmetic Workbook
Table of Contents

This material corresponds to the Virtual Classroom Instructions in the
PowerPrep DVD/Internet/iApp for Arithmetic

<u>Virtual Classroom</u>

Arithmetic
Part 1: Vocabulary

Virtual Classroom>Arithmetic>Vocabulary

This material Corresponds to the Virtual Classroom Instructions in the
PowerPrep DVD/Internet/iApp for Arithmetic

Virtual Classroom

Important Abbreviations
These abbreviations are used throughout the program

POE: Process of Elimination
SARR: Synthesize, Analyze, Reduce, and Restate (has to do with Logical Reasoning)
AC: Answer Choice
QS: Question Stem
LOD: Level of Difficulty

Example Question: What is the least common multiple of 3, 4, and 7? **(This is the call of the question or Question Stem "QS")**

These are Answer Choices "AC" A, B, C, D, E

(A) 12
(B) 21
(C) 28
(D) 48
(E) 84

Part 1: Vocabulary

Integers: Whole numbers which are negative, zero or positive (-3,0,3)

Rational Number: Number which can be expressed in the form of a/b where *a* and *b* are integers. It is a finite quantity.

$$\left(3 = \frac{3}{1}, \frac{2}{5}, -\frac{4}{3}\right)$$

Irrational Number: Number which cannot be expressed precisely, or simply anything not rational! $(\sqrt{2}, \pi)$

Real Number: All the above. Every number you see on the exam will be a real number.

Factors: Any whole number which divides <u>evenly</u> into an integer. **Example:** Factors of 12 are (1, 2, 3, 4, 6)

Prime Number: Any positive integer which has two factors – meaning it can only be divided by 1 and itself. (2, 3, 7, 11)
- Zero is *NOT* a prime number (it can be divided by lots of numbers to get a result of zero)
- One is *NOT* a prime number (there are not two factors of 1)
- Two is the *ONLY* even prime number (its' two factors are 2 and 1)
- Not every odd number is a prime (9 has three factors $(1 * 9)$, but also $(3 * 3)$)

Composite Number: Any integer which has more than two factors; any integer which is not prime. (4, 6, 9, 12, 15)
- Zero is **NOT** a composite number (it can't be broken into factors)
- One is **NOT** a composite number (it doesn't have more than two factors)

Prime Factorization: Writing an integer as the product of its prime integers. You do this by breaking an integer down into its prime numbers. **Example:** Prime factors for $24 = 6 * 4 = 3 * 2 * 2 * 2$

Absolute Value: The magnitude of a number, or simply how far from zero it is on a number line without direction.
Example: $|13| = 13$, $|-4| = 4$, $-|-6| = -6$

Consecutive Integers: Ordered set of numbers where each number is one greater than the previous.
Example: $(n, n+1, n+2, n+3 ...) \ 5, 6, 7, 8$

Counting Consecutive Integers: To determine how many integers you have in a consecutive set, simply subtract the smallest integer from largest integer, then add 1. **Example:** Number of integers from 14 to 36 $\Rightarrow$ $(36 - 14) + 1 = 23$

Multiples: Given integer times any whole number. Multiples of 5 are (5, 10, 15, 20, 25...)

Common Multiple: Any number which is a multiple of <u>all</u> the integers in a given set. For the set (2, 3, 5) common multiples include 30, 60

Least Common Multiple: The smallest common multiple of all the integers in a set (LCM for previous example = 30)

PowerPrep Practice Questions 1-2

1. What is the least common multiple of 2, 5, and 9?

    (A)   10
    (B)   36
    (C)   45
    (D)   60
    (E)   90

2. Is *d* a prime number? If: (1) $-1 < d < 4$ (2) *d is not a composite number*
   - (A) Statement (1) BY ITSELF is sufficient to answer the question, but statement (2) is not
   - (B) Statement (2) BY ITSELF is sufficient to answer the question, but statement(1) is not
   - (C) Statement 1 and (2) TAKEN TOGETHER are sufficient to answer the question, even though NEITHER statement by itself is sufficient
   - (D) EITHER statement BY ITSELF is sufficient to answer the question
   - (E) Statement 1 and 2 TAKEN TOGETHER are NOT sufficient to answer the question, requiring more data pertaining to the problem

Explanation to PowerPrep Practice Question 1

Least Common Multiple (LCM) = 90 or $(2 * 5 * 9) = 90$

Note: you cannot always multiply all factors together--doing so will always give you a multiple, but it might not be the LCM. For example (2,3,4) $2 * 3 * 4 = 24$ However, 12 is the LCM not 24...so be careful

Example: Find the LCM of 8,9, and 21.

Prime Powers Method: First, factor out each number and express it as a product of prime number powers.

$8 = 2^3 * 3^0 * 5^0 * 7^0$
$9 = 2^0 * 3^2 * 5^0 * 7^0$
$21 = 2^0 * 3^1 * 5^0 * 7^1$

The LCM is the product of the highest power in each prime factor category. Out of the 4 prime factor categories 2, 3, 5, and 7, the highest powers from each is $2^3, 3^2, 5^0, and \ 7^1$. Thus, LCM (8,9,1) = $2^3 * 3^2 * 5^0 * 7^1 = 8 * 9 * 1 * 7 = 504$

Table Method

	2	2	2	3	3	7
8	4	2	1	1	1	1
9	9	9	9	3	1	1
21	21	21	21	7	7	1

Now, multiply the numbers on the top and you have the LCM. In this case, it is $(2 \times 2 \times 2 \times 3 \times 3 \times 7 = 504)$.
so the LCM of $(8,9,21)$ *is* $2^3 * 3^2 * 7$ *or* $8 * 9 * 7$ *or* $72 * 7$ *or* 504

Process of Elimination: in the given problem, we were asked to find the LCM of (2,5,9)
10 is a multiple of 2 and 5, but not 9
36 is a multiple of 2 and 9, but not 5
45 is a multiple of 5 and 9, but not 2
60 is a multiple of 2 and 5, but not 9
90 is multiple of 2, 5 and 9

ANSWER: (E)

Explanation to PowerPrep Practice Question 2

What are you looking for? The numerical value of *d*.

Statement 1: *First we need to review the definition of a Prime number.*

Prime Number: Any positive integer which has exactly two factors – meaning it can only be divided by 1 and itself. (2, 3, 7, 11)
•Zero is *NOT* a prime number (it can be divided by lots of numbers to get a result of zero)
•One is *NOT* a prime number (there are not two factors for 1)
•Two is the *ONLY* even prime number (its two factors are 2 and 1)
• Not every odd number is a prime (9 has three factors $(1 * 9)$, but also $(3 * 3)$)

Given this information *d* could be 0, 1, 2, or 3 (not a prime number) or (a prime number). "2" and "3" are prime, but zero and "1" are not. Since we can't narrow down our choices, we **DO NOT** have sufficient information.

Statement 2: *First we need to remember the definition of composite numbers.* **Composite Number:** Any integer which has more than two factors; any integer which is not prime. (4, 6, 9, 12, 15)
• Zero is **NOT** a composite number (it can't be broken into factors)
• One is **NOT** a composite number (it doesn't have more than two factors)

We are told that *d* is **NOT** a composite number…therefore statement 2 tells us that *d* **does not have more than two factors**.

Given this information *d* could still be "1" (not a composite or a prime number) or 3 (not a composite but is a prime number) or it could be 0 (not prime and not composite). Since we can't narrow down our choices, we **DO NOT** have sufficient information.

Both Statements: Combining both statements still does not allow us to narrow our choices enough to answer the question. *d* could be 0, 1, 2 or 3 all of which fit the restrictions of Statement 1 and none are composite numbers. Further, "0" and "1" are not prime. Therefore, we **DO NOT** have sufficient information. **ANSWER: (E)**

Extra Sample Questions <u>not</u> in the Virtual Classroom on the DVD

Extra Sample Questions 1-4

1. Which point on the number line below has the least absolute value?

   (A) A
   (B) B
   (C) C
   (D) D
   (E) E

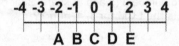

2. If x, y and z are positive integers such that $x = 15, y = 3, and\ z = 3,$ which of the following must be an integer?

   (A) $\frac{x}{y+z}$

   (B) $\frac{x}{yz}$

   (C) $\frac{y+z}{x}$

   (D) $\frac{yz}{x}$

   (E) $\frac{x}{y} + \frac{x}{z}$

3. What is the least common multiple of $3, 4, and\ 7$?

   (A) 3
   (B) 7
   (C) 12
   (D) 28
   (E) 84

4. Which of the following is the lowest prime number?

    (A) 0
    (B) 1
    (C) 2
    (D) 4
    (E) 5

Explanation to Extra Sample Question 1

Because we are looking for ABSOLUTE VALUE we ignore signs.

$A = -2$ *and absolute value of* $-2 = 2$
$B = -1$ *and absolute value of* $-1 = 1$
$C = 0$ ***and absolute value of*** $0 = 0$
$D = 1$ *and absolute value of* $1 = 1$
$E = 2$ *and absolute value of* $2 = 2$

> The lowest number of among all the possible answers is AC C or 0.
>
> **ANSWER: (C)**

Explanation to Extra Sample Question 2

Pick numbers: *Let* $y = 3$ *Let* $z = 3$ *Let* $x = 15$
Substitute these numbers into AC's:

(A) $\dfrac{15}{3+3} = \dfrac{15}{6} =$ not an integer

(B) $\dfrac{15}{3*3} = \dfrac{15}{9} = 1\dfrac{6}{9} = 1\dfrac{2}{3} =$ not an integer

(C) $\dfrac{3+3}{15} = \dfrac{6}{15} = \dfrac{2}{5} =$ not an integer

(D) $\dfrac{3*3}{15} = \dfrac{9}{15} = \dfrac{3}{5} =$ not an integer

(E) $\dfrac{15}{3} + \dfrac{15}{3} = 5+5 = 10$ **= integer** <u>ANSWER: (E)</u>

Explanation to Extra Sample Question 3

Multiples, Factors, and primes are heavily tested. They are usually tested in word problems. Even thought the math is relatively straightforward, the verbiage or language can be confusing. Make sure you have studied these concepts and can identify them.

Multiples: The product between two integer—for example, the first four multiples of 5 are: 5, 10, 15, and 20 because $(5*1) = 5$, $(5*2) = 10$, $(5*3) = 15$, and $(5*4) = 20$.

Least Common Multiple (LCM): The Least Common Multiple or LCM is the lowest multiple that two numbers share. For example, the LCM of 5 and 8 is:

Multiples for 5: 5, 10, 15, 20 , 25, 30, 35, **40**, 45, 50, 55, 60, 65, 70, 75, **80**
Multiples for 8: 8, 16, 24, 32, **40**, 48, 56, 64, 72, **80,**

So the LCM of 5 and 8 is 40, it 's the first multiple they both share. These two numbers (5 and 8) share other common multiples, like 80…but 40 is the lowest or Least Common Multiple. **So what is the LCM for 3, 4, and 7?**

Short Way: Multiple the numbers together $(3*4*7) = 84$

Then double check by calculating the factors of the largest number of the group…in this case that is 7.

Start counting by 7 and at each multiple calculate if either 3 or 4 has the same multiple.

Long Way: To find this, we calculate the multiples for each integer:

Multiples of 3: 3, 6, 9, 12, 15, 18, 21, 24, 27, 30, 33, 36, 39, 42, 45, 48, 51, 54, 57, 60, 63, 66, 69, 72, 75, 78, 81, **84**
Multiples of 4: 4, 8, 12, 16, 20, 24, 28, 32, 36, 40, 44, 48, 52, 56, 60, 64, 68, 72, 76, 80, **84**
Multiples of 7: 7, 14, 21, 28, 35, 42, 49, 56, 63, 70, 77, **84**

<u>ANSWER: (E)</u>

Explanation to Extra Sample Question 4

A prime number is divisible by one 1 and itself.

Note: The number one (1) is NOT considered a prime number. The number two (2) is the smallest prime number.

The number 29 is prime because the only factors are 1 and 29.

List of Primes: 2, 3, 5, 7, 11, 13, 17, 19, 23, 29, 31, 37, 41, 43, 47, 53, 59, 61, 67, 71, 73, 79, 83, 89…1847…2861 … 3079…4493…5477…6011…7001…7757…7919

The 10,000th prime is 104,729.

By definition the smallest prime number is always 2. Therefore, the correct answer is C. <u>**ANSWER : (C)**</u>

Arithmetic
Part 2: Operations & Signs
Virtual Classroom>Arithmetic>Operations & Signs
This material corresponds to the Virtual Classroom Instructions in the
PowerPrep DVD/Internet/iApp for Arithmetic

Virtual Classroom

Part 2: Operations & Signs

Adding/Subtracting Numbers with Signs

To add positive and negative numbers: Find the difference between the two numbers, add sign of the larger number.
Example: $7+(-18) \Rightarrow$ difference is 11, larger sign is negative $\Rightarrow -11$

To subtract positive and negative numbers: When subtracting a positive number from a negative number, simply combine and keep the negative sign. **Example:** $-6 - 9 \Rightarrow -15$
Note: When subtracting a negative number from another negative number, turn the subtraction sign into addition using the two negatives equals a positive rule. Follow addition rules. **Example:** $-6 - (-9) \Rightarrow -6 + 9 \Rightarrow$ difference is 3, larger sign is + $\Rightarrow +3$

Multiplying/Dividing Numbers w/Signs: Complete the operation (multiply/divide the numbers) first; then add the appropriate sign by the following rules:
- If the number of total negative signs is <u>odd</u>, the answer is negative.
- If the number of total negative signs is <u>even</u>, the answer is positive.

Examples: $(-5*2*-3 =?)$ *just multiply the numbers without the signs* $(5)(2)(3) = 30$, there are two negative signs and two negatives signs cancel to positive...therefore the over sign is positive. Therefore, the answer is positive 30.

$\frac{20}{-4} = 5$, *but there is a single negative sign so the result is negative or* -5

$(-5)*2*(-3) \Rightarrow 30$, two (-) = positive answer = 30

$\frac{20}{-4} \Rightarrow 5$, one (-) = negative answer = -5

Order of Operations: PEMDAS

| Parenthesis |
| Exponents |
| Multiplication |
| Division |
| Addition |
| Subtraction |

When you have more than one operation in a problem, there is a definite order in which you should perform the operations:

Following PEMDAS you would:
1. Parentheses come first. But also note that when you are working within a parentheses, you still follow PEMDAS, so multiplication before addition etc. In this case, it would look like this:

> When working with math terms, you should first calculate the math inside the Parentheses, then do the exponents, then do the multiplication and division working from left to right, and finally you would do the addition and subtraction working left to right.
>
> **For example:** $\frac{(25-5)*5^2}{10} +10 - (5*3-5)$

$$\frac{(25-5)*5^2}{10} + 10 - (5*3-5) \Rightarrow \frac{(20)*5^2}{10} + 10 - (15-5) \Rightarrow \frac{(20)*5^2}{10} + 10 - (10)$$

2. Exponents: $\frac{(20)*5^2}{10} + 10 - (10) \Rightarrow \frac{(20)*25}{10} + 10 - (10)$

3. Multiplication: $\frac{500}{10} + 10 - (10)$

4. Division: $50 + 10 - (10)$

5. Addition and Subtraction: $50 + 0 = \mathbf{50}$

PowerPrep Practice Questions Also in the Virtual Classroom on DVD

PowerPrep Practice Questions 3-4

3. $6[13 + (-7)] - \frac{4^3}{(22-6)} + 15 =$

   (A) 220
   (B) 200
   (C) 65
   (D) 50
   (E) 47

4. What is the value of $(x - 4)$ if:
   (1) $|x| = 9$
   (2) x is a negative number

   (A) 5
   (B) -13
   (C) 13
   (D) -5
   (E) 0

Explanation to PowerPrep Practice Question 3

Start with parentheses: $6[13 + (-7)] - \frac{4^3}{(22-6)} + 15 = 6[13 - 7] - \frac{4^3}{(16)} + 15 = 6[6] - \frac{4^3}{(16)} + 15$ **Next**

exponents: $6[6] - \frac{4^3}{(16)} + 15 = 6[6] - \frac{64}{16} + 15$ **Then multiplication:** $6[6] - \frac{64}{16} + 15 = 36 - 4 + 15$ **And finally**

addition: $36 - 4 + 15 = 36 + 11 = \mathbf{47}$ (note that subtraction is just addition of a negative)   **ANSWER: (E)**

Explanation to PowerPrep Practice Question 4

What are you looking for? *The value of x so you can solve for* $(x - 4)$.
Statement 1: $|x| = 9$, therefore, *x equals both 9 and* -9. This means $(x - 4)$ could equal 5 *or* - 13.
Combine Statements 1 & 2: $|X| = 9$ so X is either 9 *or* -9, Statement 2 says *X is negative*, therefore, *X must be* -9.
Plug it into the given $(x - 4)$ becomes $(-9 - 4) = -13$ **ANSWER: (B)**

Extra Sample Questions not in the Virtual Classroom on the DVD

Extra Sample Questions 5-6

5. $5(7 - 3)^2 + \left(\frac{24}{6}\right)^0 = ?$

   (A) 404
   (B) 400
   (C) 81
   (D) 80
   (E) 40

6. If $|x| = 9$ then which is greater? $(x - 4)$ *or* 0

   (A) $(x - 4)$ is greater
   (B) 0 is greater
   (C) They are equal
   (D) Not sufficient information

Explanation to Extra Sample Question 5

Follow PEMDAS: **P**arenthesis, **E**xponents, **M**ultiplication, **D**ivision, **A**ddition, **S**ubtraction
Reminder: $x^0 = 1$. $1 = \frac{x^4}{x^4} = x^{4-4} = x^0$ *therefore,* $x^0 = 1$

Start with parenthesis: $5(7 - 3)^2 + \left(\frac{24}{6}\right)^0 = 5(4)^2 + (4)^0 =$ **Next comes exponents:** $5(4)^2 + (4)^0 = (5 * 16) +$
1 = **Then multiplication:** $(5 * 16) + 1 = 80 + 1$ **And finally addition:** $80 + 1 = 81$ For all numbers except
0...IOW, x cannot = 0...you can't have 0^0 *that is undefinable.*
You need to commit this to memory.   **ANSWER: (C)**

Explanation to Extra Sample Question 6

Review Absolute Value
The absolute value of x, denoted "$|x|$" (and which is read as "the absolute value of x"), is the distance of x from zero. This is why absolute value is never negative; absolute value only asks "how far?", not "in which direction?". This means not only that $|3| = 3$, because 3 is three units to the right of zero, but also that $|-3| = 3$, because -3 is three units to the left of zero.

It is important to note that the absolute value bars do NOT work in the same way as do parentheses.
$-(-3) = +3$, but absolute value does not work this way **Given** $-|-3|$
First handle the absolute value part, the absolute value of -3 *is* $+3$ **and** $-|-3| = -(+3)$
Now apply the negative through the parentheses: $-|-3| = -(3) = -3$
As this illustrates, if you take the negative of an absolute value, you will get a negative number for your answer.
While $-(-3) = 3$ but $-|-3| = -3$

Explanation Question 6: We are given $|x| = 9$ So this means that x can be either 9 *or* -9
If $x = (9, -9)$ *Then* $(x - 4)$ *is* $(9 - 4)$ *or* $(-9 - 4)$ That means the quantity could be -13 *or* 5   **Therefore,** $-13 <$
$0, but\ 5 > 0$ This means we cannot tell which is greater $(x - 4)$ or 0, because x is both 9 *and* -9.
Therefore, AC D (unknown because insufficient information) **ANSWER: (D)**

Arithmetic
Part 3: Fractions
Virtual Classroom>Arithmetic>Fractions

This material corresponds to the Virtual Classroom Instructions in the
PowerPrep DVD/Internet/iApp for Arithmetic

Virtual Classroom

Part 3: Fractions

$$\frac{3}{5} = \frac{numerator}{denominator}$$

Numerator = top number
Denominator = bottom number

Reducing Fractions: When you reduce a fraction you reduce both the numerator and the denominator by the same amount. You can do this by canceling out common integers found in both. **Example:** $\frac{24}{36} = \frac{6*4}{6*6} = \frac{4}{6} = \frac{2*2}{2*3} = \frac{2}{3}$

Adding/Subtracting Fractions: You can **only** add or subtract fractions when they have common denominators. When fractions have the same denominator, simply add/subtract the numerators. **Example:** $\frac{1}{6} + \frac{4}{6} = \frac{5}{6}$
When fractions don't have the same denominator, you must **first** find a common denominator, convert each fraction, **then** can add the numerators. (To find the smallest common denominator, identify the largest denominator, then look at its multiples to find the one that is a multiple of all the denominators.) **Example:** $\frac{3}{8} + \frac{7}{20} \Rightarrow$ common denominator is 40 convert both fractions, $\frac{3}{8}\left(\frac{5}{5}\right) + \frac{7}{20}\left(\frac{2}{2}\right) = \frac{15}{40} + \frac{14}{40} = \frac{9}{40}$

Multiplying Fractions: Multiply numerators together, multiply denominators together. **Example:** $\frac{3}{7} * \frac{4}{5} = \frac{3*4}{7*5} = \frac{12}{35}$

Dividing Fractions: Invert the **second** fraction (the number you are dividing by), then treat it just like a multiplication problem. **Example:** $\frac{1}{5} \div \frac{2}{3} = \frac{1}{5} * \frac{3}{2} = \frac{1*3}{(5*2)} = \frac{3}{10}$

Reciprocal: It is what we call a fraction that has been inverted. **Example:** Reciprocal of $\frac{3}{5}$ is $\frac{5}{3}$

Mixed Number: Whole number combined with a fraction $5\frac{1}{2}$

Improper Fraction: Fraction where the numerator is greater than the denominator $\frac{7}{3}$

Converting a Mixed Number to an Improper Fraction:
1. Multiply the whole number in front by the denominator, then add the numerator.
2. Place that new number over the old denominator. **Example:** $3\frac{1}{4} \Rightarrow 3 \times 4 = 12 \Rightarrow (12 + 1) \Rightarrow \frac{13}{4}$

Converting an Improper Fraction to a Mixed Number:
1. Divide denominator into numerator to get a whole number and a remainder.
2. Record whole number and then place the remainder over the denominator to create the fraction.
    Example: $\frac{17}{5} \Rightarrow (5 \times 3)$ plus remainder 2 $= 3\frac{2}{5}$

Comparing Fractions: When comparing one fraction with another (often to determine which is greater), convert each fraction to one with a common denominator for direct comparison. **Example:** $\left(\frac{4}{5} \text{ and } \frac{5}{7}\right) \Rightarrow \left(\frac{4*7}{5*7} \text{ and } \frac{5*5}{7*5}\right) \Rightarrow \left(\frac{28}{35} \text{ and } \frac{25}{35}\right)$

PowerPrep Practice Questions Also in the Virtual Classroom on DVD

PowerPrep Practice Questions 5-6

5. Reduce: $\dfrac{\left(\frac{1}{7}\right)+\left(\frac{1}{2}\right)}{\left(\frac{1}{3}\right)}$

   (A) 1/9
   (B) 1/3
   (C) $1\,^3/_7$
   (D) $1\,^{13}/_{14}$
   (E) 3

6. $(1/2)(1/3) - \left(\dfrac{1}{6}\right)^2 =$

   (A) 1/36
   (B) 5/36
   (C) 1/6
   (D) 7/36
   (E) 2/3

Explanation to PowerPrep Practice Question 5

Find the least common denominator for the numerator. To add the numerator $\frac{1}{7}$ and $\frac{1}{2}$ you have to find the LCD (least common denominator) $(1/7 + 1/2)$ Multiply the denominators $(7 \times 2) = 14$ (this will be the LCD) $\frac{1}{7} = \frac{2}{14}$ *and*

$\frac{1}{2} = \frac{7}{14}$ becomes $\left(\frac{2}{14} + \frac{7}{14}\right) = \frac{9}{14}$ (the new numerator) **So you now have** $\left(\dfrac{\frac{9}{14}}{\frac{1}{3}}\right)$

> Now you invert and multiply...Multiply the numerator by the reciprocal of the denominator.
> Like this: $\frac{9}{14} * \frac{3}{1} = \frac{27}{14} = 1\frac{13}{14}$

ANSWER: (D)

Explanation to PowerPrep Practice Question 6

Exponents: $\left(\frac{1}{2}\right)\left(\frac{1}{3}\right) - \left(\frac{1}{6}\right)^2 =$ **Let's work with** $\left(-\frac{1}{6}\right)^2$ **first convert the fraction like this:** $-\frac{1}{6} * -\frac{1}{6} = \frac{1}{36}$

Now let's work with: $\frac{1}{2} * \frac{1}{3} = \frac{1}{6}$ **We now have:** $\frac{1}{6} - \frac{1}{36}$ Create common denominator for $\frac{1}{6}$ and then

subtract: $\frac{1}{6} = \frac{6}{36}$ **Complete subtraction:** $\frac{6}{36} - \frac{1}{36} = \frac{5}{36}$ **ANSWER: (B)**

Extra Sample Questions <u>not</u> in the Virtual Classroom on the DVD

Extra Sample Questions 7-8

7. $\left(\dfrac{\frac{3}{9}+\frac{1}{3}}{\frac{1}{3}}\right) * \dfrac{4^2}{\left(\frac{1}{16}\right)} = ?$

   (A) 512
   (B) 256
   (C) $105\frac{1}{3}$
   (D) $16\frac{1}{9}$
   (E) 9

8. $\left(\frac{1}{6} * \frac{2}{3}\right) - \left(\frac{4}{12}\right)^2 + \frac{3}{4} + \frac{4}{12^2} = ?$

   (A) 7/144
   (B) 7/9
   (C) 27/36
   (D) 3/4
   (E) 144

Explanation to Extra Sample Question 7

Find the least common denominator for the numerator of the left fraction. *numerator of the first fraction is* $\left[\frac{3}{9} + \frac{1}{3}\right]$
Notice $\frac{3}{9}$ can reduce to $\frac{1}{3}$ now you can add $\left(\frac{1}{3} + \frac{1}{3}\right) = \frac{2}{3}$ **invert and multiply. The overall fraction becomes** $\frac{2}{3} / \frac{1}{3}$
$= \frac{2}{3} * \frac{3}{1} = \frac{6}{3}$ *or* 2 (the left fraction is 2) **Now the right side of the calculation:** $4^2 = 16$ so it's $16/(\frac{1}{16})$ that's 16
divided by $\frac{1}{16}$. Invert and multiply again $\frac{16}{1} * \frac{16}{1} = \frac{256}{1}$ *or* 256 **Now multiply the left and right** $(2 * 256 = \mathbf{512})$
ANSWER: (A)

Explanation to Extra Sample Question 8

There are four terms; let's do each one separately: $\left(\frac{1}{6} * \frac{2}{3}\right) = \frac{2}{18} = \frac{1}{9}$ **Next** $\left(\frac{4}{12}\right)^2 = \frac{4}{12} * \frac{4}{12} = \frac{16}{144} = \frac{1}{9}$ or you

could reduce first $\frac{4}{12} = \frac{1}{3}$ and $\frac{1}{3} * \frac{1}{3} = \frac{1}{9}$ **Next** $\frac{3}{4}$ *nothing to do here...yet.* **Next** $\frac{4}{12^2} = \frac{4}{144} = \frac{1}{36}$ **Now put them all back**

together $\frac{1}{9} - \frac{1}{9} + \frac{3}{4} + \frac{1}{36}$ find the LCD and simplify: $\frac{4}{36} - \frac{4}{36} + \frac{27}{36} + \frac{1}{36} = \frac{28}{36}$ reduce $\frac{28}{36} = \frac{14}{18} = \frac{7}{9}$ **ANSWER: (B)**

Arithmetic
Part 4: Decimals & Percents

Virtual Classroom>Arithmetic>Decimals & Percents

This material corresponds to the Virtual Classroom Instructions in the
PowerPrep DVD/Internet/iApp for Arithmetic

Virtual Classroom

Important Abbreviations
These abbreviations are used throughout the program

POE: Process of Elimination
SARR: Synthesize, Analyze, Reduce, and Restate (has to do with Logical Reasoning)
AC: Answer Choice
QS: Question Stem
LOD: Level of Difficulty

Example Question: What is the least common multiple of 3, 4, and 7? (**This is the call of the question or Question Stem "QS"**)

These are Answer Choices "AC" A, B, C, D, E

   (A)   12
   (B)   21
   (C)   28
   (D)   48
   (E)   84

Part 4: Decimals & Percents

Adding/Subtracting Decimals: Line up decimal points. Add zeros to fill in empty spaces if needed. Add or subtract.

Example: $(45.6 + 79.23)$ becomes
```
 45.60
+79.23
124.83
```

Multiplying Decimals: The most important part of this operation is to keep track of the number of decimal places you have. First, ignoring the decimals, multiply the numbers. Next, count the number of digits behind the given decimals and place decimal there in your multiplied number. **Example:** $(3.25 * 5) \Rightarrow 325 * (5) \Rightarrow 1625 \Rightarrow$ two digits behind decimals $\Rightarrow 16.25$

Dividing Decimals: You want to turn the decimals into integers by moving the decimal to the right for **all** numbers. Then you can divide the whole numbers directly. **Example:** $(13.25 \div .4) \Rightarrow (1325 \div 40) \Rightarrow \left(\frac{1325}{40}\right) \Rightarrow 33.125$

Repeating Decimals: A series of digits that repeat themselves. To find a specific digit within the repeating series:
• Note the number of repeating digits.
• Find the multiple just smaller than the digit you are looking for;
• Count the remainder of places to determine specific digit.
   Example: $.18651865\ldots$ has 4 repeating digits. What is the $42nd$ digit? $(4 * 10) = 40 \Rightarrow$ this series would repeat completely 10 times for 40 digits, giving us a remainder of 2 for desired specific digit $\Rightarrow 2^{nd}$ digit in repeating series is 8.

Converting Decimals to Percent: Move decimal two places to the right. **Example:** $.23 = 23\%$

PowerPrep Practice Questions Also in the Virtual Classroom on DVD

PowerPrep Practice Question 7

7. What is the value of $(x \div y)$ if: $x = 2.5 - 1.9$ and $y = (.1)^2$

    (A) .06
    (B) .6
    (C) 6
    (D) 60
    (E) 600

Explanation to PowerPrep Practice Question 7

Solve for x: $x = (2.5 - 1.9) = .6$ **Then solve for y:** $y = (.1)^2 = .01$ **Solve for $x \div y$:** $(x \div y) = (.6 \div .01)$

Move the decimal point to the right two places on both numbers by multiplying by 100. This gives you: $(.6 * 100) = 60$ and $(.01 * 100) = 1$ **Now you have** $60 \div 1 = $ **60** **ANSWER: (D)**

Extra Sample Question <u>not</u> in the Virtual Classroom on the DVD

Extra Sample Question 9

9. If $(x = 2.5 - 1.9)$, and $y = (.1)^2$ Which is greater, $\frac{x}{y}$ or 6 ?

    (A) $\frac{x}{y}$ is greater
    (B) 6 is greater
    (C) They are equal
    (D) Unknown—insufficient information

Explanation to Extra Sample Question 9

What we know: $x = (2.5 - 1.9)$ and $y = (.1)^2$ **Let's first solve for x:** $x = 2.5 - 1.9$ **becomes:** $x = .6$ **Now solve for y:** $y = (.1)^2$ becomes: $y = .01$ **Now solve for $x \div y$ or $\frac{x}{y}$** (they are equal) you get: $x = .6$ and $y = .01$ ***Plug it into the given:*** $x \div y$ **Becomes:** $.6 \div .01$ **Move the Decimals two places to the right to clear them, so it becomes**: $60 \div 1$ **Which is the same as:** $\frac{60}{1} = 60$ **Now we know that** $\frac{x}{y} = 60$ **The other option was 6. Since** $60 > 6$ **the correct**

Answer is A, $\frac{x}{y}$ is greater than 6 **ANSWER: (A)**

Percents

% = Part/Whole

Percent Increase/Decrease: To increase or decrease a number by a certain percent, calculate the part increase/decrease; then add/subtract it from the original value. Simply convert the percent to decimal form for calculations.

Example: Increase 60 by 20%
Part = .2(60)   Part = 12
Original + part for increase = $60 + 12 = 72$

$(Increase/Decrease)$ *of the Part* $= \%(Original\ Whole)$
New Whole $= Original\ Whole \pm Increase/Decrease\ of\ Part$

$$\% = \frac{inc\ or\ dec\ of\ Part}{Original\ Whole}$$

Calculating Certain Percent: To calculate what percent a part of a whole is, or to calculate by what percent something increased or decreased—divide the part gained/lost/given by the original whole. Multiply final fraction by 100 to convert to percent form.

Example: John had five pennies. He now has seven. What is his percent increase?

Part increase (gain) $\Rightarrow$ $(7 - 5) = 2$ (2 pennies is the increase) $\% = \frac{2}{5} = .4$

Convert to percentage: .(4 $*$ 100) $\Rightarrow$ **40%**
The two pennies represents a 40% increase over the 5 that he had.
Original Whole: To find the original whole before an increase or decrease, add the percent in decimal form to 1, multiply it by the unknown original whole (x) and set it equal to the new given whole.

Example: After a 10% increase, Joe has $44. What was the original amount?
10% is .1   **Add the 10% to the whole:** $.1 + 1 = 1.1$ or $1.10(x) = 44$ **Solve for x:** x = 40
The original amount was $40, then 10% increase of $4.00, led to a total of $44.00

PowerPrep Practice Questions   Also in the Virtual Classroom on DVD

PowerPrep Practice Questions 8-9

8. At a certain deli, 14 percent of the sandwiches sold at lunchtime were turkey sandwiches. If 28 turkey sandwiches were sold at lunchtime, how many sandwiches were sold at lunch in total?

   (A)   2
   (B)   20
   (C)   50
   (D)   100
   (E)   200

9. How many honors students in a chemistry class with 40 students plan to study for the final? If:
   (1) 25 percent of the chemistry students are honors students.
   (2) 75 percent of the chemistry students plan to study for the final.

   (A) Statement (1) BY ITSELF is sufficient to answer the question, but statement (2) is not
   (B) Statement (2) BY ITSELF is sufficient to answer the question, but statement (1) is not
   (C) Statement 1 and (2) TAKEN TOGETHER are sufficient to answer the question, even though NEITHER statement by itself is sufficient
   (D) EITHER statement BY ITSELF is sufficient to answer the question
   (E) Statement 1 and 2 TAKEN TOGETHER are NOT sufficient to answer the question, requiring more data pertaining to the problem

Explanation to PowerPrep Practice Question 8

The deli sold 28 turkey sandwiches at lunch. Those 28 sandwiches represented 14% of all the sandwiches sold at lunch. That means 14% of all the sandwiches equals 28. Or $14\%\ of\ X = 28$ (where "X" = total number of sandwiches sold at lunch)
14% *is written as* .14 So ($.14\ of\ X) = 28$ also written as $(.14x) = 28$

Now divide both sides by .14 **becomes**: $x = \frac{28}{.14}$

$28 \div .14$ = move the decimal to the right two places, then multiply both by 100, **becomes** $2800 \div 14 = 200$

Short way: % = Part/Whole: % sandwiches sold $= \frac{turkey\ sandwiches\ sold}{total\ \#\ sandwiches\ sold}$

$14 = \frac{28}{x}$ $.14x = 28$ $x = \frac{28}{.14}$ $x = \frac{2800}{14}$ **So, x = 200 total sandwiches ANSWER: (E)**

Explanation to PowerPrep Practice Question 9

What are you looking for? The number of chem. honors students who plan to study for the exam.
Facts: 40 students in chem. class, 25% or 10 are honors, 75% of the total class plans to study—that's 30 students. But we need to know how many of the 10 honors students are going to study.
Statement 1: we can calculate the number of students in the chemistry class who are honors students—that's
10 or (.25 x 40) = 10. But, we do not know how many of these plan to study for the final. We **DON'T** have enough information.
Statement 2: we calculate the number of students who plan to study for the final—that's 30 or (.75 x 40 = 30). However, we do not know how many of these studiers are honors students. We **DO NOT** have sufficient information.

Both Statements: We know how many students are honors students (10) and we know how many students plan to study for the final (30), but we do not know how many of this group of 30 studiers are honors kids…it could be none, or 10 or any number in between…**we don't have sufficient information to figure that out.** <u>ANSWER: (E)</u>

Extra Sample Questions not in the Virtual Classroom on the DVD

Extra Sample Questions 10-13

10. If 25 percent of my iPod apps don't work and if the total number of apps that don't work is 6, how many total iPod apps do I have?

    (A) 5
    (B) 12
    (C) 18
    (D) 24
    (E) 48

11. Last year Sara had 15 stuffed animals on her bed. This year she has 18. What is her percent increase?

    (A) 10
    (B) 17
    (C) 20
    (D) 80
    (E) 83

12. At a certain high school there are 1200 boys and 1250 girls. 40% of the boys play sports and 30% of the girls play sports. 22% of boys that play sports are also honors students and 27% of girls that play sports are also honors students. Which is least? (round to the nearest whole number)

    (A) Boys that play sports
    (B) Girls that play sports
    (C) Boys who play sports and are also honors students
    (D) Girls who play sports and are also honors students
    (E) You cannot tell.

13. A runner doubled his number of wins this year from last year. Which is greater? The percent by which the runner's wins increased this year over last or 50%

    (A) The percent by which the runner's wins increased this year over last
    (B) 50%
    (C) They are equal
    (D) Unknown—insufficient information

Explanation to Extra Sample Question 10

What we know: 25% of the apps don't work and the total number of broken apps is 6.
Call of the Question: How many total iPod apps do I have?

Formula to calculate percent: $\% = \dfrac{Part}{Whole}$ $\% \text{ of apps that don't work} = \dfrac{broken\ apps}{number\ of\ total\ apps}$

$.25 = \dfrac{6}{x}$ => $.25x = 6$ => $x = \dfrac{6}{.25}$ => $x = \dfrac{600}{25}$ => $x = 24$ **total iPod apps** <u>ANSWER: (D)</u>

Explanation to Extra Sample Question 11

What we know: Sara had 15 animals and Now she has 18
Call of the Question: What is the percent increase of stuffed animals?

Formula: $\% = \dfrac{part\ increase}{oringal\ whole}$ Part increase = ending number – starting number = (18 – 15) = 3

Part increase = 3 (plug it into the formula) $\% = \dfrac{3}{15} = \dfrac{1}{5} = .20 = 20\%$ <u>ANSWER: (C)</u>

Explanation to Extra Sample Question 12

What we know:
Total Boys = 1200
Total Girls = 1250

- 40% of boys play sports $(.40 * 1200 = 480\ boys\ who\ play\ sports)$
- 30% of girls play sports $(.30 * 1250 = 375\ girls\ who\ play\ sports)$ So far this is the least number
- 22% of the boys who play sports are also honors students $(.22 * 480 = 105.6)$ *round up to* 106
- 27% of the girls who play sports are also honors students $(.27 * 375 = 101.25)$ *round down to* **101**
  (this is the lowest number)

<u>ANSWER: (D)</u>

Explanation to Extra Sample Question 13

What we know: A runner doubled his wins.
What does that mean? If the runner won three times last year, then according to the information, he won six times this year. Six is twice three…so this information shows he won twice as many races as last year.

The number of wins increased by 3. $\% \ increases = \dfrac{part\ increase}{original\ whole}$ $\dfrac{3\ (increase)}{3\ (original\ whole)}$ **or** $\dfrac{3}{3} = 1.0\ or\ 100\%$

$100\% > 50\%$ Therefore AC A is greatest <u>ANSWER: (A)</u>

Arithmetic
Part 5: Mean/Median/Mode/Range
Virtual Classroom>Arithmetic>Mean Median Mode Range

This material corresponds to the Virtual Classroom Instructions in the
PowerPrep DVD/Internet/iApp for Arithmetic

Virtual Classroom

Part 5: Mean/Median/Mode/Range

Average (Mean): In general the average of a set of numbers is the sum of all the terms divided by the total number of terms.

$$Average = \frac{x_1 + x_2 + x_3 + x_4}{n}$$

Example: Average of (5, 7, 39) $\Rightarrow \frac{5+7+39}{3} = \frac{51}{3} = 17$

Average of Even Spaced Numbers: The average number in a set of evenly spaced numbers is the middle term. This is easy to keep track of for small number sets. If you have a large number set and don't want to risk finding the exact middle, you can simply add the first and last numbers, then divide by two.

Example: Average of (20, 24, 28, 32, 36, 40, 44) $\Rightarrow \frac{20+44}{2} = 32$

Missing Term in Set: If you are given an overall average for a set of numbers and then given specific values of some of the numbers in that set, you can solve for a specific unknown number. Use the same formula given above and simply solve for one of the *x*'s.
Example: Five boys have an average age of 8. If four are 4, 9, 11, and 6, how old is the fifth?

$$8 = \frac{4+9+11+6+x}{5} \Rightarrow \text{ Multiply both sides by 5 (to clear the denominator)}$$

$8(5) = (30 + x) \Rightarrow 40 = 30 + x$ Add -30 to both sides **x = 10**

Average & Sum: The sum of a set of terms is equal to the average for that set multiplied by the number of terms in that set
Example: If the average of 6 numbers is 9, then the sum of that set is $(9 * 6 = 54)$

Sum = (average) • (# of terms)

PowerPrep Practice Questions Also in the Virtual Classroom on DVD

PowerPrep Practice Questions 10-11

10. The average of 3, 4, 8, and 11 is equal to the sum of 8, 1.3, 2.7 and *x*. What is the value of *x*?
    (A) −5.5
    (B) −3.5
    (C) 7/4
    (D) 3.5
    (E) 6.5

11. What is the total cost of a stack of magazines? IF:
    (1) The magazines cost an average of $4 each.
    (2) The stack contains six magazines.

    (A) Statement (1) BY ITSELF is sufficient to answer the question, but statement (2) is not
    (B) Statement (2) BY ITSELF is sufficient to answer the question, but statement (1) is not
    (C) Statement 1 and (2) TAKEN TOGETHER are sufficient to answer the question, even though NEITHER statement by itself is sufficient
    (D) EITHER statement BY ITSELF is sufficient to answer the question
    (E) Statement 1 and 2 TAKEN TOGETHER are NOT sufficient to answer the question, requiring more data pertaining to the problem

Explanation to PowerPrep Practice Question 10

1st set of numbers is (3,4,8,11) and 2nd Set of numbers is (8, 1.3, 2.7, x) *Average of first set = Sum of second set*
Set the first group equal to the second group and solve for x.

First find the average of the 1st set: $Average = \frac{3+4+8+11}{4} = \frac{26}{4} = 6.5$

Now you know the value of the 1st set is 6.5...plug it into the equation

6.5 is equal to the sum of the 2nd set of numbers:

$$6.5 = 8 + 1.3 + 2.7 + x$$
$$6.5 = 12 + x$$
$$6.5 - 12 = x$$
$$-5.5 = x$$

ANSWER: (A)

Explanation to PowerPrep Practice Question 11

What are you looking for? The cost of the entire stack of magazines—but, if you know The average cost and number of magazines, you can figure out the total cost. When calculating the average cost of the magazines, you would add up the cost of each magazine and then divide by the number of magazines.

In this case we are told the average cost is $4 and the total number is 6. If you set the sum of the six (6) mags = to X, you get: $\frac{x}{6} = \$4.00$
(where x is the sum of all the magazine prices) becomes: $x = (\$4.00 * 6)$ So $x = \$24$
So all the magazines added together cost $24.00, we need the information in both statements to figure this out.

Statement 1: From this statement, we know the average cost is $4.00.   However, we do not know how many magazines there are and how much the entire stack costs. We DO NOT have sufficient information.
Statement 2: From this statement, we know how many magazines there are (6). However, we do not know what the average cost of each is or the cost of the entire stack. We DO NOT have sufficient information.
Both Statements: From Statement 1 we know the average cost of the magazines ($4.00) and from Statement 2 we know how many magazines there are (6). We can calculate the sum by multiplying the average cost by the number of magazines in the stack ($24.00). **We have sufficient information. ANSWER: (C)**

Extra Sample Questions *not* in the Virtual Classroom on the DVD

Extra Sample Questions 14-16

14. The average of group A is equal to one-half the sum of group B
    What is the value of x?

    Group A: $(6, \ 2^4, \ \frac{9}{6}, \ 100.5)$

    Group B: $(7, 10.5, \ \frac{4}{8}, 5x, 10^2, -1)$

    (A) −11
    (B) −55
    (C) 31
    (D) 100.5
    (E) 117

16. Sam hit four home runs that were an average of 400 feet long. If his first two were 426 and 412, what was the average distance for the other two?

    (A) 400
    (B) 417
    (C) 381
    (D) 388
    (E) 394

15. The average of 4,7,13,5, and x is 9.2. Which is larger, x or 11?

    (A) x
    (B) 11
    (C) They are equal
    (D) Insufficient information

Explanation to Extra Sample Question 14

What we know: $Average \ A = \frac{1}{2}(sum \ of \ B)$ **First, find average of A.** Add the members of A and divide by 4 (the number of members) $6 + 2^4 + \frac{9}{6} + \frac{100.5}{4} = (6 + 16 + 1.5 + 100.5)/4 = \frac{124}{4}$ or 31 **Now find Group B sum** $\left(7 + 10.5 + \frac{4}{8} + 5x + 10^2 - 1\right) = 7 + 10.5 + \frac{1}{2} + 5x + 100 - 1 = 117 + 5x$ (as far as we can go) **Plug into formula:** $Avg \ A = \frac{1}{2}B$ *becomes* $31 = \frac{1}{2}(117 + 5x)$ *Now simplify* $62 = (117 + 5x)$. *Simplify* $-55 = 5x$ *or* $x = -11$ **Answer: (A)**

Explanation to Extra Sample Question 15

What we know: The average of the list of numbers is 9.2   So let's solve for x: $Average \ is \ \frac{4+7+13+5+x}{5} = 9.2$

Add the numerator: $\frac{29+x}{5} = 9.2$ **Multiply both sides by 5 to clear the denominator:** $29 + x = 5(9.2)$ **Multiply:** $29 + x = 46$ **Add** -29 **to both sides:** $x = 46 - 29$, **Simplify:** $x = 17$ The other option was 11, but since 17 > 11
ANSWER: (A)

Explanation to Extra Sample Question 16

Average = $\frac{426+412+x+x}{4} = 400$ **Simplify numerator:** $\frac{838+2x}{4} = 400$

Multiply both sides by 4 (to clear denominator) $838 + 2x = 4(400)$ *becomes:* $838 + 2x = 1600$

Add negative 838 to both sides: $2x = 1600 - 838$ **then simplify:** $2x = 762$

Divide both sides by 2 to isolate x: $(x = \frac{726}{2} = 381)$ **Finally:** $x = 381$ **ANSWER: (C)**

Statistics (median-mode-range)

Median: The *middle* number in a set of numbers. (Make sure they are in ascending/descending order.)
- Even number of items 3, 17, 42, 50, 51 ⇒ middle is 42
- Odd number of items 3, 17, 42, 50, 51, 70 ⇒ middle numbers are 42 & 50 ⇒ $\frac{42+50}{2} = 46$

Note: When you have an even number of data points, add the two numbers together and then divide by two.

Mode: The number that occurs most often in a set of numbers.
Questions can be bi-modal (have two numbers which occur most frequently).
Questions can have no mode (no number occurs more than once).

Example: 2, 5, 7, 5, 3, 9 ⇒ mode is 5

Range: The distance from the biggest to smallest number. Simply subtract the two.
Example: 11, 18, -2, 6, 0, 9 ⇒ **range is (biggest – smallest)** ⇒ $\{18 - (-2)\} = 20$

PowerPrep Practice Questions Also in the Virtual Classroom on DVD

PowerPrepPractice Questions 12-13

12.   {2, 4, 4, 6, 7, 9, 11}
For the set of numbers above, what is the difference between the range and the mode?

(A)   2
(B)   4
(C)   5
(D)   9
(E)   11

13. For the group of numbers {32, 41, 23, 23, 16, 31} Which number is the largest?

(A) The Mean
(B) The Mode
(C) The Median
(D) The Range
(E) None

Explanation to PowerPrep Practice Question 12

This question tests your knowledge of the definitions for:

Range: the distance between the biggest and smallest number (subtract smallest from biggest) **Example:**
(1,1,2,10,100,4,6,40,25,4,2,2,1,54) in this case the smallest number is "1" and the largest number is "100". It does not matter how many times a number repeats, just find the smallest and biggest numbers and subtract them. Here $(100 - 1 = 99)$...so the Range is 99 in this example.

Mode: the number that repeats the most, there can be more than one mode. **Example:** (1,1,1,4,3,5,4,6,5,4) in this case the number 4 and the number 1 both repeat three times each. So the Mode is both 1 and 4 in this case.

Median: the number in the middle—list all the numbers in order (include multiples—if the same number appears more than one time) find the middle number in the list/group, if there is an even number, add the two middle numbers and divide by two.
Examples: Odd number in the group: (1,3,8,10,12,12,15) There are seven (7) numbers in the group and 10 is the Median because it's in the middle.   Even number in the group: (1,3,8,8,10,12,12,15) there are eight (8) numbers in the group, so add the 4th and 5th numbers in the group, in this case $(8 + 10) = 18$, divide by two (2) = 9. In this example "9" is the Median.

Mean: another word for "Average". To find the mean, add all the numbers in the list/group together and divide the total by the number in the list. **Example:** (1,3,8,10,12,12,16) the sum of these numbers is 64. Divide this by the number in the group, in this case it's seven (7). The average or *Mean is* 9.14
To answer the question, you must first calculate the Range and the Mode from the list of given numbers: {2, 4, 4, 6, 7, 9, 11}
What is the Range? Largest less smallest number—in this case $(11 - 2)$ *or* 9. So the Range is 9.
What is the Mode? The number that appears most often. All the numbers appear one time only, except the number "4" which appears twice. So the Mode = 4 **The question asks, "What is the difference between the Range and the Mode?"** Range = 9 and Mode = 4
Difference between them is: $9 - 4 = 5$ **ANSWER: (C)**

Explanation to PowerPrep Practice Question 13

This question directly tests your knowledge of the definitions for:
Range: the distance between the biggest and smallest number (subtract smallest from biggest) **Example:**
(1,1,2,10,100,4,6,40,25,4,2,2,1,54) in this case the smallest number is "1" and the largest number is "100". It does not matter how many times a number repeats, just find the smallest and biggest numbers and subtract them. Here $100 - 1 = 99$...so the Range is 99 in this example.

Mode: the number that repeats the most, there can be more than one mode. **Example:** (1,1,1,4,3,5,4,6,5,4) in this case the number 4 and the number 1 both repeat three times each. So the Mode is both 1 and 4 in this case.

Median: the number in the middle—list all the numbers in order (include multiples—if the same number appears more than one time) find the middle number in the list/group, if there is an even number, you add the two middle numbers and divide by two. **Examples:** Odd number in the group: (1,3,8,**10**,12,12,15) There are seven (7) numbers in the group and 10 is the Median because it's in the middle. Even number in the group: (1,3,8,8,10,12,12,15) there are eight (8) numbers in the group, so add the 4th and 5th numbers in the group, in this case (8 + 10) = 18, divide by two (2) = 9. In this example "9" is the Median.

Mean: another word for "Average". To find the mean, add all the numbers in the list/group together and divide the total by the number in the list. **Example:** (1,3,8,10,12,12,16) the sum of these numbers is 64. Divide this by the number in the group, in this case it's seven (7). The average or Mean is 9.14

To answer the question, you must first calculate the Range, Mean, Median, and Mode for the list of given numbers: {32, 41, 23, 23, 16, 31}

Range: The distance between the Largest and Smallest numbers in the list. The biggest number in our list is 41. The smallest number is 16. Therefore, the Range is (41 – 16) *or* **25**

Mean: The average of $(32 + 41 + 23 + 23 + 16 + 31) = 166$ *Divide* 166 *by* 6 *like this:* $\left(\frac{166}{6}\right) = \mathbf{27.66}$

Median: The number in the middle—list them in order (16, 23,23, 31, 32, 41), there is no middle number because we have an even number (6). So you have to add the 3rd and 4th numbers (23 and 31) = 54, then divide by 2, like this: $\frac{54}{2} = \mathbf{27}$

Mode: The number that repeats the most. In this case the only number that repeats is **23**.
Range is 25   **Mean** is 27.66   **Median** is 27   **Mode** is 23

The largest number is the Mean 27.66

ANSWER: (A)

Extra Sample Questions <u>not</u> in the Virtual Classroom on the DVD

Extra Sample Questions 17-18

17. {3, 10, 7, 3, 3, 10}

   For the set of numbers above, what is five times the mean divided by the median?

   (A) 3
   (B) 4
   (C) 5
   (D) 6
   (E) 12

18. For the group {7, 5, 7, 5, 7, 3, 2} Which is least?

   (A) *Mode minus Range*
   (B) *Median plus Mean*
   (C) *Mean plus Range*
   (D) *Mode^2 minus Range^2*
   (E) *Median plus median*

Explanation to Extra Sample Question 17

Call of the Question: Find $\frac{5(mean)}{median}$

First, the Mean: $\frac{3+3+3+7+10+10}{6} = \frac{36}{6} = 6$

Next find the Median: (the number in the middle) (3, 3, **3, 7**, 10, 10) Since there are an even number of numbers, average the middle two numbers like this: $\frac{3+7}{2} = \frac{10}{2} = 5$

Now we know: Mean = 6   Median = 5

Now calculate the formula we were given: $\frac{5(mean)}{median} => \frac{(5)(6)}{5} = \frac{30}{5} = 6$

ANSWER: (D)

Explanation to Extra Sample Question 18

What we know: *{7, 5, 7, 5, 7, 3, 2} rearrange to (2,3,5,5,7,7,7) seven members in the group*

Call of the Question: which of the Answer Choices is **LEAST**

Mean $= \frac{36}{7}$ *or* 5.14   **Median** = 5 (the 4th number, the one in the middle), **Mode** = 7 (the most), **Range** = (7 – 2) *or* 5

   (A) *Mode minus Range* :(7 – 5) = **2**
   (B) *Median plus Mean:* (5 + 5.14) = 10.14
   (C) *Mean plus Range:* (5.14 + 5) = 10.14
   (D) *Mode^2 minus Range^2* : (7^2 – 5^2) => (49 – 25) = 24
   (E) *Median plus median:* (5 + 5) = 10

ANSWER: (A)

Arithmetic

Part 6: Ratios/Proportions/Probabilities

Virtual Classroom>Arithmetic>Ratios Proportions Probabilities

This material corresponds to the Virtual Classroom Instructions in the
PowerPrep DVD/Internet/iApp for Arithmetic

Virtual Classroom

Important Abbreviations
These abbreviations are used throughout the program

POE: Process of Elimination
SARR: Synthesize, Analyze, Reduce, and Restate (has to do with Logical Reasoning)
AC: Answer Choice
QS: Question Stem
LOD: Level of Difficulty

Example Question: What is the least common multiple of 3, 4, and 7? **(This is the call of the question or Question Stem "QS")**

These are Answer Choices "AC" A, B, C, D, E

(A)   12
(B)   21
(C)   28
(D)   48
(E)   84

Part 6: Ratios/Proportions/Probabilities

<u>Ratio:</u> Comparison of two numbers by division (similar to a fraction). You set it up as $\frac{of}{to}$ or (of : to) **Example:** Ratio of 8 boys to 2 girls $\Rightarrow \frac{8}{2} = \frac{4}{1}$ or $4:1$

<u>Possible Total (Whole):</u> The two parts of the ratio add up to give you the total. On a question which asks you for a possible total number of a ratio, the correct answer choice must be a multiple of this total. **Example:** The ratio of dogs to cats is 2 : 3. Possible totals would be multiples of 5.

<u>Parts and Whole:</u> Remember that a ratio is comparing two parts. Together they give you a total (or whole). When you are given one ratio of parts and are asked to find a second ratio based on a whole number you:
- Add the two parts in the ratio together.
- Divide that number into the total given in the question.
- Multiply that integer by each term in the ratio.
- Add the two new parts of the ratio to verify they equal the total given in the problem.

   Example: Ratio of cars to trucks is (1 : 3) If there are 28 autos, how many are cars?

Add two parts $\Rightarrow$ 1 + 3 = 4   **Divide into total** $\Rightarrow \frac{28}{4} = 7$ **Multiply ratio** $\Rightarrow$ 1(7) = 7, 3(7) = 21
Add parts $\Rightarrow$ 7 + 21 = 28   **Answer** = 21 cars

<u>Proportion:</u> You create a proportion by setting two ratios equal to each other. Solve for the unknown value in the equation by cross-multiplying. **Example:** 12 stacked boxes are 18 ft tall. If 4 more boxes are added, what is the new height?

Ratio 1st Set =   Ratio 2nd Set $\frac{12}{18} = \frac{16}{x}$ **Multiply both sides by 18 to clear the denominator on the left.** $12 = \frac{288}{x}$
Multiply both sides by x to clear the denominator on the right: 12x = 288 **Divide both sides by 12:** x = 24

PowerPrep Practice Questions Also in the Virtual Classroom on DVD

PowerPrep Practice Questions 14-15

14. A pool cleaning business services a total of three pools on Tuesday (one residential, one hotel, one community). These are the only three pools the company cleans on Tuesdays. The company's total Tuesday revenue generated by these three pools is represented as a ratio of 2:3:4 from the residential, hotel, and community pools respectively. If the hotel paid $99.00 for Tuesday cleaning, what is the pool cleaner's total revenue for Tuesday?

   (A) $99
   (B) $297
   (C) $349
   (D) $691
   (E) $89

15. How many hamburgers did Stephanie and Jessica sell in a day, if the ratio of hamburgers to hot dogs sold on that day was 3:7 and they sold 49 hotdogs.
   (A) 7
   (B) 25
   (C) 49
   (D) 21
   (E) 147

Explanation to PowerPrep Practice Question 14

What we know: The division of revenue between the three Tuesday pools is 2:3:4
That means: The residential pool is a 2 share of Tuesday's revenue, hotel pool is a 3 share, and community pool is a 4 share. It also means the total share of revenues for Tuesday is 9 (2+3+4). Finally we know the hotel pool was $99.00 for Tuesday.

If the hotel pool is a 3 share of the total 9 shares and it made $99.00, then we know something. We know that if we divide $99.00 by 3 (hotel pool's share) we can find out what a single share is worth and then we can multiply each pool's share by the amount of single share. **We could do this work manually, but we can also create a formula like this:** Hotel pool's ratio: $99.00 is a 3 share or 3 ratio That means $99 : 3 or $\frac{99}{3}$. **The total Tuesday revenue shares:** $2 + 3 + 4 = 9$ That means we know the total ratio or share is 9. **If we set the total dollar amount into this ratio we get:** $x : 9$ or $\frac{x}{9}$

Now we can create a proportion of hotel pool to the total Tuesday pools: $\left(\frac{99 \, (hotel \, \$)}{3 \, (hotel \, shares)} = \frac{x \, (total \, tues.\$)}{9 \, (total \, shares)} \right)$

Now solve: First multiply both sides by 3 => $\left(99 = \frac{3x}{9} \right)$ **Now multiply** both sides by 9 => $9(99) = 3x$
Simplify: $891 = 3x$ **now divide by 3** => $x = 297$ <u>ANSWER: (B)</u>

Check your work: *hotel is 3 shares which generate* $99.00. So 1 share $= \$33$ **NEXT:** total shares are 9 so $(9x33 = 297)$

$Hotel \; revenue : 3(hotel \; shares) = x \,(total \; reveue):9 \,(total \; shares)$ => $\frac{hotel \, \$}{3 \,(hotel \, shares)} = \frac{x \,(total \, \$)}{9 \,(total \, shares)}$ => $\frac{99}{3} = \frac{x}{9}$

now simplify $3x = 99(9)$ => $3x = 891$ **simplify** $x = \frac{891}{3}$ **finally** $x = \$297$

Explanation to PowerPrep Practice Question 15

The ratio of hamburgers to hot dogs is $3:7$
This means for every 3 hamburgers the girls sold 7 hot dogs
Put another way, they sold 7 hot dogs for every 3 hamburgers
They sold **2.33** hotdogs for every hamburger.   They sold **.43** hamburgers for every hotdog.
Bottom line—the hotdogs are going over twice as fast as the hamburgers **But** you need to know how many hamburgers they sold if they sold 49 hot dogs.   **Set up the ratio this way:** [3 hamburgers : 7 hotdogs] = [X hamburgers : 49 hotdogs]

You can also set up the ratio this way: $[3:7] = [X:49]$ Or $\frac{3}{7} = \frac{x}{49}$

Where "X" is the number of hamburgers sold in a day. **Now solve for "X":** 1st multiply both sides by 49 to isolate X on the

right-hand side of the equation. $\frac{49}{1} * \frac{3}{7} = x$ becomes $\frac{147}{7} = x$ becomes $21 = X$ They sold 21 hamburgers on

that day. **Note: POE + Logic = Speedy answers**
Using some basic logic, you can check the answer—just looking at the ratio of $3:7$ you know that hotdogs sold a little better than 2 to 1. A Ratio of $3:6$ would be two hotdogs for each hamburger…but we were given $3:7$ so we know the hotdogs sold a little better than 2 for each hamburger.

We also know the girls sold 49 hotdogs…so you can guess the hamburgers would have to be somewhere slightly less than half—something less than 24 but more than 20. You should be able to estimate that within 10 seconds.

This is a good example of POE, if you were running low on time, you could have immediately eliminated three of the Answer Choices, 7, 49, and 147…that would leave you a guess between 25 and 21.   You could eliminate 25 because 25 is more than half of 49 and you know $3:7$ ratio is slightly less than half, not more than half.

So if you understood ratios, you could have glanced at this problem and eliminated all four of the wrong answers without even working the problem.   Even if you are not pressed for time, if you can answer a question like this it will save you a minute or two that you can use somewhere else in the section. **ANSWER: (D)**

Extra Sample Questions not in the Virtual Classroom on the DVD

Extra Sample Questions 19-22

19. Ryan, Kelly, and Josh work a lemonade stand on the weekend. The three decide to divide all of their profit in the ratios 3 : 4 : 5, respectively, based on the amount of work each did. If Kelly received $3.20 in profit for a certain weekend, what was the total profit for the weekend?

    (A) $0.60
    (B) $0.80
    (C) $6.40
    (D) $8.40
    (E) $9.60

20. After a soccer game, Kim checks her legs and finds that she has two bruises for every three cuts. Which of the following could be the total number of bruises and cuts on Kim's legs?

    (A) 6
    (B) 15
    (C) 19
    (D) 23
    (E) 24

21. Mario has only dimes and quarters in a glass jar at home. The ratio of dimes to quarters is 3:9.   How many dimes does he have in the jar if he has 27 quarters?

    (A) 3
    (B) 6
    (C) 8
    (D) 9
    (E) 12

22. A certain farmer owns only sheep and horses.

Which is greater, the total number of animals the farmer owns if the ratio of sheep to horses is $4:9$ *or* 13.

    (A) The total number of animals the farmer owns is greater
    (B) 13 is greater
    (C) They are equal
    (D) Unknown—insufficient information

Explanation to Extra Sample Question 19

What we know: The division of profit will be 3:4:5
That means: Ryan gets 3 shares and Kelly gets 4 shares and Josh gets 5 shares. These means there is a total of 12 total shares. We also know that Kelly got $3.20 in profit.

If Kelly gets a 4 share of the total 12 shares and he got $3.20, then we know something. We know that if we divide $3.20 by 4 (Kelly's share) we can find out what a single share is worth and then we can multiply each boy's share by the amount of single share. **We could do this work manually, but we can also create a formula like this:** Kelly's ratio: $3.20 is a 4 share or 4 ratio That means $3.20 :

4 or $\frac{3.20}{4}$ **Total team ratio:** $3 + 4 + 5 = 12$ That means we know the total ratio or share is 12 **If we set the total dollar**

amount into this ratio we get: $x : 12 or $\frac{x}{12}$ **Now we can** create a proportion of Kelly to the total team: $[Kelly : Team]$

$\left(\frac{3.2}{4} = \frac{x}{12}\right)$ **Now solve…**First multiple both sides by 4: **becomes:** $\left(3.2 = \frac{4x}{12}\right)$ **Now multiply** both sides by 12: **becomes:**

$12(3.2) = 4x$ **Simplify:** $38.4 = 4x$, **then divide by 4, becomes:** $x = 9.6$ **ANSWER: (E)**

Check your work: This tells us the total profit for the week was $9.60 and Kelly got a 4 share or $3.20. To check this, divide the total profit by 12 to find a single share value of $.80 Now multiply each boy's total shares by $0.80 to find the value of their shares.   If Kelly has a 4 ratio or 4 share, then $(4*80) = 3.20$ (which is exactly what we expected.) **Ryan** gets a 3 share or $(3*80) = 2.40 **Josh** gets a 5 share or $(5*80) = 4.00 **Now add them all up:** $2.40 + 3.20 + 4.00$ **Total amount is $9.60, So it all checks**

Another Way:
The key to correctly answering this question is to first understand exactly what the question asks and what it tells you.
What does it mean to divide the profits in a ratio of 3:4:5 respectively? The problem lists the boys in the order Ryan, Kelly, Josh. Then it says they divided their profit in a 3:4:5 ratio, respectively...
This means they divided the total profit-pot into twelve (12) even shares $(3 + 4 + 5)$. Then Ryan got three (3) shares, Kelly got four (4) shares and Josh got five (5) shares. Once you understand the set up, the question gets a lot easier.
We know Kelly got $3.20 and he has four (4) shares. **How much is each share worth?** **Divide** $3.20 by four (4) to get the value of a single share. $3.20/4 = .80$ (80 cents) per share on the weekend in question.
If a single share on the given weekend was worth 80 cents, what was the total pot that weekend worth? ($12\ shares *$ $80\ cents/share$) **Multiply** the single share value of 80 cents times the total number of shares 12. $.80\ x\ 12 = \$9.60$

Explanation to Extra Sample Question 20

Add the two parts to find the total. The bruises and cuts come in groups of 5 are 2 bruises and 3 cuts $2 + 3 = 5$
Therefore, the answer must be a multiple of 5. The only AC that is a multiple of 5 is AC B which is 15. All the other AC's are NOT multiples of 5 and therefore, do not respond to the question. **ANSWER: (B)**

Explanation to Extra Sample Question 21

What do we know: dimes: 3, quarters: 9 , total units:12 $(3 + 9)$. Out of every 12 coins, 3 are dimes and 9 are quarters.
Note: you could also simplify the ratio from 3:9 to 1:3 and the math will work the same way
Create a proportion: (3 dimes : 9 quarters). The question is the given ratio of $x\ dimes : 27\ quarters$
This means: $\frac{3}{9} = \frac{x}{27}$ Now solve...Multiply both sides by 9 => $3 = \frac{9x}{27}$ **Multiply both sides by 27:** $27(3) = 9x$
Multiply: $81 = 9x$ **Divide by 9:** $9 = x$ This tells us that if Mario has 27 quarters then he also has 9 dimes. **ANSWER: (D)**
If you simplified the initial ratio from $\frac{3}{9}\ to\ \frac{1}{3}$ the math would be: $\frac{1}{3} = \frac{x}{27}$ => $27 = 3x$ => $9 = x$ **This works the same way.**

Explanation to Extra Sample Question 22

What we know: The ratio of sheep to horses is 4 : 9
What we don't know: We don't know how many sheep or horses the farmer has, we only know the ratio. This means he could have 13 total animals or he could have 130 or 1300 or 13,000 or any number...but we are not told anything that locks us down to a number...only a ratio. This means we don't have sufficient information to solve this question. **ANSWER: (D)**

Possibility & Probability

$$P = \frac{\#\ of\ desired\ outcomes}{\#\ of\ total\ possible\ outcomes}$$

Probability: A ratio of the number of desired outcomes divided by the total number of possible outcomes.

Numerator: number of things you want—called **"Desired Outcomes"**
Example of possible desired outcomes:
Heads on a coin: 1   The number Three on a dice: 1   Draw a six in a deck of cards: 4
Denominator: everything possible, the total number of outcomes. **Examples** of "Total Outcomes" If you flip a coin – 2 possible outcomes (heads or tails) Roll a dice – 6 possible outcomes (1,2,3,4,5,6) Draw a card from a deck – 52 possible outcomes (52 cards in a standard deck)

Example: 4 quarters, 6 dimes, 14 pennies – what is probability of drawing a dime? $P = \frac{6\ (dimes)}{4Q+6D+14P} = \frac{6}{24} = \frac{1}{4}$ or 25%

Consecutive Probabilities: When you have several probabilities combined, calculate each separately then multiply probabilities together. **Example:** Probability of drawing a six and then an eight from a deck of cards?

$P_1 = \frac{4}{52} = \frac{1}{13},\quad P_2 = \frac{4}{52} = \frac{1}{13},\quad total\ P = \left(\frac{1}{13}\right) * \left(\frac{1}{13}\right) = \frac{1}{169}$

$P_1 = \frac{4(total\ cards\ in\ the\ deck\ with\ a\ 6)}{52\ (total\ cards)} = \frac{1}{13}$ $P_2 = \frac{4\ (total\ cards\ in\ the\ deck\ with\ an\ 8)}{52\ (total\ cards)} = \frac{1}{13}$ **Total P** $= \frac{1}{13} * \frac{1}{13} = \frac{1}{169}$

The possibility of drawing a 6 followed by an 8 is 1 in 169.
Possibility: The total number of possible outcomes when combining certain situations. If you have *a* objects and a separate set of *b* objects and you want to know how many different ways of combining those objects there are, simply multiply the quantity of each situation together. **Example:** 4 crayons, 3 colored papers $\Rightarrow 4\ x\ 3 = 12$ crayon/paper combinations

Variation: Now we are talking about ordering groups of items rather than combining objects. Suppose there are three horses in a race. How many different finishing possibilities are there?

Horse 1 in first place	Horse 2 in first place	Horse 3 in first place
1, 2, 3	2, 1, 3	3, 1, 2
1, 3, 2	2, 3, 1	3, 2, 1

There are 6 variations. You can create a chart or matrix like this or you can take a shortcut by using a **factorial** (written like 3!) A factorial is a number multiplied by every number smaller than it. Any horse can come in first place, so there are three possibilities. Once that horse is in first place, it leaves two possibilities for second place. After the horse is set in second place, there is only one possibility for third place. So the formula is called 3 Factorial and is written **3!** $= 3 * 2 * 1 = 6\ variations$

Let's say there were eight horses in the race and we wanted to know how many combinations for first, second and third place there were. The same logic shows us eight possible combinations for first, seven combinations for second and six combinations for third. $(8)(7)(6) = 336$ variations

PowerPrep Practice Questions Also in the Virtual Classroom on DVD

PowerPrep Practice Questions 16-17

16. A bag contains marbles of only three colors as follows: 20 red, 15 yellow and 12 green. Each time Mike reaches into the bag, he removes one marble and tosses it onto his bed. One-at- a-time, he removes six (6) marbles— a red marble, a green marble, a yellow marble, a green marble, a red marble and a yellow marble.

What is the probability that on the next reach he will remove a green marble?
- (A) 15/47
- (B) 13/41
- (C) 10/41
- (D) 13/15
- (E) 11/15

17. Your friend Mustafa, has a trick deck of cards. There are only 42 cards in this deck and they are either green or red and each card has the picture of animal on one side and a number between 1 and 10 on the other side. There are twice as many green cards as red cards in the stack.

How many green cards are there?
- (A) 14
- (B) 28
- (C) 21
- (D) 35
- (E) 7

Explanation to PowerPrep Practice Question 16

This problem demonstrates a trap that the test-makers use all the time. They try to make a problem appear to be more difficult than it really is. They constantly try to mix you up. This problem may seem complex at first, but it's very straight forward.
First, make a quick chart that shows number of marbles and their colors before Mike starts throwing them on his bed:

$20 : 47\ red \quad 15 : 47\ yellow \quad 12 : 47\ green$

There are 47 total marbles. The probability of picking any given color is the total number of that color compared to the total number of all the marbles. Mike has pulled out two red marbles, two yellow marbles and two green marbles. Now he has 18 red, 13 yellow and 10 green left in the bag. The total number of marbles is now 41.

To start:	After 6 times
$20 : 47\ red$	$18 : 41\ red$
$15 : 47\ yellow$	$13 : 41\ yellow$
$12 : 47\ green$	$10 : 41\ green$

So the probability of picking a green marble the next time is 10 to 41 or $[10 : 41]\ or\ \left(\frac{10}{41}\right)\ or\ (10/41)$

$\text{Probability} = \dfrac{\#\ desired\ outcomes}{\#\ total\ outcomes}$ $\qquad \text{Probability} = \dfrac{10}{41}$ $\qquad$ **ANSWER: (C)**

Explanation to PowerPrep Practice Question 17

What do you know? And what do you know that is relevant to the question?
There are only three (3) pieces of relevant information:
Total number of cards = 42 Total number of red cards = X Total number of green cards = 2X
The equation you need to solve is this: $x\ (total\ red\ cards) + 2x\ (total\ green\ cards) = 42\ (total\ cards)$
Therefore, if you add the total number of red cards and green cards you'll get the total number of cards. $X + 2X = 42$
Solve...$3X = 42$ becomes $X = 14$ *There are* $14\ red\ cards$ $2X = green\ cards$
Therefore, we have **28 green cards** **ANSWER: (B)**

Extra Sample Questions not in the Virtual Classroom on the DVD

Extra Sample Questions 23-26

23. A deck of cards contains 52 cards, 13 from each suit. If a card is flipped over, what is the probability that it is an even card?
Count the jacks =11, Queens=12, Kings=13 and Aces=1.

- (A) 1/2
- (B) 7/13
- (C) 28/52
- (D) 6/13
- (E) 26/52

24. A volleyball team has four women and two men. If one member is selected at random to be captain, and a second member is selected at random to be co-captain, what is the probability that both are women?

- (A) 1/6
- (B) 1/3
- (C) 1/2
- (D) 1/4
- (E) 2/5

25. A used car salesman must place four cars in a row of four parking spaces. How many different arrangements could the salesman place the cars in?

- (A) 4
- (B) 8
- (C) 16
- (D) 24
- (E) 36

26. A group of cards has one of two markings on each card--either a plus or a minus sign: $+\ or\ -$
There are 8 plus signs (+) and 17 minus signs (−). The cards are shuffled and Markus selects a random card. He keeps his card and then Maria selects a card from the remainder. What is the probability that Markus draws a plus (+) and Maria draws a minus (−) ?

- (A) 24/75
- (B) 17/25
- (C) 17/24
- (D) 8/25
- (E) 17/75

Explanation to Extra Sample Question 23

What we know: 4 suits (spades, clubs, diamonds, hearts) and 13 cards per suit (Ace,2,3,4,5,6,7,8,9,10,j,q,k) total of 52 cards.

There is a slight trick to this question. If you consider the deck as 1-52, then the odds of turning an even or an odd is 50-50 or 1/2. Between 1 and 52 there are 26 even numbers and 26 odd numbers. BUT, that's not the case with a deck of cards.

The cards are divided among four (4) suits of 13 cards each. Each of the four sets has 6 even and 7 odd cards. Therefore, six(6) even cards multiplied by four (4) sets is 24 even cards and seven (7) odd multiplied by four (4) sets is 28 total odd cards. So the odds of drawing an even card is 24/52 or 6/13 and the odds of drawing an odd card are 28/52 or 7/13.

You could also evaluate a single suit of cards as your sample, since each suit is identical in terms of even and odd cards. Pick any suit (it won't matter) and look at the even and odd cards. $\{Ace(1), 2, 3, 4, 5, 6, 7, 8, 9, 10, jack(11), queen(12), king(13)\}$.

That's six(6) even cards (2, 4, 6, 8, 10, Queen12) and seven(7) odd cards (ace1, 3, 5, 7, 9, 11jack, 13king).

The odds of selecting an even card from a single suit is 6/13 and those odds remain the same for the entire deck. **Answer (D)**

Explanation to Extra Sample Question 24

What we know: A team has 6 total members, 4 women, 2 men
Call of the question: What is the probability that two random choices will result in two (2) women
Remember for questions that ask about two consecutive probabilities, you calculate each probability separately and then multiply.

The probability of the first woman being chosen: $P = \frac{4}{6} = \frac{2}{3}$ $P = \frac{4}{6} = \frac{2}{3}$ So the probability of a first random choice being a woman is $66\% \, or \, \frac{2}{3}$ **Now we have 5 total players and 3 women left to choose from. so the probability of the second woman being chosen :** $P = \frac{3}{5}$ $or \, 60\%$ **Now calculate what the probability is for both selections to happen—select one woman and then another:** $\frac{2}{3} * \frac{3}{5} = \frac{6}{10} = \frac{2}{5} \, or \, 40\%$ ANSWER: (E)

Explanation to Extra Sample Question 25

What we know: Four cars: **Car** 1, **Car** 2, **Car** 3, **Car** 4
Call of the Question: How many different arrangements of these?

Car 1 in first place	Car 2 in first place	Car 3 in first place	Car 4 in first place
1, 2, 3, 4	2, 1, 3, 4	3, 1, 2, 4	4, 3, 2, 1,
1, 2, 4, 3	2, 1, 4, 3	3, 1, 4, 2,	4, 3, 1, 2,
1, 3, 2, 4	2, 3, 1, 4	3, 2, 1, 4	4, 2, 1, 3
1, 3, 4, 2	2, 3, 4, 1	3, 2, 4, 1	4, 2, 3, 1
1, 4, 2, 3	2, 4, 1, 3	3, 4, 1, 2	4, 1, 2, 3
1, 4, 3, 2	2, 4, 3, 1	3, 4, 2, 1	4, 1, 3, 2

24 total possibilities **ANSWER: (D)**

But there is a much easier way to calculate this using Factorials. Possible outcomes = $4! = (4)(3)(2)(1) = 24$
Also results in the same outcome, which is 24

Explanation to Extra Sample Question 26

The group of cards have eight (8) plus sign (+) cards and 17 minus sign (-) cards or a total of 25 cards

To find a basic probability, with all outcomes equally likely, we make a fraction like this: $\frac{number \ of \ chances \ of \ our \ event}{number \ of \ total \ chances}$

In this case we have two events that combined make up the single event for which we want to find a probability.

Keep it clearly in your mind that we want to find the probability of Markus drawing a + **AND** Maria drawing a −. Each event has a probability and the combination has a probability.

First let's find the probability of Markus drawing a plus (+): there are 8 plus (+) sign cards and 25 total cards so the probability is $\frac{8}{25}$

Next Maria: there are 17 minus sign (−) cards but after Markus picked a card the total is one less, so the probability is now $\frac{17}{24}$ $(not \ 25)$ We have the two individual events: Markus is $\frac{8}{25}$ and Maria is $\frac{17}{24}$

In two successive picks there are four (4) possible combinations:

$Markus \ + \ and \ Maria \ +$
$Markus \ + \ and \ Maria \ -$
$Markus \ - \ and \ Maria \ -$
$Markus \ - \ and \ Maria \ +$

we want option two (2) above: $Markus \ + \ and \ Maria \ -$

To do this you multiply the two individual probabilities.

So it's: Markus $\frac{8}{25} * Maria \ \frac{17}{24} = \frac{136}{600}$ reduce $\frac{68}{300}$ reduce $\frac{34}{150}$ reduce $\frac{17}{75}$ Answer: (E)

Arithmetic

Part 7: Powers & Roots

<u>Virtual Classroom>Arithmetic>Powers & Roots</u>
This material corresponds to the Virtual Classroom Instructions in the
PowerPrep DVD/Internet/iApp for Arithmetic

<u>Virtual Classroom</u>

Important Abbreviations

These abbreviations are used throughout the program

POE: Process of Elimination
SARR: Synthesize, Analyze, Reduce, and Restate (has to do with Logical Reasoning)
AC: Answer Choice
QS: Question Stem
LOD: Level of Difficulty

Example Question: What is the least common multiple of 3, 4, and 7? **(This is the call of the question or Question Stem "QS")**

These are Answer Choices "AC" A, B, C, D, E

(A)   12
(B)   21
(C)   28
(D)   48
(E)   84

Part 7: Powers & Roots

Base: The big number or letter. **Example:** x^2 (*x is the base*)
Exponent: Little number or letter. **Example:** x^2 (2 is the exponent)

- Any base raised to the zero power equals one. ($5^0 = 1$, $b^0 = 1$)
- Any negative number raised to an even power ends up positive $(-4)^2 = 16$
- Any negative number raised to an odd power ends up negative $(-4)^3 = -64$
- Any fraction, pos. or neg., raised to a positive exponent becomes smaller $\left(\frac{1}{3}\right)^2 = \frac{1}{9}$

Square: A base number multiplied by itself. **Example:** $b * b = b^2$ **NOTE:** When you see b^2 it could be broken down into $(b * b)$ or $(-b)(-b)$

Reciprocal: A base number with a negative exponent is equal to the reciprocal of something. **Example:** $b^{-2} = \frac{1}{b^2}$

Square Root: For a given number (x) the square root is a number (y) that, when multiplied by itself, gives us (x). **Example:** x = 9, $\sqrt{9} \Rightarrow 3 = y \Rightarrow \sqrt{x} = y$, or 3 is the $\sqrt{9}$ Square root is also represented with a fractional exponent. $9^{1/2} = \sqrt{9} = 3$

Multiplying Like Bases: To multiply bases that are the same, simply add the exponents. **Example:** $(a^3 * a^5) = a^{3+5} = a^8$ **Note:** You **cannot** multiply different bases. $(a^3 * b^5) = (a^3 * b^5)$ (you cannot simplify this any further, because the bases are different (*a and b are different bases*)

Dividing Like Bases: To divide bases that are the same, simply subtract exponents. **Example:** $(b^9 \div b^3) = b^{(9-3)} = b^6$ **or** $\frac{b^9}{b^3} = b^{9-3} = b^6$

Adding/Subtracting like Bases w/like Exponents: To add like bases raised to exponents that are the same, (same base value, same exponent value) simply add or subtract the coefficient of the base. **Example:** $5x^3 - 2x^3 = 3x^3$ **Note:** You cannot add/subtract like bases with different exponents **or** different base with like exponents.

Exponents Raised to Exponents: When you have one exponent inside a set of parenthesis and another exponent outside the parentheses, simply multiply the exponents together. **Example:** $(c^2)^3 = c^{(2*3)} = c^6$

PowerPrep Practice Questions Also in the Virtual Classroom on DVD

PowerPrep Practice Questions 18-19

18. Which of the following numbers is the reciprocal of $3^{-\frac{1}{2}}$?

   (A) -4.5
   (B) -1.5
   (C) $1/\sqrt{3}$
   (D) 1.5
   (E) $\sqrt{3}$

19. If *a* is a prime number and (*na*) is both the square of an integer and the cube of an integer, where *n* is a positive integer, what is the greatest value of $\frac{1}{na}$?

   (A) 1
   (B) 1/32
   (C) 1/64
   (D) 1/81
   (E) 1/729

Explanation to PowerPrep Practice Question 18

This question tests your knowledge of the rules of exponents and reciprocal. **Negative exponents:** A negative exponent is equivalent to the inverse of the same number. $x^{-7} = \frac{1}{x^7}$

Samples: $3^{-2} = \frac{1}{9}$ $4^{-1} = \frac{1}{4}$ $7^{-5} = \frac{1}{7^5}$ $\frac{1}{2^{-2}} = 2^2$ $\frac{1}{5^{-1}} = 5^1$

If a negative exponent is equal to the reciprocal of the integer, then:
The rule of fractional exponents: A fractional exponent like 1/n means you take the nth root of the number.
In our case, an integer with an exponent of ½ is equal to the square root of the integer:

The last part of the question tells us to take the reciprocal. So what is the reciprocal of $\frac{1}{\sqrt{3}}$?

In making a reciprocal you just flip the fraction—the reciprocal of ½ is 2, the reciprocal of 3 is $\frac{1}{3}$.

So the reciprocal of $\frac{1}{\sqrt{3}}$ is $\sqrt{3}$
ANSWER: (E)

$3^{-\frac{1}{2}} = \frac{1}{2^{\frac{1}{2}}}$

$\frac{1}{3^{1/2}} = \frac{1}{\sqrt{3}}$

Rule of fractional exponents
$X^{1/n} = \sqrt[n]{X}$

Explanation to PowerPrep Practice Question 19

Realize that the greatest value of $\frac{1}{na}$ will coincide with the smallest value of *na*.

Take a look at each AC to determine if it has a square root and a cube root. Then determine if there is a prime factor.

(A) 1 $\Rightarrow$ square root = 1, cube root = 1, doesn't have a prime factor

(B) 32 $\Rightarrow$ doesn't have square root

(C) **64 $\Rightarrow$ square root = 8, cube root = 4, prime factor = 2 ANSWER: (C)**

(D) 81 $\Rightarrow$ square root = 9, doesn't have cube root

(E) 729 $\Rightarrow$ even if it has a square and cube root $\frac{1}{729} < \frac{1}{64}$

Roots

<u>Square Root:</u> The square root of m (positive number) is a number that, when you multiply it by itself, gives you m. **Example:** $\sqrt{6.25} = 2.5\ because\ (2.5)*(2.5) = 6.26$ **Note:** A perfect square is a square root that gives you an integer result. ($\sqrt{9} = 3$)

<u>Simplifying a Square Root:</u> To simplify a square root, breakup the value into smaller parts and possible perfect squares; remove the square root of the perfect square; leave any possible remainder under the square root sign. **Example:** $\sqrt{45} = \sqrt{9*5} = 3\sqrt{5}$

<u>Adding/Subtracting Radicals:</u> To add/subtract numbers with like radicals, simply add/subtract the coefficients (number in front). **Example:** $4\sqrt{5} + 3\sqrt{5} = 7\sqrt{5}$ **Note:** You cannot add/subtract different radicals. $4\sqrt{5} + 3\sqrt{6} = ?$

<u>Multiplying Radicals:</u> Multiply numbers inside each radical then place the product inside the radical. **Example:** $\sqrt{7} * \sqrt{3} = \sqrt{(7*3)} = \sqrt{21}$

<u>Dividing Radicals:</u> Divide numbers inside the radicals; then place the product inside the radical. **Example:** $\frac{\sqrt{8}}{\sqrt{4}} = \sqrt{\frac{8}{4}} = \sqrt{2}$

Note: If you have coefficients, multiply or divide them as well.

$$
\begin{array}{l}
(8\sqrt{30})*(2\sqrt{3}) \\
(8)(2)\sqrt{30}*\sqrt{3} \\
16\sqrt{(30*3)} \\
16\sqrt{90}
\end{array}
\Rightarrow
\begin{array}{l}
\text{Factor 90} \\
16\sqrt{(9*10)} \\
(16)(3)\sqrt{10} \\
48\sqrt{10}
\end{array}
$$

PowerPrep Practice Questions Also in the Virtual Classroom on DVD

PowerPrep Practice Questions 20

20. Which of the following is equivalent to $(\sqrt{6a^2b}) * (3\sqrt{4c^2})$ in its simplest form?

(A) $24abc$

(B) $3\sqrt{24a^2bca^2}$

(C) $6abc\sqrt{6}$

(D) $6ac\sqrt{6b}$

(E) $12ac\sqrt{3b}$

Explanation to PowerPrep Practice Question 20

Let's reduce the left side first: $\sqrt{6a^2b}$ The $\sqrt{a^2} = a$ So we now have: $a\sqrt{6b}$ Now let's **reduce** the right side: $3\sqrt{4c^2}$ The $\sqrt{4c^2}$ reduces to 2c. So we have: $(3 \bullet 2c)$ or $6c$ Now **combine** the two reduced sides: $(a\sqrt{6b}) * (6c)$ **Becomes: $6ac\sqrt{6b}$ ANSWER: (D)**

Extra Sample Questions <u>not</u> in the Virtual Classroom on the DVD

Extra Sample Question 27

27. Which is greater, $(\sqrt{6} * \sqrt{4})$ or $2\sqrt{6}$

A) $(\sqrt{6}*\sqrt{4})$ is greater

(B) $\sqrt{6}$ is greater

(C) They are equal

(D) Unknown—insufficient information

Explanation to Extra Sample Question 27

We need to simplify both terms and then compare them to which is greater. Simplify First Term: $(\sqrt{6} * \sqrt{4})$ becomes $(\sqrt{6*4})$ Now factor because 4 is a perfect square: $2\sqrt{6}$ The 2nd term is already simplified and turns out to be **equal to the first term:** $2\sqrt{6}$ **They are equal:** $2\sqrt{6} = 2\sqrt{6}$ **ANSWER: (C)**

Arithmetic

Part 8: Rates

Virtual Classroom>Arithmetic>Rates

This material corresponds to the Virtual Classroom Instructions in the
PowerPrep DVD/Internet/iApps for Arithmetic

Virtual Classroom

Important Abbreviations
These abbreviations are used throughout the program

POE: Process of Elimination
SARR: Synthesize, Analyze, Reduce, and Restate (has to do with Logical Reasoning)
AC: Answer Choice
QS: Question Stem
LOD: Level of Difficulty

Example Question: What is the least common multiple of 3, 4, and 7? (**This is the call of the question or Question Stem "QS"**)

These are Answer Choices "AC" A, B, C, D, E

(A) 12
(B) 21
(C) 28
(D) 48
(E) 84

Part 8: Rates

<u>**Rate:**</u> A measure of how fast you do something. The most common rate you will see is speed. Our rate, 40 miles/hour – is a measure of how long it takes (1 hour) to travel a certain distance (40 miles).

$$Distance = (Rate) * (Time)$$

$$Time = \frac{Distance}{Rate}$$

$$Rate = \frac{Distance}{Time}$$

These are your three main formulas. They will allow you to calculate how far something travels (at a given rate), how fast something is going or how long it takes something to travel a certain distance. The only trick comes in remembering that you must use the *total* distance traveled and the *total* time taken to find the rate for an entire trip.

Note: Make sure your units match each other! **Example:** Alex runs at a rate of $4 \frac{meters}{sec}$ (also written as 4 meters/sec)

How far has he gone after two minutes? $D = (R)(T)$ D = $(4 \frac{meters}{sec})$(120 seconds) = $\frac{480 \; meters \; seconds}{seconds}$

Cancel the seconds from the numerator and denominator and it becomes: D = 480 meters

In general, a rate is a measure of some quantity divided by time – a measure of how quickly you complete a given task.

PowerPrep Practice Questions Also in the Virtual Classroom on DVD

PowerPrep Practice Questions 20-21

21. Hose A sprays water at a uniform rate of 2 gallons every 30 seconds and Hose B sprays water at a uniform rate of 3 gallons every 40 seconds. If the two hoses run simultaneously how many minutes will it take for them to fill an empty pool with a capacity of 153 gallons?

(A) 8.5 minutes
(B) 18 minutes
(C) 30 minutes
(D) 31 minutes
(E) 72.25 minutes

22. Before Race 2, Kelly's best time in biking 6 miles was 20 minutes. Did Kelly beat this time in Race 2? IF:

(1) Kelly biked Race 2 at a rate of 16 miles/hour.
(2) It took Kelly between 1100 and 1300 seconds to finish Race 2.

(A) Statement (1) BY ITSELF is sufficient to answer the question, but statement (2) is not
(B) Statement (2) BY ITSELF is sufficient to answer the question, but statement (1) is not
(C) Statement 1 and (2) TAKEN TOGETHER are sufficient to answer the question, even though NEITHER statement by itself is sufficient
(D) EITHER statement BY ITSELF is sufficient to answer the question
(E) Statement 1 and 2 TAKEN TOGETHER are NOT sufficient to answer the question, requiring more data pertaining to the problem

Explanation to PowerPrep Practice Question 21

Hose A: **2 gallons/30 seconds**   **Hose B**: **3 gallons/40 seconds**
Now we need to convert the water output for both hose A and B in similar terms so we can compare them.
Hose A = 2 gallons/30 seconds (2 gallons every 30 seconds—you should be able to see this is the same as 4 gallons per minute—but let's go about solving the problem using straight math.

2 gallons per 30 seconds can be written as either: $2 \; gallons / \left(\frac{30}{60}\right) min$ **or** $\frac{2 \; gallons}{\left(\frac{30}{60}\right) min}$

Either way it means 2 gallons every half minute. Now convert this to gallons per min. If hose A can fill 2 gallons every 30 seconds then it can fill 4 gallons per min. **Hose A = 2 gallons / 30 seconds =** $2 \; gallons / \left(\frac{30}{60}\right) min$ = $4 \; gallons/min$

Now let's look at hose B: We know it produces 3 gallons/40 seconds: We can write it this way: $3 \; gallons / \left(\frac{40}{60}\right) min$ or

$\frac{4 \; gallons}{\left(\frac{40}{60}\right) min}$, $\frac{40}{60}$ *of a minute is the same as* $\frac{4}{6}$ *which is the same as* $\frac{2}{3}$. In $\frac{2}{3}$ *of a min* Hose B produces 3 gallons—if we divide 1 min (60 seconds) into 20 second intervals we can see that Hose B is producing 1.5 gallons every 20 seconds.
Check the work: if it produces 1.5 gallons every 20 seconds, then it produces 3 gallons in 40 seconds (that matches the given information), but it also means Hose B produces 4.5 gallons in 60 seconds. Now we have a rate for both hoses that we can compare: **Hose A** = 4 gallons/min   **Hose B** = 4.5 gallons/min   **Together:** A + B spray 8.5 gallons/minute Now we have a full rate (8.5 gallons/min). Convert the standard Rate formula to solve for T (time)

Since we know that (R)(T)=D (rate x time = distance), we can manipulate the formula to solve for T (time) like this: $T = \left(\frac{Distance}{Rate}\right)$, but "distance" is not a variable, we need "volume" or how much total water. Hopefully you can see that "total

water" in this case is the same as "total Distance" in a typical RT=D equation. $T = \left(\frac{Volume}{Rate}\right)$ substitute what we know. Pool

Volume is 153 gallons and the rate is 8.5 gallons/min. $Time = \frac{153 \; gal}{8.5 \; gal/min} = \frac{153 \; gal}{1} * \frac{min}{8.5 \; gal} = \frac{153 \; min}{8.5} = 18 \; min$

Time = 18 minutes <u>ANSWER: (B)</u>

Explanation to PowerPrep Practice Question 22

What are you looking for? Kelly's time (or rate) for Race #2.

What we know:
> Kelly's prior best time was 20 mins for 6 mile course
> Kelly biked Race #2 at the rate of 16 mph
> Kelly finished Race #2 between 1100 and 1300 seconds

Statement 1: If Kelly's best time before race 2 was 6 miles in 20 minutes, we can figure out what that rate would be.

$$(Rate * Time) = Distance \; (RT = D) \quad \text{or} \quad Rate = \frac{Distance}{Time} \quad \text{or} \quad \left(R = \frac{D}{T}\right)$$

In this case the distance was 6 miles and the time was 20 minutes. 20 minutes is 1/3 of an hour.

So plug this information into the formula to find Rate. $\frac{Distance}{Time}$ becomes $\frac{6 \; miles}{\frac{1}{3} \; hour}$ **Invert and multiply:** $\frac{6 \; miles}{1} *$

$\frac{3 \; hours}{1}$ becomes $(6 \; miles \; x \; 3 \; hours) = 18 \; miles/hour$ If she completed Race #2 at a rate of only $16 \; miles/hour$ then we know at this slower rate she did not beat her previous best time. We **DO** have sufficient information.

Another way to figure this problem, is to find out how far Kelly travels in one (1) minute

We know Kelly went 6 miles in 20 minutes. **Divide** 6 miles by 20 minutes to find how far in 1 min. $6/20 = .30 \; (miles/min)$

Now multiple the miles per min by 60 mins (1 hour) to find MPH: $(60 * .30 = 18 \; mph)$

Either way Kelly's prior personal best was $18mph$ and Race #2 was 16mph. So Race #2 was NOT faster than the prior best time. So this statement alone will answer the question...but let's see if statement #2 also is sufficient to answer the question

Statement 2: Kelly's previous best time was 20 minutes, or 1200 seconds ($20 * 60 = 1200$). Statement #2 tells us that Kelly rode Race #2 some place between 1100 and 1300 seconds.

So, we cannot tell from this statement whether Race #2 was competed faster or slower than 1200 seconds. This statement does not give us specific enough information to determine if it took more time or less time than 1200 seconds. We DO NOT have sufficient information.

Statement #1 gave us sufficient information to answer the question, but statement #2 did not give sufficient information...therefore... **ANSWER: (A)**

Extra Sample Questions not in the Virtual Classroom on the DVD

Extra Sample Question 28

28. Which is greater: The number of miles Kelly can bike in one hour if she can bike 6 miles in 20 minutes, or the number of miles David can bike in 2 hours if he can bike 8 miles in 30 minutes.

(A) The number of miles Kelly can bike is greater
(B) The number of miles David can bike is greater
(C) They are equal
(D) Unknown—insufficient information

Explanation to Extra Sample Question 28

What do we know: Kelly bikes 6 mi in 20 mins.   David bikes 8 mi in 30 mins.
Call of the question: Which is greater, Kelly's distance in one hour or David's distance in two hours.

We know each biker's rate so we have to calculate how far they can bike in the given amount of time.

Let's start with Kelly: 6 miles in 20 mins. Since 20 mins is 1/3 of an hour, Kelly can bike 18 miles in 1 hour. $18 \; is \; (3 * 6)$ ...so Kelly's rate is 18mph

Let's look at David: He can bike 8 miles in 30 mins. and 30 mins is ½ of an hour...so we just need to double the distance to find out David's rate in hours. David can bike at 16mph

Now we have rates for both bikers that we can compare: Kelly is 18mph   David is 16mph
So the call of the question asks us to compare how far Kelly can bike in one hour (which we now know is 18 miles) to David's distance in two hours (which we can tell is 32 miles)

Compare: Now we can compare the two--Kelly 18 miles < David's 32 miles
So David wins because: 32 is more than 18 ANSWER: (B)

CONGRATULATIONS!!!
You have completed the Arithmetic Workshop!

Take a break before moving on to the Arithmetic Drills!

Arithmetic Index

Knowledge
Freedom to Learn

Algebra Workbook
Table of Contents
This material corresponds to the Virtual Classroom Instructions in the
PowerPrep DVD/Internet/iApp for Algebra

Virtual Classroom

Algebra
Part 1: Vocabulary
Virtual Classroom>Algebra>Vocabulary
This material corresponds to the Virtual Classroom Instructions in the
PowerPrep DVD/Internet/iApp for Algebra

Virtual Classroom

Important Abbreviations
These abbreviations are used throughout the program

POE: Process of Elimination
SARR: Synthesize, Analyze, Reduce, and Restate (has to do with Logical Reasoning)
AC: Answer Choice
QS: Question Stem
LOD: Level of Difficulty

Example Question: What is the least common multiple of 3, 4, and 7? **(This is the call of the question or Question Stem "QS")**

These are Answer Choices "AC" A, B, C, D, E

  (A)   12
  (B)   21
  (C)   28
  (D)   48
  (E)   84

Part 1: Vocabulary

Vocabulary

Basics

Constant: Any number , **Example:** 3, 21, ½
Variable: A letter which represents some unknown constant or constants. **Example:** $x, 2y, 3z$
Algebraic Expression: Any combination of constants and variables. **Example:** $2x + y, z - 3$
Algebraic Equation: Any expression that is set equal to something else. **Example:** $2x + y = 3, z - 3 = 0$

Exponent Review

Squared: A variable raised to the second power (squared) is that variable multiplied by itself. **Example:** $b^2 = (b * b)$

Negative Exponents: A variable raised to a negative power is a reciprocal of something **Example:** $b^{-3} = \frac{1}{b^3}$

Multiply like variables: To multiply like variables, add exponents: **Example:** $(b^2)(b^3) = b5$
Power to Power: To raise an exponent by a power, multiply exponents: **Example:** $(b^2)^4 = b^8$
Combining variables: To add or subtract variables with like exponents, add or subtract the coefficients of the variables
Example: $21b^2 - 11b^2 = 10b^2$

You cannot add or subtract variables with *different* exponents: **Example:** While $(b^2 + b^2 = 2b^2)$
$b^2 + b^3$ *cannot be added together*
You cannot add or subtract *different* variables with the same exponents: **Example:** $b^2 + c^2$

Combining Like-Terms

Like terms are those with common variables (like x and $2x$). If the variables are raised to some power, then the power value must be the same as well (like $3b^2$ and $4b^2$). Numbers are considered like terms. You can combine like terms by adding or subtracting. **Example:** $3d - 4f - d + 6f + 2d^2 = (3d - d) + (-4f + 6f) + 2d^2 = 2d + 2f + 2d^2$

Expressions

Combining Expressions by $(+/-)$ When adding or subtracting expressions (combinations of terms), make sure all negative signs are distributed first, then combine like terms.
Example: $(2r - 3) - (4r + 6) = 2r - 3 - 4r - 6 = (2r - 4r) + (-3 - 6) = -2r - 9$

PowerPrep Practice Questions Also in the Virtual Classroom on DVD

PowerPrep Practice Questions 1-2

1. If $(x^2 - 2x)$ is subtracted from $(2x^2 + 5x)$, what is the result in terms of x?

    (A) $\quad x^2 + 3x$
    (B) $\quad 3x^2 + 3x$
    (C) $\quad -x^2 - 7x$
    (D) $\quad x^2 + 7x$
    (E) $\quad 2 + 7x$

2. If $y = (-2x^2 + x)$, $then$, $(x^2 - 3x + y) = ?$

    (A) $\quad -3x^2 - 2x$
    (B) $\quad -x^2 - 4x$
    (C) $\quad -x^2 - 2x$
    (D) $\quad -x^2 + 2x$
    (E) $\quad 3x^2 - 2x$

Explanation to PowerPrep Practice Question 1

Quick Answer: Distribute negative sign: $2x^2 + 5x - (x^2 - 2x) = (2x^2 + 5x - x^2 + 2x)$
Combine like terms: $(2x^2 - x^2) + (5x + 2x) = (x^2 + 7x)$
Longer Explanation: If the **1st** quantity $(x^2 - 2x)$ **Is subtracted from the 2nd** quantity $(2x^2 + 5x)$ **Set up like this:**
$(2x^2 + 5x) - (x^2 - 2x)$ **Now distribute negative sign to the 2nd** quantity: $-(x^2 - 2x)$ **becomes** $(-x^2 + 2x)$ **Now you have:** $2x^2 + 5x - x^2 + 2x$ **Now combine the like terms:** $(2x^2 - x^2) + (5x + 2x)$ **Now add and subtract the like terms:** $(2x^2 - x^2)$ **becomes** x^2 **and** $(5x + 2x)$ $becomes$ $7x$ **Final result is:** $x^2 + 7x$ **Answer: (D)**

Explanation to PowerPrep Practice Question 2

Explanation: First, substitute the given value for y in the 1st equation into the 2nd equation.
1st Equation $y = -2x^2 + x$ (gives us "y" in terms of x), **2nd Equation:** $x^2 - 3x + y = ?$

New equation becomes: $x^2 - 3x + (-2x^2 + x) = ?$ **Combine like terms:** $(x^2 - 2x^2) + (-3x + x)$ **Now add and subtract the like terms:** $(x^2 - 2x^2)$ **becomes** $-x^2$ **and** $(-3x + x)$ **becomes** $-2x$ **New term becomes:**
$-x^2 - 2x,$ So $x^2 - 3x + y = -x^2 - 2x$ **Answer: (C)**

Bonus Sample Questions <u>not</u> in the Virtual Classroom on the DVD

Bonus Sample Question 1-3

1. What is the product of $(a)(b)(c)$ if $c = \frac{1}{2ab}$

   (A) 4

   (B) 2

   (C) 0

   (D) $\frac{1}{2}$

   (E) $\frac{3}{4}$

2. Which is greater, the average of $(60 + 2z)$ and $(z - 14)$ or the average of $(y + 8 - z)$ and $(4z + 38 - y)$?

   (A) The average of $(60 + 2z)$ and $(z - 14)$ is greater
   (B) The average of $(y + 8 - z)$ and $(4z + 38 - y)$ is greater
   (C) They are equal
   (D) Unknown—insufficient information3. If $2x + z = 2y \ and \ 2x + 2y + z = 20$ what is the value of y ?

3. If $2x + z = 2y \ and \ 2x + 2y + z = 20$ what is the value of y ?

   (A) 5
   (B) 8
   (C) 10
   (D) 15
   (E) It cannot be determined from the information given.

Explanation to Bonus Sample Question 1

We are given $\left(c = \frac{1}{2ab} \right)$ and then asked what does $(abc) =$? So we must simplify $\left(c = \frac{1}{2ab} \right)$ **and see.** First clear the denominator by multiplying both sides by $(2ab)$ like this: $\left(\frac{2ab}{1} * c \right) = \frac{1}{2ab} * \frac{2ab}{1}$ **Becomes:** $2ab(c) = 1$ (Be sure you understand this concept because it is tested repeatedly) $2abc = 1$ Clear the (2) from the left side so that only abc is left, **becomes:** $\left(\frac{1}{2} * \frac{2}{1} \right)(abc) = \left(\frac{1}{1} * \frac{1}{2} \right)$ **Multiply:** $1(abc) = \frac{1}{2}$ **same as:** $abc = \frac{1}{2}$ <u>**Answer: D**</u>

Explanation to Bonus Sample Question 2

Simplify 1st Average: $\frac{(60+2z)+(z-14)}{2} = \frac{(60-14+2z+z)}{2} = \frac{46+3z}{2}$

Simplify 2nd Average: $\frac{(y+8-z)+(4z+38-y)}{2} = \frac{y-y+8+38-z+4z}{2} = \frac{46+3z}{2}$ <u>**Answer: (C)**</u>

Explanation to Bonus Sample Question 3

If $2x + z = 2y \ and \ 2x + 2y + z = 20$ what is the value of y ?

This is considered a very high level of difficulty. So be sure you understand the reasoning behind this explanation.

We are given two equation with three variables and asked to find the value of y. It is not possible to find the value of three variables with only two equations. At least that's what the test makers are counting on with this sort of question. But there is a trick that you should know.

While the general premise is correct that it takes three (3) equations to solve for three (3) variables or it takes two (2) equations to solve for two (2) variables, it can be solved with fewer equations IF the equations themselves can act as the missing variable.

It's a little tricky, but look at this: $2x + 2y + z = 20$ with just a little manipulation we can make the left side of this equation the same as the left side of the other given equation. **Like this:** $add - 2y$ to both sides, **becomes:** $2x + (2y - 2y) + z = 20 - 2y$ **or** $2x + z = 20 - 2y$

Now we have two equations where the left sides are equal so we can drop out the left side entirely and set the right sides equal. **Like this:** $2x + z = 2y$ and $2x + z = 20 - 2y$ therefore, the $(2x + z)$ *is the same in both equations. So drop it.* **The new equation becomes:** $2y = 20 - 2y$

NOTE: If you don't understand this, look at it this way. If you had a string of equalities, like: $a = b = c = d = x = y = z$, you could drop out the middle and simply say $a = z$ That's what we've done in this case. We had $2y = (2x + z) \ and \ (2x + z) = 20 - 2y$ so we can drop the middle and leave the two ends equal to each other.

$2y = \cancel{(2x + z) \ and \ (2x + z)} = 20 - 2y$ **becomes:** $2y = 20 - 2y$

Now solve $2y = 20 - 2y$ **becomes:** $4y = 20$ **divide:** $y = 5$ <u>**Answer A**</u>

Algebra
Part 2: Factoring

Virtual Classroom> Algebra >Factoring

This material corresponds to the Virtual Classroom Instructions in the
PowerPrep DVD/Internet/iApps for Algebra

Virtual Classroom

Important Abbreviations
These abbreviations are used throughout the program

POE: Process of Elimination
SARR: Synthesize, Analyze, Reduce, and Restate (has to do with Logical Reasoning)
AC: Answer Choice
QS: Question Stem
LOD: Level of Difficulty

Example Question: What is the least common multiple of 3, 4, and 7? (**This is the call of the question or Question Stem "QS"**)

These are Answer Choices "AC" A, B, C, D, E
   (A)   12
   (B)   21
   (C)   28
   (D)   48
   (E)   84

Part 2: Factoring

Factoring Expressions

When you factor an expression, you are finding common coefficients and variables present in every term and removing those commonalities from the expression.

Example: $5x + 25 = [5(x) + 5(5)] = 5(x + 5)$ **Example**: $2x^2 + 6x = [2(x)(x) + 2(3)(x)] = 2x(x + 3)$

PowerPrep Practice Questions Also in the Virtual Classroom on DVD

PowerPrep Practice Questions 3-4

3. If $(2x^2)$ is factored out of $(2x^2 + 6x^4)$, what is the result in terms of x?

   (A) $1 + 3x^2$
   (B) $6x^2$
   (C) $3x^2$
   (D) 4
   (E) $1 + x^2$

4. Given: $(x = 9 - 3y)$ and $(2x + 8y = 36)$, Solve for y.

   (A) 72
   (B) 14
   (C) 36
   (D) 18
   (E) 9

Explanation to PowerPrep Practice Question 3

$2x^2 + 6x^4 = 2(x)(x) + (2)(3)(x)(x)(x)(x)$ Factor out the "like terms": Similar terms are "2" and $(x)(x)$ or x^2
That means we can factor out a $2x^2$ **You write it this way**: $2x^2(1 + 3x^2)$
If you multiplied this back, it would result in $2x^2 + 6x^4$ which is where we started
This problem tests your understanding of multiplying and factoring terms with exponents.

Multiplying Powers: when the bases are the same, find the new power by just **adding the exponents**:$(x^a)(x^b) = x^{(a+b)}$
What you know: First term: $2x^2 = 2(x)(x)$ Second term: $6x^4 = 2(3)(x)(x)(x)(x)$
Factor the 1ˢᵗ Term: If we factor out $2x^2$ from the first term we get **1** because factoring $2x^2$ from $2x^2$ means $2x^2$ can be factored one time from itself.
Factor the 2ⁿᵈ Term: If we factor out $2x^2$ from the second term we are left with $3x^{2\cdot}$ $(2x^2)(3x^2) = 6x^4$ or $2x^2(3)(x)(x) = 6x^4$.
Final result: $2x^2(1 + 3x^2) = 2x^2 + 6x^4$ **Therefore the answer is**: $(1 + 3x^2)$ **Answer: (A)**

Explanation to PowerPrep Practice Question 4

Put the 2ⁿᵈ equation in terms of y. In other words, substitute the value of X in first equation into the "X" term in the 2ⁿᵈ equation.
Like this: 1ˢᵗ equation: $(x = 9 - 3y)$ **2ⁿᵈ equation**: $(2x + 8y = 36)$
Put the value of X in the first equation here: $2x + 8y = 36$ **becomes:** $2(9 - 3y) + 8y = 36$ **Now solve for y:**
$2(9 - 3y) + 8y$ 36 **Multiply:** $18 - 6y + 8y = 36$ **Subtract 18 from both sides:** $-6y + 8y = 18$ **Add like terms:**
$2y = 18$ **Divide by 2 on both sides:** $Y = 9$ **Answer: (E)**

Bonus Sample Questions <u>not</u> in the Virtual Classroom on the DVD

Bonus Sample Question 4-5

4. $(x^2 - 5x + 3) - (5x^2 - 5x - 3)$ is equivalent to:

   (A) $-4x^2 + 10x + 6$
   (B) $6x^2 + 10x + 6$
   (C) $4x^2 + 6$
   (D) $2(x^2 + 6)$
   (E) $-2(2x^2 - 3)$

5. If $6y + 15x = 36$, which is greater, $5x + 2y$ or 13 ?
   (A) $5x + 2y$ is greater
   (B) 13 is greater
   (C) They are equal
   (D) Unknown—insufficient information

Explanation to Bonus Sample Question 4

You are asked to simplify the expression and find its equivalent among the answer choices. This problem tests your ability to multiply expressions, add like terms, and factor.
We start with the given information: $(x^2 - 5x + 3) - (5x^2 - 5x - 3)$ then distribute the negative sign through the second parenthesis. So $5x^2 becomes - 5x^2, -5x becomes 5x, and - 3 becomes 3$
Like this: $(x^2 - 5x + 3) - 5x^2 + 5x + 3$
Now combine the like terms…first we group them together, like this: $(x^2 - 5x^2) + (-5x + 5x) + (3 + 3)$
Next we combine them, like this: $-4x^2 + 6$
It's possible the answer choice could be simply $-4x^2 + 6$ because that is as far as we can go by just combining terms and in some cases this would be the final answer. However, checking the AC's shows this is not one of the AC's. So we have to do more. **Factor out −2 becomes:** $-2(2x^2 - 3)$ This is **Answer E**

You should also notice it is possible to factor out a positive 2. It would look like this: $2(-2x^2 + 3)$ but that is not one of the AC's. The test makers would not give you two answers that could both be correct. <u>Answer E</u>

Explanation to Bonus Sample Question 5

This is a little tricky, but here is how you figure it out: If we factor 3 out of the given equation, we find: $\frac{6y}{3} + \frac{15x}{3} = \frac{36}{3}$

Becomes: $2y + 5x = 12$ **Now we know that:** $2y + 5x = 12$, so the second term (13) is greater than the first term, $2y + 5x$, because that term is equal to 12. <u>Answer: (B)</u>

Multiplying Expressions

FOIL Method

When multiplying one expression by another expression, the order of multiplication is referred to as the FOIL Method. FOIL stand for:

F = First (Multiply first terms in each expression)
O = Outside (Multiply outside terms in each expression)
I = Inside (Multiply inside terms in each expression)
L = Last (Multiply last terms in each expression)

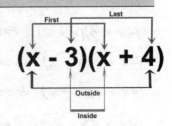

> You use this specifically when multiplying TWO expressions containing TWO terms each. Once you have multiplied the expressions, combine like terms to simplify.
>
> **Example** $(x - 3)(x + 4)$
>
> $F = (x)(x) = x^2$
> $O = (x)(4) = 4x$
> $I = (-3)(x) = -3x$
> $L = (-3)(4) = -12$
>
> $x^2 + 4x + (-3x) + (-12)$ **Becomes:** $x^2 + x - 12$

Example $(2w + 4)(w - 1)$
   $F = (2w)(w) = 2w^2$
   $O = (2w)(-1) = -2w$
   $I = (4)(w) = 4w$
   $L = (4)(-1) = -4$

   $2w^2 + (-2w) + 4w + (-4) = 2w^2 + 2w - 4$

Example $(3a + b)(a + 2b)$
   $F = (3a)(a) = 3a^2$
   $O = (3a)(2b) = 6ab$
   $I = (b)(a) = ab$
   $L = (b)(2b) = 2b^2$

   $3a^2 + 6ab + ab + 2b^2 = 3a^2 + 7ab + 2b^2$

There are three standard FOIL problems you should memorize:

1. $(a + b)^2 = (a + b)(a + b) = (a^2 + 2ab + b^2)$
   $(a + 3)^2 = (a + 3)(a + 3) = a^2 + 2a(3) + 3^2 = a^2 + 6a + 9$

2. $(a - b)^2 = (a - b)(a - b) = a^2 - 2ab + b^2$
   $(a - 3)^2 = (a - 3)(a - 3) = a^2 - 2a(3) + (-3)^2 = a^2 - 6a + 9$

3. $(a - b)(a + b) = a^2 - b^2$
   $(a - 3)(a + 3) = a^2 - (3)(a) + (a)(3) + (-3)^2 = a^2 + 9$

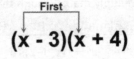

PowerPrep Practice Questions Also in the Virtual Classroom on DVD

PowerPrep Practice Questions 5-6

5. $x(2x + y)^2 =$

   (A) $2x^2 + xy$
   (B) $2x^3 + y^2x$
   (C) $x^3 + x^2y + y^2x$
   (D) $4x^3 + 4x^2y + y^2x$
   (E) $4x^3 + 4x^2y - y^2x$

6. Given: $a = (x + 2)$, $b = (x - 2)$, and $(ab) = 12$,
   Solve for X

   (A)   12
   (B)   4
   (C)   8
   (D)   2
   (E)   -2

Explanation to PowerPrep Practice Question 5

Quick Answer: $x(2x + y)^2$ **Becomes:** $x(2x + y)(2x + y)$
Multiply the binomials first (FOIL): $x[4x^2 + 2xy + 2xy + y^2]$

Combine like terms inside brackets: $x[4x^2 + 4xy + y^2]$
Multiply the x through the entire bracket: $4x^3 + 4x^2y + y^2x$

Full Explanation: This question tests your understanding of quantities raised to an exponent and your ability to distribute using the FOIL method.

First, expand the quantity squared, like this: $x(2x + y)^2$ **Becomes:** $x[(2x + y)(2x + y)]$
Next use FOIL. Reminder: You use FOIL to multiply the terms inside the parenthesis in a specific order: **first, outside, inside, last.** Here's how to solve $(4x + 6)(x + 2)$:

$(4x + 6)(x + 2)$ **First** - multiply the first term in each set of parenthesis: $(4x * x) = 4x^2$

$(4x + 6)(x + 2)$ **Outside** - multiply the two terms on the outside: $(4x * 2) = 8x$

$(4x + 6)(x + 2)$ **Inside** - multiply both of the inside terms: $(6 * x) = 6x$

$(4x + 6)(x + 2)$ **Last** - multiply the last term in each set of parenthesis: $(6 * 2) = 12$

Now just add everything together to get $4x^2 + 14x + 12$.
FOIL in our case: $x(2x + y)^2$ is the same thing as: $x[(2x + y)(2x + y)]$
   First: $2x * 2x = 4x^2$
   Outside $2x * y = 2xy$
   Inside $y * 2x = 2xy$
   Last $= (y * y) = y^2$
Add them all up: $4x^2 + 2xy + 2xy + y^2$ **Combine again:** $4x^2 + 4xy + y^2$
Don't forget the "x" at the beginning of the combine like terms inside: $x[4x^2 + 4xy + y^2]$
Multiply the x through the entire bracket: $4x^3 + 4x^2y + y^2x$ **Answer: (D)**

Explanation to PowerPrep Practice Question 6

Given: $a = (x + 2)$, $b = (x - 2)$, $(ab) = 12$
Explanation: This question tests your ability to distribute binomials using FOIL.
First, substituted what you know about "a" and "b" in terms of x. Like this: $(ab) = 12$
Becomes: $(x + 2)(x - 2) = 12$ **Next, distribute using FOIL**
   First $= (x)(x)$ or x^2
   Outside $= (-2)(x)$ or $-2x$
   Inside $= (2)(x)$ or $2x$
   Outside $= (2)(-2)$ or -4
Now add them up: $(x^2 - 2x + 2x - 4) = 12$ **Combine the middle terms** $(-2x + 2x)$ **Becomes:** $x^2 - 4 = 12$
Add 4 to each side: $x^2 = 16$ **Take square root of each side:** $x = 4$ **Answer (B)**
You can test it by plugging it back into the equation: $(4 + 2)(4 - 2) = 12$ **Becomes:** $6 \times 2 = 12$ **Becomes:** $12 = 12$

Bonus Sample Questions not in the Virtual Classroom on the DVD

Bonus Sample Question 6-8

6. $\left(\frac{1}{4}x^2 - xy + y^2\right) = ?$

   (A) $\left(\frac{1}{4}x - y\right)\left(\frac{1}{4}x - y\right)$

   (B) $\frac{1}{4}x^2 + y^2$

   (C) $x^2 + 2xy + y^2$

   (D) $\left(\frac{1}{2}x - y\right)^2$

   (E) $\left(\frac{1}{4}x - y\right)^2$

7. Which of the following is the product of $(a + 3)$ and $(a + 2)$?

   (A) $2a + 5$
   (B) $7a + 6$
   (C) $a^2 + 5a + 6$
   (D) $a^2 + 6a + 5$
   (E) $a^2 + 6a + 6$

8. Which is greater: $(a + 3)(b - 2)$ or $(ab - 2a + 3b + 6)$?
   (A) $(a + 3)(b - 2)$ is greater
   (B) $(ab - 2a + 3b + 6)$ is greater
   (C) They are equal
   (D) Unknown—insufficient information

Explanation to Bonus Sample Question 6

Quick Answer: $\left(\frac{1}{4}x^2 - xy + y^2\right) = ?$ This problem is in the general format of $(a^2 + 2ab + b^2)$ which is equivalent to

$(a + b)^2$ If $a = \frac{1}{2}x$ and $b = -1$, then $(a + b)^2 = \left(\frac{1}{2}x - y\right)^2$ which is AC D

More Detailed Answer: In the polynomial $\left(\frac{1}{4}x^2 - xy + y^2\right)$ look at the first term $\left(\frac{1}{4}x^2\right)$ You would fact this term as

$\left(\frac{1}{2}x\right) * \left(\frac{1}{2}x\right) = \frac{1}{4}x^2$ The last term is y^2 obviously that is factored as $(y * y) = y^2$ We now know we have

$\left(\frac{1}{2}x \quad y\right)\left(\frac{1}{2}x \quad y\right)$ We only need to figure out the sign in the middle.

Using FOIL it would result in: $\mathbf{F} = \frac{1}{2}x * \frac{1}{2}x = \frac{1}{4}x^2$ $\mathbf{O} = \frac{1}{2}xy$ $\mathbf{I} = \frac{1}{2}xy$ $\mathbf{L} = y * y = y^2$

Again we just need to figure out the signs $(+ or -)$ Since the original polynomial is: $\left(\frac{1}{4}x^2 - xy + y^2\right)$ we must end up with

a middle term of $-xy$ and a last term of $+y^2$ The only way to get both a negative middle term and a positive last term is to

make both signs negative, like this: $\left(\frac{1}{2}x - y\right)\left(\frac{1}{2}x - y\right)$ This would result in a middle term of

$\left(-\frac{1}{2}xy\right)$ and $\left(-\frac{1}{2}xy\right)$ which is the same as $(-1xy)$ or just $(-xy)$ it also gives us $\left(-y * -y = y^2\right)$ for our last term

(which is what we needed). $\left(\frac{1}{2}x - y\right)\left(\frac{1}{2}x - y\right)$ using **FOIL** becomes:

$\mathbf{F} = \left(\frac{1}{2}x * \frac{1}{2}x\right) = \frac{1}{4}x^2$ $\mathbf{O} = -\frac{1}{2}xy$ $\mathbf{I} = -\frac{1}{2}xy$ $\mathbf{L} = (-y * -y) = y^2$

Finally, $\left(\frac{1}{2}x - y\right)\left(\frac{1}{2}x - y\right) = \left(\frac{1}{2}x - y\right)^2$ **Answer D**

Explanation to Bonus Sample Question 7

$(a + 3)(a + 2) = ?$

$F = (a)(a) = a^2$ $O = (a)(2) = 2a$ $I = (3)(a) = 3a$ $L = (3)(2) = 6$

$a^2 + 2a + 3a + 6$ **Combine like terms :** $a^2 + 5a + 6$
POE: always remember to POE. In this case, you could look quickly at the First and Last terms…those are easy to quickly
calculate(a^2 and 6), that means the first term must be a^2 and the last term must be 6…only AC (C) and (E) correctly include
these. so if you had to guess, you could eliminate A,B,D… **Answer: (C)**

Explanation to Bonus Sample Question 8

First expression: Multiply binomials to create expression **FOIL:** $(a + 3)(b - 2)$

$F = (a)(b) = ab$ $O = (a)(-2) = -2a$ $I = (3)(b) = 3b$ $L = (3)(-2) = -6$

$ab - 2a + 3b - 6$

The other term in the given information is: $(ab - 2a + 3b + 6)$
Compare the two terms and eliminate like terms: **First expression=** ~~ab - 2a + 3b~~ $- 6$
Second expression = ~~ab - 2a + 3b~~ $+ 6$ The only terms that are not the same and do not cancel are $(6 \text{ and } -6)$ and
$-6 < 6$ **Therefore, the second expression is greater** **Answer: (B)**

Reverse FOIL

Factoring expression into two binomials

This is simply the reverse of what we just did in the section on FOIL(Multiplying Expressions). Rather than taking two binomials
and multiplying them together to get a final quadratic expression, we will do just the opposite – **start with a quadratic
expression and factor it into two binomials.** **Example** $x^2 + 8x + 12$
1. **First, draw two sets of parenthesis:** ( )( )
2. To get x^2, figure out what two FIRST terms need to be multiplied together to give you this expression?
In this case it is (x)(x). **Fill in the parenthesis.** (x)(x)
3.To calculate the 12, what LAST terms need to be multiplied together to give you this?. **IOW, what are the FACTORS of 12?**

It could be $(1 * 12)$ or $(2 * 6)$ or $(3 * 4)$. Here's where it gets a bit tricky. Next, we need to find the magical numbers which,
when **added** together also give us our middle part of the equation (8x). This is a combination of the **INNER** and **OUTER** terms.
Look at $(2 * 6)$ This will give us the 12 term when multiplied, and also it will give us the 8x middle term when added together

Fill in the parenthesis and check your work. $(x + 6)(x + 2)$
$F = (x)(x) = x^2$
$O = (x)(2) = 2x$
$I = (6)(x) = 6x$
$L = (6)(2) = 12$

$x^2 + 2x + 6x + 12 = x^2 + 8x + 12$ **Looks good!**

$F = (x)(x) = x^2$
$O = (x)(4) = 4x$
$I = (-5)(x) = -5x$
$L = (-5)(4) = -20$

$x^2 + 4x + (-5x) + (-20) = x^2 - x - 20$

Reverse FOIL Example $x^2 - x - 20$

1. ( )( )
2. $x^2 = (x)(x)$ **Becomes:** $(x\ )(x\ )$
3. $-20 = -(1)(20), -(2)(10), -(5)(4)$

What combination of factors, when added together gives us –1?
Answer: $(-5 * 4)$ the product is -20, *the sum is* -1,
Becomes: $(x - 5)(x + 4)$

You can verify your answer by using the **FOIL** method to multiply the binomials and verify the result is the same as your starting equation:

PowerPrep Practice Questions Also in the Virtual Classroom on DVD

PowerPrep Practice Questions 7-8

7. Factor the quadratic into two binomials: $3x^2 - x - 2 =$

(A) $(x - 1)(x + 2)$
(B) $(x + 2)(3x - 1)$
(C) $(2x + 2)(x + 1)$
(D) $(3x + 1)(x - 2)$
(E) $(3x + 2)(x - 1)$

8. What is the value of y in terms of x? IF, y is equal to a factor of $(2x^2 + x - 6)$ *and* y is also equal to a factor of $(x^2 - 4)$.

(A) Statement (1) BY ITSELF is sufficient to answer the question, but statement (2) is not
(B) Statement (2) BY ITSELF is sufficient to answer the question, but statement(1) is not
(C) Statement 1 and (2) TAKEN TOGETHER are sufficient to answer the question, even though NEITHER statement by itself is sufficient
(D) EITHER statement BY ITSELF is sufficient to answer the question
(E) Statement 1 and 2 TAKEN TOGETHER are NOT sufficient to answer the question, requiring more data pertaining to the problem

Explanation to PowerPrep Practice Question 7

Quick Answer: Reverse FOIL is needed to factor this expression.

1. To get $3x^2$ we need to multiply $3(x)(x)$ or $(3x)(x)$ **Becomes:** $(3x\ )(x\ )$
2. The only combination of factors which, when multiplied, give us $- 2$ are either $(-1)(2)$ or $(1)(-2)$. Now we have to decide which combo, when placed in the parenthesis, will give us inner and outer terms that will add to give us $-1x$.
The two options are: $(3x\ 1)(x\ 2)$ or $(3x\ 2)(x\ 1)$
3. $(3x + 2)(x - 1)$ **Answer: (E)**

More Detailed Answer: Factor the quadratic into two binomials: $3x^2 - x - 2 =$ This question tests your ability to factor a quadratic into the product of two binomials--sometimes referred to as REVERSE FOIL.

Factoring: To factor a quadratic, you must express it as the product of two binomials. Factoring a quadratic involves a reverse-FOIL process.

Explanation: Reverse FOIL to factor this expression into two binomials: $x^2 - x - 2 = (?\ x?)(?\ x?)$
First: FOIL, "F" means the first terms, in this case we reverse and ask what do you multiply together to get $3x^2$?
$3x^2 - x - 2$ You need to find the factors of $3x^2$. There are only two factors (1 and 3) Therefore, we know the following: $(3x\ )(x\ )$ The first terms in the binomial we are building would multiply together to give us $3x^2$. which is what we want.

Next, skip to the "L" in FOIL—find the last combination. The last two numbers in each binomial when multiplied give us the term without a variable—in this case we are looking for -2. $(3x^2 - x - 2)$
So, what are the only factors of "$- 2$" = $(1, -2)$ or $(-1, 2)$

Now we know it will look like: $(3x\ 1)(x\ 2)$ or $(3x\ 2)(x\ 1)$
Next, we have to decide which combo, when placed in the parenthesis, will give us inner and outer terms that will add to give us $-x$. **Becomes:** $3x^2 - x - 2$ Therefore, we know it will be one of these: $(3x\ 1)(x\ 2)$ or $(3x\ 2)(x\ 1)$
Remember, the goal is this: $3x^2 - x - 2$ **Let's try the first option:** $(3x\ 1)(x\ 2)$
We've used the "F" and "L" Now we need to do the Inner (I) and Outer (O)—in this case it will result in

inner
$(3x\ 1)(x\ 2)$ **We get:** *Inner* $= 1x$ **and** *Outer* $= 6x$
Outer Outer
Whether we add or subtract these two terms it won't give us the "-x" we need. **Let's try the other option:** $(3x\ 2)(x\ 1)$

inner
$(3x\ 2)(x\ 1)$ **We get:** *Inner* $= 2x$ **and** *Outer* $= 3x$
Outer outer
If $3x$ is negative and $2x$ is positive, it will give us the "$- x$" we need. This means the final binomial will be: $(3x + 2)(x - 1)$
Answer: (E)

Explanation to PowerPrep Practice Question 8

Explanation: What are you looking for? The solution of y in some terms of x.

Statement 1: If we use Reverse FOIL to factor the expression, we find: $(2x^2 + x - 6) =$
First term is $2x^2$. What are the factors of 2? Only 1 and 2.
Therefore, we know: $(2x\quad)(x\quad)$ **Factor the Last term which is 6:** $2x^2 + x - 6$

The factors are (1, 6) (2,3) But bear in mind, while they have to multiply to give us 6, they also have to add to give us 1—the middle term of the quadratic $2x^2 + x - 6$ (multiply to = 6, add to 1) So the factors (2,3) work>

Next we figure out the order—we have two options: $(2x\quad 3)(x\quad 2)$ **or** $(2x\quad 2)(x\quad 3)$
Option 2 will result in 2x and 6x—we cannot add or subtract those to give us 1x
Option 1 will give us 3x and 4x—this will work

Now figure out the right place for the negative sign $(-3x)$ and positive $4x$ are what we want. $(2x\quad - \quad 3)(x\quad + \quad 2)$
If you use FOIL on this binomial, it will result in the quadratic we started with: $2x^2 + x - 6$
Now we have the correct binomials: $(2x\quad - \quad 3)(x\quad + \quad 2)$ **Statement 1** in the given information tells us that y is equal to one of these factors.
Therefore, y is equal to either: $(2x\quad - \quad 3)$ **or** $(x\quad + \quad 2)$ This helps us answer the question, but it's not sufficient on its own. So let's move on to statement 2

Statement 2: we use Reverse FOIL to factor the expression, $(x^2 - 4)$ This time the math is more straightforward.
$(x\quad)(x\quad)$ This will give us x^2
So what are the factors of 4? Two options again $(1,4)$ *and* $(2,2)$

Bear in mind, this quadratic does not have a middle term. Any combination of 1 and 4 will result in a middle term, so that leaves the factors of 2 and 2 as the only viable options.
Now we know: $(x\quad 2)(x\quad 2)$ In this case it won't matter whether the first factor gets the negative sign or the 2nd one gets it…just as long as one "2" is negative and one is positive. That way they multiply to make -4 and they add to 0 and drop out.

So we are left with: $(x - 2)(x + 2)$ Statement 2 in the given information tells us that y is equal to one of these factors.
Therefore, y is equal to either: $(x - 2)(x + 2)$ This helps us answer the question, but it's not sufficient on its own.
Both Statements: But, if we combine the information in Statement 1 and Statement 2, we can see that they share one of the factors. $(x + 2)$ is a factor in both the first and second equations. If y is a factor of both equations, then **y must equal** $(x + 2)$ So if we add the information in statement 1 with the information in statement 2, we can answer the question. **Answer: (C)**

Bonus Sample Questions not in the Virtual Classroom on the DVD

Bonus Sample Question 9-11

9. Which of the following quadratic equations has solutions $x = 5a,\ x = -4b$?

    (A) $x^2 - 2ab = 0$
    (B) $x^2 - x(4b - 5a) - 20ab = 0$
    (C) $x^2 - x(4b + 5a) + 20ab = 0$
    (D) $x^2 + x(4b - 5a) - 20ab = 0$
    (E) $x^2 + x(4b + 5a) + 20ab = 0$

10. Which of the following is equal to the expression $\frac{x^2 - 16}{x - 4}$

    (A) 2
    (B) $\left(\frac{2}{x-4}\right)$
    (C) $x + 4$
    (D) $x - 4$
    (E) x^2

11. If $(a - b = -1)$, then which is greater, $4(a - b) + 6$ or $a^2 - 2ab + b^2$

    (A) $4(a - b) + 6$ is greater
    (B) $a^2 - 2ab + b^2$ is greater
    (C) They are equal
    (D) Unknown—insufficient information

Explanation to Bonus Sample Question 9

There are at least two basic ways to solve this problem. If you understand the underlying form of quadratics just put this in proper form and solve or you could backsolve using the answer choices

First, you will recall how we factor expressions into two binomials in the form:
$(x \pm constant)(x \pm conststant)$ **for example:** $(x + 6)(x + 2) = 0$ where the solution is $(-6, -2)$

F: x^2
O: $4bx$
I: $-5ax$
L: $-20ab$

The call-of-the-question is: Which of the following quadratic equations has solutions: $x = 5a,\ x = -4b$? This tells us the corresponding binomial must be: $(x - 5a)(x + 4b) = 0$ so the solution for x *would be either* $(5a)$ *or* $(-4b)$ (what we were given). Either of these makes the binomial equal zero, which is what we want.
Now use FOIL to expand the binomial: $(x - 5a)(x + 4b) = 0$ (see box on left)
Put these terms together, becomes: $x^2 + 4bx - 5ax - 20ab = 0$

A quick search of the ACs shows this form of the answer is not given, so there is still another step left. That is to factor out an "x" from the middle two terms. **Like this:** $x^2 + 4bx - 5ax - 20ab = 0$ **becomes:** $x^2 + x(4b - 5a) - 20ab = 0$
See AC D. Answer D

Backsolving: Test each possible AC by plugging in either the $(x = 5a)$ or $(x = -4b)$. Unfortunately, you may have to check BOTH answers if you get two results that seem to work. In that case, you'll need to check the second option. When you check the 2nd option, one of the answer choices will fall out. If it returns a zero, then it's a keeper until you check them all. We'll use $(x = 5a)$ to start with (but you could use $(-4b)$ for x also).

Test each possible AC:
(A) $x^2 - 2ab = 0$,
(B) $x^2 - x(4b - 5a) - 20ab = 0$,
(C) $x^2 - x(4b + 5a) + 20ab = 0$,
(D) $x^2 + x(4b - 5a) - 20ab = 0$,
(E) $x^2 + x(4b + 5a) + 20ab = 0$

Test = 5a :

(A) $x^2 - 2ab = 0$ becomes: $(5a)^2 - 2ab = 0$ becomes: $25a^2 - 2ab = 0$ becomes: $a(25a - 2b) = 0$ that's as far as you can go.

(B) $x^2 - x(4b - 5a) - 20ab = 0$ becomes: $(5a)^2 - (5a)(4b - 5a) - 20ab = 0$ becomes: $25a^2 - 20ab + 25a^2 - 20ab = 0$ becomes $50a^2 - 40ab = 0$ **that's as far as you can go.**

(C) $x^2 - x(4b + 5a) + 20ab = 0$ becomes $(5a)^2 - 5a(4b + 5a) + 20ab = 0$ becomes: $25a^2 - 20ab - 25a^2 + 20ab = 0$ **both terms fall out $(25a^2 - 25a^2) + (20ab - 20ab) = 0$ *becomes* $0 = 0$
So AC C is a keeper so far, but we should check the other AC's and see if they return zero for $x = 5a$

**(D) $x^2 + x(4b - 5a) - 20ab = 0$ becomes $(5a)^2 + 5a(4b - 5a) - 20ab = 0$
becomes: $25a^2 + 20ab - 25a^2 - 20ab = 0$ becomes: $(25a^2 - 25a^2) + (20ab - 20ab) = 0$ or $0 = 0$
This AC also is a keeper so far for $x = 5a$ **we'll need to check it for** $x = -3a$

(E) $x^2 + x(4b + 5a) + 20ab = 0$ becomes: $(5a)^2 + 5a(4b + 5a) + 20ab = 0$
becomes: $25a^2 + 20ab + 25a^2 + 20ab = 0$ becomes: $(25a^2 + 25a^2) + (20ab + 20ab) = 0$ **or**
$50a^2 + 40ab = 0$ becomes: $10a(5a + 4b) = 0$ **that's as far as you can go**

We have two possible candidates: **AC C and D**…all the other AC's have been eliminated. So now we should test the two remaining AC's with the other option that was provided: $(x = -4b)$

Test $(x = -4b)$:

(C) $x^2 - x(4b + 5a) + 20ab = 0$ becomes: $(-4b)^2 - (-4b)(4b + 5a) + 20ab = 0$ becomes:
$(16b^2 + (4b)(4b + 5a) + 20ab = 0$ becomes: $(16b^2 + 16b^2 + 20ab + 20ab) = 0$ becomes:
$(32b^2 + 40ab) = 0$ **factor:** $8b(4b + 5a) = 0$ **that's as far as you can go**

Since $(x = -4a)$ *did not work on AC C it* **should work on AC D**…let's see:

(D) $x^2 + x(4b - 5a) - 20ab = 0$ becomes: $(-4b)^2 + (-4b)(4b - 5a) - 20ab = 0$ becomes:
$16b^2 - 16b^2 + 20ab - 20ab = 0$ as you can see, the terms all cancel and become
$(16b^2 - 16b^2) + (20ab - 20ab) = 0$ or $0 = 0$

So AC D returns zero for BOTH possible options: $(x = 5a)$ and $(x = -4b)$ <u>Answer D</u>

Explanation to Bonus Sample Question 10

Factor the difference of perfect squares in the numerator first, $(x^2 - 16)$ becomes: $\dfrac{(x+4)(x-4)}{x-4}$
Now cancel the like terms in the numerator and denominator $(x - 4)$ cancels. **This leaves:** $(x + 4)$ <u>Answer: (C)</u>

Explanation to Bonus Sample Question 11

Simplify the First expression: **Substitute** $(a - b) = -1$ becomes: $4(a - b) + 6$ **Becomes:** $4(-1) + 6$
Simplify: $4(-1) + 6$ **Simplify:** $-4 + 6 = 2$ **Factor the second expression:** $a^2 - 2ab + b^2$ **Becomes:** $(a - b)(a - b)$
Substitute $(a - b) = -1$ **Becomes:** $(a - b)(a - b)$ **Substitute becomes:** $(-1)(-1) = 1$ **Now compare:** $4(a - b) + 6$
= 2 and $a^2 - 2ab + b^2 = 1$

Therefore, $2 > 1$ <u>Answer: (A)</u>

Algebra
Part 3: Solving Equations

Virtual Classroom> Algebra >Solving Equations

This material corresponds to the Virtual Classroom Instructions in the
PowerPrep DVD/Internet/iApps for Algebra

Virtual Classroom

Important Abbreviations
These abbreviations are used throughout the program

POE: Process of Elimination
SARR: Synthesize, Analyze, Reduce, and Restate (has to do with Logical Reasoning)
AC: Answer Choice
QS: Question Stem
LOD: Level of Difficulty
Example Question: What is the least common multiple of 3, 4, and 7? **(This is the call of the question or Question Stem "QS")**
These are Answer Choices "AC" A, B, C, D, E

Part 3: Solving Equations

Linear Equations, one variable

Example: $3x - 7 = x + 5$

Add 7 and –x to both sides
$$3x - 7 = x + 5$$
$$\underline{-x + 7 \quad -x + 7}$$
$$2x + 0 = 12$$

A linear equation is defined as one with no exponents on the variables. (It's highest degree →1st order). Solving the equation means figuring out what the value or values of the variables are. To do this, you combine all the like variables on one side and all the constants (numbers) on the other side of the equation.

Divide both sides by 2: $\frac{2x}{2} = \frac{12}{2}$ Becomes: $x = 6$ **Test it:** If x=6, substitute it back into the equation $3x - 7 = x + 5$ becomes: $3(6) - 7 = 6 + 5$ **Becomes**: $18 - 7 = 11$ **Finally**: **11 = 11**

PowerPrep Practice Questions Also in the Virtual Classroom on DVD

PowerPrep Practice Questions 9-10

9. What is the area of a square if one side equals $(12 - x)$ and one side equals $2x$?

(A) 4
(B) 8
(C) 16
(D) 32
(E) 64

10. If $\frac{2}{5}$ of y is 70, what number is 10 percent of y?

(A) 15
(B) 17.5
(C) 35
(D) 44
(E) 175

Explanation to PowerPrep Practice Question 9

What is the area of a square if one side equals $(12 - x)$ and one side equals $2x$? In order to solve for the area, we need to know the length of one side of the square. Since we know all sides of the square are equal, we can set the two expressions equal to each other. We are told that one side of the square is $(12 - x)$ We are told that one side of the square is $(2x)$ Since all sides of a square are equal, we can conclude that: $(12 - x) = (2x)$ Now we have an equation with a variable and we can solve for that variable:

$(12 - x) = (2x)$ **Add x to both sides:** $12 - x = 2x$ **Becomes:** $12 = 3x$ **Now Divide by 3:** $\frac{12}{3} = \frac{3x}{3}$ **Simplify:** $4 = x$ This just tells us the value of x, but we can't stop there. We have to plug this value back into either or both of the expressions to find out what the length of the side is. **Solve for one side:** If $x = 4$ then, $(2x) = 2(4) = 8$ **Check it with the other expression:** If $x = 4$ then, $12 - x = 8$ **Solve for area:** $Area = (side)^2 = (8)^2 = 64$ **Answer: (E)**

Explanation to PowerPrep Practice Question 10

10. If $\frac{2}{5}$ of y is 70, what number is 10 percent of y? **Explanation: First**, Write the given information as an equation and solve: $70 = \frac{2}{5}(y)$ **Multiply** both sides by 5/2 to clear the fraction from the right side and isolate y: $70\left(\frac{5}{2}\right) = y$ **Multiply:** $\frac{350}{2} = y$ **Divide:** 175 = y Now we know y is 175. **Now we have to find 10% of 175.** This tests your knowledge of percents. 10% is also .10 **Therefore**, .10 x 175 is the proper equation. **Move the decimal 1 place to get the correct answer** 175 becomes **17.5** **Answer: (B)**

Bonus Sample Questions <u>not</u> in the Virtual Classroom on the DVD

Bonus Sample Question 12-13

12. If $x^2 = d$ and $x = 2$, then in simplest terms what is $\dfrac{x^2}{\left(\sqrt{d}\right)^3}$?

(A) $\frac{1}{\sqrt{x}}$
(B) $\frac{1}{2}$
(C) $\frac{x^3}{x^2}$
(D) 2
(E) $\frac{1}{2}x^2$

13. If $(2.4 + .6 + .3 + 1.7 + .5y) = 7.5$, then which is greater, 2.5 or y?

(A) 2.5 is greater
(B) y is greater
(C) They are equal
(D) Unknown—insufficient information

Explanation to Bonus Sample Question 12

11. $\dfrac{x^2}{\left(\sqrt{d}\right)^3} = \dfrac{x^2}{\left(\sqrt{x^2}\right)^3} = \dfrac{x^2}{(x)^3} = \dfrac{x*x}{x*x*x} = \dfrac{1}{x}$ (Substitute $x = 2$ becomes) $\dfrac{1}{x} = \dfrac{1}{2}$ You could also substitute $x = 2$ at the

second step when we got rid of the "d" $\frac{x^2}{(\sqrt{d})^3} = \frac{x^2}{(\sqrt{x^2})^3}$ $\frac{x^2}{(\sqrt{x^2})^3}$ if you substituted $x = 2$ here it

becomes: $\frac{2^2}{\sqrt{2^2}^3} = \frac{4}{2^3} = \frac{4}{8} = \frac{1}{2}$ Either way we get $\frac{1}{2}$ **Answer B**

Explanation to Bonus Sample Question 13

Solve the linear equation for y: $2.4 + .6 + .3 + 1.7 + .5y = 7.5$ Simplify: $5 + .5y = 7.5$

Add -5 to both sides: $5y = 2.5$ **Now Divide by** .5 $\frac{.5y}{.5} = \frac{2.5}{.5}$ Becomes: $y = 5$ **Now compare the two options**

2.5 *and* $y = 5$, **obviously, 2.5 < 5** Answer: (B)

Linear Equations, two variables

Sometimes you need to solve for one variable in terms of another variable. This is similar to solving Linear Equations, one variable. Now you simply combine all the like variables (the one you are solving for) on one side of the equation, and everything else (variables and constants) on the other side.

Example: What is the value of a in terms of b if, $4a + 12b - 6 = 2 + 2a + 4b$

$4a + 12b - 6 = 2 + 2a + 4b$ **Add $-2a$:** $(2a + 12b - 6 = 2 + 4b)$ **Now Add $-12b$ Becomes:** $2a - 6 = 2 - 8b$ **Add 6:**

$2a = 8 - 8b$ **Divide by 2:** $a = \frac{8 - 8b}{2}$ **Becomes:** $a = 4 - 4b$

PowerPrep Practice Questions Also in the Virtual Classroom on DVD

PowerPrep Practice Questions 11-12

11. If $4x + 3y = x - \frac{1}{2}y$, what is x in terms of y?

   (A)   -7/6y
   (B)   -6/7y
   (C)   y
   (D)   6y
   (E)   7y

12. If $2x + 5y = 2$, then x =

   (A)   ½ (-5y)
   (B)   1 – 5y
   (C)   2 – 5y
   (D) $\frac{2+5y}{2}$
   (E) $\frac{2-5y}{2}$

Explanation to PowerPrep Practice Question 11

Quick Answer: If $4x + 3y = x - \frac{1}{2}y$, what is x in terms of y?

We need to isolate x on one side of the equation to find what it equals: $4x + 3y = x - \frac{1}{2}y$

Add $-x$: $3x + 3y = -\frac{1}{2}y$ **Add $-3y$:** $3x = -3.5y$ **Divide by 3:** $x = -\frac{3.5y}{3} = -\frac{7}{6}y$ Answer: (A)

Detailed Explanation: This question tests your understanding of solving one variable in terms of another. If you did not understand "in terms of y", you could look at the answer choices and see they are all in terms of y. Solve the equation with x isolated on one side and y on the other.   When you simplify the equation like this, it results in an equation that says X is expressed in terms of Y.

First, we need to isolate x on one side of the equation to find what it equals in terms of y

$4x + 3y = x - \frac{1}{2}y$ You could begin clearing either the left or right side, but we will begin by clearing x from the right-hand side. **Subtract x from both sides:** $(4x - x) + 3y = (x - x) - ½(y)$ **Now Add becomes:** $3x + 3y = -½(y)$ **Subtract 3y**

from both sides: $3x + 3y - 3y = -3y - ½(y)$ **Add** $3x = -3½ y$ **Divide both sides by 3:** $\frac{3x}{3} = \frac{-3\frac{1}{2}y}{3}$ **Becomes**;

$x = \frac{-3\frac{1}{2}y}{3}$ We've isolated x and answered the equation for y in terms of x. **We still have to simplify the fraction.**

This can be tricky if you are a little rusty. First make the numerator $-3½$ into a fraction $-7/2$ (this is the same as $-3\,½$)

We also have to divide $-3\,½$ by 3. But, dividing the numerator by 3 is the same as multiplying by $\frac{1}{3}$ **Therefore,** $\frac{-7}{2}$ *

$\frac{1}{3} = -\frac{-7}{6}$ **Finally,** $x = -\frac{7}{6}y$ Answer: (A)

Explanation to PowerPrep Practice Question 12

If $2x + 5y = 2$, then x =? **Explanation: Solve for x in terms of y, which means just solve for x:**
First, we have to isolate x on one side of the equation. We'll use the left side: **Subtract 5y from**

both sides: Now divide both sides by 2 to isolate the x: $\frac{2x}{2} = \frac{(2-5y)}{2}$ **Simplify:** $x = \frac{2-5y}{2}$

Answer: (E)

$$2x + 5y = 2$$
$$\underline{\quad -5y \quad -5y \quad}$$
$$2x \qquad = 2 - 5y$$

Bonus Sample Questions <u>not</u> in the Virtual Classroom on the DVD

Bonus Sample Question 14-15

14. If $x + 5 = y$ then $5x + 25 =?$

(A) $y + 5$
(B) $y + 25$
(C) $5y$
(D) $5y + 5$
(E) $5y + 25$

15. If $\frac{3x}{2} = \frac{y}{8}$ then which is greater, x or $\frac{y}{12}$

(A) x is greater

(B) $\frac{y}{12}$ is greater

(C) They are equal

(D) Unknown—insufficient information

Explanation to Bonus Sample Question 14

We are told that $(x + 5) = y$ **and then asked what would** $5x + 25 =?$

This is a case of two equations and two variables. So we should calculate one variable in terms of the other and then substitute. In this case, we convert the first equation as follows:

$x + 5 = y$ **add** -5 *to both sides,* **becomes**: $x = (y - 5)$ **Now substitute** this value into the second equation and simplify: $5x + 25 =?$ **substitute** $x = (y - 5)$ into $5x + 25 =?$ **becomes**: $5(y - 5) + 25 =?$ **Now simplify,**: $5y - 25 + 25$ **add, the 25's cancel each other and it becomes:** $5y$ which is **AC C** <u>Answer C</u>

Explanation to Bonus Sample Question 15

If we cross multiply the two ratios, we find: $\frac{3x}{2} = \frac{y}{8}$ **Now Multiply by 2:** $3x = \frac{2y}{8}$

Multiply by 8: $24x = 2y$ **Divide by 2:** $12x = y$ **Divide by 12:** $x = \frac{y}{12}$ If $= \frac{y}{12}$, which is greater $\frac{y}{12}$ or $\frac{y}{12}$, they are equal. <u>Answer: (C)</u>

Linear Equations, inequalities

Inequalities are very similar to regular equations. You want to combine your variable on one side of the equation and constants on the other. There is one trick to watch out for. When you multiply or divide the inequality by a **NEGATIVE NUMBER,** you **MUST** change the direction of the inequality.

(Remember an inequality means you are usually solving for a range of answers, not just one.)

Example: If $x + 6 > 3x - 4$, solve for x.

$x + 6 > 3x - 4$ **Add** $-x$: $6 > 2x - 4$ **Add 4:** $10 > 2x$ **Divide by 2:** $\frac{10}{2} > x$ **Becomes:** $5 > x$ **or** $x < 5$

Example: If $5x + 3 < 2x + 12$ *is x* > 6?

$5x + 3 < 2x + 12$ **Add** $-2x$: $3x + 3 < 12$ **Add** -3: $3x < 9$ **Divide by 3:** $x < \frac{9}{3}$ or $x < 3$

So we've found out that $x < 3$ *and NOT greater than* 6

PowerPrep Practice Questions Also in the Virtual Classroom on DVD

PowerPrep Practice Questions 13-14

13. If $-3x + 4 > 5$, which of the following is true?
(A) $x \neq -1$
(B) $x = 0$
(C) $x < -1/3$
(D) $x > 1/3$
(E) $-3x < 1$

14. Solve $4(x - 2) + 4 \geq 3(2x - 3)$

(A) $\frac{5}{2} \leq x$
(B) $x \geq -4$
(C) $x \leq \frac{5}{2}$
(D) $-x < 4$
(E) $4 \leq x$

Explanation to PowerPrep Practice Question 13

If $-3x + 4 > 5$, which of the following is true? We need to isolate x on one side of the equation to find what it equals:

Simplify: $-3x + 4 > 5$ **Add** -4: $-3x > 1$ **Divide by** -3 **(WATCH OUT!!!! SWITCH THE SIGN)** $x < -\frac{1}{3}$

** Remember when you divide an inequality by a negative number, you MUST switch the inequality. <u>Answer: (C)</u>

More Explanation: solving an inequality is no different (except for one issue) than solving a regular equation. The one difference is when you multiply or divide across the inequality sign—remember to switch the direction of the sign. **See the note below**. **We need to isolate x on one side of the inequality to find what it equals:**

Subtract 4 from both sides: Now divide both sides by -3: $-\frac{3x}{-3} > \frac{1}{-3}$ **BUT SWITCH THE**

SIGN: $-\frac{3x}{-3} < \frac{1}{-3}$ **Simplify, This becomes:** $x < -\frac{1}{3}$ <u>**Answer: (C)**</u>

$$\begin{array}{r} -3x + 4 > 5 \\ \underline{-4 \quad -1} \\ -3x \quad > 1 \end{array}$$

Notice that in the last example, the inequality had to be reversed because we dived by a negative number. Remember the rule that anytime you multiply or divide across the inequality, you have to change its direction.

If it helps, try to visualize this: start with $x > y$, then what happens if you multiply (or divide) both sides with a negative number (in this case -1) $x > y$ becomes $-x < -y$, just as $10 > 5$ so is $-10 < -5$.

Intuitively, this idea makes sense, and it might help you remember this special rule of inequalities. Multiplication by a negative is an abstraction that is visualized best by imagining a reflection.

If an airplane is flying above the tree tops, and you look at the reflection, you have an airplane flying below the treetop. What was "above" (greater than) becomes "below" (less than) in the reflection.

** **Remember** when you divide an inequality by a negative number, you MUST switch the inequality.

Explanation to PowerPrep Practice Question 14

Solve $4(x - 2) + 4 \geq 3(2x - 3)$ **Explanation:** First we will multiply through and simplify; then we'll solve:
Multiply to expand the quantities $4(x - 2)$ and $3(2x - 3)$ => $4(x - 2) + 4 \geq 3(2x - 3)$ **Becomes:** $4x - 8 + 4 \geq 6x - 9$
Simplify (add $-8 + 4$) => $4x - 8 + 4 \geq 6x - 9$ **Becomes**: $4x - 4 \geq 6x - 9$ **Subtract $4x$ from both sides *:** $4x - 4 \geq$
$6x - 9$ Becomes: $-4 \geq 2x - 9$ **Add 9 to both sides:** $-4 \geq 2x - 9$ Becomes: $5 \geq 2x$ *Divide by 2:* $\frac{5}{2} \geq x$ **Switch**

direction ** $x \leq \frac{5}{2}$ <u>**Answer (C)**</u>

*Important Notes: Why did we move the "$3x$" over to the right-hand side, instead of moving the "$4x$" to the left-hand side? Because moving the smaller term avoids having a negative coefficient on the variable, which lessens the chance of forgetting to flip the sign when you multiply/divide by a negative. Either way works, if this makes sense use if—if not, don't worry.

** Why did we switch the inequality in the last line and put the variable on the left? Because some people are more comfortable with inequalities when the answers are formatted this way—with the variable on the left. But, this did not change the value and is not the same thing as flipping the inequality sign when multiplying/dividing by a negative. This flip was for aesthetic purposes only.

 Again, it's only a matter of taste. The form of the answer as, $\frac{5}{2} \geq x$, is perfectly acceptable.

As long as you remember to flip the inequality sign when you multiply or divide through by a negative, you shouldn't have any trouble with solving linear inequalities.

Bonus Sample Questions <u>not</u> in the Virtual Classroom on the DVD

Bonus Sample Question 16-18

16. If $(a + b) = 30$ and $a > 15$, then which of the following must be true?

    (A) $b > 0$
    (B) $b < 15$
    (C) $b = 15$
    (D) $b > 15$
    (E) $a < 45$

17. If $(11 + 3y > 29)$, then which is greater, y or 6

    (A) y is greater
    (B) 6 is greater
    (C) They are equal
    (D) Unknown—insufficient information

18. If $(-\frac{1}{2}x^2 + 10 > 4)$ then which is greater, -24 or x^2

    (A) -24 is greater
    (B) x^2 is greater
    (C) They are equal
    (D) Unknown—insufficient information

Explanation to Bonus Sample Question 16

Quick Answer: $a + b = 30$ and $a > 15$
Substitute $a > 15$ *into the first equality and it becomes*: *(all numbers greater than* 15) + b = 30.
Subtract (all numbers greater than 15) from both sides: $b = 30 -$ (all numbers greater than 15)
$b = 30 - (< 15)$ This means if we subtract all numbers greater than 15...that is 16,17,18,19,20...
We are left with $b = $ *(all numbers less than* 15) which is the same as saying ($b < 15$) all numbers less than 15.

Test a sample just to prove it: if *b is all numbers less than* 15, pick one. let's say 14 and plug it into the original equation $a + b = 30$ **becomes** $a + 14 = 30$ **add -14 *to both sides*:** $a = 30 - 14$ or $a = 16$ Which is also greater than 15, which was the other requirement.

Hopefully you can see that as *b gets smaller and smaller (less than* 15) it means we subtract less and less from 30, which means the final outcome for the variable "a" will get larger and larger. We just tested the pivotal case where $b = 14$ and the result was $a = 16$ (which fits the 2nd requirement of $a > 15$) As "b" gets smaller, "a" will get larger.

The bottom line answer is *b must be less than* 15 which is written as $b < 15$ **Answer B**

Backsolve: This is a Must Be True (MBT) style question. These questions test your logic skills as much as anything. We are given two facts: 1. $(a + b) = 30$ and, 2. $(a > 15)$, We must accept these two facts and then decide which of the following AC's MBT based on the set of two facts we are given.

MBT question can be tricky so be careful. There are a few ways to approach this question. Here we will backsolve by first solving for "a" and then testing each AC. $(a + b) = 30$ add $-b$ to each side to isolate the "a", it becomes: $a = (30 - b)$ **and** $a > 15$ Now we test each AC.

(A) $b > 0$ **Does b have to be greater than zero**. IOW, can we find a "b" that is less than zero that still meets the two criteria above. Let's test $b = -1$. Remember we're looking for a single case that DOES NOT FIT. If this works then this AC is not true "all the time". Remember we are looking for AC's that MBT 100% of the time…so if we can find a single case that does not work then it nullifies the entire AC.   If $b = -1$ what result? Plug it into the **first given:**
$a = (30 - b)$ substitute $b = -1$ becomes: $a = \big(30 - (-1)\big)$ the two negative signs cancel and we are left with: $a = (30 + 1)$ or $a = 31$
So what does this mean? This is where they test your reasoning skills and logic. There's a lot happening all at once. We tested a situation that was against AC A. AC A said *b must be greater than zero*, and we just tested a situation where *b was LESS than zero*. But it still resulted in an outcome that was consistent with our given information…that "*a*" *MUST BE greater than* 15. Our result was ($a = 31$) which is obviously greater than 15.

So we proved AC A is false for the case ($b = -1$)…it is NOT a MBT—there are cases that disprove it…So knock this AC out.

(B) $b < 15$ **Does "b" have to be LESS THAN 15 so that "a" is always GREATER THAN 15. Let's test this case. If $b = 14$ what result? $a = 30 - b$ becomes: $a = 30 - 14$ or $a = 16$ Obviously this returned a result greater than 15, which it must if this is to be MBT.   If you look at this equation: $a = (30 - 14)$, 14 is b and as we subtract ever smaller numbers from 30, the result will be an ever increasing "a". We just tested the pivotal case, where $b = 14$ and it gave us a true result. Therefore, this AC MBT for every number *b* that is LESS THAN 15.

(C) $b = 15$ **We just showed in AC B, that the case of $b = 14$ is the limit or pivotal case.** Therefore, $b = 15$ will return a false result. But test it to see. $a = (30 - 15)$ *becomes* $a = 15$, but 15 is not GREATER THAN 15, which is the requirement in the given information that $a > 15$. Therefore, $b = 15$ returns a FALSE answer and is NOT a MBT.

(D) $b > 15$ **We just showed that $b < 15$ is a MBT and $b = 15$ is false.** Therefore, it should be easy to see that $b > 15$ will always be false. But check it out. $a = 30 - 16$ becomes: $a = 14$ and 14 is NOT GREATER than 15. So this is false. In fact it will always be false. It's a MBF and not a MBT

(E) $a < 45$ **This AC is not relevant.** It contradicts the given information that $a > 15$ *in all cases*. You can't restrict "a" to be *between* 15 *and* 45 which is what this AC says. The variable "a" would have to be $15 < a < 45$ ("a" greater than 15 but less than 45) There is nothing that forces this conclusion as a MBT. **Answer B**

Explanation to Bonus Sample Question 17

Solve the inequality for y: $(11 + 3y > 29)$
Add -11: $3y > 18$ **Divide by 3:** $y > \frac{18}{3}$ *or* $y > 6$ **Becomes:** *y is greater than* 6   **Answer: (A)**

Explanation to Bonus Sample Question 18

First: Solve for x^2: $\left(-\frac{1}{2}x^2 + 10 > 4\right)$ **Add -10:** $-\frac{1}{2}x^2 > 4 - 10$ **Becomes:** $-\frac{1}{2}x^2 > -6$
Multiply by -2 (SWITCH THE SIGN!!) $x^2 < 12$
Less than 12 means all number to the left (on a number line) of 12…but not negative because no real number squared can be negative…that would require imaginary numbers which is beyond the scope of the SAT 1 Math.

The question asks which is GREATER: -24 or x^2
We know that x^2 is between 0 and 12. So which is GREATER -24 *or or a number between* 0 *and* 12?
Answer: x^2 is Greater. You could also notice that any number squared must be greater than -24 because no real number squared can be negative. Either way the answer is x^2 is greater **Answer: (B)**

Two equations, two unknowns

This type of problem gives you two equations, each containing two variables. It asks you to either solve for one of the variables, or both of the variables. Solving for a variable requires two steps:
1. Use one equation to convert one variable in terms of the other—Which is exactly what we just did in linear equations with two variables.
2. Substitute this variable equality into the second equation and solve for the second variable
    (If needed, plug the value of the first variable into either equation to solve for the second variable.)

Example What is the value of y if: $(x + 2y = 10)$ and $(2x - 3y = -8)$
1. Use the first equation to solve for x: $(x + 2y = 10)$ **Add $-2y$ becomes**: $x = 10 - 2y$ (now we have y in terms of x)
2. Substitute this in for x in the first equation: 2nd equation: $2x - 3y = -8$ Becomes: $2(10 - 2y) - 3y = -8$, Now we have an equation with only one variable and we can solve it $2(10 - 2y) - 3y = -8$ **Multiply:** $20 - 4y - 3y = -8$
Combine like-terms: $20 - 7y = -8$ **Add -20:** $-7y = -28$ **Divide by -7:** $y = -\frac{28}{-7} = 4$

PowerPrep Practice Questions Also in the Virtual Classroom on DVD

PowerPrep Practice Questions 15-16

15. Given: $(2x + 3y = 9)$ and $(x + 4y = 7)$ What is the value of x?

   (A) -1
   (B) $1/3$
   (C) $7/4$
   (D) $9/5$
   (E) 3

16. Given: $(6x + 3y = 42)$ and $(5y - 2x = -2)$ What is the value of x and y ?

   (A) 6, 2
   (B) 2, 6
   (C) 4, 2
   (D) 4, 6
   (E) 6, 4

Explanation to PowerPrep Practice Question 15

Given: $2x + 3y = 9$ *and* $x + 4y = 7$ What is the value of x?
Select one equation and solve for a variable. The easiest is to solve for x in: $x + 4y = 7$ **Add** $-4y$: $x = 7 - 4y$
Now we have y in terms of x and we can substitute into the other equation.

Sub into Equation 1: $2x + 3y = 9$ Put $x = 7 - 4y$ **into the x term**: $2(7 - 4y) + 3y = 9$
Now we only have y terms (the x term has been converted to y) Now we can solve it. $2(7 - 4y) + 3y = 9$

Multiply: $14 - 8y + 3y = 9$ **Add** -14: $(-8y + 3y = -5)$ **Combine like-terms**: $-5y = -5$ **Divide by** -5: $y = \left(-\frac{5}{-5}\right) = 1$
Now find the x variable: Sub $(y = 1)$ into either equation, solve for x: $(x + 4y = 7)$ **Becomes**: $x + 4(1) = 7$ **Simplify**:
$x + 4 = 7$ **Simplify**: $x = 3$

Now we know the x and the y: $x = 3$, $y = 1$ **Check these answers in either or both original equations:**

1st **equation**: $2x + 3y = 9$ **Becomes**: $2(3) + 3(1) = 9$ **Becomes**: $6 + 3 = 9$ **Becomes**: $9 = 9$
2nd **equation**: $x + 4y = 7$ **Becomes**: $3 + 4(1) = 7$ **Becomes**: $3 + 4 = 7$ **Becomes**: $7 = 7$
They both check out.   Answer: (E)

More Detailed Explanation: This question tests your ability to solve for two variables with two equations. We need to solve one equation for x or y and then use that information to solve the other equation.

Like this: We think the easier way is to begin solving for x in the equation $x + 4y = 7$
In this equation the x is already alone without a coefficient (the number in front of the variable)

FYI: In the first equation, the x coefficient is 2 and the y coefficient is 3.
Let's start: $x + 4y = 7$ **Subtract 4y from both sides:** $x + 4y = 7$ **Becomes:** $x = 7 - 4y$
Now we have an equation where x is in terms of y. So let's substitute what we know about x into the other
equation. **Like this:** $2x + 3y = 9$ **Becomes:** $2(7 - 4y) + 3y = 9$ **Multiply:** $2(7 - 4y) + 3y = 9$ **Becomes:**
$14 - 8y + 3y = 9$ **Subtract 14 from both sides:** $14 - 8y + 3y = 9$ **Becomes:** $-8y + 3y = -5$
Add the y's: $-8y + 3y = -5$ **Becomes:** $-5y = -5$ **Divide by** -5: $-5y = -5$ **Becomes:** $y = -\frac{5}{-5}$

Note: a negative numerator and a negative denominator makes the fraction a positive: So you have: $y = \frac{5}{5}$ or $y = 1$
Now substitute y = 1 into either equation and solve for x: $(2x + 3y = 9)$ or $(x + 4y = 7)$

Equation 1: $(2x + 3y = 9)$ **Becomes:** $(2x + 3(1) = 9)$ **Subtract 3:** $2x = 6$ **Divide by 2:** $x = 3$
Equation 2: $x + 4y = 7$ **Becomes:** $x + 4(1) = 7$ **Subtract 4:** $x = 3$

Either way you test it, $x = 3$ **Answer: (E)**

Explanation to PowerPrep Practice Question 16

16. Given: $(6x + 3y = 42)$ **and** $(5y - 2x = -2)$ **What is the value of** x **and** y
Explanation: We have two equations and two unknowns. We are being asked to solve for both unknowns. We therefore need to solve for the values of both x and y.

You can begin with either equation and either x *or* y. But once you select an equation and a variable, you need to solve the other equation for the OTHER variable. We will start with the first equation and solve for x (remember, you could solve for y)

Solve the first equation for x: $6x + 3y = 42$ **Subtract 3y from both sides:** $6x + 3y = 42$

Becomes: $6x = 42 - 3y$ **Divide both sides by 6:** $6x = 42 - 3y$ **Becomes:** $x = 7 - \left(\frac{3}{6}\right)y$

Simplify: $x = 7 - \left(\frac{3}{6}\right)y$ **Becomes:** $x = 7 - \frac{1}{2}y$ **You now have x in terms of y**. Plug what you know about x back into the 2nd equation and solve for y.

2nd **equation:** $5y - 2x = -2$ **Substitute the value of x from first equation:** $x = 7 - \frac{1}{2}y$

Becomes: $5y - 2(7 - \frac{1}{2}y) = -2$ **Multiply:** $5y - 2(7 - \frac{1}{2}y) = -2$ (remember the order of operation—multiply before
add) **Becomes:** $5y - 14 + 1y = -2$ (note: negative 2 times negative ½ is 1) **Add 14 to both sides:** $5y - 14 +$

$1y = -2$ **Becomes:** $5y + y = -2 + 14$ **Becomes:** $5y + y = 12$ **Add the y's:** $5y + y = 12$ **Becomes:** $6y = 12$ **Divide by 6:** $6y = 12$ **Becomes:** $y = 2$ Now we know the real value of y. We can plug that value into either equation and find x.

Like this: First equation: $6x + 3y = 42$ *Plug $y = 2$:* **Becomes:** $6x + (3)(2) = 42$ **Becomes:** $6x + 6 = 42$ **Becomes:** $6x = 36$ **Becomes:** $x = 6$
Second equation: $5y - 2x = -2$ *Plug $y = 2$* **Becomes:** $5(2) - 2x = -2$ **Becomes:** $10 - 2x = -2$
Becomes: $-2x = -12$ **Becomes:** $x = -\frac{12}{-2}$ the negatives in the numerator and denominator cancel each other: $x = \frac{12}{2}$ **Becomes:** $x = 6$ **Either way you check it,** $x = 6 \ and \ y = 2$ Answer (A)

Bonus Sample Questions not in the Virtual Classroom on the DVD

Bonus Sample Question 19-20

19. If $\left(\frac{xy+y}{9}\right) = \left(\frac{x+1}{3z}\right)$, what is the value of y when $(x = 2) \ and \ (z = 3)$?

(A) $-\frac{1}{3}$

(B) 0

(C) $\frac{1}{3}$

(D) 1

(E) 3

20. If $(q = 10r)$, for what value of r is $(q = r)$?

(A) q can never equal r

(B) 10

(C) 1

(D) $\frac{1}{5}$

(E) 0

Explanation to Bonus Sample Question 19

If $\left(\frac{xy+y}{9}\right) = \left(\frac{x+1}{3z}\right)$, **what is the value of y when** $(x = 2) \ and \ (z = 3)$?

First substitute the supplied information $(x = 2) \ and \ (z = 3)$, $\left(\frac{xy+y}{9}\right) = \left(\frac{x+1}{3z}\right)$ **becomes:** $\left(\frac{2y+y}{9}\right) = \left(\frac{2+1}{(3)(3)}\right)$

Simplify: $\left(\frac{3y}{9}\right) = \left(\frac{3}{9}\right)$ **Divide:** $\left(\frac{1y}{3}\right) = \left(\frac{1}{3}\right)$ **Same as:** $\frac{1}{3}y = \frac{1}{3}$ **Multiply by 3:** $\left(\frac{3}{1} * \frac{1}{3}\right)(y) = \left(\frac{1}{3} * \frac{3}{1}\right)$ **Simplify:** $1y = 1 \ or \ y = 1$ Answer D

Explanation to Bonus Sample Question 20

If $(q = 10r)$, for what value of r is $(q = r)$?

This tests your logic skills. Can you think of any situation where you can increase a number 10 fold and it still equals the number you started with. IOW, if you start with 5 and multiply it by 10, it will always be more than where you started (in this example 5), so 50 is greater than 5.
Is there any situation where $10x = x$ (where you multiply by 10, but remain the same)

Is there any number that fits? What happens if you try a fraction? For example $\frac{1}{10}$,

If you start with $\frac{1}{10} \ and \ multiply \ by$ 10 you get 1, but 1 does not equal your starting point of $\frac{1}{10}$
Try 1: If you multiply 1 by 10, you get 10. But 10 is not equal to the starting point of 1.

The only situation that satisfies the condition is zero. If you begin with zero and multiply it by 10, you end up where you started (zero), because zero times any number is still zero.
This question came directly from a real exam, so this is something they have tested in the past. Answer E

Algebra

Part 4: Quadratics

Virtual Classroom> Algebra >Quadratics
This material corresponds to the Virtual Classroom Instructions in the
PowerPrep DVD/Internet/iApp for Algebra

Virtual Classroom

Important Abbreviations

These abbreviations are used throughout the program

POE: Process of Elimination
SARR: Synthesize, Analyze, Reduce, and Restate (has to do with Logical Reasoning)
AC: Answer Choice
QS: Question Stem
LOD: Level of Difficulty

Example Question: What is the least common multiple of 3, 4, and 7? **(This is the call of the question or Question Stem "QS")**

These are Answer Choices "AC" A, B, C, D, E

    (A)   12
    (B)   21
    (C)   28
    (D)   48
    (E)   84

Part 4: Quadratic Equations

Quadratics

When you are asked to *solve* a quadratic equation (find the possible values of the variable), you are basically going through the Reverse FOIL process, factoring the equation into its' two binomials and then taking it one step further by solving for those variables.

Example If $(x^2 + 2x - 15 = 0)$, what is x = ?

1. $(x\quad)(x\quad)$
2. $-15 = -(1)(15)\ \ or\ -(5)(3)$ Also, to get $2x$ we need to add $+5\ and\ -3$
3. $(x + 5)(x - 3) = 0$

Now, set EACH binomial equal to zero and solve for the variable.

$(x + 5 = 0)\ so\ x = -5$ and $(x - 3 = 0)\ so\ x = 3$ $\quad$ *Therefore, x* $= +3\ or\ -5$

PowerPrep Practice Questions Also in the Virtual Classroom on DVD

PowerPrep Practice Questions 17-18

17. Which of the following is a solution to the equation:
$(y + 3)(y - 1) = 5$?

(A) -4
(B) -3
(C) -2
(D) 1
(E) 4

18. Given: $(c^2 - c - 2 = 0)$ and $(c > 0)$, What is the value of C?

(A) -1
(B) 0
(C) 1
(D) 2
(E) -2

Explanation to PowerPrep Practice Question 17

Which of the following is a solution to the equation $(y + 3)(y - 1) = 5$
Quick Answer; First, we need to create a quadratic equation. This means multiplying the binomials (FOIL), then move the 5 to the left side: $(y + 3)(y - 1) = 5$
FOIL: First, Outside, Inside, Last: $y^2 + 3y - y - 3 = 5$ **Combine Like-terms:** $y^2 + 2y - 3 = 5$ **Add - 5:** $y^2 + 2y - 8 = 0$ **Now, we need to factor the equation to find possible solutions:** $y^2 + 2y - 8 = 0$ **Becomes:** $(y + 4)(y - 2) = 0$ **Therefore,** $(y + 4 = 0)$, $(y - 2 = 0)$ **Becomes:** $y = -4, 2$ **Answer: (A)**
More Detailed Explanation: This question tests your ability to FOIL and reverse FOIL
First, we need to create a quadratic equation. This means multiplying the binomials (FOIL), then moving the 5 to the left side.
Here's how: Start with the given equation: $(y + 3)(y - 1) = 5$

FOIL: First $= (y)(y)\ or\ y^2$ $\quad$ Outside $= -1y$ $\quad$ Insides $= 3y$ $\quad$ Lasts $= -3$
Put it all together: $y^2 - y + 3y - 3 = 5$ (don't forget the 5 on the right side of the equation)
Now combine the y terms: $y^2 - y + 3y - 3 = 5$ **Becomes:** $y^2 + 2y - 3 = 5$
Now move the 5 to the left side to get the equation into a quadratic form: $y^2 + 2y - 3 = 5$
Becomes: $y^2 + 2y - 8 = 0$

Now, we need to factor the equation to find possible solutions. REVERSE FOIL $y^2 + 2y - 8 = 0$
What do you know? $(y\quad)(\quad y)$
What are the factors of 8 (the last term)? $(1,8)\ and\ (2,4)$
They have to multiply to 8 and add/subtract to 2 (the middle term 2y)
The (8,1) factors won't add/subtract to 2
They have to add up to positive 2, therefore, the 4 must be positive and the 2 negative: $+4\ and\ -2$
$(y\ 4)(y\ 2)\quad or\quad (y\ 2)(y\ 4)$
So we have two possibilities to check:
$(y + 4)(y - 2)\ gives\ you\ the\ -8\ and\ the\ 2y$
$(y + 2)(y - 4)\ gives\ you\ the\ -8\ but\ also\ -2y$

So we select: $(y + 4)(y - 2) = 0$
Now we set both factors equal to zero and solve (remember, for the equation to equal zero, one of the factors has to equal zero.
First Factor: $(y + 4) = 0$ Solve, Subtract 4 **Becomes:** $y = -4$
Second Factor: $(y - 2) = 0$ Solve, Add 2 **Becomes:** $y = 2$
The two possible answers are $y = (-4, 2)$ $\quad$ Check the answer choices and we see that $AC\ (A)\ is\ -4$

None of the answer choices is 2, but that does not matter. The call of the question asks us which of the following answer choices is a solution to the equation. Either $-4\ or\ 2$ is a solution to the equation. **Answer: (A)**

Explanation to PowerPrep Practice Question 18

Given: $(c^2 - c - 2 = 0)$ **and** $(c > 0)$, **What is the value of C?**

Explanation: We have to use REVERSE FOIL again. **What do we know:** $c^2 - c - 2 = 0$

So we start with the c^2 term like this: $(c \quad)(c \quad)$

Next, what are the factors of 2? **They are** $(1, 2)$ So now you know: $(c \quad 1)(c \quad 2)$

You know the middle term is negative and the last term is negative 2: $(c^2 - c - 2 = 0)$

So you know the 2, must be negative to make the middle term -1.

Therefore: $(c + 1)(c - 2)$ This gives you the (-2) and the $(-c)$ that you need.

Now you have: $(c + 1)(c - 2) = 0$ Set each factor equal to zero and solve for each.

First Factor: $(c + 1 = 0)$ **Becomes:** $(c = -1)$ **Second Factor:** $(c - 2 = 0)$ **Becomes:** $(c = 2)$ Now you know that c must be -1 or 2. Apply the given information that c must be greater than 0 $(c > 0)$ Therefore, of the two possible answer $(-1 \ and \ 2)$ **only 2** is greater than zero and is, therefore, the correct answer. **Answer (D)**

Bonus Sample Questions not in the Virtual Classroom on the DVD

Bonus Sample Question 21-22

21. If $xy = 7$ and $(x - y) = 5$, then $x^2 y - xy^2 = ?$

   (A) 2
   (B) 12
   (C) 24
   (D) 35
   (E) 70

22. The figure is a right triangle. What is the value of $\left(\frac{100}{x^2} + x^3 - 100\right)$?

   (A) .11
   (B) 1
   (C) 10
   (D) 99
   (E) 100

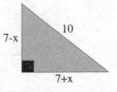

Explanation to Bonus Sample Question 21

If $xy = 7$ and $(x - y) = 5$, then $x^2 y - xy^2 = ?$

The first step is to factor. This is the key to the entire problem. Keep in mind, this problem is considered very high level of difficulty. So if you can answer this one, you are doing well and you understand factoring.

$x^2 y - xy^2 = ?$ **Factor as much as you can from this, becomes:** $xy(x - y)$ We've been given the value of each term: $xy = 7$ and $(x - y) = 5$, so all that's left is to substitute: $xy(x - y)$ **becomes:** $7(5) = 35$ **Answer D**

Explanation to Bonus Sample Question 22

This question combines some geometry with algebra (Quadratics). You can solve this problem with all Geometry (mostly Pythagorean theorem) or if you recognize the triangle is a 3-4-5 triangle doubled, you can skip the geometry.

Pythagorean Triples: 3:4:5 Triangle

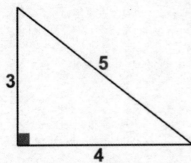

Ratio of sides 3:4:5
If legs have ratios of 3 and 4 then the hypotenuse has a ratio of 5.

For example, a triangle with sides 9:12:15, are 3 times a 3:4:5

Therefore, a 9:12:15 will have the same properties of a 3:4:5

Any triangle whose sides are in the ratio **3:4:5** is a right triangle. These are called **Pythagorean Triples**. There are an infinite number of them, and **3:4:5** is just the smallest.

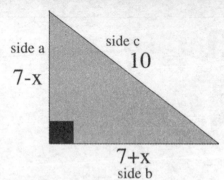

side a

7-x

side c

10

7+x

side b

In the information provided, we have sides a,b,c where side c is the hypotenuse and is 10.

If side "a" is 6, because it's a 3-4-5 triangle doubled, then side "a" would be *side 3 doubled or 6*   that means the side "a" is $(7 - x)$ and since side a is 6, then $(7 - x) = 6$ or $-x = -1$ or $x = 1$

We now know everything we need to know in order to solve the problem. But you should realize you could have solved this by looking at side "b" and doubled that side in the 3-4-5 triangle to give you a result of 8 for side b. If side b is 8, that means $7 + x = 8$ *or* $x = 8 - 7$ *or* $(x = 1)$

Either way $x = 1$. Now we can plug $x = 1$ *into the given equation and solve*:

$$\left(\frac{100}{x^2} + x^3 - 100\right) = \left(\frac{100}{1^2} + 1^3 - 100\right) = \left(\frac{100}{1} + 1 - 100\right) = (100 + 1 - 100) = 1 \quad \underline{\textbf{Answer B}}$$

If you did not recognize the Pythagorean Triple for the 3-4-5 triangle, you could still solve the problem, but it takes a little more calculating and you still must remember the **Pythagorean Theorem: $a^2 + b^2 = c^2$ where c is the hypotenuse**

Side a $= (7 - x)$, *Side b* $= (7 + x)$, and *Side c* $= 10$
Therefore, $a^2 + b^2 = c^2$ *becomes*: $(7 - x)^2 + (7 + x)^2 = 10^2$ **expand and simplify:**
$(7 - x)(7 - x) + (7 + x)(7 + x) = 100$
$49 - 7x - 7x + x^2 + 49 + 7x + 7x + x^2 = 100$ **Now organize like terms**
$49 + 49 - 14x + 14x + 2x^2 = 100$ **becomes:** $2x^2 + 98 = 100$
$2x^2 = 2$ **becomes:** $x^2 = 1$ *becomes*: $x = \sqrt{1}$ *or* $x = 1$

Any way you approach this problem you will still get the final answer of $x = 1$, then plug it into the given:
$$\left(\frac{100}{x^2} + x^3 - 100\right) = \left(\frac{100}{1^2} + 1^3 - 100\right) = \left(\frac{100}{1} + 1 - 100\right) = (100 + 1 - 100) = 1 \quad \underline{\textbf{Answer B}}$$

Algebra
Part 5: Word Problems
Virtual Classroom> Algebra >Word Problems
This material Corresponds to the Virtual Classroom Instructions in the
PowerPrep DVD/Internet/iApp for Algebra

Virtual Classroom

Part 5: Word Problems

Approach

Read through entire question: •Make sure you locate the *specific* question.   •Write it down on your scratch paper

Look for the best approach: •Translate words into an equation.   •Translate words into a diagram.   •Consider Backsolving or picking numbers if appropriate Also, **Solve or make an educated guess**

Translation Table

Problem Type	Term	Translation
Equation	equal to	$=$
	block A <u>is as</u> tall <u>as</u> block B	$A = B$
Inequality	less than greater than	$<$ $>$
	less than or equal to greater than or equal to	$\leq$ $\geq$
Addition	number <u>increased</u> by 4	$x + 4$
	six <u>more than</u> a number	$x + 6$
	the sum of a number and two	$x + 2$
Subtraction	three <u>less than</u> a number	$x - 3$
	eight <u>decreased by</u> a number	$8 - x$
	four <u>fewer than</u> a number	$x - 4$
	the <u>difference of</u> 16 and two times a number	$16 - 2x$
Multiplication	<u>twice</u> a number <u>one half</u> a number	$2x$ $\frac{1}{2}x$
	ten <u>percent of</u> a number	$0.1x$
	a number is four <u>times the amount</u> y–2	$4(y - 2)$
Division	four <u>divided into</u> a number	$x/4$
	five apples for every two bananas	$a/b = 5/2$
	twelve miles <u>per</u> hour	$12\,mph$

PowerPrep Practice Questions Also in the Virtual Classroom on DVD

PowerPrep Practice Questions19-20

19. Sharon has 17 coins amounting to $2.00. The number of nickels she has is three times the number of dimes. She has two more quarters than dimes. How many dimes does she have?

(A) 2
(B) 3
(C) 5
(D) 10
(E) 15

20. Twenty-one days from now the puppy will be three times as old as he was one week ago. In terms of weeks, how old is the puppy now?

(A) 3
(B) 6
(C) 12
(D) 24
(E) 42

Explanation to PowerPrep Practice Question 19

Sharon has 17 coins amounting to $2.00. She only has Nickels, Dimes, and Quarters. The number of nickels she has is three times the number of dimes. She has two more quarters than dimes. How many dimes does she have?

Quick Answer: Realize that the dollar amount we are given is extra information we don't need. We are only concerned with the number of coins equaling 17.

We are told two things about the money: 1. Three times as many nickels as dimes is $N = 3D$
2. Two more quarters than dimes is $Q = D + 2$

We also know that the total number of N, D, Q *is* 17 or $(N + D + Q = 17)$
We also have an equation for each coin in terms of Dimes: Nickels = 3 Dimes, Quarters = Dimes plus 2

So everything is in terms of Dimes. So we can substitute this information into the main equation and solve for the number of Dimes: $(3D) + D + (D + 2) = 17$ **Combine like-terms:** $5D + 2 = 17$ **Add** -2**:** $5D = 15$ **Divide by 5:** $D = \frac{15}{5} = 3$, **Therefore,** $D = 3$ Now compare the two options, the number of dimes or 4. $3 < 4$ **Answer: (B)**

More Detailed Explanation: Realize that the dollar amount we are given is extra information we don't need. We are only concerned with the number of coins equaling 17.

First, itemize what you know from the given information
- 17 coins
- Total $2.00
- $N = 3D$ (nickels are three times dimes)
- $Q = D + 2$ Be Careful! **it's not** $(Q + 2 = D)$

This is the trickiest part—you have to add 2 extra dimes to equal the quarters—IOW, count all your dimes, you have to add two more to equal the number of quarters. So if she added two more dimes she would have the same number of dimes and quarters. Or you could say $(D = Q - 2)$. Count up all the quarters, take two away and that equals the number of dimes. If you wrote $(Q + 2 = D)$, it would mean you could count all your quarters, then add two more and that would be the number of dimes—IOW two more dimes than quarters (not what the information says). It's a little difficult to keep straight. $N + D + Q = 17$

What is D? How many dimes does she have? This can seem tricky, but once you get the logic it's straight forward.

Next, add up what you know: Bear in mind, you don't really care about the dollar value, you just want to know how many dimes.

If there are 3 times as many dimes as nickels, we can replace N with (3D) in the equation.
$N = 3D$, N + D + Q = 17, **Therefore,** $(3D + D + Q = 17)$

What do we know about Quarters and Dimes? $Q = D + 2$
So replace Q in our equation with $(D + 2)$
$3D + D + Q = 17$
$3D + D + (D + 2) = 17$
Getting the equation set up is the difficult part. If we get it set up correctly, solving it is easier. Now we're ready to solve the equation. 3D + D + D + 2 = 17
Combine the D's: $(5D + 2 = 17)$ **Subtract 2 from both sides:** $(5D + 2) = 17$ **Becomes:**
$5D = 15$ **Divide by 5:** 5D = 15 **Becomes:** $D = 3$

This tells us there are 3 dimes in the group of 17 Answer: (B)
Check your work: Plug what we know about Dimes back into the given information:
Nickels: $N = 3D$ We now know we have 3 dimes: *Therefore,* $N = (3)(3)$ or $N = 9$ Sharon has 9 nickels
Quarters: $Q = D + 2$ We know we have 3 dimes: *Therefore,* $Q = (3 + 2)$ *or* $Q = 5$ Sharon has 5 quarters
Nickels = 3, Dimes = 9, Quarters = 5 Becomes: $(3 + 9 + 5) = 17$ or $17 = 17$

ALTERNATIVE METHOD: Backsolving. Backsolving is where you check the answer choices and use POE (process of elimination) From the given answer choices, you know that one of them correctly identifies how many dimes Sharon has.
The options are: 2, 3, 5, 10, 15

If you plugged the AC information into what you know, you would get the following:
(A) dimes =2, quarters = 2 + 2 = 4, nickels = 3(2) = 6, total = 2 + 4 + 6 = 12 ≠ 17
(B) dimes =3, quarters = 2 + 3 = 5, nickels = 3(3) = 9, total = 3 + 5 + 9 = 17 = 17
(C) dimes =5, quarters = 2 + 5 = 7, nickels = 3(5) = 15, total = 5 + 7 + 15 = 27 ≠ 17
(D) dimes =10, quarters = 2 + 10 = 12, nickels=3(10) = 30, total = 10 + 12 + 30 = 52 ≠ 17
(E) dimes =15, quarters = 2 + 15 = 17, nickels=3(15) = 45, total = 15 + 17 + 45 = 77 ≠ 17

Once you got the right answer, you would stop and move to next question **Answer: (B)**

Explanation to PowerPrep Practice Question 20

Twenty-one days from now the puppy will be three times as old as he was one week ago. In terms of weeks, how old is the puppy now?

Quick Answer: $(21\ days = 3\ weeks)$, and $(x = the\ puppy's\ current\ age\ in\ weeks)$ "Three weeks (21 days) from now" is written as the puppy's current age (x), plus 3 or $x + 3$ **"The puppy will be" is written "="** $x + 3 =$

"Three times as old as he was one week ago": Start with the puppy's current age (x) and subtract 1 week $(x - 1)$ that's his age one week ago. But this tells us one week ago the puppy was three times as old as one week ago. If one week ago is $(x - 1)$ then three times one week ago will be $3(x - 1)$

Now put it all together and solve for x (the current age): $x + 3 = 3(x - 1)$ **Multiply:** $x + 3 = 3x - 3$ **Now Group variables and constants and** Add 3: $x + 3 + (3) = 3x$ **Add:** $x + 6 = 3x$ **Add** $-x$ $6 = 2x$ **Divide by 2:** $3 = x$

The puppy's current age is 3 weeks, but that is not the answer to the question. The problem wants to know which is greater between the two options. We have just shown the two options 3 and x are equal, because x also equals 3. **Answer: C**

More Detailed Explanation: These kinds of questions require a methodical, step by step approach. Don't try and absorb the entire problem—take it in chunks.

What do you know?
  21 days = 3 weeks
  x = the puppy's current age in weeks
  $X\ (now) + 21\ days =$ in three weeks
  $3x$ = three times as old
  $x\ (now) - 7\ (days)$ = 1 week or 7 days ago.

Do the problem in days or weeks, but be consistent and then convert if you need to at the end. We are going to use weeks (but you could use days.) $x + 3 = 3(x - 1)$
This says, in three weeks $(x + 3)$ the puppy will be three times as old as he was 1 week ago $3(x - 1)$

Now solve for x: $x + 3 = 3(x - 1)$ **Multiply the 3:** $x + 3 = 3(x - 1)$ **Becomes:** $x + 3 = 3x - 3$ **Subtract an x from the left and right:** $x + 3 = 3x - 3$ **Becomes:** $3 = 2x - 3$ **Move the -3 on the right:** $3 = 2x - 3$ **Becomes:** $6 = 2x$ **Divide by 3:** $6 = 3x$ **Becomes:** $3 = x$ _Answer (A)_

Bonus Sample Questions not in the Virtual Classroom on the DVD

Bonus Sample Question 23-25

23. If Lindsay is twice as tall as Kristin and Amy's height is $\frac{2}{3}$ of Lindsay's height, then
  which is greater, Amy's height or Kristin's height

  (A) Amy's height is greater
  (B) Kristin's height is greater
  (C) They are equal
  (D) Unknown—insufficient information

24. A painter is hired to paint a fence. He was paid $160 total for all the hours of work and it took a total of five hours to paint the fence. If he is paid $3 more for each hour of painting than he was paid for the hour before, how much was he paid for his second hour of work?

  (A) $3.00
  (B) $9.00
  (C) $20.00
  (D) $26.00
  (E) $29.00

25. In a certain downtown area, the bank and the library stand next to each other. At mid-morning the bank casts a shadow that is 25 feet long and the library casts a shadow that is 20 feet long. Assuming the height of the individual stories is the same for both buildings, how many stories high is the library? We also know that:

  (1) The building across the street casts a shadow that is 32 feet long.
  (2) The bank is 20 stories high.

  (A) 16
  (B) 18
  (C) 20
  (D) 25
  (E) 26

Explanation to Bonus Sample Question 23

Write the statements in terms of algebraic equations: Lindsay is twice as tall as Kristin: $L = 2K$
Amy is $\frac{2}{3}$ as tall as Lindsay: $A = \frac{2}{3} L$ Find the value of both in terms of the same variable: Since $L = 2K$ and $A = \frac{2}{3} L$
Substitute the 2K (which is Lindsay) into the Amy equation for L. Like this: $A = \frac{2}{3}(2K)$ In this equation the 2K represents L,
Now simplify: $A = \frac{4}{3} K$ This means that Amy is taller than Kristen because Amy is $\frac{4}{3}$ Kristin's height **Answer: (A)**

Explanation to Bonus Sample Question 24

First we should figure out what we know from the given information:

Fact 1: We know the total amount of money he was paid for all the hours of work--$160.
Fact 2: We know the total number of hours the painter worked—5 hours.
Fact 3: Each hour he was paid $3.00 more than the prior hour

"Call-of-the-Question" or "What are you looking for?" The amount the painter was paid for the first hour of work so we can figure out how much he was paid for the second hour.

All Statements: We know the total number of hours he worked (5) and the total amount of money he was paid for the work ($160). We know each hour he made $3.00 more than the prior hour. We can now set up an equation: Set x equal to hour 1: each succeeding hour will be $3.00 more for a total of 5 hours of work and a total sum of $160. **Like this:**
*(**Hour 1** he made x)* + *(**hour 2** he made x + 3)* + *(**hour 3** he made x + 6)* + *(**hour 4** he made x + 9)* + *(**hour 5** he made x + 12) for a total of $160.*

$x + (x + 3) + (x + 6) + (x + 9) + (x + 12) = 160$
Simplify by adding up all the variables (the x's) and all the constants (the numbers)
$5x + 30 = 160$ ***Add* -30 becomes:** $5x = 130$ **Divide by 5 becomes:** $x = 26$

Check your work: If $x = 26$, then $(\$26 + (26 + 3) + (26 + 6) + (26 + 9) + (26 + 12) = \$160$
Do the math and find out if it checks: $(26 + 29 + 32 + 35 + 38) = 160$ Becomes $160 = 160$
It checks out. This means the original first hour the painter received $26 for that hour.

But we wanted to know how much he was paid for hour number two (2). That would be $(x + 3)$ or $\$26 + 3 = \$29$ <u>Answer E</u>

Explanation to Bonus Sample Question 25

First we should review what we know:

Fact 1: The individual stories are the same height in the bank and library. This is important so we know a ratio is possible. If the individual stories where different heights then we could not set up a ratio. Imagine one story in the bank was 10 feet, but one story in the library was 100 feet. It would not work. This fact is actually very important and shows you must pay attention to details.

On the other hand, they will also give you information that is not relevant. In this case, they told us that the building across the street cast a shadow of 32 feet. This information does not help us and is just given to mess you up and see if you can weed out extraneous information that is not relevant.

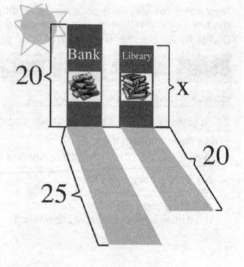

Fact 2: The bank is 20 stories tall
Fact 3: The bank shadow is 25 feet
Fact 4: The library shadow is 20 feet

We want to know the height of the library in stories.

Now we can set up two proportionate ratios for the height of the buildings and the length of their shadows. Let x be the height, in stories, of the library.

$\frac{20 \ bank \ stories}{25 \ foot \ shadow} = \frac{16 \ library \ stories}{20 \ foot \ shadow}$ or $\left(\frac{20}{25} = \frac{16}{20}\right)$ **Next, clear the**

fractions by multiplying both sides by 25 and by 20 $\left(\frac{25}{1} * \frac{20}{25}\right) =$

$\left(\frac{x}{20} * \frac{25}{1}\right)$ **Becomes:** $20 = \frac{25x}{20}$ **Now multiply both sides by 20,**

becomes: $(20 * 20) = 25x$ or $400 = 25x$ **Divide both sides by 25,**

becomes: $\frac{400}{25} = x$ **or** $16 = x$

Recall that x represents the height of the Library. So the library is 16 stories tall. <u>Answer A</u>

Check your work: If the bank is 20 stories and casts a 25 foot shadow, then the library is 16 stories and casts a 20 foot shadow.
$\frac{20 \ bank \ stories}{25 \ foot \ shadow} = \frac{16 \ library \ stories}{20 \ foot \ shadow}$ or $\frac{20}{25} = \frac{16}{20}$ Simplify by dividing left side by 5 so $\frac{20}{25} \ becomes \ \frac{4}{5}, \ \frac{20}{25} \ simplified \ is \ \frac{4}{5}$
Now simplify the right side by dividing by 4: $\frac{16}{20} \ becomes \ \frac{4}{5}$ Therefore, $\frac{20}{25} = \frac{16}{20} \ is \ the \ same \ as \ \frac{4}{5} = \frac{4}{5}$ so the ratio holds

Algebra

Part 6: Functions

Virtual Classroom> Algebra >Functions
This material corresponds to the Virtual Classroom Instructions in the
PowerPrep DVD/Internet/iApps for Algebra

Virtual Classroom

Part 6: Functions

Scatter Plot

A scatter plot shows the relationship between two variables. Unlike the graph of a function, they don't form a perfect line, but vary.

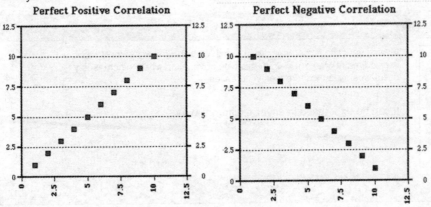

Scatter Plot
A scatter plot shows the relationship between two variables. They are used to plot real-life data. Usually the data is "scattered" like you see below, and does not form a perfect line (real life is that way), you will be asked to interpret the data and create a line that best fits the data.

Students are expected to identify the general characteristics of the line of best fit for a given scatter plat. You might determine the slope of the line of best fit, but would not be expected to use formal methods of finding the equation of the line of best fit.

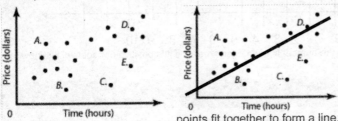

This scatter plot is more like the type you will see on the exam. You will need to figure out the best fit line.
Do this by drawing a line right on the graph that best fits the data. Like this:
Obviously it doesn't correspond perfectly, but you can now analyze it and make decisions about slope. This line has a positive slope and it is probably equal to 1.   The more the points fit together to form a line, the higher or more perfect the correlation is.

This graph has a low correlation. This helps you to understand how strong a relationship there is between the two variables. The exam may ask you more complicated questions about the scatter plot, but if you can estimate the slope with a best fit line, you will be able to make predictions about the equation of the line and correlation between the two variables.

Domain and Range

The **domain** of a function is all the values where the function can be defined; these are all the x values. The **range** of a function is all the values that are possible outputs of the functions, or the y values. A number is outside the domain, or undefined, if x cannot be that number.

For example: For the function f(x) = 1/(x-3). 3 is outside the domain because it would make the denominator 0 and the denominator of a fraction cannot be 0, it is an undefined value. You can find out the range of a function by graphing it or by analyzing the equation. Look for a lower limit and upper limit. Check for holes left by an undefined x. **Example:** $f(x) = x^2$

The **domain** of this function is $[-\infty, +\infty]$ or all real numbers. There are no undefined x values.
The **range** is $[0, +\infty]$ or all numbers from 0 to infinity.
This type of question usually just requires some careful analysis. Try plugging in -100, -2, -1, 0, 1, 2, and 100 to get a good idea of the behavior of the function.

Direct Variation

x	y
-1	-2
0	0
1	2
2	4
3	6
4	8

If x and y vary directly, then x = (yk) where k is a constant. This means that as x increases y increases, as x decreases y decreases.

If k were 1, then x = y. And if you increase x you increase y.
But x and y don't have to be the same number to vary directly. If k were 2, then $x = 2y$. And if $x = 1$, then $y = \frac{1}{2}$. If $x = 2$, then $y = 1$. If $x = \frac{1}{4}$ then $y = \frac{1}{8}$. If $x = 100$, then $y = 50$. There are several different ways to express direct variation.

$$x = \frac{1}{2}y, \quad x = \frac{y}{2}, \quad 2x = y, \frac{x}{y} = \frac{1}{2},$$ so you need to carefully analyze it, plugging in numbers to make sure what type of variation it is.

Direct variation problems often show up as graphs.
For the equation above $x = \frac{y}{2}$

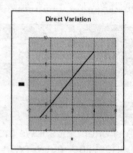

Direct Variation

The graph for inverse variation is more complex because as one value increases the other decreases. Direct variation and inverse variation problems can also be snuck in as word problems.
For example, a problem about speed and time might be an inverse variation problem because as speed increases time decreases.

Inverse Variation

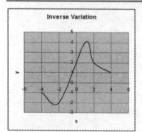

Inverse Variation

Inverse variation is the opposite of direct variation. Two numbers x and y vary indirectly when $xy = k$. In this type of variation when x increases y decreases, when x decreases y increases.

It can be expressed in several different ways. $x = \frac{k}{y}, \quad \frac{xy}{k} = 1,$
$\frac{x}{k} = \frac{1}{y}. \quad xy = 4$

x	y
-4	-1
-2	-2
1	4
2	2
4	1

Absolute Value

This is the symbol for absolute value: | |. Whatever is inside the two brackets becomes positive.
So $|9| = 9$ and $|-9| = 9$. $|a| = a$ and $|-a| = a$.

If you have a number line:

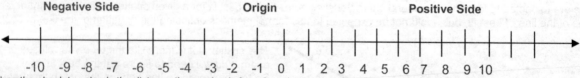

Negative Side   Origin   Positive Side

-10 -9 -8 -7 -6 -5 -4 -3 -2 -1 0 1 2 3 4 5 6 7 8 9 10

Then the absolute value is the distance the number is from 0 on the number line. It doesn't matter if it is positive or negative, just how far away it is; -9 and 9 are both 9 away from 0.

Inequality or Equation

For example: $|x| > 7$. The trick is x could be greater than +7 or less than −7; both have an absolute value greater than 7.
$|x| > 7$ and $|x| < -7$

The process is the same for an equation except of course $x = 7$ and -7. Try $|x + 3| > 7$
Just like in the first example, x could be a positive or negative number. Also, like the first example, we make 7 positive and negative; **BUT** we change the sign for the negative!!! $|x + 3| > 7$ and $|x + 3| < -7$

After that we don't need to worry about the absolute value signs anymore. $x + 3 > 7$ and $x + 3 < -7$
Solve both inequalities for x like any other algebraic expression. $x > 4$ and $x < -10$
Let's check this: $x > 4, try\ 6$ $|6 + 3| = 9$ which is greater than 7. $x < -10, try -14$
$|-14 + 3| = |-11| = 11$ which is also greater than 7.

Now try $|x + 3| < 7$, 1. $x + 3 < 7$ and $x + 3 > -7$, 2. $x < 4$ and $x > -10$

Let's check this: An $x < 4\ is\ 1, |1 + 3| = 4$, which is less than 7. An $x > -10\ is -2$, $|-2 + 3| = 1$, which is less than 7.
Notice that in this type of problem if the | x |is > y than the answers are going to be pointing out both ends of the number line towards infinity. On the other hand, if the | x | is < y then the answers are going to be in between two points on the number line.   So; in the first question the answer was all the numbers less than -10 and all the numbers greater than 4. And in the second question, the answers were all the values in between -10 and 4. This is a pattern that is consistent throughout this type of question.

Integer and Rational Exponents

Positive integers are easy to deal with. $3^4 = 3\ x\ 3\ x\ 3\ x\ 3 = 81$.
Negative integer exponents like 3^{-4} are easily made positive and simple as well. A negative exponent sends its base

number to the denominator of a fraction. 3^{-4} is the same as $\left(\frac{1}{3}\right)^4$ or $\frac{1}{81}$

Fraction exponents like $3^{(2/3)}$ can be expressed in a simpler way. The numerator works like the integer exponent, that's the power it's raised to. The denominator takes the root. For $3^{2/3}$, 3 is raised to the second power and the cube root. In other

words $\sqrt[3]{3}^2$ **Remember any number raised to the zero power is one.** $3^0 = 1,\ 4^0 = 1,\ .976^0 = 1$

Simplify $\left[\left(3x^4y^7z^{12}\right)^5\left(-5x^9y^3z^4\right)^2\right]^0$ The entire thing is just 1

Any number raised to the first power remains the same number. $3^1 = 3$, $4^1 = 4$, $.976^1 = .976$
The denominator of an exponent is a root.

$8^{\frac{1}{4}} = 3$, 81 to the fourth root or $\left(\sqrt[4]{81}\right)$

$16^{\frac{1}{2}} = 4$,   16 to the square root, $\left(\sqrt[2]{16}\right)$

$81^{\frac{1}{2}} = 9$, 81 to the square root, $\left(\sqrt[2]{81}\right)$

   You can simplify exponents with like bases. $\frac{x^5}{x^4}$ is the same as $x^{(5-4)}$ **When you raise an exponent to an exponent,**

you multiply: $(x)^{2^4} = (xx)(xx)(xx)(xx) = x^8$ Note that x^8 also equals $x^{(2\cdot4)}$. This demonstrates the second exponent rule: Whenever you have an exponent expression that is raised to a power, you can multiply the exponent and power:

$\left(x^m\right)^n = x^{mn}$ But if you multiply a number with an exponent by a number with an exponent, you add the exponents.

$x^5 * x^4 = (xxxxx)(xxxx) = x^{(5+4)}$ $(x^m)(x^n) = x^{m+n}$

However, we can NOT simplify $(x^4)(y^3)$, because the bases are different

Another example would be: $\left(\frac{x}{y}\right)^2 = \frac{x^2}{y^2}$

Warning: This rule does NOT work if you have a sum or difference within the parentheses. Exponents, unlike multiplication, do NOT "underline distribute" over addition. For instance, given $(3 + 4)^2$, do NOT succumb to the temptation to say "This equals $3^2 + 4^2 = 9 + 16 = 25$", because this is wrong. Actually, $(3 + 4)^2 = (7)^2 = 49$, not 25. When in doubt, write out the expression according to the definition of the power. Given $(x - 2)^2$, don't try to do this in your head. Instead, write it out: "squared" means "times itself", so $(x - 2)^2 = (x - 2)(x - 2) = xx - 2x - 2x + 4 = x^2 - 4x + 4$.

Functions

An equation in function notation is an equation starting with f(x). It is read "f of x". If you are unfamiliar with this concept, think of it as a box, you put in some number (the x) and you get out another number. For the function, $f(x) = x^2 + 2$ you put in 0, you take out 2, you put in 1, you take out 3, and on and on. Values are plugged in for x and the result is called the y value.

In the above function $f(3) = 3^2 = 2 = 11$.   A single x value can only result in one y value, but identical y values are possible. $f(-3) = 11$ just as $f(3) = 11$, but we can't have a function where $f(3) = 11$ and $f(3) = 6$.

An x and an f(x) form a set of ordered pairs. From the above we have the ordered pairs (3, 11) and (-3, 11), each with an x coordinate and a y coordinate. These can be graphed on a coordinate plane.

Linear functions form a line and if two points are given, you can find out the slope, the midpoint of those points, and the distance between those two points by identifying the x and y coordinates and using them in the slope formula, midpoint formula, or distance formula. You do not need the function to analyze details of the function.

Linear Functions are often in the slope intercept form: $y = mx + b$, or $f(x) = mx + b$

m and b are constants, b is the y intercept and m is the slope of the line. If you are given two points on a line you can plug them in to solve for the slope and the y intercept.

Example: (3, 0) and (4, 2) are on a line, find the slope and y intercept. **Use the slope formula:** $\frac{y_2 - y_1}{x_2 - x_1} = \frac{2 - 0}{4 - 3} = 2$

This gives us $y = 2x + b$, then we just plug in one of the coordinate pairs.
$2 = 2(4) + b$, $2 = 8 + b$, $b = -6$

CONGRATULATIONS!!!
You have completed the Algebra Workshop!

Take a break before moving on to the Algebra Drills!

Algebra Index

Geometry Workbook

Table of Contents

This material corresponds to the Virtual Classroom Instructions in the
PowerPrep DVD/Internet/iApp for Geometry

Virtual Classroom

68

Geometry
Part 1: Angles

Virtual Classroom>Geometry>Angles

This material corresponds to the Virtual Classroom Instructions in the
PowerPrep DVD/Internet/iApps for Geometry

Virtual Classroom

Important Abbreviations
These abbreviations are used throughout the program

POE: Process of Elimination
SARR: Synthesize, Analyze, Reduce, and Restate (has to do with Logical Reasoning)
AC: Answer Choice
QS: Question Stem
LOD: Level of Difficulty

Example Question: What is the least common multiple of 3, 4, and 7? (**This is the call of the question or Question Stem "QS"**)

These are Answer Choices "AC" A, B, C, D, E

(A)   12
(B)   21
(C)   28
(D)   48
(E)   84

Part 1: Angles

Generally

- There are no negative angles
- There are no zero angles
- You should only see angles as whole numbers

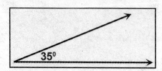

Acute Angle – Angles smaller than 90°

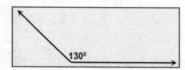

Obtuse Angle – Angles larger than 90°

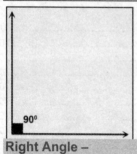

Angles equal to 90°
(squares, rectangles,
and perpendicular
lines all form right
angles)

Right Angle –

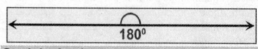

Straight Angle – Angle measures 180°

Multiple Angles

Reflex Angles –

Angle greater than 180° but less than 360°
$180° < x° < 360°$

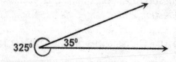

Supplementary Angles-

Two angles that total 180° $x° + y° = 180$

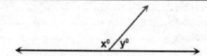

Complimentary Angles –

Two angles which total 90° $x° + y° = 90$

Vertical Angles--

form Intersecting lines – **When two lines intersect, the opposite angles at the point of intersection equal each other (vertical angles). Adjacent angles are supplementary.**
$x° = y°$, $x° + a° = 180$, $x° + b° = 180$

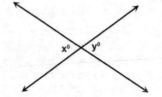 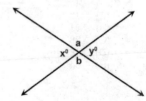

Corresponding Angles

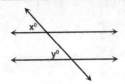

When a transversal line intersects two parallel lines, the angles in the same position are equal.

| x and y are congruent, x=y |

Rules of Corresponding Angles

- 2 = 4 = 6 = 8, all obtuse, all equal
- 1 = 3 = 5 = 7, all acute, all equal
- 1 & 2, 3 & 4, 5 & 6, 7 & 8 → supplementary
- 1 & 4, 2 & 3, 5 & 8, 6 & 7 → supplementary
- 1 & 8, 2 & 7, 3 & 6, 4 & 5 → supplementary
- 3 & 5, 4 & 6 → alternate interior angles → Equal

PowerPrep Practice Questions   Also in the Virtual Classroom on DVD

PowerPrep Practice Questions 1-2

1. Lines L, M, and N intersect. What is the value of $a° + b°$?

    (A) 47°
    (B) 105°
    (C) 118°
    (D) 120°
    (E) 137°

2. If lines M and N are parallel, what is the value of ½ c°?

    (A) 73°
    (B) 107°
    (C) 180°
    (D) 53.5°
    (E) 36.5°

Explanation to PowerPrep Practice Question 1

This question tests your understanding of "Straight Angles" and "Supplementary Angles"--remember that straight angles = 180°

Then you know that: $a° + 43° + b° = 180°$

Now solve for $a° + b°$ becomes: $a° + b° + 43° = 180°$ **Then, subtract 43° from both sides:**

$$a° + b° + 43° = 180°$$
$$\underline{-43 \quad\quad -43}$$

Becomes: $a° + b° = 137°$

Answer: (E)

Explanation to PowerPrep Practice Question 2

There are several ways to answer this question. This question tests your general understanding of the relationships of angles and parallel lines.

Quick Review: Vertical angles are opposite pairs of congruent (or equal) angles that are made when 2 lines intersect (cross at a point). In the figure below, opposite angles 1 and 3 (and also opposite angles 2 and 4) are called vertical angles.

Supplementary Angles: Angles 1 and 2 are supplementary angles, because they add up to 180 degrees. You'll also notice that (2 and 3) are a pair of supplementary angles, as are (3 and 4) and (4 and 1). There's 4 sets of supplementary angles.

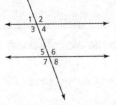

When a line (called a transversal) cuts through a set of parallel lines, it creates certain properties of angles.   What they are called, is not as important as understanding their relationships.

Interior and exterior angles: Angles 3,6 and 4,5 are *alternate interior angles*; angles 1,8 and 2,7 are *alternate exterior angles*. These pairs are all equal. If we use this information and apply it to the given information we have several ways of answering the question.

First: Let's look at straight angles and supplementary angles (add up to 180°). We know that $a° + b° = 180$ And we know that $73° + a° = 180°$ **Let's solve $73° + a° = 180°$**

Subtract 73 from both sides **Becomes:** $a° = 107°$ **If we know a° = 107°** Now we can solve: $a° + b° = 180$ **Substitute a° = 107°** **Becomes:** $107° + b° = 180°$ **Subtract 107°** **Becomes:** $b° = 73°$ **Now we know a° = 107° and b° = 73°**

Now apply the concepts of alternating interior and exterior angles.   Here's where there are several ways to proceed.   Angles 1 and 8 are equal. We were given the value of angle 1 in the material (73°) so angle c is also 73° (alternate exterior angles) and ½ of 73 is 36.5° We could have stopped right there.

But let's apply other aspects of the relationship. For example, angles 4 & 5 are alternate interior angels and also equal. In our case angle 4 is b° = 73°   Angel c in our given information would also be 73° because it is vertical. So we can solve the problem: ½ **of 73° is also 36.5°**

See how many other relationships you can find that would result in the correct answer.
NOTE: It's important that you understand the relationship between angles because it will be tested repeatedly on the exam.

Bonus Sample Questions   not in the Virtual Classroom on the DVD

Bonus Sample Question 1-4

1. What is the value of $(x \div y)$?
    (A) −1
    (B) 1
    (C) 5
    (D) 85
    (E) 95

2. In the figure above, lines *l*, *m*, and *n* intersect. What is the value of $a° + b°$?
    (A) 47°
    (B) 105°
    (C) 118°
    (D) 120°
    (E) 137°

3. In triangle ABC above, BV bisects $\angle ABC$. Therefore, which is greater?
    (A) The segment AV is greater
    (B) The segment VC is greater
    (C) They are equal
    (D) Unknown—insufficient information

4. If lines m and n are parallel, which is greater, $2(a - b)$ or $(b - \frac{1}{2}c)$?
    (A) $2(a - b)$ is greater
    (B) $\left(b - \frac{1}{2}c\right)$ is greater
    (C) They are equal
    (D) Unknown—insufficient information

Explanation to Bonus Sample Question 1

x and y are vertical angles.   By definition x = y   If x = y, Then $\frac{x}{y} = 1$
Correct answer: (B)

Explanation to Bonus Sample Question 2

Because these angles are supplementary angles, then: $a° + 43° + b° = 180°$ **Solve for (a° + b°)**
$a° + b° + 43° = 180°$ **Add -43** $a° + b° = (180° - 43°)$ becomes $a° + b° = 137°$
Correct answer: (E)

Explanation to Bonus Sample Question 3

If BV bisects $\angle ABC$, and it is perpendicular to segment AC, then point V will be the midpoint of line AC.
Therefore, AV = VC
Answer: (C)

Explanation to Bonus Sample Question 4

Options 1: $2(a - b)$ The angle corresponding to $a°$ is equal to 107°, $b°$ is vertical to the angle with measure 73°.
    Now substitute for $a°$ and $b°$, $2(a - b)$ **Becomes** $2(107 - 73)$, $2(34) = 68°$
Option 2: $\left(b - \frac{1}{2}c\right)$, We know the measure of b is 73°. c is an angle corresponding to b so it also has a measure of 73°
    Now substitute for $b°$ and $c°$. $\left(b - \frac{1}{2}c\right)$, $73 - \frac{1}{2}(73)$ becomes $73 - 36.5 = 36.5$ **36.5°**
Now compare option 1 and 2
    $68° > 36.5°$ Therefore, Option 1 is greater
Answer: (A)

Geometry
Part 2: Triangles

Virtual Classroom> Geometry >Triangles

This material corresponds to the Virtual Classroom Instructions in the
PowerPrep DVD/Internet/iApps for Geometry

Virtual Classroom

Important Abbreviations
These abbreviations are used throughout the program

POE: Process of Elimination
SARR: Synthesize, Analyze, Reduce, and Restate (has to do with Logical Reasoning)
AC: Answer Choice
QS: Question Stem
LOD: Level of Difficulty

Example Question: What is the least common multiple of 3, 4, and 7? (**This is the call of the question or Question Stem "QS"**)

These are Answer Choices "AC" A, B, C, D, E

(A)   12
(B)   21
(C)   28
(D)   48
(E)   84

Part 2: Triangles

Generally

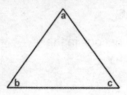

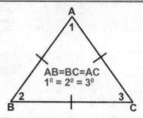

Interior Angles –

Sum of 3 interior angles = 180° for any shape or size of triangle.   a° + b° + c° = 180

Equilateral Triangle—

All sides are equal, all Angles are equal.   AB = BC = AC
1° = 2° = 3°

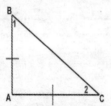

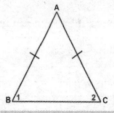

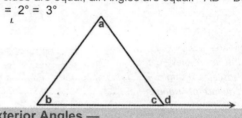

Isosceles Triangles –

An Isosceles Triangle has two equal sides.   The two angles opposite the equal sides are also equal.
Reminder: a Right triangle can also be Isosceles.
AB = AC,   1° = 2°

Exterior Angles —

An exterior angle "d" = sum of remote interior angles
$d° = a° + b°$ **All 3 exterior angles summed= 360°**

Right Triangle –

One angle measures 90° Side opposite = 90° **Hypotenuse =** longest side

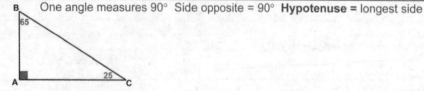

Proportional Triangles –

If two triangles of different size have the same interior angles, then their side lengths are **proportional**.

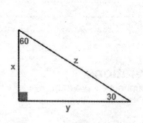

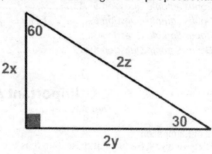

If two triangles are proportional, the ratio of their areas is equal to the ratio of their sides squared. Side of B is 3 times as long as side of A, therefore the area of B is $(3)^2$ or 9 times larger than the area of A (27 is 9 times larger than 3).

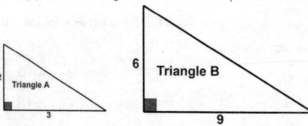

Note: *In any triangle, the largest angle is opposite the largest side.*

Area of a Triangle

$area = \frac{1}{2}(base)(height)$ The height of a triangle is a line dropped from the heights point and perpendicular to the base. In a right triangle, the height is the side. The dashed lines below show the height of other triangles created by dropping a perpendicular line.

 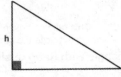 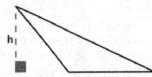

Perimeter of a Triangle

$Perimeter = sum\ of\ all\ three\ sides$
$P = a + b + c$

Pythagorean Theorem

Pythagorean Theorem is used to find the length of one side of a triangle when you know the other two lengths. Remember, this only works on right triangles! To calculate LN (hypotenuse) use Pythagorean Theorem → $a^2 + b^2 = c^2$ Or $(side\ 1)^2 + (side\ 2)^2 = H^2$

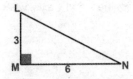

$$c = \sqrt{a^2 + b^2} = \left(\sqrt{(3)^2}\right) + \left(\sqrt{(6)^2}\right) = \sqrt{9 + 36} = \sqrt{45} = \sqrt{9 * 5} = 3\sqrt{5}$$

Therefore, $c = 3\sqrt{5}$

Special Right Triangles

3 : 4 : 5 Triangles

Ratio of sides 3:4:5
If legs have ratios of 3 and 4 then the hypotenuse has a ratio of 5. For example, a triangle with sides 9:12:15. are 3 times a 3:4:5 Therefore. a 9:12:15 will have the same properties of a 3:4:5

Any triangle whose sides are in the ratio **3:4:5** is a right triangle. These are called **Pythagorean Triples**. There are an infinite number of them, and **3:4:5** is just the smallest. If you multiply all the sides by the same number (any number), the result will still be a right triangle whose sides are in the ratio **3:4:5**. For example **6:8:10** or **9:12:15**

Interior Angles: Because we have a right triangle one angle is obviously 90°. The other two are approximately 36.86° and 53.13°.

5 : 12 : 13 Triangle

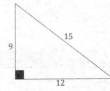

If one leg has a ratio of 5 and the other leg has a ratio of 12, then the hypotenuse has a ratio of **10: 24: 26 is two times 5: 12: 13**

45° : 45° : 90° or Isosceles Right Triangle

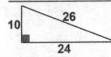

Side: x
Side: x
Hypotenuse: x√2
Ratio of sides: x : x : x√2

If the two legs have the same length x, then the hypotenuse will have a length of x √2. **Example** 45°, 45°, 90° has a ratio of sides **x : x : x√2**. In this example side a = 4. Therefore, the triangle is **4 : 4 : 4√2**

30° 60° 90° triangle

Side: x, **Side:** $x\sqrt{3}$, **Hypotenuse:** $2x$

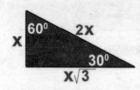

30° – 60° – 90° **Ratio of sides:** $x : x\sqrt{3} : 2x$

If one leg is length x and the second leg is length $x\sqrt{3}$, then the hypotenuse will be length of 2x.

* Notice the hypotenuse is twice the length of the smaller side (one opposite the 30 degree angle). This is a 'standard' triangle you should be able recognize on sight. **Commit to memory:** *The sides are always in the ratio* $(1 : 2 : \sqrt{3})$

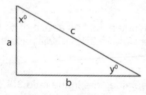

With the '2' being the hypotenuse (longest side). This ratio comes in handy later in the study of trigonometry. Also notice that the smallest angle is always opposite the smallest side.

Here is an example of a $30° - 60° - 90°$ **triangle with Ratio of sides:** $x : x\sqrt{3} : 2x$, but scaled so x=5. Therefore, the sides are $5 : 5\sqrt{3} : 10$.

Triangle Reminders

- **If you know the sum of any two angles, yo**u can find the third.
- **If you know two of the following** – Height, Base, Area, then you can find the third.
- **For a right triangle;** if you know the length of any two sides you can find the third.
- **For special right triangles like:** 45-45-90, 30-60-90

If you know the length of any one side and its opposite angle, you can find the length of both other legs.

PowerPrep Practice Questions   Also in the Virtual Classroom on DVD

PowerPrep Practice Questions 3-4

3. In the rectangular coordinate system above, if the line segment shown created a right triangle with the x and y axis, what would be the perimeter of the triangle?

(A) $\sqrt{146}$
(B) $6 + 2\sqrt{73}$
(C) $11 + 2\sqrt{73}$
(D) $16 + 2\sqrt{73}$
(E) $16 + \sqrt{146}$

(11,0)

(0,-5)

4. Given: 1. $y = ½ x$, and 2. $a^2 + b^2 = c^2$

What is the value of *x*?

(A) 30
(B) 45
(C) **60**
(D) 90
(E) 120

Explanation to PowerPrep Practice Question 3

This question tests your knowledge of the Pythagorean Theorem.

Quick Review: The sum of two squares whose sides are the two legs (a and b) is equal to the area of the square whose side is the hypotenuse (c)

Where "a" and "b" are the sides of the triangle forming the right angle and "c" is the hypotenuse:
$a^2 + b^2 = c^2$ or solved for "c" it becomes: $c = \sqrt{a^2 + b^2}$

If you already know the hypotenuse and one leg of the triangle, you can solve for the other leg.
As follows: $a^2 - c^2 = b^2$ or $c^2 - b^2 = a^2$ This equation provides a simple relationship among the three sides of a right triangle. If the length of any two sides is known, the length of the third side can be discovered.

Answer to Question #3: Since the angle where the two axis' meet is a right angle, we can use the Pythagorean Theorem to solve for the length of the line segment. **We know one leg of the triangle = 11 and the other leg = 5**

Therefore, plug the information into the Pythagorean Theorem and solve for side c (the hypotenuse) $a^2 + b^2 = c^2$
Substitute a=11 and b=5 becomes: $11^2 + 5^2 = c^2$ **Multiply the squares:** $121 + 25 = c^2$ **Then add:** $146 = c^2$
Simplify by taking square root of c^2 : $\sqrt{146} = c$ **Plug this information back into the question. What is the perimeter of the triangle?** Perimeter of triangle = sum of all three sides = $11 + 5 + \sqrt{146}$ add $16 + \sqrt{146}$ **Answer: (E)**

Explanation to PowerPrep Practice Question 4

This question tests your understanding of both the Pythagorean Theorem and solving equations for x in terms of y. You cannot assume that the triangle is a right triangle. However, in the given information it says that $a^2 + b^2 = c^2$ This tells us the triangle is, in fact, a right triangle— because the Pythagorean Theorem only applies to right triangles.

If the given triangle is "right", what more do we know? We know the angle formed by legs a and b is $90°$
Fact: all the interior angles of a triangle must add to 180°

We now know that one angle is $90°$ We also know that the sum of the angles is $180°$

And we were given a third piece of information: $y = \frac{1}{2}x$ **Now we can substitute what we know and solve the problem.**
$x^o + y^o + 90^o = 180^o$ becomes $y^o = \frac{1}{2}x^o$

Substitute for y: $x^o + \frac{1}{2}x^o + 90^o = 180^o$ **Subtract 90 from both sides:** $x^o + \frac{1}{2}x^o + 90^o = 180^o$ **Becomes:**
$x^o + \frac{1}{2}x^o = 90^o$ **Add the x's:** $x^o + \frac{1}{2}x^o = 90^o$ **Becomes:** $1\frac{1}{2}x^o = 90^o$ **Convert 1 ½ to fraction:** $1\frac{1}{2} = \frac{3}{2}$
Invert and multiply both sides by $\frac{2}{3}$: $\frac{3}{2}x^o = 90^o$ **Becomes:** $x^o = 90^o * \frac{2}{3}$ **Simplify:** $x^o = 90^o * \frac{2}{3}$ becomes:
$x = \frac{180}{3}$ becomes: **x = 60** <u>Check your work:</u> If x = 60 **Then :** $x^o + y^o + 90^o = 180^o$ **becomes** $60^o + y^o +$
$90^o = 180^o$ **becomes** $y^o + 150^o = 180^o$ **becomes** $y^o = 30^o$ **Therefore,** $x^o + y^o + 90^o = 180^o$ **SO** 60 + 30 +
90 = 180 **and** 180 = 180 <u>Answer: (C)</u>

Bonus Sample Questions   not in the Virtual Classroom on the DVD

Bonus Sample Question 5-8

5. At two o'clock in the afternoon the pole represented by segment AB casts a shadow that ends at point C. At four o'clock the pole casts a shadow that ends at point D, a distance of 9 feet from the bottom of the pole. If the distance from A to C is (square root 61 feet), what is the distance, in feet, from C to D?

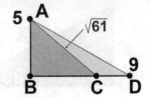

(A) 2
(B) 3
(C) 4
(D) 6
(E) 7

6. You are given three (3) points in a coordinate system on the x and y axis plane $(-4,0)$, $origin$, $(0,-3)$. If the three points are connected to form a triangle, what is the hypotenuse of that triangle?

(A) 3
(B) $2\sqrt{3}$
(C) $\sqrt{3}$
(D) $\sqrt{5}$
(E) 5

7. If side GH of equilateral triangle FGH is 6, which is greater; the area of triangle FGH or the perimeter of triangle FGH

(A) The area of triangle FGH is greater
(B) The perimeter of triangle FGH is greater
(C) They are equal
(D) Unknown—insufficient information

8. In the right triangle, if x=3, what is the value of y?
(A) $\sqrt{13}$
(B) $\sqrt{15}$
(C) 4
(D) $\sqrt{17}$
(E) 5

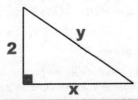

Explanation to Bonus Sample Question 5

Analysis: The triangle formed with points ABC is a right triangle. Use the Pythagorean Theorem to solve for the length of BC.
$a^2 + b^2 = c^2$ **becomes** $5^2 + b^2 = \left(\sqrt{61}\right)^2$ **becomes** $25 + b^2 = 61$ **So** $b^2 = 36$ **becomes** $b = 6 = BC$
Solve for the length of CD: $BD = BC = CD$ Becomes: $9 - 6 = 3$ <u>Correct answer:</u> **(B)**

Explanation to Bonus Sample Question 6

Analysis: First we must correctly diagram the image given to us in the stimulus material...connect the three points $(-4,0)$, $origin$, $(0,-3)$.

Since the angle where the two axes meet is a right angle, we can use the Pythagorean Theorem to solve for the length of the hypotenuse. $a^2 + b^2 = c^2$ **Becomes** $3^2 + 4^2 = c^2$
Becomes $9 + 16 = c^2$ **Finally** $25 = c^2$ becomes $\sqrt{25} = c$ or $c = 5$ **Hypotenuse is 5**

<u>Correct answer:</u> **(E)**

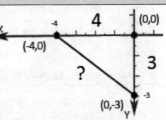

Explanation to Bonus Sample Question 7

Option 1 Make a sketch.

What we know: Triangle GHF is equilateral. This means all the sides are equal and all the angles are equal. We are told that segment GH = 6

Therefore, GH = 6, HF= 6, and FG = 6

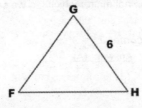
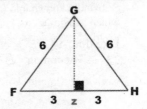

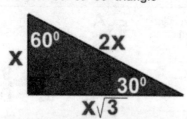

Next, drop a perpendicular line from point G so that it intersects the base FH at point Z. **See diagram.**

Since all sides are equal in an equilateral triangle, all angles are also equal. We also know that every triangle has 180^0 total degrees. If all angles are equal in an equilateral triangle and they total 180^0, then each angle must equal 60^0.

Now notice that perpendicular line GZ bisects angle G. If angle G was 60^0 and then it was bisected into two equal parts, each side is a 30^0 angle. The line GZ also creates a 90^0 angle where it intersects FH at point Z.

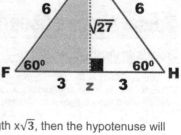

We started with all angles in the triangle equal to 60^0. Angle F is the only remaining 60^0 angle. Angle G has been bisected into two 30^0 angles and the angle at point Z is 90^0.

So we now have a triangle GFZ and it is a 30 – 60 – 90 triangle.

Review: 30° 60° 90° triangle

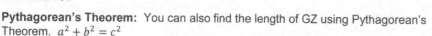

Side: x, **Side:** $x\sqrt{3}$, **Hypotenuse:** $2x$
Ratio of sides: $x : x\sqrt{3} : 2x$

If one leg has length x and the second leg has length $x\sqrt{3}$, then the hypotenuse will have a length of 2x.

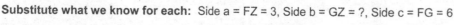

If you apply the ratios of sides for a 30 – 60 – 90 triangle, you find out that the sides of this triangle are: $x = 3$, $2x = 6$, and $x\sqrt{3} = 3\sqrt{3}$ The height or second side (GZ) has a length of $3\sqrt{3}$. The diagram shows the height or side GZ as $\sqrt{27}$ but if you factor that, it becomes $3\sqrt{3}$

Pythagorean's Theorem: You can also find the length of GZ using Pythagorean's Theorem. $a^2 + b^2 = c^2$

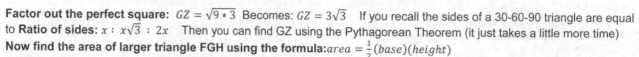

Substitute what we know for each: Side a = FZ = 3, Side b = GZ = ?, Side c = FG = 6

$a^2 + b^2 = c^2$ **Becomes** $3^2 + GZ^2 = 6^2 => 9 + GZ^2 = 36 => GZ^2 = 27 => GZ = \sqrt{27}$

Factor out the perfect square: $GZ = \sqrt{9*3}$ Becomes: $GZ = 3\sqrt{3}$ If you recall the sides of a 30-60-90 triangle are equal to **Ratio of sides:** $x : x\sqrt{3} : 2x$ Then you can find GZ using the Pythagorean Theorem (it just takes a little more time)

Now find the area of larger triangle FGH using the formula: $area = \frac{1}{2}(base)(height)$

We went through the process of finding the length of GZ, because GZ is the height of the larger triangle FGH

Substitute what we know: $Area\ FGH = \frac{1}{2}(bh)$ Becomes:

$Area = \frac{1}{2}(6)(3\sqrt{3})$ becomes $area = (3)(3)(\sqrt{3})$ becomes $area = 9\sqrt{3}$

The final value of Option 1: $area = 9\sqrt{3}$

Option 2: Perimeter of FGH. The formula for perimeter is, $side\ a + side\ b + side\ c$ Substitute what we know:
Becomes: $6 + 6 + 6 = 18$. So, the value of Options 2 is 18

Compare Option 1 and Option 2: Which is greater between $9\sqrt{3}$ and 18?

After all this work to get to this point, we still have to figure out how to put these two terms in a format that allows comparison.

Note that 18 can be factored like this: $9 * 2 = 18$
Now we have something that looks easier to compare: $9\sqrt{3}$ and 9(2)
Since both terms have (9), so we can eliminate the (9) and compare: $\sqrt{3}$ and (2)
The $\sqrt{3}$ is less than 2 because $2^2 = 4$

So Option 2: which is 18 is greater than Option 1, which turned out to be $9\sqrt{3}$ or $\sqrt{27}$

Answer: (B)

Explanation to Bonus Sample Question 8

In any right triangle, you can use Pythagorean Theorem to solve for any side once you know the length of two sides. In this case, we are given the length of two sides: The image shows us the height is 2 and the text information tells us that x= 3.

We are asked to find y, the hypotenuse. We just need to plug this information into Pythagorean's Theorem: $a^2 + b^2 = c^2$
Substitute known info (it does not matter which leg we set as side "a" or "b", as long as we have side "y" as the hypotenuse which is side "c"

Like this: $a^2 + b^2 = c^2$ **Becomes** $2^2 + 3^2 = c^2$
$13 = c^2$ **becomes** $\sqrt{13} = c$ **Answer: (A)**

Geometry
Part 3: Quadrilaterals
Virtual Classroom>Geometry>Angles
This material corresponds to the Virtual Classroom Instructions in the
PowerPrep DVD/Internet/iApps for Geometry

Virtual Classroom

Part 3: Quadrilaterals

Generally

Any object with four sides is called a quadrilateral.
Its interior angles total 360 degrees. It can be cut into two triangles, each having a total 180 degrees.

Types of quadrilateral

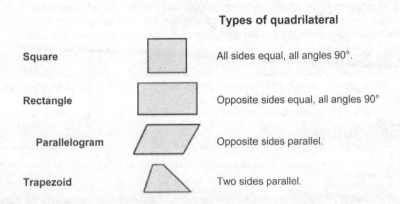

Square	All sides equal, all angles 90°.
Rectangle	Opposite sides equal, all angles 90°
Parallelogram	Opposite sides parallel.
Trapezoid	Two sides parallel.

Square

A square is a quadrilateral with four equal sides and all four interior angles are right angles.
Perimeter: *Sum of sides* $= 4x$
Area: *length* $*$ *width* $= side^2 = x^2$

Rectangle

A rectangle is a quadrilateral that has two sets of equal sides which are opposite each other: top and bottom, left and right.
All four interior angles are right angles.

Perimeter: *sum all sides* = $2(l + w)$

Area: *length* $*$ *width* = lw

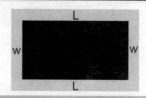

Parallelogram

A parallelogram is a quadrilateral that is similar to a rectangle in that it has two sets of equal sides that are opposite each other (top and bottom, left and right)
They are also parallel to each other. Also, its opposite angles are equal.

Perimeter: *sum all sides* = $2(b + w)$

Area: *base* $*$ *height* = $(b)(h)$

Properties of a parallelogram

These facts are true for parallelograms and the descendant shapes: square, rectangle and rhombus.

The diagonals bisect each other
Each diagonal cuts the other diagonal into two equal parts.

Opposite angles are equal
In the figure on the right notice, the opposite angles are always equal. For example ∠CAB = ∠BDC.

Consecutive angles are supplementary
Consecutive angles are always supplementary (add to 180°) For example ∠ABD + ∠BDC =180°. This is a result of the line BD being a transversal of the parallel lines AB and CD

Trapezoid

A trapezoid is a quadrilateral that has two parallel and two non-parallel sides.

Area: $\frac{1}{2}(base_1 + base_2)(height) = \frac{1}{2}(b_1 + b_2)h$ **Perimeter**: *Sum all sides* = $(b_1 + b_2 + s_1 + s_2)$ **The area of a trapezoid is given by the formula**

$$area = a\left(\frac{b_1 + b_2}{2}\right)$$ *Where* b_1, b_2 *are the lengths of the two bases and "a" is the altitude of the trapezoid*

Recall that the bases are the two parallel sides of the trapezoid. The altitude (or height) of a trapezoid is the **perpendicular** distance between the two bases. This is equivalent to the altitude times the average length of the bases. Since the **median of a trapezoid** is also the average length of the two bases, the area is also the altitude times the median length.
Area as a compound shape: Another way to find the area of a trapezoid is to treat it as some simpler shapes, and then add or subtract their areas to find the result. For example, a trapezoid could be considered to be a smaller rectangle plus two right triangles:

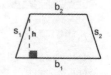

Quadrilateral Reminders

Square: if you know any one of the three – length of side, area, or perimeter – you can find the other two.
Rectangle: if you know length and width, you can find area and perimeter.
Rectangle: if you know area or perimeter, you cannot find length and width unless you know the relationship between the two.

Data Sufficiency Reminders

Base	Any side can be considered a base. Choose any one you like. If used to calculate the area the corresponding altitude must be used.
Altitude (height)	The altitude (or height) of a parallelogram is the perpendicular distance from the base to the opposite side (which may have to be extended). In the figure above, the altitude is show by the dashed line.
Area	The area of a parallelogram can be found by multiplying a base by the corresponding altitude.
Perimeter	The distance around the parallelogram. The sum of its sides.

For a square, if you know any of the following: •Length of any side •Area •Perimeter
Then you can find the other two: For a rectangle, if you know length and width, you can find area and perimeter. For a rectangle, if you know area or perimeter, you cannot find length and width **unless** you know the relationship between the two.

PowerPrep Practice Questions   Also in the Virtual Classroom on DVD

PowerPrep Practice Questions 5-6

5. What is the area of the square?

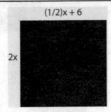

(A) 4
(B) 8
(C) 16
(D) 32
(E) 64

6. In parallelogram ABCD $\angle A$ = 60°. Find the remaining angles ($\angle B$, $\angle C$, $\angle D$)
(A) (60,60,60)
(B) (120, 60, 60)
(C) (60, 120, 60)
(D) (120,60,120)
(E) (180, 60, 180)

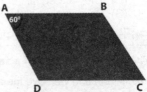

Explanation to PowerPrep Practice Question 5

There are two facts about squares that we need to know to answer this problem. 1. The sides of a square are equal 2. Area = side^2

Because the sides of a square are equal you can set the two sides equal. Like this: $2x$ $(given)$ = $\frac{1}{2} x$ + 6 $(given)$
Now solve: $2x$ = $\frac{1}{2} x$ + 6   first, **subtract ½ x from both sides**: becomes: $1 \frac{1}{2} x$ = 6

Convert 1 ½ to a fraction: $1 \frac{1}{2}$ = $\frac{3}{2}$ then **Invert and multiply to clear** $\frac{3}{2}$ from the left side. $\frac{3}{2} x$ = 6 invert and

multiply becomes: x = $6 x \frac{2}{3}$ **Simplify**: $x = \frac{12}{3}$ becomes: x = 4

Don't stop there, you have to plug this information into the given. You can use either given fact ($\frac{1}{2} x$ + 6) Or ($2x$)
Now plug in the value for x: x = 4 **Therefore**, 2x becomes 2(4) = 8 **Or** ½ x + 6 becomes: ½ (4) + 6 **becomes**
2 + 6 = 8 **Either way, you find the length of one side of the square is 8.** But don't stop yet. Now you have to use the
formula for **Area of a square = side^2** Since side = 8 then Area = 8^2, therefore **Area = 64 Answer: (E)**

Explanation to PowerPrep Practice Question 6

Quick Review: A parallelogram is a quadrilateral where the opposite sides are parallel to each other.
Properties of a Parallelogram:
• Opposite sides of a parallelogram are equal.
• Opposite angles of a parallelogram are equal.
• Any two consecutive angles are supplementary (add up to 180°)
• The area, A, of a parallelogram is $A = bh$, where b is the base of the parallelogram and h is the height.
• The area of a parallelogram is twice the area of a triangle created by one of its diagonals.
• Each diagonal bisects the parallelogram into two congruent triangles.
• The diagonals bisect the other: IOW—each diagonal cuts the other diagonal into two equal parts.

Explanation: What do we know?   1. the figure is a parallelogram 2. $\angle A$ = **60°**
When we combine the given information with the basic properties of Parallelograms, we can solve the problem.
Since opposite angles of a parallelogram are equal, and $\angle A$ = **60°** then $\angle C$ = **60°**
Since consecutive angles are supplementary (add to 180°) If $\angle A$ = **60°** Then, both $\angle D$ = **120°** and $\angle B$ = **120°** Answer: (D)

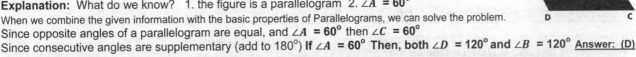

Bonus Sample Questions   <u>not</u> in the Virtual Classroom on the DVD

Bonus Sample Questions 9-12

9. If the area of a square is 324 sq. inches, what is the length of one side of the square in feet?

(A) 8748
(B) 18
(C) 9
(D) 1.5
(E) 1

10. If the distance from W to V is 10 feet, what is the area of the trapezoid?
(A) 8
(B) 24
(C) 40
(D) 80
(E) 96

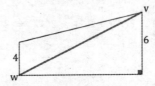

11. If the perimeter of square A and the area of square B are equal, then which is greater, $(4ac)$ or (b^2c) ?

    (A) $(4ac)$ is greater
    (B) (b^2c) is greater
    (C) They are equal
    (D) Unknown—insufficient information

12. If parallelogram ABCD, AB + BC = 12, then which is greater, $2(BC + DC)$ or Perimeter of ABCD?

    (A) $2(BC + DC)$ is greater
    (B) *Perimeter of ABCD* is greater
    (C) They are equal
    (D) Unknown—insufficient information

Explanation to Bonus Sample Question 9

The formula for area of a square is: $side^2$ *or* l^2

In this question we have the answer for the area and we have to work backwards. If $side^2 = area$ and we we know the area is 324, then the formula is $l^2 = 324$. Now simplify $l = \sqrt{324}$ the square root of 324 is 18.

But now we have to answer the second part of the question. We know the side of the square is 18 inches, but we have to convert to feet. 18 inches is 1.5 feet **Correct Answer (D)**

Explanation to Bonus Sample Question 10

Analysis: Segment WV divides the trapezoid into two triangles.
Use the Pythagorean Theorem to find the third side of the bottom triangle. $a^2 + b^2 = c^2$
$6^2 + b^2 = 10^2$, $36 + b^2 = 100$, $b^2 = 64$ becomes $b = \sqrt{64}$ becomes $b = 8$

Now find the area of the trapezoid. $area = a\left(\dfrac{b_1 + b_2}{2}\right)$ *Where b1, b2 are the lengths of the two bases a is the altitude of the trapezoid*

The key to answering this question is realizing the two parallel segments are considered the bases (even if they are vertical, like this case).

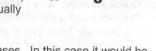

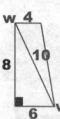

This image shows all the information we have at this point.
It might help to imagine the trapezoid rotated so that the base (side with length 6) is on the bottom. That will help you visualize that the side with length 8 is actually the height because it intersects the base with a perpendicular right angle.

Also, remember that the altitude or height is the distance between the two bases. In this case it would be the line segment that ends at point W and is one of the legs of the 90° angle. In the Pythagorean Theorem this is side b (in this case)

Solve for Area: $area = \frac{1}{2}(base_1 + base_2) * height$ **Substitute what we know:** $area = \frac{1}{2}(6+4)*8$ becomes: $area = 5 * 8 = 40$ **Correct answer: (C)**

Explanation to Bonus Sample Question 11

If the perimeter of square A equals area of square B, then: *Perimeter A = Area B*
Perimeter of a square is $(side\ 1 + side\ 2 + side\ 3 + side\ 4) = 4s$
Area of a square $= side * side = side^2$

Square A has side a and Square B has side b
Therefore square A's perimeter is: $a + a + a + a = perimeter\ of\ square\ A$. This is the same as $4a$
The Area of square B is: $4b$ which is also b^2. Now we know that: $4a = b^2$ **But we are asked to compare:**
$(4ac)\ and\ (b^2c)$ **Since we have shown that:** $4a = b^2$ The only difference between this equality and $(4ac)\ and\ (b^2c)$
The difference is "c" If we multiply the same variable to each side of an already equal comparison, we do not change anything. **Therefore, if $4a = b^2$ then $(4ac)\ and\ (b^2c)$ are also equal** **Answer: (C)**

Explanation to Bonus Sample Question 12

Option 1: Since ABCD is a parallelogram, $AB + BC = BC + DC$
Therefore, $2(BC + DC = 2(AB + BC)$
We are told that $AB + BC = 12$ Therefore $2(AB + BC)$, must be $(2 * 12)$ or 24

Option 2 : Perimeter of ABCD = AB + BC + CD + DA
We already know that $AB + BC = 12$, *so that means*, $2(AB + BC) = 2(12) = 24$
Compare both options: Option 1: 24   Option 2: 24
$24 = 24$ **Answer: (C)**

Geometry
Part 4: Polygons

Virtual Classroom>Geometry>Polygons

This material corresponds to the Virtual Classroom Instructions in the
PowerPrep DVD/Internet/iApps for Geometry

Virtual Classroom

Important Abbreviations
These abbreviations are used throughout the program

POE: Process of Elimination
SARR: Synthesize, Analyze, Reduce, and Restate (has to do with Logical Reasoning)
AC: Answer Choice
QS: Question Stem
LOD: Level of Difficulty

Example Question: What is the least common multiple of 3, 4, and 7? **(This is the call of the question or Question Stem "QS")**

These are Answer Choices "AC" A, B, C, D, E

(A)   12
(B)   21
(C)   28
(D)   48
(E)   84

Part 4: Polygons

Generally

A polygon with equal sides and equal angles is called a **regular polygon**.
Example: equilateral triangle, square

5 sides – pentagon	7 sides – heptagon	9 sides – nonagon
6 sides – hexagon	8 sides – octagon	10 sides – decagon

Types of Polygon

 Regular A polygon with all sides and interior angles the same. Regular polygons are always convex

 Irregular Each side may a different length, each angle may be a different measure—The opposite of a regular polygon.

 Radius The radius is the distance from the center to any vertex. It is also the radius of the polygon's circumcircle, the circle that passes through every vertex.

Central Angle: The angle at the center of the polygon made by two adjacent radius lines. There are a total of 360^0 in the central angel for every regular polygon. To find the exact measure of any given central angle, divide 360^0 by the number of sides in the polygon (remember the number of sides also equals the total number of possible angles) In the example here, the total number of sides is 8, the total number of central angles is 8, so the central angle is equal to $\frac{360^0}{8}$ or 45^0

This means that every Polygon with eight (8) sides has central angle equal to 45^0.

A **central angle** is an angle whose **vertex** is the center of a circle, and whose sides pass through a pair of points on the circle, thereby subtending an arc between those two points whose angle is (by definition) equal to the central angle itself. It is also known as the arc segment's angular distance.

Vertex The vertex (plural: vertices) is a corner of the polygon. In any polygon, the number of sides and vertices are always equal.

Side The sides are the straight line segments that make up the polygon.

Being equilateral is not enough

 For a polygon to be 'regular' it must have all sides the same length <u>and</u> all interior angles the same. The figure on the right is actually an example of an equilateral polygon since it has all sides the same length, but it is *not* a regular polygon because its interior angles are not all the same

Properties of all Polygons (regular and irregular)

 Interior angles The interior angles of a polygon are those angles at each vertex on the inside of the polygon.

 Exterior Angles The angle on the outside of a polygon between a side and the extended adjacent side.

 Diagonals The diagonals of a polygon are lines linking any two non-adjacent vertices.

Area For regular polygons there are various ways to calculate the area. See Area of a Regular Polygon
For irregular polygons things are a little harder since there are no general formulas.
Perimeter The distance around a polygon—The sum of its side lengths.

Area

There are several formulas we use for finding the area of a regular polygon, but most require advanced trigonometry that is beyond what will be tested on the exam. So we will subdivide the polygon into shapes (usually triangles).
   •To find the area of a polygon, divide it into 3-sided figures (triangles), then find the area of the figures and add them up.
   • The number of triangles formed will always be two less than the number of sides.
One approach is to break the shape up into pieces that you <u>can</u> solve - usually triangles, since there are many ways to calculate the area of triangles. Exactly how you do it depends on what you are given to start. Since this is highly variable there is no easy rule for how to do it. The examples below give you some basic approaches to try.

 1. Break into triangles, then add: Divide the figure it into triangles by drawing all the diagonals from one of the vertices. If you know enough sides and angles to find the area of each, then you can simply add them up to find the total. Do not be afraid to draw extra lines anywhere if they will help find shapes you can solve. Here, the irregular pentagon is divided in to 4 triangles by the addition of the red lines.

2. Find 'missing' triangles, then subtract: In the figure on the right, the overall shape is a regular hexagon, but there is a triangular piece missing. (in white) We know how to find the area of a regular polygon so we just subtract the area of the 'missing' triangle created by drawing the red line.

 3. Consider other shapes: In the figure on the right, the shape is an irregular hexagon, but it has a symmetry that lets us break it into two parallelograms by drawing the red dotted line. (Assuming the lines that look parallel really are parallel!)

We know how to find the area of a parallelogram so we just find the area of each one and add them together.

As you see, there are myriad ways to divide shapes into pieces that are easier to manage. You then add or subtract the areas of the more manageable shapes. Exactly how you do it depends on personal preference and what information you have.

Sum Interior Angles

Sum of <u>all interior angles</u> inside a polygon : $sum = 180(n - 2) \, degrees$
Where n equals the number of sides.

Example: Square (has four sides) therefore, $180(4 - 2) = 180(2) = 360^o$
Average measure of a <u>single inside angle</u> for a REGULAR polygon:

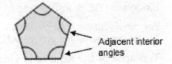
Adjacent interior angles

$\dfrac{180(n-2)}{n} \, degrees$	**Where** n is the number of sides

All we did is find the sum of the all the interior angles using the formula: $sum = 180(n - 2) \, degrees$

Then we divide this total by the number of angles (or sides—which is the same)

But this only works for Regular Polygons where all the angles are congruent.

More about Interior Angles: The interior angles of a polygon are those angles at each **vertex** that are on the inside of the polygon. There is one per vertex. So for a polygon with N sides, there are N **vertices** and N interior angles.

For a **regular polygon**, by definition, all the interior angles are the same

For an **irregular polygon**, each angle may be different.

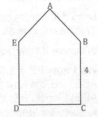

Sum of Interior Angles: The interior angles of any polygon always add up to a constant value, which depends only on the number of sides. For example the interior angles of a **pentagon** always add up to 540° no matter if it regular or irregular, **convex** or **concave**, or what size and shape it is. The sum of the interior angles of a polygon is given by the formula

$sum = 180(n - 2) \, degrees$ **Where** n is the number of sides

A **square**	has 4 sides,	so interior angles add up to 360°
A **pentagon**	has 5 sides,	so interior angles add up to 540°
A **hexagon**	has 6 sides,	so interior angles add up to 720°
... etc		

In Regular Polygons: For a regular polygon, the total described above is spread evenly among all the interior angles, since they all have the same values. So for example the interior angles of a pentagon always add up to 540°, so in a regular pentagon (5 sides), each one is one fifth of that, or 108°. Or, as a formula, each interior angle of a regular polygon is given by: $\dfrac{180(n-2)}{n} \, degrees$ **Where** n is the number of sides

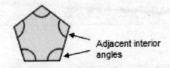
Adjacent interior angles

Adjacent angles: Two interior angles that share a common side are called "adjacent interior angles" or just "interior angles".

PowerPrep Practice Questions Also in the Virtual Classroom on DVD

PowerPrep Practice Questions 7-8

7. Given:

1. Triangle ABE is equilateral
2. $\angle EAB = 60^\circ$
3. Segment AB = 5
4. Polygon BCDE is a square

What is the area of polygon   ABCDE?

(A) $2.5\sqrt{18.75}$
(B) 45
(C) $\sqrt{18.75}$
(D) $2.5\sqrt{18.75} + 25$
(E) $(2.5\sqrt{18.75}) / 25$

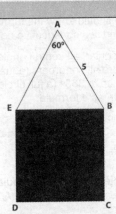

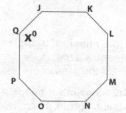

8. Given: Polygon JKLMNOPQ is regular. What is the value of *x*?
   (A) 135°
   (B) 145°
   (C) 95°
   (D) 100°
   (E) 150°

Explanation to PowerPrep Practice Question 7

First, itemize what we know and what it means.

The given information tells us the triangle sitting on top of the square is equilateral.
This means all the angles are the same (60°) and all the sides are the same (5)
BCDE is a square. This means all the sides are the same.

Since triangle ABE is equilateral, and side AB is 5, then side BE is also 5.
Since side BE is also a side of the square, and all sides of a square are equal, then all four sides of the square are 5

We can divide the polygon ABCDE into a square BCDE and a triangle ABE
To find the area of the polygon ABCDE we find the area of the square BCDE and the triangle ABE and add them together.

The area of the square is side^2. Since BE = 5 we know the area = 5^2 then, the **Area of BCDE = 25**
Now we have to find the area of the triangle ABE: **Area of triangle = $(\frac{1}{2})(base * height)$**

Base of ABE = 5 (because equilateral triangle) **Therefore**, AE also = 5
Now we have to find the height of ABE

Drop a line from point A to line BE (this represents the height of ABE
This new line is also a leg of a right triangle. Call the new point where it intersects BE, point Z.

We have a new triangle called AZE (or AZB, does not matter)

We know EZ = 2.5 or BZ = 2.5 because AZ bisects BE. We also know that EA = 5 (equilateral ABE). EA is now the hypotenuse of AZE. We also know that the vertical line AZ (the height of ABE) bisects BE, therefore angle AZE and AZB is a right angle. Since AZE is right, we can use the Pythagorean Theorem to solve for length of AZ (which will be height of ABE). **So using Pythagorean Theorem we know:** $a^2 + b^2 = c^2$ (where c is the hypotenuse)
But we need to solve for a leg (AZ) of the triangle (AZE). We also know c (the hypotenuse) = 5

Subtract b^2 from both sides of the Theorem so we can solve for one side. $a^2 = c^2 - b^2$
Now plug in what we know: Hypotenuse $c = 5$ and Base $b = 2.5$

Therefore: $(a^2 = 5^2 - 2.5^2)$ **Multiply** $(a^2 = 25 - 6.25)$ **Add** $a^2 = 18.75$ **Square root** $a = \sqrt{18.75}$
Bear in mind that we just solved the height of ABE by finding the length of line AZ which was side *A* in our Pythagorean Theorem for triangle AZE.

If that's confusing, look it over until it makes sense.
Now we return to the big triangle ABE to find the area: $\frac{1}{2}(b \times h) = area$
Plug in what we know: Base = 5 and Height = $\sqrt{18.75}$
Therefore: $\frac{1}{2}(5 * \sqrt{18.75})$ **Multiply** $2.5\sqrt{18.75}$ **Therefore, area of the triangle ABE is** $2.5\sqrt{18.75}$
But we were asked for area of the polygon ABCDE. We already know the area of the square BCDE= $(5 * 5)$ or 25
Therefore, polygon ABCDE area = area of triangle ABE and square BCDE $(2.5\sqrt{18.75} + 25)$ **Answer: (D)**

Explanation to PowerPrep Practice Question 8

There are several important concepts dealing with **polygons** and their angles.
Quick Review:
Regular Polygons: First you should know that a regular polygon has equal sides, and equal interior angles.
It is NOT sufficient to have all sides equal. For a polygon to be 'regular' it must have all sides the same length and all interior angles the same. The figure on the right shows an equilateral polygon, since it has all sides the same length, but it is **not** a regular polygon because its interior angles are not all the same

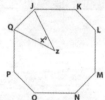

Central Angle: Next, you should know the formula to find the **central angle** created by the mid-point (Z) of a regular polygon and two consecutive points on the polygon.

Because this polygon is regular, all central angles are equal (in this case x°). It does not matter which angle you choose—they are all congruent (equal)
All the central angles add up to 360° (a full circle), so the measure of the central angle is 360 divided by the number of sides. Or, as a formula:

The measure of the central angle, thus, depends only on the number of sides.

<u>**Note:** do not confuse central angles with interior angles.</u>

$$central\ angle = \frac{360}{n}\ degrees$$

where **n** is the number of sides

Interior Angles: Interior angles of a regular

polygon are equal. To find the measure of one interior angle of a regular polygon, use the formula $\frac{(n-2) * 180}{n}$,
where n = # of sides.

Solve Question 8: We won't need all the information above, but we will need much of it.
The question asks for the value of $\angle x$. We know the 8 sided polygon is REGULAR (given). From this information we know that all sides and all interior angles are equal. Once we know the polygon is regular, we just need to apply the formula for finding interior angles of regular polygons. $\frac{(n-2)*180}{n}$, where n = # of sides. Plug in the information we know about the number of sides: $\frac{(n-2)*180}{n}$ becomes $\frac{(8-2)(180)}{8}$ **Simplify:** $\frac{(180)(6)}{8}$ **Multiply** $\frac{1080}{8}$ **Divide** $135°$ **So we know that Each interior angle is 135°** **Answer: (A)**

Bonus Sample Questions   not in the Virtual Classroom on the DVD

Bonus Sample Questions 13-14

13. If BCDE forms a square and the height of triangle ABE is 1.5, what is the area of polygon ABCDE?

    (A) 3
    (B) 12
    (C) 15
    (D) 16
    (E) 19

14. If Z is the center of regular octagon ABCDEFGH, then which is greater, twice the measure of $\angle AZB$ or the measure of $\angle ABC$?

    (A) Twice the measure of $\angle AZB$ is greater
    (B) The measure of $\angle ABC$ is greater
    (C) They are equal
    (D) Unknown—insufficient information

Explanation to Bonus Sample Questions 13

Analysis: Area of square BCDE = $side^2$ **becomes** $4^2 = 16$

Area of triangle ABE = $\frac{1}{2}(base * height) = \frac{1}{2}(4 * 1.5)$ **becomes**

$\left(\frac{1}{2}(6) = 3\right)$ **So** $Area = 3$

Area of polygon ABCDE = $Area\ BCDE + Area\ ABE$ **Becomes** $16 + 3 = 19$

Correct answer: (E)

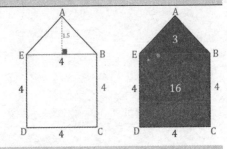

Explanation to Bonus Sample Questions 14

To answer this question, you can either calculate the exact value of the angles using the formulas related to Polygons, or you can use logic and reason.

Let's look at the Polygon formulas first:

Option 1:
You need to know how to find **Central Angles** and **Interior Angles**. First let's look at the **Central Angle**.

Central Angle: The angle at the center of the polygon made by two adjacent radius lines. There are a total of $360°$ in the central angel for every regular polygon. To find the exact measure of any given central angle, divide $360°$ by the number of sides in the polygon (remember the number of sides also equals the total number of possible angles) In the example here, the total number of sides is 8, the total number of central angles is 8, so the central angle is equal to $\frac{360°}{8}$ or $45°$ **This means that every Polygon with eight (8) sides has central angle equal to 45°.**

In our case, the regular polygon has eight (8) sides, therefore, the central angle represented by $\angle AZB = 45°$

The rule or formula related to central angles Measure of

$\angle AZB = \frac{360°}{number\ of\ sides}$ or $\frac{360°}{8} = 45°$

Option 1 tells us: $2(\angle AZB) = 2(45°) = 90°$, The value of Option 1 is 90°

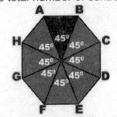

Total degrees in a regular polygon = $360°$

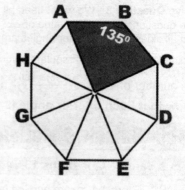

Option 2:
This option asks us to find the value of an **Interior Angle**. The formula for Interior Angles is:

Interior Angle $= \frac{(number\ of\ sides - 2)180}{number\ of\ sides}$

Substitute what we know: Measure of Interior Angle $\angle ABC = \frac{(8-2)180}{8}$

Measure of $\angle ABC = \frac{1080}{8} = 135^0$

Value of Option 2: 135^0

Compare value of Option 1 and Option 2: Option 1 = 90,   Option 2= 135
90 < 135   **Answer: (B)**

Geometry

Part 5: Volume & Surface Area

Virtual Classroom>Geometry>Volume & Surface Area

This material corresponds to the Virtual Classroom Instructions in the
PowerPrep DVD/Internet/iApps for Geometry

Virtual Classroom

Important Abbreviations
These abbreviations are used throughout the program

POE:	Process of Elimination
SARR:	Synthesize, Analyze, Reduce, and Restate (has to do with Logical Reasoning)
AC:	Answer Choice
QS:	Question Stem
LOD:	Level of Difficulty

Example Question: What is the least common multiple of 3, 4, and 7? (**This is the call of the question or Question Stem "QS"**)

These are Answer Choices "AC" A, B, C, D, E

  (A)   12
  (B)   21
  (C)   28
  (D)   48
  (E)   84

Part 5: Volume & Area

Volume Generally

In general, the volume of any right polygon (also called right prism) is: (*Area of base*) ∗ (*height*)
This is also the same as: (*length*) ∗ (*width*) ∗ (*height*)

Right Prism Volume: The volume V of any right prism is the product of B, the area of the base, and the height h of the prism.

Formula Volume $= (B)(h)$ and where $B = lw$

Notice the BASE in the formula represented by capital B, is NOT the length of a side (the way we have seen in measuring the base of a triangle or any other two dimensional object). As we move into the three dimensional objects, when the term BASE is used, it means the surface area of the base, NOT the length of a side.

When you calculate the area of the BASE to find B, you multiply the length of the (width) and (length) so you will have already calculated the surface area or the two dimensional area of the BASE, then when you multiply the surface are of the BASE times the height, it gives you the three dimensional volume.

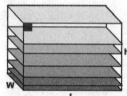

Once you find the surface area of the base (represented by the bottom slice of the darkest green), then multiply the surface are of the base times the height. The height multiplied by each slice results in the volume area of the three (3) dimensional object with right angles (commonly called a prism)

This is a very important formula that is heavily tested on the exam. You should commit this to memory and make sure you understand it.

Volume Cube

Six-sided object, all with equal sides: **Volume: (*area of base*) ∗ (*height*) $= s^2(s) = s^3$**

How to find the volume of a cube
Recall that a cube has all edges the same length. The volume of a cube is found by multiplying the length of any edge by itself twice. So if the length of an edge is 4, the volume is $(4 ∗ 4 ∗ 4 = 64)$

$$volume = s^3 \quad \text{Where } s \text{ is the length of any edge of the cube}$$

Some notes on the volume of a cube: Recall that a cube is like an empty box. It has nothing inside, and the walls of the box have zero thickness. So strictly speaking, the cube has zero volume. When we talk about the volume of a cube, we really are talking about how much liquid it can hold, or how many unit cubes would fit inside it. Think of it this way: if you took a real, empty metal box and melted it down, you would end up with a small blob of metal. If the box was made of metal

with zero thickness, you would get no metal at all. That is what we mean when we say a cube has no volume.

The strictly correct way of saying it is "the volume enclosed by a cube" - the amount space there is inside it. But many textbooks simply say *"the volume of a cube"* to mean the same thing. However, this is not strictly correct in the mathematical sense. What they usually mean when they say this is the volume enclosed by the cube.

Parts of a cube

Face: Also called facets or sides. A cube has six faces which are all squares, so each face has four equal sides and all four interior angles are right angles.
Edge: A line segment formed where two edges meet. A cube has 12 edges.
Because all faces are squares and congruent to each other, all 12 edges are the same length.
Vertex: A point formed where three edges meet. A cube has 8 vertices.
Volume: The volume is s^3 where s is the length of one edge.
Surface Area: The surface area of a cube is $6s^2$ where s is the length of one edge.

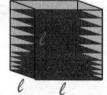

Vertex (8)
Edge (12)
Face (6)

Volume Rectangular Solid

Six-sided object with sets of equal sides: Top and bottom, left and right, front and back.

Volume: (*area of base*) ∗ (*height*) or (lw) ∗ (h) = lwh

This is actually the same formula as for a cube. With rectangle solids the width and length are different so we have to multiple length x width to find the area of the base. With a cube, the length, width and height are equal, so we can use the formula x^3 However, the process is actually (*length ∗ width ∗ height*)

Volume Cylinder

This shape is like a can of soup. The top and bottom are equal circles separated by some height.

Definition: The number of cubic units that will exactly fill a cylinder
Volume: $(Area\ of\ base) * (height)\ or\ Area = \pi r^2\ h$

How to find the volume of a cylinder: The volume of a cylinder is found by multiplying the area of one end of the cylinder by its height. **Or as a formula:**

$volume = \pi r^2 h$ **Where** π is **Pi**, approximately 3.142
r is the **radius** of the circular end of the cylinder h height of the cylinder

Some notes on the volume of a cylinder

Recall that a cylinder is like an empty soup can. It has nothing inside, and the walls of the can have zero thickness. So strictly speaking, the cylinder has zero volume. When we talk about the volume of a cylinder, we really are talking about how much soup it can hold.

Think of it this way: if you took a real, empty metal can and melted it down, you would end up with a small blob of metal. If the can was made of metal with zero thickness, you would get no metal at all. That is what we mean when we say a cylinder has no volume.

The strictly correct way of saying it is "the volume enclosed by a cylinder" - the amount of soup it holds. *But many textbooks simply say "the volume of a cylinder"* to mean the same thing. However, this is not strictly correct in the mathematical sense. What they usually mean when they say this is the volume *enclosed* by the cylinder.

Volume: $(area\ of\ base) * (height) =$
$\pi r^2 * h = h\pi r^2$
$volume = \pi r^2 h$

Find the area of one circle and then multiply that "slice" of the cylinder times the height
The image above demonstrates the idea of slicing the cylinder into many pieces and then adding them up...so find the area of one slice (usually the top or bottom) and then multiply by the height of the cylinder.

PowerPrep Practice Questions   Also in the Virtual Classroom on DVD

PowerPrep Practice Questions 9-10

9. Your dad assigns you the job of figuring out the correct size for a room air conditioner to purchase for your bedroom. Your room has the following shape and the ceiling is nine feet tall (all measurements in the diagram are in feet and all corners are right angles). What is the volume of air in your bedroom?

(A) 1620
(B) 1260
(C) 1080
(D) 180
(E) 360

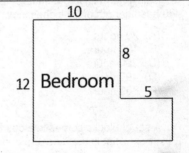

10. What is the volume enclosed by the cylinder below if the radius is 6 and height is 10?

(A) 60
(B) 1,131.12
(C) 600
(D) 18.85
(E) 3140

Explanation to PowerPrep Practice Question 9

This question tests your understanding of volume. The formula for volume of a prism is $(length * width * height)$

There are two ways to view this diagram: 1. a single rectangle size $15x12$ feet with a cutout of size $8x5$ OR a single rectangle of size $12x10$ with an addition of size $5x4$. We can solve the problem either way.

First, let's find the volume of the bigger rectangle prism: Since volume $= lwh$, **plug in what we know:**
$v = lwh$ **becomes**: $v = (12)(10)(9)$ **becomes**: $v = 1,080$ cubic feet of air
Now add the smaller rectangle prism with dimensions $(5x4x9) = 180$ cubic feet of air

Now add the two to get the volume of air for the entire room: $1,080 + 180 = 1,260$ cubic feet of air.

We could also calculate the answer the other way: full size rectangle prism is $12x15x9 = 1620$ cubic feet of air
Less the cut out that is $(8x5x9)$ or 360 cubic feet of air
Total volume is $1620 - 360 = 1260$ Same answer **Answer (B)**

Explanation to PowerPrep Practice Question 10

This question tests your understanding of the formula for finding volume of a cylinder. **Quick Review how to find the volume of a cylinder:** The volume of a cylinder is found by multiplying the area of one end of the cylinder by its height.

	where:
$volume = \pi r^2 h$	π or Pi is approximately 3.142 r is the radius of the circular end of the cylinder h height of the cylinder

Some notes on the volume of a cylinder: A cylinder is like an empty soda can and the walls of the can have zero thickness. When we talk about the volume of a cylinder, we really are talking about how much soda the can hold—not the can itself.

Diameter is the circle's 'width'. The diameter is two times the radius.
Circumference The circumference is the distance around the edge of the circle.

Answer to Question 10: We are asked to find the volume of a cylinder with radius 6 and height 10.

We plug this information into the formula for volume: $volume = \pi r^2 h$
$V = (3.142)(6^2)(10)$ becomes $V = 3.14(36)(10)$ becomes $V = 3.14(360)$
$V = 1,131.12$
Answer: (B)

Note: since π or pi is used to calculate the volume and π is a number that we cannot exactly calculate, the end result of volume is an approximation. It's a good approximation, but still an approximation. When picking an answer, you should select the answer choice that is closest. The test makers will not give you two answer choices that are equally possible. One answer choice will be obviously correct.

Bonus Sample Questions   not in the Virtual Classroom on the DVD

Bonus Sample Questions 15-17

15. Rainwater falls into a square basin at a constant rate of 2 cubic inches per hour. If the basin is 4 inches deep and one side has a length of 20 inches, how long will it take to fill the basin?

    (A) 20 hours
    (B) 100 hours
    (C) 200 hours
    (D) 400 hours
    (E) 800 hours

16. A set of blocks comes in a box that is 14 inches long, 8 inches wide, and 12 inches tall. If 168 cubic blocks fit perfectly in the box, what is the measure of one edge of one block?

    (A) 2
    (B) 3
    (C) 6
    (D) 12
    (E) 14

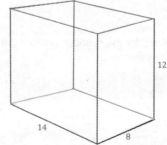

17. Which is greater, the volume of a cylinder with height 5 and radius 2 or the volume of cube with edge 5? **Note:** $\pi = 3.14$

    (A) The volume of a cylinder with height 5 and radius 2 is greater
    (B) The volume of cube with edge 5 is greater
    (C) They are equal
    (D) Unknown—insufficient information

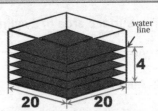

Explanation to Bonus Sample Question 15

Analysis: Find the volume of the square basin.
Volume = (width)•(length)•(height)
Volume = (20)•(20)•(4)
Volume = 1600 cubic inches

Time to fill = $\dfrac{volume\ of\ basin}{rate\ of\ fill}$ **Time** $= \dfrac{1600\ in^3}{2\ in^3/hr} = 800\ hours$

Don't let the inches cubed throw you. It just means the rain is falling at a rain of 2 inches cubed (that's a cubic inch-the volume) per hour and the basin holds rain in units called inches cubed—again that's the volume. <u>**Correct answer: (E)**</u>

Explanation to Bonus Sample Question 16

Analysis: Find the volume of the box of blocks. $V = (l)(w)(h)$ becomes $= (14)(8)(12) = 1,344\ cubic\ inces$

Determine the volume of one block by dividing the total volume by total number of blocks. $\dfrac{1,344}{168} = 8\ cubic\ inces$

This means each block is 8 cubic inches—but we are asked to find the length of a single edge of one of those blocks. So if we know the volume is equal to 8, what do we know?

Volume of a single block: $8\ cubic\ inches$
Volume of cube with side l: $volume = (length\ of\ a\ single\ side)^3$ or $V = l^3$

   $Substitute\ what\ we\ know$: $l^3 = 8$ **becomes** $l = \sqrt[3]{8}$ **becomes** $l = 2\ (length\ of\ a\ single\ side)$
Summary: We have a box with sides (14)(8) and (12) inches. The box has a volume of 1,344 cubic inches, the box contains 168 blocks and each block has sides $(lwh) = 2 * 2 * 2$ or 8 cubic inches. 168 blocks, each block 8 cubic inches $(size\ 2 * 2 * 2)$

Correct answer: (A)

Explanation to Bonus Sample Question 17

Option 1
First we have a cylinder with dimensions: Height = 5, Radius =2
We are asked to find the volume: *Formula for finding the volume of a cylinder is:* $v = \pi r^2 h$
Substitute what we know: Height = 5, Radius = 2
$v = \pi r^2 h$ **Becomes:** $v = \pi(2^2)5$ **Simplify**: $v = \pi(4)5$ Simplify: $v = 20\pi$ Simplify: $v = 20(3.14)$
$v \cong 62.8$ *(Because we π is approximate)*
Option 1 = approximately 62.8

Option 2
We have a cube with dimensions: One side = 5,   We are asked to find the volume
Formula for volume of a cube: $volume\ cube = (one\ side)^3$ or $volume\ cube = l^3$
Substitute what we know: One side = 5, $volume\ cube = l^3$ Becomes $v = 5^3$
$volume\ cube = 5 * 5 * 5 = 125$, therefore, **option 2 = 125**
Compare option 1 and 2: Option 1 is approximately 62.8 and Option 2 is 125 and **$62.8 < 125$**

Correct Answer: (B)

Surface Area Cube

In general, the surface area is the sum of the areas of each surface of the figure.

Cube: A cube has six identical sides, each being a square.

Area of each square: (with all sides equal) $Area\ of\ one\ side = l^2$

Surface Area: Where all sides equal: $6(area\ of\ one\ side) = 6(l)^2$

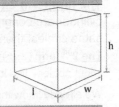

Surface Area of a Solid Rectangle

In general, the surface area is the sum of the areas of each surface of the figure.

Rectangular Solid: A rectangular solid, like a box, has an identical top and bottom, identical left and right sides, and an identical front and back.

Surface Area: $2(area\ bottom) + 2(area\ front) + 2(area\ side) = 2(lw) + 2(lh) + 2(wh)$

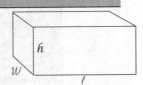

Surface Area of a Cylinder

$Surface\ Area$: $\mathbf{2(area\ top) + area\ retaglular\ body = 2(\pi r^2) + length * height = \ 2\pi r^2 + circumference * height)}$

Note: *that circumference = length of the rectangle*

The surface area of a cylinder is made up of three parts:

1. Area of the top circle

2. Area of the bottom circle

3. Area of the outside lateral surface (The wrapper)

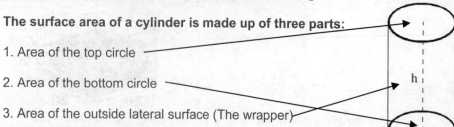

The area of a circle is calculated πr^2

In a cylinder, there is a top and a bottom circle. So, the area is twice, or double, the area of the top or bottom circle by itself. In other words, the area of the top and bottom circles of the cylinder is $2(\pi r^2)$

The lateral side area (the wrapper)

If you can see the cylinder as a soup can with a paper label around it, then you can see the wrapper is a rectangle. What would happen if you were to cut the paper label and then unwrap the soup can, what would the paper label look like?

It would look like a rectangle where the Area of the top circle = πr^2

Area of the wrapped around label = *(length * width)*

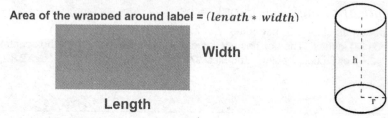

Width

Length

Area of the bottom circle = πr^2

The rectangle above represents the soup can label (cylinder wrapper). If you were to unglue the edge of the label and then unroll it from the can, you would see this rectangle.

Also, you should notice that the circumference of the top or bottom circle is equal to the length of the rectangle. So if you know the circumference of the circle of a cylinder and the height, you can calculate the surface area.

Add the top circle + bottom circle + rectangle wrapper: $\pi r^2 + \pi r^2 +$ (length • width of rectangle)

$2\pi r^2 +$ (length • width of rectangle)

Length of the rectangle is equal to the circumference of the top or bottom circle, and the circumference of any circle is $2\pi r$ therefore: $2\pi r^2 + (2\pi r)(width)$

Width of the rectangle is equal to the height of the cylinder, therefore: $2\pi r^2 + (2\pi r)(width)$

Becomes: $2\pi r^2 + (2\pi r)(h)$

Area of a cylinder : Area = $2\pi r^2 +$ (length • width of rectangle): Becomes $2\pi r^2 + (2\pi r)(h)$

Explanation: In the formula for the area of the cylinder you add up the area of the top circle, the bottom circle, and the side of the cylinder (the label wrapped around the outside of the cylinder) see above.

The first term $2\pi r^2$: Is nothing more than twice the area of a single circle (since the top and bottom of the cylinder are congruent circles—the same circles). Since πr^2 is the formula for a circle, and you have two of the same circles, then $2(\pi r^2)$ is the formula for the top and bottom area of the cylinder.

The 2nd term $(2\pi r)(h)$: This is nothing more than (length • width) of the rectangle label that wraps around the cylinder. It might not look like it, but it is.

We already know that the area of a rectangle is found by multiplying length times width. If you unwrap the label from around the cylinder, it is a rectangle

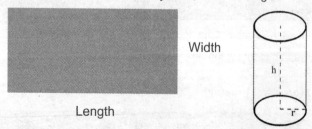

Width

Length

Here's the tricky part: The length of the rectangle is equal to the circumference of the top or bottom circles. Study the cylinder until you can see this fact clearly. So what is the formula for finding the circumference of a circle?

Circumference = $2\pi r$ Or **Circumference** = πd (where d is the diameter—or twice the radius)

You should study these relationships until you understand them clearly. So all we have to do is multiply length or circumference $2\pi r$ times the width of the rectangle (which is also the height of the cylinder)

This gives us the 2nd term: $(2\pi r)(h)$ Now add the area of the circles to the area of the rectangle wrapper
Surface Area of a Cylinder = $2\pi r^2 + (2\pi r)(h)$

Summary

Add the top circle + bottom circle + rectangle wrapper
$\pi r^2 + (\pi r) + (length * width\ of\ rectangle)$
$2\pi r^2 + (length * width\ of\ rectangle)$
Length of the rectangle is equal to the circumference of the top or bottom circle, and the circumference of any circle is $2\pi r$

therefore, $2\pi r^2 + (2\pi r)(width)$. Width of the rectangle is equal to the height of the cylinder,

therefore, $2\pi r^2 + (2\pi r)(width)$ **Becomes:** $2\pi r^2 + (2\pi r)(h)$

PowerPrep Practice Questions   Also in the Virtual Classroom on DVD

PowerPrep Practice Questions 11-12

11. How much paper is needed to make a cylindrical paper cup with an open top whose radius is 2 inches and whose height is 4 inches?

   (A) 2π + 4 square inches
   (B) 4π square inches
   (C) 4π + 6 square inches
   (D) 4π + 8 square inches
   (E) 20π square inches

12. What is the surface area of a cube with length 4 and a rectangle with height and width of 3 and length of 9?

   (A)   (96,126)
   (B)   (64, 96)
   (C)   (64, 126)
   (D)   (96, 96)
   (E)   (64, 81)

Explanation to PowerPrep Practice Question 11

Quick Review:

The surface area of a cylinder is made up of three parts:

1. Area of the top circle

2. Area of the bottom circle

3. Area of the outside lateral surface (the wrapper)

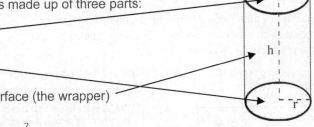

The area of a circle is calculated: πr^2
In a cylinder, there is a top and a bottom circle. So, the area is twice, or double, the area of the top or bottom circle by itself. In other words, the area of the top and bottom circles of the cylinder is $2(\pi r2)$

The lateral side area (the wrapper): If you can see the cylinder as a soup can with a paper label around it, then you can see the wrapper is a rectangle. What would happen if you were to cut the paper label and then unwrap the soup can, what would the paper label look like? It would look like a rectangle (see below)

Three parts. 1. Area of the top circle = πr^2 2. Area of label = $length\ x\ width$ 3. Area of the bottom circle = πr^2

1. Area of the bottom circle = πr^2

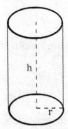

2. Area of the wrapped around label = $length\ x\ width$

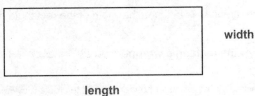
width

length

3. Area of the bottom circle = πr^2

The rectangle above represents the soup can label (cylinder wrapper). If you were to unglue the edge of the label and then unroll it from the can, you would see this rectangle.

Also, you should notice that the circumference of the top or bottom circle is equal to the length of the rectangle. So if you know the circumference of the circle of a cylinder and the height, you can calculate the surface area.

Add the top circle + bottom circle + rectangle wrapper
$\pi r^2 + \pi r^2 + (length * width\ of\ rectangle)$ becomes: $2\pi r^2 + (length\ x\ width\ of\ rectangle)$
Length of the rectangle is equal to the circumference of the top or bottom circle, and the circumference of any circle is $2\pi r$
therefore: $2\pi r^2 + (2\pi r)(width)$
Width of the rectangle is equal to the height of the cylinder, therefore: $2\pi r^2 + (2\pi r)(width)$
Becomes: $2\pi r^2 + (2\pi r)(h)$

Here are the formulas you need to know for area of a circle

If you know the radius: Given the radius of a circle, the area inside it can be calculated using the formula

	where:
$area = \pi r^2$	R is the radius of the circle
	π or Pi, approximately 3.142

If you know the diameter: If you know the diameter of a circle, the area inside it can be found using the formula

	where:
$area = \dfrac{\pi D^2}{4}$	D is the diameter of the circle
	π or Pi, approximately 3.142

If you know the circumference
If you know the circumference of a circle, the area inside it can be found using the formula

	where:
$area = \dfrac{C^2}{4\pi}$	C is the circumference of the circle π or Pi, approximately 3.142

Circumference of a circle: Given the radius of a circle, the circumference can be calculated using the formula

	where:
$circumference = 2\pi R$	R is the radius of the circle π or Pi, approximately 3.142

Surface Area of a cylinder: $Area = 2\pi r^2 + (length * width\ of\ rectangle)$ **Becomes:** $Area = 2\pi r^2 + 2\pi r(h)$

Explanation Question 11:

In the formula for the area of the cylinder you add up the area of the top circle, the bottom circle, and the side of the cylinder (the label wrapped around the outside of the cylinder) see above.

The first term $2\pi r^2$: Is nothing more than twice the area of a single circle (since the top and bottom of the cylinder are congruent circles—the same circles). Since $\pi r2$ is the formula for a circle, and you have two of the same circles, then $2(\pi r2)$ is the formula for the top and bottom area of the cylinder.

The 2nd term $2\pi r(h)$: This is nothing more than $(length\ x\ width)$ of the rectangle label that wraps around the cylinder. It might not look like it, but it is.

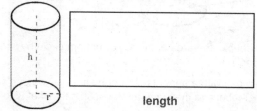

width

length

We already know that the area of a rectangle is found by multiplying length times width. If you unwrap the label from around the cylinder, it is a rectangle

Here's the tricky part: The length of the rectangle is equal to the circumference of the top or bottom circles. Study the cylinder until you can see this fact clearly.

So what is the formula for finding the circumference of a circle?
$Circumference = 2\pi r$ or $circumference = \pi d$ (where d is the diameter—or twice the radius)

You should study these relationships until you understand them clearly.

So all we have to do is multiply length or circumference $(2\pi r)$ times the width of the rectangle (which is also the height of the cylinder) This gives us the 2nd term: $2\pi r(h)$

Now add the area of the circles to the area of the rectangle wrapper: $Area = 2\pi r^2 + 2\pi r(h)$

Answer to Question 11
Trick: You needed to recognize that the question asked for the amount of paper needed to create a cylinder with the given dimensions. This is the same as asking "what is the surface area" Also, you should notice that the question asks for the area of a cylinder **WITH AN OPEN TOP**. This means we only have to find the area of the bottom circle and the area of the rectangle wrapped around the outside of the cylinder.

Plug in what we know: $Area\ of\ a\ cylinder\ =\ 2\pi r^2\ +\ 2\pi r(h)$ But this question only asks for the area of one of the circles, so Area $= 2\pi r^2\ +\ 2\pi r(h)$ **Remove the 2**

For this problem the formula will be: $Area\ =\ \pi r^2\ +\ 2\pi r(h)$
Given: Radius = 2, Height = 4

Plug in: Area $= \pi r^2\ +\ 2\pi r(h)$ **Becomes:** $Area\ =\ \pi 2^2\ +\ 2\pi 2(4)$

Simplify: $Area\ =\ \pi 2^2\ +\ 2\pi 2(4)$ Simplify: $Area\ =\ \pi 4\ +\ 2\pi 8$
Simplify: $Area\ =\ 4\pi\ +\ 16\pi$
$Area\ =\ 20\pi$ **Answer: (E)**

Explanation to PowerPrep Practice Question 12

This question tests your understanding of surface area and cubes and rectangles.
The formulas are: Surface area of a $cube\ =\ 6a^2$ (where a is the length of one side)

the surface area of a cube is the area of the six squares that cover it. The area of one of them is $(a * a)$, or a^2. Since these are all the same, you can multiply one of them by six, so the surface area of a cube is 6 times one of the sides squared. $6a^2$

In our case, we are told that the cube in question has a length of 4.

Therefore: $6a^2$ (where a = 4)
Plug in: $(6)(4^2)$ Becomes: $6 * 16\ =$ **Area = 96**
Surface area of a cube with one side equal to 4 is 96

Now find the surface area of the rectangle (called a prism)
Surface area of rectangle with different dimensions is: $SA\ =\ 2(wh\ +\ lw\ +\ lh)$
The surface area of a rectangular prism is the area of the six rectangles that cover it. But we don't have to figure out all six because we know the top and bottom are the same, the front and back are the same, and the left and right sides are the same.

The area of the top and bottom (side lengths a and c) $= (a * c)$. Since there are two of them, you get $(2ac)$. The front and back have side lengths of b and c. The area of one of them is $(b * c)$, and there are two of them, so the surface area of those two is $(2bc)$. The left and right side have side lengths of $a\ and\ b$, so the surface area of one of them is $(a * b)$. Again, there are two of them, so their combined surface area is $(2ab)$.

In our case we were told: length = 9, Width = 3, Height = 3
Plug into the formula: $Area\ =\ 2(wh\ +\ lw\ +\ lh)$ Becomes: $Area\ =\ 2(3 * 3\ +\ 9 * 3\ +\ 9 * 3)$
Simplify: $2(9\ +\ 27\ +\ 27)$ **Simplify:** $2(63)\ =\ 126$ **Area = 126**
Area of the cube = 96, Area of the rectangle = 126 (96,126)

Answer: (A)

Bonus Sample Questions not in the Virtual Classroom on the DVD

Bonus Sample Questions 18-19

18. What is the surface area of a giant can of peaches with a diameter is 10 inches and whose height is 15 inches?

    (A) $150\pi\ square\ inches$
    (B) $200\ square\ inches$
    (C) $75\pi\ +\ 6\ square\ inches$
    (D) $517.4\ square\ inches$
    (E) $628.3\ square\ inches$

19. Which is greater, the amount of cardboard needed to create a cubical box with edge 6 or the amount of cardboard needed to create a rectangular box with height and width of 3 and length of 9.

    (A) The amount of cardboard needed to create a cubical box with edge 6 is greater
    (B) The amount of cardboard needed to create a rectangular box with height and
        width of 3 and length of 9 is greater
    (C) They are equal
    (D) Unknown—insufficient information

h=3 L=9 w=3

Explanation to Bonus Sample Question 18

1st Key: knowing the full surface area formula: **Surface Area of a Cylinder** $= 2\pi r^2\ +\ (2\pi r)(h)$
2nd key: recognizing the radius is one-half the diameter. We know the diameter is 10 so the radius is 5

Plug the information into the formula: $2\pi r^2\ +\ (2\pi r)(h)$ **becomes:** $2\pi 5^2\ +\ 2\pi(5)(15)$ **multiply:** $2\pi 5^2\ +\ 2\pi(75)$
multiply: $2\pi 5^2\ +\ 150\pi$ **exponent:** $2\pi 25\ +\ 150\pi$ **multiply:** $50\pi\ +\ 150\pi$ **add:** 200π **now check the answer choices to see if they are in terms of pi or decimal. Since we don't see our answer of** 200π**, finish by multiplying** 200 and π
or $(200 * 3.14159)\ =\ 628.318$

Correct Answer: (E)

Explanation to Bonus Sample Question 19

<u>Option 1</u>
When the test or question asks "how much cardboard is needed to make…", it is their "tricky"(or not so tricky) way of asking, "What is the surface area of…"

In this question they ask, "What is the amount of cardboard needed to create a cubical box with edge 6."
This is the same as asking: What is the surface area of a cube with side = 6

The formula for surface area of a cube is: $\text{side}^3 = $ surface area of a cube
Remember that a cube is a solid rectangle with 6 equal sides. IOW, all sides are square. You can think of this as a dice (single die) or a block or box.

Plug in what we know: $\text{side}^3 = $ surface area of a cube
Becomes: $6^3 = 6 * 6 * 6$ **Simplify** = 216 **Area of the cube with side = 6 is 216**

<u>Options 2</u>
We are asked to find the surface area (amount of cardboard…) of a rectangle with the following dimensions: Width = 3, Length = 9, Height = 3

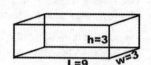

The formula for surface area of a rectangle solid with six faces is:
$SA\ rectangle\ solid = 2(lw) + 2(lh) + 2(wh)$
Plug in what we know to: $2(lw) + 2(lh) + 2(wh)$, Becomes: $2(9 * 3) + 2(9 * 3) + 2(3 * 3)$

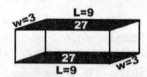

Becomes $2(27) + 2(9 * 3) + 2(3 * 3)$
$2(27) + 2(27) + 2(3 * 3)$
$$2(27) + 2(27) + 2(9)$$
Now add up the sides: $2(27) + 2(27) + 2(9)$ **becomes** 54+54+18 = 126

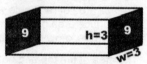

Compare Options: Option 1 = 216, Option 2 = 126
216 > 126

Answer: (A)

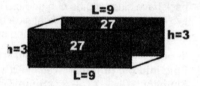

Geometry
Part 6: Circles

Virtual Classroom>Geometry>Circles

This material corresponds to the Virtual Classroom Instructions in the
PowerPrep DVD/Internet/iApps for Geometry

Virtual Classroom

Important Abbreviations
These abbreviations are used throughout the program

POE: Process of Elimination
SARR: Synthesize, Analyze, Reduce, and Restate (has to do with Logical Reasoning)
AC: Answer Choice
QS: Question Stem
LOD: Level of Difficulty

Example Question: What is the least common multiple of 3, 4, and 7? **(This is the call of the question or Question Stem "QS")**

These are Answer Choices "AC" A, B, C, D, E

   (A)   12
   (B)   21
   (C)   28
   (D)   48
   (E)   84

Part 6: Circles

Vocabulary

Center: A point inside the circle and all points on the circle are equidistant (same distance) from the center point.

 Radius – Distance from center to edge

Diameter – Line from edge to edge, through center (equal 2radius) $d = 2r$

 Chord – Line segment that connects any two points on the circle's perimeter.

The longest chord is the diameter.

Radius

The radius is the distance from the center to any point on the circle.

$$radius = \frac{D}{2}$$

where:
D is the **diameter** of the circle

It is half the diameter. Given the diameter of a circle, the radius is simply half the diameter:

If you know the area of a circle, the radius can be found using the formula

$$radius = \sqrt{\frac{A}{\pi}}$$

where:
A is the **area of the circle**
π or **Pi**, approximately 3.142

Diameter

The distance across the circle—Diameter is the length of any chord passing through the center. It is twice the radius.

$$diameter = 2R$$

where:
R is the **radius** of the circle

Given the radius of a circle, the diameter can be calculated using the formula:

If you know the **circumference** of a circle, the diameter can be found using the formula:

$$diameter = \frac{c}{\pi}$$

where:
C is the **circumference** of the circle
π or **Pi**, approximately 3.142

$$diameter = \sqrt{\frac{4A}{\pi}}$$

where:
A is the **area of the circle**
π or **Pi**, approximately 3.142

If you know the area of a circle, the diameter can be found using the formula:

Circumference

Circumference: Distance around circle (perimeter) = $Circumference = 2\pi R$
Where: R is the **radius** of the circle
π or **Pi**, approximately 3.142
The circumference is the distance around the circle.

$$Circumference = 2\pi R$$

where:
R is the **radius** of the circle
π is **Pi**, approximately 3.142

Given the radius of a circle, the circumference can be calculated with the formula:

If you know the diameter of a circle, the circumference can be found using the formula:

$$Circumference = \pi D$$

where:
D is the **diameter** of the circle
π or **Pi**, approximately 3.142

$$Circumference = \sqrt{4\pi A}$$

where:
A is the **area of the circle**
π is **Pi**, approximately 3.142

If you know the area of a circle, the circumference can be found using the formula:

Distance around circle = $2\pi r$
Area of Circle – πr^2

Find the Circumference: *If d = 12*
If d = 12, then r = 6,
   If r = 6 then c = $2\pi r$
      c = $2\pi 6 = 12\pi$

Find the Area: Area = πr^2
$\pi 6^2 = 36\pi$

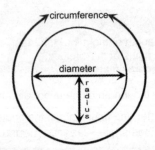

Area

Area of Circle: $area = \pi R^2$
Where: R is the **radius** of the circle and π is **Pi**, approximately 3.142

Strictly speaking a circle is a line, and so has no area. What is usually meant is the area of the region enclosed by the circle.

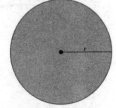

$$area = \pi R^2$$
where:
R is the **radius** of the circle
π or Pi, approximately 3.142

Given the radius of a circle, you can calculate the area inside it using the formula:

If you know the diameter of a circle, the area inside it can be found using the formula:

$$area = \frac{\pi D^2}{4}$$
where:
D is the **diameter** of the circle
π or **Pi**, approximately 3.142

$$area = \frac{C^2}{4\pi}$$
where:
C is the **circumference** of the circle
π or **Pi**, approximately 3.142

If you know the circumference of a circle, the area inside it can be found using the formula:

Circle Arcs and Angles

The Central angle and Arc are a portion of the circumference of the circle defined by an angle. The degree measure (angle) of the intercepted arc equals the center angle.

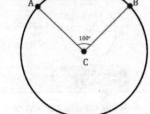

Given two points A and B, lines from them to center of the circle form the central angle ∠AOB. The central angle is the smaller of the two at the center. It does not mean the **reflex angle** ∠AOB.

Arcs and Chords: The two points A and B can be isolated points, or they could be the end points of an arc or chord. When they are the end points of an arc, the angle is sometimes called the "arc central angle".

The Central Angle Theorem states that the measure of inscribed angle (∠APB) is always half the measure of the central angle ∠AOB.

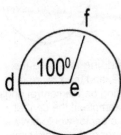

Central angle and Arc – are a portion of the circumference of the circle defined by an angle. The degree measure (angle) of the intercepted arc equals the center angle.

Degree measure of arc df = 100⁰

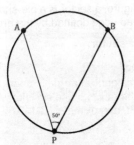

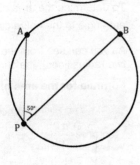

Inscribed Angle and Arc

An inscribed angle and arc is an angle with center and endpoints of the angle on the circumference of the circle. The angle of the intercepted arc equals TWICE the inscribed angle. Degree measure of arc pr = 110°

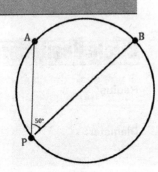

Definition Inscribed Angle: Given two points A and B, lines from them to a third point P form the inscribed angle ∠APB. If you drag the point P, the inscribed angle would remain constant. It only depends on the position of A and B.
The inscribed angle is only defined for points on the **major arc** (the longest path around the circle between the two given points).

$$angle = \frac{90L}{\pi R} \; degrees$$

where:
L is the length of the minor (shortest) arc AB
R is the radius of the circle
π is **Pi**, approximately 3.142

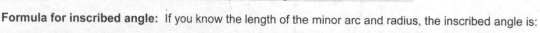

Formula for inscribed angle: If you know the length of the minor arc and radius, the inscribed angle is:

Inscribed Angle and Arc: An angle with center and endpoints of the angle on the circumference of the circle. The angle of the intercepted arc equals *TWICE* the inscribed angle. Degree measure of arc *pr* = 110°

Length of Arc

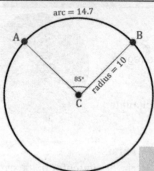

To find the numerical length of an arc, find the circumference and then multiply it by the fraction of its angle relative to the entire circle $\left(\frac{angle}{360}\right)$

Length of arc ab $= 2\pi r + \left(\frac{C}{360}\right)$

Definition: *The distance along the curved line making up the arc*
The arc length is the measure of the distance along the curved line making up the arc. It is longer than the straight line distance between its endpoints (which would be a **chord**)

The formula the arc measure is:

$$arc \; length = 2\pi R \left(\frac{C}{360}\right)$$

where:
C is the **central angle** of the arc in degrees
R is the radius of the arc
π or **Pi**, approximately 3.142

Recall $2\pi r$ is the circumference of the whole circle, so the formula simply reduces this by the ratio of the arc angle to a full angle (360^0). By transposing the formula, you solve for the radius, central angle, or arc length if you know any two of them.

An interesting side note: Notice that the radius and arc length are the same – they are both 10.0 when the initial central angle is set to one radian. (57° when rounded to the nearest degree), thus demonstrating a definition of a radian: "the angle subtended at the center by an arc whose arc length is equal to the arc's radius".

Length of Arc – To find the numerical length of an arc, find the circumference, then multiply it by the fraction of its angle relative to the entire circle $\left(\frac{angle}{360}\right)$. **lengh of arc ac** $= 2\pi r \left(\frac{x}{360}\right)$

Sector

A sector is a portion of the area of a circle formed by an arc.
To determine the area of a sector, find the area of the entire circle, then multiply by the fraction of the arc angle to the entire circle. **Area of sector abc:** $= \pi r^2 \left(\frac{C}{360}\right)$

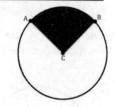

As you can see from the figure, a sector is a pie-shaped part of a circle. It has two straight sides (the two radius lines), the curved edge defined by the **arc**, and touches the center of the circle.

Formula for the area of a sector:

$$area = \frac{C\pi R^2}{360}$$

Where:
C is the **central angle** in degrees
R is the radius of the circle of which the sector is part.
π is **Pi**, approximately 3.142

What this formula is doing is taking the area of the whole circle, and then taking a fraction of that depending on the central angle of the sector. So for example, if the central angle was 90°, then the sector would have an area equal to one quarter of the whole circle.

Sector – Portion of the area of a circle formed by an arc. To determine the area of a sector, find the area of the entire circle, then multiply by the fraction of the arc angle to the entire circle.
Area of sector abc $= \pi r^2 \left(\frac{x}{360}\right)$

Circle Reminder

Radius:

$$radius = \frac{D}{2}$$

where: D is the **diameter** of the circle

Diameter:

$$diameter = 2R$$

where: R is the **radius** of the circle

| Circumference: | $Circumference = 2\pi R$ | **where:**
R is the **radius** of the circle
π is **Pi**, approximately 3.142 |

| Area: | $area = \pi R^2$ | **where:**
R is the **radius** of the circle
π is **Pi**, approximately 3.142 |

If you know any one of those, you can find all other three.

PowerPrep Practice Questions   Also in the Virtual Classroom on DVD

PowerPrep Practice Questions 13-14

13. In the figure, side *DB* of square *ABCD* is also the diameter of circle *E*. What is the area of the shaded region?

(A) $9 - 3\pi$
(B) $9 - 2.25\pi$
(C) $9 - 1.125\pi$
(D) $9 + 1.125\pi$
(E) $9 + 9\pi$

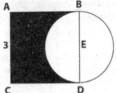

14. A rolling pin makes 360-degree rotations while flattening a ball of dough. The rolling pin has a circumference of 4.5 inches. If it takes 14 full rotations to flatten every ball of dough, how many inches does the pin roll while flattening 12 balls of dough?

(A) 168
(B) 756
(C) 1,467
(D) 95
(E) 155

Explanation to PowerPrep Practice Question 13

This question tests your ability to find the area of a square and a circle using logic to find the area of the unshaded region.

First find the area of each individual figure. Let's start with the circle.
The formula for area of a circle is: $Area\ of\ circle = \pi r^2$
Plug in what you know: Diameter = 3, **Radius** $= \frac{1}{2}$ of the diameter. **Therefore,** $r = (\frac{1}{2})(3)$
So, $r = 1.5$ **Plug in what you know:** $Area = \pi r^2$, Therefore Area $= \pi(1.5)^2$
Simplify: $Area = \pi(1.5)(1.5)$ So, $Area = \pi(2.25)$ or $Area = 2.25\pi$

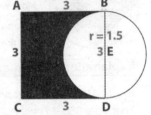

Now find the area of the square: $Area\ of\ square = side^2$
Plug in what we know: Area of square = $(3)2$ Simplify: Area of square = 9

square $= 3^2$
Circle $= pi\ r^2 = pi(1.5)^2$
$3^2 - (pi)(1.5^2)$
$9 - (1.125)(pi)$

Now we know the area of the square and the area of the circle. Since the diameter of the circle is also one side of the square, we know that the side of the square passes through the midpoint of the circle. In other words, it bisects the circle.

Therefore, one half of the circle is inside the square. **So,** if we subtract one-half the area of the entire circle from the area of the square, we will know the area of the unshaded region. **Like this:** The area of the unshaded region =
$\{Area\ of\ square - \frac{1}{2}\ (Area\ of\ circle)\}$ **Plug in what we know:** $9 - (\frac{1}{2}(2.25\pi))$ Becomes: $(9 - 1.125\pi)$

Answer: (C)

Explanation to PowerPrep Practice Question 14

This question tests your basic knowledge of circumference and your ability to logically analyze.

What do we know: The rolling pin is 4.5 inches in circumference—this means that every 360 degree rotation, the rolling pin travels 4.5 inches. It takes 14 of these 360 degree rolls to flatten a single ball of dough. We want to know how far, in inches, the rolling pin travels if it flattens 12 dough balls. **The math on this one is rather straight forward.**

1. A single 360 degree rotation = 4.5 inches. 2. 14 rotations for 1 dough ball, 3. 12 dough balls
In other words: $(4.5\ inches * 14 * 12)$ **Simplify:** $(4.5 * 14 = 63)$ **Simplify:** $(63 * 12) = 756\ inches$

Answer: (B)

Extra Sample Questions not in the Virtual Classroom on the DVD

Bonus Sample Questions 20-23

20. Determine the area of the square inscribed in the circle (the shaded area) where the circumference of the circle is $6\pi\ cm$.

(A) $\sqrt{18}\ cm^2$
(B) $9\ cm^2$
(C) $18\ cm^2$
(D) $6\pi\ cm^2$
(E) $3\pi\ cm^2$

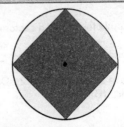

21. If H is the center of the circle above and the circumference of the circle is 12π, what is the measure of the arc AB?

   (A) $\frac{1}{4}\pi$
   (B) 2π
   (C) 3π
   (D) $12\pi - 4$
   (E) $12\pi + 4$

22. If the area of circle $A = 9\pi$ and the circumference of circle $B = 6\pi$ then which is greater, the radius of circle A or the radius of circle B?

   (A) The radius of circle A is greater
   (B) The radius of circle B is greater
   (C) They are equal
   (D) Unknown—insufficient information

23. Which is greater, the area of a 36° sector of a circle with radius 4 or the area of a 40° sector of a circle with radius 5.

   (A) The area of a 36° sector of a circle with radius 4 is greater
   (B) The area of a 40° sector of a circle with radius 5 is greater
   (C) They are equal
   (D) Unknown—insufficient information

Explanation to Bonus Sample Question 20

Key: understand the relationship between circumference, radius, Pythagorean theorem and area of a square. If you saw these relationships the problem is straight forward. However, if you did not see these relationships this problem probably gave you trouble.

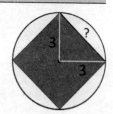

Analysis: First, we know the circumference is $6\pi\ cm$ and the formula for circumference is $2\pi r$. So we can set up an equation and solve for radius: $2\pi r = 6\pi$ divide both sides by π becomes $2r = 6$ divide by 2 becomes $r = 3$ now we know the radius is 3

Now we can draw a triangle with two legs of 3cm (the radius of the circle)

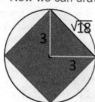

Because the lines that bisect the center of the square form a right angle, we now have a right triangle and the Pythagorean Theorem will work: $a^2 + b^2 = c^2$ (where side c is the hypotenuse, which we are looking for)
So plug in the information for the radii, **becomes:** $3^2 + 3^2 = c^2$ **becomes:** $9 + 9 = c^2$ **or** $18 = c^2$ **or** $\sqrt{18} = c$
Now we know one side of the square has length $\sqrt{18}$ and the formula for area of a square is $side^2$. That means this square has area of $\left(\sqrt{18}\right)^2$ which is the same as 18.
The area of the shaded square is $18cm^2$ **Answer: (C)**

Explanation to Bonus Sample Question 21

angle AHB = 90⁰ **Becomes:** $90^0 = \frac{1}{4}(360^0)$ Also, $Arc\ AB = \frac{1}{4}(circumference\ of\ circle)$
There are 360^0 in every circle: The given angle AHB is 90^0, which is ¼ of 360^0
We are given the circumference of the circle as 12π. Since ARC AB is ¼ of the circumference of the circle, then we can say:
$Arc\ AB = \frac{1}{4}circumference\ of\ circle\ H$ **We know that circumference of circle H = (12π), therefore,** $Arc\ AB = \frac{1}{4}$ of (12π),
$Arc\ AB = \frac{1}{4}(12\pi)$ **or** $Arc\ AB = 3\pi$ **Answer: (C)**

Explanation to Bonus Sample Question 22

Option 1: We are asked to find the radius of a circle with the following dimensions: $Area\ of\ A = 9\pi$
Formula for area of a circle is: $Area\ of\ a\ cirlce = \pi r^2$ **Substitute what we know:** $Area\ of\ A = 9\pi$ **Becomes:**
$\pi r^2 = 9\pi$ **Divide by** π, $r^2 = \frac{9\pi}{\pi}$ **Becomes:** $r^2 = 9$ **Becomes:** $r = \sqrt{9}$ **Finally:** $r = 3$

Option 2: We are asked to find the radius of circle B, given the following info: $circumference\ circle\ B = 6\pi$
Formula for circumference is: $2(\pi)(r)$ **Substitute what we know:** $2(\pi)(r) = 6\pi$ **Divide by** π **Becomes:** $2(r) = \frac{6\pi}{\pi}$
Cancel π: $2(r) = 6$ **Divide by 2:** $r = 3$ **Compare Option 1 and Option 2:** Option 1 = 3, Option 2 = 3, **They are equal**
Answer: (C)

Explanation to Bonus Sample Question 23

Option 1: We are asked to find the area of a sector with the following dimensions: Sector = 36^0 Radius = 4 **The**

formula for area of a sector is: $\dfrac{\pi r^2(angle\ measure)}{360}$

Substitute what we know: area of sector = $\dfrac{\pi 4^2(36)}{360}$ and $\dfrac{\pi 4^2(36)}{360} = \dfrac{16\pi(36)}{360} = \dfrac{576\pi}{360} = \mathbf{1.6\pi}$

Column B: We are asked to find the area of a sector with the following dimensions: Sector = 40^0 Radius = 5

The formula for area of a sector is: $= \dfrac{\pi r^2(angle\ measure)}{360}$

Substitute what we know: $= \dfrac{\pi 5^2(40)}{360}$ becomes $\dfrac{25\pi(40)}{360} = \dfrac{1000\pi}{360} = \mathbf{2.777\pi}$

Compare Options 1 and 2: Option 1 = 1.6π, Option 2 = 2.777π and $\mathbf{1.6\pi < 2.8\pi}$
Answer: (B)

Geometry

Part 7: Coordinate Geometry

Virtual Classroom>Geometry>Coordinate Geometry

This material corresponds to the Virtual Classroom Instructions in the
PowerPrep DVD/Internet/iApp for Geometry

Virtual Classroom

Important Abbreviations
These abbreviations are used throughout the program

POE: Process of Elimination
SARR: Synthesize, Analyze, Reduce, and Restate (has to do with Logical Reasoning)
AC: Answer Choice
QS: Question Stem
LOD: Level of Difficulty

Example Question: What is the least common multiple of 3, 4, and 7? (**This is the call of the question or Question Stem "QS"**)

These are Answer Choices "AC" A, B, C, D, E

(A) 12
(B) 21
(C) 28
(D) 48
(E) 84

Part 7: Coordinate Geometry

Generally

The horizontal axis is called the X axis. The vertical axis is called the Y axis.
Points are labeled (x, y) where the first number represents how far the point is horizontally from the origin and the second number represents how far the point is vertically from the origin.

*A system of geometry where the position of **points** on the **plane** is described using a pair of numbers.*

Recall that a plane is a flat surface that goes on forever in both directions. If we were to place a point on the plane, coordinate geometry gives us a way to describe exactly where it is by using two numbers.

What are coordinates?
To introduce the idea, consider the grid on the right. The columns of the grid are lettered A,B,C etc. The rows are numbered 1,2,3 etc from the top. We can see that the **X** is in box D3; that is, column D, row 3.   D and 3 are called the *coordinates* of the box. It has two parts: the row and the column. There are many boxes in each row and many boxes in each column. But by having both we can find one single box, where the row and column intersect.

	A	B	C	D	E	F
1						
2						
3				X		
4						
5						
6						

The Coordinate Plane

In coordinate geometry, points are placed on the "coordinate plane" as shown here. It has two scales - one running across the plane called the "x axis" and another at right angles to it called the y-axis. The point where the axes cross is called the **origin** and is where both x and y are zero.

On the **x-axis**, values to the right are positive and those to the left are negative.   On the y-axis, values above the origin are positive and those below are negative.

A point's location on the plane is given by two numbers, one that tells where it is on the x-axis and another which tells where it is on the **y-axis**. Together, they define a single, unique position on the plane.
So in the diagram, the point A has an x value of 8 and a y value of 6. These are the coordinates of the point A, sometimes referred to as its **"rectangular coordinates"**.

Things you can do in Coordinate Geometry
If you know the coordinates of a group of points you can:
- Determine the distance between them
- Find the midpoint, slope and equation of a line segment
- Determine if lines are parallel or perpendicular
- Find the area and perimeter of a polygon defined by the points
- Transform a shape by moving, rotating and reflecting it.
- Define the equations of curves, circles and ellipses.

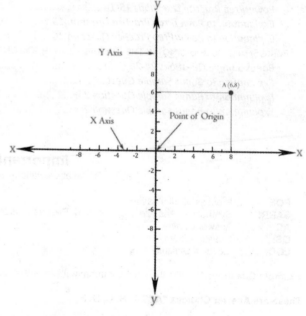

Distance Between Two Points

Distance between two points : The distance between two points is like a hypotenuse of a triangle. If we know the length of side X and the length of side Y, we can solve for the length of the hypotenuse. Use Pythagorean's theorem to do so.

*Given the **coordinates** of two points, the distance D between the points is given by:*
$$D = \sqrt{dx^2 + dy^2}$$

Where dx is the difference between the x-coordinates of the points and dy is the difference between the y-coordinates of the points

This formula is simply a use of **Pythagoras' Theorem**. As you can see, the line segment AB is the **hypotenuse** of a right triangle, where one side is *dx* - the difference in x-coordinates, and the other is *dy* - the difference in y-coordinates. $AB^2 = dx^2 + dy^2$
Solving this for AB gives us the formula: $AB = \sqrt{dx^2 + dy^2}$

Find the length of side X and Y by taking the difference between their coordinates. $a^2 + b^2 = c^2$
In this case, that means:

$$d^2_{(hypotenuse)} = x^2 + y^2 \quad \text{or} \quad d^2 = (x_1 - x_2)^2 + (y_1 - y_2)^2 \quad \text{or} \quad d^2 = (3 - (-4))^2 + (2 - (-4))^2$$

NOTE: it's very important that you realize it's the distance between the pair of x's and the pair of y's. It does not matter what order you add or subtract…look at is as the number of units apart they are. The line x is 4 units from the point to the x axis and then 3 more to the 90° point. That's a total of 7. The y line is 2 units from the (3,2) point to the y axis, and then 4 more units to the 90° point. That a total of 6 units. Don't let the positive and negative signs mess you up.

$d^2 = 7^2 + 6^2$ **Becomes:** $d^2 = 49 + 36$ **Becomes:** $d^2 = 85$ **Becomes:** $d = \sqrt{85}$ (about 9.2)

Midpoint of a Line

The coordinates of the midpoint of a line segment are the average of the coordinates of its endpoints. $\quad C_x = \dfrac{x_1 + x_2}{2}$

The y midpoint coordinate for point C is ($x_1 + x_2$) divided by 2. IOW the average of the two x coordinates.

The y midpoint coordinate for point C is ($y_1 + y_2$) divided by 2. IOW the average of the two y coordinates.

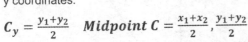

$C_y = \dfrac{y_1 + y_2}{2} \quad Midpoint\ C = \dfrac{x_1 + x_2}{2}, \dfrac{y_1 + y_2}{2}$

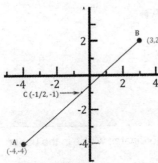

First find the *x-coordinate* of C: This is the average of the *x-coordinates* of A and B. The coordinates of A are (-4, -4) so the *x-coordinate* is -4, the first number of the pair. Similarly, the *x-coordinate* of B is 3. To find the average of these, add them together and divide the result by two: $\dfrac{-4+3}{2}$ **Becomes:** $-\dfrac{1}{2} = x$ coordinate for the new midpoint

Next, find the *y-coordinate* of C: This is the average of the *y-coordinates* of A and B. The coordinates of A are (-4,-4) so the *y-coordinate* is -4, the second number of the pair. Similarly, the *y-coordinate* of B is 2. To find the average of these, add them together and divide the result by two: $\dfrac{-4+2}{2}$ **Becomes:** $-1 = y$ coordinate for the new midpoint

So now we know that the midpoint C has the coordinates $(-\frac{1}{2}, -1)$

Slope of a line

Equation of a line: $y = mx + b, m = slope, b = y\ intercept$

Slope: $\dfrac{change\ in\ y}{change\ in\ x} = \dfrac{y_1 - y_2}{x_1 - x_2}$

Slope $= \dfrac{(2-(-4))}{(3-(-4))} = \dfrac{6}{7}$

$\dfrac{change\ in\ y}{change\ in\ x} = \dfrac{rise}{run} = \dfrac{y_1 - y_2}{x_1 - x_2}$

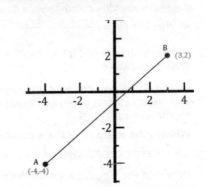

Rise 6, Run 7

Bear in mind, it does not matter whether you designate point A or B as the first coordinate when performing the calculation. But it is important that once you select one of them as your x_1 the y of the point, must also be your y_1.

Remember: The slope of a line is a number that measures its "steepness", usually denoted by the letter m. It is the change in y for a unit change in x along the line.

For any two points on a line, their slope is defined as: $slope = \dfrac{y_1 - y_2}{x_1 - x_2}$

Where (x_1, y_1) and (x_2, y_2) are points on the line

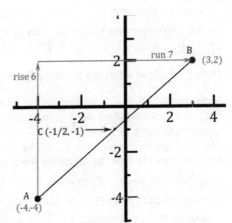

If *m* represents the slope of a line and *A* and *B* are points with coordinates (x_1, y_1) and (x_2, y_2) respectively, then the slope of the line passing through A and B is given by the following formulas

$slope = \dfrac{change\ in\ y}{change\ in\ x} = \dfrac{rise}{run} = \dfrac{y_1 - y_2}{x_1 - x_2}$

Where $x_2 \neq x_1$ All this means is that A and B cannot be points on a vertical line, so x_1, and x_2, cannot be equal to one another. If $x_1 = x_2$, then the line is vertical and the slope is undefined.

Slope intercept formula: $y = mx + b$ (where $m = slope$ of the line and $b = y\ intercept$)

	Any straight line on the coordinate plane can be described by the equation:	
$y = mx + b$	**Where:**	
	x, y	are the coordinates of any point on the line
	m	is the slope of the line
	b	is the intercept (where the line crosses the y-axis)

Recall that the slope (m) is the "steepness" of the line and b is the intercept - the point where the line crosses the y-axis.

PowerPrep Practice Questions   Also in the Virtual Classroom on DVD

PowerPrep Practice Questions 15-16

15. If segment AB is extended equally in both directions so that the new segment is twice the length of the original segment, what would be the new endpoint with only positive coordinates?
   - (B) (5.5, -3)
   - (C) (5.5, 3)
   - (D) (10, 5)
   - (E) (10.5, 5)
   - (F) (16, 2)

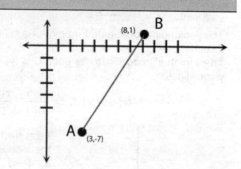

16. Given: For the line y = -2x + 10. Where does this line cross the x axis?
   - (A)   -5
   - (B)   2
   - (C)   -2
   - (D)   5
   - (E)   10

Explanation to PowerPrep Practice Question 15

AB will be extended ½ the length of AB in both directions. The endpoint with only positive coordinates will be in the upper right quadrant (a new point D).

If we find the midpoint of segment AB (point C), we can then use point B as the new midpoint of our new segment (segment CD). It would extend from the original midpoint of AB (point C) to the new endpoint we are asked to find (point D).

This problem requires the application of the Midpoint Theorem: *The coordinates of the midpoint of a line segment are the average of the coordinates of its endpoints.*

$$Midpoint\ C = \frac{x_1 + x_2}{2}, \frac{y_1 + y_2}{2}$$

In other words, to find the midpoint of any line you average the x and y coordinate for each end point. In the problem we are solving, this would mean:

To find C (the new midpoint) between point A and B, we average the x and y coordinates of both ends of the line. The two coordinate of the end points are (8,1) and (3,-7). So the two x coordinates for the endpoints are 8 and 3. The two y coordinates are 1 and -7

What is the average of the x coordinates? $\frac{8+3}{2} = x$ **Simplify:** $\frac{11}{2} = x$
5.5 = new x coordinate for the midpoint C

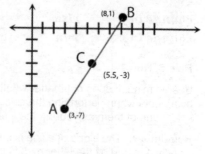

Now find the y coordinate for the new midpoint C
$\frac{1-7}{2} = y$ Becomes: $-\frac{6}{2} = y$ Becomes: $-3 = y$
So the new coordinates for the midpoint C of line AB are $(5.5, -3)$
$$Midpoint\ C = \frac{x_1 + x_2}{2}, \frac{y_1 + y_2}{2}$$

Now Substitute what we know: $Midpoint\ C = \frac{3+11}{2}, \frac{-7+1}{2}$ or $\frac{11}{2}, -\frac{6}{2}$

Midpoint C = $(5.5, -3)$ of line AB, Now we can solve for the new endpoint D (x, y)
Let's call the midpoint we just found point Z. This point Z is now the endpoint , of the new segment DZ. It's coordinates are $(5.5, -3)$
The midpoint for the new line DZ will be the old end point, $(8, 1)$
Now we have to use the midpoint theorem to find an endpoint (because we know one end point and the midpoint).

The theorem says: $Midpoint\ C = \frac{x_1 + x_2}{2}, \frac{y_1 + y_2}{2}$

In other words to find the x or y coordinate of the midpoint, where a and b are the two x coordinates or y coordinates of the endpoints and c is the midpoint $\frac{a+b}{2} = c$ Where $a = x_1$ and $b = x_2$ OR $a = y_1$ and $b = y_2$

Add the x's or y's for both end points and divide by 2 to find the new midpoint

So let's alter the formula to find an endpoint. If $\frac{a+b}{2} = c$

You could figure out an endpoint formula, but it's easier to fill in what you know to the midpoint formula.

You know the x coordinate for one end point (Z) is 5.5 and you know the x coordinate for the new midpoint (old endpoint) point B is 8

So $a = 5.5$ and $c = 8$, Where "a" is the x coordinate for point Z and C is the x coordinate for point B

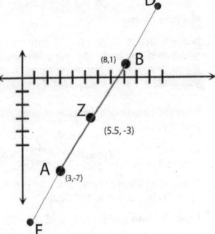

$\frac{5.5+b}{2} = 8$ **Multiply by 2 Becomes** $5.5 + b = 16$ **Subtract 5.5**

Becomes $b = 10.5$ **This is the x coordinate for the new endpoint D.**

Now repeat the process for the y coordinate for endpoint D. If $\frac{a+b}{2} = c$

You know the y coordinate for one endpoint (Z) is -3, and you know the y coordinate for the new midpoint (old endpoint, B) is 1 **Plug it in:** $\left(\frac{a+b}{2} = c\right)$

Becomes: $\left(\frac{-3+b}{2} = 1\right)$ **Multiply by 2 Becomes:** $(-3 + b = 1(2))$

Becomes: $(-3 + b = 2)$ **Add 3 Becomes:** $b = 5$

This is the new y coordinate for the new endpoint D. We now have the two new coordinates for the new endpoint D. $(10.5, 5)$ The endpoint of new segment $= (10.5, 5)$ **Answer: (D)**

Explanation to PowerPrep Practice Question 16

Brief Review of Slope of a Line: The slope of a line is a number that measures its "steepness", usually denoted by the letter m. It is the change in y for a unit change in x along the line.

For any two points on a line, their slope is defined as:

$$slope = \frac{y_1 - y_2}{x_1 - x_2}$$ Where (x_1, y_1) and (x_2, y_2) are points on the line

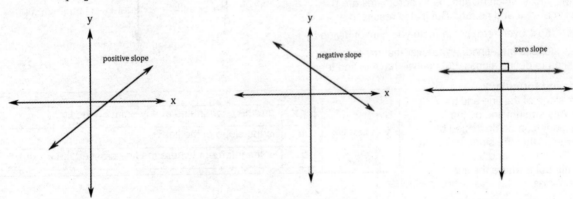

Any time the line slopes up from left to right, it is a positive slope.

When a line falls from left to right, the slope is a negative number.
The x-axis or any line parallel to the x-axis has a slope of zero.
The y-axis or any line parallel to the y-axis has no defined slope.

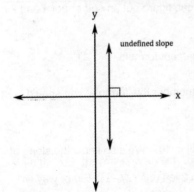

Samples
If *m* represents the slope of a line and *A* and *B* are points with coordinates (x_1, y_1) and (x_2, y_2) respectively, then the slope of the line passing through *A* and *B* is given by the following formulas

$$Slope = \frac{y_1 - y_2}{x_1 - x_2} = \frac{Rise}{Run} = \frac{\Delta x}{\Delta y}$$

where $x_2 \neq x_1$ All this means is that A and B cannot be points on a vertical line, so x_1 and x_2 cannot be equal to one another. If $x_1 = x_2$, then the line is vertical and the slope is undefined.

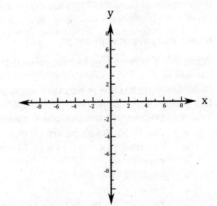

You should become very familiar with the slop, rise run concepts.
Another way to understand slope is Rise over Run
  • Rise is the y axis—how far up and down the y axis
  • Run is the x axis—how far left and right

So if we have a slope of 1, you should look at this as a fraction of $\frac{1}{1}$ where the numerator is the rise and the denominator is the run—that means for every unit to the right (positive 1), you take one up (positive 1) or 1 up and 1 right (it's the same)

Slope of ½ means one step up and 2 steps to the right (or 2 right and 1 up) While $\left(-\frac{1}{2}\right)$ means one step left and one step up—it does not matter if you put the negative on the 1 or the 2 (left 1 or down 2, as long as the other number is positive) so $\left(-\frac{1}{2}\right)$ is the same as $\left(\frac{1}{-2}\right)$. It just changes the direction of the line, but it's the same line. Test it out on the grid below

Note: there is no $((-1/-2)$, that's the same as ½ (because down one and left one is just working backwards on a positive slope line. It's the same as positive 1/2) test it out on the blank grid below
Note: also with a negative slope, it does not matter whether you make the top (rise) or bottom (run) negative, it keeps you on the same line. Test it out on the grid below.

Find the slopes of lines a, b, c, and d. **Line "a" has point** $(-7, 2)$ and $(-3, 4)$

$$M = \frac{4-2}{-3-(-7)} \quad \text{Simplify:} \quad \frac{4-2}{-3-(-7)} = \frac{2}{-3+7} = \frac{2}{4} = \frac{1}{2}$$

This means that the rise is 1 and the run is 2. For every step up, take two steps to the right.

Line "b" has point $(2, 4)$ **and** $(6, -2)$

$$M = \frac{-2-4}{6-2} = -\frac{6}{4} = -\frac{3}{2}$$

This means for every 3 steps down (-3), take 2 steps to the right (negative slope)   Note this is the same as $\left(\frac{3}{-2}\right)$ (three up and 2 to the left) it's the same slope

Line C is parallel to the x axis—it has zero for the rise $\left(\frac{0}{-6}\right)$ this means a zero slope. Line d is undefined because it is parallel to the y axis which means the x coordinates are 0. This results in all rise and no run. But it also results in a fraction like $\frac{1}{0}$ (up 1 over zero) but in math you cannot divide by zero) so this slope is undefined. (Whatever that means) You won't be asked to define slopes, but you will have to find them.

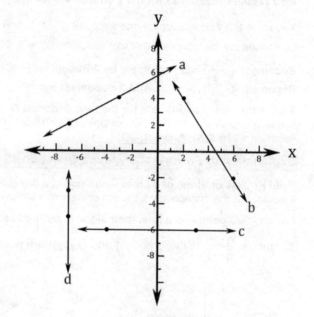

Slope intercept formula: $Y = mx + b$ (where m = slope of the line and b= y intercept)   Any straight line on the coordinate plane can be described by the equation. Recall that the slope (m) is the "steepness" of the line and b is the intercept - the point where the line crosses the y-axis.

$y = mx + b$	**Where:**	
	x, y	are the coordinates of any point on the line
	m	is the slope of the line
	b	is the intercept (where the line crosses the y-axis)

What is the equation used for? The equation of a line is used in two main ways.
1. As a simple way of defining a particular line. If you know a line is defined by y=2x+12. You could plot this line exactly.
2. To locate points on the line. Given the line's equation and a point on the line, you can figure out any other point and the slope of the line.

Given: For the line y = -2x + 10

Where does this line cross the x axis? This tests your understanding of the slope intercept formula.
$Y = mx + b$ (where m is the slope of the line and b is the y intercept)

If you remembered this formula, the problem is actually straight forward. If you don't remember this formula, you should review the content above. $y = mx + b$ **defines any line.**

In our case we are given: $y = -2x + 10$

What We Know: From this we know that one point on the line is $(0, 10)$. The y intercept is 10.   We also know the slope of the line is -2
In other words the line is negative slope and the rise/run is left two up one $(-2/1)$ or up 2 left one $(2/-1)$. Either way will find points on the same line.
You could manually calculate the x intercept using the slope information and the y intercept as 10.
- You know the slope will go down 2 right 1 and we are beginning at (0, 10)
- The next stop would be $(1, 8)$ (down 2, right 1)
- Then $(2, 6)$
- Then $(3, 4)$
- Then $(4, 2)$
- **Then $(5, 0)$ that's the x intercept**

But you could also figure out the x intercept using the formula for the line: $y = mx + b$

In our case we are given: $y = -2x + 10$

Plug in 0 for y to find out what the x coordinate will be—this would be the x intercept: $0 = -2x + 10$

Subtract 10 from both sides: $-10 = -2x$ **Divide by** -2: $\left(-\frac{10}{-2} = x\right)$ **Becomes:** $5 = x$

Answer: (D)

Bonus Sample Questions not in the Virtual Classroom on the DVD

Bonus Sample Questions 24-26

24. According to the figure, the coordinates of point G are

    (A) (-14, 6)
    (B) (14, -6)
    (C) (-6, -14)
    (D) (-6, 14)
    (E) (6, 14)

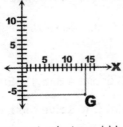

25. If segment AB is extended equally in both directions
so that the new segment is twice the length of the original segment, what would be
the new endpoint with only positive coordinates?

    (A) (5.5, -3)
    (B) (5.5, 3)
    (C) (10, 5)
    (D) (10.5, 5)
    (E) (16, 2)

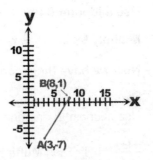

26. Which is greater, x or y?

    (A) The value for X is greater
    (B) The value for Y is greater
    (C) They are equal
    (D) Unknown—insufficient information

Explanation to Bonus Sample Question 24

This question tests your knowledge of the x and y axis. Coordinates always follow the form of (x, y) where the x coordinate is always first and always = horizontal (right for positive numbers, left for negative numbers) and the y coordinate is always second and always = vertical (up for positive numbers, down for negative numbers) .

Since the x coordinate comes first and is horizontal, we count 14 to the right x coordinate is 14
The y coordinate is second and on the vertical axis and we count down -6
Coordinates are written $(x, y) = (14, -6)$

Answer: (B)

Explanation to Bonus Sample Question 25

Midpoint Formula
AB will be extended ½ the length of AB in both directions. The endpoint with only positive coordinates will be in the upper right quadrant and we'll name that **point D. This is the coordinate we are asked to find.**
So what are the coordinate values for point D?
First we'll find the midpoint of the given AB line segment. We'll name the midpoint of AB, point C.

Here's the key, not only is point C the midpoint of the given line AB, but it will also be the opposite endpoint of the segment CD. Keep in mind we want to find the coordinates for D.

Therefore, by finding the midpoint of AB (point C) it will become the endpoint of CD. Also the midpoint of CD is the point B (8,1) (which we already know because it was given for AB)
This may sound confusing, but as you can see from the diagram, it's a little easier than it may sound

Let's start by finding the midpoint of AB (point C)

If we find the midpoint of segment AB (point C), we can then use point B as the new midpoint of our new segment (segment CD). It will extend from the original midpoint of AB (point C) to the new endpoint we are asked to find (point D).

Midpoint formula is: $midpoint\ C = \frac{x_1 + x_2}{2}, \frac{y_1 + y_2}{2}$

Substitute the coordinates we have for segment AB
A = (3,-7), B = (8,1)

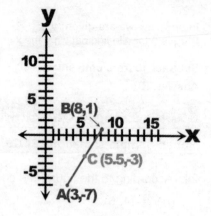

$midpoint\ C = \frac{x_1+x_2}{2}, \frac{y_1+y_2}{2}$ **Becomes** $midpoint\ C = \frac{3+8}{2}, \frac{-7+1}{2}$

$midpoint\ C = \frac{11}{2}, \frac{-6}{2}$

$\boldsymbol{midpoint\ C = (5.5, -3)}$

This point C is both the midpoint of AB and the endpoint of CD
(keep in mind, we want to find the coordinates for D)

Since we know one endpoint C and we know the midpoint B, we can find the endpoint D

Now we can solve for the new endpoint:
One endpoint = C (5.5,-3), Midpoint = B (8,1), Endpoint D = (?,?)

Use midpoint B and endpoint C to solve the x coordinate of endpoint D: $\frac{5.5+x_2}{2} = 8$

Multiply by 2: $5.5 + x_2 = 8(2)$ **Becomes**: $5.5 + x_2 = 16$ Then **Add** -5.5 **Becomes**: $x_2 + 10.5$

Now we have the x coordinate for D (10.5)

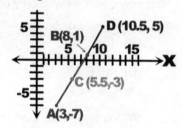

Let's solve for the y coordinate for D
Use midpoint B and endpoint C to solve for the y coordinate of endpoint D:

$\frac{-3+y_2}{2} = 1$ Then **Multiply by 2:** $(-3 + y_2 = 2)$ **Then Add 3:** $y_2 = 5$

Now we have the y coordinate for point D **(5). The** (x,y) **coordinates for the endpoint D are** $(10.5, 5)$

Answer: (D)

Explanation to Bonus Sample Question 26

Option 1
Point (x,y) in the diagram will have the same x coordinate as point $(15,9)$ because the triangle formed by the points is a right triangle.
Therefore, $x = 15$

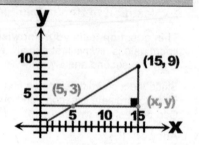

Option 2
Point (x,y) will have the same y coordinate as point $(5,3)$ because the triangle formed by the points is a right triangle. **Therefore,** $y = 3$

Compare Option 1 and 2
Option 1 is $x = 15$
Option 2 is $y = 3$
$15 > 3$

Answer: (A)

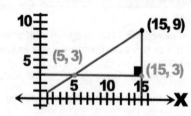

Geometry
Part 8: Geometric Probability

Virtual Classroom>Geometry>Geometry Probability

This material corresponds to the Virtual Classroom Instructions in the
PowerPrep DVD/Internet/iApp for Geometry

Virtual Classroom

Part 8: Geometric Probability

For questions involving geometric probability, rely on the area equations from geometry to find the total area and then the area of the significant part. To find probability divide the part by the total.

Example: A target with 12-inch radius has a bull's-eye with a 1-inch radius. What is the probability that a dart randomly thrown will hit the bull's-eye, assuming it will hit the target?

$area\ of\ a\ circle = \pi r^2$ $where\ r\ is\ the\ radius\ of\ the\ circle$

In our case we have two concentric circles—one with a 12 inch radius and one with a 1 inch radius.
The total area of the target is $\pi 12^2$ and the area of the center is $\pi 1^2$.

Then we divide the desired outcome by the total possible outcome: $(\pi 1^2)/\pi 12^2$

Simplify: $\frac{\pi}{144\pi}$ **Cancel π: becomes:** $\frac{1}{144}$

Note that by not rushing to multiply out the π, it is easier to divide it out at the end.

This problem could be complicated by asking the probability that one of three darts would make it in. For this type of question, you multiply the probability; you want to know the chance that exactly one will make it. So then you multiply:

$$\frac{1}{144} * \frac{1}{144} * \frac{1}{144} = \frac{1}{2,985,984}$$

If it asked what is the probability *any* of three darts make it in, you add; so

$$\frac{1}{144} + \frac{1}{144} + \frac{1}{144} = \frac{3}{144}$$

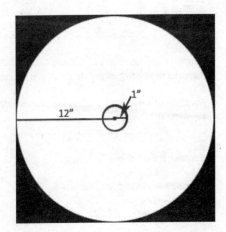

CONGRATULATIONS!!!
You have completed the Geometry Workshop!

Take a break before moving on to the Geometry Drills!

Geometry Index

Trigonometry Workbook
Table of Contents

This material corresponds to the Virtual Classroom Instructions in the
PowerPrep DVD/Internet/iApp for Trigonometry

Virtual Classroom

Important Abbreviations
These abbreviations are used throughout the program

POE: Process of Elimination
SARR: Synthesize, Analyze, Reduce, and Restate (has to do with Logical Reasoning)
AC: Answer Choice
QS: Question Stem
LOD: Level of Difficulty

Example Question: What is the least common multiple of 3, 4, and 7? (**This is the call of the question or Question Stem "QS"**)
These are Answer Choices "AC" A, B, C, D, E

    (A)   12
    (B)   21
    (C)   28
    (D)   48
    (E)   84

Trigonometry
Part 1: Angles of Triangles

Virtual Classroom>Trigonometry>Angles of Triangles

This material corresponds to the Virtual Classroom Instructions in the
PowerPrep DVD/Internet/iApp for Trigonometry

Virtual Classroom

Important Abbreviations
These abbreviations are used throughout the program

POE: Process of Elimination
SARR: Synthesize, Analyze, Reduce, and Restate (has to do with Logical Reasoning)
AC: Answer Choice
QS: Question Stem
LOD: Level of Difficulty

Example Question: What is the least common multiple of 3, 4, and 7? **(This is the call of the question or Question Stem "QS")**

These are Answer Choices "AC" A, B, C, D, E

(A)   12
(B)   21
(C)   28
(D)   48
(E)   84

Part 1: Angles of Triangles

Generally

Trigonometry is the branch of mathematics dealing with the measures of the sides and angles of a triangle. Using trigonometric ratios, one can determine the side and angle measures (i.e. "solve the triangle") using minimal information.

What is A Right Triangle?

A right triangle is any triangle where one angle measures 90°. A right triangle consists of two small sides, across from the smaller angles, and a longer side, across from the right angle. The sides of a right triangle have special names. The two smaller ones are called *legs*, and the longer side is called the **hypotenuse (pronounced hi-POT-uh-noose).**

Notice that the bottom-left angle is 90 degrees. The sides labeled "opposite" and "adjacent" are the legs, and the names are in reference to the angle "a". These terms will always be used when discussing sides of a right triangle, and will always be given in reference to some angle. Remember, **the hypotenuse is always the longest side and is always across from the right angle.**

Example

For the triangle below, fill in the blanks.

1. What is the length of the hypotenuse? _____
2. What is the length of the side opposite angle "a"?_____
3. What is the length of the side adjacent to angle "a"?_____
4. What is sin A? _____

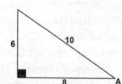

Answers: 1. $hypot = 10$, 2. $opp\ 8$, 3. $adj\ 6$, and 4. $Sin\ A = opp/hypot = \frac{6}{10}$
The values of *sin and cos* CANNOT be larger than one!

Any side of a triangle will always be smaller than the hypotenuse. Since both sin and cos are calculated by a side divided by a hypotenuse, you will always have a smaller number divided by a larger number. Make sure you immediately eliminate answer choices with fractions greater than one!!

Trigonometric Ratios

The three most common trigonometric ratios are

Sine (abbreviated "sin"),   **Cosine** (abbreviated "cos"), and   **Tangent** (abbreviated "tan").
These trigonometric ratios can be determined contingent on the information you have available. If the angle measure is given, entering $sin(x), cos(x), or\ tan(x)$ in most scientific calculators (where "x" is the angle measure) will yield the *sine, cosine, and tangent* of the given value.

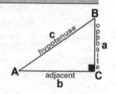

We know the side length of a triangle is directly related its' opposite angle measurement. Remember – the longer the side, the larger the angle opposite it.

We talked about two specific triangles in the geometry section: (30°- 60°- 90°) and (45°- 45°- 90°) and how their side lengths relate to the opposite angle measurements. There are obviously many other angle combinations for triangles, and we need a generic way to determine angle value based on the side lengths of a triangle—IOW, a **ratio or relationship between sides.**   So we have – **SOH CAH TOA !!!**

SOH ➜ Sine $= \dfrac{Opposite}{Hypotenuse}$ **CAH** ➜ Cosine $= \dfrac{Adjacent}{Hypotenuse}$ **TOA** ➜ Tangent $= \dfrac{Opposite}{Adjacent}$

Make sure you recognize the following relationships as well:

SEC: Secant $= \dfrac{1}{Cosine} = \dfrac{hypotenuse}{adjacent}$ CSC: Cosecant $= \dfrac{1}{tangent} = \dfrac{1}{sine} = \dfrac{hypotenuse}{opposite}$ COT: Cotangent $= \dfrac{1}{tangent} = \dfrac{adjacent}{opposite}$

Since there are three sides to the triangle, we there are several ways we can use the side lengths to solve the value of an angle.
Let's solve for the value of angle 1: $Sin\ 1 = \dfrac{Opposite}{Hypotenuse} = \dfrac{BC}{AC}$ $Cos\ 1 = \dfrac{Adjacent}{Hypotenuse} = \dfrac{AB}{AC}$ $Tan\ 1 = \dfrac{Opposite}{Adjacent} =$
$\dfrac{BC}{AB}$ We could solve the value of the angle ANY of these three ways and come up with the same answer.

SOH-CAH-TOA

In a right triangle, if you are given at least two of the side measures, you can determine the sine, cosine, or tangent using a method commonly referred to by the mnemonic device *Soh Cah Toa*. **What this refers to is: Soh: sine** $= \dfrac{opposite}{hypotenuse}$,

Cah: cosine $= \dfrac{adjacent}{hypotenuse}$, **Toa: tangent** $= \dfrac{opposite}{adjacent}$. The terms *opposite* and *adjacent* are in relation to the **reference angle**, which is the angle your calculations are based upon.

SOH-CAH-TOA

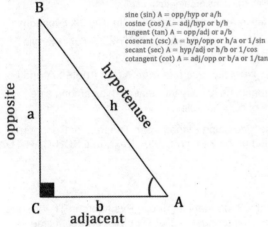

$$\sin (A) = \frac{\text{opposite}}{\text{hypotenuse}} = \frac{a}{c}$$

$$\cos (A) = \frac{\text{adjacent}}{\text{hypotenuse}} = \frac{b}{c}$$

$$\tan (A) = \frac{\text{opposite}}{\text{adjacent}} = \frac{a}{b}$$

**sine = sin
cosine = cos
tangent = tan**

In Figure 1, since angle A is the reference angle, then the side opposite of that angle is side a. While there are two sides adjacent to angle A, side b is designated as the hypotenuse so side c is the adjacent side. **Therefore, in Figure 1:** $\sin(A) = \frac{a}{b}$ $\cos(A) = \frac{c}{b}$ $\tan(A) = \frac{a}{c}$

Please note that "sin(A)" is read as "sine of A," "cos(A)" is read as "cosine of A," and "tan(A)" is read as "tangent of A." **For example,** if $a = 7$ and $c = 14$, you would need to find the tangent of angle A, as the other two ratios require the hypotenuse which is unavailable. As the tangent is the opposite divided by the adjacent, you would get $\tan A =$ $\left(\frac{7}{14}\right)$, which can be simplified to one-half.

Figure 1, angle A is the reference angle, and so side a must be the opposite side and side c the adjacent side. Side b is the hypotenuse.

Trig 6 Functions

Trigonometry Six (6) Functions Review:
A right triangle always includes a 90° (π/2 radians) angle, here labeled C. Angles A and B may vary. Trigonometric functions specify the relationships among side lengths and interior angles of a right triangle.

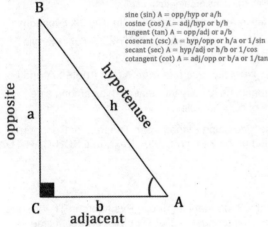

sine (sin) A = opp/hyp or a/h
cosine (cos) A = adj/hyp or b/h
tangent (tan) A = opp/adj or a/b
cosecant (csc) A = hyp/opp or h/a or 1/sin
secant (sec) A = hyp/adj or h/b or 1/cos
cotangent (cot) A = adj/opp or b/a or 1/tan

In this right triangle:
If one angle of a triangle is 90 degrees and one of the other angles is known, the third is thereby fixed, because the three angles of any triangle always add up to 180 degrees. The two acute angels therefore, add up to 90 degrees: they are complementary angles. The shape of a right triangle is completely determined, up to similarity, by the angles. This means that once one of the other angles is known, the ratios of the various sides are always the same regardless of the overall size of the triangle. These ratios are given by the following trigonometric functions of the known angle A, where a, b, and c refer to the lengths of the sides in the accompanying figure:

The sine function (sin), defined as the ratio of the side opposite the angle to the hypotenuse. $\sin A = \left(\frac{opposite}{hypotenuse}\right) = \frac{a}{c}$

The cosine function (cos), defined as the ratio of the adjacent leg to the hypotenuse $\cos A = \left(\frac{adjacent}{hypotenuse}\right) = \frac{b}{c}$

The Tangent function (tan), defined as the ratio of the opposite leg to the adjacent leg $\tan A = \left(\frac{opposite}{adjacent}\right) = \frac{a}{b} = \frac{sine\ A}{cosA}$

The **hypotenuse** is the side opposite to the 90 degree angle in a right triangle; it is the longest side of the triangle, and one of the two sides adjacent to angle *A*. The **adjacent leg** is the other side that is adjacent to angle *A*. The **opposite side** is the side that is opposite to angle *A*. The terms **perpendicular** and **base** are sometimes used for the opposite and adjacent sides respectively. Many people find it easy to remember what sides of the right triangle are equal to sine, cosine, or tangent, by memorizing the word **SOH-CAH-TOA**

$$\sin A = \frac{a}{c}$$
$$\cos A = \frac{b}{c}$$
$$\tan A = \frac{a}{b}$$

With these functions one can answer virtually all questions about arbitrary triangles by using the law of sines and the law of cosines. These laws can be used to compute the remaining angles and sides of any triangle as soon as two sides and an angle or two angles and a side or three sides are known. These laws are useful in all branches of geometry, since every polygon may be described as a finite combination of triangles.

Using a Calculator to Determine Angles. *Note: Please make sure your calculator calculates angle measures in degrees* When determining the measures of a triangle, the sines, cosines, and tangents have a function: determining the angle measure. If you entered $\tan^{-1}\left(\frac{1}{2}\right)$ into a scientific calculator, you will see that you will get the angle measure of *A*, which is approximately 26.6°. You now have two angle measures: 26.6° and 90°, since this is a right triangle. Because the sum of all angles in a triangle is 180°, subtract the two known angle measures from 180 and you will get the third angle measure: 63.4°

PowerPrep Practice Questions Also in the virtual Classroom on DVD

PowerPrep Practice Questions 1-2

1. What is sin A?

(A) 6/10
(B) 8/10
(C) 4/10
(D) 10/6
(E) 10/8

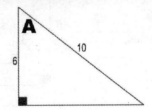

2. What is *cos B* **if** *tan B* **is** 5/12?

(A) 12/13
(B) 5/13
(C) 13/12
(D) 12/5
(E) 13/5

Explanation to PowerPrep Practice Question 1

Quick Answer: $Sin = SOH = \frac{opp}{hypot}$ **and in the provided information** $Opposite = x, Hypotenuse = 10$

Therefore: $Sin\ A = \frac{Opp}{hypot} = \frac{x}{10}$ Solve for the value of x. This triangle is a scaled up 3-4-5 triangle where the values are all doubled. The hypotenuse is 2(5), one side is 2(3), which leaves the second side with a value of 2(4), or 8.

You can also calculate the missing side by using Pythagorean Theorem: $a^2 + b^2 = c^2$ **Plug in what we know:** a = 6 (adjacent), b = x (opposite), c = 10 (hypotenuse) $a^2 + b^2 = c^2$ **Becomes** $6^2 + b^2 = 10^2$ **then,** $36 + b^2 = 100$ **then,** $b^2 = 64$ **then,** $b = 8$ $Sin\ A = \frac{Opp}{hypot} = \frac{8}{10}$

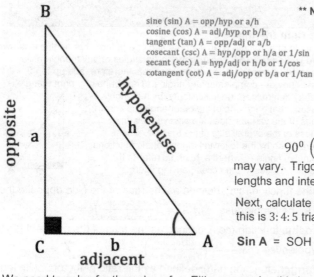

sine (sin) A = opp/hyp or a/h
cosine (cos) A = adj/hyp or b/h
tangent (tan) A = opp/adj or a/b
cosecant (csc) A = hyp/opp or h/a or 1/sin
secant (sec) A = hyp/adj or h/b or 1/cos
cotangent (cot) A = adj/opp or b/a or 1/tan

** NOTICE - The values of sin and cos CANNOT be larger than one! **

Any side of a triangle will always be smaller than the hypotenuse. Since both sin and cos are calculated by a side divided by a hypotenuse, you will always have a smaller number divided by a larger number. Make sure you immediately eliminate answer choices with fractions greater than one!!

More Detailed Answer: First Review the Trig Six Functions

Trigonometry Six (6) Functions Review: A right triangle always includes a

$90^0 \left(\frac{\pi}{2}\ radians\right) angle, here\ it's\ labeled\ C.$ Angles A and B may vary. Trigonometric functions specify the relationships among side lengths and interior angles of right triangles.

Next, calculate the missing side using Pythagorean Theorem or Recognize this is 3 : 4 : 5 triangle (scaled up by 2 to a 6 : 8 : 10) **Next, use SOH-CAH-TOA**

$Sin\ A = SOH = \frac{opposite}{hypotenuse} = \frac{x}{10}$

We need to solve for the value of x. Either recognize this is a variation of a 3:4:5 triangle, or use Pythagorean Theorem to solve. This triangle is a 3-4-5 triangle where the values are all doubled.   Hypotenuse = 2 ∗ (5) or 10,   Adjacent side = 2 ∗ (3), or 6   Opposite side value must be 2 ∗ (4), or 8.
$a^2 + b^2 = c^2$ **becomes:** $6^2 + b^2 = 10^2$ **becomes:** $36 + b^2 = 100$
$b^2 = 64$ **becomes:** $b = \sqrt{64}$ **or** **b = 8**   **Either way,** you will find that the opposite side is 8. Now we can insert the values into the formula for SOH-CAH-TOA to find sin A. $Sin\ A = SOH = \frac{opposite}{hypotenuse} = \frac{b}{10}$ **Now we know that "b" is 8**   Sin $A = SOH = \frac{opposite}{hypotenuse} = \frac{8}{10}$ **Answer: (B)**

Explanation to PowerPrep Practice Question 2

We know $tan = TOA = \frac{opposite}{adjacent}$ $tan\ b = \frac{opp}{adj}$ so the opposite side of the triangle must be 5 and the adjacent side must be 12.

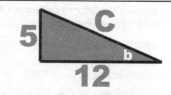

We know that $cos\ b = \frac{adj}{hypot}$ We must solve for the hypotenuse.
Two ways to solve for the hypotenuse:
1. This is a (5-12-13) triangle, so the hypotenuse has a value of 13.
2. You can also calculate the missing side by using Pythagorean Theorem: $a^2 + b^2 = c^2$

Plug in what we know: $a = 12\ (adjacent),\ b = 5\ (opposite),$
$c = x\ (hypotenuse)$
$a^2 + b^2 = c^2$ **Becomes:** $12^2 + b^2 = 10^2$ **becomes:** $36 + 5^2 = c^2$ **becomes:**
$169 = c^2$

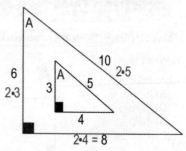

$13 = c$ **or** $cos\ b = \frac{adj}{hypot} = \frac{12}{13}$

Answer: (A)

Trigonometry
Part 2: Value of Angles
Virtual Classroom>Trigonometry>Value of Angles

This material corresponds to the Virtual Classroom Instructions in the
PowerPrep DVD/Internet/iApp for Trigonometry

Virtual Classroom

Part 2: Value of Angles

Generally

Here are some values of common angles you will want to recognize or be able to quickly calculate.

Angle	Sin	Cos	tan
0°	0	1	0
30°	$\frac{1}{2}$	$\sqrt{3}/_2$	$\sqrt{3}/_3$
45°	$\sqrt{2}/_2$	$\sqrt{2}/_2$	1
60°	$\sqrt{3}/_2$	$\frac{1}{2}$	$\sqrt{3}$
90°	1	0	undefined

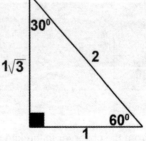

Let's take a look at a few: $cos\ 60\ = ???$

Draw a 30°- 60°- 90° triangle
Remember the ratio of the sides is $x :\ x\sqrt{3} :\ 2x$

$cos60 = \frac{adj}{hypot} = \frac{1}{2}$ $sin60 = \frac{opp}{hypot} = \frac{\sqrt{3}}{2}$ $tan60 = \frac{opp}{adj} = 1\left(\sqrt{3}/_1\right) = \sqrt{3}$ $\boldsymbol{Tan\ 45\ =????}$

Draw out a 45°- 45°- 90° triangle

$tan\ 45 = \frac{opposite}{adjacent} = \frac{1}{1} = 1$ $cos\ 45 = \frac{opposite}{hypotenuse} = \frac{1}{\sqrt{2}} = \frac{\sqrt{2}}{2}$ $sin\ 45 = \frac{opposite}{hypotenuse} = \frac{1}{\sqrt{2}} = \frac{\sqrt{2}}{2}$

Remember the ratio of the sides is $\left(x : x : x\sqrt{2}\right)$

PowerPrep Practice Questions Also in the Virtual Classroom on DVD

PowerPrep Practice Questions 3

3. From an observer on the ground, the angle of elevation to a kite flying nearby is 17°. The distance from the observer to a point on the ground directly underneath the kite is 42 feet. How far off the ground is the kite?

(A) $\dfrac{42}{\cos 17^0}$

(B) $\dfrac{42}{\tan 17^0}$

(C) $42(\sin 17^0)$

(D) $42(\cos 17^0)$

(E) $42(\tan 17^0)$

Explanation to PowerPrep Practice Question 3

$\tan 17^0 = \dfrac{opp}{adj} = \dfrac{x}{42}$ $\quad \tan 17^0 = \dfrac{x}{42}$ $\qquad x = 42(\tan 17^0)$

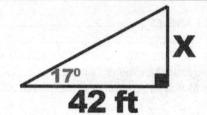

Answer: (E)

More Detailed Explanation:

If you can visualize this information, the math is rather straight forward. Don't let the information about an "observer" mess you up. We want to find out how high the kite is flying. We know one angle and the length of one side of the right triangle. This is sufficient information to calculate the height.

This red line, marked "x", is the distance we want to find—from the kite to the ground.

We are told the distance from the observer to the perpendicular line from kite to ground is 42 feet. Notice also, that our observer could be anywhere along the white circle with a radius of 42 feet. We've picked the spot on the circle where the person is standing on the left. But it could be anywhere along the circle and the math would work out…

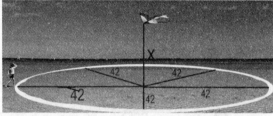

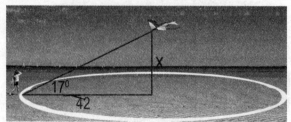

We are also told that from the observer to the kite is 17^0

Now we have sufficient information to calculate "x"

Remember SOH-CAH-TOA $\tan = TOA = \dfrac{opposite}{adjacent}$ If we apply that to our

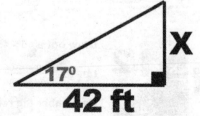

information, we get: $\tan 17^0 = \dfrac{x}{42}$

Multiply both sides by 42 to isolate x: $42(\tan 17^0) = x$
Therefore, $x = 42(\tan 17^0)$

Answer: (E)

Trigonometry
Part 3: Unit Circle

Virtual Classroom> Trigonometry >Unit Circle

This material corresponds to the Virtual Classroom Instructions in the
PowerPrep DVD/Internet/iApp for Trigonometry

Virtual Classroom

Important Abbreviations
These abbreviations are used throughout the program

POE: Process of Elimination
SARR: Synthesize, Analyze, Reduce, and Restate (has to do with Logical Reasoning)
AC: Answer Choice
QS: Question Stem
LOD: Level of Difficulty

Example Question: What is the least common multiple of 3, 4, and 7? (**This is the call of the question or Question Stem "QS"**)

These are Answer Choices "AC" A, B, C, D, E

   (A)   12
   (B)   21
   (C)   28
   (D)   48
   (E)   84

Part 3: Unit Circle

Part 1

The last step of **SOH CAH TOA** is to relate angles to a unit circle. This is a circle with a radius of 1.
Notice that the radius of the circle could become the hypotenuse of a triangle where the lengths of the two sides would be the distance along the x axis and y axis.

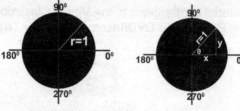
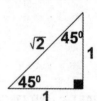

$$sin\ \theta = \frac{opposite}{hypotenuse} = \frac{y}{1} = y$$

$$cos\ \theta = \frac{adjacent}{hypotenuse} = \frac{x}{1} = x$$

$$tan\ \theta = \frac{opposite}{adjacent} = \frac{y}{x}$$

If we make θ = 45, then we have an x : x : x triangle. This is the standard $90^0{:}45^0{:}45^0$ triangle with equal sides = 1 But with the unit circle, the hypotenuse is 1, so we have to do some conversion to get to the new triangle with hypotenuse 1. Since our radius is 1 (x = 1), in order to go from x : x : $x\sqrt{2}$

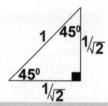

triangle to our triangle below, we divide all three parts of our ratio by: $\sqrt{2}$ to get $\left(\frac{1}{\sqrt{2}}\ :\ \frac{1}{\sqrt{2}}\ :\ \mathbf{1}\right)$

The new unit circle triangle looks like this: $\quad sin\ \theta° = \frac{opposite}{hypotenuse} = \frac{y}{1} = \frac{1}{\sqrt{2}} = \frac{\sqrt{2}}{2}$ (rationalized below)

$$\mathbf{cos\ \theta°} = \frac{adjacent}{hypotenuse} = \frac{x}{1} = x = \frac{1}{\sqrt{2}} = \frac{\sqrt{2}}{2} \qquad\qquad \mathbf{tan\ \theta°} = \frac{opposite}{adjacent} = \frac{y}{x} = \frac{\frac{1}{\sqrt{2}}}{\frac{1}{\sqrt{2}}} = 1$$

Rationalized

You might wonder how $\frac{1}{\sqrt{2}} = \frac{\sqrt{2}}{2}$, it might not look like it, but they are equal. It is a mathematical convention to rationalize the denominator--that is, to write the fraction as an equivalent expression **with no roots in the denominator.** To rationalize a denominator, multiply the fraction by a "clever" form of 1--that is, by a fraction whose numerator and denominator are both equal to the square root in the denominator. For example, to rationalize the denominator of $\frac{25}{2\sqrt{3}}$ Multiply this fraction by $\frac{\sqrt{3}}{\sqrt{3}}$

which is just 1 It becomes: $\left(\frac{25}{2\sqrt{3}}\right)\left(\frac{\sqrt{3}}{\sqrt{3}}\right) = \frac{25\sqrt{3}}{2(\sqrt{3})(\sqrt{3})} = \frac{25\sqrt{3}}{2(\sqrt{3*3})} = \frac{25\sqrt{3}}{2\sqrt{3^2}} = \frac{25\sqrt{3}}{2*3} = \frac{25\sqrt{3}}{6}$ So in the case above where

$sin\ 45 = \frac{1}{\sqrt{2}}$ So rationalize $\frac{1}{\sqrt{2}}$

$\frac{1}{\sqrt{2}} = \left(\frac{1}{\sqrt{2}}\right)\left(\frac{\sqrt{2}}{\sqrt{2}}\right) = \frac{\sqrt{2}}{\sqrt{2}*\sqrt{2}} = \frac{\sqrt{2}}{\sqrt{2*2}} = \frac{\sqrt{2}}{\sqrt{2^2}} = \frac{\sqrt{2}}{2}$ And that's how you rationalize $\frac{1}{\sqrt{2}}$ so that it equals $\frac{\sqrt{2}}{2}$. If you're still not convinced and this hints of some deep dark black magic, you can always multiply it out: $\sqrt{2} = 1.41$
$\frac{1}{1.41} = .71$ And $\frac{1.41}{2} = .71$ If this still seems problematic, it's just one of those things you'll have to accept and move on.
The cool part about the unit circle is that the hypotenuse is ALWAYS 1, so these values for sin, cos and tan are always the same. $sin\ \theta° = y \qquad cos\ \theta° = x \qquad tan\ \theta° = y/x$

Part 2

What happens at $0°$ At $0°$, our x distance is the same as the radius, so x = 1.
This means $cos\ 0° = 1$.
At zero, y = 0 (we have no height). $sin\ 0° = 0 \quad tan\ 0° = y/x = 0/1 = 0$

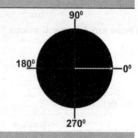

Part 3

At $180°$ things are very similar except $x = -1$
$\quad cos\ 180° = x = -1$

$\quad sin\ 180° = y = 0$

$\quad tan\ 180^0 = \frac{y}{x} = \frac{0}{-1} = 0$

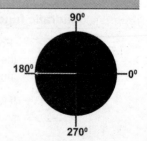

Part 4

At 90°, y is the radius and we have no horizontal distance $(x = 0)$

$cos\ 90° = x = 0$

$sin\ 90° = y = 1$

$tan\ 90° = \frac{y}{x} = \frac{1}{0}$ = Undefined. Can't divide a number by 0

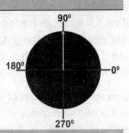

Part 5

At 270°, y is now −1

$cos\ 90 = x = 0$

$sin\ 90 = y = -1$

$tan\ 90° = \frac{y}{x} = -\frac{1}{0} = undefined$

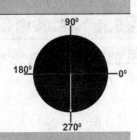

Part 6

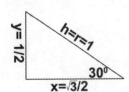

As you have seen with $180°\ and\ 270°$**, it is possible to calculate angle values (ratios) for angles greater than** $90°$

Let's start with the $150°$ angle. Although it is 150 degrees from zero, it is only 30 degrees from the $180°$ marker. We know what happens with a $30°$ angle. The only difference here is that x will be negative.

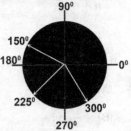

$\sin 150° = y = \frac{1}{2}$ $\cos 150° = x = -\frac{\sqrt{3}}{2}$ (Negative direction) $\tan 150° = \frac{y}{x} = \frac{\frac{1}{2}}{-\frac{\sqrt{3}}{2}} = -\frac{1}{\sqrt{3}} = -\frac{\sqrt{3}}{3}$ (rationalized)

What about 225°?

It is 45° from the 180° marker. At this position both x and y will be negative.

Remember that the sides of a 45-45-90 triangle are $(x : x : x\sqrt{2})$ Again, since the hypotenuse has a value of 1, we can divide all three parts of the ratio by $\sqrt{2}$ then substitute x = 1 for each.

$\left(\frac{x}{\sqrt{2}} : \frac{x}{\sqrt{2}} : x\right) \rightarrow \left(\frac{1}{\sqrt{2}} : \frac{1}{\sqrt{2}} : 1\right) \rightarrow \left(\frac{\sqrt{2}}{2} : \frac{\sqrt{2}}{2} : 1\right)$

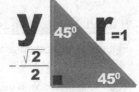

Sin 225° = $y = -\frac{\sqrt{2}}{2}$ Cos 225° = $x = -\frac{\sqrt{2}}{2}$ Tan 225° = $\frac{y}{x} = \left(\frac{-\frac{\sqrt{2}}{2}}{-\frac{\sqrt{2}}{2}}\right) = 1$

Functions by Quadrant

Quadrant II	Quadrant I
[-x, y]	[x, y]
SIN (csc) +	SIN, COS, TAN +
	(csc, sec, cot)
Quadrant III	Quadrant IV
[-x, -y]	[x, -y]
TAN (cot) +	COS (sec) +

$sin\ θ° = y$

$cos\ θ° = x$

$tan\ θ° = \frac{y}{x}$

Graphs-- quadratic functions

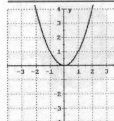

For linear functions the slope intercept form $y = mx + b$ tells us a lot about the graph. m is the slope of the line and b is the y intercept. This can be extended to quadratic functions. The most basic quadratic function is $y = x^2$

If we look at $y = x^2$ as being like $y = mx + b$, then we have $y = 1x^2 + 0$, and because the x is squared we complicate the equation by adding $y = 1(x - 0)^2 + 0$

First let's see the effect from changing the y intercept. In $y = x^2$, b is 0 and the graph crosses the y axis at 0. If we change the equation to, $y = x^2 + 1$ the graph shifts up one, and it crosses at $y = 1$.

If we think of it as having a slope then we can look at the value in front of the square as being the slope. In the above graph it is positive and the graph is concave up, meaning the bowl part faces up. If we looked at the graph $y = -x^2$ it would look like the one above, but concave down. The graph of $2x^2$ will look more narrow and steep than x^2 because it grows more quickly. On the other hand, the graph of ½ x^2 will look wide and will grow more slowly.

Changing a third part of the function, the x value, the graph shifts along the x axis. The function $y = (x + 2)^2$ shifts the graph in the negative direction. The vertex went from $(0,0)$ in the original graph to $(-2, 0)$. For the function $y = (x - 2)^2$ the graph shifts in the positive direction and the vertex is at $(2, 0)$. If we foiled this function out to $y = x^2 - 4x + 4$ it, of course, forms the same graph, but it isn't as easy to analyze. In this case you would need to factor into the original form or else graph it.

Bonus Sample Questions not in the Virtual Classroom on the DVD

Bonus Sample Question 1-2

1. $tan\ 480^0 = ?$

   (A)   1

   (B)   −1

   (C) $\sqrt{3}$

   (D) $-\sqrt{3}$

   (E) $-\sqrt{\frac{3}{2}}$

2. If angle A is between 0° an 180° and sin A = $\frac{3}{5}$, what are the possible values of tan A?

   (A) $-\frac{3}{4}$

   (B) $-\frac{3}{4}$ and $\frac{3}{4}$

   (C) $-\frac{4}{3}$ and $\frac{4}{3}$

   (D) $\frac{3}{4}$

   (E) $\frac{4}{3}$

Explanation to Bonus Sample Question 1

Figure out what quadrant this angle is in and its relative angle measurement.
$480° - 360° = 120°$

120° is in the second quadrant and is 60° from the 180° marker. We know it will have a negative value in this quadrant (positive y divided by negative x is negative).

$\tan \theta° = \frac{y}{x}$ so, $tan\ 60^0 = \frac{y}{x} = \frac{\frac{\sqrt{3}}{2}}{-\frac{1}{2}} = -\sqrt{3}$ **Answer: (D)**

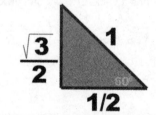

Explanation to Bonus Sample Question 2

First, think about the quadrants. From 0° to 180° is two quadrants (I and II) We are told that sin A is POSITIVE $\frac{3}{5}$. Is sin positive in quadrant I. YES.

Is sin positive in quadrant II. YES. So we have two possible locations for angle A.
Draw a picture!
Each is a 3-4-5 triangle. QI has a positive x and Q2 has a negative x.
$QI: \tan \theta° = \frac{y}{x} = \frac{3}{4}$

$QII: \tan \theta° = \frac{y}{x} = \frac{3}{-4} = -\frac{3}{4}$ **Answer: (B)**

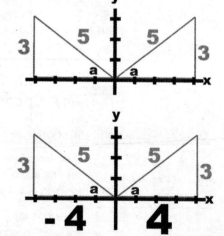

CONGRATULATIONS!!!

You Have Completed The Trigonometry Workshop!

Take A Break Before Moving On To The Drills.

Trigonometry Index

Top 10 Traps Workbook
Table of Contents

This material corresponds to the Virtual Classroom Instructions in the
PowerPrep DVD/Internet/iApp for Top 10 Traps

Virtual Classroom

Top 10 Traps

Part 1: Remainders

Virtual Classroom>Top 10 Traps>Remainders

This material corresponds to the Virtual Classroom Instructions in the
PowerPrep DVD/Internet/iApp for Top 10 Traps

Virtual Classroom

Important Abbreviations
These abbreviations are used throughout the program

POE: Process of Elimination
SARR: Synthesize, Analyze, Reduce, and Restate (has to do with Logical Reasoning)
AC: Answer Choice
QS: Question Stem
LOD: Level of Difficulty

Example Question: What is the least common multiple of 3, 4, and 7? **(This is the call of the question or Question Stem "QS")**

These are Answer Choices "AC" A, B, C, D, E

    (A)   12
    (B)   21
    (C)   28
    (D)   48
    (E)   84

Part 1: Remainders

Remainders:

Remainders: The number left over from dividing one integer by another. $(14 \div 3 = 4 \; remainder \; 2)$

Strategy:

- Pick the number given in the denominator (or multiple of the denominator)
- Add the remainder given in the problem to the denominator to determine the value of the variable
- Solve the second portion of the question for the new variable value
- Determine the remainder value

Example:

When p is divided by 5, remainder is 2. What is the remainder when $4p$ is divided by 5?

Pick a number: Let's use $Denominator = 5$ But we could pick multiples of 5 $(like \; 10)$

Add the remainder to determine the value of the variable: $5 + 2 = 7$ Therefore, $p = 7$
Or if you selected another multiple of 5, like 10, it would be: $10 + 2 = 12$ Therefore $p = 12$

Solve for second variable: $4p$ becomes $4(7) = 28$ or if you used 10 as your starting point: $4p$ becomes $4(12) = 48$

Determine remainder: $\frac{28}{5} = 5 \; remainder \; 3$ If you started with 10 it would be: $\frac{48}{5} = 9 \; remainder \; 3$. Either way you get remainder 3 <u>**Answer: (D)**</u>

PowerPrep Practice Questions Also in the Virtual Classroom on DVD

PowerPrep Practice Questions 1-2

1. If the remainder of "a" divided by 3 is 2, what is the remainder when $(a - 3)$ is divided by 3?

    (A) 0
    (B) 1
    (C) 2
    (D) 3
    (E) 4

2. When b is divided by 5 the remainder is 1. When c is divided by 5 the remainder is 2. What is the remainder when $(b + c)$ is divided by 5?
    (A) 3
    (B) 2
    (C) 1
    (D) 0
    (E) 5

Explanation to PowerPrep Practice Question 1

Remainders and Arbitrary numbers: This question tests Picking Arbitrary numbers. Sometimes the way to solve a problem begins by picking an arbitrary number. This question is a good example of this process.

Strategy for Remainders Questions:
1. Select an arbitrary number for the variable
2. Add the given remainder to the arbitrary number you selected—this will determine the value of the variable.
3. Solve the second portion of the question for the new variable value
4. Determine the remainder value.

This might sound complex, but it's not when you see it in action.

Our given information was: If "a" divided by 3 gives remainder 2, what is the remainder when $(a - 3)$ is divided by 3?
Restate this information: We are looking for a variable represented by "a" and we are told that "a" divided by 3 gives a remainder of 2

Step 1: select an arbitrary number "N". It's easiest to use a multiple of the number you chose to divide—in this case the number is 3, so we are picking a multiple of 3, like 6 for our N.
Step 2: add the remainder to the arbitrary N. In this case it would be $6 + 2$ (the given remainder).
Now we have $(6 + 2) = 8$. So 8 is the variable we were looking for. In other words, $a = 8$
Step 3: solve the 2nd part of the question. What is the remainder when $(a - 3)$ is divided by 3

Since $a = 8$, you have $\frac{8-3}{3}$ or $\frac{5}{3}$ or $1 \; remainder \; 2$

Step 4: we solved the remainder question above in step 3—the remainder is 2

First, pick any number: Make sure it's a multiple of 3 to avoid tricky math. We picked 6, N = 6
6 + (*remainder* 2) = 8 But the set consists of all multiples of 3 plus 2
IOW (3+2 =**5**, 6+2=**8**, 9+2=**11**, 12+2=**14**, 15+2=**17**, 18+2=**20**…)
(5, 8, 11, 14, 17, 20…) We are using 8, but it could be any number from this set

You might want to first check to be sure the math worked. Does 8 divided by 3 give us remainder 2? Yes: $\frac{8}{3} = 2r2$ So this fits the given information where we had a remainder 2.

Now plug this information into the given: What is the remainder when (*a* – 3) is divided by 3? $\frac{a-3}{3}$

We chose a = 8 (but remember it could be any number from the set (5, 8, 11, 14, 17, 20…) **Becomes** $\frac{8-3}{3} = \frac{5}{3}$

How many times does 3 divide into 5? Answer 1. **What is the remainder?** Answer 2, **Therefore,** $\frac{5}{3} = 1r2$

The question asks what the remainder is. So the answer is 1 with **remainder 2**
But any number from the set would also work: (5, 8, 11, 14, 17, 20…)
For example, If $a = 17$, then $\frac{17-3}{3} = \frac{14}{3} = 4\ r2$ Any number from the set will give remainder 2 **ANSWER: (C)**

Explanation to PowerPrep Practice Question 2

Strategy for Remainders Questions:
1. Select an arbitrary number for the variable
2. Add the given remainder to the arbitrary number you selected—this will determine the value of the variable.
3. Solve the second portion of the question for the new variable value
4. Determine the remainder value.

Select an arbitrary number, in this case it should be a multiple of 5 to keep the math simple.
We'll chose $N = 10$ (arbitrary multiple of 5—the number you use to divide)

Now add the given remainder to N becomes $(10 + 1) = b$ *So* $b = 11$
Do the same thing for the variable "C".
$N = 10$ (Because we are dividing by 5). Select a multiple, we could pick 15, 20 etc) try it.
We'll pick 20 just to show you. $N = 20$

Apply it to the given: $c = 20 + 2$ (*the remainder*) *So*, $c = 22$
Check it: What is 22 divided by 5? 4 **What is the remainder?** 2

So this works: If you cannot see why this works, keep reviewing these concepts before moving forward to the final step and solve. **What's the remainder of** $\left(\frac{b+c}{5}\right)$ "b" turned out to be 11 and "c" was 22 so what is $(b + c) \div 5$?

Becomes: $\frac{11+22}{5} = \frac{33}{5}$ Or **6 remainder 3   Answer (A)**

Another Example: Just to show how this works for any multiple of the given number used to divide.

Let's choose $N = 100$ **for the b part of the equation and** $N = 50$ **for the c part of the equation**
Both are multiples of 5, so the math will work out evenly.

First the "b" part of the problem: When b is divided by 5, the remainder is 1. We picked N (the random multiple of 5) as 100. So add the remainder to the random N: $(N = 100)$
$100 + (1)$ *the given remainder* $= b$ **Becomes** $b = 101$

Now solve the c part of the problem. *When c is divided by 5 the remainder is 2*
We chose N to be 50 (a random multiple of 5) So **add** the remainder to N (**the random multiple of 5**)
$N + 2$ (given remainder) = c **So** $(50 + 2 = c)$ Then, $c = 52$

Now solve the given question: What is the remainder when $(b + c)$ is divided by 5? **b=101, c = 52**

Becomes: $\frac{b+c}{5}$ => $\frac{101+52}{5}$ => $\frac{153}{5}$ = 30 **remainder 3**
As you can see the remainders are the same: In this case 3.
Bear in mind, you are only concerned about remainders in this type of question.   CORRECT ANSWER: (A)

Bonus Sample Questions <u>not</u> in the Virtual Classroom on the DVD

Bonus Sample Question 1

1. If b is divided by 5 and the remainder is 1, then which is greater, the remainder when b is divided by 3 or the remainder when b is divided by 4?
   (A) The remainder when b is divided by 3 is greater
   (B) The remainder when b is divided by 4 is greater
   (C) They are equal
   (D) Unknown—insufficient information

Explanation to Bonus Sample Question 1

You can answer this question without calculating the values of b. If you divide 3 and 4 into a series of numbers, 3 can only have remainders of 0, 1, and 2 while 4 can have remainders of 0, 1, 2, and 3.

Therefore, 4 will always have the possibility of a remainder 3 as its biggest remainder and 3 will only have the possibility of remainder 2 as its biggest remainder.

The key, is to realize that the set of possible b's will return every possible outcome (the 4 will have remainder 3, 2, 1, 0 and the 3 will have outcome 2, 1, 0)

First, if b is divided by 5 the remainder is 1. $\frac{b}{5} = x \ remainder \ 1$

Pick a multiple of the denominator: $(5, 10, 15, 20, 25 \dots)$
Next add the remainder to each possible answer for b: In this case the remainder is 1

So add 1 to each possible answer in the set: $(5, 10, 15, 20, 25, 30 \dots)$ **becomes** $(6, 11, 16, 21, 26, 31 \dots)$ So b can equal any number in the set $(6, 11, 16, 21, 26, 31 \dots)$

Now calculate the values for 3: $b = (6, 11, 16, 21, 26, 31 \dots)$ $\frac{6, \ 11, \ 16, \ 21, \ 26, \ 31\dots}{3} = a \ series \ of \ possible \ outcomes$

$\frac{6}{3} = 2 \ \boldsymbol{remainder} \ \boldsymbol{0}$, $\frac{11}{3} = 3 \ \boldsymbol{remainder} \ \boldsymbol{2}$, $\frac{16}{3} = 5 \ \boldsymbol{remainder} \ \boldsymbol{1}$

Now the pattern of 0,2,1 remainders will repeat: $\frac{21}{3} = 7 \ \boldsymbol{remainder} \ \boldsymbol{0}$, $\frac{26}{3} = 8 \ \boldsymbol{remainder} \ \boldsymbol{2}$, $\frac{31}{3} = 10 \ \boldsymbol{remainder} \ \boldsymbol{1}$
The pattern of remainders 0,2,1 repeats

Now calculate the values for 4: $b = (6, 11, 16, 21, 26, 31, 36, 41 \dots)$
$\frac{6, \ 11, \ 16, \ 21, \ 26, \ 31\dots}{4} = a \ series \ of \ possible \ outcomes$

$\frac{6}{4} = 1 \ remainder \ 2$, $\frac{11}{4} = 2 \ remainder \ 3$, $\frac{16}{4} = 4 \ remainder \ 0$, $\frac{21}{4} = 5 \ remainder \ 1$

Now the pattern of (2, 3, 0, 1) remainders will repeat.
$\frac{26}{4} = 6 \ remainder \ 2$, $\frac{31}{4} = 7 \ remainder \ 3$, $\frac{36}{4} = 8 \ remainder \ 0$, $\frac{41}{4} = 10 \ remainder \ 1$

The pattern of remainders (2, 3, 0, 1) repeats again
So you can see that the larger the number being divided, the larger the possible remainder.

The denominator 4 will always have the possibility of a larger remainder than the denominator 3   **Answer: (B)**

Top 10 Traps
Part 2: Ratio Comparison

Virtual Classroom>Top 10 Traps>Ratio Comparison

This material corresponds to the Virtual Classroom Instructions in the
PowerPrep DVD/Internet/iApp for Top 10 Traps

Virtual Classroom

Important Abbreviations
These abbreviations are used throughout the program

POE: Process of Elimination
SARR: Synthesize, Analyze, Reduce, and Restate (has to do with Logical Reasoning)
AC: Answer Choice
QS: Question Stem
LOD: Level of Difficulty

Example Question: What is the least common multiple of 3, 4, and 7? (**This is the call of the question or Question Stem "QS"**)

These are Answer Choices "AC" A, B, C, D, E

  (A)   12
  (B)   21
  (C)   28
  (D)   48
  (E)   84

Part 2: Ratio Comparison

Ratio Comparison

A ratio which compares two unknown quantities measured in different units.

Strategy:

- Pick a number for each variable
- Solve the problem using the linking value
- Substitute each variable's value into the answer choices
- Find the corresponding answer

Example:

If baseballs and softballs cost the same per ball and the cost of six baseballs is x dollars, y softballs would cost how many dollars?

- (A) $6xy$
- (B) $\frac{6x}{y}$
- (C) $\frac{6}{xy}$
- (D) $\frac{x}{6y}$
- (E) $\frac{xy}{6}$

Straight Math Way: $6B = x$ ($6\ baseballs = x\ dollars$) **Solve for B** $B = \frac{x}{6}$ $\left(1\ baseball\ costs\ \frac{x}{6}\ or\ \frac{1}{6}x\right)$ **Substitute:** If the cost of a single baseball is $\frac{x}{6}$ and baseballs and softballs cost the same, then y softballs will cost $\frac{x}{6}(y)$ **Simplify:** $\frac{yx}{6}$

Answer E

Another Way: Picking Numbers Strategy

- Pick a number for each variable,
- Solve the problem using the linking value,
- Substitute each variable's value into the answer choices,
- Find the corresponding answer.

$x = cost\ of\ 6\ baseballs$ Pick a number that makes it easy. We'll pick $12.00\ for\ x$, that way baseballs will cost $2.00 each. So let $x = 12$, 6 baseballs cost 12 dollars or $2 each

$Y = number\ of\ softballs$
Let $y = 4$, (random number) But we already know that baseballs and softballs cost the same per ball and in our sample we calculated baseballs at $2.00 each. Therefore, *Linking value* = $2.00/ball. 4 softballs (at $2.00 each) cost $8.00

Plug in: $x = 12\ and\ y = 4$ to answer choices. **The correct answer must give us a value of $8.00**

(A) $6(12)(4) = 288$ (B) $\frac{6(12)}{4} = \frac{72}{4} = 18$ (C) $\frac{6}{(12)(4)} = \frac{6}{48} = \frac{1}{8}$ (D) $\frac{12}{(6)(4)} = \frac{12}{24} = \frac{1}{2}$ **(E)** $\frac{(12)(4)}{6} = \frac{48}{6} = 8$

Answer: (E)

PowerPrep Practice Questions Also in the Virtual Classroom on DVD

PowerPrep Practice Questions 3-4

3. If fish and seahorses cost the same and the cost of $x\ fish\ is$ $2.00, then y seahorses would cost how many dollars?

   (A) $\frac{2x}{y}$

   (B) $\frac{x}{2y}$

   (C) $\frac{2y}{x}$

   (D) $2xy$

   (E) $\frac{2}{xy}$

4. If Sam ran 6 miles in x hours (at a constant speed), how many miles did Sam run, (at a constant speed), in the first y hours of his workout?

   (A) $\frac{6x}{y}$

   (B) $6xy$

   (C) $\frac{y}{6x}$

   (D) $\frac{6}{xy}$

   (E) $\frac{6y}{x}$

Explanation to PowerPrep Practice Question 3

Straight Math Way: $xF = 2(x\ fish) = 2\ dollars$ Solve for F $(fish)$, $F = \frac{2}{x}$ (1 Fish costs $\frac{2}{x}$) **Substitute:** If the cost of a single fish is $\frac{2}{x}$ and fish and seahorses cost the same, then y seahorses cost $\frac{2}{x}(y)$ **Simplify:** $\frac{2y}{x}$ **Answer C**

Another Way: Picking Numbers
This is a comparison problem. It's not a problem with a fixed answer. Your answer will be a comparison that will depend on the value of x and y that you select, however, the comparison will be constant.

First solve for the cost of fish: $If\ x\ fish\ cost$ $2
Pick an arbitrary number for the fish (**be wise, select a number that makes the math easy**) $Let's\ pick$ $2\ fish.$

Now we have 2 fish that cost a total of $2.00. How much does 1 fish cost? $1.00 (in this example)
Therefore, in this comparison fish and seahorses will cost $1 each

Now pick any number for y (the number of seahorses you want to buy—it won't matter what number you pick, but be wise and select a number that will make the math easy)

Let's pick six (6) seahorses.
Now solve. If fish and seahorses cost the same and that number for this comparison is $1.00
How much do 6 (our number) seahorses cost. **Answer: $6.00**

So the answer has to equal 6. To get the answer of $6, we found $x = 2$ $(number\ of\ fish)$ and $= 6$ $(number\ of\ seahorses)$
Plug these numbers into the answer choices and find the one that equals 6.
Plug in $x = 2$ $and\ y = 6$ **into answer choices**

(A) $\frac{2x}{y} = \frac{2(2)}{6} = \frac{4}{6} = \frac{2}{3}$ (B) $\frac{x}{2y} = \frac{2}{(2)(6)} = \frac{2}{12} = \frac{1}{6}$ **(C)** $\frac{2y}{x} = \frac{2(6)}{2} = \frac{12}{2} = 6$ (D) $2xy = 2*2*6 = 4*6 = 24$ (E) $\frac{2}{xy} = \frac{2}{2*6} = \frac{2}{12} = \frac{1}{6}$

This may be confusing, so let's look at another example to show how it works as long as you keep the comparisons right.

Given, fish and seahorses cost the same. $X = number\ of\ fish$, and $Y = number\ of\ seahorses$. $X\ fish\ cost$ $2.00 (this is our constant from which the problem is solved) It won't matter what you pick for x because we are looking for comparisons

In the last example we picked 2 fish to make the math easy. But now, let's pick something less obvious. Say $X = 4$

If we buy 4 fish for $2.00, then each fish cost .50 cents.
Since fish and seahorses cost the same, we have now figured out the cost of both. $(.50cents)$

How many seahorses do we want to buy? $Let's\ say$ 10 (random number—could be anything) So, $y = 10$ (we are buying 10 seahorses) **Solve the cost of 10 seahorses at .50cents each.** Total cost is $5.00

This is what we must find in our answer choices. It may seem odd that the answer choice (C) in the first example was 6, but in this example that same answer choice will be 5.   This is because we have new variables but the same comparison.

In this example we chose $x = 4$ **and** $y = 10$ **and the answer is $5.00**
Now plug these $x's\ and\ y's$ **into the possible answer choices and find the one that returns the answer of 5.** $X = 4, y = 10$ (find the AC that gives 5)

(A) $\frac{2x}{y} = \frac{2*4}{y} = \frac{8}{10} = \frac{4}{5}$ (B) $\frac{x}{2y} = \frac{4}{2*10} = \frac{4}{20} = \frac{1}{5}$ **(C)** $\frac{2y}{x} = \frac{2*10}{4} = \frac{20}{40} = 5$ (D) $2xy = (2)(4)(10) = 2(40) = 80$

(E) $\frac{2}{xy} = \frac{2}{(4)(10)} = \frac{2}{40} = \frac{1}{20}$

You can see, the correct AC is still "C", which in this case returned the answer of 5 $for\ the\ x, y$ combination of $x = 4, y = 10$
As long as we set the problem up correctly the answer will always be C.

Study this until you understand it clearly. Answer: (C)

Explanation to PowerPrep Practice Question 4

Straight Math: Sam runs 6 miles in x hours $\frac{6\ miles}{x\ hours}$
If you don't see this fraction, try this: If Sam runs 6 miles in 6 hours, what is his rate? 1mph. $\left(\frac{(6\ miles)}{6\ hours} = \frac{6}{6}\ or\ 1\ mph\right)$
If Sam runs 6 miles in 1 hours what is his rate? 6 mph. $\frac{6\ miles}{1\ hour} = 6\ or\ 6\ mph$ So Sam's rate in this problem is $\frac{6miles}{x\ hours}$ or $\frac{6}{x}$
Now we want to know how far he can run in y hours.
$(Rate * time) = distance$ We want to know the distance and we have the rate $\frac{6}{x}$ We have the time (sort of) y. So,
$\frac{6}{x} = rate$ and $y = time$. If $(Rate * time) = distance$ then, $\frac{6}{x} * y = distance$. **Simplify:** $\frac{6y}{x} = distance$ **Answer E**
Another Way: Picking Numbers
What are you looking for? The amount of miles Sam ran in a given amount of time.   If Sam runs $x\ fast$, how many miles will he cover in $y\ hours$.

First, find a rate (how fast he runs—bear in mind, this rate is a comparison—it's like saying, if I can improve my speed to x, then how many miles can I cover.) Another example would be losing weight. If I can lose weight at the rate of 1 pound a week, how long will it take to lose 20 lbs, what if I can lose ½ a $pound/week$, etc) these are all comparisons.

In this example we will choose a random number of hours for x: To make the math simple, let's choose $x = 6$, in other words, Sam runs $6\ miles\ in\ 6\ hours$ $(x = 6\ hours)$

So he runs $1/mph$ (we forced the math to be easy). If he runs $1/mph$ how far does he run in $1\ hour$? ...answer , $1\ mile$
$X = 6\ hours$ and $Y = 1\ hours$ $Answer\ 1\ mile$.   If he runs 6 miles in 6 hours, how far does he run in 1 hour? **Answer 1 mile**

X = 6, y = 1   Answer 1

Now plug this information back into the answers to find the (AC) that gives a result of 1.   For $x = 6\ and\ y = 1$

(A) $\frac{6x}{y} = \frac{6*6}{1} = \frac{36}{1} = 36$ (B) $6xy = 6(6)(1) = 36 * 1 = 36$ (C) $\frac{y}{6x} = \frac{1}{6*6} = \frac{1}{36}$ (D) $\frac{6}{xy} = \frac{6}{6*1} = \frac{6}{6} = 1$ **(E)** $\frac{6y}{x} = \frac{6*1}{6} = \frac{6}{6} = \mathbf{1}$

OOPS! This shows us the problem that sometimes happens when setting a variable equal to 1. You can get false positives. If you get two "correct" answers, you know they cannot both be correct. So choose another set of variables for x, y and solve it again. This time, don't choose 1 for a variable.

Let's try again and this time, what about $x = 2\ and\ y = 10$ This would mean that Sam ran $6\ miles\ in\ 2\ hours\ (our\ x)$,
How fast is 6mi in 2 hours? $3mph$
If Sam runs 3mph, then how far does he run in 10 hours (our y)? He ran $30\ miles$
Now we have a new set of numbers: $X = 2\ y = 10\ answer = 30$
So plug these numbers into the answer choices and find which one returns an answer of 30

(A) $\frac{6x}{y} = \frac{6*2}{10} = \frac{12}{10} = \frac{6}{5}$ (B) $6xy = 6*2*10 = 12*10 = 120$ (C) $\frac{y}{6x} = \frac{10}{6*2} = \frac{10}{12} = \frac{5}{6}$

(D) $\frac{6}{xy} = \frac{6}{2*10} = \frac{6}{20} = \frac{3}{10}$ **(E)** $\frac{6y}{x} = \frac{6(10)}{2} = \frac{60}{2} = \mathbf{30}$ __Answer: (E)__

This time AC (D) did not return a correct number (30). So (D) was a false positive. Now you know the correct AC is (E).

Let's do one more, just to prove the point.
In x hours he runs $6\ miles$: Set $x = 12$.   **How fast is he running now?** $.5\ mph$
Now select y: If he runs $.5\ mph$, how far does he run in $50\ hours$ $(y = 50)$.   **Answer is 25 miles**
Now we have some very different numbers: $X = 12\ Y = 50\ Answer = 25$

But if we have selected the correct AC from our prior work, then AC (E) will still work.
Check it: $X = 12\ y = 50\ answer = 25$
For this to be correct AC (E), must return 25
(A) $\frac{6x}{y} = \frac{6*12}{50} = \frac{72}{50} = 1.44$ (B) $6xy = (6)(12)(50) = 3600$ (C) $\frac{y}{6x} = \frac{50}{6*12} = \frac{50}{72} = .69$

(D) $\frac{6}{xy} = \frac{6}{12*50} = \frac{6}{600} = .01$ **(E)** $\frac{6y}{x} = \frac{6*50}{12} = \frac{300}{12} = 25$

Hopefully this proves the point. If this is not clear, please take the time to review this information.   Correct __Answer: (E)__

Top 10 Traps

Part 3: Symbols

Virtual Classroom>Top 10 Traps>Symbols
This material corresponds to the Virtual Classroom Instructions in the
PowerPrep DVD/Internet/iApp for Top 10 Traps

Virtual Classroom

Part 3: Symbols

Symbols

Unknown character representing an arithmetic symbol ($\oplus$, $\leftrightarrow$, $\blacklozenge$)

Strategy:

- The test maker's objective is to distract and confuse you with an odd looking symbol
- Read the question stem to determine the variable's value and the operation of the symbol
- Perform the necessary arithmetic operation(s)

Example:

If $(a \otimes b = a^2 + b^2)$, what is the value of $(4 \otimes 5)$?
  (A) -9
  (B) 1
  (C) 9
  (D) 41
  (E) 81

Read the question stem to understand what the symbol is representing mathematically. $a = 4 \; and \; b = 5$
Plug values into the given equation: $4^2 + 5^2 = 16 + 25 = 41$ **Answer: (D)**

PowerPrep Practice Questions Also in the Virtual Classroom on DVD

PowerPrep Practice Questions 5-6

5. If $j \lrcorner k = j(j - k)$ for all integers $(j \; and \; k)$, then
   $2 \lrcorner (3 \lrcorner 4)$ equals:
   (A) -2
   (B) 1
   (C) 7
   (D) 9
   (E) 10

6. If the symbol ξ when applied to a number results in the
   equation of 3 times 4 less than half the number, what is $\xi \, 14$
   (A) 14
   (B) 9
   (C) 84
   (D) -9
   (E) 42

Explanation to PowerPrep Practice Question 5

Look for similarities: We know that any time we see $(j \lrcorner k)$ we can replace it with $j(j - k)$ We understand multiplication and subtraction, but we don't know what crooked arrow $\lrcorner$ means. But, the information tells us that $j \lrcorner k$ is the same as $j(j - k)$. **So look for content in the same configuration as $j \lrcorner k$ and then replace it with $j(j - k)$. We will have to apply the operation twice:** Start in parenthesis: $(3 \lrcorner 4) = j(j - k)$ **Where** $j = 3 \, and \, k = 4$ **Fill in what we know:** $j(j - k)$ becomes: $3(3 - 4)$ **then,** $3(-1) = -3$. **Now apply the operation the second time where we have:** $j \lrcorner k$ **But this time** $j = 2, k = -3$. **Becomes** $2 \lrcorner (-3)$ **becomes:** $j(j - k)$ **Becomes** $2[2 - (-3)]$ **then,** $2(5) = 10$. **You could also simplify first and then substitute, like this:** $j(j - k)$ **Becomes** $j^2 - jk$. **Substitute** $j = 3 \, and \, k = 4$ becomes: $3^2 - (3 * 4) = 9 - 12 = -3$. **$2^{nd}$ part:** $2 \lrcorner (-3)$ **Becomes:** $j^2 - jk$ **Becomes** $2^2 - (2 * -3) = 4 - (-6)$ **then,** $4 + 6 = 10$ Answer: (E)

Explanation to PowerPrep Practice Question 6

First, we must express the information in math we can understand.
So what does "3 times 4 less than half the number" actually mean? Start from the end and work backwards. We have a number—*say x*. **The given says "half the number"** $\frac{1}{2} x$ **Then it says 4 less than ½ the number:** $(\frac{1}{2} x) - 4$

Then it says 3 times that amount: $3\left(\left(\frac{1}{2}x\right) - 4\right)$. That is 3 times 4 less than half the number. Then we are told the symbol ξ tells us to apply this math to a given number. **The given number is 14.** $\xi 14$. **So let's plug 14 into the equation for x and see what result.** $3\left(\left(\frac{1}{2}x\right) - 4\right)$ becomes: $3\left(\left(\frac{1}{2} * 14\right) - 4\right)$ **Multiply by ½ Becomes** $3(7 - 4)$ **Subtract becomes:** $3(3)$ **Multiply becomes:** 9 **Therefore, $\xi 14 = 9$** ANSWER: (B)

Bonus Sample Questions not in the Virtual Classroom on the DVD

Bonus Sample Question 2

2. If the symbol ‡ when applied to a number results in the equation of 5 times the result of 4 divided by 2 times the number, then which is greater, ‡ 4 or ‡ $\frac{1}{4}$

   (A) ‡ 4 is greater

   (B) ‡ $\frac{1}{4}$ is greater

   (C) They are equal

   (D) Unknown—insufficient information

Explanation to Bonus Sample Question 2

First, we must express the information in math we can understand.

So what does "5 times the result of 4 divided by 2 times the number" actually mean?
Start from the end and work backwards. We have a number—*say n*

The given says "2 times the number": $2n$. **Then it says 4 divided by 2 times the number:** $\frac{4}{2n}$. **Then it says 5 times that amount:** $5\left(\frac{4}{2n}\right)$. **So now we have "5 times the result of 4 divided by 2 times the number" in math**
Next we are told the symbol ‡ tells us to apply this math to a given number.

The given numbers are 4 and $\frac{1}{4}$ **So:** ‡ 4 =? and ‡ $\frac{1}{4}$ = ?

First, let's plug 4 into the equation for n and see what result: $5\left(\frac{4}{2n}\right)$ where $(n = 4)$. $5\left(\frac{4}{2*4}\right)$ **Multiply denominator:** $5\left(\frac{4}{2*4}\right)$ **Becomes** $5\left(\frac{4}{8}\right)$ **Multiply:** $\left(\frac{20}{8}\right)$. **Reduce** $\left(\frac{20}{8}\right) = \frac{10}{4} = \frac{5}{2} = 2\frac{1}{2}$. **Therefore,** ‡ $4 = 2\frac{1}{2}$. **Next, let's plug** $\frac{1}{4}$ **into the equation for n and see what result.** $5\left(\frac{4}{2n}\right)$ where $n = \frac{1}{4}$. $5\left(\frac{4}{\left(2*\frac{1}{4}\right)}\right)$ **Multiply denominator** $5\left(\frac{4}{\left(\frac{2}{4}\right)}\right)$ **Becomes**

$5\left(\frac{4}{\left(\frac{1}{2}\right)}\right)$ **Invert and Multiply** . $5\left(\frac{4}{\left(\frac{1}{2}\right)}\right) = 5\left(\frac{4}{(1)} * \frac{2}{1}\right) = 5\left(\frac{8}{1}\right)$ **Multiply** $5\left(\frac{8}{1}\right) = \frac{40}{1}$ **Reduce** $\left(\frac{40}{1}\right) = 40$

Therefore, ‡ $\frac{1}{4} = 40$. **Now compare** $40 > 2\frac{1}{2}$ **Therefore,** ‡ $\frac{1}{4} >$ ‡ 4 Answer: (B)

Top 10 Traps

Top 4: Multiple Percent Change

Virtual Classroom>Top 10 Traps>Multiple Percent Change

This material corresponds to the Virtual Classroom Instructions in the
PowerPrep DVD/Internet/iApp for Top 10 Traps

Virtual Classroom

Important Abbreviations

These abbreviations are used throughout the program

POE: Process of Elimination
SARR: Synthesize, Analyze, Reduce, and Restate (has to do with Logical Reasoning)
AC: Answer Choice
QS: Question Stem
LOD: Level of Difficulty

Example Question: What is the least common multiple of 3, 4, and 7? **(This is the call of the question or Question Stem "QS")**

These are Answer Choices "AC" A, B, C, D, E

   (A)   12
   (B)   21
   (C)   28
   (D)   48
   (E)   84

Part 4: Multiple Percent Change

Multiple Percentage Increase/Decrease

Some problems will give you a value which has been increased and/or decreased by a certain percent more than one time.

Strategy:

- When a quantity is increased/decreased by a percentage multiple times you CANNOT add/subtract the percentages to determine the final answer
- Calculate each percent increase/decrease individually.

Example:

Julie purchased a sweater last month. She sold it to Amy for 30 percent less than she paid for it. Amy added 40 percent to the price she paid and sold it to Beth. The price Beth paid was what percent of the original price?

- (A) 90
- (B) 95
- (C) 98
- (D) 100
- (E) 102

Straight Math:

Julie purchase price (pp) = x
Amy purchase price (pp) = EITHER: $(70\% \, of \, x)$ **same as** $.7x$ **OR:** $(x - 30\%x)$ **same as** $(x - .3x)$
Beth Purchas Price (pp) = (3 ways to show this)

1. $(1.4)(.7x) = .98x$ or 98% of original price (bear in mind that x is the original price so .98 of x is 98% of the original price).
2. $(1.4)(x - .3x) = 1.4x - .42x = .98x$ (98% of original price)
3. $[.40(x - .3x) + (x - .3x)] = (.4x - .12x + x - .3x) = (1.4x - .42x) = .98x$ (98% of original price)

In all three methods we are looking for the Beth pp so we can compare it to the original Julie purchase price of x.

This process can be tricky so be careful. Be sure you understand percentage increases and discounts. The key is to realize you MUST include the ORIGINAL amount, you cannot simply calculate the amount of the increase or decrease. You MUST include the original amount plus or minus the increase or decrease in order to find the new price.

In number one above we take 140% or (1.4) times the Amy purchase price to get to Beth pp, so that's 140% of 70% of x which is written $(1.4)(.7x) = Beth \, pp$

Also we can calculate the Beth pp by taking 140% of the Amy pp which was also described as $(x - .3x)$
That would be written $1.4(x - .3x)$

We can also demonstrate Beth's pp using the most difficult method by taking 40% of the Amy price, then adding the original Amy price. That's shown like 40% of $(x - .3x)$ $plus$ $(x - .3x)$

Another Way: Pick Numbers

Quick Pick:
Pick 100 as starting cost, calculate selling price:
$Part = \%(whole) = 30\%(100) = 30 \, decrease$
$100 - 30 = 70 \, selling \, price$

Calculate next selling price: $Part = \%(whole) = 40\%(70) = .4(70) = 28 \, increase$
$70 + 28 = 98 \, new \, selling \, price$ and 98 is what percent of the original price of 100? Answer 98%

Longer Pick Numbers:
Let's pick an original sales price of $10.00. So Julie paid $10.00 for the sweater originally.

Next she sold the sweater to Amy for 30% less than she bought it. What is 30% of $10.00
Answer: $3.00
So Amy got a $3.00 $discount$, but her purchase prices was not $3.00 it was $7.00 (that's $3.00 $less \, than \, the$ $10.00 original purchase price)

Now Amy sold her $7.00 sweater to Beth for 40% more than she paid. She paid $7.00
So she sold it to Beth for 40% $more \, than$ $7.00 she paid .4 ($7.00) = $2.80 **That's the increase $2.80**

So Beth bought from Amy for $7.00 (her purchase price) plus $2.80 (the increase.) Beth's purchase price was $7.00 + $2.80 or $9.80

Now let's compare: Julie's original purchase was $10.00> Beth's purchase prices was $9.80

$9.80 $is \, 98\% \, of \, the \, original \, price \, of$ $10.00 $\left(\frac{9.8}{10} = .98\right)$ or 98% **Answer: (C)**

PowerPrep Practice Questions Also in the Virtual Classroom on DVD

PowerPrep Practice Questions 7-8

7. Liz brought a box of candy to school. She gave Mike all but 25% of the candy she had brought and Mike gave Jim all but 40% of the candy he had received from Liz. What percent of the total amount of candy did Jim receive?

(A) 25
(B) 40
(C) 45
(D) 50
(E) 75

8. What is the total percent increase of Stephanie's savings, if Stephanie made an initial investment in her savings three and one-half years ago and she has not deposited nor withdrawn any funds since that time (except for interest) The fund adds 10% interest to her savings at the end of each year.

(A) 33.1%
(B) 30%
(C) 50%
(D) 100%
(E) 35%

Explanation to PowerPrep Practice Question 7

Straight Math: This is actually a straightforward question once you translate the given information into a consistent format.

Liz gave Mike all but 25% of the candy. What does that mean? It means she kept 25% and gave him 75%. So mike now has 75% of the candy that we started with.

Mike then gave "*all but* 40%" to Jim. That means Mike kept 40% and gave Jim 60%.

So, Jim got 60% of what Mike had. How much did Mike have? 75%   So Jim got 60% *of* 75%

How do you write 60% *of* 75%? Percents are fractions of 100. So 60 *percent is* .60 *and* 75 percent is .75. Therefore, .60 *of* .75 is written (.60 ∗ .75) or (.60)(.75) = .45   .45 *in percentage is* 45%

So Jim got 45% of the original amount of candy that Liz started with.

Another Way: Pick Numbers
We can pick any number to start with, but we should select numbers that result in "easy" math.

Let 100 be the total amount of candy Liz brought to school. This means that each piece of candy represents 1% of the total.

Liz gave Mike 75% *and kept* **25%:** What's 75% *of* 100 pieces? 75 pieces of candy went to Mike and she kept 25 pieces (not relevant)

So Mike now has 75 pieces of candy and he gives Jim 60% of those 75 pieces of candy

What is 60% *of* 75 pieces of candy? .6 ∗ 75 = 45 or 45 pieces of candy

Jim got 45 pieces of candy. Since we set the original amount of candy equal to 100, each piece of candy represented 1%. Therefore, 45 *pieces of candy is the same as* 45%

Either way, Jim got 45% of the original amount of the candy Liz brought to school **Answer: (C)**

Explanation to PowerPrep Practice Question 8

This problem demonstrates the issue of "compound interest" or interest on interest. This principle works against you when you have credit cards and it can work in your favor when you have investments.

Once you see the formula, it should be straightforward. But there are a couple of tricks to keep in mind that can cause trouble on the test.

What do we know?
• Three and one-half years ago she made an initial investment
• She has not added or subtracted anything to that investment
• The investment pays 10% interest at the end of each year
• There have been 3 interest payments so far

Solve:
First, select any amount of initial principle $100, $1, $4,297.34, $10,000, $1,000,000 it won't matter what you select as the starting point, because we are calculating the total **INTEREST** increase over the 3 *years*.
It's always best to pick a number that you think will make the math turn out easy. **Let's pick $100** (it's always a simple way to work with percents, because each dollar or unit is also a percent)

We have three payment periods where the investment will pay 10% on the principal

Start of year 1: $100
End of year 1 interest payment: $100 *x* .10 (10%) = $10

Start of year 2: $100 + year one's interest of $10 = $110
End of year 2 interest payment: $110 x .10 (10%) = $11

Start of year 3: $110 + $11 = $121
End of year 3 interest payment: $121 x .10 (10%) = $12.10

Start of year 4: $133.10

Now calculate the total increase from opening the account to present.

Ending amount = $133.10
Beginning amount = $100
Amount of increase = $33.10

What is the percent increase?
Selecting $100 as our starting point makes it easy to calculate the percent increase. Since we increased
$33.10 *dollars, the percent increase is* 33.10%

If we had not selected $100 for the starting point, we would have: $\dfrac{\$33.10}{\$100}$ (total gain divided by starting amount) **Equals .331 or 33.1%**

We also could have just added up the yearly dollar increases ($10, $11, *and* $12.10) and divided by 100 $\left(\dfrac{33.10}{100}\right)$

Let's try it with a different beginning balance to prove the point that this is a percentage increase and it does not matter
what you choose as the beginning balance.

Let's start with $500
   Interest year 1: $50
   Interest year 2: ($500 + 50)x .10 = $55
   Interest year 3: ($500 + 50 + 55) x .10 = $60.50
   Total interest = 50 + 55 + 60.5 = 165.50

$\dfrac{165.5}{500}$ = . **331** *or* **33.** 1%   <u>**ANSWER: (A)**</u>

Top 10 Traps
Part 5: Weighted Averages

Virtual Classroom>Top 10 Traps>Weighted Averages

This material corresponds to the Virtual Classroom Instructions in the
PowerPrep DVD/Internet/iApp for Top 10 Traps

Virtual Classroom

Part 5: Weighted Averages

Weighted Averages

A problem with two or more groups, each containing their own average, that requires you to calculate an OVERALL group average is called a weighted average.

Strategy:

- You cannot combine two separate averages together to get an overall average
- Calculate the sum of each group
- Calculate an overall average for the groups combined
- Total average = $\dfrac{sum_1 + sum_2}{total\ number\ of\ objects}$

Example:

In a group of nine students, six girls have an average of $9.00 and three boys have an average of $7.00. What is the average amount, in dollars, of the whole group?

(A) 7.50
(B) 8.00
(C) 8.25
(D) 8.33
(E) 8.50

$Total\ average = \dfrac{sum_1 + sum_2}{total\ number\ of\ objects}$

$sum = (number)(average),$

$sum_1 = (number\ of\ girls) * (\$ Avg) = (6\ girls * \$9.00) = \$54,$

$sum_2 = (number\ of\ boys) * (\$ Avg) = (3\ boys * \$7.00) = \$21$

$Total\ average = \dfrac{54+21}{9} = \dfrac{75}{9} = \$8.33$ **Answer: (D)**

PowerPrep Practice Questions Also in the Virtual Classroom on DVD

9. Dave purchased 10 watermelons at an average of 2.5 pounds each and 7 cantaloupes at an average of 1.2 pounds each. What is the average weight, in pounds, of one piece of the fruit that Dave purchased?
   (A) 1.75
   (B) 1.80
   (C) 1.96
   (D) 2.10
   (E) 2.15

10. If Melissa bought 4 roses at $6 each and 6 tulips at $4 each, what is the average price per flower for the all roses and tulips Melissa bought?
    (A) $5.00
    (B) $4.80
    (C) $5.80
    (D) $6. 00
    (E) $5.10

Explanation to PowerPrep Practice Question 9

Quick Answer: $sum_1 = (number\ of\ wm)(weight\ per\ wm) = (10)(2.5) = 25,$
$sum_2 = (number\ of\ c)(weight\ per\ c) = (7)(1.2) = 8.4$

$$total\ average = \frac{(10*2.5)+(7*1.2)}{17} = \frac{33.4}{17} = 1.96 \quad \underline{\textbf{Answer: (C)}}$$

Detailed Answer: What are we looking for to answer this question? We want to know what the overall average weight of all 17 pieces of fruit (watermelons and cantaloupes.)
We know: Dave has 10 watermelons that average 2.5 pounds each. He has 7 cantaloupes with average weight of 1.2 pounds each. So there is a total of 17 watermelons and cantaloupes.
How do you write the math? If 10 watermelons *avg 2.5lbs ea* and 7 cantaloupes *avg 1.2 lbs ea*

Then, $Total\ average = \frac{sum_1 + sum_2}{total\ number\ of\ objects}$. **Substitute what we know:** $wm = 10,\ wm\ avg\ weight = 2.5,\ c =$

$7,\ c\ avg\ weight = 1.2.$ $\frac{(10*2.5)+(7*1.2)}{17}$ = the average weight of all 17 fruits (wm and c). **Simplify,** $\frac{25+8.4}{17}$ **Add,** $\frac{33.4}{17}$

Divide, 1.965 lbs = average weight of the 17 combined watermelons and cantaloupes **Answer: (C)**

Explanation to PowerPrep Practice Question 10

Calculate how much Melissa spent on all the flowers and then divide by the total number of flowers she purchased.
This will give you the average price per flower. Roses were $6 * 4 = $24 Tulips were $4 * 6 = $24. **Total spent $48.**
Total number of flowers purchased = 10. *Average price* = ($48 ÷ 10) **Or** ($4.80)/*flower* **ANSWER: (B)**

Bonus Sample Questions not in the Virtual Classroom on the DVD

Bonus Sample Question 3

3. An internet company spent $21,000 to purchase new laptop and desktop computers. They purchased 5 new laptops for $593.60 each. The Desktop computers cost $1,127 each. What was the average cost of all the computers they purchased?

   (A) $593.60 each
   (B) $827.00 each
   (C) $1,000.00 each
   (D) $1,127.00 each
   (E) $2,000.00 each

Explanation to Bonus Sample Question 3

What do we know: Total cost = $21,000, Cost of laptops = $593.60 each   Number of laptops = 5
   Cost of Desktops = $1127 each   Number of Desktops = ?
First figure out the number and total cost of the Desktop computers
   The total cost of all computers = $21,000, total number of laptops = 5, price per laptop = $593.60
Therefore, (5 * $593.60 = $2,968) So, the total cost of all laptops = $2,968
Calculate cost of all desktops: Total cost of all computers = $21,000 and total cost of all laptops = $2,968 **Therefore,**
$21,000 − $2,968 = $18,032   So the total cost of desktops = **$18,032**

Now calculate the cost of each desktop: Total cost of desktops = $18,032 **and** Individual cost of desktops = $1,127
Therefore, $\frac{\$18,032}{\$1,127} = 16$ this means **16 total desktop computers.**

Now we can calculate the combined average of all the computers: $Total\ average = \frac{sum_1 + sum_2}{total\ number\ of\ objects}$

$$Total\ average = \frac{(5\ laptops*\$593.60)+(16\ desktops*\$1127)}{5\ laptops+16\ desktops} = \frac{(5*593.60)+(16*1127)}{21}$$

$$\frac{(2968)+(18,032)}{21} = \frac{21,000}{21} = \$1,000$$

Note: You should note that you already had the numerator. The numerator is the total combined amount of money spent or $21,000. The key to this problem was calculating the total number of desktop computers. Once you figure out there are 16 Desktop computers you can answer the question. **Answer: (C)**

Top 10 Traps

Part 6: Ratio:Ratio:Ratio

Virtual Classroom>Top 10 Traps>Ratio:Ratio:Ratio
This material corresponds to the Virtual Classroom Instructions in the
PowerPrep DVD/Internet/iApp for Top 10 Traps

Virtual Classroom

Part 6: Triple Ratio

Triple Ratio

A triple ratio gives you two sets of ratios that contain a common term. You are asked to compare a term in the first ratio to a term in the second ratio.

Strategy:

- Realize the different ratios don't refer to the same whole, so they are not in proportion to each other
- Scale both ratios so the numbers representing the common terms are the same
- Compare scaled terms directly

Example:

The store parking lot contains cars, trucks and SUV's. If the ratio of cars to trucks is 5:2, and the ratio of trucks to SUV's is 3:4, what is the ratio of cars to SUV's?

    (A) $5:4$
    (B) $7:5$
    (C) $10:6$
    (D) $12:7$
    (E) $15:8$

Quick Answer: Cars to trucks $= 5:2$, Trucks to SUV's $= 3:4$, Ratio of trucks in first $= 2$, Ratio of trucks in second $= 3$, Common multiple is 6. Cars to trucks $= 5(3):2(3) = 15:6$. Trucks to SUV's $= 3(2):4(2) = 6:8$
   Cars to trucks to SUV's $= 15:6:8$ *or* $15:8$ *for cars* : *SUV's* **Answer E**

Detailed Answer: These ratio questions require some logical reasoning. We know two of the relationships and have to find the third relationship.
We know cars to trucks is 5 to 2 or *Cars : Trucks is* $5:2$ This means out of 7 vehicles 5 will be cars and 2 will trucks
We also know trucks to SUV's is 3 to 4 or *Trucks : SUV is* $3:4$
This means out of 7 vehicles 3 will be trucks and 4 will be SUV's

Now we need to figure out the ratio of Cars to SUV's. We know Cars to Trucks and Trucks to SUV's is $5:2$ *and* $3:4$
The 2 and the 3 both represent Trucks. We need to convert the ratios the same way we convert fractions. What is the LCM of 2 and 3 *Answer 6*

So let's convert the Cars to Trucks first: $5:2$ **Multiply by 3, becomes** $15:6$
So 15 to 6 is the same as 5 to 2, but now we have a common number for Trucks
Now let's do Trucks to SUV's: $3:4$ Multiply by 2, becomes $6:8$

So 6 *to* 8 *is the same as* 3 *to* 4, but now we have a common number for Trucks
The common number for trucks is 6. We have 6 trucks in both ratios. Now that we have a common number for trucks we can drop it out and relate Cars to SUV's

Cars to Trucks and Trucks to SUV's: 15 *to* 6 *and* 6 *to* 8
Drop out the trucks (both are 6), becomes **15 *to* 8 *or* 15 : 8** <u>**Answer: (E)**</u>

PowerPrep Practice Questions Also in the Virtual Classroom on DVD

PowerPrep Practice Questions 11-12

11. For every mile that Bob runs, Fred runs 2 miles. For every 4 miles that Fred runs, Harry runs 5 miles. If Bob runs 5 miles, how many miles does Harry run?

   (A) 5
   (B) 9
   (C) 10
   (D) 12.5
   (E) 14.5

12. If Jordan has 2 cats for every dog and 3 fish for every cat and he also owns 6 fish. How many fish and dogs does Jordan own?

   (A) 1fish and 6 dogs
   (B) 6 fish and 2 dogs
   (C) 6 fish and 3 dogs
   (D) 6 fish and 6 dogs
   (E) 6 fish and 1 dog

Explanation to PowerPrep Practice Question 11

Quick Answer: $Bob : Fred = 1 : 2$ $Fred : Harry = 4 : 5$
Ratio of Fred's mileage in *first* = 2
Ratio of Fred's mileage in *second* = 4

The common multiple is 4. Bob's mileage : Fred's mileage = $1(2) : 2(2) = 2 : 4$
Fred's mileage : Harry's mileage = $4 : 5$ Bob's mileage : Harry's mileage = $2 : 5$
Create a proportion to find the mileage: $\frac{2}{5} = \frac{5}{x}$ or ($x = 12.5$) <u>**Answer: (D)**</u>

Detailed Answer: What do we know: Bob runs 1 and Fred runs 2 or B *and* $F = 1 : 2$ *ratio*
Fred runs 4 and Harry runs 5 or F *and* $H = 4 : 5$ *ratio*

Question: If Bob runs 5, how many does Harry run? If Bob runs 5, what does Fred run?
The ratio between Bob and Fred is 1 : 2 For every mile Bob runs, Fred runs 2

Therefore, if Bob runs 5, then Fred runs 10. **Now we have the first half of the problem, Fred is at 10 miles**
If Fred runs 10, what does Harry run? We have a ratio for that one too. The ratio between Fred and Harry is 4 : 5 For every 4 miles Fred runs, Harry runs 5. So if Fred runs 10 how many does Harry run?

4 *goes into* 10, 2 times with remainder 2. So if Fred runs two groups of 4 (8 total) then Harry runs two groups of 5 or 10 total. But we have a remainder of 2. If Fred runs 2 (which is half his ratio of the 4 : 5, his is the 4), then Harry runs half his ratio of the 4 : 5 (his is the five, or 2.5). Therefore, if Fred runs 10 (2 groups of 4, plus a half of the final group of 4) then Harry runs 12.5 (2 groups of 5, plus a half of the final group of 5). *Now we know that if Bob runs* **5**; *then Harry runs* **12.5** *miles.* <u>**Answer: (D)**</u>

Explanation to PowerPrep Practice Question 12

Quick Answer: Set up the ratio: $Cats : Dogs = 2 : 1$ $Fish : Cats = 3 : 1$ $6\,Fish$

Double the Fish to Cats *ratio of* $3 : 1$ to reflect 6 fish
$Fish : Cats = 3 : 1$ *becomes* $(2)(3) : (1)(2) = 6 : 2$
If 2 cats, we know dogs = 1, Therefore, $Dogs : Cats : Fish = 1 : 2 : 6$ $Dogs : Fish = 1 : 6$
6 fish and 1 dog

George will always own 6 times as many fish as he will own dogs.

Detailed Answer: What do we know? $Cats : Dogs = 2 : 1$ $Fish : Cats = 3 : 1$ $6\,Fish$
What are you looking for? *Answer:* The number of fish and dogs.

We already know part of the answer, he has 6 fish.
But now we need to find how many dogs he has. We'll use the ratios and the fact that he has 6 fish.

So let's start plugging in information: Start with fish. He has 6 fish. The ratio of fish to cats is 3 : 1 (3 fish for every cat)

Therefore, If he has 6 fish, he has 2 cats, because every 3rd fish equals 1 cat. If we double the fish (from 3 to 6) then we also double the cats (from 1 to 2). **Now we know:** $Fish = 6$ $Cats = 2$

So let's figure out dogs. If he has 2 cats, then how many dogs does he have?
The ratio of cats to dogs is 2 : 1 Every 2 cats equal 1 dog. We have just figured out that if he has 6 fish, he has 2 cats

Applying the Cats to Dogs ratio of 2 : 1, we can now calculate the dogs. If he has 2 cats he must have 1 dog. Now we know that Jordan has 2 cats, 1 dog and 6 fish.

We also know the following ratios: $Cats : Dogs = 2 : 1$, $Fish : Cats = 3 : 1$, $Dogs : Cats : Fish = 1 : 2 : 6$, $Fish : Dogs = 6 : 1$
We know he has one dog and 6 fish <u>**Answer: (E)**</u>

Top 10 Traps
Part 7: Multiple Order of Points

Virtual Classroom>Top 10 Traps>Multiple Order of Points

This material corresponds to the Virtual Classroom Instructions in the
PowerPrep DVD/Internet/iApp for Top 10 Traps

Virtual Classroom

Part 7: Multiple Order of Points

Multiple Order of Points

Strategy:

- Don't assume there is only one arrangement of points
- Look for alternative setups

Example:

If Point A is 14 units away from B on line X and Point B is 9 units away from C on line X, what is the distance from point A to C on line X? Don't assume there is only one arrangement of points. Look for alternative setups.

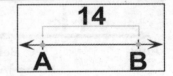

We know that the distance between points A and B is 14.

We know that the distance between points B and C is 9.

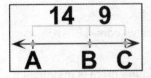

Draw a diagram: There are two possible solutions to the information. **First points ABC could be sequential as you see here.** *In this case A to C is* $14 + 9 = 23$
Look for second alternative: In this case the distances are overlaid A to B and then backwards B to C. *In this case A to C is*
$14 - 9 = 5$. So the distance from A to C could be 23 or 5

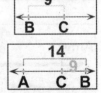

PowerPrep Practice Questions Also in the Virtual Classroom on DVD

PowerPrep Practice Questions 13

13. Given: Line segment $EF = 5$ and Line segment $FG = 8$. If line segment EF is juxtaposed immediately to the left of segment FG on a number line, what is the distance from E to G?

   (A) 3
   (B) 6
   (C) 13
   (D) 14
   (E) 24

Explanation to PowerPrep Practice Question 13

We know that the segments will be arranged in the following way:
Line segment EF ends at point F.   Line segment FG, begins with point F
They share point F in common
EF is 5 units long and at the point it ends, line segment FG begins and is 8
more units in length.   **Therefore,** $(EF + FG = (5 + 8) = 13$ ANSWER: (C)

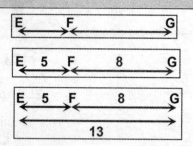

Bonus Sample Questions not in the Virtual Classroom on the DVD

Bonus Sample Question 4

4. **If Sam lives 4 miles from Beth while Beth lives 11 miles from Amy, then which is greater, the distance from Sam's house to Amy's house or 15 miles?**

   (A) The distance from Sam's house to Amy's house is greater
   (B) 15 miles is greater
   (C) They are equal
   (D) Unknown—insufficient information

Explanation to Bonus Sample Question 4

We know the distance between Sam and Beth is 4 miles and Beth lives 11 miles from Amy.

   SB = 4 miles and   BA = 11 miles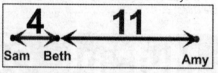

There are two possible configurations:
Consecutive as you see above or overlaid where you travel from Sam to Beth (4 miles) and then you reverse course to Amy's house (11 miles)

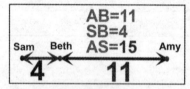

Option 1: Consecutive--Sam to Beth, Beth to Amy in a straight line consecutive:
In this case, the distance from Sam to Beth is 4 miles and then from Beth to Amy is 11 miles. The combined distance is 4 + 11 = 15

Option 2: Overlaid--In this option Sam to Beth and then reverse to Amy, the distance between Sam and Amy is 7 miles (11 − 4 = 7) **So there are two possible answers:** Amy to Sam is either 15 miles or 7 miles depending how you arrange the locations of Amy Sam and Beth. But to answer the question we want to know which is greater: 15 miles or the distance between Amy and Sam

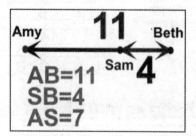

Amy to Sam = 15 miles or 7 miles: So the two options are either equal (15 = 15) or Sam to Amy is less than 15.

But since there are two conflicting answers we must conclude there is insufficient information to answer the overall question. Answer: (D)

Top 10 Traps
Part 8: Length to Area Ratios

Virtual Classroom>Top 10 Traps>Length to Area Ratios

This material corresponds to the Virtual Classroom Instructions in the
PowerPrep DVD/Internet/iApp for Top 10 Traps

Virtual Classroom

Important Abbreviations
These abbreviations are used throughout the program

POE: Process of Elimination
SARR: Synthesize, Analyze, Reduce, and Restate (has to do with Logical Reasoning)
AC: Answer Choice
QS: Question Stem
LOD: Level of Difficulty

Example Question: What is the least common multiple of 3, 4, and 7? **(This is the call of the question or Question Stem "QS")**

These are Answer Choices "AC" A, B, C, D, E

   (A)   12
   (B)   21
   (C)   28
   (D)   48
   (E)   84

Part 8: Length to Area Ratios

Length to Area Ratios

Strategy:

- Ratio of areas is not the same as ratio of lengths—it is the SQUARE of the ratio of the length

Example:

A certain square picture frame has an area of $36cm^2$. If each side of the frame is doubled in length, what would be the new area of the new larger frame?

(A) $6cm^2$
(B) $42cm^2$
(C) $48cm^2$
(D) $72cm^2$
(E) $144cm^2$

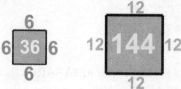

Ratio of areas is not the same as ratio of lengths, rather, it is the SQUARE of the ratio of the length.   If length is doubled then ratio of area is $(doubled)^2 \; or \; (2)^2 \; = 4$ times larger $4(36) \; = \; 144$.   **Double check using area formula:** *Area of Square =* $side^2 = 6*6 = 36. \quad side = \sqrt{36} = 6$.   **Now double the length of the sides of the square.**   Side 6 becomes side 12.
Area of Square $= side^2 = 12 * 12 = 144$ **Answer: (E)**

PowerPrep Practice Questions Also in the Virtual Classroom on DVD

PowerPrep Practice Questions 14-15

14. Circle A has diameter X and area Y. If the diameter of circle A is reduced to $\frac{1}{3}$ of the original diameter, what is the new area of the reduced circle?

(A) $\frac{1}{9} Y$

(B) $\frac{1}{3} Y$

(C) Y
(D) 3 Y
(E) 9 Y

15. If the perimeter of square A is twice the perimeter of square B, is the area of square A more than twice the area of square B?
(A) no
(B) yes
(C) unknown

Explanation to PowerPrep Practice Question 14

Quick Answer: If diameter is cut in $\frac{1}{3}$, radius is cut in $\frac{1}{3}$.   If radius is cut in $\frac{1}{3}$, then the ratio of the area is cut in $\left(\frac{1}{3}\right)^2 = \frac{1}{9}$ New area is $\frac{1}{9}$ of original area.   New area $= \frac{1}{9}y$ **Answer A**

Detailed Answer: The diameter is twice the radius or you can also say the radius is $\frac{1}{2}$ the Diameter. **The formula for area of a circle** $= \pi r^2$ What happens to the area of a circle if you reduce the radius? Is the area reduced proportionately?
Let's try some real numbers and see what happens: Assume the diameter of circle A is 6.   If we reduce it to $\frac{1}{3}$ that size, the new diameter would be 2. We now have two circles and we can compare their areas: The larger circle has diameter 6 and the smaller is $\frac{1}{3}$ that diameter or (2)
What happens to their respective areas? First the larger circle with diameter 6

Radius = 3
πr^2
$\pi 3^2$
9π

So the area of circle A with diameter 6 is 9π

Now let's look at the smaller circle that is $\frac{1}{3}$ the size with diameter 2

Radius = 1
πr^2
$\pi 1^2$
π

So the area of the new smaller circle with radius 1 is 1π and the larger circle is 9π

That means if you reduce the radius (or diameter) to $\frac{1}{3}$ you reduce the area to $\frac{1}{9}$ or $\left(\frac{1}{3}\right)^2$

This fraction or ratio holds for all cases where one circle has a diameter or radius $\frac{1}{3}$ that of another circle. The smaller circle

will always have an area that is $\frac{1}{9}$ or $\left(\frac{1}{3}\right)^2$ or a 9th the size of the larger circle. **ANSWER: (A)**

Explanation to PowerPrep Practice Question 15

This question tests your understanding of calculating perimeters and areas.

What are we asked? We are asked to find the correlation between perimeter and area. Specifically, what happens if we double (or halve) the perimeter, what effect on the area? **Let's pick some numbers and find out what the correlation is between perimeter and area.** Let's set square A perimeter = 24 (*each side is 6*)

Then set square B perimeter = 12 (*each side is 3*) Square B is half the perimeter of square A
Now let's calculate the area of both. Area of Square $A = s^2$ therefore, $s = 6$

Therefore, $6^2 = 36$ The area of square $A = 36$ (where sides are equal to 6, and perimeter = 24)
Now let's find the area of Square B. $Area = s^2$ and $s = 3$ So $Area = 3^2$ or $Area = 9$. **Therefore,** the area of square $B = 9$ (*with sides* $= 3$ *and perimeter* $= 12$). **Now let's compare the areas of the two squares.** $A = 36$ *and* $B = 9$

What can we conclude about the relationship between the two squares where one square has twice the perimeter of the other square?. If we double the perimeter, does the area also double? When the perimeter of A is twice the perimeter of B, the area is $4x$ *or* 2^2

Therefore, to answer the actual question-- is the area of square A more than twice the area of square B? **Answer = yes** (the area of A is more than twice the area of B, in fact it's $4x$ as large) **ANSWER: (B)**

Bonus Sample Questions <u>not</u> in the Virtual Classroom on the DVD

Bonus Sample Question 5

5. If square A has a perimeter of 16 and square B has a perimeter of 8, then which is greater, the area of square A or twice the area of square B.

    (A) The area of square A is greater
    (B) Twice the area of square B is greater
    (C) They are equal
    (D) Unknown—insufficient information

**This is very similar to PPQ 15 but there is sufficient information here to warrant a close review by the student.

Explanation to Bonus Sample Question 5

Quick Answer: Square A—Perimeter of Square $A = 16$ or Side $= \left(\frac{16}{4}\right) = 4$. $Area = side^2 = 4^2 = 16$
Square B—Perimeter of Square $B = 8$ Side $= \left(\frac{8}{4}\right) = 2$ or $2(Area) = 2(side^2) = 2(2^2) = 8$. $16 > 8$ **Answer A**

Detailed Answers: This question tests your understanding of calculating perimeters and areas.
What are we asked? We are asked to find the correlation between perimeter and area.
Specifically, what happens if we double (or halve) the perimeter, how does that affect the area?

Let's pick some numbers and find out what the correlation is between perimeter and area
Let's set square A perimeter = 16 (each side is 4)
Then set square B perimeter = 4 (each side is 2)
Square B is half the perimeter of square A

Now let's calculate the area of both **Area of Square $A = s^2$ where $s = 4$**
Therefore, $4^2 = 16$ so *Area of square $A = 16$*
(Where sides are *equal to 4, and perimeter* $= 16$)
Now let's find the area of Square B: $Area = s^2$ where $s = 2$
So Area $= 2^2$ *or Area* $= 4$

Therefore, the area of square $B = 4$ (*with sides* $= 2$ *and perimeter* $= 8$)
Now let's compare the areas of the two squares.
Square $A = 16$ and Square $B = 4$
What can we conclude about the relationship between the two squares where one square has twice the perimeter of the other square? If we double the perimeter, does the area also double? **If the perimeter of A is twice the perimeter of B, the area is $4x$ or 2^2** Is the area of square A more than twice the area of square B? **Answer** = yes (the area of A is more than twice the area of B—in fact it's $4x$ as large) **Answer: (A)**

Top 10 Traps
Part 9: Negative Variables

Virtual Classroom>Top 10 Traps>Negative Variables
This material corresponds to the Virtual Classroom Instructions in the
PowerPrep DVD/Internet/iApp for Top 10 Traps

Virtual Classroom

Part 9: Negative Variables

Not All Variables Are Positive

Strategy:

• When picking number, include negative numbers and fractions

Example:

If n ≠ 0, which of the following must be true:

  I. $n^2 > n$
  II. $2n > n$
  III. $n + 1 > n$

  (A) I
  (B) II
  (C) III
  (D) I and III
  (E) I, II, and III

Options I: $n^2 > n$. If $n = 2$ then $2^2 > 2$, true . If $n = -1$ then $-1^2 = 1$ and $1 > -1$, true.

If $n = 1$ then $1^2 = 1$, but 1 is not > 1, false. If $n = \frac{1}{2}$ then $\frac{1^2}{2} = \frac{1}{4}$ and $\frac{1}{4}$ not $> \frac{1}{2}$ false

Therefore, I is NOT always true

Option II: $2n > n$. if $n = 2$ then $(2 * 2)$ or $4 > 2$ True. if $n = -1$ then $(-1 * 2)$ or -2 is NOT greater than -1 False

Therefore, II is NOT always true

Option III: $n + 1 > n$. If $n = 2$, then $2 + 1 = 3$ and $3 > 2$ True. if $n = -1$ then $1 + (-1) = 0$ and $0 > -1$ True
if $n = \frac{1}{2}$ then $\frac{1}{2} + 1 = 1\frac{1}{2}$ and $1\frac{1}{2} > \frac{1}{2}$ True

Adding 1 to any number results in a greater number than what you started with...you will always be one greater than where you started. **Therefore, III is ALWAYS true Answer: (C)**

PowerPrep™ Practice Questions Also in the Virtual Classroom on DVD

PowerPrep™ Practice Questions 16-17

16. Given: $a^2 > b$ If $b = 4$, which of the following is/are possible value(s) for "a"?

    I.   2

    II. $|-2|$

    III. $\frac{4}{3}$

  (A) I only
  (B) III only
  (C) I and II only
  (D) I, II, and III
  (E) None of the above

17. If $a^2 > b^2$, then which is greater, a^3 or b^3 ?
  (A) a^3 is greater
  (B) b^3 is greater
  (C) They are equal
  (D) Unknown—insufficient information

Explanation to PowerPrep Practice Question 16

Quick Answer: **Option 1 (a = 2).** $a^2 > b$ so, $2^2 > 4$ But 4 is not greater than 4 : **So this is FALSE**
Option 2 (a = | − 2|). $a^2 > 4$ *where a is* $|-2|$ so $|-2|^2 = 2^2 = 4$ but, 4 is not greater than 4: **So this is FALSE**

Option 3 $\left(a = \frac{4}{3}\right)$. $a^2 > 4$ *where a is* $\frac{4}{3}$ so, $\frac{4^2}{3} = \frac{16}{9} = 1\frac{7}{9}$ but, $1\frac{7}{9}$ is not greater than 4: **So this is FALSE**
All three options are false <u>Answer E</u>
Detailed Answer: $a^2 > b$ *and* $b = 4$
Which of the following is/are a possible value for "a"? We have to solve for each possible answer choice.
Option 1 ($a = 2$). Plug it into the given information: $a^2 > b$ where $b = 4$ *and* $a = 2$ Becomes $a^2 > 4$
Since $a = 2, therefore, \ 2^2 > 4$ but $4 > 4$ *which is Not True*

Option 2 ($a = |-2|$). What is the absolute value of -2? Answer: 2

Quick review of absolute value: The absolute value of a number is its numerical value without regard to its sign. So for example, 3 is the absolute value of both 3 and -3. The absolute value of a number "a" is denoted by $|a|$. The absolute value is never negative. Since absolute value of -2 *is* 2, plug it into the given information. $a^2 > b$ *where* $b = 4$ *and* $a = 2$ *or* $|-2|$ so, $a^2 > 4$. $a = 2, therefore \ 2^2 > 4$ but $4 > 4$ *which is NOT True*

Option 3 $\left(a = \frac{4}{3}\right)$. Before doing the math, you should be able to look at this and realize that $\frac{4}{3}$ is less than 2 and we just figured out that if $a = 2$, the answer is False. Therefore, if we square a number less than 2, the result cannot be more than 4. So we can tell this choice will not work. **But let's do the math to show:** $a^2 > b$ *where* $b = 4$ *and* $a = \frac{4}{3}$ so, $a^2 > 4$ and

$a = \frac{4}{3}$ *therefore,* $\left(\frac{4}{3}\right)^2 > 4$ becomes, $\frac{16}{9} > 4$ but, $1\frac{7}{9} > 4$ *which is NOT True*
Summary:
I. $a^2 = 2^2 = 4$ and 4 *is not greater than* 4, *therefore this is false*
II. $a^2 = |-2|^2 = 4$ *and* 4 *is not greater than* 4, *therefore this is false.*

III. $a^2 = \left(\frac{4}{3}\right)^2 = \frac{16}{9} = 1\frac{7}{9}$ *and* $1\frac{7}{9}$ *is NOT greater than* 4, *so this is false*
Conclusion: If all three options are false, then the correct choice is (E) None of the above <u>Answer: (E)</u>

Explanation to PowerPrep Practice Question 17

This problem may look obvious, but it's testing your understanding of what happens when we raise negative numbers to exponential powers.

At first blush, it may seem obvious that if a^2 is larger than b^2, then a^3 will be larger than b^3.
In fact, it would seem that "**a**" raised to any power will always be greater than "**b**" raised to the same power.

If "**a**" and "**b**" are positive numbers, our initial assumption will be correct. If a^2 is greater than b^2, then "**a**" raised to any power will always be greater than "**b**" raised to that same power—IFF (If and only If) "**a**" and "**b**" are POSITIVE

But, look a little closer at what happens when "**a**" and "**b**" are raised to odd powers and "**a**" and "**b**" are negative.
If a = 3 and b = 2 then $3^2 > 2^2$ becomes, $9 > 4$ **Also,** $3^3 > 2^3$ is $27 > 8$ **This proves the point about positive numbers**

Now let's look at negative numbers: *If a = −3 and b = −2* . **Even though** -3 *is less than* -2
-3^2 *is greater than* -2^2 , here's why, $-3*-3 = 9$ and $-2*-2 = 4$ So -3^2 *is greater than* -2^2

So for any two negative numbers for example, $a = -3$ *and* $b = -2$, **it fits our given setup of** $a^2 > b^2$
But now use those same two numbers $(-3, -2)$ **and cube them:** *If a = −3 and b = −2 then* a^3 *and* b^3 *becomes:*
$(-3*-3*-3) = (9*-3) = -27$, $(-2*-2*-2) = (4*-2) = -8$. But -8 *is greater than* -27

Therefore, for two negative numbers like $a = -3$ *and* $b = -2$: a^2 *is greater than* b^2 **But,** a^3 *is NOT Greater than* b^3
So the answer to the question is "It Depends". For some a *and* b where $a^2 > b^2$. It is also true that $a^3 > b^3$ **But for some other** "a *and* b": $a^2 > b^2$ *but* a^3 *is NOT Greater than* b^3.**Therefore, the correct answer is "Unknown"** <u>Answer: (D)</u>

Top 10 Traps

Part 10: Average Rates

Virtual Classroom>Top 10 Traps>Average Rates
This material corresponds to the Virtual Classroom Instructions in the
PowerPrep DVD/Internet/iApp for Top 10 Traps

Virtual Classroom

Part 10: Average Rates

Average Rates

Strategy:

- You cannot average two rates together to get the overall average
- Find the total distance traveled and the total time taken
- Then solve for the average rate
- $Formula\ for\ Average\ Rate = \dfrac{total\ distance}{total\ time}$

Example:

Jill drove to the store at an average speed of 20 miles per hour, then immediately drove back home at an average speed of 40 miles per hour. What was the car's average speed for the entire trip, in miles per hour?

   (A) 25.5
   (B) 26.67
   (C) 30
   (D) 35.45
   (E) 60

NOTE: These questions will trick the vast majority of test takers. However, the math is not really that difficult as long as you recognize what the problem is asking and then apply the rules below. These questions will give you extra points that most test takers will not get. So learn this approach. $\boldsymbol{Average\ Rate = \dfrac{total\ distance}{total\ time}}$

If you have trouble memorizing this formula, just remember the standard formula of $\boldsymbol{(rate) * (time) = distance}$

You learned this formula very early in your math career and it's easier to remember. All you have to do is convert it to solve for the Rate. $(rate) * (time) = distance$ **Becomes** $rate = \dfrac{distance}{time}$

Next pick a distance: You can pick any distance but use smart math numbers. Since we know they gave us 20mph and 40mph, we'll chose 40 miles as our random distance.

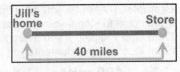

Distance from Jill's home to the store is 40 miles.
We've chosen our random distance between Jill's home and the store to be 40 miles

First Trip to the store: First leg of trip is 20 mph and the distance is 40 miles, therefore:
$rate * time = distance$. We already know the rate: 20mph
We already know the distance 40 miles

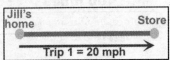

So let's calculate the time: $rate * time = distance$ Therefore, $\boldsymbol{time} = \frac{distance}{rate} = t = \frac{d}{r}$

Plug in what we know: $R = 20\,mph$ and $D = 40\,mi$ **Therefore,** $t = \frac{d}{r}$ **so,** $t = \frac{40}{20}$
$\boldsymbol{Time} = \boldsymbol{2\,(hours)}$

Second Trip back home: Second leg of trip is 40 mph and the distance is still 40 miles, therefore: $rate * time = distance$
We already know the rate: 40mph, We already know the distance 40 miles

So let's calculate the time: $rate * time = distance$. $\boldsymbol{time} = \frac{distance}{rate} = t = \frac{d}{r}$

Plug in what we know: $R = 40\,mph$ and $D = 40\,mi$, **therefore,** $t = \frac{d}{r}$ **so,** $t = \frac{40}{40}$ $\boldsymbol{Time} = \boldsymbol{1\,(hour)}$
Now we can find the AVERAGE RATE between the two trips.

Note: You CANNOT average the two averages—like this: Trip $1 = 20mph$ and Trip $2 = 40mph$. $\frac{20+40}{2} = \frac{60}{2} = 30\,mph$

Many students will make this mistake...Here is how you do it: **Begin with the standard formula:** $(rate) * (time) = distance$. This time we want to calculate "Rate" $rate = \frac{distance}{time}$

The distance is the sum of the two trips: 40 miles one way, 40 miles back home—total trip 80 miles
Time: Trip one was 2 hours and trip back home was 1 hour...total trip time 3 hours

Plug it into the formula: $rate = \frac{distance}{time}$ **becomes** $r = \frac{40+40}{2+1}$ **becomes:** $r = \frac{80}{3}$. $r = 26.67\,mi/hour$ **Answer: (B)**

PowerPrep Practice Questions Also in the Virtual Classroom on DVD

PowerPrep Practice Questions 18-19

18. Sara is a server at a restaurant. She serves an average of 12 tables per hour in the morning. Claire works at the same restaurant and serves an average of 24 tables per hour in the morning. What is Sara's and Claire's combined average rate of tables served?

    (A)   2
    (B)   4
    (C)   16
    (D)   18
    (E)   22

19. What is the average rate of cars washed per hour by Fred's Car Wash on Tuesdays and Wednesdays? If:

    (1) Fred's Car Wash washes an average of 15 cars per hour on Tuesdays.
    (2) Fred's Car Wash washes an average of 20 cars per hour on Wednesdays.

    (A)   17.5
    (B)   35
    (C)   20
    (D)   17.14
    (E)   15

Explanation to PowerPrep Practice Question 18

Quick Answer: Pick a number of tables to be served: 48

Sara: $12 = \frac{48}{x}$ **becomes**: $12x = 48$ **becomes**: $x = 4\,hours$

Claire: $24 = \frac{48}{x}$ **becomes**: $24x = 48$ **becomes**: $x = 2\,hours$

Combined Average rate: $\frac{48+48}{6} = \frac{96}{6} = 16\,tables/hour$ **Answer C**

Detailed Answer: When finding the average rate, you cannot simply average the rates together.

This is not intuitive and might take some concentrated review before it makes sense. $\boldsymbol{Averge\,Rate} = \frac{total\,distance}{total\,time}$ or $r = \frac{d}{t}$

This problems is just a variation of the common formula of $rt = d$ or $(rate * time = distance)$
Example1: A dog walks 8 miles at 4 mph, and then chases a rabbit for 2 miles at 20 mph. What is the dog's average rate of speed for the distance he traveled? The total distance traveled is $8 + 2 = 10\,m$.
Now we must calculate the total time he was traveling.

For the first part of the trip, he walked $(8 \div 4) = 2\,hours$. He chased the rabbit $(2 \div 20) = 0.1\,hour$.

The total time for the trip is $(2 + 0.1) = 2.1\,hours$.

The average rate of speed for his trip is $(10 \div 2.1) = (100 \div 21\,mph)$ or $4.75\,mph$.

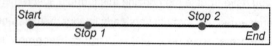

Example 2: Assume you drive from your home to your grandparent's home.
From home to stop 1 you average 50 mph
From stop 1 to stop 2 you average 75 mph
From stop 2 to grandparents you average 85 mph

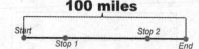

Total distance from home to grandparents is 100 miles. What is the average rate?
Answer: you can't tell yet.

You cannot do the following: $\frac{50+75+25}{3} = \frac{150}{3} = 50$ and say the average speed was 50 mph

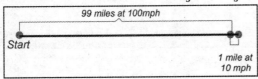

To prove the point logically—assume you average 100 mph for 99 miles and then the last mile your car has engine trouble and you average 10 mph.

Does it seem reasonable that the average rate is the sum of the two rates divided by two? $(100 + 10) \div 2 \; or \; 55 mph$?

Or does 91.7 mph sound more reasonable? 99 miles at 100 mph would take .99 hours and 1 mile at 10 mph would take .1 hour so, the *average rate = total distance ÷ total time*

In this example it would be: $100 \div 1.09 = 91.7 \; mph$ (does this seem more reasonable)

To solve the distance problem we need to know how far, how fast, and for what amount of time we traveled each leg.

Therefore, assume:

Home to stop 1 $= 25 \; miles \; and \; 50 \; mph \; avg$
Stop 1 to stop 2 $- 50 \; miles \; and \; 75 \; mph \; avg$
Stop 2 to grandmas is $25 \; miles \; and \; 25 \; mph \; avg$.

Now calculate the time for each leg of the trip:

Time for First Leg of trip: 25 mi at 50 mph would take $\frac{25 \; miles}{50 mph} = same \; as \; saying$ $\frac{25 \; miles}{\frac{50 \; miles}{hour}}$ invert and multiply $\frac{25 \; miles}{1} *$ $\left(\frac{hours}{50 \; miles}\right)$ miles drop out and you are left with $\frac{25}{50} hours = \frac{1}{2} hour \; or$ .5 hrs

Time for Second Leg of trip: 50 mi at 75 mph would take $\frac{50 \; miles}{75 mph} = ame \; as \; saying$ $\frac{50 \; miles}{\frac{75 \; miles}{hour}}$ invert and multiply $\frac{50 \; miles}{1} *$ $\left(\frac{hours}{75 \; miles}\right)$ miles drop out and you are left with $= \frac{50}{75} hours \; or \; \frac{10}{15} \; or \; \frac{2}{3} \; or$ .6666 hours

Time for Third Leg of trip: 25 miles at 25 mph would take $\frac{25 \; miles}{25 mph} = same \; as \; saying$ $\frac{25 \; miles}{\frac{25 \; miles}{hour}}$ invert and multiply $\frac{25 \; miles}{1} *$ $\left(\frac{hours}{25 \; miles}\right)$ miles drop out and you are left with $\frac{25}{25} \; hours = 1 \; hour$

$\frac{Total \; Distance}{total \; time} = \frac{100 \; miles}{(.5 + .666 + 1) hours} = \frac{100 \; miles}{2.166 \; hours} = 46.16 \; mph$

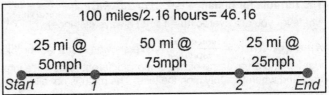

Back to Sara and Claire and their restaurant

In the problem we were told Sara and Claire serve tables at a restaurant. We were told the rate and time, but not the amount. In the car example above, we had both the rate and the distance and had to solve for **time** before solving the problem.

Average rate = *total distance ÷ total time* or $r = \frac{d}{t}$ In the table serving problem we are not driving a car miles per hour; we are serving tables per hour. So in place of "distance" or "miles" in the formula above, we have "tables served"

We are provided a rate for both Sara and Claire, but not total "distance" or "tables served"

Average rate = $\frac{total \; distance}{total \; time}$ or $\left(r = \frac{d}{t}\right)$ We are missing total distance (in our case, it's total tables served) *Average rate =* (total tables served *÷ total time*)

So we will have to assume a number. Let's pick a number of tables to be served: 48
This is a random number, but we put some thought behind it. The numbers we have in the given info are 12 and 24...so we've selected a number that is related to those two numbers. It's just smart to pay attention to these situations and select numbers that make the math easier.

Sara: 12 *tables/per hour* so, how long would it take her to serve 48 tables at 12 per hour? Start with the basic formula of $(r * t) = d$ *convert to solve for time it becomes* $\left(t = \frac{d}{r}\right)$ **Plug in what we know:** *Total tables (or distance)* $= 48$ **and** *Rate* $= 12 \; tables/hour$ **Becomes:** $\frac{48}{12} = x$ **Multiply by 12** $(12x = 48)$ **Divide by 12 so,** $x = 4 \; hours$

It would take Sara 4 hours to serve 48 tables. **Now let's calculate how many hours Claire needs to serve 48 tables** Claire's rate is 24 *tables/hour* and the formula for time is $t = \frac{d}{r}$ also, *total tables* (*distance*) $= 48$. so, *Rate* $= 24 \; tables/$ *hour* becomes $\frac{48}{24} = x$ becomes $x = 2 \; hours$. It would take Claire 2 hours to serve 48 tables. **Now we know Sara can serve 48 tables in 4 hours and Claire can serve 48 tables in 2 hours** Now find the Average Rate of both servers combined: Formula for Average rate is: *Average rate =* (total distance ÷ total time) **or** $r = \frac{d}{t}$. Where "d" in this case is the total combined tables from both servers. **Plug in what we know:** Total combined tables for Clair and Sara is 48 +

48 *or* 96. Total time for Clair was 2 hours and for Sara 4 hours $(2 + 4 = 6 \ hours)$. $r = \frac{d}{t}$ **Becomes** $\frac{48+48}{4+2} = \frac{96}{6} = 16$

average rate $= \frac{48+48}{6} = \frac{96}{6} = 16 \ tables/hour$ **Answer: (C)**

Explanation to PowerPrep Practice Question 19

Quick Answer: Pick a number of cars: 60

Tuesdays: $15 = \frac{60}{x}$ **becomes** $15x = 60$ **becomes** $x = 4 \ hours$

Wednesdays: $20 = \frac{60}{x}$ **becomes** $20x = 60$ **becomes** $x = 3 \ hours$

Combined Average Rate: $rate = \frac{60+60}{7}$ **becomes** $\frac{120}{7} = 17.4 \ cars \ per \ hour$ **Answer D**

Detailed Answer: In order to solve these average rate questions, we have to keep it very straight in our minds what is being asked. Let's look at what is NOT being asked.

These questions do NOT ask for the total number of cars washed, miles driven, or tables served in an hour. In other words, in this question, 35 is not the answer (15 cars per hour + 20 cars per hour)

Next, they do not ask for an arithmetic mean (straight average) where you add up the total miles, tables, cars, etc, and divide by two (typically)—if two people wash cars, wait tables, etc.
In this case, you cannot find a straight average or mean simply by adding 15 + 20 and then dividing the result (35) by 2 and solve for the mean 17.5.

The test makers love to trick people this way.
When we work with varying, or weighted, rates (mph, tables/hour, cars washed/hour, or any other rate) we have to consider each factor is not equal—we are actually finding a sort of weighted average.

In the prior problem we gave the example of a trip from your home to your grandma's home. If you traveled 99 miles at 100 mph and then traveled the last mile at 10 mph, you should be able to see that

a straight arithmetic mean or average will not give a valid result. $\frac{99+10}{2} = 54.5 \ mph$ (this is the straight mean or straight average)…it's a valid number, but it's not very useful. These questions ask us to find the Average Rate, or Weighted Average. We need to average the distance and time of each rate.

The formula for distance is: $Average \ Rate = \frac{total \ distance}{total \ time}$ (where total distance could be total tables, total cars or total whatever you are averaging—it's not always distance)

$Average \ Rate = \frac{total \ distance}{total \ time}$ We showed in the last problem how this formula can be modified for any situation where we want to find an average of two or more different rates. It's important that you spend time with this information and understand how and when to apply it on the test. The math is not all that difficult, but it is logically challenging to be sure.

Let's solve the problem at Fred's Car Wash

What are you looking for? The average rate of cars washed, if we know Fred's washes cars at two different rates (15 *cars/hour* and 20 *cars/hour*) **We'll use the formula:** $Average \ Rate = \frac{total \ distance}{total \ time}$ But we will change "total distance" to "cars washed" $Average \ Rate = \frac{total \ cars \ washed}{total \ time}$ To successfully do this we have to pick a random (sort of) number of cars to wash and then calculate how much time it took to wash that random number of cars given the two different rates.

We will use 60 as our "random" number. We truly can use any random number, but be wise about selecting random numbers—choosing a number that will result in easy math is always smart.

We chose 60 because it's the lowest common multiple of both 15 and 20.

If Fred's washes 60 cars on Tuesday, how long will it take? Tuesday's rate is 15/*hour*. Therefore it will take 4 hours on Tuesday $(60 \div 15 = 4)$. **Wednesday:** How long will it take Fred's to wash 60 cars on Wednesday? Wednesday's rate is 20/*hour*. Therefore, it will take 3 hours on Wednesday $(60 \div 20 = 3)$

Now we have total cars and total time. Plug it in to the formula: $Average \ Rate = \frac{total \ cars \ washed}{total \ time}$

$Average \ Rate = \frac{60+60}{4+3}$, $Average \ Rate = \frac{120 \ cars}{7 \ hours} = 17.14 \ cars/hour$

This is the new average rate of cars given the information in the question. **Answer: (D)**

CONGRATULATIONS!!!

You have completed the Top 10 Traps Workshop!

Take a break before moving on to the Drills!

Top 10 Traps Index

Problem Solving Workbook

Table of Contents

This material Corresponds to the Resources in the Virtual Classroom
PowerPrep DVD/Internet/iApp for Math Problem Solving Strategies

Virtual Classroom

Math Problem Solving

Part 1: Generally

Virtual Classroom>Math>Problem Solving Strategies

This Material Corresponds to the Resources in the
PowerPrep DVD/Internet/iApp for Math Problem Solving

Virtual Classroom

Important Abbreviations
These abbreviations are used throughout the program

POE: Process of Elimination
SARR: Synthesize, Analyze, Reduce, and Restate (has to do with Logical Reasoning)
AC: Answer Choice
QS: Question Stem
LOD: Level of Difficulty

Example Question: What is the least common multiple of 3, 4, and 7? **(This is the call of the question or Question Stem "QS")**

These are Answer Choices "AC" A, B, C, D, E

   (A)   12
   (B)   21
   (C)   28
   (D)   48
   (E)   84

Part 1: Generally

Directions

Unless otherwise indicated, the figures accompanying questions have been drawn as accurately as possible and may be used as sources of information for answering the questions.

All figures are lines in a plane except where noted.

All numbers used are real numbers. You won't see any imaginary numbers like $\sqrt{-3}$

Approach

1. **Read entire question**
   Make sure you understand EXACTLY what you are solving
   Record important information on your scratch paper

2. **Choose best approach to problem**
   Make sure to think about shortcuts and strategies if the problem looks complicated or confusing

3. **Solve the problem, eliminate answers which are unrealistic,** Constantly using POE

4. **If you can't solve the problem, make an educated guess**
   Use logic to eliminate unreasonable answer choices
   On roman numeral problems, try to eliminate choices which appear in more than one answer
   Try to estimate the final answer and eliminate those far from it

Math Problem Solving

Part 2: Backsolving

Virtual Classroom>Math>Problem Solving Strategies
This Material Corresponds to the Resources in the
PowerPrep DVD/Internet/iApp for Math Problem Solving

Virtual Classroom

Part 2: Backsolving

Generally

This may be the single most useful tip in the entire program.

Most students don't realize the full power and potential of this tool. Almost every problem on the exam can be completely or partially solved with this technique and its cousins.

What: Solving the question, using the given answers.

How:
• Start in the middle of the answer choices.
• Plug AC (C) into the problem and solve
• If AC (C) does not give you a correct solution; move on to the next AC.
• Eliminate smaller/larger AC's depending on the answer (C) gives you.
• If you eliminate (C) and aren't sure which direction to move, select an answer that looks easy to use.

When:
• All answer choices are numbers.
• You are confused on how to solve a problem.
• Your approach seems it will take a long time

Actually you can use Backsolving on almost every problem—keep it mentally ready.

Sample Question 1—Equations

1. If $c + d + e = 30$, $c = 3d$, and $2c = 3e$, then $d = ?$

   (A) 5
   (B) 6
   (C) 10
   (D) 12
   (E) 15

Tests: Solving for 1 Variable, Substitution

Quick Answer

Backsolve when it is quicker than the standard approach of solving the problem.

1. **Plug in (C) and solve:** If d = 10, c = 3(10) = 30, 2(30) = 3e, 60 = 3e, e = 20
2. **Check first equality:** c + d + e = 30 + 10 + 20 = 60, 60 ≠ 30
3. **Move to smaller value:** Answer choice B...If d = 6, c = 3(6) = 18, 2(18) = 3e, 36 = 3e, e = 12
4. **Check first equality:** c + d + e = 18 + 6 + 12 = 36, 36 ≠ 30
5. **Move to smaller value:** Answer Choice A...If d = 5, c = 3(5) = 15, 2(15) = 3e, 30 = 3e, e = 10
6. **Check first equality:** c + d + e = 15 + 5 + 10 = 30, 30 = 30

Correct answer: (A)

Detailed Answer

Goal: Find correct value of d by proving first equality statement.

When we use the Problem Solving Tool called Backsolving, we typically begin with Answer Choice C and plug that value into the given information and solve.

In this case, AC C is 10, so let's plug 10 into the given information and solve to see if we get a true statement.

What we know: c = 3d **and** 2c = 3e **and** c + d + e = 30
Call of the Question: d = ?
Answer Choice C is d = 10
  If d = 10, solve for c in the given (c = 3d) **Becomes:** c = 3(10) or c = 30
  For AC C if d = 10, then C = 30, Now we can solve for e because we have a value for c and d.
  Solve for e: If c = 30, Plug it into the given: 2c = 3e **Becomes** 2(30) = 3e, => 60 = 3e, => e = 20

Now we have all the variables solved based on AC C which is d=10
  So we have d=10, c=30, and e =20, Plug it all into the given and see if it works
  Given information: c + d + e = 30 , Plug in the values for c, d, e, 30 + 10 + 20 = 30 Becomes 60 ≠ 30

So we know that AC C (d=10 does not work because it returned a number that was significantly too big—60. But we need the answer to be 30)

Note: The smart thing would be to move to AC A (d=5) because AC C (d=10) was significantly high. Also, since AC A (d = 5) is one-half of AC C (d = 10) and since the final outcome for AC C (where d = 10) was twice as large (60 ≠ 30), all this points to skipping AC B (d = 6) and moving right to AC A (d = 5)

As it turns out, AC A (d = 5) will be the correct answer, but even if you did not see these connections and you only saw that the AC C (d = 10) was too large and you moved to AC B (the next smaller answer), the only bad result is a little wasted time. No big deal if you did not see this connection.

Answer Choice A (d=5)
  If d=5, first solve for c: given: $c = 3d$ => c = 3(5) => c = 15

Now Solve for e: 2c =3e and c = 15 Therefore, 2(15) = 3e, => 30 = 3e, => e = 10
Now we know that AC A gives us: $c = 15, d = 5, and\ e = 10$

Plug this information into the given equality: $c + d + e = 30$, 15 + 5 + 10 = 30 so 30 = 30
It proves AC A where d = 5 is the correct Answer **Correct answer: (A)**

Another Way: Logic

Focus on the "Big Picture" "What are they really asking?" Try not to get bogged down in the natural rush to find the right math formula---if you can do all that, you will find **Logic** can be a great friend.

It's like solving a puzzle or a mystery. They give you lots of clues in the "given" information. But most students don't use all the clues. The AC's provide additional information that will help you solve questions.

It's like coming to a crime scene but only focusing on the hard evidence inside the yellow "Crime Scene" tape—but failing to talk to the eye witnesses.

You won't be able to solve every problem all the way to a final answer using only logic. But you can almost always eliminate AC's and get close. If nothing else, it can help you save precious time.

For example, we were given: If $c + d + e = 30$ And $c = 3d$, and $2c = 3e$, Then $d = ?$

  (A) 5
  (B) 6
  (C) 10
  (D) 12
  (E) 15

We have 3 numbers (c,d,e) that must add up to 30. We also have some combinations and relationships between those numbers. But we also have all the AC's (the eye witnesses)

Look at the relationship they gave us regarding C: $c = 3d$

When you couple that piece of information with the group of AC's, we can see a pattern.

AC E is 15....but 3 *times* 15 *is* 45...which is more than the total sum of 30...that means AC E is out.
AC D is 12...same problem...3 x 12 = 36...too big...throw it out
AC C is 10...same problem 3 x 10 = 30...too big...if *C is* 30 *and D is* 10...that's 40...

Immediately we have narrowed it down to AC A and B...this process took about 30 second and it got us 80% of the way. It also gives you confidence when you can see the logic of a problem.

Logic is another incredibly useful tool. It's a cousin of Backsolving and together they can help you throughout the exam.

Sample Question 2—Diagrams

2. If the surface area of a cube is 37.5, what is the length of one side?
  (A) 1
  (B) 2
  (C) 2.25
  (D) 2.5
  (E) 2.75

Explanation

Tests: Formula for Surface Area of a Cube

Goal: To find the length of a side by proving the surface area of the object is 37.5 by substituting the value of an AC into the formula until we find the right answer.

Quick Answer

If the surface area of the cube is 54, what is the length of AB? *(A)* 1   *(B)* 2   *(C)* 2.25   *(D)* 2.5   *(E)* 2.75

Backsolve

1. **Plug in AC (C) (2.25) and solve:** If length of one side of the square = 2.25,

   Formula of Surface area = 6(area of one surface of the square) = $6(l)^2$

Formula is: $6(l)^2 = surface\ area\ of\ a\ square$

2. **Check AC C where side = 2.25:** $6(2.25)^2 = 6(5.0625) = 30.375$ BUT $30.375 \neq 37.5$

3. **Move to next larger value which is AC D where side = 2.5.** If side = 2.5, Surface area = 6(area of one surface of the square) = $6(l)^2$

4. **Substitute side = 2.5**

   $6(2.5)^2 = 6(6.25) = 37.5$ AND   **37.5 = 37.5   Answer D**

Detailed Answer

What we know: The formula for surface area of a cube is:
$6(L^2)$ where L = the length of one side/edge of a cube.

Remember a cube has six (6) faces or surfaces and each one has a surface area which is calculated as l^2 and each edge/side of cube is equal, therefore the surface area of a cube is:

$Surface\ Area\ of\ a\ cube = (6)(l^2)$

Straight Math: We could solve this problem like this: $6(L^2) = 37.5$
$L^2 = \frac{37.5}{6}$ => $L^2 = 6.25$ => $L = \sqrt{6.25}$ => L = 2.5 **The length of one side/edge of a cube that has surface area of 37.5 is**

2.5...or AC (D)   Answer D

Backsolving

AC C where side = 2.25
We know the entire surface area is 37.5,   We know the formula is $6(l^2)$,   We know $l = 2.25$
Therefore, $6(l^2) = 37.5$, $6(2.25^2) = 37.5$, $6(5.0625) = 37.5$, $30.375 \neq 37.5$

So AC C where side is 2.25 returns a surface area answer of 30.375, but we are looking for an answer that returns 37.5. So AC C is too SMALL...this means we should move to the next larger option which is AC D where side D = 2.5

So AC (C) was too small, move to AC (D) 2.5

AC D where side = 2.5
We know the entire surface area is 37.5,   We know the formula is $6(l^2)$,   We know $l = 2.5$
Therefore, $6(l^2) = 37.5$, $6(2.5^2) = 37.5$, $6(6.25) = 37.5$, $37.5 \neq 37.5$ This AC proves correct...with a side = 2.5, the surface area is 37.5 **Correct answer: (D)**

Another Way: Logic + Backsolving

You might have noticed that the given surface area of 37.5 is a fraction, it's not a whole number integer. That tells us immediately that the length of a side cannot be a whole number or integer because any whole number squared and then multiplied by 6 will always return another whole number integer.

$AC\ A\ (6)(l^2) = 6(1^2) = 6 * 1 = 6$

$AC\ B\ (6)(l^2) = 6(2^2) = 6 * 4 = 24$

IOW, AC A and B cannot be true because they are whole number integers….therefore, the correct answer must be either C, D, or E

With this information in mind, you could alter the normal Backsolving approach where we normally start with AC C…instead, in this case the logical approach would be to start with AC D…Between C and E By quickly eliminating AC A and B and then splitting the remaining possible answers and starting with AC D, we guarantee that we only have to Backsolve a single AC (that's AC D)…if AC D returned a response that is too small, then by POE we know the correct answer must be AC E (because it is the next and only answer that is larger than D.) If however, you solve AC D and it gives a response that is too large, then we automatically know the correct answer must be C, because AC C is the only possible AC that is smaller than AC D.

```
Logic
(A) 1 (can't be a whole number)
(B) 2 (can't be a whole number)
Backsolve
(C) 2.25
(D) 2.5 (split these and start with AC D)
(E) 2.75
Logic and POE: If AC D is too big, then select
C, if AC D is too small, then select AC E
```

So by combining LOGIC and Backsolving, we can shave off precious time in answering this question.

Sample Question 3—Complex Word Problems

3. A high school has 37 teachers. If there are seven more women than men at the school, how many employees are women?

  (A) 13
  (B) 15
  (C) 19
  (D) 22
  (E) 25

Explanation:

Tests: Word Problem, substituting one variable for another, Solving Equations,
Goal: To find the number of women by proving the total number of teachers is 37.

Backsolve
1. **Start with AC C and Plug in the value where AC $C = 19$ and solve:** If women = 19,
   Then men are: $m = 19 - 7 = 12$
2. **Check original number:** Total teachers = m + w must equal 37
   Plug in what we found for AC C where value for women was 19
   $W = 19$ and $M = 12$
   $m + w = 37 => 19 + 12 = 37$ **BUT** $31 \neq 37$ So this does not prove out.
   The result is too small, we need a value that is greater (more women), so move to AC D where $women = 22$
3. **Move to larger value:** AC D says women would be 22
   $If\ w = 22, then\ m = 22 - 7 = 15$
4. **Check original number:** $W = 19$ and $M = 12$
   $m + w = 37 => 22 + 15 = 37$ **AND** $37 = 37$
   So this proves out. Therefore the number of women is 22 and the number of men is 15 **Correct answer: (D)**

Another Way: Straight Math

What we know: 37 total teachers and 7 more women than men
Set up the equation this way: $37 = m + w$
   If we sent the number of men equal to "m" , then the number of women would be $(m + 7)$

Now add these two terms together: $37 = m + (7 + m)$ *add* -7 *to both sides*: $20 = 2m$ Divide by 2: $15 = m$
   Men = 15. If men = 15, the given information tells us that women are 7 more, so Women = $15 + 7 = 22$ Either way you answer this question, it turns out to be 22 women **Answer D**

Math Problem Solving

Part 3: Pricking Numbers

Virtual Classroom>Math>Problem Solving Strategies

This Material Corresponds to the Resources in the
PowerPrep DVD/Internet/iApp for Math Problem Solving

Virtual Classroom

Part 3: Picking Numbers

Generally

What: Similar to Backsolving, Picking Numbers uses the same approach, but with random numbers (not given AC numbers). You substitute a random number for a variable into the question and answer choices to find the correct answer.

How:
- Choose an easy number (one that gives easy math) to work with—WRITE IT DOWN! Understanding the problems "logic" will help you in selecting the right number.
- Substitute your value into the problem, then into the AC's. Look for the AC value that matches the problem value.
- If more than one AC matches the problem, choose another number.

When: Problems contain variables in question and/or answer.

Sample Question 4: Variables

4. If x is an odd integer and y is an even integer, which of the following must be odd?
  (A) xy^2
  (B) x^2y
  (C) xy
  (D) $x + 2y$
  (E) $2x + y$

Explanation

Tests: integers, even and odd, powers
Goal: After, substituting a random number for the variable, find an answer solution that matches the problem-solution.
Quick Answer: Find the answer choice that matches the problem question (which of the following must be odd?)
1. **Pick numbers:** $x = odd$, $y = even$: We'll pick $x = 3\ and\ y = 4$

2. **Substitute x and y into answer choices:**

(A) $(3)(4^2) = 3 * 16 = 48 = even$

(B) $(3^2)(4) = 9 * 4 = 36 = even$

(C) $(3) * (4) = 12 = even$

(D) $3 + (2 * 4) = 3 + 8 = 11 = odd$

(E) $(2 * 3) + 4 = 6 + 4 = 10 = even$

Correct Answer: (D)

Another Way: Logic

If you remember the following's rules or facts about even and odd numbers you could answer this question without picking up your pencil. **We know that x is odd and y is even. Therefore**, $even * even = even$, $Even^2 = even$, $Even * odd = even$, $Even + odd = odd$, $Odd + odd = even$, $Odd * odd = odd$

x = odd, y = even

(A) $xy^2 = odd(even^2) = (odd * even) = even$

(B) $x^2y = (odd^2 * even) = (odd * even) = even$

(C) $xy = odd * even = even$

(D) $x + 2y = odd + 2(even) = odd + even = odd$

(E) $2x + y = 2(odd) + even = even + even = even$

Therefore, AC (D) will always return odd and the others will always return even answers.

Sample Question 5—Percent Problems

4. If m is a positive number, which of the following is the equivalent of decreasing m by 20 percent then increasing the result by 50 percent?

   (A)   increase m by 10%

   (B)   increase m by 20%

   (C)   increase m by 30%

   (D)   decrease m by 10%

   (E)   decrease m by 30%

Explanation:

Tests: percentage of percentage, word problem,

Goal: To find an answer solution which matches the problem question by substituting values for the variable in the question and solving for its value.

Quick Answer: If you aren't given the original whole, pick 100.

1. **Pick numbers:** m = 100
2. **1st increase m by 20%:** part = %(whole) = 20%(100) = 20: New whole = (old whole – part decrease) = (100 – 20) = 80
3. **2nd percentage change:** part = %(whole) = 50%(80) = 40: New whole = (old whole + part increase) = (80 + 40) = 120
4. **120 (new whole) – 100 (original whole) = 20 percent increase Correct Answer: (B)**

Detailed Answer

We could solve the problem using straight math: $(m - (.2m)) * 1.5 \Rightarrow (.8m) * 1.5 \Rightarrow 1.2m$ 20% increase over m

First take 80% of m (the same as decreasing m by 20%) then adding 50% of that total back, or 1.5. This results in: $.8m \times 1.5 = 1.2m$ **IOW**, a 20% overall increase of m or AC (B)

But that might be confusing…so let's pick a number and see

So, let's set m = 100

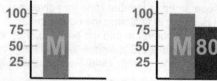

1st either find out what 20% of 100 is and then deduct it: $20\% \ of \ 100 = 20$ $100 - 20 = 80$ We are left with 80 after the first part. **Or**

We could also see that decreasing a number by 20% is also the same as saying "what is 80% of that number". Since m =100, then 80% of 100 = 80

Either way, the first part of the question returns the answer of 80 (if m=100)

2nd Part: Now move to second part of the question—increase the result by 50%

We can either take 50% of 80 (.5 x 80) = 40
And add it back to the 80
40 + 80 = 120

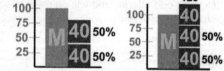

Then compare our given number m = 100 to our ending number after decreasing by 20% and increasing by 50% and we end with 120. **Therefore, the % increase is 20…AC B.**

Or we can take the 80 and multiply by 1.5, (this saves a step) and see the total is 120, then compare 100 to 120 and see the percent increase is 20… or AC (B).

Either way it's a 20% increase…AC (B) If you work with percents a few times, this will become second nature and you'll like these kinds of questions. **Correct Answer: (B)**

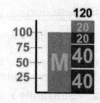

Sample Question 6—Simplify Algebraic Expressions

6. If $x = \frac{y}{4} + 3$, what is y in terms of x?

(A) $x + 3$

(B) $4x + 3$

(C) $\frac{x}{4} + 6$

(D) $x - 3$

(E) $(4x - 12)$

Explanation

Tests: One variable in terms of another, Solve Equation Variable,

Goal: To find an answer solution which matches the problem solution by substituting values for the variables.

Quick Answer: Pick numbers when you need to simplify algebraic expressions.   Example: If $x = \frac{y}{4} + 3$, what is y

in terms of x?   (A) $x + 3$ (B) $4x + 3$ (C) $\left(\frac{x}{4}\right) + 6$ (D) x - 3   (E) $4x - 12$

1. **Pick numbers:** $y = 4$ (this is just a random number) solve the given information with a random number and then plug that information back into the answer choices.

2. **Substitute y into question and answer choices:** $x = \frac{4}{4} + 3$ $x = 1 + 3$ $x = 4$

So we picked a random value for y: $y = 4$ (but you could pick anything) Then we plugged $y = 4$ into the given equation and solved for x and we found that $x = 4$. So if we set $y = 4$, we find x also ends up 4. Now plug $x = 4$ into the AC's and find the one that returns a correct result.

3. **Answer choice solutions:** Plug x=4 and we look for a result of 4: $x + 3\ becomes\ (4 + 3) = 7\ and\ 7 \neq 4$

(A) $4x + 3\ becomes\ (4) * (4) + 3 = 16 + 3 = 19\ and\ 19 \neq 4$

(B) $(4x - 3)$ becomes 4(4) – 3 becomes 13   13 $\neq$ 4 (false)

(C) $\frac{x}{4} + 6\ becomes\ \frac{4}{4} + 6 = 1 + 6 = 7\ and\ 7 \neq 4$

(D) $x - 3\ becomes\ (4 - 3) = 1\ and\ 1 \neq 4$

(E) $(4x - 12)\ becomes\ (4 * 4) - 12 = 16 - 12 = 4\ \ and\ 4 = 4\ True$

Correct Answer: (E)

Detailed Answer

We could solve this problem using math: $x = (y/4) + 3$, $(x - 3) = y / 4$, $4(x - 3) = y$, $4x - 12 = y$

But, you could easily make the mistake of clearing the $y/4$ first and solving the problem incorrectly like this:
$x = (y/4) + 3$, $4x = y + 3$, $4x - 3 = y$

Logic and POE

Sometimes, it pays to either figure out a problem initially by picking numbers, or at least checking your answer with sample numbers.   You can also use some logic to reduce the AC's. Since y is divided by 4, you know the right answer can't be $(x + 3)\ or\ (x - 3)$. Those would be correct answers if y were just alone. So by looking at the information and absorbing it just a little, we can quickly eliminate AC's (A) and (D).

You might also realize that you have to multiply by 4 to clear the right side, so AC (C) with $x/4$ is probably not in the correct form.   So in a pinch you could probably feel safe eliminating AC D.

That leaves us with AC (B) and (E). We either have to solve the problem using math (see above) or pick a number and see. Either way, will give us a correct answer.

Remember: When picking numbers use logic to give you the easiest math. In this case, that means picking y=4 and solving for x. We picked 4 because (y/4) will give us (4/4) or 1.

Goal: After, substituting a random number for the variable, find an answer solution which matches the problem-solution.

First, Substitute y = 4 and solve: $x = 4/4 + 3$ $= 1 + 3$ $= 4$

So with our random number 4 for y, we get x = 4

Next, plug x =4 into the given AC's and see which one is true (that's our correct answer)

Keep in mind, that if we used logic, we would only test AC B because we already used POE and logic to eliminate AC's (A), (C), and (D). If AC B proves false, we could just mark E as the correct one and move on. But if we have time, we should check it; just to be sure our approach was correct.

But, we'll check them all here just to give you all the information.

(A) Given: $(x + 3)$ becomes   4 + 3 = 7 becomes   7 $\neq$ 4 (false)

(B) Given: $(4x - 3)$ becomes 4(4) – 3   becomes 13   13 $\neq$ 4 (false)

(C) Given: $(x/4 + 6)$ becomes $(4/4) + 6$ becomes 7 $7 \neq 4$ (false)
(D) Given: $(x - 3)$ becomes $4 - 3$ becomes 1 $1 \neq 4$ (false)
(E) Given: $(4x - 12)$ becomes $4(4) - 12$ becomes 4 $4 = 4$ **(true)**

Correct answer: (E)

Sample Question 7—Word Problems

7. If w books cost x dollars, then y books would cost how many dollars?
   (A)   wx/y
   (B)   wy/x
   (C)   xy/w
   (D)   w/xy
   (E)   x/wy

Goal: To find an answer solution which matches the problem solution by substituting values for the variables.

Quick Answer

1. **Pick numbers:** w = 2 books, and x = 10 dollars → $5 each

2. **Substitute y into question and answer choices:** Question solution: y = 4 books → 4 books (at $5 each) cost $20

3. **Answer choice solutions:**
   (A) 2(10)/4 = 5   5 ≠ 20
   (B) (2)(4)/10 = .8   .8 ≠ 20
   (C) (10)(4)/2 = 20   20 = 20
   (D) 2/(10)(4) = .05   .05 ≠ 20
   (E) (10)/(2)(4) = 1.25   1.25 ≠ 20

Find the answer choice solution that matches the question solution. Correct Answer: (C)

Detailed Answer

We could solve this with math:

If w books costs x dollars, what is the rate or per/book cost? w (number of books) times some rate (per book cost) = x dollars (total) **Number times rate = total:** $w(r) = x$ (where w = total books, r = rate or per/book cost, and x = total $)
So, if : w(r) = x   **Then,** $r = x/w$ (rate or per book cost is the total price of all books divided by total number of books)

Now we know the rate is x/w: Therefore, how much does some other amount of books, like y, cost? We would multiply the number of books times the rate, or $y(x/w)$ **Or** $(yx) / w$ **See AC C**

Picking numbers: If we did not see this, then we could just as easily solve the problem by picking numbers.
First, list what we know: w = total books, x = how much w books cost, y = another group of book
We want to know how much the stack of y books costs.

Goal: After, substituting a random number for the variable, find an answer solution which matches the problem-solution.
Pick a random number of books…let's say 2 books. Pick a random cost/book…let's say $5.00 each

Now we have our variables picked
If w (total books) = 2,   Then what is their total cost if they cost $5 each?   Answer $10.00
In this imaginary case with w = 2 and the cost/book = $5.00. x (total cost) would be $10.00

Now using that information, how much would another group of books cost?
Say y (another group) is 4 books. If y = 4, And they cost $5.00 each (see above), The total cost would be $20.00

So, we plug this information into the AC's and find out which one proves true.
w = number of first group of book (2),   y = number of 2nd group of books (4),   x = total cost of first group of books ($10.00)
The new total cost is $20. If y = 4 books; 4 books (at $5 each) cost $20

Plug value into AC's and solve:
   (A) Given: (wx/y) becomes   2(10)/4   becomes 20/4   becomes 5   5 ≠ 20 (false)
   (B) Given: (wy/x) becomes (2)(4)/10 becomes 8/10   becomes .8   .8 ≠ 20 (false)
   (C) Given: (xy/w) becomes (10)(4)/2 becomes 40/2   becomes 20   20 = 20 (true)
   (D) Given: (w/xy) becomes 2/(10)(4) becomes   2/40   becomes .05   .05 ≠ 20 (false)
   (E) Given: (x/wy) becomes (10)/(2)(4) becomes 10/8 becomes 1.25   1.25 ≠ 20 (false)

Correct answer: (C)

Math Problem Solving
Part 4: Grid-ins (**SAT ONLY**)

Virtual Classroom>Math>Problem Solving Strategies
This Material Corresponds to the Resources in the
PowerPrep DVD/Internet/iApp for Math Problem Solving

Virtual Classroom

Part 4: Grid-Ins (SAT ONLY)

Generally

Not all Math questions on the SAT are multiple-choice. For one type--called **Student-Produced Response** or **Grid-in**--you have to find and fill in your own answer. Unlike the rest of the questions on the SAT, there is no penalty for wrong answers on the grid-in section. Since there are no answers to choose from, guessing is practically impossible. But if you want to guess, go for it, no points will be subtracted for an incorrect answer.

The grid-ins are like regular math questions--they cover the same subject areas, and they range in difficulty from easy to hard. Make sure to double check your answers with a calculator for this section--without answers to choose from it's easy to make careless mistakes.

There are 10 Grid-ins on the quantitative section of the SAT, so **Grid-Ins account for one-sixth of your quantitative score**. To answer a Grid-in question, you must fill out a grid with four boxes and a column of ovals beneath each. It's recommended that you first write your numerical answer in the boxes above and then shade in the corresponding ovals below. **You must fill out the grid properly to get credit for a correct answer**. So take some time to learn the directions for Grid-ins

Directions: For each of the following questions, solve the problem and indicate your answer by darkening the ovals on the special grid. For example: If the correct answer is 1 1/4, then grid-in the number as **1.25** or **5/4**, like so

- It is recommended, through not required, that you write your answer in the boxes at the top of the columns. However, you will receive credit only for darkening in ovals correctly.

- Grid only one answer to a question, even though some problems may have more than one correct answer.

- Darken no more than one oval per column. $1\frac{1}{4}$

- No answers are negative.

- Mixed numbers cannot be gridded. For example: the number $1\frac{1}{4}$ must be gridded as 1.25 or 5/4

If it is gridded as 11/4, it will be interpreted as $\frac{11}{4}$, not $1\frac{1}{4}$.

Either position is acceptable

Write Answers in boxes

Grid in results

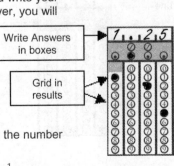

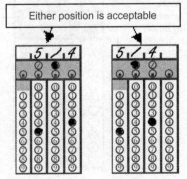

- **Decimal accuracy:** Decimal answers must be entered as accurately as possible. For example, if you obtain an answer such as 0.1666. . ., you should record the result as .166 or .167. **Less accurate values such as .16 or .17 are not acceptable.**

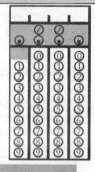

Acceptable ways to grid $\frac{1}{6} = .16666 \ldots$

1 / 6   .166   .167

What all this means to you:

- Your answer must have at most 4 characters, including the decimal point or fraction bar.
- The grid cannot accommodate negative numbers, mixed numbers, or numbers greater than 9,999.
- A fractional number with 4 digits won't fit.
- Mixed numbers must be changed to decimals or fractions before you grid.
- Decimals must be as complete as possible (for long or repeating decimals, use as many columns as possible) but do not have to be rounded up for accuracy's sake.
- Many questions may have more than one correct answer, and there may be many ways to fill in the grid correctly (just choose a single safe one).
- You will only get credit for filling in the ovals correctly—if you fill in two ovals in the same column, the computer reads this as an omission.

The Grid (Student Produced Responses)

1. Each question requires you to solve the problem and enter your answer by marking the ovals in the special grid.
2. Mark no more than one oval in any column.
3. You will only receive credit if the ovals are filled in correctly.
4. It is suggested you write your answer in the boxes at the top to help fill in the ovals correctly. BUT, the computer will only grade answers that you grid-in (blacken the ovals) if you write the answers in the boxes but fail to grid, you won't receive credit. Also, if you write a correct answer, but grid-in a different response, the computer grades the grid. So be careful!
5. Some problems may have more than one correct answer. In such cases, grid only one answer.
6. No question has a negative answer.
7. Mixed numbers such as 2 ½ must be gridded as 2.5 or 5/2. 2 1/2 will be interpreted as 21÷2.
8. You may start your answers in any column, space permitting. Columns not needed should be left blank.
9. If you obtain a decimal answer, enter the most accurate value the grid will accommodate. For example, if your answer is .7777 ..... you should record the result as .777 or .778. Less accurate values such as .77 or .78 are not acceptable.

Filling in the grid

- You cannot fill in negative numbers, variables, commas, mixed numbers
- Fill out grid left to right
- Only gridded answers are scored, but you may write in answers if you like
- Convert mixed numbers (5 ½ = 11/2)
- Fill out decimals to end of grid (.222 cannot be rounded to .2)
- Choose any one of a set of multiple correct answers
- Grid in signs (/ and .)
- Never fill in 0 before a decimal point (0.25 should be gridded as .25)
- Fill in only one oval per column

Directions

For Student-Produced Response questions 9-18, use the grids at the bottom of the answer sheet page on which you have answered questions 1-8. Each of the remaining 10 questions requires you to solve the problem and enter your answer by marking the circles in the special grid, as shown in the examples below. You may use any available space for scratch work.

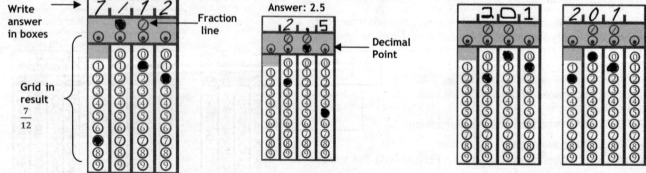

Answer: 201
Either position is correct

Decimal Answers: If you have a decimal answer with more digits than the grid can accommodate, you may round or truncate, but it must fill the entire grid. For example, if your answer is 0.66666..., you should record your result as .666 or .667. A less accurate value such as .66 will be scored incorrect. **Note**: You may start your answers in any column, space permitting. Columns not needed should be left blank.

Acceptable ways to score $\frac{2}{3}$ are:

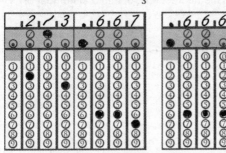

- Mark no more than one circle in any column
- Because the answer sheet will be machine-scored, **you will receive credit only if the circles are filled in correctly and completely.**
- Although not required, it is suggested that you write your answer in the boxes at the top of the columns to help you fill in the circles accurately.
- Some problems may have more than one correct answer. In such cases, grid only one answer.
- No question has a negative answer.
- **Mixed numbers** such as $3\frac{1}{2}$ must be gridded as 3.5 or 7/2

If you grid it as [3 1 / 2] it will be interpreted by the machine as $\frac{31}{2}$ not $3\frac{1}{2}$

Review

1. Remember that only the answer entered on the grid will count...the handwritten answer that you enter in the space provided will not count. So be very careful as you grid in the answer.
2. Don't grid zeros before the decimal point.
3. Take each question one step at a time because some questions that seem difficult are just a series of easy questions.
4. Think about what you need to know in order to answer a question.
5. Make sure you answer the question that has been asked.
6. Double-check your answers, especially on grid-in questions, if you have time.
7. Remember that some questions have more than one correct answer; grid any of the correct answers and get full credit.
8. State an answer as a fraction or a decimal: you can grid $\frac{1}{2}$ as $\frac{1}{2}$ or .5.
9. Write mixed numbers as improper fractions. For example, $1\frac{3}{5}$ is $\frac{8}{5}$. The grid-reading system cannot distinguish between $1\frac{3}{5}$ and $\frac{13}{5}$
10. Grid as much of a repeating decimal as will fit in the grid. You may need to round a repeating decimal, but round only the last digit; grid $\frac{2}{3}$ as $\frac{2}{3}$ or .666 or .667. Do not grid the value of $\frac{2}{3}$ as .67 or .66.
11. Use a calculator to help speed up getting an answer.
12. Jot down your calculations in your test booklet.
13. Write relevant facts (about angles, lengths or sides, etc.) on figures as you pick up more information.
14. Look for special properties that may help you answer questions.
15. Grid zero by entering 0 in a single column (any column where 0 appears.)

Sample Question 8

8. In the line at right, $AC = 5$. If $BC = \left(\frac{1}{2}AC\right)$ and $BD = 8$, what is the length of CD?

$\underset{\bullet\quad\bullet\quad\bullet\qquad\qquad\bullet}{A\ B\ C\qquad D}$

Explanation:

Tests: Number line, Solve for 1 variable

What we know: $AC = 5$, $BC = \frac{1}{2}AC$, and $BD = 8$

Call of the question: What is the length of segment CD

Answer: If AC=5 and BC $= \frac{1}{2}AC$, then BC $= \left(\frac{1}{2}\right) * (5) = 2.5$, So BC = 2.5

Now solve for length CD: $CD = BD - BC$. **Substitute what we know:** BD = 8, BC = 2.5

$CD = BD - BC$ Becomes $CD = 8 - 2.5$ **OR** CD = 5.5

Now Grid the answer: You can grid 5.5 or $\frac{11}{2}$

Answer: Grid-in $\frac{11}{2}$ or 5.5 **NOT** $5\frac{1}{2}$ because it would be written 51/2 and this would be scored by the machine as $\frac{51}{2}$ and not $5\frac{1}{2}$

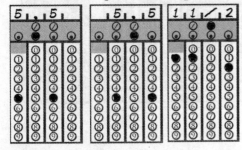

NOTE: Each of these is an acceptable way of gridding the answer

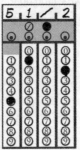

NOTE: Do not grid like this (51/2) because that will be graded as $\frac{51}{2}$ and not $5\frac{1}{2}$

Sample Question 9—Percentages

9. A bookshelf holds 14 books with green covers and 18 books with red covers. If 5 of the books with green covers have gold lettering and 4 of the books with red covers have gold lettering, what percent, to the nearest unit, of the total number of books have gold lettering?

Explanation:

Tests: Percentages

14 books with green covers + 18 books with red covers = 32 books total
5 books with green covers + 4 books with red covers = 9 books with gold lettering

Total books = 32 and Gold letter = 9

9 books with gold lettering ÷ 32 books total $= \frac{9}{32} = .28 = 28\%$

This question asks "What PERCENT to the nearest unit…"
The answer is 28% not .28 (even though .28 is another way to write it, they asked for the actual percent.) If you were to grid .28, that would mean .28 of a single percent.

Answer: Grid-in   28 **not** .28

> **NOTE:** Do **not** grid like this .28 because that will be graded as .28 *percent or* .28% and not 28%

You can grid 28% any of the three ways below

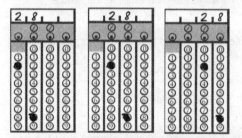

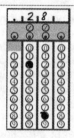

Sample Question 10—Averages

Grove Number	Average Number of Oranges per Tree
Grove 1	23
Grove 2	47
Grove 3	36
Grove 4	61

10. According to the chart above, what is the average number of oranges per tree for all 4 groves combined? (Round to the nearest integer)

Explanation:

Tests: Averages, Integers, Rounding

This problem requires an understanding of averages and it requires an understanding of the term "integer"
Average (Mean): In general the average of a set of numbers is the sum of all the terms divided by the total number of terms.
Substitute what we know: Grove 1 = 23 oranges, **Grove 2** = 47 oranges
Grove 3 = 36 oranges, **Grove 4** = 61 oranges

$$Average = \frac{x_1 + x_2 + x_3 + x_4}{n}$$

$Average = \frac{x_1+x_2+x_3+x_4}{n}$ **Becomes:** $\frac{23+47+36+61}{4} = 41.75 = 42$ *oranges per tree for all groves combined*

Integers: Whole numbers which are negative, zero or positive (-3,0,3)   In our case 41.75 is not an integer because integers are whole numbers. The question tells us to "Round to the nearest integer"

Rounding: We round numbers up or down depending on the fraction (or decimal) .50 or higher you round up, .49 or lower you round down. In this case we have .75, so we round up to the next higher number which is 42

Answer: Grid-in 42 (any of the following will be accepted)

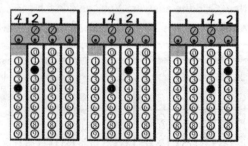

Sample Question 11—powers

11. If $6^{2^x} = 6^{4^2}$ what is the value of x?

Explanation:

Tests: Powers, Base, Exponents, Solve for 1 Variable, square root

Base: The big number or letter. **Example:** x^2 (x is the base)   **Exponent:** Little number or letter. **Example:** x^2 (2 is the exponent)   We have two terms in the equation:

Term 1: 6^{2^x} $Base_1 = 6$ $Exponent_1 = 2$ and $Base_2 = 2$ $Exponent_2 = x$

Term 2: 6^{4^2} $Base_1 = 6$, $Exponent_1 = 4$ and $Base_2 = 4$, $Exponent_2 = 2$

Notice that the first exponent in each term is also the base for the next level. In the first term, 2 is both the exponent for 6 and the base for x. In the second term, 4 is both the exponent for 6 and the base for 2.

Eliminate similar bases: Eliminate the base of 6 from both sides of the equation. (if $5^3 = 5^3$ then 3 = 3)

The easiest way to solve this problem is to realize that 6 is the $base_1$ for both terms. Since it is equal, we can eliminate it.

Like this: $6^{2^x} = 6^{4^2}$

Eliminate the same base of 6, becomes: $2^x = 4^2$ Multiply $2^x = 16$ Two raised to what power equals 16?

$2^x = 16$ same as $2 \cdot 2 \cdot 2 \cdot 2 = 16$

$2^4 = 16$ **Therefore** $x = 4$

Another Way

Exponents Raised by Exponents: When you have one exponent inside a set of parenthesis and another exponent outside the parentheses, simply multiply the exponents together. **Example:** $(c^2)^3 = c^{(2 \cdot 3)} = c^6$

$6^{2^x} = 6^{4^2}$ **Becomes** $6^{2x} = 6^{(4*2)}$ **Becomes** $6^{2x} = 6^8$

Now we have the same base of 6 so we can eliminate it. $2x = 8$ OR $x = 4$

Another Way: Multiply everything
We could also just multiply everything and use the calculator.

Start with the second term: 6^{4^2} Becomes $6^4 = 6 * 6 * 6 * 6$ **Becomes** $36 * 36 = 1296$

Therefore $6^4 = 1,296$

Now square that number: $1296^2 = 1,679,616$ **SO** The 2nd term is 1,679,616

Now set first term equal to 2nd term: $6^{2^x} = 1,679,616$

Multiply the first part of the first term: $6^2 = 36$

Now we know: $36^x = 1,679,616$

The easiest way is to use your calculator and start multiplying 36 by 36 and see how many times it takes to arrive at 1,679,616

$36 * 36 * 36 * 36 = 1,679,616$, So $36^4 = 1,679,616$, Therefore $x = 4$ **Anyway you try it, x will always be 4**

Answer: Grid-in 4 (any of the following will work)

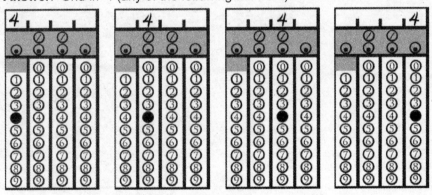

CONGRATULATIONS!!!
You Have Completed The Question-Type Workshop!

Take a break before moving on to the next section.

Problem Solving Index

Reading Workbook
Table of Contents

This material corresponds to the Virtual Classroom Instructions in the
PowerPrep DVD/Internet/iApp **for Critical Reading**

Virtual Classroom

182

Critical Reading
Part 1: SAT Overview & Directions

Classroom> Reading>Overview & Directions

This material corresponds to the Virtual Classroom Instructions in the
PowerPrep DVD/Internet/iApp for Reading

Virtual Classroom

Important Abbreviations
These abbreviations are used throughout the program

POE: Process of Elimination
SARR: Synthesize, Analyze, Reduce, and Restate (has to do with Logical Reasoning)
AC: Answer Choice
QS: Question Stem
LOD: Level of Difficulty

Example Question: What is the least common multiple of 3, 4, and 7? (**This is the call of the question or Question Stem "QS"**)

These are Answer Choices "AC" A, B, C, D, E

   (A)   12
   (B)   21
   (C)   28
   (D)   48
   (E)   84

Part 1: SAT Overview & Directions

SAT General Information Critical Reading

Time: 70 min (two 25 min sections and one 20 min section)
Sills Tested: Critical reading and sentence-level reading. Question Types: Reading Comprehension and sentence completion and paragraph-length critical reading-
Scoring: 200 to 800

The critical reading section, formerly known as the verbal section, includes short as well as long reading passages. Questions can be based on one, or sometimes two, reading passages. Some questions are not based on reading passages, but ask you to complete sentences.

There are two types of Multiple-Choice Critical Reading Questions:
- Sentence Completions
- Passage-based Reading

With attribution to SAT, ETS, and College Board

Sample Passage & Questions

The reading questions on the SAT measure a student's ability to read and think carefully about several different passages ranging in length from about 100 to about 850 words. Passages are taken from a variety of fields, including the humanities, social studies, natural sciences, and literary fiction. They vary in style and can include narrative, argumentative, and expository elements. Some selections consist of a pair of related passages on a shared issue or theme that you are asked to compare and contrast.

The following kinds of questions may be asked about a passage:

- **Vocabulary in Context**: These questions ask you to determine the meanings of words from their context in the reading passage.

- **Literal Comprehension**: These questions assess your understanding of significant information directly stated in the passage.

- **Extended Reasoning:** These questions measure your ability to synthesize and analyze information as well as to evaluate the assumptions made and the techniques used by the author. Most of the reading questions fall into this category. You may be asked to identify cause and effect, make inferences, recognize a main idea or an author's tone, and follow the logic of an analogy or an argument.

Approaching Passage-based Reading: Below are samples of the kind of reading passages and questions that may appear on your test. For each set of sample materials, you should:
- read the passage carefully,
- decide on the best answer to each question, and then
- read the explanation for the correct answer.

Directions: The passages below are followed by questions based on their content; questions following a pair of related passages may also be based on the relationship between the paired passages. Answer the questions on the basis of what is stated or implied in the passages and in any introductory material that may be provided.
The questions below are based on the following passage.

	"The rock was still wet. The animal was glistening, like it was still swimming," recalls Hou Xianguang. Hou discovered the
Line 5	unusual fossil while surveying rocks as a paleontology graduate student in 1984, near the Chinese town of Chengjiang. "My teachers always talked about the Burgess Shale
Line 10	animals. It looked like one of them.
	My hands began to shake." Hou had indeed found a Naraoia like those from Canada. However, Hou's animal was 15 million years
Line 15	older than its Canadian relatives.

Some of the reading passages in the SAT are as short as a paragraph or two, about 100 words in length. You will also find one or more pairs of related short passages in each edition of the test. Such material can be followed by two to five questions that measure the same kinds of reading skills as are measured by the questions following longer passages.

Questions

Some questions ask you to recognize the meaning of a word as it is used in the context of the passage.

Question 1:

In line 5, "surveying" most nearly means

(A) calculating the value of
(B) examining comprehensively
(C) determining the boundaries of
(D) polling randomly
(E) conducting a statistical study of

Explanation 1

The word "surveying" has a number of meanings, several of which are included in the choices above. In the context of this passage, however, only (B) makes sense. A student in the field of "paleontology" is one who studies prehistoric life as recorded in fossil remains. One of the activities of such a student would be to examine rocks carefully and "comprehensively" while looking for fossils.

(A), (C), and (E) are incorrect because someone who studies fossils would not calculate the "value" of rocks, or determine the "boundaries" of rocks, or conduct a "statistical study" of rocks.

(D) is wrong because "polling" rocks makes no sense at all.

You may be asked to make an inference or draw a conclusion about a statement made in the passage.
Correct answer: (B)

Question 2:

It can be inferred that Hou Xianguang's "hands began to shake" (line 11) because he was
(A) afraid that he might lose the fossil
(B) worried about the implications of his finding
(C) concerned that he might not get credit for his work
(D) uncertain about the authenticity of the fossil
(E) excited about the magnitude of his discovery

Explanation 2

In the passage, Hou states that the fossil that he found "looked like" certain other fossils that his "teacher always talked about." He understands almost immediately, therefore, the significance of what he has found, and so (E) is the correct answer: Hou's hands were shaking because he was "excited about the magnitude of his discovery."

(A) is wrong because there is no suggestion that Hou was "afraid that he might lose the fossil."
(B) and (C) are wrong because Hou was not "worried about" his discovery or "concerned that he might not get credit." The passage indicates only that Hou recognized that he had found something valuable.
(D) is wrong because Hou's immediate reaction is that he thinks he has found an important fossil. The first two sentences of the passage dramatize the discovery; it is Hou's excitement that causes him to tremble, not his uncertainty.
Correct answer: (E)

With attribution to SAT, ETS, and College Board

Approaches to the Critical Reading Section

- Work on sentence completion questions first. They take less time to answer than the passage-based reading questions.
- The difficulty of sentence completion questions increases as you answer them in order.
- Reading questions do not increase in difficulty from easy to hard. Instead, they follow the logic of the passage.
- The information you need to answer each reading question is always in the passage(s). Reading carefully is the key to finding the correct answer. Don't be misled by an answer that looks correct but is not supported by the actual text of the passage(s).
- Reading questions often include line numbers to help direct you to the relevant part(s) of the passage. If one word or more is quoted exactly from the passage, the line number(s) where that quotation can be found will appear in the test question. You may have to read some of the passage before or after the quoted word(s), however, in order to find support for the best answer to the question.
- Do not jump from passage to passage. Stay with a passage until you have answered as many questions as you can before you proceed to the next passage.
- If you don't know what a word means in a sentence completion or reading passage, consider related words, familiar sayings and phrases, roots, prefixes, and suffixes. Have you ever heard or seen a word that may be related to it?
- In your test booklet, mark each question you don't answer so that you can easily go back to it later if you have time.
- Remember that all questions are worth the same number of points regardless of the type or difficulty.

With attribution to SAT, ETS, and College Board

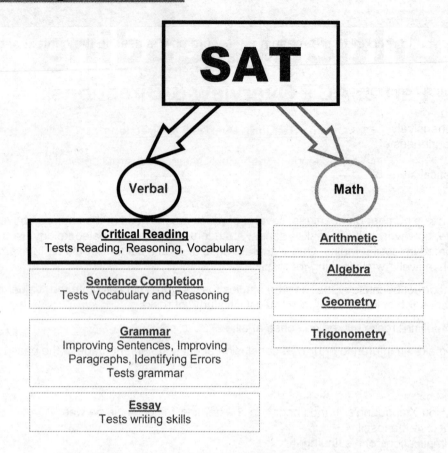

More about "Critical Reading"

48 Critical Reading Questions 70 minutes.

Four Passages—
- ♦ Two short (100-450 words)
- ♦ One long—800 to 850 words
- ♦ One Compare and Contrast—consists of two passages in one (about 800 words)

Critical Reading

Part 2: ACT Overview & Directions

Classroom> Reading>Overview & Directions

This material corresponds to the Virtual Classroom Instructions in the
PowerPrep DVD/Internet/iApp for Reading

Virtual Classroom

Important Abbreviations
These abbreviations are used throughout the program

POE: Process of Elimination
SARR: Synthesize, Analyze, Reduce, and Restate (has to do with Logical Reasoning)
AC: Answer Choice
QS: Question Stem
LOD: Level of Difficulty

Example Question: What is the least common multiple of 3, 4, and 7? **(This is the call of the question or Question Stem "QS")**

These are Answer Choices "AC" A, B, C, D, E

  (A) 12
  (B) 21
  (C) 28
  (D) 48
  (E) 84

Part 2: ACT Overview & Directions

ACT Reading Test Description

The Reading Test is a 40-question, 35-minute test that measures your reading comprehension. You're asked to read four passages and answer questions that show your understanding of:

- what is directly stated
- statements with implied meanings

Specifically, questions will ask you to use referring and reasoning skills to:

- determine main ideas
- locate and interpret significant details
- understand sequences of events
- make comparisons
- comprehend cause-effect relationships
- determine the meaning of context-dependent words, phrases, and statements
- draw generalizations
- analyze the author's or narrator's voice and method

The test comprises four prose passages that are representative of the level and kinds of reading required in first-year college courses; passages on topics in social studies, natural sciences, fiction, and the humanities are included.

Each passage is accompanied by a set of multiple-choice test questions. These questions do not test the rote recall of facts from outside the passage, isolated vocabulary items, or rules of formal logic. Instead, the test focuses on the complementary and supportive skills that readers must use in studying written materials across a range of subject areas.

With attribution to www.act.org

The Reading Test is based on four types of reading selections: social studies, natural sciences, prose fiction, and humanities. The Social Studies/Sciences subscore is based on the questions on the social studies and natural sciences passages, and the Arts/Literature subscore is based on the questions on the prose fiction and humanities passages.

- **Social Studies (25%).** Questions in this category are based on passages in the content areas of anthropology, archaeology, biography, business, economics, education, geography, history, political science, psychology, and sociology.
- **Natural Sciences (25%).** Questions in this category are based on passages in the content areas of anatomy, astronomy, biology, botany, chemistry, ecology, geology, medicine, meteorology, microbiology, natural history, physiology, physics, technology, and zoology.
- **Prose Fiction (25%).** Questions in this category are based on intact short stories or excerpts from short stories or novels.
- **Humanities (25%).** Questions in this category are based on passages from memoirs and personal essays and in the content areas of architecture, art, dance, ethics, film, language, literary criticism, music, philosophy, radio, television, and theater.

Reading Sample Questions

Select the letter choices to determine if you have the correct answer and for question explanations.
An actual ACT Reading Test contains 40 questions to be answered in 35 minutes.

Directions:

The passage in this test is followed by several questions. After reading the passage, choose the best answer to each question and fill in the corresponding oval on your answer document. You may refer to the passage as often as necessary.

Passage

Prose Fiction:

This passage is adapted from Elizabeth Bishop's short story "The Housekeeper" (©1984 by Alice Methfessel).

      Outside, the rain continued to run down the
screened windows of Mrs. Sennett's little Cape Cod
cottage. The long weeds and grass that composed the
front yard dripped against the blurred background of
5 the bay, where the water was almost the color of the
grass. Mrs. Sennett's five charges were vigorously
playing house in the dining room. (In the wintertime,
Mrs. Sennett was housekeeper for a Mr. Curley, in
Boston, and during the summers the Curley children

10   boarded with her on the Cape.)
      My expression must have changed. "Are those
      children making too much noise?" Mrs. Sennett
      demanded, a sort of wave going over her that might
      mark the beginning of her getting up out of her chair. I
15   shook my head no, and gave her a little push on the
      shoulder to keep her seated. Mrs. Sennett was almost
      stone-deaf and had been for a long time, but she could
      read lips. You could talk to her without making any
      sound yourself, if you wanted to, and she more than
20   kept up her side of the conversation in a loud, rusty
      voice that dropped weirdly every now and then into a
      whisper. She adored talking.
      To look at Mrs. Sennett made me think of eigh-
      teenth-century England and its literary figures. Her hair
25   must have been sadly thin, because she always wore,
      indoors and out, either a hat or a sort of turban, and
      sometimes she wore both. The rims of her eyes were
      dark; she looked very ill.
      Mrs. Sennett and I continued talking. She said she
30   really didn't think she'd stay with the children another
      winter. Their father wanted her to, but it was too much
      for her. She wanted to stay right here in the cottage.
      The afternoon was getting along, and I finally left
      because I knew that at four o'clock Mrs. Sennett's "sit
35   down" was over and she started to get supper. At six
      o'clock, from my nearby cottage, I saw Theresa coming
      through the rain with a shawl over her head. She was
      bringing me a six-inch-square piece of spicecake, still
      hot from the oven and kept warm between two soup
40   plates.
      A few days later I learned from the twins, who
      brought over gifts of firewood and blackberries, that
      their father was coming the next morning, bringing
      their aunt and her husband and their cousin. Mrs.
45   Sennett had promised to take them all on a picnic at the
      pond some pleasant day.
      On the fourth day of their visit, Xavier arrived
      with a note. It was from Mrs. Sennett, written in blue
      ink, in a large, serene, ornamented hand, on linen-finish
50   paper:
           . . . Tomorrow is the last day Mr. Curley has and
           the Children all wanted the Picnic so much. The Men
           can walk to the Pond but it is too far for the Children. I
           see your Friend has a car and I hate to ask this but
55   could you possibly drive us to the Pond tomorrow
           morning? . . .
           Very sincerely yours,
           Carmen Sennett
      After the picnic, Mrs. Sennett's presents to me
60   were numberless. It was almost time for the children to
      go back to school in South Boston. Mrs. Sennett
      insisted that she was not going; their father was coming
      down again to get them and she was just going to stay.
      He would have to get another housekeeper. She said
65   this over and over to me, loudly, and her turbans and
      kerchiefs grew more and more distrait.
      One evening, Mary came to call on me and we sat
      on an old table in the back yard to watch the sunset.
      "Papa came today," she said, "and we've got to go

70 back day after tomorrow."
    "Is Mrs. Sennett going to stay here?"
    "She said at supper she was. She said this time she
    really was, because she'd said that last year and came
    back, but now she means it."
75 I said, "Oh dear," scarcely knowing which side I
    was on.
    "It was awful at supper. I cried and cried."
    "Did Theresa cry?"
    "Oh, we all cried. Papa cried, too. We always do."
80 "But don't you think Mrs. Sennett needs a rest?"
    "Yes, but I think she'll come, though. Papa told
    her he'd cry every single night at supper if she didn't,
    and then we all *did*."
    The next day I heard that Mrs. Sennett was going
85 back with them just to "help settle." She came over the
    following morning to say goodbye, supported by all
    five children. She was wearing her traveling hat of
    black satin and black straw, with sequins. High and
    somber, above her ravaged face, it had quite a Spanish-
90 grandee air.
    "This isn't really goodbye," she said. "I'll be back
    as soon as I get these bad, noisy children off my
    hands."
    But the children hung on to her skirt and tugged at
95 her sleeves, shaking their heads frantically, silently
    saying, *"No! No! No!"* to her with their puckered-up
    mouths.

Questions 1-10

1. According to the narrator, Mrs. Sennett wears a hat because she:
   A. is often outside.
   B. wants to look like a literary figure.
   C. has thin hair.
   D. has unique taste in clothing.

2. Considering the events of the entire passage, it is most reasonable to infer that Mrs. Sennett calls the children bad (line 92) because she:
   F. is bothered by the noise they are making.
   G. doesn't like them hanging on her skirt.
   H. doesn't want to reveal her affection for them.
   J. is angry that they never do what she tells them.

3. Considering how Mrs. Sennett is portrayed in the passage, it is most reasonable to infer that the word *ravaged*, as it is used in line 89, most nearly means that her face reveals:
   A. irritation and annoyance.
   B. resentfulness and anger.
   C. age and fatigue.
   D. enthusiasm and excitement.

4. What is the main insight suggested by the conversation in lines 69-83?
   F. The Curley family cries to manipulate Mrs. Sennett into doing what they want.
   G. The narrator regrets that she is not going to Boston and is a little jealous of Mrs. Sennett.
   H. Mrs. Sennett is happy to leave the Curley family because they are always whining and crying.
   J. Mrs. Sennett intends to return to the Cape soon because she has discovered that they have been manipulating and taking advantage of her.

5. Which of the following does the passage suggest is the result of Mrs. Sennett's loss of hearing?
   A. She is often frustrated and short-tempered.
   B. She can lip-read.
   C. She dislikes conversation.
   D. She is a shy and lonely woman.

6. Given the evidence provided throughout the passage, the children probably silently mouth the word "no" (lines 94-97) because:
   F. Mrs. Sennett has just called them bad, noisy children, and they are defending themselves.
   G. they do not want to leave the Cape before the summer is over and are protesting.
   H. they are letting the narrator know that Mrs. Sennett is thinking about returning to the Cape.
   J. they are continuing their battle against Mrs. Sennett's intention to return to the Cape.

7. It is reasonable to infer from the passage that Mrs. Sennett asked "Are those children making too much noise?" (lines 11-12) because Mrs. Sennett:

  A. concerns herself about the well-being of others.
  B. wishes to change the subject to literary figures.
  C. cannot supervise the children without the narrator.
  D. is bothered by the noise the children make.

8. The details and events in the passage suggest that the friendship between the narrator and Mrs. Sennett would most accurately be described as:

  F. stimulating, marked by a shared love of eccentric adventures.
  G. indifferent, marked by occasional insensitivity to the needs of the other.
  H. considerate, notable for the friends' exchange of favors.
  J. emotional, based on the friends' long commitment to share their burdens with one another.

9. As it is used in line 3, the word *composed* most nearly means:

  A. contented.
  B. unexcited.
  C. satisfied.
  D. constituted.

10. At what point does Mr. Curley cry at the supper table?

  F. Before Mary and the narrator sit and watch the sunset
  G. Before Mrs. Sennett tells the narrator she doubts she will stay another winter with the children
  H. Before the children spend a rainy afternoon playing house in the dining room
  J. After the narrator learns that Mrs. Sennett will return to Boston

With attribution to www.act.org

Reading Answer Key to Sample Questions

1. The best answer is C
Lines 24-25 express the narrator's opinion that "Her hair must have been sadly thin," and other evidence in support of this view appears in the third paragraph (lines 23-28). While the narrator thinks of literary figures (line 24), there is no indication that Mrs. Sennett wears a hat for this reason, so B is a choice not supported by the passage. She wears a hat all the time, "indoors and out," which rules out A. There is no evidence that she has unique taste in clothing, which blocks D as a good answer.

2. The best answer is H
It is clear from the passage that Mrs. Sennett has affection for the children; we know that while she needs to and would rather rest, she has returned with the children before, and will do so again now. While the children do hang onto her skirt, there is no indication that Mrs. Sennett is bothered by this (G). Because Mrs. Sennett is "almost stone-deaf" (lines 16-7), she would not be disturbed by their noise, which rules out F. G and J are choices contradicted by Mrs. Sennett's apparent affection for the children, and by her generous personality; th1ere is no evidence to suggest that the children are disobedient or that their behavior bothers her.

3. The best answer is C
We know that Mrs. Sennett is old, looked ill (line 28), and is tired (lines 31-32). There is no indication that Mrs. Sennett feels annoyance (A) or anger (B); she has agreed to go, and must know that she is wanted. D is too strong; while she is willing, she probably is not "enthusiastic" about going. Her words in lines 91-93 do not show enthusiasm.

4. The best answer is F
There are indications provided by lines 79 and 81-83 that the Curleys cry on cue to get what they want. There is no evidence in the passage that Mrs. Sennett is aware of their manipulation, which rules out J. Neither is there any evidence available to support G or H.

5. The best answer is B
The key is clearly supported by lines 16-18. All of the other foils are contradicted by the passage: C by line 22, and A and D by her personality as it is revealed over the course of the passage.

6. The best answer is J
The last 30+ lines of the passage focus on this issue. H is simply not true: the children are speaking to Mrs. Sennett, not the narrator. There is no indication that they are reluctant to leave, which rules out G. F can be eliminated because the children do not seem offended by Mrs. Sennett's words; it is more likely that they are merely continuing their manipulative behavior (see lines 79, 81-83).

7. The best answer is A
This choice is consistent with Mrs. Sennett's generous personality, and Mrs. Sennett's action comes in direct reaction to the narrator's change of expression (line 11). There is no evidence anywhere in the passage in support of B; C is obviously not true (she has performed her duties to the Curleys' satisfaction); and there is never any evidence that Mrs. Sennett is bothered by the noise the children make--she is "almost stone-deaf," after all, which rules out D.

8. The best answer is H
Both characters are considerate and exchange favors: the narrator lends Mrs. Sennett the car (lines 51-56) and Mrs. Sennett gives the narrator many presents (lines 59-60). There is no indication that their relationship has been anything but a relatively short-term, neighborly friendship, which makes both F and J choices that are not supported by the passage. G is contradicted by examples of both characters' sensitivity to the other (lines 11-16, 80).

9. The best answer is D
A, B, and C do not make sense in the context of the sentence.

10. The best answer is F
Mary tells the narrator of this earlier event as they sit watching the sunset (lines 67-68). Mrs. Sennett had told the narrator of her intentions before Mr. Curley even arrived (lines 61-63), so G cannot be correct. There is no evidence in the passage that supports H, which makes it implausible. The narrator learns of Mrs. Sennett's plans to return to Boston the next day, which rules out J.

ACT Reading Review

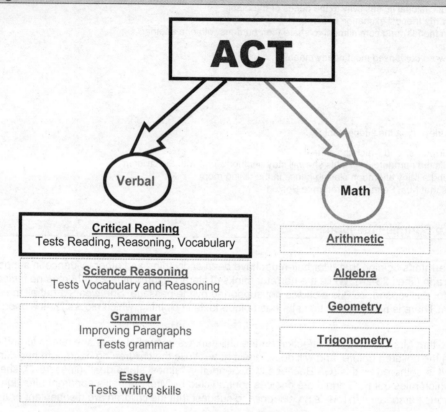

More about "Critical Reading"

There are four reading passages in the categories of fiction, humanities, social science, and natural science with 10 questions about each passage.

The Reading Test is a 40-question, 35-minute test that measures your reading comprehension. You're asked to read four passages and answer questions that show your understanding of:
   • What is directly stated
   • Statements with implied meanings

Critical Reading

Part 3: Instruction

Virtual Classroom> Reading>Instruction

This material corresponds to the SAT and ACT Virtual Classroom Instructions in the
PowerPrep DVD/Internet/iApp for Reading

Virtual Classroom

Important Abbreviations
These abbreviations are used throughout the program

POE: Process of Elimination
SARR: Synthesize, Analyze, Reduce, and Restate (has to do with Logical Reasoning)
AC: Answer Choice
QS: Question Stem
LOD: Level of Difficulty

Example Question: What is the least common multiple of 3, 4, and 7? **(This is the call of the question or Question Stem "QS")**

These are Answer Choices "AC" A, B, C, D, E

   (A)   12
   (B)   21
   (C)   28
   (D)   48
   (E)   84

Part 3: Instruction

Quick Overview

Here's what the folks who write the exam say about the Reading Assessment (Reading Comprehension or Critical Reading):

"Critical Reading does not depend on knowledge you already have but on your ability to understand and make sense of the information given to you in the passages... A few questions in each test will ask you to demonstrate that you have understood what the author is saying... And a few other questions will ask you to figure out the meaning of a word as it is used in the passage. But the great majority of the Critical Reading questions will require "extended reasoning." You'll have to do more than just absorb information and then recognize a restatement of it. You'll have to be an active reader and think carefully about what you're reading.

Whatever you call it—it tests the same skill—ability to **analyze** written text.

Reading Comprehension or Critical Reading tests two basic skill sets:

1. Vocabulary—substantive (defined content) **2. Analytical Reading**—your ability to understand what you read

Good News! ***They tell you what kind of passage you are reading.***
- Prose Fiction (personal short stories)
- Humanities (art, music, dance, film etc.)
- Social Studies (economics, political science, history, business)
- Natural Science (astronomy, biology, chemistry, medicine, physics)

DIRECTIONS: The passage below is followed b y questions based on its content. Answer the questions on the basis of what is stated or implied in the passage and in any introductory material that may be provided.

The Directions: Read them once and don't waste any time with them on the test.

Helpful Hints

Questions come in EASY, MEDIUM and DIFFICULT levels.

All questions worth same value—one point. Don't waste time on questions you find too difficult. You don't want to run out of time when there are easy questions waiting to be answered.

Eliminate as many wrong Answer Choices as you can and then guess between those that are left.

Try not to leave any blanks—but remember there is a slight penalty that amounts to a fraction of a point for wrong answers. They say the small penalty is to compensate for random guessing—that's guessing without any clue which Answer is Correct.

Check your AC and bubbles often.

The Seven Types of CR Questions

1. Main idea or Primary purpose 2. Identify important detail. 3. Comparisons between characters and ideas 4. Cause and effect 5. Generalizations about event or characters 6. Inferences about events, ideas, or characters 7. Point of view
They can be reduced to two (2) main categories: 1. Explicit 2. Inference

Form of Question	Level of Information Referred To	Frequency (number/percent)
Main Idea	Level 1 only	1.5 questions or 3.75%
Purpose	Level 2 and 3	6.4 questions or 16%
Interpretation	Level 3	1.7 questions or 4.25%
Summary	Levels 2 & 3	.8 questions or 2%
Explicit	Levels 1, 2 & 3	3.7 questions or 9.25%
Word Meaning	Level 3	4 questions or 10%
Inference	Levels 1, 2, 3	16.8 questions or 42%
Technique	Levels 1, 2, 3	1.7 questions or 4.25 %
For Two (2) Passage Only--all of the above plus the following:		
Compare	2 passage only	2.1 questions or 5.25%
Contrast	2 passage only	.9 questions or 2.25 %
Reaction	2 passage only	.2 questions or .5%
Tone	2 passage only	.1 questions or .25%
Total		40 Questions

Points of Interest

1. **Main Idea and Purpose Questions : About 20% or 8 questions**
2. **Inference questions :** 42% or 17 questions
3. **Explicit questions :** 20% or 8 questions
4. **Compare and Contrast :** 8% or 3 questions

So far that's 90% of the test or 36 questions of the 40

The remaining 4 questions will come from: Interpretation, Summation, Technique, Reaction, Tone etc

Other Question Types

Vocabulary in Context: These ask you to determine the meanings of words from their context in the reading passage.

Literal Comprehension: These assess your understanding of significant information directly stated in the passage.

Extended Reasoning: These measure your ability to synthesize and analyze information as well as to evaluate the assumptions made and the techniques used by the author. Most of the reading questions fall into this category. You may be asked to identify cause and effect, make inferences, recognize a main idea or an author's tone, and follow the logic of an analogy or an argument.

Passages taken from: Prose Fiction, Humanities, Social Studies, Natural Science

Further points of Interest: 1. 8 of the 40 questions are EXPLICIT   2. The remaining 32 questions ARE INFERENCE

Review

☑ 3 graded sections
☑ Four (4) passages
☑ Total about 80 lines per passage
☑ Average about 10 questions per passage
☑ 40 total questions

BOTTOM LINE: Total of 320 lines of text (1600 words) and 40 questions

The Details

Critical Reading is Detective Work:

 We all filter and analyze information all day long, every day. It does not matter where the information comes from—we take in information through all of our senses 24-7-365.

As we take in information, whether through our eyes or ears or any of our senses, we organize and apply meaning to the information by taking that information through our individual filters—sometimes called a frame of reference.

This filter is unique to each of us and it is nothing more than the sum total of all of our experiences. Whether we are aware of the process or not, all day long every day we analyze a constant stream of information.

For our purposes, we will refer to the filtering process as SARRing. On the exam you will take the information you read and then SARR it through your own analytical system which creates your understanding. How well you understand the information will depend on the amount and quality of the SARRing that goes on in your own mind.

In the image below you can see the **"SARR"** situated in the middle. The information is represented by the "blah, blah, blah". Understanding is dependent on the quality of the SARRing. or filtering

The more you refine and improve your ability to **Simplify, Analyze, Reduce, and Restate**, the more questions you'll answer correctly on the exam.

SARR (**S**implify **A**nalyze **R**educe **R**estate)

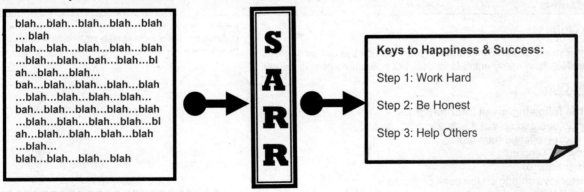

This diagram shows what happens when you SARR.
   The professor talks..blah, blah, blah, or
   You read words in a text book…blah, blah, blah, or
   You read words on the exam…blah, blah, blah

SARRing   **S**IMPLIFY **A**NALYZE **R**EDUCE **R**ESTATE

Distracters Generally

In addition to your ability to analyze or SARR, there are factors that get in the way of understanding. We will call these "Distracters".

Distracter can be many things. In general, they are anything that gets in the way of your understanding. Some distracters you won't be able to control on exam day. But some distracters can be overcome. A distracter could be external: the noise of the traffic outside the exam room window that "distracts" you and takes your mind away from what you are doing. Distracters can be internal—hunger pains or thoughts about anything not related to the material. In addition to these kinds of distracters, the people who make the exam also include written distracters in the questions. These are intended to draw your attention away from the important or correct information.

The following are some fun examples that tests your SARRing.
(You won't have actual questions like these on the exam, but some of the skills used are the same).

Paris Quiz

What does this say?

PARIS IN THE
THE SPRING

Did you get: Paris in the Spring

> **Look closer:** it says "Paris in **THE** **THE** Spring

Distracters—here, the shape of the lines in the triangle distract. The lines of the triangle move your eyes down so you focus on the last line that says, "The Spring"…your eyes don't want to move back up the phrase because the lines subconsciously push your eyes down. So the physical shape of the triangle "**distracts**" from what it actually says—**Paris in the the Spring**

Your eye misses the double "The The" because the lines force your eyes down.

In the exam, you will encounter many distracters that push your reasoning towards or away from something. The test writers are expert at misdirection.

The F Quiz

Count the number of F's

FINISHED FILES ARE THE RESULT OF YEARS OF FRANTIC EFFORT OF NFORTUNATE OFFICERS.

Finished **f**iles are the result o**f** years o**f** **f**rantic e**ff**ort o**f** un**f**ortunate o**ff**icers.

> **Answer: 11**

Verbal Distracters

The Moses Quiz

> **Answer**: Moses didn't take any. It was Noah.

Given: How many of each animal did Moses take on the ark with him?
Distracter: Not, how many animals in total, but how many of each kind?

The Rooster Quiz

Assume the following given information:
   A barn is oriented so that it is facing north and south
   A 60 degree pitched barn roof
   Exactly 12:00 noon
   Summer equinox
   A rooster lays an egg on the peak of that roof…
Q: Will it roll left or right (east or west) off the peak?

> **Answer**: Roosters don't lay eggs, hens do.

Answer: WEEDING - Distracter (ROOSTER)

"Who Can I Marry" Quiz

Q: In the United States, is it legal for a man to marry his widow's sister?

Analysis: work backwards from the inside out to see what it really is saying
KEY: What does widow mean? A widow is a woman whose husband has died.

> **Answer**: Who is his widow - His wife - if and only if he is already dead. So the question really asks: Can a dead man marry his living wife's sister?

NOTE: You won't actually see questions like these on the exam. However, the analytical skills they require to answer is very similar to the skills you must use.

General Approach

Process of Elimination: This approach is different from math or vocabulary where there is a "right" answer. In Critical Reading, usually you are not looking for the "right" answer as much as eliminating Answer Choices (AC's) that for some reason are wrong (cannot be true) until you are left with one AC that you cannot eliminate and therefore, is the most correct or best AC.

There are two (2) major categories of questions:

1. **Explicit**—relates to specific detail of information provided in the passage.
2. **Inference**—requires you to logically extend information provided in the passage.

Also, Critical Reading requires that you become very familiar with both, **Process** and **Substance** of questions:
- **Process**—the way they ask the questions
- **Substance**— your ability to analyze critically, and carefully **the content of the question.**

POEing: In Answering a Critical Reading Question, you must eliminate each of the alternative AC's in an effort to locate the most correct AC. This approach differs dramatically from the approach you would use on a math problem, where you would work out the problem and then search the AC's for the "right" AC.

Good news: no knowledge of a particular subject is needed. The information necessary to answer every question is provided in the passage. You do not need outside understanding of the subject covered in the passage. In fact, outside information can become a distraction because you may unwittingly begin to rely on your "outside" knowledge.

Skill Improvement: The most important skill is **critically analyzing written text**. The length of the Passages ultimately is not relevant—you analyze information the same whether it comes in short, medium or long passages. Nevertheless, at this point, most of your practice in the Workshop and the Drills will be on Longer Passages because they promote more consistent detailed analysis. We can build and improve your analytical skills more efficiently with longer, more weighty passages.

You will read a passage and answer questions about the passage:

Question Categories

Explicit Questions: • Repeat facts contained in the passage. • Typically less difficult. • Less common.
Example: If the passage explained that the United States fought a war with England in 1812: An **explicit** fact question would be:

When was the war mentioned in the passage fought?

A. 1811
B. 1812
C. 1912
D. 1776
E. 1945

Inference Questions
- **More common**
- **More difficult**—answers come from logically extending information provided in the material—you'll have to think (analyze) rather than regurgitate information:

Example: When the author of the passage states:
"Even before the hot war and hostilities began in 1812, there were battles between the mother country and the colonies..."

He most likely meant:
○ Americans never accepted England as their "mother country".
○ The British Ambassador to the United States had offended the President, creating a cooling of the relationship between the two countries.
○ The British were boarding American merchant ships and impressing the sailors into England's military against their will.
○ The British were not allowing free trade of American made goods in England.
○ Even after America won the Revolutionary war of 1776, Britain continued to view America as her "colonies," which infuriated the President of the United States.
  Something within each AC makes it false, except one.

Number and Types of Questions

Two ways to look at the type of questions:
1. The **amount of the passage** they refer to:
2. The form of the question or the **type of information** the question deals with:

Amount of Information Referred to:

Level I: Questions that deal with the entire passage.
Level II: Questions that deal with an entire paragraph.
Level III: Questions that deal with a sentence, phrase or a word.

Form of the Question:
- ☑ Main Idea or Purpose
- ☑ Supporting Ideas
- ☑ Interpretation
- ☑ Inference
- ☑ Summary
- ☑ Application to New Information
- ☑ Explicit

- ☑ Structure Word Meaning (vocabulary)
- ☑ Technique
- ☑ Compare
- ☑ Contrast
- ☑ Reaction
- ☑ Tone

Points of Interest:

Main Idea and Purpose questions are the same kind focused at different amounts of information:
- Main Idea of entire passage.
- Purpose of a Paragraph or part of a paragraph.

Inference questions make up the largest group of questions:
- Which of the following assumptions…
- It can be inferred from the passage, or paragraph,…
- The author suggests
- The author implies
- The author…most probably to…
- Which of the following, if true would (strengthen, weaken…)

Explicit:
- The passage states:
- According to the passage:
- At line ___ the use of the word or phrase…means

Question Stems

Some questions cross over between categories, having elements of both **inference and explicit.** We want to familiarize you with the way the questions stems will look and how to get at the information the TEST MAKERS want to test. Do NOT memorize the question stems, because it won't help. Just take a few minutes to review these so you are familiar with them.

Level #1: Passage as a Whole

Main Idea:
- The passage serves primarily to...
- Which of the following titles best summarizes the content of the passage?
- The passage serves mainly to ...
- The passage is primarily concerned with...
- The passage is best described as...

Explicit Information:
- According to the passage...
- The _____ include all of the following except
- Which question about _____ is NOT answered in the passage?

Inference:
- The passage as a whole suggests ....
- The author's apparent assumption ....
- Which of the following _____ most likely agree
- For the author, the experience _____ can be best described as
- The primary motive...
- Which statement, if true, would most directly weaken the author's argument regarding…
- On the whole, the author's attitude toward _____ is one of...

Technique:
- In creating an impression _____ the author makes use of...
- Which of the following best describes the approach of Passage 1?
- Which _____ best describes the structure of the author's discussion in this passage?

LEVEL #2: Parts of Passage

Main Idea:
- In the 4th paragraph the author's most important point is that…
- The first paragraph primarily explores the contrast between...

Purpose:
- The author describes (event) in order to...
- The example in the last paragraph is used to illustrate how ...
- The first 2 paragraphs serve all of the following purposes except ...

Summarization Of Paragraph:
- Which statement _____ the author's argument in the last paragraph?

Explicit Information:
- According to the passage
- According to the author
- In the third paragraph, the author criticizes _____

Inference:
- The final paragraph suggest that the author probably believes _____
- The author implies that _____
- The author's reference to_____ to indicate _____
- In the second paragraph, the _____ is portrayed as exemplifying _____

Technique:
- The argumentative strategy _____ can best be described as _____
- In the fourth paragraph, the idea of telling a story is used as _____
- In the third paragraph, the narrator emphasizes _____
- In the last paragraph, the author is _____
- Which _____ best describes the relationship between the 4th and 5th paragraphs?
- How does the second paragraph function in relation to the first paragraph?
- The primary function of the second paragraph is to show that _____

Level #3: Words, Short Phrases

Purpose of Words/Lines:
- The author refers to _____ chiefly to illustrate the _____
- The author includes the detail of _____ primarily to emphasize _____
- In line 32, _____ the author uses the word _____ to emphasize _____
- The narrator most likely mentions _____ to suggest _____
- The author mentions _____ in order to _____
- The author presents _____ as an example of _____
- The description of _____ serves primarily to _____
- The effect of the sentence _____ is to _____
- The author uses the words _____ to express _____
- The author uses the term _____ in order to _____

Interpreting Quotes/Lines:
- Which could best be substituted for the words _____ without changing meaning
- The quotation in lines ☐can best be interpreted to mean
- The phrase _____ can be best interpreted
- The term _____ refers
- In lines 32-35 the _____ is characterized as

Summarization of Lines:
- The author's views ☐can best be summarized as which of the following
- Which best summarizes the idea
- Which example most accurately illustrates what is being described in lines
- Which statement best summarizes point made in lines

Explicit Information:
- The contrast mentioned in lines 32-36 specifically concerns the
- The author describes_____ primarily in terms of

Word Meaning:
- In line 32 , _____ means
- The author indicates that _____ differs from _____ in that
- In line 32, _____ most nearly means

Inference:
- Which does the author consider the best example of _____ mentioned in line
- The discussion of _____ suggests that she was
- It can be inferred
- In lines32-36 the author suggests
- If the claim made by _____ should turn out to be true, which of the following must also be true?
- The reference _____ in lines 32-36 differs from that in lines 15-18. in that the first reference is an example of
- The author's description suggests the author views them
- The author's attitude toward _____ is one of
- Which statement is a logical extension of the argument
- If the author had wished to explain
- The quotation in lines ☐most probably reflects the point of view of
- The terms _____ and _____ suggest the author would agree with which statement?

• Which statement, if true, would most effectively challenge the view of _____

Technique:
• In line 32-36 metaphorically compares _____ to
• In lines 32-36, the author is doing which of the following?
• The sentence beginning at line 32 the author does which of the following

Two Passages

Sometimes you will be asked to compare and contrast the content in two passages

All of the above, plus:

TONE:
• In comparison to the tone of P-1, the tone of P-2 is more

CONTRAST:
• The contrast between the two descriptions
• Unlike P-2, P-1 assumes
• Which point made in P-1 does the author of P-2 fail to address?

COMPARE:
• Both authors' discussion assume
• The two authors would most likely agree with which statement
• Both passages discuss
• Both passages indicate
•The authors of the two passages would apparently agree

REACTION:
• The author of P-2 would most likely respond _____ in P-1, by

Plan of Attack

General Process

Generally speaking the process has four (4) Steps:

1. Assimilate the Information: (Pre-Read & Read)

Methods of Reading:
• Skim.
• Read the question Stems—look for line numbers and mark those in the passage.
• Read the first and last paragraphs first.
• Read the first and last lines of each paragraph.
• Read the entire passage.

2. Analyze the Information (SARR)
• AC's.
• The first thing you have to understand is the QS.
• Equal parts Passage and AC.

3. Understand the Information (SARR)
• Passage
• QS
• AC's

4. Test Your Understanding (POE)
• The QS with AC's.

Two Important Tools (SARR & POE)

Tool 1
SARR
Simplify, Analyze, Reduce, and Restate
Constantly asking "So what's your point"

Tool 2
POE
Process Of Elimination
Search and Rescue

These two (2) tools work in tandem to answer every question.

Tool 1: SaRR

Which means, constantly asking: "So what's your point?" This is where the logic, analysis, reasoning, and thinking comes in.

It is important to critically read and understand:
* The QS—so you are answering the question being asked.
* Each AC –so you are answering the way you think you are.

An AC could contain factually accurate information, yet not be responsive to the QS. Each AC will be eliminated because of something it contains and you have to find it.

Tool 2: POE

As you analyze or SARR information, you use POE to answer questions. Every AC has something in it that makes it incorrect — except one. Use POE to eliminate all the MBF (must be false) answers until you get to the one remaining answer that you cannot eliminate. Remember, you are not looking for the Right Answer (like Math). You are looking for the AC that cannot be eliminated.

The CORRECT AC is the AC that is NOT wrong.

General Review

* All of the question appear at the start.   • The AC's appear as letters e.g., AC "A"...   • You can skip around and return to more difficult questions if need be.   • You can return to a question after you have answered it if you determine later that it may not be correct.

Once you leave a section and time expires, you cannot return to that section.   **Questions usually go from general to specific:**

> **Level 1** (questions about the entire passage)
> ⇓
> **Level II** (questions about paragraphs and parts of (paragraphs),
> ⇓
> **Level III** (questions about words or short phrases)

The test makers also tend to spread the questions out to cover some aspect from each part of the passage.   In other words, you won't get 6 questions from information in one paragraph.

Good News! All Questions Are of Equal Value!

Easy questions are worth the exact same as difficult questions—make sure you get the easy ones and the curve is created by the more difficult ones.

Spend more time on **SARRing**—outlining or filtering to be sure you understand.

Two Part Plan

How to answer a Critical Reading question: First, outline the reading material using the two step Outlining process and then answer the questions using the POE process explained below.

Two (2) Steps to Answer a Reading Question:
1. **Outline (SARR):** Pre-Read and Read to: Filter out non essential information and gain understanding
2. **Answer (POE)**—test your understanding

We will start by reviewing the Outlining Process (Don't be confused that each part of the process has two steps)
How to Answer a Critical Reading Question has two steps
1. Outline (Read and Pre-Read)
2. Answer

Also, Outlining has two steps (Pre-read and Read)

<u>**Step 1: Outline**</u>

1. **Pre-Read: creates context**
   * Find space in your booklet to make notes.
   * Paragraph by paragraph written summary using **SaRR**
   * Preview
   * First sentence, paragraph 1
   * First sentence, paragraph 2
   * First sentence, paragraph 3
   * QS 1st question

2. **Read**
   * Read the entire passage for understanding, **SaRR** ing as you go.
   * Take notes in the column.
   * Circle
   * Underline
   * Notes on free space in your booklet.
   * Arrows

- Abbreviations
- Full Summary, Analysis, Review Using **SARR**
  - Build on preview of Paragraph 1
  - Build on Preview of Paragraph 2
  - Build on Preview of Paragraph 3...

Outline Review: On the test, you have an average of about one (1) minute per question—The Outlining process may take half of your total available time or even more. Directed, focused time at the beginning—pays off in the end. Further if you are at the beginning of the section, you may wish to borrow time from future questions to be sure you start off strong. You can't short change the outlining process. The point is, you can't skim this stuff and expect to answer questions correctly.

BOTTOM LINE: Outlining and SARR ing takes time—but it is worth it.

Step 2: Answer POE SEARCH & RESCUE

1. **Carefully read and analyze the first QS :** Refer to your outline and the passage as necessary

2. **Carefully Read each AC:** Refer to your outline and the passage as necessary

3. **Answer**—Using POE develop a response to the QS

Eliminate AC's by finding the error or mistake that makes each one unacceptable—this may require a lot of scrolling and reviewing.

Note: Even though these steps are listed 1,2,3, they are happening almost simultaneously as you go.

Sample Template

The two step outline process

Step 1: Paragraph 1 (Review 1st sentence), **Paragraph 2 (**Review 1st sentence), **Paragraph 3** Review 1st sentence
Step 2: Paragraph 1 (Using SARR outline the paragraph), **Paragraph 2 (**Using SARR outline the paragraph)
   Paragraph 3 (Using SARR outline the paragraph)

Critical Reading Outlining Example "Entropy"

Now let's practice the skill of outlining written material. Read the following article on "Entropy"

Follow the Outlining Two step approach:
1. **Pre-Read:** Preview the first sentence of each paragraph
2. **Read:** dig into the content and SARR

Entropy

Entropy is a measure of the degree of disorder in a system—that is how much energy in the system has become so dispersed (usually as low-quality heat) that it is no longer available to do work. When we transfer energy from one type to another, we are changing the quality of the energy to do work.

Consider an old-school overhead projector for example. Electric energy is transformed to make the bulb shine. The energy conversion from electric energy to light is not perfect. That is, if 100 units of electrical energy from the power socket are put into the bulb, maybe only 50 units of energy units are emitted from the bulb as light. Were the other 50 units of energy lost? No. The law of energy transformations says that we can never destroy energy. So where did those other 50 units of energy go? They were converted to heat energy and sent into the environment (the classroom in our example).

Entropy measures a system's efficiency. If 100 units of energy are put into a system, does that system use all 100 units to its advantage? Or, does the system use only part of the available energy and lose part to heat or waste. Entropy measures efficiency. We say an "inefficient" system is <u>disordered</u>—it goes from order to disorder—because it does not take full advantage of all the available energy.

Human's for example, are only about ten percent efficient. For every hundred units of energy we ingest (through food) we use only about 10% and loose 90% to waste or heat. Entropy calls this "disorder" losing energy in the form of heat during the transformation process. The only way to avoid disorder is to continually add energy.

Step 1 "Entropy"

Step 1 of Outline—Pre-Read Passage about Entropy:

Paragraph 1 – SARR 1st Sentence: *Entropy is the loss of energy, usually in terms of heat.*
Paragraph 2 – SARR 1st Sentence: *Example of an overhead projector.*
Paragraph 3 – SARR 1st Sentence: *Entropy measures a system's efficiency*
Paragraph 4 – SARR 1st Sentence: *People are only 10% efficient—high entropy*
Notes: *1st Q—Primary purpose of passage*

Step 2 "Entropy"

Completed "Entropy" Outline—Read

Paragraph 1: SARR 1st Paragraph –
Entropy is the loss of energy, usually in terms of heat.
- When energy is "lost" it is not available to do work.
- Not really lost, just not used for the desired purpose

Paragraph 2: SARR 2nd Paragraph –
Example of an overhead projector.
- Electric energy => light
- There is some loss of energy…it's not 1 to 1
- The energy was not lost…just changed to heat
- Useful work energy => light
- Wasted energy =>lost in heat (not used to make light)

Paragraph 3: SARR 3rd Paragraph
Entropy measures a system's efficiency
- How much energy is used to advantage…
- How much is wasted in heat
- Inefficient system = disordered
- Goes from ordered=>disordered because of wasted energy

Paragraph 4: SARR 4th Paragraph
People are only 10% efficient—high entropy
- About 90% of our food energy is wasted in lost heat
- Only 10% is used for work
- Losing energy in the form of heat = Disorder
- To avoid "Disorder" requires constant adding of energy

First question stem notes: *1st Q—Primary purpose of passage.*

You would now begin to answer questions…

Helpful Hints for Successful SARRing

 So What's Your Point ???

Active Reading
- Anticipate where the author is going
- Engage in the passage
- Expect
- Predict

Structure—Watch out for:
- Lists—Punctuation (colons and semi-colons usually indicate a list).
- Names
- Quotes
- Key or Transitional words (however, but, also, etc)
- Keep track of who is talking —often you will find two or three different voices in the same passage—e.g. the test writer is talking about a review done by an analyst about a book written by an author. It can become very confusing sorting out who is talking.
- Topic Sentences
- Last paragraph can sum up.
- Avoid trying to remember too much detail until the QS demands it.
- Spend the time initially with your outline—Don't be in a hurry to get to the Questions.

Use Abbreviations: Use arrows or other "notations" that mean something to you that will save time.

Symbol:	Meaning:
X ⇒ y	x "caused or led to" y
B/4	Before
≠	Does not follow or unequal
¶	Paragraph
§	Section
$	Money
&	And
#	Number
...	Break in the action
/	Break in the action
≈	About--approximate
>	Greater than
<	Less than
=	Equal
"..."	Quote
!	Important point
w/	With
@	At
ea	Each

Remember To

☑ **Make a Template** — Write on the test book.

☑ **Outline** — Make your notes where you can in the booklet.

☑ **Pre-Read** — Read the first sentence of each paragraph and the first QS - fill in your template or beside the location in the passage as you go.   (circle, highlight, underline, use arrows and abbreviations)

☑ **Read** — Read carefully for meaning, SARRing all the way - fill in the remainder of the template doing the same as in the Pre-read.

Critical Reading

Part 4: Practice Questions

Virtual Classroom> Reading>Overview & Directions

This material corresponds to the SAT & ACT Virtual Classroom Instructions in the
PowerPrep DVD/Internet/iApp for Reading

Virtual Classroom

Important Abbreviations

These abbreviations are used throughout the program

POE: Process of Elimination
SARR: Synthesize, Analyze, Reduce, and Restate (has to do with Logical Reasoning)
AC: Answer Choice
QS: Question Stem
LOD: Level of Difficulty

Example Question: What is the least common multiple of 3, 4, and 7? **(This is the call of the question or Question Stem "QS")**

These are Answer Choices "AC" A, B, C, D, E

(A) 12
(B) 21
(C) 28
(D) 48
(E) 84

Part 4: Practice Questions

The following passage about the history and meaning of conservative political philosophy was adapted from an essay by a modern conservative writer.

The ideology of modern conservatism seeks to reestablish the ancient conviction of the necessity of a moral or virtuous <u>polity</u> as the guardian of the unalienable right of self-government. This political
5 philosophy traces its ancestry to at least 500 B.C. to Cicero and Plato, with subsequent incarnations known variously as <u>neo-scholastics</u>, Aristotelians, traditionalists, realists and further into the 1700's when it was rediscovered by American
10 Revolutionaries and became their dominant political ideology providing the philosophical basis for the revolution, the Declaration of Independence and the Constitution. This "<u>new</u>" doctrine permeated their political discourse. It can be followed through the
15 writings of George Washington, John Adams, Thomas Jefferson, James Madison, Thomas Paine and many others, to the early 1900's in the political convictions of President Theodore Roosevelt and to the 1920's through President Calvin Coolidge to the
20 1980's through President Ronald Reagan. Finally, the early 21st century's most vocal neo-conservative proponent is Republican presidential candidate, Dr. Alan Keyes.

As reflected in the Federalist Papers and the
25 writings of early American leaders, conservatives have always had a healthy suspicion of government, "...but government, even in its best state is but a necessary evil, in its worst state an intolerable one"[1], "Government is not reason, it is not eloquence--it is
30 force! Like fire, it is a dangerous servant and a fearful master!"[2] They sought to control this potentially dangerous master by dividing and limiting it, thus heeding the warnings of Thomas Jefferson found in a letter to Joseph C. Cabell, dated February 2, 1816,
35 "<u>What has destroyed liberty...in every government which has existed...? The generalizing and concentrating all cares and powers into one body.</u>" Additionally, they believe solutions to social problems exist in the private social realm and are
40 beyond the purview of government intervention. People should be left free to, "...regulate their own pursuits of industry and improvement, and [the government] shall not take from the mouth of the laborer the bread it has earned."[3] Henry David Thoreau
45 in *Civil Disobedience,* 1849, concurred: "This government never of itself furthered any enterprise, but by the <u>alacrity</u> with which it got out of its way." As late as the 1960's the liberal and conservative ideologies were not as divergent on this issue as illustrated by the
50 famous quote of President John F. Kennedy, "Ask not what your country can do for you..."

The demands of self-government are considerable, requiring self-discipline and a moral character--what the early leaders referred to as
55 "public virtue". In its absence, Plato believed liberty degenerates into license and is soon lost: "<u>That freedom which knew no bounds must now put on the livery* of the most harsh and bitter servitude..</u>".
60 Morality, or the virtue of the people is a fundamental principle of conservatism and requirement of the American system of government: John Adams, the 2nd President of the United States, believed, "Our Constitution was made only for a
65 moral and religious people. It is wholly inadequate to the government of any other."; George Washington referred to religion and morality as the, "indispensable supports of political prosperity"; James Madison, the "Father of the Constitution"
70 said, "It must be assumed that people will have sufficient virtue and intelligence to select men of virtue and wisdom or no theoretical check, no form of government, can render us secure."; The famous French historian Alexis de Tocqueville noted this in
75 his work, *Democracy in America,* as he sought for what he considered the source of "American greatness", and did not find it until, "...I went to the churches of America and heard her pulpits aflame with righteousness did I understand the secret of her
80 genius and power. America is great because she is good, and if America ever ceases to be good, America will cease to be great."

More modern leaders have echoed the same conclusion. President Calvin Coolidge: "We do not
85 need more material development, we need more spiritual development ...more moral power...more character...more religion..." Most recently, presidential candidate, Dr. Alan Keyes, reiterated the same conservative principles in Iowa July 4,
90 1999: "The key to this nation's strength has not been a government that does everything for us, but a people with the character, the strength, the willingness, and responsibility to do what they have to for themselves...placing number one on the
95 agenda of our concerns, the restoration of this Nations moral principles, of its moral conscience, of its moral character...we will then reclaim our control over...government which is not to be our master, but our servant and our tool."

100

1 Thomas Paine --Common Sense, January 1776

2 George Washington--

3 Thomas Jefferson--First Inaugural Address 1801

* A distinctive uniform worn by the male servants of a household

Passage: "Conservatism" Sample Questions

1. **The passage is primarily concerned with**
   (A) Advancing a political agenda.
   (B) Arguing against the liberal political ideology.
   (C) Reviewing the history and meaning of conservative political ideology.
   (D) Debunking false impressions of conservative political ideology.
   (E) Recruiting readers to a conservative political philosophy.

2. **The author would most likely disagree with which one of the following statement about government?**
   (A) Government is a necessary evil.
   (B) Religion is an indispensable support of political prosperity.
   (C) Freedom requires moral and ethical limitations.
   (D) Government has obtained too much control over citizens' lives.
   (E) Modern conservatives believe the current condition of government, while not perfect, is acceptable.

3. **In line 3 "polity" means**
   (A) Society
   (B) Conviction
   (C) Political leadership
   (D) Constitution
   (E) Governor

4. **As used in line 7 "neo-scholastic" refers to**
   (A) A new method of scholarship.
   (B) A specific political philosophy.
   (C) A group of disparate political ideologies.
   (D) Cicero and Plato.
   (E) The dominant political philosophy of 500 B.C.

5. **By describing the doctrine, which permeated their discourse as "new", at line 13, the author suggests**
   (A) The new doctrine provided the philosophical basis for the American Revolution.
   (B) The philosophical basis of the American Revolution emerged for the first time in the1700's.
   (C) This newly discovered political doctrine caused the American Revolution.
   (D) The new political doctrine was not new at all.
   (E) The ancient political doctrine of Cicero and Plato was repudiated with the discovery of a new political doctrine.

6. **According to the second paragraph, Thomas Paine would most likely disagree with which of the following descriptions about government?**
   (A) A reasonable compromise
   (B) An essential element
   (C) An eternally intolerable evil
   (D) A fearful master
   (E) A necessary evil

7. **The quotation from Thomas Jefferson found at line 35 to line 38 is used to provide--**
   (A) A warning about the tenuous nature of liberty.
   (B) A summation on how to concentrate governmental powers to avoid the destruction of liberty.
   (C) A generalization about government.
   (D) An admonition about the excesses of governmental power.
   (E) A description of what destroys liberty.

8. **In line 47, "alacrity" means**
   (A) Success
   (B) Quickness
   (C) Reluctance
   (D) Hesitation
   (E) Completeness

9. **The author's primary reason in quoting President John Kennedy at the end of the second paragraph was to support the idea that**
   (A) Liberals and conservatives have not always disagreed on the level of government intervention in private affairs.
   (B) conservatives and liberals do not currently agree about how involved the government should be in social issues.
   (C) President Kennedy's liberal political ideology diverged from the conservative philosophy.
   (D) Citizens should not ask the government to provide for them.
   (E) President Kennedy was not a conservative political leader.

10. **The quotation from Plato at lines 57-59 emphasizes the author's point that**
   (A) It is a harsh and bitter struggle for freedom.
   (B) Those who live without freedom suffer under harsh constraints of servitude.
   (C) The bitter conditions of slavery result from unexercised freedom.
   (D) Liberty without license will result in servitude.
   (E) Freedom without constraint leads to slavery.

11. The author primarily employs which persuasion technique to make the principle point of the fourth paragraph?
   (A) Appeal to logic.
   (B) Appeal to emotion.
   (C) Appeal to morality.
   (D) Appeal to authority.
   (E) Appeal to political science.

Review of Passage

Step 1: Outline
NOTE: You will not have time on the test to do this in depth analysis, sentence by sentence.
Introductory Material: *The history and meaning of conservatism as presented by a modern conservative.*

Paragraph 1:

Sentence #1: *The ideology of modern conservatism seeks to reestablish the ancient conviction of the necessity of a moral or virtuous polity as the basis of the unalienable right of self-government.*
Take Away Points: • Modern Conservatism   • Reestablish   • Moral virtuous nation   • Basis of • Freedom

Sentence #2: *This political philosophy traces its ancestry to at least 500 B.C. to Cicero and Plato, with subsequent incarnations known variously as neo-scholastics, Aristotelians, traditionalists, realists and further into the 1700's when it was rediscovered by American Revolutionaries and became their dominant political ideology providing the philosophical basis for the revolution, the Declaration of Independence and the Constitution.*
Take Away Points: • This political philosophy • Morality and virtue required for self-government • Ancient • Several incarnations • Rediscovered by founders • Became their philosophy

Sentence #3: *This "new doctrine" permeated their political discourse.*
Take Away Points: • The "new" doctrine is actually an ancient one •permeated the politics of the 1700's

Sentence #4: *It can be followed through the writings of George Washington, John Adams, Thomas Jefferson, James Madison, Thomas Paine and many others, to the early 1900's in the political convictions of President Theodore Roosevelt and to the 1920's through President Calvin Coolidge to the 1980's through President Ronald Reagan.*
Take Away Points: It (the idea that freedom requires a virtuous nation) can be traced through:....founders to Reagan.

Sentence #5: *Finally, the early 21st century's most vocal neo-conservative proponent is Republican presidential candidate, Dr. Alan Keyes.*
Take Away Points: the same ideology traced to current day "Alan Keyes"

Summary of Paragraph 1: Modern conservatives seek to reestablish old idea that freedom requires virtuous nation--this ideology at foundation of America and traced from 500 BC to today.

Paragraph 2:

Sentence #1: *As reflected in the Federalist Papers and the writings of early American* **leaders,** *conservatives have always had a healthy suspicion of government, "...but government, even in its best state is but a necessary evil, in its worst state an intolerable one"[1], "Government is not reason, it is not eloquence--it is force! Like fire, it is a dangerous servant and a fearful master!"[2]*
Take Away Points: •conservatives suspicious of government • support from Thomas Paine • support from George Washington

Sentence #2: *They sought to control this potentially dangerous master by dividing and limiting it, thus heeding the warnings of Thomas Jefferson found in a letter to Joseph C. Cabell, dated February 2, 1816, "What has destroyed liberty...in every government which has existed...? The generalizing and concentrating all cares and powers into one body."*
Take Away Points: • governmental power should be divided • support from Thomas Jefferson

Sentence #3: *Additionally, they believe solutions to social problems exist in the private social realm and are beyond the purview of government intervention.*
Take Away Points: social problems and issues not for government

Sentence #4: *People should be left free to, "...regulate their own pursuits of industry and improvement, and [the government] shall not take from the mouth of the laborer the bread it has earned."[3]*
Take Away Points:- support from Thomas Jefferson for idea that government should not get involved and redistribute wealth

Sentence #5: *Henry David Thoreau in Civil Disobedience, 1849, concurred: "This government never of itself furthered any enterprise, but by the alacrity with which it got out of its way."*
Take Away Points: support from Thoreau--government should get out of way

Sentence #6: *As late as the 1960's the liberal and conservative ideologies were not as divergent on this issue as illustrated by the famous quote of President John F. Kennedy, "Ask not what your country can do for you..."*
Take Away Points: Conservatives and liberals did not diverge on this point--JFK quote

Summary of Paragraph 2: • conservatives are suspicious of government • government power should be divided •government should not be involved in private social issues • conservatives and liberals have not always disagreed on these points

Paragraph 3:

Sentence #1: *The demands of self-government are considerable, requiring self-discipline and a moral character--what the early leaders referred to as "public virtue".*

Take Away Points: public virtue required

Sentence #2: *In its absence, Plato believed liberty degenerates into license and is soon lost: "That freedom which knew no bounds must now put on the livery* of the most harsh and bitter servitude..".*
Take Away Points: freedom without limits leads to slavery

Summary of Paragraph 3: public virtue required freedom without limits leads to slavery--Plato

Paragraph 4:

Morality, or the virtue of the people is a fundamental principle of conservatism and requirement of the American system of government: John Adams, the 2nd President of the United States, believed, "Our Constitution was made only for a moral and religious people. It is wholly inadequate to the government of any other."; George Washington referred to religion and morality as the, "indispensable supports of political prosperity"; James Madison, the "Father of the Constitution" said, "It must be assumed that people will have sufficient virtue and intelligence to select men of virtue and wisdom or no theoretical check, no form of government, can render us secure."; The famous French historian Alexis de Tocqueville noted this in his work, Democracy in America, as he fought for what he considered the source of "American greatness", and did not find it until, "...I went to the churches of America and heard her pulpits aflame with righteousness did I understand the secret of her genius and power. America is great because she is good, and if America ever ceases to be good, America will cease to be great."

Summary of Paragraph 4:
- virtue/morality of the people basis of American system of government
- supported by John Adams, GW, James Madison, Tocqueville

Paragraph 5:

Sentence # 1: *More modern leaders have echoed the same conclusion. President Calvin Coolidge: "We do not need more material development, we need more spiritual development ...more moral power...more character...more religion..."*
Take Away Points: • modern conservatives echoed same ideas • Coolidge--more religion

Sentence #2: *Most recently, presidential candidate, Dr. Alan Keyes, reiterated the same conservative principles in Iowa July 4, 1999: "The key to this nation's strength has not been a government that does everything for us, but a people with the character, the strength, the willingness, and responsibility to do what they have to for themselves...placing number one on the agenda of our concerns, the restoration of this Nations moral principles, of its moral conscience, of its moral character...we will then reclaim our control over...government which is not to be our master, but our servant and our tool."*
Take Away Points: same ideas brought to present day--Alan Keyes

Summary of Paragraph 5: modern conservatives express the same ideas--virtue required to continue freedom

OVERALL SUMMARY

Summary of Introductory Material: the history and meaning of conservatism as presented by a modern conservative
Summary of Paragraph 1: modern conservatives seek to reestablish old idea that freedom requires virtuous nation--this ideology at foundation of America and traced from 500 BC to today

Summary of Paragraph 2:
- conservatives are suspicious of government
- government power should be divided
- government should not be involved in private social issues
- conservatives and liberals have not always disagreed on these points

Summary of Paragraph 3:
- public virtue required
- freedom without limits leads to slavery--Plato

Summary of Paragraph 4:
- virtue/morality of the people basis of American system of government
- supported by John Adams, GW, James Madison, Tocqueville

Summary of Paragraph 5:
- modern conservatives express the same ideas--virtue required to continue freedom
BOTTOM LINE: The passage deals with: *The following passage about the history and meaning of conservative political philosophy was adapted from an essay by a modern conservative writer.*

Step 2: Answer (Using Poe)

Explanatory Answers

EXPLANATION TO QUESTION #1:

Question Type: Level I: Inference
Explanation:
    Key: This is a good example of the need to read the introductory or supplemental information. The introductory information tells you the passage is about the history and meaning of conservative political philosophy (conservatism) We also learn it was written by a modern conservative writer.
    Conclusion: The passage is about the history and meaning of conservatism as presented by a modern conservative.

Reminder: Key material waiting to be found in the Introductory, Topic Sentences, and Conclusions. Think of it as a gift from the test makers to you.

(A) Advancing a political agenda. The passage does not advocate a position.

(B) Arguing against the liberal political ideology. Nothing in the passage says anything negative about liberalism.

(C) Reviewing the history and meaning of conservative political ideology. * Correct Response. See explanation above.

(D) Debunking false impressions of conservative political ideology. Nothing in the passage mentions that a false impression exists.

(E) Recruiting readers to a conservative political philosophy. Nothing in the passage states to choose this ideology. It is simply an explanation of a political ideology and its history.

EXPLANATION TO QUESTION #2:

Question Type: Level I: Explicit
Explanation:
Key: This is a thought reverser—which AC would author disagree with? You have to keep in mind.
- **author is a conservative writer**
- **main point is the history and meaning of conservatism**
- **virtue/morals required for self government and is at the foundation of American system**

(A) Government is a necessary evil. This is a quote from Thomas Paine—and the author would agree with it because it was included as support for the point that Conservatism has a "healthy suspicion of government."

(B) Religion is an indispensable support of political prosperity. This is a quote from George Washington. The author would probably agree with this because the quote was included as support for the point that public virtue is a requirement of the American System of Government.

(C) Freedom requires moral and ethical limitations. This restates the Plato quote. The author would most likely agree with this.

(D) Government has obtained too much control over citizens' lives. This point is implied by the information at the end of the second paragraph: • that gov't should not be involved in the private sector • and liberals and conservatives did not begin to diverge on this until sometime around the JFK time. However, you could not say unequivocally that the author would agree with this statement. But you cannot say unequivocally that the author would disagree either. We do not have sufficient information for this AC to say one or the other.

(E) Modern conservatives believe the current condition of government, while not perfect, is acceptable. The contrary to this point is implied in the first sentence of the passage where it states: *Modern conservatives seek to re-establish* ...(this implies that things are not currently ok.) Of all the AC, this is the one the author most likely would disagree with.

EXPLANATION TO QUESTION #3:

Question Type: Level III: Explicit
Explanation: Answer A
Key: Vocab
Polity: an organized society such as a nation, having a specific form of government.
...supported by the ancient conviction of the necessity of a moral of virtuous polity.

EXPLANATION TO QUESTION #4:

Question Type: Level II or I: Inference
Explanation: This political philosophy (which one?) traces its ancestry to at least 500 B.C. to Cicero and Plato, with subsequent incarnations known variously as neo-scholastics, Aristotelians, traditionalists, realists and further into the 1700's...
The same idea that self-government (freedom) requires a virtuous people was known as:
neo-scholastics, Aristotelians, traditionalists, realists and further into the 1700's...
First answer the question—Which political philosophy?
The answer is found in the preceding sentence: *The ideology of modern conservatism seeks to reestablish the ancient conviction of the necessity of a moral or virtuous polity as the basis of the unalienable right of self-government.*
In other words—self-government requires virtuous people.
The political philosophy that self-government (freedom) requires a virtuous people can be traced back to at least 500 B.C. (Cicero and Plato). From that point, the same ideas had subsequent incarnations (resurface through history). The same idea that self-government requires a virtuous people was known as: neo-scholastics, Aristotelians, etc.
Therefore, to answer the question: As used in line 7, "neo-scholastics" refers to a specific political philosophy.

(A) a new method of scholarship. This would be a direct translation of the words "neo" and "scholastic" but taken out of context. The question asks you to respond to it in context "as used in line 7." Be careful and analyze the QS so you answer the correct question.

(B) a specific political philosophy.   * Correct Response.   See explanation above.

(C) a group of disparate political ideologies. This AC might entice because "neo-scholastics" is used in a list of other terms. It is a reference to a political ideology and it is in a group. But those terms are all names for the same ideology and not disparate political ideologies.

(D) Cicero and Plato. This AC attempts to mislead those who did not have time to closely read and skimmed and saw the names of Cicero and Plato and the word incarnation. This gets at the idea that the AC is a name for something that preceded it, but not Cicero and Plato.

(E) the dominant political philosophy of 500 B.C. The passage tells us that the philosophy existed as far back as 500 B.C., but it does not say it was dominant at that time. It eventually became dominant in the 1700's in American Political Thought

EXPLANATION TO QUESTION #5:

Question Type: Level II: Inference
Explanation:
First Sentence: Modern conservatism reestablish... idea of the need for a moral people (nation) as the basic necessity for self-government (freedom)

Second Sentence: LONG.   This political philosophy (freedom requires virtue of the people)--goes back to Plato and Cicero--500 B.C. Then traces it through ...to the 1700s where this old political ideology resurfaces again (anew) and becomes the dominant political philosophy of the American Revolution era.
Third Sentence: Conclusion. This "new" ideology permeated—was evidenced throughout the time, Dec of Ind, Constitution etc.
   • Taken together—Sentence 1,2, and 3...
The "new" political idea that self-government (freedom) requires a virtuous or moral society is actually an ancient idea. **The author puts "new" in quotes to indicate that it means something different. However, the concept was not new. It was rediscovered during the 1700's in America.**

(A) the new doctrine provided the philosophical basis for the American Revolution. A tempting distracter. The AC correctly restates information provided in the Passage. However, it does not respond to the Question—Why did the author use the word "new"?
(B) the philosophical basis of the American Revolution emerged for the first time in the 1700's. A misstatement.
(C) this newly discovered political doctrine caused the American Revolution. This AC fails for two reasons: 1. It was newly discovered—it was more correctly "rediscovered." 2. Nothing in the passage states the ideology "caused" the Revolution.
(D) the new political doctrine was not new at all.   * Correct Response.   See explanation above.
(E) the ancient political doctrine of Cicero and Plato was repudiated with the discovery of a new political doctrine. A misstatement—the ancient political doctrine was re-born not repudiated.

EXPLANATION TO QUESTION #6:

Question Type: Level II: Implicit
Explanation:
Key: You first have to find the quote by Thomas Paine in the Second Paragraph.
"...but government, even in its best state is but a necessary evil, in its worst state an intolerable one"[1],

Analysis of quote:
        Paine creates a spectrum for government
        BEST CASE: necessary evil
        WORST CASE: intolerable evil
        Watch out for thought reversers!
(A) A reasonable compromise. *...but government, even in its best state is but a necessary evil, in its worst state an intolerable one*[1] We don't have enough information to conclude he would either agree or disagree with this description of government.
(B) An essential element.   From the quote, we would probably conclude that government can be necessary or essential, but it is still capable of creating a lot of problems. At its best, it is a necessary evil. But we can't logically conclude that he would disagree with that. In fact, the quote argues that he would agree.
(C) an eternally intolerable evil.   This AC adds the word "eternally," which makes the difference. The quote tells us that Paine would agree that gov't can be an intolerable evil—that's the worst case above. However, this AC adds the adverb "eternally." Eternally, as used here, indicates that gov't is always, forever, endlessly an intolerable evil. We can logically conclude from the quote that Paine would have to disagree with the statement that government is always, eternally an "intolerable evil."
(D) A fearful master. This AC combines words from the quote below by Washington. *Government is not reason, it is not eloquence—it is force! Like fire, it is a dangerous servant and a fearful master.* But from Paine's quote, you would probably have to conclude he would agree with this—government can be a fearful master. In Paine's mind, it can be an intolerable evil. Nothing would allow us to conclude logically that he must disagree with the "fearful master" idea.
(E) A necessary evil. This is a restatement of the first part of the dichotomy. Paine would agree with this because he said it—government can be a necessary evil.

EXPLANATION TO QUESTION #7:

Question Type: Level II: Inference
Explanation: 1. Find the quote: *"What has destroyed liberty...in every government which has existed...? The generalizing and concentrating all cares and powers into* one body."
2. Restate the meaning in your own words: So What 's Your Point?
Generalizing governmental powers into one body destroys, has always destroyed liberty, freedom.
3. Move onto the AC and see if you can POE, Search and Rescue

REMEMBER: something in each AC except one makes it not acceptable.
(A) a warning about the tenuous nature of liberty.
        Warning—ok , but is he warning about the tenuous (delicate, fragile) nature of freedom? It may be true that freedom is tenuous, but that is not the point of the Jefferson quote—he is pointing out that concentration of power destroys freedom.

(B) a summation on how to concentrate governmental powers to avoid the destruction of liberty.
1. Summation—ok.
2. How to concentrate power—the quote does not explain how to concentrate power—it warns that concentrating it will destroy liberty.
3. To avoid destruction of liberty
Opposite-concentrating government power does not avoid the destruction of liberty. It causes the destruction of liberty.
This AC misses on several counts.
(C) a generalization about government.
1. Generalization—ok – but about what?
2. Government—the quote does generalize that the concentration of power has always led to the destruction of liberty—that is definitely a generalization.
However, it is not a generalization about "government" as a whole. This AC is way too broad.
(D) an admonition about the excesses of governmental power. 1. Admonition—what is he admonishing? 2. Excesses of governmental power. Once the power is centralized, it becomes excessive is true. But the passage is talking about how you get to the point of excessive governmental power in the first place—by concentrating it. The resulting loss is liberty. But the process occurs by first concentrating power—losing the checks and balances, the divisions of power.
(E) a description of what destroys liberty. 1. Description—ok—but what is he describing? 2..What destroys liberty Exactly—the concentration of power destroys liberty. The passage is a description of what destroys liberty—concentrating power.

EXPLANATION TO QUESTION #8:

Question Type: Level III: Explicit
Explanation: Answer B
Key: Vocab. Alacrity: cheerful willingness; eagerness, speed or quickness
Henry David Thoreau in *Civil Disobedience*, 1849, concurred: "This government never of itself furthered any enterprise, but by the alacrity with which it got out of its way."

All of the AC's make sense, but only QUICKNESS is a synonym for ALACRITY. Thoreau's quote supports the idea that governmental involvement in most cases does not help: The government never furthered (helped) any enterprise (undertaking) except by getting out of the way of the private sector as quickly as possible.

EXPLANATION TO QUESTION #9:

Question Type: Level II: Inference
Explanation: This question requires an understanding of the passage beginning with line 38 where the sentence begins with "Additionally" to the end of the JFK quote.

Relevant part of passage: *Additionally, they believe solutions to social problems exist in the private social realm and are beyond the purview of government intervention.   People should be left free to, "...regulate their own pursuits of industry and improvement, and [the government] shall not take from the mouth of the laborer the bread it has earned."[3] Henry David Thoreau in Civil Disobedience, 1849, concurred: "This government never of itself furthered any enterprise, but by the alacrity with which it got out of its way."   As late as the 1960's the liberal and conservative ideologies were not as divergent on this issue as illustrated by the famous quote of President John F. Kennedy, "Ask not what your country can do for you..."*

Sentence 1: Additionally they (conservatives) believe private social issues are not for the government
Sentence 2: The GW quote supports this idea--government out, people left alone to regulate themselves— and the government should not redistribute wealth or take bread from the laborer who earned it
Sentence 3: Thoreau quote supports the idea that government just gets in the way of the private sector. **The best way the government can help--get out of the way quickly.**

Sentence 4: Conclusion--Liberals and Conservatives have not always disagreed about this idea--limited government involvement in private social issues.
Author Supports the Conclusion by Using the JFK Quote
Liberal Democratic President JFK stated people should not ask the government for support

The Call of the Question: The author's primary reason in quoting President John Kennedy was to support the idea that:
• Liberals and Conservatives have not always disagreed,
• The divergence between the liberal and conservative point of view regarding governmental involvement is relatively recent
• As noted by the early 1960 quote from JFK
Note: Each part of the paragraph is built by the succeeding part

(A) liberals and conservatives have not always disagreed on the level of government intervention in private affairs.
Note: This may not be historically accurate, however, that is not the issue. The question you have to answer is: "How was the quote used, what idea did the author intend to support by using this JFK quote?"--not whether it is historically accurate.
(B) conservatives and liberals do not currently agree about how involved the government should be in social issues. This is a true statement. However, it does not respond to the question.
(C) President Kennedy's liberal political ideology diverged from the conservative philosophy. This AC uses the word "diverged" to distract you. The JFK quote was not used to support the idea that JFK's policies were: • liberal • diverged from conservative policy. The quote was meant to show the two sides used to be more in agreement.
(D) citizens should not ask the government to provide for them. The quote standing alone is accurately described in AC (D)—that's what the plain language of the quote means. But you were asked to decide what point the author wanted

to make by using the quote—that conservative and liberal ideology was not always so divergent on the issue of governmental involvement in people's lives.

(E) President Kennedy was not a conservative political leader.   This may be a true statement historically, but it is not the reason the author used the JFK quote.

EXPLANATION TO QUESTION #10:

Question Type: Level II: Inference and Explicit
Explanation: What is the author's point in using the Plato Quote?
Freedom—the ability to make decisions (self determination)
License—permission or excessive freedom, excuse without responsibility which ultimately results in slavery.

PLATO: *"That freedom which knew no bounds must now put on the livery* of the most harsh and bitter servitude.."*.
LIVERY: a distinctive uniform worn by the male servants of a household

Plato's Logic: Freedom which knew no bounds (freedom exercised without internal constraints) must now put on the livery of (the distinctive uniform of a servant) the most harsh and bitter servitude.

The author's point: A certain level of moral character and self—discipline must exist in people if they are to remain free. Without it, the people will self destruct and freedom is lost. The author uses Plato's quote to support this point.

(A) it is a harsh and bitter struggle for freedom.   This might be a true statement, but it is not the meaning of the Plato quote.
(B) those who live without freedom suffer under harsh constraints of servitude.   This might be a true statement but it is not the meaning of the Plato quote.
(C) the bitter conditions of slavery result from unexercised freedom.   This might be a true statement but it is not the meaning of the Plato quote.
(D) liberty without license will result in servitude.   This actually has the opposite meaning from the Plato quote. This AC uses "liberty" and "license" to mislead.
(E) freedom without constrains leads to slavery.   * Correct Response.   Freedom exercised without an internal code of ethics leads to slavery.

EXPLANATION TO QUESTION #11:

Question Type: Level II: Inference

Explanation: Analysis of the fourth paragraph: What is the principle point?
• **Morality, or the virtue of the people is a fundamental principle of conservatism and**
  requirement of the American system of government

NOTE: this sentence is followed by a colon—this indicates a list that relates back to what was just said-

Look for punctuation as a key to help you.
The remainder of the paragraph supports this idea by quoting famous, historical, expert authorities

NOTE: each quote is separated by a semi-colon—the list continues which relates back to the original first statement.

1. John Adams
"Our Constitution was made only for a moral and religious people. It is wholly inadequate to the government of any other."

2. George Washington referred to religion and morality as the, *"indispensable supports of political   prosperity"*;
Basically—morality, or the virtue of the people is a fundamental principle of conservatism and requirement of the American system of government.

3. James Madison, the "Father of the Constitution" said,
"It must be assumed that people will have sufficient virtue and intelligence to select men of virtue and wisdom or no theoretical check, no form of government, can render us secure."

4. Alexis de Tocqueville
"...I went to the churches of America and heard her pulpits aflame with righteousness did I understand the secret of her genius and power. America is great because she is good, and if America ever ceases to be good, America will cease to be great."

This is a much longer quote, but conveys the same idea: Morality, or the virtue of the people, is a fundamental principle of conservatism and the American system of government.

The author supports this main point by an appeal to the authority of famous experts or authorities.
(A) Appeal to logic. There is some logic to the delivery of the argument, but it is not the primary way the author makes the point.

(B) Appeal to emotion. The quotes cited in the paragraph may cause emotional reaction in the reader—but again, it is not the primary way the author attempts to make his point.

(C) Appeal to morality. This AC attempts to mislead by using the word "morality," which appears in the first sentence. But the author is not appealing to the reader's sense of right and wrong as the primary method of making the point that morality is required.

(D) Appeal to authority. * Correct Response.   See explanation above.

(E) Appeal to political science. The quotes in the paragraph come from those who one might logically consider political scientists of some nature, because they created a country. However, the main point is not made by appealing to the authors of the quotes as political scientists—rather as experts in Nation Building on the one hand and as a famous historian in the case of Tocqueville.

English Grammar Workbook

Question Types

Table of Contents

This material corresponds to the Virtual Classroom Section in the
PowerPrep DVD for English

Virtual Classroom

English Questions
Part 1: ***SAT*** Overview & Directions

Virtual Classroom>English>Overview & Directions
This material corresponds to the Virtual Classroom in the
PowerPrep DVD/Internet/iApp for English

Virtual Classroom

Part 1: SAT Overview & Directions

IMPROVING SENTENCES

Directions: *For each question in this section, select the best answer from among the choices given. The following sentences test correctness and effectiveness of expression. Part of each sentence or the entire sentence is underlined; beneath each sentence are five ways of phrasing the underlined material. Choice A repeats the original phrasing; the other four choices are different. If you think the original phrasing produces a better sentence than any of the alternatives, select choice A; if not, select one of the other choices. In making your selection, follow the requirements of standard written English; that is, pay attention to grammar, choice of words, sentence construction, and punctuation. Your selection should result in the most effective sentence—clear and precise, without awkwardness or ambiguity.*

Improving Sentences Sample Questions

1. According to the study, as the body ages, the chance that medications will cause harmful side effects <u>are on the increase</u>.
   - (A) are on the increase
   - (B) are increasing
   - (C) has increased
   - (D) increase
   - (E) increases

2. The most versatile skin in nature helps squid ambush prey, <u>avoiding predators, as well as courting mates, and signaling</u> one another.
   - (A) avoiding predators, as well as courting mates, and signaling
   - (B) avoiding predators, courting mates, and they signal
   - (C) to avoid predators, court mates, and for signaling
   - (D) avoid predators, court mates, and they signal
   - (E) avoid predators, court mates, and signal

3. Six stories high, with portholes for eyes and a spiral staircase in each hind leg, <u>is the elephant-shaped building known as "Lucy," which towered over Margate City, New Jersey, since 1881</u>.
   - (A) is the elephant-shaped building known as "Lucy," which towered over Margate City, New Jersey, since 1881
   - (B) since 1881 it has towered over Margate City, New Jersey, the elephant-shaped building known as "Lucy"
   - (C) the elephant-shaped building known as "Lucy" has towered over Margate City, New Jersey, since 1881
   - (D) towering over Margate City, New Jersey, since 1881 has been the elephant-shaped building known as "Lucy"
   - (E) there is an elephant-shaped building known as "Lucy," and it has towered over Margate City, New Jersey, since 1881

4. Male cicadas have a white, drum-like plate called a tymbal on either side of their abdomen, <u>vibrating</u> rapidly to make a variety of calls.
   - (A) vibrating
   - (B) and vibrates
   - (C) and vibrating it
   - (D) which they vibrate
   - (E) and they make it vibrate

5. Researchers have found that the eyes of tropical nocturnal sweat bees are about 30 times more sensitive to light than <u>it is with honeybees</u>.
   - (A) it is with honeybees
   - (B) those of honeybees
   - (C) honeybees can be
   - (D) honeybees are
   - (E) honeybees

6. A war is raging between experts who see psychotherapy as an art <u>as well as them calling for</u> scientifically proven methods.
   - (A) as well as them calling for
   - (B) as well as the ones who want
   - (C) or those that are calling for
   - (D) and those who call for
   - (E) and others, wanting

7. Where the Illinois and Missouri Rivers feed into the Mississippi, the rivers meander, <u>forming swamps and oxbow lakes and creating a flood plain environment known as</u> the American Bottom.
   - (A) forming swamps and oxbow lakes and creating a flood plain environment known as
   - (B) forming swamps and oxbow lakes, creating a flood plain environment known that it is
   - (C) and it forms swamps and oxbow lakes and creating a flood plain environment known that it is
   - (D) form swamps and oxbow lakes and it creates a flood plain environment known as
   - (E) form swamps and oxbow lakes and they create a flood plain environment known as

8. As postmaster general, Benjamin Franklin sped up mail service between Boston and <u>Philadelphia, he required</u> post riders to continue day and night, thus making the round trip in six days instead of three weeks.
   - (A) Philadelphia, he required
   - (B) Philadelphia, it required
   - (C) Philadelphia and requiring
   - (D) Philadelphia by requiring
   - (E) Philadelphia to require

Answer Key

1. E 2.E 3.C 4D. 5.B 6.D 7.A 8.d

IDENTIFYING SENTENCE ERRORS

Directions: For each question in this section, select the best answer from among the choices given. The following sentences test your ability to recognize grammar and usage errors. Each sentence contains either a single error or no error at all. No sentence contains more than one error. The error, if there is one, is underlined and lettered. If the sentence contains an error, select the one underlined part that must be changed to make the sentence correct. If the sentence is correct, select choice E. In choosing answers, follow the requirements of standard written English.

Identifying Errors Sample Questions

1. When a major flood destroyed most of the Hohokam canal networks in 1358, people who <u>had struggled</u> for centuries <u>to water</u> their
    A   **B**

    lands <u>at last in the end</u> abandoned them   <u>because there was</u> too much water. <u>No error</u>
         C   D   E

2. In 1937, Louis Agassiz, a Swiss naturalist, proposed <u>the then</u> radical idea that in the   <u>not too distant</u> past <u>much of</u> Europe
                                                          A   B   C

    <u>had been covered</u> by glaciers. <u>No error</u>
         D   E

3. In 1772, four <u>years before</u> the Declaration of Independence, Mercy Otis Warren <u>published</u> *The Adulateur*, a satiric play that cast the
                   A   B

    colonial governor <u>to be a</u>   villain intent <u>on robbing</u> the colony. <u>No error</u>
                      C   D   E

4. The modern roller coaster is descended <u>from</u> a gravity ride called the Russian Mountain, <u>which</u> <u>was</u> a popular amusement in St.
                                            A   B   C

    Petersburg <u>as soon as</u> the sixteenth century. <u>No error</u>
               D   E

Answer Key

   1.C 2.E 3.C 4D

IMPROVING PARAGRAPHS

Directions: The following passage is an early draft of an essay. Some parts of the passage need to be rewritten.
Read the passage and select the best answers for the questions that follow. Some questions are about particular sentences or parts of sentences and ask you to improve sentence structure or word choice. Other questions ask you to consider organization and development. In choosing answers, follow the requirements of standard written English.

Improving Paragraphs Sample Questions

Questions 1 – 2 are based on the following passage.

(1) Many types of frogs hibernate, essentially sleeping through the winter. (2) They protect themselves from the cold by burrowing into the dirt or camping out under piles of leaves. (3) Some frogs are even equipped with mechanisms that allow them to survive being frozen. (4) One type of frog, the wood frog, can survive even when 65% of its total body water turns to ice. (5) These frogs appear to be dead but, it seems miraculous, they are not.

(6) Frozen frogs have extensive ice formation in their body cavities and in the spaces between their cells. (7) The reason that these frogs survive, however, is that no ice forms within their cells. (8) Ice crystals form within cells, they can kill an animal by puncturing certain specialized parts of the cells. (9) These frogs are protected from the harmful effects of freezing by a chemical reaction. (10) When the first ice crystals begin to form on the skin of a hibernating frog, an internal alarm goes off. (11) This causes the frog's cells to fill with glucose. (12) Precisely the opposite occurs in the spaces between the cells. (13) There special proteins promote the formation of ice crystals. (14) This draws water away from the cells so it does not freeze there.

1. In context, which word should be inserted at the beginning of sentence 8?
    (A) Because
    (B) Although
    (C) While
    (D) If (E) Since

2. Which of the following facts about glucose is most important to add to sentence 11?
    (A) Glucose acts as an antifreeze.
    (B) Glucose can be stored in the liver.
    (C) Glucose is regulated by two hormones, insulin and glucagon.
    (D) Glucose is used by the cells for energy.
    (E) Glucose is a blood sugar found in vertebrates.

Answer Key

English Questions

Part 2: ***ACT*** Overview & Directions

<u>Virtual Classroom>English>Overview & Directions</u>
This material corresponds to the Virtual Classroom in the
PowerPrep DVD/Internet/iApp for English

<u>Virtual Classroom</u>

Part 2: ACT Overview & Directions

ACT ENGLISH TEST DESCRIPTION

The English test is a 75-question, 45-minute test that covers:

Standard Written English	**Rhetorical Skills**
punctuation	strategy
grammar and usage	organization
sentence structure	style

- Spelling, vocabulary, and rote recall of rules of grammar are not tested.
- The test consists of five prose passages, each one followed by multiple-choice test questions. Different passage types are included to provide variety.
- Some questions refer to underlined portions of the passage and offer several alternatives to the portion underlined. You must decide which choice is most appropriate in the context of the passage.
- Some questions ask about an underlined portion, a section of the passage, or the passage as a whole. You must decide which choice best answers the question posed.
- Many questions include **"NO CHANGE"** to the passage as one of the choices.
- The questions are numbered consecutively.
- Each question number corresponds to an underlined portion in the passage or to a box located in the passage.

Content Covered by the ACT English Test

Six elements of effective writing are included in the English Test: punctuation, grammar, sentence structure, strategy, organization, and style. The questions covering punctuation, grammar, and sentence structure make up the Usage/Mechanics subscore. The questions covering strategy, organization, and style make up the Rhetorical Skills subscore.

Usage/Mechanics
- **Punctuation (13%).** Questions in this category test your knowledge of the conventions of internal and end-of-sentence punctuation, with emphasis on the relationship of punctuation to meaning (for example, avoiding ambiguity, indicating appositives).
- **Grammar and Usage (16%).** Questions in this category test your understanding of agreement between subject and verb, between pronoun and antecedent, and between modifiers and the word modified; verb formation; pronoun case; formation of comparative and superlative adjectives and adverbs; and idiomatic usage.
- **Sentence Structure (24%).** Questions in this category test your understanding of relationships between and among clauses, placement of modifiers, and shifts in construction.

Rhetorical Skills
- **Strategy (16%).** Questions in this category test how well you develop a given topic by choosing expressions appropriate to an essay's audience and purpose; judging the effect of adding, revising, or deleting supporting material; and choosing effective opening, transitional, and closing sentences.
- **Organization (15%).** Questions in this category test how well you organize ideas and judge the relevance of statements in context (making decisions about order, coherence, and unity).
- **Style (16%).** Questions in this category test how well you select precise and appropriate words and images, maintain the level of style and tone in an essay, manage sentence elements for rhetorical effectiveness, and avoid ambiguous pronoun references, wordiness, and redundancy.

DIRECTIONS: In the passage that follows, certain words and phrases are underlined and numbered. In the right-hand column, you will find alternatives for the underlined part. In most cases, you are to choose the one that best expresses the idea, makes the statement appropriate for standard written English, or is worded most consistently with the style and tone of the passage as a whole. If you think the original version is best, choose "NO CHANGE." In some cases, you will find in the right-hand column a question about the underlined part. You are to choose the best answer to the question.

You will also find questions about a section of the passage, or about the passage as a whole. These questions do not refer to an underlined portion of the passage, but rather are identified by a number or numbers in a box. For each question, choose the alternative you consider best and fill in the corresponding oval on your answer document. Read the passage through once before you begin to answer the questions that accompany it. For many of the questions, you must read several sentences beyond the question to determine the answer. Be sure that you have read far enough ahead each time you choose an alternative.

Bessie Coleman: In Flight

[1]

After *the final performance of one last* [1] practice landing, the French instructor nodded to the young African-American woman at the controls and jumped down to the ground. Bessie Colman was on her own now. She lined *up* [2] the nose of the open cockpit biplane on the runway's center *mark, she* [3] gave the engine full throttle, and took off into history.

[2]

It was a long journey from the American *Southwest she'd been* [4] born in 1893, to these French skies. The year in which se was born was about a century ago. [5]

There hadn't been much of a future for her in Oklahoma then. After *both semesters of the two-semester year* [6] at Langston Industrial College, Coleman headed for Chicago to see what could be done to realize a dream. Ever since she saw her first airplane when she was a little girl, Coleman had known that someday, somehow, she would fly.

[3]

Try as she might, however, Coleman could not obtain flying lessons anywhere in the city. Then she sought aid from Robert S. *Abbott* [7] of the Chicago Weekly Defender. The newspaperman got in touch with a flight school in France that was willing to teach this determined young woman to fly.

[4] {11}

[1] While *they're, she had as* [8] one of her instructors Anthony Fokker, the famous aircraft designer. [2] Bessie Coleman took a quick course in French, *should she settle* [9] her affairs, and sailed for Europe. [3] Coping with a *daily* [10] foreign language and flying in capricious, unstable machines held together with baling wire was daunting, but Coleman persevered.

[5]

On June 15, 1921, Bessie *Coleman, earned an international pilot's license,* [12] issued by the International Aeronautical Federation. Not only was she the first black woman to win her pilot's wings, she was the first American woman to hold this coveted license.

[6]

She was ready for a triumphant return to the United States to barnstorm and *lecture proof* [13] that if the will is *strong enough for* [14] one's dream can be attained.

Question 15 asks about the preceding passage as a whole: The writer intends to add the following sentence to the essay in order to provide a comparison that would help underline the challenges that Bessie Coleman faced: *"Her dream of becoming the world's first black woman pilot seemed as remote in Chicago as it had been in Oklahoma.'*
In order to accomplish this purpose, it would be most logical and appropriate to place this sentence after the:

1. A. NO CHANGE
   B. one finally ultimate
   C. one final
   D. one last final

2. F. NO CHANGE
   G. off
   H. along
   J. OMIT the underlined portion.

3. A. NO CHANGE
   B. mark,
   C. mark, Colman
   D. mark that

4. F. NO CHANGE
   G. Southwest that she'd been
   H. Southwest, where she'd been
   J. Southwest, she was

5. A. NO CHANGE
   B. It is now just about a century since the year of her birth.
   C. Just about a century has passed since the year of her birth.
   D. OMIT the underlined portion.

6. F. NO CHANGE
   G. a year
   H. a year like two full semesters
   J. one year filled with two semesters

7. A. NO CHANGE
   B. Abbott;
   C. Abbot, whose
   D. Abbot;

8. F. NO CHANGE
   G. they're
   H. there,
   J. there, she had as

9. A. NO CHANGE
   B. as if to settle
   C. to settle
   D. settled

10. F. NO CHANGE
    G. (place after *with*)
    H. (Place after *flying*)
    J. (Place after *in*)

11. Which of the following sequences of sentences will make Paragraph 4 most logical?
    A. NO CHANGE
    B. 1,3,2
    C. 2,1,3
    D. 3,2,1

12. F. NO CHANGE
    G. Coleman earned an international pilot's license
    H. Coleman, earned an international pilot's license
    J. Coleman earned an international pilot's license;

13. A. NO CHANGE
    B. lecture and proof
    C. lecture, proof
    D. lecture proof,

14. F. NO CHANGE
    G. stronger than
    H. strongly enough,
    J. strong enough,

15. A. first sentence in Paragraph 2
    B. first sentence in Paragraph 3.
    C. last sentence in Paragraph 3.
    D. first sentence in Paragraph 5.

Answer Key: Bessie Coleman in Flight

Question 1: Correct Answer C
The best answer is C, which concisely conveys the idea that the practice landing referred to was the last one in a series. In contrast, the other choices are redundant. Choice A belabors the point that "the final performance" was indeed the "last" performance (and confusingly suggests that there was more than one performance of a single landing). Choice B pointlessly repeats the notion of finality in the redundant phrase "finally ultimate" (and confusingly suggests that all the landings strove to be ultimate, but only the last landing succeeded). Choice D is simply redundant because the words *last* and *final* in the sentence are synonymous.

Question 2: Correct Answer F
The best answer is F. It offers the only idiomatically acceptable wording. The verb phrase *line up* is often used to mean "align." Choices G and H are clearly wrong here. We would never hear someone say that "she lined off the nose of the . . . biplane on the runway's center mark" or that "she lined along the nose of the . . . biplane on the runway's center mark." Choice J, which proposes deleting the underlined portion, also sounds improbable: "She lined the nose of the . . . biplane on the runway's center mark." This sentence suggests that Bessie Coleman is doing something with the nose of the plane, but whatever it is, it doesn't make sense in terms of the rest of the information in the sentence.

Question 3: Correct Answer B
The best answer is B. This sentence presents a series of three verb phrases-three things that Bessie Coleman did. The subject for all three of the verb phrases is the pronoun *She* at the beginning of the sentence. The third verb phrase in the series ("took off into history") has no subject, so it would be inconsistent and illogical to state the subject of the second verb phrase in the series, as Choices A and C propose. Choice D proposes that, rather than being the second in the series of verb phrases, this should be a subordinate adjective clause describing the preceding noun, but there's no logical support for saying, "the runway's center mark . . . gave the engine full throttle."

Question 4: Correct Answer H
The best answer is H. It provides the relative pronoun and the punctuation that effectively relates this subordinate adjective clause to the main clause of this sentence. The main clause is as follows: "It was a long journey from the American Southwest to these French skies." The subordinate clause is describing or defining the American Southwest: "where she'd been born in 1893." Since this clause occurs in the middle of the main clause and is not essential or restrictive information, it must be set off from the main clause. Choices F and G fail to do so. Choice J does set the phrase off with commas but fails to provide a pronoun that would effectively relate this clause to the main clause.

Question 5: Correct Answer D
The best answer is D. The most appropriate decision is to delete the information-presented in Choices A, B, and C in different phrasings-that Bessie Coleman was born about a century ago. This information is a mere digression in terms of the focus or development of this essay. It sidetracks the readers. Besides, it provides information that readers could easily infer on their own, since they are told in the previous sentence that Coleman was born in 1893.

Question 6: Correct Answer G
The best answer is G. It is the only choice that doesn't propose irrelevant or redundant information. Choices F, H, and J all propose unnecessarily long-winded and wordy ways of saying that Coleman headed for Chicago after a year at Langston Industrial College. It is just not important for readers to know that a year at Langston consisted of two semesters of schooling.

Question 7: Correct Answer A
The best answer is A. No punctuation is needed here between the noun ("Robert S. Abbott") and the prepositional phrase describing that noun ("of the *Chicago Weekly Defender*"). The use here of the colon (Choice B) or the semicolon (Choice D) is not called for. Choice C incorrectly proposes setting this prepositional phrase off from the main clause and introducing it with the relative pronoun that expresses possession *(whose)*.

Question 8: Correct Answer J
The best answer is J. It proposes the correct form of the adverb *(there)* and ensures that the main clause is a complete sentence. Choices F and G are both wrong because they propose using the contracted form of *they are*. Although *they're* sounds like *there*, it has a different meaning, which would not make sense in the context of this sentence. Choice H proposes the correct adverb but also proposes deleting "she had as," which would create a sentence fragment: "While there, one of her instructors Anthony Fokker, the famous aircraft designer."

Question 9: Correct Answer D
The best answer is D. It logically presents this sentence as a series of three verb phrases, all in the simple past tense. Choices A, B, and C all incorrectly attempt to relate the second phrase in this series to the first phrase. There is no information in this essay nor any logic to support the idea that "Bessie Coleman took a quick course in French, to settle her affairs" (Choice C) or "took a quick course in French, as if to settle her affairs" (Choice B). Likewise, the sense of probability or expectation or futurity that might be expressed by "should she settle her affairs" has no logical support in the context of this essay.

Question 10: Correct Answer H
The best answer is H. This question asks the test-taker to decide the best placement of the word *daily* in the sentence. This word has the flexibility to serve as either an adverb or an adjective. Here, the most logical and appropriate place for this word would be after the word *flying*. In this arrangement, the word *daily* serves as an adverb modifying the verb preceding it: "Coping with a foreign language and flying daily in capricious, unstable machines held together with baling wire was daunting, but Coleman persevered." None of the other proposed placements make sense in the context of this sentence: Choice F would have *daily* functioning as an adjective ("a daily foreign language"). Choice G would seem to have the word functioning as an adverb, but it's hard to tell what the adverb would be describing ("Coping with daily a foreign language"). Choice J would have *daily* functioning as an adverb defining an adjective ("in daily capricious, unstable machines").

Question 11: Correct Answer C
The best answer is C. It is the only choice that places Sentence 2 as the first sentence in the paragraph. Sentence 2 should logically precede Sentences 1 and 3 because, while Sentences 1 and 3 describe Bessie Coleman's experiences in Europe, Sentence 2 tells readers that she sailed for Europe (and describes the things she did prior to making the trip). Choices A and D are wrong because they keep Sentence 2 in the second position, and Choice B is wrong because it puts Sentence 2 in the final position.

Question 12: Correct Answer G
The best answer is G. It offers the correct punctuation decisions for this sentence. Choices F and H are incorrect because they propose putting a comma between the subject ("Bessie Coleman") and the predicate or verb phrase ("earned an international pilot's license"). Choice J is incorrect because it proposes putting a semicolon between the direct object noun ("an international pilot's license") and the subordinate clause defining that noun ("issued by the International Aeronautical Federation"). It might help to realize that, between the words *license* and *issued*, the words *that were* are not expressed but are understood or implied.

Question 13: Correct Answer C

The best answer is C. This is a difficult question in a rather complex sentence. The clause beginning with *proof* serves as an appositive, a phrase that describes or defines a preceding noun. Appositives are set off from the main clause with commas and, in most cases, immediately follow the noun they are describing. Here, the appositive occurs at the end of the sentence but describes the subject at the beginning of the sentence *(She)*. "She was ready for a triumphant return to the United States to barnstorm and lecture, proof that . . . one's dream can be attained." The punctuation decisions offered by Choices A and D would both produce an illogical phrasing because they propose that *proof* should serve as the direct object of the verb *lecture* ("She was ready . . . to barnstorm and lecture proof . . ."). Choice B is equally illogical because it proposes that *proof* could function as a verb ("She was ready . . . to barnstorm and lecture and proof that . . . one's dream can be attained.")

Question 14: Correct Answer J

The best answer is J. It effectively coordinates the various elements of this noun clause, which is functioning as an appositive for the subject of the main clause of this sentence. The entire noun clause should read: "proof that if the will is strong enough, one's dream can be attained." You will see that within this noun clause, which is already serving a secondary role in terms of the main clause of the sentence, there is a main clause ("one's dream can be attained") and a subordinate clause related to that main clause by the conjunction if ("the will is strong enough"). Choice H is wrong because it proposes an adverb *(strongly)* where a predicate adjective is required. Choices F and G are both wrong because they coordinate these clauses in ways that don't make sense and that make clause fragments: "if the will is strong enough for one's dream can be attained" (Choice F) and "if the will is stronger than one's dream can be attained" (Choice G).

Question 15: Correct Answer B

The best answer is B, which provides the intended comparison by placing the sentence in the most logical location. Choice B underlines or emphasizes the challenges Coleman faced by comparing her hopes and expectations with the reality she met in Chicago. On the contrary, Choice A spoils the logical sequence that Choice B establishes, because the end of the first sentence in Paragraph 2-"these French skies"-does not support the intended comparison. Choices C and D delay making the comparison until too late in the essay. In Choice C, the comparison is weakened because, by the end of Paragraph 3, Coleman is already on her way toward flight school. In Choice D, a comparison intended to "underline the challenges" no longer is pertinent, because Coleman has already met the challenges.

English
Part 3: Grammar Details

<u>Virtual Classroom>English>Grammar Details</u>
This material corresponds to the Virtual Classroom in the
PowerPrep DVD/Internet/iApp for English

Virtual Classroom

Important Abbreviations
These abbreviations are used throughout the program

POE: Process of Elimination
SARR: Synthesize, Analyze, Reduce, and Restate (has to do with Logical Reasoning)
AC: Answer Choice
QS: Question Stem
LOD: Level of Difficulty

Example Question: What is the least common multiple of 3, 4, and 7? (**This is the call of the question or Question Stem "QS"**)

These are Answer Choices "AC" A, B, C, D, E
    (A)   12
    (B)   21
    (C)   28
    (D)   48
    (E)   84

Part 3: Grammar Details

PUNCTUATION & MARKS

Capital Letters Rules

- First word in every sentence
- March v. march, May v. may
- "I","O"' and interjections (*O'Captain, My Captain*)
- The title or position of respect (*President Clinton*)
- Family relationships (*mother v. Aunt Mabel*)
- "First and last word in titles of works of Art"
- References to the Deity (*God, and His universe*)
- Proper Nouns and Adjectives
- Geographical Names
- Persons

- Organizations
- Business Firms
- Government Bodies
- Historical Events and Periods
- Special Events
- Calendar Items
- Nationalities, Races and Religions
- Business Products
- Ships, Planets, Monuments, Awards
- The first letter in a Quote

Common noun	Proper Noun	Proper Adjective
A poet	Homer	Homeric simile
A goddess	Athena	Athenian wisdom

End Marks

1. **Period--** Sentences that are statements end in a period. (Also used for abbreviations, adv.) *It is snowing.*
2. **Question Mark** – used after all interrogative sentences. *Is it snowing?*
3. **Exclamation Mark** – used following all exclamations. *Oh my gosh, it is snowing!*

Commas

- Separate items in a series (*pencil, pen, and paper*)
- Two or more adjectives preceding a noun   (*A vain, talkative DJ annoys me.*)
- Before and, but ,or, nor, for, yet when they join an independent phrase.
- Setting off non-essential clauses and phrases (*appositive phrases as an example*)
- Use after Well, Yes, No, Why when they are introductory elements.
- To set off elements that interrupt the sentence (*He , of course, won't be attending tonight.*)
- Parenthetical Phrases (*consequently, however, moreover, nevertheless, therefore, as a matter of fact*)
- Separate dates and addresses
- After Salutations and Closings
- After a name with Jr., Sr., Dr, etc

Semicolons

- Between independent clauses if not joined by a conjunction
- Between independent clauses joined by such words as however, therefore, consequently, instead, hence, otherwise
- May be used to separate independent clauses of a compound sentence if comma's are used in the clause
- Items in a series if the items contain commas

Colons

- Use a colon to mean- "Note what follows"
- Use a colon for time, Bible reference of verse, business letter salutations

Italics

- Titles of books, plays, movies, periodicals, works of art, and musical compositions. (*The Screwtape Letters, Star Wars, Flight of the Bumblebee*)
- When the sentence refers to the word.
- For foreign words. (*Dónde esta el baño?*)

Quotation Marks

- Direct quote—a person's exact words. *"I believe," Dan said, "that she is ill."*   *Rodney whispered under his breath, "Does she really love me?"*
- Punctuation rules: commas and periods inside the quote—colons and semicolons outside the quote.
- Paragraph quotes not at the end of a paragraph where the quote continues into the next paragraph.
- Quote within a quote is a ('). *Jill exclaimed, "My mom always says, 'Put the cap back on the toothpaste.'"*

- Enclosing titles of short stories, articles, poems, songs, chapters, or other parts of books/periodicals. *"Screwtape Letters"*, *"Star Wars"*, *"Of Mice and Men"*

Apostrophes

- Possessive case of singular nouns, add apostrophe and "s" to the end of the word
    Mom's car   a hard day's work   a dollar's worth
- Possessive case of a plural noun ending in s, add only the apostrophe to the end of the word
    Both girls' behavior   Two weeks' vacation   Knives' edges

Singular	Singular Possessive	Plural	Plural Possessive
Friend	friend's home	friends	friends' home
Month	month's work	months	two months' work
Dollar	dollar's worth	dollars	three dollars' worth
Box	box's lid	boxes	boxes' lid

- Possessive personal pronouns do not need an apostrophe: *Our, ours Their, theirs Your, yours Their, their*
- Indefinite pronouns in the possessive case require an apostrophe and an "s.": *Everyone's idea, Somebody's pencil*
- Compound words, organizations, names, joint possessions—only the last word is possessive in form.
    School board's decision,   Nobody else's business,   American Medical Association's endorsement
- When two or more persons possess something individually, each of their names are in possessive form.
    Mrs. Wheeler's and Mrs. Stuart's children were in the same class.
- To show where letters and numbers have been omitted: *lets, let's they are, they're,   don't, do not*
- Use an apostrophe and "s" to form plurals of letters, signs, numbers, and of words referred to as words.
    The word grammar has two r's, two a's and two m's.   The weather today calls for lows in the 40's.

Other Punctuation Marks

Hyphen Rules: • Used to divide a word at the end of a line • Used with numbers twenty-one to ninety-nine • Used with ex-, self-, all-, -elect: *ex-champ, self-esteem, all-star, pre-revolution, President-elect*

Dash Rules: Use a dash to indicate an abrupt break in thought: *"I hope—" Audrey began and then stopped. Stephans—Ms. Stephans, I mean--was waiting for me in her office.*

Parentheses Rules: To enclose matter which is added to a sentence, but is not considered of major importance *During the middle ages (from about A.D. 500 to A.D. 1500) Moslems and Vikings invaded Europe.*

Ellipsis Rules: • Shows that one or more words has been omitted in a quote. *We the people. . .in order to establish a more perfect Union . . . establish this constitution of the United States of America.* • May be used to show a pause: *I brought my trembling hand to my focused eyes. It was red, it was. . .it was. . .a tomato.*

Brackets Rules: • Used before and after material that has been added when quoting another writer. • Used when adding a word to a quote: *Sometimes I think <**my writing**> sounds like I walked out of the room and left the typewriter running.*

- Material that was added by someone else: *"Congratulations to the astronomy clubs softball team which put in a 'stellar' performance. <groans>*
- Use around an editorial correction: *Brooklyn alone has eight percent of lead poisoning <victims> in the county.*
- Use around the letters *"sic"* to indicate that an error appearing in the quoted material was made by the original speaker/writer: *No parent can dessert <sic> his child without damaging a human life.*

CONSTRUCTION PROBLEMS

Wordiness

Wordiness means using more words than necessary to convey the point of the sentence. (also called Superfluous wording). You should work to eliminate words that don't add meaning or add redundancy

Examples: *"When Pete and the guard were finally alone they spoke <u>to each other</u> in a relaxed manner."* If Pete and the guard are alone and they speak, of course it will be to each other…no one else is present. *"The smoke from the camp fire rose softly <u>through the air</u>.* The smoke must rise "through the air" it's not rising through the water or any other substance…so that phrase is redundant.

Superfluous Phrases: *"half of an hour" better said (half hour).   "neighbor of mine" better said (my neighbor).   "in an appropriate manner better said (appropriately)*

Sentence Fragments: • Identify sentences that are dependent/subordinate clauses: *Immediately after the fall of the Roman Empire in the 5th century.* (more is needed to complete the thought)

Sentence Run-Ons: • The sentence appears, or sounds, bulky and cumbersome in communicating its message clearly.
- The sentence contains more than two or more independent clauses without a conjunction. (not an absolute, but certainly a clue): *I will give you directions for the shortest way here, the traffic is heavy along that route.* (a comma alone can't connect two independent clauses)

Comparative vs. Superlative Use

A modifier in the **comparative** degree would compare a person, a thing, an action, or an idea with another one. A modifier in the **superlative** degree would be used to compare a person, a thing, an action, or an idea with at least two others.

Comparative: *That line is longer than the one for the other movie.*
Superlative: *That line is the longest one that I have ever seen.*

Incorrect:	*Jim is more funnier than anyone else in the group.*
Correct:	*Jim is funnier than anyone else in the group.*
Confusing:	*Richard plays the oboe better than anyone in the class.*
	This sentence says either that Richard plays the oboe better than anyone in the class, including himself, or that Richard plays the oboe better than anyone in a class of which he is not a part.
Less Confusing:	*Richard can play the oboe better than anyone else in the class.* **OR...** *Richard is the best oboe player in his class.*

Idiomatic Words and Phrases

What is an idiom? An **idiom** is any English phrase that is natural and normal, and clearly understandable to a native speaker.
"Did you hear that Madison got a scholarship?"   *"Yes, I heard it through the grapevine."*

Of course, the second speaker does not mean he heard the news about Madison by putting his ear to a grapevine! He is conveying the idea of information spreading around a widespread network, usually similar to a grapevine.
We use idioms to express something that other words do not express as clearly or as cleverly. Idioms tend to be informal and are best used in spoken rather than written English.

Idioms: The Good News--Sometimes idioms are very easy for learners to understand because there are similar expressions in the speakers' mother tongue. For example: He always goes at things like a bull in a china shop! Unfortunately, the test does not favor the use of idiomatic language, and recognizing an idiomatic phrase will help you find mistakes.

Here "B" some Idioms:

bad-mouth (verb)	beat around the bush	break someone's heart
be a piece of cake	beat one's brains out	broke
be all ears	Beats me.	bug (verb)
be broke	bent out of shape	bull-headed
be fed up with	before long	buck(s)
be in and out	bite off more than one can chew	a bundle
be on the go	blabbermouth	burn the midnight oil
be on the road	blow one's top	bushed
be over	boom box	by one's self
be up and running	the bottom line	by the skin of one's teeth
be used to	blow one's top	
beat (adj.)	Break a leg!	

Paired Words of Confusion

Important Note See the extensive list of words in the Big Book of Grammar Drills

1.	accept	vs.	except	9.	good	vs.	well	
2	affect	vs.	effect	10.	learn	vs.	teach	
3.	and	vs.	etc.	11.	leave	vs.	let	
4.	beside	vs.	besides	12.	rise	vs.	raise	
5.	between	vs.	among	13.	shall	vs.	will	
6.	bring	vs.	take	14.	sit	vs.	set	
7.	discover	vs.	invent	15.	than	vs.	then	
8.	fewer	vs.	less	16.	way vs.		ways	
				17.	cite	vs.	site	
				18.	complement	vs.	compliment	
				19.	conscience	vs.	conscious	
				20.	council	vs.	counsel	

21. delusion vs.	illusion
22. disinterested vs. uninterested
23. farther vs.	further
24. hanged vs.	hung
25. loose vs.	lose
26. maybe vs.	may be
27. moral vs.	morale
28. passed vs.	past
29. quiet vs.	quite
30. principal vs.	principle

Single Words and Phrases Of Confusion

Important Note See the extensive list of words in the **Big Book of Grammar Drills (pages 269-424)**

- **sick** should not be used for displeased, bored, disgusted
- **party** should only be used for legal references
- **alibi** again legal term, a formal defense descriptive term
- **dilemma** two unsatisfactory choices
- **average** computation needs to be made
- **essential** necessary for the existence of
- **per** only in standard business expressions (per diem)
- **plus** does not mean "and"
- **sadistic** form of sexual perversion
- **irregardless** nonstandard
- **could of / would of** nonstandard

- **unique** only one of a kind
- **vital** that which is necessary for existence
- **get** informal; use arrive, recover, receive
- **thing** too broad, should be avoided
- **finalize** nonstandard, "fad word"
- **firm up** nonstandard, "fad word"
- **if and when** impossible phrase
- **ought** nonstandard, should not
- **want in / want out** nonstandard
- **a lot** nonstandard

Sentence Structure

Simple Sentence (SS) contains: One independent clause.
Compound Sentence (CS) contains: **Two or more independent clauses that are joined.**
Complex Sentence (CXS) contains: **One independent clause and one or more subordinate clauses.**
Compound-Complex Sentence (CCS) contains: **Two or more independent clauses and one or more subordinate clauses.**

Exercise: Identify the type of sentence structure for each example listed below by placing the abbreviation in the blank.
1. *George Vancouver was exploring the northwest territory.* **Simple Sentence**
2. *Since it was not a harbor, Vancouver had been deceived, and Deception Pass became its name.* **Complex Sentence**
3. *Vancouver originally thought the channel was a harbor.*   **Simple Sentence**

4. *In 1792 Vancouver discovered a channel, and he gave it an unusual name.* **Compound Sentence**
5. *The play Les Miserables, which we are producing ourselves, had better be a success, or we cannot afford another one.* **Complex Compound Sentence**

Misplaced Phrases & Clauses

Misplacement of phrases can significantly change the meaning of the sentence.

Exercise: Identify the phrase or clause that is misplaced, and correctly rearrange the sentence.

1. *Plunging more than 1,000 feet into the gorge, we saw Yosemite Falls.*
   Corrected Sentence: We saw Yosemite Falls plunging more than 1,000 feet into the gorge.
2. *Please take time to look over the brochure that is enclosed with your family.*
   Corrected Sentence: Please take some time with your family to look over the enclosed brochure.
3. *The patient was referred to a psychiatrist with a severe emotional problem.*
   Corrected Sentence: The patient with a severe emotional problem was referred to a psychiatrist.

Comma Splices & Run-On Sentences

The comma-splice and run-on sentence (and the fused sentence, as a variant is called) are all examples of the problem in which two or more sentences are improperly joined. In the typical ***comma-splice*** sentence, two sentences are joined by a comma without an intervening coordinating conjunction (*and, or, nor, but, yet*). Technically, the ***run-on*** sentence is a sentence that goes on and on and needs to be broken up; it's likely to be a comma splice as well. A ***fused*** sentence is two complete sentence just jammed together without any punctuation and without a conjunction.

Example: *Sometimes, books do not have the most complete information, it is a good idea then to look for articles in specialized periodicals.*
Correct: *Sometimes, books do not have the most complete information; it is a good idea then to look for articles in specialized periodicals.*

Example: *Most of the hours I've earned toward my associate's degree do not transfer, however, I do have at least some hours the University will accept.*
Correct: *Most of the hours I've earned toward my associate's degree do not transfer. However, I do have at least some hours the University will accept.*

Example: *Some people were highly educated professionals, others were from small villages in underdeveloped countries.*
Correct: *Some people were highly educated professionals, while others were from small villages in underdeveloped countries.*

Example: *This report presents the data we found concerning the cost of the water treatment project, then it presents comparative data from other similar projects.*
Correct: *This report first presents the data we found concerning the cost of the water treatment project and then comparative data from other similar projects.*

Modifiers

Modifier problems occur when the word or phrase that a modifier is supposed to modify is unclear or absent, or when the modifier is located in the wrong place within the sentence. A **modifier** is any element--a word, phrase, or clause--that adds information to a noun or pronoun in a sentence. Modifier problems are usually divided into two groups: misplaced modifiers and dangling modifiers.

Misplaced modifier
1. *They found out that the walkways had collapsed on the late evening news.* (Was that before or after the sports news?)
2. *The committee nearly spent a hundred hours investigating the accident.* (Did they spend even a minute?)
3. *The supervisor said after the initial planning the in-depth study would begin.*
(Just when did she say that, and when will the study begin?)

Dangling modifier
4. *Having damaged the previous one, a new fuse was installed in the car.* (damaged the fuse or the car?)

5. *After receiving the new dumb waiter, it was immediately installed.*
(Who received the dumb waiter?)

6. *Using a grant from the Urban Mass Transportation Administration, a contraflow lane was designed for I-45 North.*
(Who used that money?)

To correct misplaced modifier problems, you can usually relocate the misplaced modifier (the word or phrase). To correct dangling modifiers, you can rephrase the dangling modifier, or rephrase the rest of the sentence that it modifies. This usually means converting the sentence from passive to active voice.

1. *On the late evening news, we heard that the walkways had collapsed.*
2. *The committee spent nearly a hundred hours investigating the accident.*
3. *The supervisor said that the in-depth study would begin after the initial planning.*
4. *Because the previous fuse had been damaged, a new one had to be installed.* **OR...** *Having damaged the previous fuse, I had to install a new one in my car.*
5. *After we received the dumb waiter, it was immediately installed.* **OR...***After receiving the dumb waiter, we immediately installed it.*
6. *When the Urban Mass Transportation Administration granted funds to the city, planners began designing a contraflow lane for I-45 North.* **OR...***Using a grant from the Urban Mass Transportation Administration, city planners designed a contraflow lane for I-45 North.*

Fragments

Fragments are simply incomplete sentences—grammatically incomplete.

Example: Mary appeared at the committee meeting last week. And made a convincing presentation of her ideas about the new product.
Revision: Mary appeared at the committee meeting last week and made a convincing presentation of her ideas about the new product.

Example: *The committee considered her ideas for a new marketing strategy quite powerful. The best ideas that they had heard in years.*
Revision: *The committee considered her ideas for a new marketing strategy quite powerful, the best ideas that they had heard in years.*

Example: *In a proposal, you must include a number of sections. For example, a discussion of your personnel and their qualifications, your expectations concerning the schedule of the project, and a cost breakdown.*
Revision: In a proposal, you must include a number of sections: for example, a discussion of your personnel and their qualifications, your expectations concerning the schedule of the project, and a cost breakdown.

Example: *The research team has completely reorganized the workload. Making sure that members work in areas of their own expertise and that no member is assigned proportionately too much work.*
Revision: The research team has completely reorganized the workload. They made sure that members work in areas of their own expertise and that no member is assigned proportionately too much work.

Example: *She spent a full month evaluating his computer-based instructional materials. Which she eventually sent to her supervisor with the strongest of recommendations.*
Revision: She spent a full month evaluating his computer-based instructional materials. Eventually, she sent the evaluation to her supervisor with the strongest of recommendations.

Shifts in Construction

A **shift in construction** is a change in the structure of style midway through a sentence. One example of this covered earlier is Subject/Verb agreement. On the test, you will be expected to identify shifts in the construction of the sentence. The test will offer you selections, and you will need to pick the best possible solution to correct the shift that occurs in the sentence.

There is more than one way to correct these problems. Each suggested change offered below is probably not the only correct one for the sentence.

Sample Questions: Shift in verb construction

1. If the club <u>limited</u> its membership, it <u>will have to raise</u> its dues.
2. As Barbara <u>puts</u> in her contact lenses, the telephone <u>rang</u>.
3. Thousands of people <u>will see</u> the art exhibit by the time it <u>closes</u>.
4. By the time negotiations <u>began</u>, many pessimists <u>have expressed</u> doubt about them.
5. After Capt. James Cook <u>visited</u> Alaska on his third voyage, he <u>is killed</u> by Hawaiian islanders in 1779.
6. I <u>was</u> terribly disappointed with my grade because I <u>studied</u> very hard.
7. The moderator <u>asks</u> for questions as soon as the speaker <u>has finished</u>.
8. Everyone <u>hopes</u> the plan <u>would work</u>.
9. Harry <u>wants</u> to show his friends the photos he <u>took</u> last summer.
10. Scientists <u>predict</u> that the sun <u>will die</u> in the distant future.
11. The boy <u>insisted</u> that he <u>has paid</u> for the candy bars.
12. The doctor <u>suggested</u> bed rest for the patient, who <u>suffers</u> from a bad cold.

Answers: 1. (change will to would) 2. (change puts to put) 3. No change 4. (change have to had) 5. (change is to was) 6. (change studied to had studied) 7. (asks as habitual action; will ask is also possible) 8. (change hopes to hoped) 9. No Change 10. No Change 11. (change has to had) 12. (change suffers to was suffering)

English

Part 4: Practice Questions
Virtual Classroom>English> Practice Questions

This material corresponds to the Virtual Classroom in the
PowerPrep DVD/Internet/iApp for English

Virtual Classroom

Part 4: Practice Questions

QUESTIONS AND ANSWERS 1-4

Questions 1-4

1. Of all the potential occurrences that can endanger the world economy, the possibility of famine <u>is maybe the more difficult for prediction</u>.
   - (A) is maybe the more difficult for prediction
   - (B) is probably the most difficult to predict
   - (C) is maybe the most difficult for prediction
   - (D) is probably the more difficult to predict
   - (E) is, it may be, the prediction that is most difficult

2. The most important decision for many star athletes playing in a struggling league undergoing <u>being reconfigured to be competitive is if to sign</u> for a professional team or to stay in school.
   - (A) being reconfigured to be competitive is if to sign
   - (B) being reconfigured to be competitive is whether they should be signing
   - (C) being reconfigured to be competitive is whether or not they sign
   - (D) reconfiguration to be competitive is if to sign
   - (E) reconfiguration to be competitive is whether to sign

3. The beginning of the eighteenth century saw the emergence of the industrial revolution, with advances fabricating textiles, creating a need for an unprecedented amount of factories, and <u>produced</u> an economic boom that spread across the world.
   - (A) produced
   - (B) it produced
   - (C) would produce
   - (D) producing
   - (E) it had produced

4. A study conducted by the Berkeley National Laboratory Environmental Division has concluded that <u>much of the presently problematic pollutants to which Californians are exposed comes</u> from the combustion of hydrocarbons and oxidation of nitrogen gas.
   - (A) much of the presently problematic pollutants to which Californians are exposed comes
   - (B) much of the presently problematic pollutants that Californians are exposed to come
   - (C) much of the pollutants that are presently problematic and that Californians are exposed to comes
   - (D) many of the pollutants that are presently problematic and Californians are exposed to come
   - (E) many of the presently problematic pollutants to which Californians are exposed to come

Answers to Questions 1-4

Explanation Question #1: Choice B is best. The sentence compares one thing, *famine*, to *all potential occurrences that can endanger the world economy*; therefore, the sentence requires the superlative form of the adjective, *most difficult*, rather than the comparative form, *more difficult*, which appears in choices A and D. In A and C, the use of *maybe* is unidiomatic, and *difficult* should be completed by the infinitive *to predict*. Choice E is awkwardly phrased and produces an illogical structure when inserted into the sentence: *the possibility…is…the prediction that*.

Explanation Question #2: In A, B, and C the phrase *being reconfigured* is awkward and redundant, since the sense of process indicated by *being* has already been conveyed by *undergoing*. A and D incorrectly use *if* where it is necessary to employ *whether* since the sentence poses alternative abilities, to sign or not to sign. Only E idiomatically completes *whether* with an infinitive, *to sign*, that functions as a noun equivalent of *decision*. Choice E also uses the noun *reconfiguration*, which grammatically completes the phrase begun by *undergoing*.

Explanation Question #3: Choice D is best. The third verb phrase in the series describing the *advances* should have the same grammatical form as the first two. Only D uses the present participle (or "-ing") form that is parallel with the two preceding verbs *fabricating* and *creating*. A and B incorrectly use the past tense (*produced*), C uses an auxiliary verb (*would produce*), and E uses the past perfect tense (*had produced*). In addition, B and E introduce incorrect verb tenses with the pronoun *it*, which lacks a logical referent.

Explanation Question #4: Choices A, B and C are faulty because the countable noun *pollutants* should be modified by *many* rather than *much*, which is used with uncountable nouns such as "joy" or "hardship". Additionally, A and C incorrectly use the singular verb *comes* with the plural noun *pollutants*. Choices C and D are needlessly wordy, and D requires *that* before *Californians* to be grammatically complete and to retain meaning. **Choice E is correct and concise.**

ENGLISH—IMPROVING PARAGRAPHS

PQ #1 "Love & War" Passage

Directions: *Correctly Edit The Paragraph* Read the Passage #1 below called **Love and War**. <u>see if you can find all 32 errors</u> keep in mind there are several ways to fix every sentence. make sure you identify problems, but don't worry if your proposed fix is slightly different from the one provided in the answer. Use the chart below to assist with tracking the errors. Use a pencil to mark-up the passage identifying the mistakes. Once you have identified all the errors you can find, check it against the provided answers.

Correction 1	Correction 2	Correction 3	Correction 4	Correction 5	Correction 6	Correction 7	Correction 8
Correction 9	Correction 10	Correction 11	Correction 12	Correction 13	Correction 14	Correction 15	Correction 16
Correction 17	Correction 18	Correction 19	Correction 20	Correction 21	Correction 22	Correction 23	Correction 24
Correction 25	Correction 26	Correction 27	Correction 28	Correction 29	Correction 30	Correction 31	Correction 32

LOVE AND WAR--Passage

In ancient greek mythology helen and meneleaus was married to each other in marriage. The wedding was disrupted however when a man named paris fell in love with helen who's face was considered the most buautifulest in the world. Paris kidnapped helen some say she didn't mind and together they fled to the city of Troy. Disgraced and deceived meneleaus was pretty much fit to be tied and sent the whole greek army to troy to get helen back. This timeless tale is written down in The Iliad, and epic work by homer. Reading the story today you might think how ridiculous it was to fight a war over a lost love, on the other hand we don't have no photographs of helen whose face has been called the face that launched a thousand ships.

PQ #1 "Love & War" Answer

Sentence 1: In ancient greek mythology Helen and meneleaus was married to each other in marriage.

Corrections: In Ancient Greek mythology, Helen and Meneleaus WERE married.
Explanations:
- "Ancient Greek", "Helen", and "Meneleaus" need to be capitalized because they are proper nouns.
- Replace "was" with "were" because the subject "Helen and Meneleaus" is a plural subject.
- A comma is need after "*mythology*" to separate dependent clauses.
- "*to each other in marriage*" is taken out because it is redundant.--bear in mind it's possible to argue "to each other" adds some information (what if they are married, but not "to each other"). But you get the point--be careful about word usage and make sure each word has a job and adds to your writing.

Sentence 2: The wedding was disrupted however when a man named paris fell in love with helen who's face was considered the most buautifulest in the world..
Corrections: The wedding was disrupted however, when Paris fell in love with Helen, WHOSE face was considered the most beautiful.
Explanations:
- A comma is needed after "*however*" to **separate dependent clauses.**
- "*a man named*" is taken out because it is **superfluous wording**.
- "*Paris*" and "*Helen*" need to be **capitalized** because they are proper nouns.
- "*who's*" is changed to "*whose*" because it should be a **pronoun**, not a contraction.
- The –est is taken off of "*beautifulest*" because it is **improper**.
- "*in the world*" is taken out because it is **superfluous wording**.

Sentence 3: Paris kidnapped helen some say she didn't mind and together they fled to the city of Troy.
Corrections: Paris kidnapped Helen; some say she didn't mind and THEY FLED to the City of Troy.
Explanations:
- "*Helen*" and "*City*" need to be **capitalized** because they are proper nouns.
- A semicolon is needed after "*Helen*" to **separate independent clauses**.
- "*together*" is taken out because it is **superfluous wording**.

Sentence 4: Disgraced and deceived meneleaus was pretty much fit to be tied and sent the whole greek army to troy to get helen back.
Corrections: Disgraced and deceived, Meneleaus was ANGRY and sent the Greek army to Troy to FIND Helen.
Explanations:
- A comma is needed after "*deceived*" to **separate dependent clauses**.
- "*Meneleaus*", "*Greek*", "*Troy*", and "*Helen*" need to be **capitalized** because they are proper nouns.

- "*pretty much fit to be tied*" is replaced with "*angry*" because we want to avoid using **clichés**.
- "*whole*" and "*back*" are taken out because it is **superfluous wording**.
- "*to get*" is replaced with "*find*" because we want to avoid **general words**.

Sentence 5: This timeless tale is written down in The Iliad, and epic work by homer.
  Correction: This timeless tale is written in *THE ILIAD*, AN epic work by Homer.
  Explanations:
- "*down*" is taken out to reduce **wordiness**.
- "*The Iliad*" is **italicized** because it is a title.
- "*and*" is replaced with "*an*" because an **article** is needed in its place.
- "*Homer*" is **capitalized** because it is a proper noun.

Sentence 6: Reading the story today you might think how ridiculous it was to fight a war over a lost love, on the other hand we don't have no photographs of helen whose face has been called the face that launched a thousand ships.
  Correction: Reading the story, ONE might think how ridiculous it was to fight a war over a lost love. On the other hand, we don't have photographs of Helen, whose face has been called "the face that launched a thousand ships."
  Explanations:
- A comma is added after "*story*" to **separate dependent clauses**.
- "*today*" is taken out to reduce **wordiness**.
- "*you*" is replaced with "*one*"
- A period is added after "*love*" to **finalize the sentence**.
- "*On*" is **capitalized** because it is the start of a new sentence.
- A comma is added after "*hand*" to **separate dependent clauses**.
- "*no*" is taken out to correct a **double negative**.
- "*Helen*" is **capitalized** because it is a proper noun.
- Quotation marks are placed around "*the face that launched a thousand ships*" because it is a quote.

The Final Passage Should Look Like This: *LOVE and WAR* **(corrections)**
In Ancient Greek mythology, Helen and Meneleaus were married. The wedding was disrupted however, when Paris fell in love with Helen, whose face was considered the most beautiful. Paris kidnapped Helen; some say she didn't mind and they fled to the City of Troy. Disgraced and deceived, Meneleaus was angry and sent the Greek army to Troy to find Helen. This timeless tale is written in *The Iliad*, an epic work by Homer. Reading the story, one might think how ridiculous it was to fight a war over a lost love. On the other hand, we don't have photographs of Helen, whose face has been called "the face that launched a thousand ships."

LOVE AND WAR (alternative corrections)

In ancient Greek mythology Helen and Meneleaus were married to each other ~~in marriage~~. The wedding was disrupted ~~however~~ when ~~a man named~~ Paris fell in love with Helen—whose ~~who's~~ face was considered the most beautiful in the world. Some say Helen did not mind when Paris kidnapped her, and together they fled to the city of Troy. Disgraced and deceived, Meneleaus ~~was pretty much fit to be tied and~~ sent the whole Greek army to Troy to get Helen back. **Homer told this story in his epic work called the Iliad.** ~~This timeless tale is written down in The Iliad, and epic work by homer.~~ ~~Reading the story~~ Today ~~you~~ some might think ~~how~~ it ridiculous ~~it was~~ to fight a war over a lost love. On the other hand, we do not have ~~no~~ photographs of Helen, whose face ~~has been called the face that~~ was said to have launched a thousand ships.

PQ #2 "Popcorn An All-American Snack" Passage

Directions: *Correctly Edit The Paragraph   Read the Passage #1 below called **Popcorn--An All-American Snack**. **see if you can find all 27 errors** keep in mind there are several ways to fix every sentence. make sure you identify problems, but don't worry if your proposed fix is slightly different from the one provided in the answer. Use the chart below to assist with tracking the errors.   Use a pencil to mark-up the passage identifying the mistakes. Once you have identified all the errors you can find, check it against the provided answers.*

Correction 1	Correction 2	Correction 3	Correction 4	Correction 5	Correction 6	Correction 7	Correction 8
Correction 9	Correction 10	Correction 11	Correction 12	Correction 13	Correction 14	Correction 15	Correction 16
Correction 17	Correction 18	Correction 19	Correction 20	Correction 21	Correction 22	Correction 23	Correction 24
Correction 25	Correction 26	Correction 27					

Popcorn—An All-American Snack--*Passage*

There's many different types of corn, and popcorn is one of the oldest, it looks a lot like other corn, but it's kernels are more smaller and harder then the other types. Inside the hard outer shell are a mass of moist starch. When the kernel is heated. The shell bursts and the starch puffed out. Popcorn is native to both north and south America. It was used by native americans for food and decoration and in religious ceremonies. Thousand's of years before europeans arrived in the americas. According to legend the puritans ate bowls of popcorn at the first thanksgiving and ever since than it has been 1 of our most popularish snack foods.

PQ #2 "Popcorn—An All-American Snack" Answer

Sentence 1: There's many different types of corn, and popcorn is one of the oldest, it looks a lot like other corn, but it's kernels are more smaller and harder then the other types.
  Correction: THERE ARE many types of corn, and popcorn is one of the oldest. It looks a lot like other corn, but ITS kernels are smaller and harder THAN the other types.
  Explanations:
- "*There's*" is replaced with "*There are*" because the **subject is plural**.
- A period is added after "*oldest*" to **finalize the sentence**.

- "*It*" is **capitalized** because it is the start of a new sentence.
- "*it's*" is replaced with "*its*" because a **possessive noun** is needed.
- "*more*" is taken out because it is redundant.
- "*then*" is replaced with "*than*" because we need a word for **comparison**.

Sentence 2: Inside the hard outer shell are a mass of moist starch.
  Correction: Inside the hard outer shell IS a mass of moist starch.
  Explanations:
- "*are*" is replaced with "*is*" because the subject "*shell*" is **singular**.

Sentence 3: When the kernel is heated. The shell bursts and the starch puffed out.
  Correction: When the kernel is heated, THE shell bursts and the starch PUFFS out.
  Explanations:
- A comma is added after "*heated*" to **connect the dependent clause** with the next sentence.
- "*the*" is no longer capitalized because it isn't the start of a new sentence.
- "*puffed*" is changed to "*puffs*" to have **parallel** structure.

Sentence 4: Popcorn is native to both north and south America.
  Correction: Popcorn is native to both NORTH and SOUTH America.
  Explanations:
- "*North*" and "*South*" need to be **capitalized** because they are proper nouns.

Sentence 5: It was used by native Americans for food and decoration and in religious ceremonies.
  Correction: It was used by Native Americans for food, decorations, and religious ceremonies.
  Explanations:
- "*Native*" is **capitalized** because it is a proper noun.
- Commas are added after "*food*" and "*decoration*" because **a list** is given.
- "*and*" and "*in*" are taken out to have **parallel** structure.

Sentence 6: Thousand's of years before Europeans arrived in the Americas.
  Correction: It was used by Native Americans for food, decorations, and religious ceremonies THOUSANDS OF YEARS BEFORE EUROPEANS ARRIVED IN AMERICA.
  Explanations:
- "*Thousand's*" is changed to "*thousands*" because it is a **plural** case.
- "*the*" is taken out and "*Americas*" is changed to "*America*"
- "*thousands of years before Europeans arrived in America*" is added to the previous sentence to **complete the thought**.

Sentence 7: *According to legend the puritans ate bowls of popcorn at the first thanksgiving and ever since than it has been 1 of our most popularish snack foods.*
  Correction: According to legend, the Puritans ate bowls of popcorn at the first Thanksgiving and since THEN, it has been ONE of our most POPULAR snack foods.
  Explanations:
- A comma is added after "*legend*" because it indicates a **clause**.
- "*Puritans*" and "*Thanksgiving*" is **capitalized** because they are proper nouns.
- "*ever*" is taken out to reduce **wordiness**.
- "*than*" is replaced with "*then*" to indicate **sequence**.
- A comma is added after "*then*" to indicate **a natural pause**.
- "*1*" is spelled out "*one*"
- "*popularish*" is replaced with "*popular*"

The final passage should look like the following:

Popcorn—An All-American Snack (corrections)

There are many types of corn, and popcorn is one of the oldest. It looks a lot like other corn, but its kernels are smaller and harder than the other types. Inside the hard outer shell is a mass of moist starch. When the kernel is heated, the shell bursts and the starch puffs out. Popcorn is native to both North and South America. It was used by Native Americans for food, decorations, and religious ceremonies. It was used by Native Americans for food, decorations, and religious ceremonies thousands of years before Europeans arrived in America. According to legend, the Puritans ate bowls of popcorn at the first Thanksgiving and since then, it has been one of our most popular snack foods.

Popcorn—An All-American Snack (alternative corrections)

~~There's~~ There are many different types of corn. But popcorn is one of the oldest. Although it looks **a lot** like other corn, **its** kernels are ~~more~~ smaller and harder ~~then~~ **than** the other types. Inside the hard outer shell ~~are~~ is a mass of moist starch. When the kernel is heated, **the** shell bursts and the starch **puffs** out. Popcorn is native to both North and South America. Thousands of years before Europeans arrived in the Americas it was used by Native Americans for food, ~~and~~ decoration, and ~~in~~ religious ceremonies. According to legend, the Puritans ate bowls of popcorn at the first Thanksgiving and ever since ~~than~~ **then** it has been ~~1~~ one of our most popular snack foods.

CONGRATULATIONS!!

You Have Completed the English Workbook!!

Take a Break Before Moving on to the Next Section.

Essay Writing Workbook
Table of Contents

This Material Corresponds to the Virtual Classroom Section in the
PowerPrep DVD/Internet/iApp for Essay Writing

Virtual Classroom

234

Essay Writing

Part 1: How to Write

Virtual Classroom>Essay Writing> How to Write
This Material Corresponds to the Virtual Classroom in the
PowerPrep DVD/Internet/iApp for Essay Writing

Virtual Classroom

Important Abbreviations

These abbreviations are used throughout the program

POE: Process of Elimination
SARR: Synthesize, Analyze, Reduce, and Restate (has to do with Logical Reasoning)
AC: Answer Choice
QS: Question Stem
LOD: Level of Difficulty

Example Question: What is the least common multiple of 3, 4, and 7? **(This is the call of the question or Question Stem "QS")**

These are Answer Choices "AC" A, B, C, D, E

(A) 12
(B) 21
(C) 28
(D) 48
(E) 84

Part 1: How to Write

GOALS

This workshop will:

- ☑ Familiarize you with each type of essay question, helping you understand exactly what is being asked.
- ☑ Explain clearly a methodology for test day.
- ☑ provide rubrics, covering the key components of an excellent, average and poor response.
- ☑ help you develop a greater understanding of the process in creating a quality opinionated essay.
- ☑ highlight essential characteristics and elements which make up effective analytical essays.
- ☑ help you break down an argument, thus creating an effective critical analysis.
- ☑ provide sample essay questions, responses, and analysis of these responses based on the rubrics.
- ☑ provide opportunities for you to write responses to some sample questions.

DESCRIPTION OF QUESTIONS

Analysis of an Issue

Objective: In this section you are to take a particular position and thoroughly explain your viewpoint.
- There is no "correct" answer.
- There is no specific stance on any given issue that will increase your score.

Example: "Regardless of the person's position in life, be it president or pauper, everyone should have the same right to privacy. In this regard, as long as the public is not in danger, the media should stay out of people's personal lives."

Discuss the extent to which you agree or disagree with the opinion stated above. Support your view with relevant information from your own background, education or experience.

Analysis of an Argument

Objective: In this section you are to analyze a specific, already formulated argument.
- Do not express your own views regarding the subject.
- Assess only the validity of the argument.
- Exhibit clear reasoning when refuting or defending the writer's claims.

Example: The following editorial appeared in a local newspaper:

"During spring break, 50 high school students from Sycamore Unified School District protested at the state capital against mandated exit tests. The other 10,000 students, evidently unconcerned about this issue, decided to stay home or do something more important. Since the group that decided not to protest was far more numerous it is obvious that this issue is not that important to the vast majority of SUSD high school students. Therefore, the State Board of Education should not heed the appeals of such a few disgruntled students."

Discuss how compelling you find the above argument. Analyze the reasoning presented, using the evidence that supports the author's claims. Explain what may strengthen or refute the assertions made, what changes would make the argument more sound or what evidence would change the conclusion.

GENERAL ESSAY FORMAT

Opening Paragraph

Objective: The opening paragraph should gain the reader's attention and it should identify the thesis statement.
- Thesis is the controlling idea.
- Thesis focuses the essay, identifying what you are trying to prove, assert or claim.
- Thesis is the most vital part of the essay.

> **Simple thesis formula:** Subject + specific feeling or characteristic = thesis

Some possible starting points:
- Present a brief background to your subject or topic.
- Define a key term or concept that leads you to more specifics.
- Provide a personal account or history that relates to the topic.
- Challenge the reader to look at the topic in a different light, thus gaining interest.
- Use a brief quote that leads the reader to your topic.
- Begin with a brief taste of your conclusion teasing the reader.
- Open with some drama to emphasize some key ideas you will discuss later.

Supporting Paragraphs

Objective: The supporting paragraphs provide the evidence that clearly and logically proves your thesis.
- Contains a topic sentence.
- Contains facts, ideas or concepts that support the thesis.

• Clearly arranged and organized.

Some possible arrangements:
• **Chronological:** Order your details according to which happened first.
• **Classify:** Explain your concept generally and then provide specifics explaining its unique features.
• **Location:** Arrange details left to right, front to back, top to bottom, east to west, etc.
• **Compare or contrast:** Measure one idea or concept to another within the same category. State the likeness or difference between the two.
• **Cause and effect:** Make connections between results and the events that produced or proceeded that result.
• **Deduction:** State the main idea (topic sentence) give specific details, examples or facts supporting the main idea.
• **Induction:** Provide details, examples or facts building towards a general supporting statement (topic sentence).

Levels of detail:
1. **Topic sentence:** A statement that focuses the paragraph.
2. **Clarifying sentence:** Makes the topic clearer and puts the topic in context.
3. **Completing sentence:** This adds specifics that further explain or describe the topic.

Transitional Statements

Objective: Transitional statements help connect ideas and help the reader follow your proof.

Location					
above	*across*	*against*	*along*	*among*	*around*
away from	*behind*	*below*	*beneath*	*beside*	*between*
beyond	*by*	*down*	*in back of*	*in front of*	*inside*
into	*near*	*off*	*on top of*	*onto*	*outside*
over	*throughout*	*to the right*	*under*		
Time					
about	*first*	*meanwhile*	*soon*	*then*	*after*
second	*later*	*next*	*at*	*before*	*during*
until	*finally*	*as soon as*	*when*	*afterward*	
Similarities					
likewise	*like*	*in the same way*	*as*	*also*	*similarly*
Differences					
however	*otherwise*	*although*	*on the other hand*	*but*	*yet*
still	*even though*				
Emphasis					
again	*for this reason*	*truly*	*to repeat*	*in fact*	*to emphasize*
Summarize					
as a result	*finally*	*in conclusion*	*to sum up*	*therefore*	*last*
in summary	*all in all*				
Detail					
again	*another*	*for instance*	*also*	*and*	*besides*
additionally	*next*	*likewise*	*along with*	*for example*	*moreover*
Clarification					
in other words	*for instance*	*put another way*	*that is*		

Concluding Paragraph

Objective: The concluding paragraph restates the main ideas that support your thesis.
• Brief and concise.
• Tie essential points together.
• Make clear connections to thesis.

IMAGE OF GENERAL ESSAY

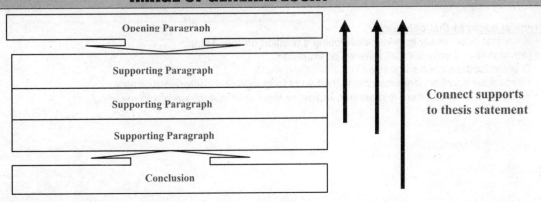

Tell 'em what you're going to tell 'em, tell 'em, and then tell 'em what you told 'em

METHODOLOGY: 5-STEPS

Objective: A 5-step process in formulating an effective essay under testing and time constraints.

1. **Absorb the Issue or Argument:** • Understand the task • Define key terms or points (t-chart) • Look at explicit and implied meaning • Form questions
2. **Develop/Recognize Key Points:** • Look at both sides • Look at depth or extent of proof • Identify flaws or weak points
3. **Arrange Proof:** • Create thesis • Quick outline • Connect to thesis
4. **Write/Type:** • Use assertive language • Be clear and concise • Use transitions to connect ideas • Provide a strong summary
5. **Final Editing:** • Look for problems in logic/understanding • Any obvious grammar problems?

SCORING & GRADING RUBRICS

Scoring

Objective: *show* ability to logically formulate and clearly articulate ideas in writing. • Human and "e-rater" • Holistic scoring

Keys:
- **Structure:** Clear organization (see diagram).
- **Thesis:** What you are going to prove.
- **Beginning/conclusion:** Set the tone and provide the final impression.
- **Clarity:** Omit needless words.
- **Correct grammar/punctuation:** Avoid spelling errors and awkward sentences.
- **Transitions:** Use words and phrases that connect ideas.
- **Reasonable:** Exhibit clear logic that is sensible and rational.

"E-rater" Keys:
- Be careful about being too creative.
- Use keywords that indicate a progression of ideas.

Grading

Score 6:
A 6 paper presents a cogent, well-articulated analysis of the complexities of the issue and demonstrates mastery of the elements of effective writing.

A typical paper in this category:
- develops a position on the issue with insightful reasons and/or persuasive examples.
- sustains a well-focused, well-organized discussion.
- expresses ideas clearly and precisely.
- uses language fluently, with varied sentence structure and effective vocabulary.
- demonstrates superior facility with the conventions of standards written English but may have minor flaws.

Score 4:
A 4 paper presents a competent analysis of the issue and demonstrates adequate control of the elements of writing.

A typical paper in this category:
- develops a position on the issue with relevant reasons and/or examples.
- is adequately organized.
- expresses ideas clearly.
- demonstrates adequate control of language but may lack sentence variety.
- demonstrates control of the convention of standard written English but may have some flaws.

Score 2:
A 2 paper demonstrates serious weaknesses in analytical writing. A typical paper in this category exhibits one or more of the following characteristics:

A typical paper in this category:
- is unclear or seriously limited in developing a position on the issue.
- provides few, if any, relevant reasons or examples.
- is unfocused and/or disorganized.
- has serious and frequent problems in the use of language and sentence structure.
- contains numerous errors in grammar, usage, or mechanic that interfere with meaning.

Essay Writing

Part 2: Comparing SAT and ACT Writing

<u>Virtual Classroom>Essay Writing>Compare SAT & ACT Writing</u>

This Material Corresponds to the Virtual Classroom in the
PowerPrep DVD/Internet/iApp for Essay Writing

Virtual Classroom

Important Abbreviations
These abbreviations are used throughout the program

POE: Process of Elimination
SARR: Synthesize, Analyze, Reduce, and Restate (has to do with Logical Reasoning)
AC: Answer Choice
QS: Question Stem
LOD: Level of Difficulty

Example Question: What is the least common multiple of 3, 4, and 7? (**This is the call of the question or Question Stem "QS"**)

These are Answer Choices "AC" A, B, C, D, E

    (A)   12
    (B)   21
    (C)   28
    (D)   48
    (E)   84

Part 2: Compare SAT & ACT Writing

SAT ESSAY INSTRUCTIONS & PROMPT

SAT Essay Instructions

For additional information about the SAT, visit our site http://eknowledge.com/TOC_SAT_MAIN_PAGE.asp

The essay measures your ability to:
- Develop a point of view on an issue presented in an excerpt
- Support your point of view using reasoning and examples from your reading, studies, experience, or observations
- Follow the conventions of standard written English

The essay will be scored by trained high school and college teachers. Each reader will give the essay a score from 1 to 6 (6 is the highest score) based on the overall quality of the essay and your demonstration of writing competence.

SAT Sample Essay Prompt

Assignment: Do memories hinder or help people in their effort to learn from the past and succeed in the present? Plan and write an essay in which you develop your point of view on this issue. Support your position with reasoning and examples taken from your reading, studies, experience, or observations.

http://eknowledge.com/toc_sat_Sample_Essay_Scores_1-6.asp   attribution to SAT, ETS, and College Board

ACT ESSAY INSTRUCTIONS & PROMPT

ACT Essay Instructions

For additional information about the ACT, visit http://eknowledge.com/TOC_ACT_MAIN_PAGE.asp

The following instructions are printed on the cover of the Writing Test booklet.

DIRECTIONS

This is a test of your writing skills. You will have thirty (30) minutes to write an essay in English. Before you begin planning and writing your essay, read the writing prompt carefully to understand exactly what you are being asked to do. Your essay will be evaluated on the evidence it provides of your ability to express judgments by taking a position on the issue in the writing prompt; to maintain a focus on the topic throughout the essay; to develop a position by using logical reasoning and by supporting your ideas; to organize ideas in a logical way; and to use language clearly and effectively according to the conventions of standard written English.

You may use the unlined pages in this test booklet to plan your essay. These pages will not be scored. **You must write your essay in pencil on the lined pages in the answer folder**. Your writing on those lined pages will be scored. You may not need all the lined pages, but to ensure you have enough room to finish, do NOT skip lines. You may write corrections or additions neatly between the lines of your essay, but do NOT write in the margins of the lined pages.

Illegible essays cannot be scored, so you must write (or print) clearly.

If you finish before time is called, you may review your work. Lay your pencil down immediately when time is called.

DO NOT OPEN THIS BOOK UNTIL YOU ARE TOLD TO DO SO.

ACT Sample Essay Prompt

Prompts used for the ACT Writing Test:
- describe an issue relevant to high school students
- ask examinees to write about their perspective on the issue

As a starting place, two different perspectives on the issue will be provided. Examinees may choose to support one of these perspectives or to develop a response based on their own perspective. Sample Prompt Educators debate extending high school to five years because of increasing demands on students from employers and colleges to participate in extracurricular activities and community service in addition to having high grades. Some educators support extending high school to five years because they think students need more time to achieve all that is expected of them. Other educators do not support extending high school to five years because they think students would lose interest in school and attendance would drop in the fifth year. In your opinion, should high school be extended to five years? In your essay, take a position on this question. You may write about either one of the two points of view given, or you may present a different point of view on this question. Use specific reasons and examples to support your position.

The standard directions in the second paragraph above are a part of all prompts used on the Writing Test.

Sample essays and scores available at http://eknowledge.com/toc_ACT_Writing_Sample_Scored_Essays.asp
With attribution to www.act.org

SAT/ACT ADDITIONAL INFORMATION FOR THE ESSAY WRITING

For additional information about the SAT or ACT exam, visit our site http://eknowledge.com/TOC_SAT_MAIN_PAGE.asp

There are many ways to prepare for the Writing Test (either SAT or ACT). You may be surprised that these include reading newspapers and magazines, listening to news analyses on television or radio, and participating in discussions and debates about issues and problems. These activities help you become more familiar with current issues, with different perspectives on those issues, and with strategies that skilled writers and speakers use to present their points of view.

Of course, one of the best ways to prepare for the Essay Writing is to practice writing. Practice writing different kinds of texts, for different purposes, with different audiences in mind. The writing you do in your English classes will help you. So will practice in writing essays, stories, poems, plays, editorials, reports, letters to the editor, a personal journal, or other kinds of writing that you do on your own. Because the Essay Test asks you to explain your perspective on an issue in a convincing way, writing opportunities like editorials or letters to the editor of a newspaper are especially helpful. Practicing a variety of different kinds of writing will help make you a versatile writer able to adjust to different writing assignments.

It's also a good idea to get some practice writing within a time limit. This will help build skills that are important in college-level learning and in the world of work.

Here are some ways you can strengthen your writing skills:
- Read and write frequently. Read as much as you can from a variety of sources, including plays, essays, fiction, poetry, news stories, business writing and magazine features.
- Practice writing in different formats and in as many real situations as possible. Write letters to the editor, or letters to a company requesting information. Writing emails is good practice, but realize that writing for school and business is usually more formal than an email to a friend.
- Share your writing with others and get feedback. Feedback helps you anticipate how readers might interpret your writing and what types of questions they might have. This can help you anticipate what a reader might want to know.
- Become familiar with current issues in society and develop your own opinions on the issues. Think of arguments you would use to convince someone of your opinion. Taking speech and debate classes can help you think through issues and communicate them to others.
- Try some extracurricular writing. School newspapers, yearbooks, and creative writing clubs offer opportunities to express ideas in writing.
- Learn to see writing as a process-brainstorming, planning, writing and then editing. This applies to all writing activities.
- Listen to the advice your English teacher gives you about your writing.
- Strive for your writing to be well developed and well organized, using precise, clear and concise language.
- Remember that everyone can improve writing skills. You might think others are more talented, but you know more than you think. Confidence and skill will grow with the more writing you do. Practice and work lead to achievement.

attribution to SAT, ETS, and College Board

SAT/ACT Writing Essay Writing Tips

For additional information about the SAT or ACT exam, visit our site http://eknowledge.com/toc_SAT_More_Faq.asp

- Carefully read the instructions on the cover of the test booklet.
- Do some planning before writing the essay-You will be instructed to do your prewriting in your Writing Test booklet. You can refer to these notes as you write the essay on the lined pages in your answer folder. Do not skip lines.
  - **Carefully consider the prompt** and make sure you understand it-reread it if you aren't sure.
  - **Decide how you want to answer** the question in the prompt.
  - **Then jot down your ideas** on the topic: this might simply be a list of ideas, reasons, and examples that you will use to explain your point of view on the issue.
  - **Write down what you think** others might say in opposition to your point of view and think about how you would refute their arguments.
  - **Think of how best to organize** the ideas in your essay.
- At the beginning of your essay, make sure readers will see that you understand the issue.
- Explain your point of view in a clear and logical way.
- If possible, discuss the issue in a broader context or evaluate the implications or complications of the issue.
- Address what others might say to refute your point of view and present a counterargument.
- Use specific examples.
- Vary the structure of your sentences, and use varied and precise word choices.
- Make logical relationships clear by using transitional words and phrases.
- Do not wander off the topic.
- End with a strong conclusion that summarizes or reinforces your position.
- If there is time, do a final check of the essay when it is finished.

- o Correct any mistakes in grammar, usage, punctuation, and spelling.
- o If you find any words that are hard to read, recopy them so your readers can read them easily.
- o Make any corrections and revisions neatly, between the lines (but not in the margins).

SAT Essay scoring Guide

For additional information about the SAT, visit our site http://eknowledge.com/TOC_SAT_MAIN_PAGE.asp

The essay is scored by experienced and trained high school and college teachers. Each essay is scored by two people who won't know each other's score. They won't know the student's identity or school either. Each reader gives the essay a score from 1 to 6 (6 is the highest score) based on the SAT essay Scoring Guide.

These scored essays were written in response to the essay question above.

Score	Essay
6	An essay in this category demonstrates clear and consistent mastery, although it may have a few minor errors. A typical essay • effectively and insightfully develops a point of view on the issue and demonstrates outstanding critical thinking, using clearly appropriate examples, reasons, and other evidence to support its position • is well organized and clearly focused, demonstrating clear coherence and smooth progression of ideas • exhibits skillful use of language, using a varied, accurate, and apt vocabulary • demonstrates meaningful variety in sentence structure • is free of most errors in grammar, usage, and mechanics
5	An essay in this category demonstrates reasonably consistent mastery, although it will have occasional errors or lapses in quality. A typical essay • effectively develops a point of view on the issue and demonstrates strong critical thinking, generally using appropriate examples, reasons, and other evidence to support its position • is well organized and focused, demonstrating coherence and progression of ideas • exhibits facility in the use of language, using appropriate vocabulary • demonstrates variety in sentence structure • is generally free of most errors in grammar, usage, and mechanics
4	An essay in this category demonstrates adequate mastery, although it will have lapses in quality. A typical essay • develops a point of view on the issue and demonstrates competent critical thinking, using adequate examples, • reasons, and other evidence to support its position • is generally organized and focused, demonstrating some coherence and progression of ideas • exhibits adequate but inconsistent facility in the use of language, using generally appropriate vocabulary • demonstrates some variety in sentence structure • has some errors in grammar, usage, and mechanics
3	An essay in this category demonstrates developing mastery, and is marked by ONE OR MORE of the following weaknesses: • develops a point of view on the issue, demonstrating some critical thinking, but may do so inconsistently or use inadequate examples, reasons, or other evidence to support its position • is limited in its organization or focus, or may demonstrate some lapses in coherence or progression of ideas • displays developing facility in the use of language, but sometimes uses weak vocabulary or inappropriate word choice • lacks variety or demonstrates problems in sentence structure • contains an accumulation of errors in grammar, usage, and mechanics
2	An essay in this category demonstrates little mastery, and is flawed by ONE OR MORE of the following weaknesses: • develops a point of view on the issue that is vague or seriously limited, and demonstrates weak critical thinking, providing inappropriate or insufficient examples, reasons, or other evidence to support its position • is poorly organized and/or focused, or demonstrates serious problems with coherence or progression of ideas • displays very little facility in the use of language, using very limited vocabulary or incorrect word choice • demonstrates frequent problems in sentence structure • contains errors in grammar, usage, and mechanics so serious that meaning is somewhat obscured
1	An essay in this category demonstrates very little or no mastery, and is severely flawed by ONE OR MORE of the following weaknesses: • develops no viable point of view on the issue, or provides little or no evidence to support its position • is disorganized or unfocused, resulting in a disjointed or incoherent essay • displays fundamental errors in vocabulary • demonstrates severe flaws in sentence structure • contains pervasive errors in grammar, usage, or mechanics that persistently interfere with meaning

Essays not written on the essay assignment will receive a score of zero.
attribution to SAT, ETS, and College Board

ACT Essay Scoring Guide

For additional information about the ACT, visit http://eknowledge.com/TOC_ACT_MAIN_PAGE.asp

These are the descriptions of scoring criteria that the trained readers will follow to determine the score (1-6) for your essay. Papers at each level exhibit *all* or *most* of the characteristics described at each score point.

Score = 6   Essays within this score range demonstrate effective skill in responding to the task.

The essay shows a clear understanding of the task. The essay takes a position on the issue and may offer a critical context for discussion. The essay addresses complexity by examining different perspectives on the issue, or by evaluating the implications and/or complications of the issue, or by fully responding to counterarguments to the writer's position. Development of ideas is ample, specific, and logical. Most ideas are fully elaborated. A clear focus on the specific issue in the prompt is maintained. The organization of the essay is clear: the organization may be somewhat predictable or it may grow from the writer's purpose. Ideas are logically sequenced. Most transitions reflect the writer's logic and are usually integrated into the essay. The introduction and conclusion are effective, clear, and well developed. The essay shows a good command of language. Sentences are varied and word choice is varied and precise. There are few, if any, errors to distract the reader.

Score = 5   Essays within this score range demonstrate competent skill in responding to the task.

The essay shows a clear understanding of the task. The essay takes a position on the issue and may offer a broad context for discussion. The essay shows recognition of complexity by partially evaluating the implications and/or complications of the issue, or by responding to counterarguments to the writer's position. Development of ideas is specific and logical. Most ideas are elaborated, with clear movement between general statements and specific reasons, examples, and details. Focus on the specific issue in the prompt is maintained. The organization of the essay is clear, although it may be predictable. Ideas are logically sequenced, although simple and obvious transitions may be used. The introduction and conclusion are clear and generally well developed. Language is competent. Sentences are somewhat varied and word choice is sometimes varied and precise. There may be a few errors, but they are rarely distracting.

Score = 4   Essays within this score range demonstrate adequate skill in responding to the task.

The essay shows an understanding of the task. The essay takes a position on the issue and may offer some context for discussion. The essay may show some recognition of complexity by providing some response to counterarguments to the writer's position. Development of ideas is adequate, with some movement between general statements and specific reasons, examples, and details. Focus on the specific issue in the prompt is maintained throughout most of the essay. The organization of the essay is apparent but predictable. Some evidence of logical sequencing of ideas is apparent, although most transitions are simple and obvious. The introduction and conclusion are clear and somewhat developed. Language is adequate, with some sentence variety and appropriate word choice. There may be some distracting errors, but they do not impede understanding.

Score = 3   Essays within this score range demonstrate some developing skill in responding to the task.

The essay shows some understanding of the task. The essay takes a position on the issue but does not offer a context for discussion. The essay may acknowledge a counterargument to the writer's position, but its development is brief or unclear. Development of ideas is limited and may be repetitious, with little, if any, movement between general statements and specific reasons, examples, and details. Focus on the general topic is maintained, but focus on the specific issue in the prompt may not be maintained. The organization of the essay is simple. Ideas are logically grouped within parts of the essay, but there is little or no evidence of logical sequencing of ideas. Transitions, if used, are simple and obvious. An introduction and conclusion are clearly discernible but underdeveloped. Language shows a basic control. Sentences show a little variety and word choice is appropriate. Errors may be distracting and may occasionally impede understanding.

Score = 2   Essays within this score range demonstrate inconsistent or weak skill in responding to the task.

The essay shows a weak understanding of the task. The essay may not take a position on the issue, or the essay may take a position but fail to convey reasons to support that position, or the essay may take a position but fail to maintain a stance. There is little or no recognition of a counterargument to the writer's position. The essay is thinly developed. If examples are given, they are general and may not be clearly relevant. The essay may include extensive repetition of the writer's ideas or of ideas in the prompt. Focus on the general topic is maintained, but focus on the specific issue in the prompt may not be maintained. There is some indication of an organizational structure, and some logical grouping of ideas within parts of the essay is apparent. Transitions, if used, are simple and obvious, and they may be inappropriate or misleading. An introduction and conclusion are discernible but minimal. Sentence structure and word choice are usually simple. Errors may be frequently distracting and may sometimes impede understanding.

Score = 1 Essays within this score range show little or no skill in responding to the task.

The essay shows little or no understanding of the task. If the essay takes a position, it fails to convey reasons to support that position. The essay is minimally developed. The essay may include excessive repetition of the writer's ideas or of ideas in the prompt. Focus on the general topic is usually maintained, but focus on the specific issue in the prompt may not be maintained. There is little or no evidence of an organizational structure or of the logical grouping of ideas. Transitions are rarely used. If present, an introduction and conclusion are minimal. Sentence structure and word choice are simple. Errors may be frequently distracting and may significantly impede understanding. No Score

Blank, Off-Topic, Illegible, Not in English, or Void will receive no credit
attribution to SAT, ETS, and College Board

Essay Writing

Part 3: Practice Questions

Virtual Classroom>Essay Writing> Practice Questions

This material Corresponds to the Virtual Classroom in the
PowerPrep DVD/Internet/iApp for Essay Writing

Virtual Classroom

Important Abbreviations
These abbreviations are used throughout the program

POE: Process of Elimination
SARR: Synthesize, Analyze, Reduce, and Restate (has to do with Logical Reasoning)
AC: Answer Choice
QS: Question Stem
LOD: Level of Difficulty

Example Question: What is the least common multiple of 3, 4, and 7? (**This is the call of the question or Question Stem "QS"**)

These are Answer Choices "AC" A, B, C, D, E

(A)   12
(B)   21
(C)   28
(D)   48
(E)   84

Part 3: Practice Essays

PQ #1 "YEAR 'ROUND SCHOOL"

Practice Essay Writing: Issue

Directions: *Discuss your perspective on the issue presented below. Support your view with relevant information from your own background, education or experience. Remember that there is no one "correct" response to the essay topic.*

Prompt: Year 'Round School

Many parents and educators believe that the traditional, 180-day school year is inadequate in meeting the educational requirements of today's students. From June to September many students forget much of what they learned during the school year. Many teachers link their disciplinary problems to vacation-starved students. Moreover, current statistics show that crime increases among teens during the summer months, thus further solidifying a justification for an increase in the number of school days. It is the local district administrators who often oppose the extended-year calendar solely on the basis that funding is simply not available

Answer: Year 'Round School: Score 6

1

Based on and developed during the agrarian age of U.S. history, the traditional 180-day school year seems outdated, no longer relevant to today's high-tech world, ready to be replaced. On the other hand, this calendar has been a consistent social and economic force providing a reliable track for progression. Therefore, to consider the traditional school calendar without placing it in its proper context would be inaccurate, as this issue does not occur in a vacuum. The school calendar must be discussed as but one part of a dynamic entity impacting other aspects of society.

2

In today's fast paced world, more and more people are demanding quality time with their families. Traditional family vacations, often taken over the summer months when school is out, provides much needed quality time, and therefore should not be dismissed so lightly. Many parents employed in a variety of industries and businesses also schedule vacations when school is out, favoring these months as the weather allows for better and safer travel. These "off-months" fulfill that needed social interaction among family members without requiring children to miss school. Corresponding a child's vacation with their parents' would limit the amount of remediation inevitability caused by absences thus undermining the purposes of the year-round calendar. Furthermore, reducing summers to only one month would cause a mad scramble for time off among workers, subsequently impacting the efficiency of businesses and industries.

3

Even though not every family automatically enters the tourist status during the summer, these months do provide time for students to work and earn money. During these months, students are provided with economic opportunities in which they may otherwise pass on during the hectic school year. Without these summer months, students and their families would be deprived of this needed income, an income some families need to live. A factor that must also be addressed is that some forms of education can only occur during the summer. For example, remediation courses are best utilized and suited for the summer. Summer school, although embarrassing to some, provides students the needed opportunity to catch up and avoid even greater indignity of repeating an entire school year.

4

Also, some learning cannot take place in traditional classroom settings. Trips provide unique experiences that textbooks cannot duplicate. Summer camps help students explore nature while helping them develop life-skills so valuable for success in today's society. Summer jobs provide the setting for many to practice their business skills learned previously during the school year.

5

Unfortunately, educational budgets inhibit the feasibility of year-round schooling. Considering the negative sociological and economic effects of year-around school, any minor positives are inconsequential. The traditional, effective school calendar enables many to earn an income otherwise unavailable. Families have time for quality interaction. Additionally, traditional calendars offer opportunities for remediation and time for learning by first hand and not by proxy.

Methodology:

Before you began, did you?

Absorb the Issue or Argument
- ❑ Understand the task
- ❑ Define key terms or points (t-chart)
- ❑ Look at explicit and implied meaning
- ❑ Form questions

Develop/Recognize Key Points
- ❑ Look at both sides
- ❑ Look at depth or extent of proof
- ❑ Identify flaws or weak points

Arrange Proof
- ❑ Create thesis
- ❑ Quick outline
- ❑ Connect to thesis

As you were writing, did you?

Write/Type
- ❑ Use assertive language
- ❑ Be clear and concise
- ❑ Use transitions to connect ideas
- ❑ Provide a strong summary

When finished, did you?

Edit
- ❑ Look for problems in logic/understanding
- ❑ Any obvious grammar problems?

Sample Image: Year Round School

Arrangement: Background & compare/contrast
Thesis: The school calendar must be discussed as only one part of a dynamic setting impacting other aspects of society.

Topic sentence: People demand quality time
Support: Summer provides that time for both parents and children; students would not miss school, no crunch for time off

Topic sentence: These months provide an opportunity to earn money
Support: School too hectic, families need money and would be deprived of this

Topic sentence: There are types of education besides one received in a classroom
Support: Remediation, trips provide experience, life-skills, and practice

Conclusion: Restates main ideas in different words

Analysis: Score 6

Based on the scoring rubric, this paper earns a rating of 6 because:

- It displays a command of the English language.
- It is well organized and reasonable in its assertions.
- The author selects a firm position arguing it persuasively and insightfully.
- It addresses the complexities of the issue.
- The argument addresses both societal and economical effects.
- Transitions are smooth between key ideas.

PQ #2 "LICENSE TO DRINK"

Practice Essay Writing: Argument

Directions: *Discuss how compelling you find the above argument. Analyze the reasoning presented, using the evidence that supports the author's claims. Explain what may strengthen or refute the assertions made, what changes would make the argument more sound or what evidence would change the conclusion.*

Prompt: 'License to Drink'

Even though the Prohibition of liquor failed in America during the 1920s, now may be the time to license the consumption of alcohol. The popular acceptance of alcohol, promoted and advocated by the media, has caused many Americans to ignore and leave unexamined the significant role that alcohol plays in their lives. Statistics show that alcohol directly contributes to violent crime. Furthermore, alcohol continues to be a major contributor to our nation's current health care predicament. A license to consume alcohol could be revoked when an individual is involved in an alcohol-related crime or accident. Similar to obtaining a driver's license in which an individual must study a manual, a consumption license would require drinkers to become educated about alcohol's disturbing effects on individuals and on society in general.

Answer: "License to Drink": Score 6

1

This idea to legislate the consumption of alcohol is essentially a plan to force education on adults. However, alcohol education is already available and easily accessible just as it is for most drugs, even illegal ones. Even though this legislative proposal attempts to remove itself from the unsuccessful policies employed during Prohibition, it too would make alcohol a "controlled" substance subjected to a variety of new rules and regulations. This new "controlled" status placed on alcohol is, at its foundation, a means to give legal leverage, forcing alcohol education on the American populace.

2

The argument implies that the difference between drinking and non-drinking is simply a matter of education – that the privileged status alcohol enjoys blinds the public to its real dangers. Conceptually, this may or may not be true. However, this perceived status has no distinct connection as to whether the government has the right to force an educational agenda on adults. People have the right, if they so choose, to remain ignorant of any subject they choose just as they have the right to become more educated. Cigarette smokers have no desire to be force-fed cancer statistics teaching them the dangers of smoking.

3

Making reference to an "owner's manual" and implied mandatory testing weakens the writer's argument. At this point the support for the argument takes a major turn. A consumption license is not a counterpart to a liquor license, but parallel to a driver's license. The purpose of a driver's license is to verify proficiency at safely controlling an automobile. A consumption license would not prove proficiency of safely operating an inebriated device. This implied metaphor does not support the argument.

4

Reference to violence and health care issues are the author's strongest points. They indicate that drinking affects not only the participating individual, but also others on a much larger societal scale, both physically and financially. Conversely, by referring to alcohol as a "contributor" to crime, the author personifies alcohol as an independent agent actively assisting violence. By exaggerating alcohol's role in violence, the argument becomes weakened. While the reality of health care and violence issues create a need to educate the public about the consequences of alcohol consumption, it does not validate the proposed enforcement of education.

5

To be a valid argument, this proposal needs to demonstrate that drinking imposes an entirely new set of conditions on individuals and on society compared with sobriety. It fails to do so. Drinking simply inhibits judgment. The goal of the written examination is obviously to teach people terrifying information that would pressure them not to drink. The objective of a driver's test is simply to teach people to drive.

Methodology

Before you began, did you?

Absorb the Issue or Argument

- ❏ Understand the task
- ❏ Define key terms or points (t-chart)
- ❏ Look at explicit and implied meaning
- ❏ Form questions

Develop/Recognize Key Points

- ❏ Look at both sides
- ❏ Look at depth or extent of proof
- ❏ Identify flaws or weak points

Arrange Proof
- ☐ Create thesis
- ☐ Quick outline
- ☐ Connect to thesis

As you were writing, did you?

Write/Type
- ☐ Use assertive language
- ☐ Be clear and concise
- ☐ Use transitions to connect ideas
- ☐ Provide a strong summary

When finished, did you?

Edit
- ☐ Look for problems in logic/understanding
- ☐ Any obvious grammar problems?

Sample Image: License to Drink

Arrangement: Compare and contrasting ideas
Thesis: Alcohol consumption license is an attempt to force education on adults

Topic sentence: Status warps the true problems associated with drinking
Support: Connection between status and legislation not valid

Topic sentence: A mandatory test weakens the argument
Support: Consumption license not equal to liquor license, more similar to a driver's license, would not be reasonable

Topic sentence: Author makes a good point about relation to problems
Support: However, author exaggerates the role of alcohol, does not validate legislation

Conclusion: To be valid, the author needs to demonstrate connection between consumption license and other relevant licenses, he/she fails to do so, author uses a poor analogy

Analysis: Score 6

Based on the scoring rubric, this response would rate 6 because:

- It effectively analyzes and critiques the main points of the argument.
- The author uses strong, persuasive English.
- Identifies the argument's attempt to liken its proposed license to a driver's license proceeding to discredit this fallacy.
- The author challenges the idea of legislating behavior.
- The author varies sentence lengths and uses transitions between ideas.

PQ #3 "SECOND-HAND SMOKE"

Practice Essay: Issue

Directions: *Discuss your perspective on the issue presented below. Support your view with relevant information from your own background, education or experience. Remember that there is no one "correct" response to the essay topic.*

Prompt: Second-hand Smoke
Many non-smokers feel that secondhand smoke is hazardous to their health; recent medical research supports their allegations. Smokers feel that they have a right to enjoy this pastime, and that it would be a violation of their constitutional rights to deny them this privilege. The first group wants smoking made illegal, while the second group feels that they are being treating unfairly.

Answer: "Second-Hand Smoke" Score: 6

1

Having family members who are heavy smokers, I can understand how difficult it is to quit this difficult habit. Chronic smokers continually assert the enjoyment they receive from smoking, but they often ignore the harmful effects that result for themselves and others around them. It is obvious that smoking is a powerful addiction; however why should others need to suffer the consequences of another's medical problem? I agree that smoking should be made illegal.

2

I have witnessed children cough and wheeze after their parents have smoked for several hours while in the same room with them. In fact, I too have often choked in a smoke-filled room, even though I was not the smoker. As well as an assault on your lungs, the odor of a cigarette smoker's clothes causes discomfort. The odor precedes him or her into every place that he or she goes. It becomes uncomfortable to visit a friend's home when it has the peculiar odor of old smoke consequently making it difficult for any visitor to breathe freely.

³
Until cigarettes are classified as the dangerous, addictive drug that they are, smokers will not seek the help they need. Those who smoke must realize, through clear legislation, that they are harming not only themselves, but also those with whom they come into daily contact (car pools, apartment houses, restaurants, etc.). The romanticized view of smoking, often witnessed in the late 40's and 50's, is over. Currently, it seems that only smokers are blind to the dangers of this habit. Smokers are "in denial." It is the responsibility of the nonsmokers to show this by making smoking illegal, offering smokers the health they deserve.

⁴
Coupled with this legislation, nicotine addiction should be addressed in the same manner as other drug addictions. Even though there are always personal, private clinics, these tend be extremely expensive and not affordable to everyone. City and state run clinics can best service the vast majority of the smoking population. To offset the inevitable cost of this care, government agencies could accept Medicare and Medicaid to subsidize any expense. Anti-smoking patches, psychotherapy, support groups and even cigarette surrogates such as chewing gum could be offered free of charge.

⁵
In making smoking illegal, we must not abandon these addicted people, deserting them to find their own method of quitting. This would simply lead to an illegal and dangerous "smokers' market" -- similar to today's drug market. It is our responsibility to make certain that this does not happen as the addicted smoker forced into this position might be your mother, father, brother, sister, or even your child.

⁶
Those addicted to any drug often feel desperate and lie, claiming that their habit was not harming anyone. No amount of reading newspaper articles about the rise in lung cancer deaths could convince addicts of their unhealthy habit. Like reading the Surgeon General's warning on the side of a cigarette box, the addict knows smoking is dangerous, yet their addiction never lets them fully understand the words' significance. It is a kind of unawareness that lets smokers practice their addiction in crowded places, near little children, invalids or animals who, either cannot remove themselves or have no say in the matter. I firmly agree that smoking should be made illegal, but we must provide resources for those former smokers who are suddenly left empty-handed, addicted and perplexed as to where to get help.

Sample Image: Second Hand Smoke

Arrangement: Personal account & brief background
Thesis: Smoking should be made illegal

Topic sentence: Wheezing from 2ⁿᵈ hand smoke
Support: children cough, etc. Bad odor, difficult to breathe

Topic sentence: Classify as an addictive drug
Support: Laws to show harmful effects, blind to effects, responsibility of those who do not smoke.

Topic sentence: Treat nicotine addiction
Support: City/State clinics, Medicare/Medicaid, free aides

Topic sentence: Do not abandon these people
Support: Lead to "black market", family in danger

Inductive conclusion: Restates main supporting ideas and ends with thesis

Analysis: Score 6

Based on the scoring rubric, this paper earns a rating of 6 because:

- It deals with the complexities of the issue.
- The thesis is clear, as are the topic sentences supporting the writer's views.
- The examples are relevant (children, animals, family members) and persuasively appeal to the reader's emotions.
- Suggestions to help smokers quit are well developed and insightful.
- The essay is clearly organized, logical and concise.
- The writer provides both points of view.
- The language, including diction and syntactic variety, is clear and controlled.
- Sentence structure, grammar, spelling, and punctuation do not inhibit understanding.

PQ #4 "RECYCLING"

Practice Essay: Argument

Directions: *Discuss to what extent you find the above argument persuasive. Analyze the reasoning presented and evidence that supports the author's claims. Explain what may strengthen or refute the assertions, what changes would make the argument sounder or what evidence would change the conclusion.*

Prompt: Recycling

America's recycling campaign has not prevented newspapers from filling our nation's garbage dumps. Rather, it has only made them more neatly stacked, at a cost which most towns must pass on to their already overloaded taxpayers. The amount of collected paper is so profuse that less than ten percent is ever put to a second use. Few dealers have the time, inclination or ability to deal with such a large amount of paper, thus unable to effectively survive the over-supplied market. Newspaper recycling is a wasteful exercise that should be abandoned.

Answer: Recycling: Score 6

1

The idea that recycling may be a myth, ineffective and a waste of time and energy is very captivating. A drive through any town on "newspaper day" certainly gives credibility to the author's suggestion that an overabundance of recyclable newspaper is occurring, thus furthering the burden on the taxpayer. The author's reference to dealers in newspaper recycling does reveal some genuine concerns on how these markets can work. While bottles and aluminum cans are easily melted down and put to use again, limitations do present themselves in the efforts to recycle paper. Moreover, many households can go for days without producing an empty can or bottle. How can one effectively sell used paper when seemingly every daily newspaper in America is being turned in for recycling?

2

Despite the implications fashioned by this argument, a more analytical look at the essay finds obvious flaws. For example, the phrase "less than ten percent" is far too vague to be convincing. Ten is a round number and yet the real world is never that clear cut or perfectly smooth. A more specific number, such as a "10.0", is required to persuade today's statistic-saturated public. Even with a figure of two decimal places this statistic requires a specific source from which it was derived, and, more significantly, a timeframe to which it applies. In not addressing the timeframe, the author implies that new advances in technology are not relevant. However, current advances in technology, most likely, will make recycling paper more reasonable and profitable - especially if this resource is reportedly so cheap.

3

The writer finishes with an effective plea, painting a picture in which newspapers, despite recycling campaigns, land in our dumps anyway, "neatly stacked" at the cost of the taxpayer. While emotionally influential, this image should be supported by relevant statistics demonstrating the minimal effect that recycling has on the amount of garbage amassed. Waste disposal locations are required to keep a tonnage record, which note sources and specifies content. If the claims of the argument were true, the data would be available to show significant deposits of newspapers from "recycling" municipalities. This absence of hard data undermines the impact of this emotionally charged assertion.

4

The argument's line of reasoning equates the absence of extensive recycling with a need to discontinue paper collection. Such a position fails to realize the significance of "recycling" as a philosophy and an ideal and how its practice may transcend into different arenas. Establishing the habit of reuse is more than half the battle in learning to insure a cleaner tomorrow. Even if ineffective, the practice of recycling is valuable because it conditions the public to accept the chore as meaningful thus establishing relevance to other recycling issues. More importantly, collecting recyclables makes the resource readily available, inviting industry to find a use for it.

5

A more persuasive argument would have provided support for its evidence. The assertion that only ten percent of paper is actually recycled requires more detail and sources, thereby reinforcing its credibility. The sole reliance on emotional images to persuade without adequate supporting statistics minimizes the impact that most newspapers still retire to garbage dumps. Furthermore, the author should have anticipated and discredited the idea that recycling may have some inherent value beyond just profit. On the whole, the argument was reasonable but skeletal.

Sample Image: Recycling

Arrangement: Credits the author's assertions
Deductive support: Waste of time, overabundance, limitations of paper recycling, etc.

Thesis: Argument has obvious flaws
Support: Too vague, no timeframe, does not take into account technology

Topic sentence: Argument based on emotion
Support: No relevant statistics or hard data leaves questions

Topic sentence: Recycling in and of itself is good
Support: Good practice, applicable to other habits, invites industry

Inductive conclusion: Restates main problems with argument
Restates thesis: On the whole, the argument was reasonable but skeletal

Analysis: Score 6

Based on the rubric, this analysis would rate a 6 because:

- It organizes its ideas logically and intelligently with smooth transitions.
- It distinctly identifies and sharply analyzes the crucial points of the argument.
- It exhibits a strong command of the English conventions with few errors.
- It credits the initial effectiveness of the argument to demonstrate its strengths yet points out the lack of depth of the main points.
- The essay provided a smooth and well-organized structure for the analysis.

Essay Writing

Part 4: Review

Virtual Classroom>Essay Writing> Review

This material Corresponds to the Virtual Classroom in the
PowerPrep DVD/Internet/iApp for Essay Writing

Virtual Classroom

Important Abbreviations

These abbreviations are used throughout the program

POE: Process of Elimination
SARR: Synthesize, Analyze, Reduce, and Restate (has to do with Logical Reasoning)
AC: Answer Choice
QS: Question Stem
LOD: Level of Difficulty

Example Question: What is the least common multiple of 3, 4, and 7? **(This is the call of the question or Question Stem "QS")**

These are Answer Choices "AC" A, B, C, D, E

(A) 12
(B) 21
(C) 28
(D) 48
(E) 84

Part 4: Review

TYPES OF ESSAYS

Issue Essay

• Questions are not based on pre-existing knowledge • No "correct" answer • Take a particular position
• Address the complexities • "It's not what you say but how you say it!"

Argument Essay

• Analyze an argument • Do not express your views • Exhibit clear reasoning • Refute and defend claims
• What changes could be made

WRITING THE ESSAY

General Essay Format

Opening Paragraph: • Draws reading in • _Focuses the essay_ • _States the thesis_

Supporting Paragraphs: • _Gives "meat" to your essay_ • _Topic sentences focus the support_ • _Variety of arrangements_
Transitional Statements: • _Add to flow_ • _Show clear connections_ • _Helps reader_
Concluding Paragraph: • _Brief and concise_ • _Leave with an image_ • _Restate key points_ • _Connect to thesis_

5-Step Methodology

1. Absorb the Issue or Argument 2. Develop and recognize key points 3. Arrange poof 4. Write or type 5. Final Editing

Scoring & Grading

• Human and Computer grading • Holistic scoring (0 to 6) • Use grading rubrics

Essentially looking for key characteristics:
• Structure • Thesis • Beginning and conclusion • Clarity • Correct grammar/punctuation • Transitions • Reason or logic

Remember computer grades: • Careful with creativity • Use keywords

Sample Essay: Issue

• Support your view with relevant information • Take into account the complexities of the issue
• Clear structure with thesis, topic sentences and conclusion (see image)

Sample Essay: Argument

• Do not present your opinion • To what extent (degree) you find the argument valid & analyze reasoning
• Explain what may strengthen the argument • What questions would make this more meaningful
• Clear structure with thesis, support and conclusion (see image)

Practice Essay: Issue

• Apply the 5-Step Methodology • Plug into image organizer • Look at sample response and analysis • Compare your essay

Practice Essay: Argument

• Apply the 5-Step Methodology • Plug into image organizer • Look at sample response and analysis • Compare your essay

CONGRATULATIONS!!

You Have Completed the Essay Writing Review!!
Take a Break Before Moving on to the Next Section.

Sentence Completion
Workbook
SAT Only
Table of Contents
This material corresponds to the SAT Virtual Classroom Instructions in the
PowerPrep DVD/Internet/iApp for Sentence Completion

Virtual Classroom

Important Abbreviations
These abbreviations are used throughout the program

POE: Process of Elimination
SARR: Synthesize, Analyze, Reduce, and Restate (has to do with Logical Reasoning)
AC: Answer Choice
QS: Question Stem
LOD: Level of Difficulty

Example Question: What is the least common multiple of 3, 4, and 7? (**This is the call of the question or Question Stem "QS"**)

These are Answer Choices "AC" A, B, C, D, E

    (A)   12
    (B)   21
    (C)   28
    (D)   48
    (E)   84

Sentence Completion
Part 1: Overview & Directions

SAT Classroom>Sentence Completion>Overview & Directions

This material corresponds to the SAT Virtual Classroom Instructions in the
PowerPrep **DVD/Internet/iApp** for Sentence Completion

Virtual Classroom

Important Abbreviations
These abbreviations are used throughout the program

POE: Process of Elimination
SARR: Synthesize, Analyze, Reduce, and Restate (has to do with Logical Reasoning)
AC: Answer Choice
QS: Question Stem
LOD: Level of Difficulty

Example Question: What is the least common multiple of 3, 4, and 7? (**This is the call of the question or Question Stem "QS"**)

These are Answer Choices "AC" A, B, C, D, E

   (A)   12
   (B)   21
   (C)   28
   (D)   48
   (E)   84

Part 1: Overview & Directions

Overview and Directions

1. Logical Analysis
2. Definitions of Words—VOCABULARY

General Overview of Sentence Completion

Time	Question Types	Score
70 min. (two 25-min. sections and one 20-min. section)	Passage-based reading and sentence completion	200-800

19 total questions-Sentence Completions   48 total questions-Critical Reading

The critical reading section, formerly known as the verbal section, includes short as well as long reading passages. Questions can be based on one, or sometimes two, reading passages. Some questions are not based on reading passages, but ask you to complete sentences.
There are two types of Multiple-Choice Critical Reading Questions: • Sentence Completions •Passage-based Reading
Skills Tested: Vocabulary and Analytical Thinking

Analytical Thinking: Requires you to analyze information (WEED OUT THE NON-IMPORTANT): Tests your VOCABULARY
1. Logical Analysis
2. Definitions of Words--VOCABULARY
3. Think like a Detective searching for clues
POE--Search for Details.

Sentence Completion: Sentence completion questions test your vocabulary and your understanding of sentence structure. (19 questions) 1 blank and 2 blank, but the count as only one question whether 1 or 2 blanks
- Avg. 1 min per question
- But, you want to do the Sentence Completion faster because you want to preserve as much time as possible for the Critical Reading which typically takes longer.

Important Key:
Reading Comprehension typically takes more time to answer than do the Sentence Completion. If possible, you want to answer the Sentence Completion more quickly to preserve as much time as possible for the Critical Reading.

Sentence Completion Sample Question

Sentence Completion questions measure your:
1. knowledge of the meanings of words   2. ability to understand how the different parts of a sentence fit logically together

Directions: Each sentence below has one or two blanks, each blank indicating that something has been omitted. Beneath the sentence are five words or sets of words labeled A through E. Choose the word or set of words that, when inserted in the sentence, best fits the meaning of the sentence as a whole.

2 blank Example:

Hoping to _____ the dispute, negotiators proposed a compromise that they felt would be _____ to both labor and management.
   (A) enforce . . useful
   (B) end . . divisive
   (C) overcome . . unattractive
   (D) extend . . satisfactory
   (E) resolve . . acceptable

Explanation: One way to answer a sentence completion question with two words missing is to focus first on just one of the two blanks. If one of the words in an answer choice is logically wrong, then you can eliminate the entire choice from consideration.
Look at the first blank in the example above. Would it make sense to say that "negotiators" who have "proposed a compromise" were hoping to enforce or extend the "dispute"? No, so neither (A) nor (D) can be the correct answer.

Now you can focus on the second blank. Would the "negotiators" have proposed a compromise that they believed would be divisive or unattractive to "both labor and management"? No, so (B) and (C) can be eliminated and only choice (E) remains.
Always check your answer by reading the entire sentence with your choice filled in. Does it make sense to say "Hoping to resolve the dispute, the negotiators proposed a compromise that they felt would be acceptable to both labor and management"? Yes.

With attribution to SAT, ETS, and College Board

Approaches to the Sentence Completion & Critical Reading Section

- Work on sentence completion questions first. They take less time to answer than the passage-based reading questions.
- The difficulty of sentence completion questions increases as you answer them in order.
- Reading questions do not increase in difficulty from easy to hard. Instead, they follow the logic of the passage.

- The information you need to answer each reading question is always in the passage(s). Reading carefully is the key to finding the correct answer. Don't be misled by an answer that looks correct but is not supported by the actual text of the passage(s).
- Reading questions often include line numbers to help direct you to the relevant part(s) of the passage. If one word or more is quoted exactly from the passage, the line number(s) where that quotation can be found will appear in the question. You may have to read some of the passage before or after the quoted word(s) in order to find support for the best answer.
- Do not jump from passage to passage. Stay with a passage until you have answered as many questions as you can before you proceed to the next passage.
- If you don't know what a word means in a sentence completion or reading passage, consider related words, familiar sayings and phrases, roots, prefixes, and suffixes. Have you ever heard or seen a word that may be related to it?
- In your test booklet, mark each question you don't answer so that you can easily go back to it later if you have time.
- Remember that all questions are worth the same number of points regardless of the type or difficulty.

With attribution to SAT, ETS, and College Board

How Those Skills Are Tested - "The Car Wreck"

Critical skill: the ability to WEED OUT the less important or distracting information (Analyze)

Remember to focus only on the RELEVANT Facts:

Driver #1's Story: I turned left at the light and traveled a few seconds until I was 100 feet away from the next intersection where I changed lanes and then traveled the remaining 100 feet to the intersection where the light had changed to yellow so I stopped. After being stopped for 20 seconds, a car hit me from behind.

Driver #2's Story: I turned left at the signal and about 100 feet before the next light, Driver #1 changed lanes immediately in front of me, which caused the accident.

Independent Facts: (accept these as true)

☑ Speed limit 45 mph.
☑ Heavy Traffic.
☑ Winter day.
☑ 6:45 p.m.
☑ First vehicle was a truck.
☑ Second vehicle was a van.

☑ When the police arrived, the cars were on the roadside about 80 feet before the intersection.
☑ Neither vehicle had been moved subsequent to the accident.
☑ No rain or snow on road.
☑ Male driver of the truck with no passengers.
☑ Female driver of the van with one passenger.

Question: Which driver do you think is telling the truth and why?
Pause and analyze the situation. **What do you know? What is relevant?**
Draw a diagram of what we know from each driver and from the Independent Facts.

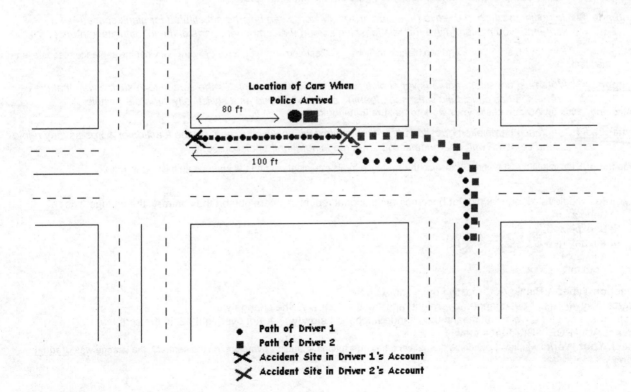

The relevant fact: The cars are parked very near the scene of the accident as reported by driver number 2. Therefore, the account by number 2 is probably more accurate.

Sentence Completion Attempts to Test This Same Logical Reasoning Skill By:

1. Giving you lots of non-critical or distracting information. To solve these questions you have to weed through the distractions and get to the core. SARR will teach you how. You will learn how to "SARR" later in the materials.
2. Adding difficulty by way of vocabulary—which is in addition to the logical reasoning.

Test Maker's Explanation and a "Real" Question

Sentence Completion Instructions from Test Makers:

Each sentence below has one or two blanks, each blank indicating that something has been omitted. Beneath the sentence are five words or sets of words. Choose the word or set of words that, when inserted in the sentence, best fits the meaning of the sentence as a whole.

Here is how the Test Makers explain the Sentence Completion:

> *The purpose of the sentence completion is to measure the ability to use the various kinds of cues provided by syntax and grammar to recognize the overall meaning of a sentence. In deciding which of the five (5) words or sets of words can best be substituted for blank space(s) in a sentence, you must analyze the relationships among the component parts of the incomplete sentence. You must consider each answer choice and decide which completes the sentence in such a way that the sentence has a logically satisfying meaning and can be read as a stylistically integrated whole.*

Sentence completion questions provide a context within which to analyze the function of words as they relate to and combine with one another to form a meaningful unit of discourse.

Analysis:

Sentence #1: *The purpose of the sentence completion is to measure the ability to use the various kinds of cues provided by syntax and grammar to recognize the overall meaning of a sentence.*

  Meaning: You are supposed to figure out what the sentence means—even with the blanks.

  If you look at the first sentence a little closer, it becomes fairly confusing: *"…use… cues provided by syntax and grammar…"*

  Syntax: The way in which words or other elements of sentence structure are combined to form grammatical sentences.

  Grammar: The system of inflection, syntax, and word formation of a language. It becomes circular and more confusing than it needs to be.

  Basically, Sentence Completion tests your ability to figure out the missing word(s).

Sentence #2: *In deciding which of the five (5) words or sets of words can best be substituted for blank space(s) in a sentence, you must analyze the relationships among the component parts of the incomplete sentence.*

  Meaning: 1. Five (5) AC's 2. One and two blank questions 3. Restatement: You have to figure out what the sentence means-even with the blank(s)

Sentence #3: *You must consider each answer choice and decide which completes the sentence in such a way that the sentence has a logically satisfying meaning and can be read as a stylistically integrated whole.*
  Meaning: Pick an AC and check your work to be sure it fits logically.

Sentence #4: *Sentence completion questions provide a context within which to analyze the function of words as they relate to and combine with one another to form a meaningful unit of discourse.*

  Meaning: This is just a restatement—analyze the sentence for its meaning and find the appropriate missing word(s).

Example: Medieval kingdoms did not become constitutional republics overnight; on the contrary, the change was_____.
   ○ unpopular
   ○ unexpected
   ○ advantageous
   ○ sufficient
   ○ gradual

Question Type: 1 Blank, Adj., mostly Logic, some Vocab
Logic: Key words: "not change…overnight" and ""to the contrary" the change was _____.
Proposal: Look for a word that means the change happened **slowly**.   1. not overnight   2. to the contrary
Vocab: AC—POE   Gradual = slowly
Check Your Work: Medieval kingdoms did not become constitutional republics overnight; on the contrary, the change was **gradual** (slowly).

Sentence Completion

Part 2: Instruction

<u>SAT Classroom>Sentence Completion>Instruction</u>

This material corresponds to the SAT Virtual Classroom Instructions in the PowerPrep DVD/Internet/iApp for Sentence Completion

Virtual Classroom

Important Abbreviations

These abbreviations are used throughout the program

POE:	Process of Elimination
SARR:	Synthesize, Analyze, Reduce, and Restate (has to do with Logical Reasoning)
AC:	Answer Choice
QS:	Question Stem
LOD:	Level of Difficulty

Example Question: What is the least common multiple of 3, 4, and 7? (**This is the call of the question or Question Stem "QS"**)

These are Answer Choices "AC" A, B, C, D, E

(A) 12
(B) 21
(C) 28
(D) 48
(E) 84

Part 2: Instructions

Plan of Attack

Step 1: Read sentence using the word "blank" where it appears.

Step 2&3: Weed using "SARR" and propose a response. Look for your predicted response or a synonym of that prediction. If your prediction is not among the AC's, use more SARR. Go back and forth between the AC's and the sentence until you "get" the logic. If you run out of time on a particular question—guess using POE.

Step 4: Check your work. If you have time, go back and plug your choice into the sentence to be sure it makes sense.

EXTRA STEP FOR TWO (2) BLANKS:
Answer two (2) blank question, one (1) blank at a time, using POE.

1. **Read Sentence using the word "blank" where it appears**
2. **Use SARR (The "WEEDING" = SARR)**
3. **Propose a Response**
4. **Check Your Work**

Simplify the information contained in the given sentence

Analyze the information

Reduce it

Restate it in your own words

Learn and Remember the Acronym: **SARR**

Helpful Hints to Select a Response

- **Read the sentence** carefully using the word "blank" where it appears.
- **Look out for transitional words** and thought reversers--*but, although, however, even though, also, therefore,* etc.
- **Look for clues** regarding the missing word.
- **Figure out what the sentence means** (SARR!).
- **Figure out** what part of speech is missing (Noun, Verb, Adj.). Look at AC for hints because a word can be all three parts of speech depending on how it is used.
- **Propose a word**—just the idea. Look for it or (synonym) –if it's there-you're done. If the exact word or similar word is not there, use more SARR until you're out of time and forced to POE.
- **Try plugging each AC into the blank** to see if they fit with meaning of the sentence.
- **Check your work**—If you have time, you should be able to offer a reason why every AC except one is not correct.

Quick Review
1. **Read sentence using "blank."**
2. **"Weed" using "SARR" and "POE."**
3. **Propose a word.**
   Repeat steps 2 and 3 until you get an answer or run out of time and then guess.
4. **Check your work.**

Extra Step for Two Blank Questions: Answer two (2) blank questions one (1) blank at a time using POE

Miscellaneous Issues (FYI)

On Two Blank Questions:
➢ If the AC fails for either blank—the entire AC is wrong.

Types of Questions:
➢ About 33% Vocabulary or Definitions
➢ About 66% logical or context

Parts of Speech Tested:

One Blank	Two Blanks:
Adjectives	Adj/Adj.
Nouns	Verb/Adj. (either order)
Verbs	Verb/Verb
	Noun/Adj. (either order)
	Noun/Verb (either order)

Remember: Questions increase or decrease in LOD (level of difficulty) depending on whether you answer prior questions correctly.

Sentence Completion
Part 3: Practice Questions

SAT Classroom>Sentence Completion>Practice Questions

This material corresponds to the SAT Virtual Classroom Instructions in the
PowerPrep DVD/Internet/iApp for Sentence Completion

Virtual Classroom

Important Abbreviations
These abbreviations are used throughout the program

POE: Process of Elimination
SARR: Synthesize, Analyze, Reduce, and Restate (has to do with Logical Reasoning)
AC: Answer Choice
QS: Question Stem
LOD: Level of Difficulty

Example Question: What is the least common multiple of 3, 4, and 7? (**This is the call of the question or Question Stem "QS"**)

These are Answer Choices "AC" A, B, C, D, E

    (A)   12
    (B)   21
    (C)   28
    (D)   48
    (E)   84

Part 3: Practice Questions

Pause The Program.

You Should Have In Front Of You: Clean Questions #1-6.
Do Question #1 and then return to the program to hear the answer.

SPEED IS NOT IMPORTANT AT THIS TIME—TAKE YOUR TIME

QUESTIONS #1-6

1. The _____ attire of the society's newest member clashed formidably with the simple elegance of the president's estate.

   ○ genteel
   ○ garish
   ○ decorous
   ○ unadorned
   ○ dynamic

2. Despite his son's participation, Thomas could not enjoy the musical number; the music was so loud and harsh that it was _____.

   ○ resplendent
   ○ cacophonous
   ○ gallant
   ○ sonorous
   ○ inappropriate

3. The invention of the Kinetograph, the first camera to record movement, by William K. L. Dickson in 1891 _____ the development of the motion picture industry in the early 1900's.

   ○ canvassed
   ○ facilitated
   ○ mottled
   ○ prohibited
   ○ relegated

4. William angrily lectured the teenagers on the responsibility of driving, but his _____ did nothing to correct their misconception of traffic laws as a hindrance rather than a defense.

   ○ tirade
   ○ recitation
   ○ query
   ○ anecdote
   ○ guise

5. Though the Red Cross was founded primarily for the purpose of _____ both physical and emotional anguish of injured soldiers in war, during times of peace the agency also offers relief to _____ of natural disasters.

   ○ exacerbating...survivors
   ○ alleviating...victims
   ○ appeasing...criminals
   ○ observing...leaders
   ○ alarming... culprits

6. Despite his _____ from years of schooling, his _____ disposition would never let him attain greater success than his more aggressive brother.

   ○ obtuseness...meek
   ○ erudition...docile
   ○ refinement...gracious
   ○ joviality...humorous
   ○ enlightenment...assertive

EXPLANATORY ANSWERS #1-6

Answer to Question 1

Question Type: 1 blank, Adj, Logic and Vocab

Call of the Question: The _____ attire of the society's newest member clashed formidably with the simple elegance of the president's estate.

Logic: The "blank" attire (of the society's newest member) clashed formidably with the simple elegance (of the president's estate). The _____ attire… **clashed**… with the **simple elegance**…   Genteel, Garish, Decorous, Unadorned, Dynamic

Proposal: Look for a word that means the opposite of simple elegance.   **Example:** Flashy, overstated, flamboyant, Las Vegas

Vocab

- ○ genteel: refined in manner, well-bred, polite, elegantly stylish
- ● **garish: excessively or stridently decorated, flashy, gaudy, ostentatious, showy, loud**
- ○ decorous: marked by decorum, proper, civilized, demure, dignified, prim & proper
- ○ unadorned: plain, simple, austere, modest, unembellished
- ○ dynamic:

1. of or relating to energy or to objects in motion, 2. marked by continuous change of activity, 3. marked by intensity and vigor, forceful

Check Your Work: The <u>garish</u> (excessively or stridently decorated) attire of the society's newest member clashed formidably with the simple elegance of the president's estate.

Answer to Question 2

Type of Question: 1 blank, Adj, little Logic and mostly Vocab.

Call of the Question: Despite his son's participation, Thomas could not enjoy the musical number; the music was so loud and harsh that it was _____.

Logic: (Despite his son's participation, Thomas could not enjoy the musical number;) the music was so loud and harsh that it was _____. …the music was so **loud and harsh** that it was _____.   **Resplendent, Cacophonous, Gallant, Sonorous, Inappropriate**

Proposal: Look for a word that means loud or harsh.

Vocab -- AC—POE

- ○ Resplendent: dazzling in appearance, brilliant, effulgent, luminous, lustrous, shiny, splendorous
- ● **Cacophonous: jarring, discordant sound; dissonance, noisy, raucous, inharmonious**
- ○ Gallant: 1. smartly dashing,   2. courageous, valiant, chivalrous , courteous, brave, heroic, quixotic
- ○ Sonorous: 1. having or producing sound. 2. having a full, deep, or rich sound.
- ○ Inappropriate: unsuitable or improper, not appropriate, indecorous, unseemly

Check Your Work: Despite his son's participation, Thomas could not enjoy the musical number; the music was so loud and harsh that it was <u>**cacophonous**</u> (jarring, noisy, raucous).

Answer to Question 3

Question Type: 1 blank, Verb, Logic and Vocab

Call of the Question: The invention of the Kinetograph, the first camera to record movement, by William K. L. Dickson in 1891 _____ the development of the motion picture industry in the early 1900's.

Logic: The invention of (the Kinetograph), the first camera to record movement, (by William K. L. Dickson in 1891) _____ the development of the motion picture industry (in the early 1900's.)

The invention of …. the first camera to record movement, _____ the development of the motion picture industry…

Proposal: Look for words like helped, started, enhanced or promoted.

Vocab -- AC—POE

- ○ Canvassed: 1. to scrutinize   2. to go through an area to solicit votes or orders
- ● **Facilitated: to make easier or assist the progress of, to aid or promote**
- ○ Mottled: to mark with spots or shades of different colors
- ○ Prohibited: to forbid by use of authority, constrained, enjoined, hindered, impeded, prevented
- ○ Relegated: to assign to an obscure place or position, to exile or banish

Check Your Work: The invention of the Kinetograph, the first camera to record movement, by William K. L. Dickson in 1891 <u>facilitated</u> (aid or promoted) the development of the motion picture industry in the early 1900's.

Answer to Question 4

Question Type: 1 blank, Noun, little Logic and more Vocab

Call of the Question: William angrily lectured the teenagers on the responsibility of driving, but his _____ did nothing to correct their misconception of traffic laws as a hindrance rather than a defense.

Logic: (William) angrily lectured (the teenagers on the responsibility of driving,) but his _____ (did nothing to correct their misconception of traffic laws as a hindrance rather than a defense.)

Proposal: Look for a word that resembles angry lecture. **Example**: talk, address, sermon, speech.

Vocab -- AC—POE

● **tirade:** an angry, often denunciatory speech; diatribe, denunciation, harangue, invective, ranting, tongue-lashing, vituperation
○ **recitation:** 1. the act of reciting 2. oral delivery of prepared lessons by pupil
○ **query:** 1. a question or inquiry 2. a doubt in the mind or reservation 3. a notation, a question mark
○ **anecdote:** a short account of an interesting or humorous incident
○ **guise:** 1. outward appearance 2. false appearance or facade 3. mode of dress

Check Your Work: William angrily lectured the teenagers on the responsibility of driving, but his **tirade** (angry speech) did nothing to correct their misconception of traffic laws as a hindrance rather than a defense.

Answer to Question 5

Question Type: 2 blank, Verb/Noun, lots of Logic and little Vocab

Call of the Question: Though the Red Cross was founded primarily for the purpose of _____ both physical and emotional anguish of injured soldiers in war, during times of peace the agency also offers relief to _____ of natural disasters.

1st BLANK--Logic: Though Red Cross' primary purpose is _____ing anguish of soldiers _____ing anguish

Proposal: Look for words like relieving or reducing.
Vocab -- AC—POE

    exacerbating: makes it worse, to increase the severity of, aggravate
✓**alleviating:** to make more bearable
✓ **appeasing:** to satisfy or pacify or relieve, usually by granting a concession
    observing: to be or become aware of, esp. through special attention
    alarming: to frighten or warn

2nd BLANK: Logic: During peace time, it offers relief to _____ of natural disasters
    Offers relief to _____ of disasters (Victims, Criminals) Obviously, "victims" works and "criminals" does not.

Check Your Work: Though the Red Cross was founded primarily for the purpose of **alleviating** (to make more bearable) both physical and emotional anguish of injured soldiers in war, during times of peace the agency also offers relief to **victims** of natural disasters. **NOTE:** You could have started with the 2nd blank first and worked through it and still get the right answer. It does not matter which blank you begin with.

Answer to Question 6

Question Type: 2 blank, Noun/Adj., lots of Logic and lots of Vocab

Call of the Question: Despite his _____ from years of schooling, his _____ disposition would never let him attain greater success than his more aggressive brother.

1st BLANK: Logic: Despite his _____ (Something that comes from years of schooling)
Proposal: Look for a word that describes something that comes from years of schooling.

Vocab -- AC—POE

    Obtuseness lack of intellect, perception, or quickness of mind
✓ **Erudition:** deep extensive learning or scholarship
✓ **Refinement:** the act of refining, an improvement
    Joviality: mirth, happiness, etc.
✓ **Enlightenment:** spiritual or intellectual insight

2nd BLANK: Logic: His _____ disposition
    Proposal: Look for a word that describes a characteristic opposite of aggressive. **Example:** passive, timid, mild.

Remaining AC:

✓ **Docile:** easily managed, submissive, gentle, meek, compliant
    Gracious: cordial, sociable, kind, considerate
    Assertive: bold, forceful, aggressive

Check Your Work: Despite his **erudition** (deep extensive learning) from years of schooling, his **docile** (submissive, gentle, meek) disposition would never let him attain greater success than his more aggressive brother. **NOTE:** You can answer 2 blank question beginning with either blank first.

Sentence Completion

Section 4: Review

SAT Classroom>Sentence Completion>Review

This material corresponds to the SAT Virtual Classroom Instructions in the PowerPrep DVD/Internet/iApp for Sentence Completion

Virtual Classroom

Important Abbreviations
These abbreviations are used throughout the program

POE: Process of Elimination
SARR: Synthesize, Analyze, Reduce, and Restate (has to do with Logical Reasoning)
AC: Answer Choice
QS: Question Stem
LOD: Level of Difficulty

Example Question: What is the least common multiple of 3, 4, and 7? (**This is the call of the question or Question Stem "QS"**)

These are Answer Choices "AC" A, B, C, D, E

(A)   12
(B)   21
(C)   28
(D)   48
(E)   84

Part 4: Review

1. Learn Directions.

2. Remember Four Step Approach:
   1. Read Sentence using "blank."
   2. WEED, SARR, POE.
   3. Propose a Response.
   4. Check your Answer.

The extra step: Answer 2 blank questions one blank at a time. Using POE . If one blank is wrong-entire AC is wrong.

3. Guess if you need to using POE to eliminate some AC's.

CONGRATULATIONS!

You Have Completed The Sentence Completion Workshop.

Take A Break Before Moving On To The Sentence Completion Drills.

Big Book of Grammar

Student Study Guide

Table of Contents

This material corresponds to the Virtual Classroom Instructions in the
PowerPrep DVD/Internet/iApp for English Grammar

Virtual Classroom

Grammar Study Guide

Part 1: Introduction

Virtual Classroom>Grammar Study Guide>Introduction

This material corresponds to the Virtual Classroom Instructions in the
PowerPrep DVD/Internet/iApp for English Grammar

Virtual Classroom

Important Abbreviations
These abbreviations are used throughout the program

POE:	Process of Elimination
SARR:	Synthesize, Analyze, Reduce, and Restate (has to do with Logical Reasoning)
AC:	Answer Choice
QS:	Question Stem
LOD:	Level of Difficulty

Example Question: What is the least common multiple of 3, 4, and 7? **(This is the call of the question or Question Stem "QS")**
These are Answer Choices "AC" A, B, C, D, E

    (A)   12
    (B)   21
    (C)   28
    (D)   48
    (E)   84

Part 1: Introduction

The Good News

Understanding the directions ahead of time will prove to be a valuable time saver on the test.
Once you identify ways to fix the sentence, you will have the upper hand on the test.
The test-makers stick to the basic rules and don't implement controversial grammar rules.

The Bad News

The "best" answer may not sound correct to you: **Example:** Hopefully, we will learn the answer to that question tomorrow." Even though we speak this way, it's not correct or accepted written grammar and the examiners test "written formal English". In fact, they rely on the fact that you will likely confuse things that "sound good" with what "is accepted". So be careful.

Corrected Sentence: We hope to learn the answer to that question tomorrow.
The exam tests your understanding of formal written English grammar and not solely on your ear.

Question Types: grammar concepts

SAT

Improving Sentences (IS)
Identifying Sentence Errors (ISE)
Improving Paragraphs (IP)

Usually appear in sections 3,4,6, and 7
Improving Sent: Questions 1-11
Identifying Sent Errors: questions 12-29
Improving Paragraphs: questions 30-35

Section 10
Improving Sentences: questions 1-14

Totals 49 questions
IS = 25 questions per test
IP= 6 questions per test
ISE = 18 questions per test

LOD (Level of Difficulty)
Easy 42% (21 questions on avg)
Med 53% (26 questions on avg)
Hard 6% (3 questions on avg)

ACT

English Test:
Correcting Sentences in a Passage
You have 45 minutes to read five (5) passages and answer 75 grammar questions. Tests your ability to revise and edit a piece of writing. Subscore from 40 Usage/mechanics questions and 35 Rhetorical Skills questions.

SAT Identifying Sentence Errors

Directions

You will have about 18 questions of this type on your exam and they will range in level-of-difficulty from Easy, Medium, and Hard (LOD E, M, H)

Directions: The following sentences test your ability to recognize grammar and usage errors. Each sentence contains either a single error or no error at all. No sentence contains more than one error. The error, if there is one, is underlined and lettered. If the sentence contains an error, select the one underlined part that must be changed to make the sentence correct. If the sentence is correct, select choice E. In choosing answers, follow the requirements of standard written English.

SAT Identifying Sentence Errors Sample Question 1

The other players and him happily accepted the trophy presented by the league president. No error.
A   B   C   D   E

Type of Question: ISE   **LOD:** Easy
Concepts tested: Subject Verb Agreement, Pronoun Use

The simple test for <u>Subject Verb Agreement</u> is to find the verb (in this case "accepted") and then locate the subject. The test makers love to split the subject –in this case "the other players" and "he/him". The easiest way to figure this out is to take each subject and put it next to the verb, like this:
The other players accepted (sounds good) **or** him accepted (not so good) **or** he accepted (sounds correct) **Correct Answer B.** You can even reduce "the other players" to "they" and then test it again:
they and him accepted (not correct) **or** they accepted (correct) he accepted (correct) they and he accepted (correct)

Samples: <u>Pronoun Use</u> and <u>Subject Verb Agreement</u> Generally
The form of the marked pronoun needs to reflect its function in your sentence and match the verb.
Instead of: They wanted to punish <u>I</u>. **Consider**: They wanted to punish me.
Instead of: <u>Them</u> are the saddest boys on earth. **Consider**: They are the saddest boys on earth.
Instead of: <u>Us</u> movie-goers went home when the show ended. **Consider**: We movie-goers went home when the show ended.

SAT Identifying Sentence Errors Sample Question 2

Leonardo da Vinci <u>completely</u> transformed <u>traditional design</u>, <u>and they had been</u> used by many other
                     A   B   C

artists simply <u>to create</u> beautiful paintings. <u>No Error</u>
              D   E

Type of Question: ISE   **LOD**: Easy
Concept tested: Wordiness
Correct AC "C" "and they had been" is <u>wordy</u> and can be eliminated entirely without changing the meaning of the sentence: Leonardo da Vinci completely transformed traditional design, used by many other artists simply to create beautiful paintings. Or you could add the word "previously". Leonardo da Vinci completely transformed traditional design, previously used by many other artists simply to create beautiful paintings.

SAT Improving Sentences

Directions (25 Questions per test)

The following Sentences test correctness and effectiveness of expression. Part of each sentence or the entire sentence is underlined; beneath each sentence are five ways of phrasing the underlined material. Choice A repeats the original phrasing; the other four choices are different. If you think the original phrasing produces a better sentence than any of the alternatives, select choice A; if not, select one of the other choices.

In making your selection, follow the requirements of standard written English; that is, pay attention to grammar, choice of words, sentence construction, and punctuation. Your selection should result in the most effective sentence—clear and precise, without awkwardness or ambiguity.

SAT Improving Sentences Sample Question 1

George Washington became the first president of the United States <u>and he was fifty-seven years old then</u>.

- (A) and he was fifty-seven years old then
- (B) when he was fifty-seven
- (C) at age fifty-seven years old
- (D) upon the reaching of fifty-seven years
- (E) at the time when he was fifty-seven

Type of Question: IS   **LOD**: Easy
Concept tested: Redundant, Wordy

Correct: George Washington became the first president of the United States when he was fifty-seven.

- (A) is <u>wordy</u> and ends the sentence with "then"…the better adverb is "when" as in AC (B)
- **(B) Correct**
- (C) "years old" at the end of the phrase is <u>redundant</u>. If it was "at age fifty-seven", it would be a viable choice.
- (D) <u>wordy</u> "upon the reaching of…"
- (E) <u>wordy</u> "at the time when he was…"

SAT Improving Sentences Sample Question 2

Jessica had just sat down at her desk <u>and that was when she was told</u> that her project had finally been graded.
- (A) and that was when she was told
- (B) and then she learned
- (C) when it was learned by her
- (D) and then they told her
- (E) when she learned

Type of Question: IS   LOD: Easy
Concept tested: Wordiness, Active vs. passive voice
Correct answer AC (E) Jessica had just sat down at her desk <u>when she learned</u> that her project had finally been graded.

Correct AC "E" The shortest "when she learned" is precise. The <u>active voice</u> does not change the meaning, eliminates <u>useless words</u>...eliminates 'is' and "was" and puts the sentence in <u>active voice</u>.

SAT Improving Paragraphs

Directions (6 questions per test)

Directions: the following passage is an early draft of an essay. Some parts of the passage need to be rewritten. Read the passage and select the best answers for the questions that follow. Some questions are about particular sentences or parts of sentences and ask you to improve sentence structure or word choice. Other questions ask you to consider organization and development. In choosing answer, follow the requirements of standard written English.

SAT Improving Paragraphs Sample Question 1

(1) Many customers complain about the poor quality of service provided by cell phone companies that are happening during the contract period. (2.) But really, what cell phone company is ever going to say they don't provide good service. (3.) Their goal, after all, is if you buy their contract.

    (A)   Delete "customers"
    (B)   Change "complain" to "complained"
    (C)   Change "are happening" to "is happened"
    (D)   Delete "that are happening"
    (E)   Insert "the course of" after "during"

Type of Question: IP   LOD: Medium
Concept tested: Wordy, Concise
Correct AC "D"

<u>Wordy</u>, the fragment "that are happening" can be deleted from the sentence and the meaning stays the same. You should always try to write <u>concise</u>, tight, and precise sentences.

SAT Improving Paragraphs Sample Question 2

In context, which is the best version of sentence 3? "Their goal, after all, is if you buy their contract."

    (A) No change
    (B) Their goal, after all, would be if you did not buy a plan from another cell phone company.
    (C) A cell phone company's goal, after all, is when contract is purchased.
    (D) The goal of cell phone companies, after all, is to sell service contracts.
    (E) The goal of cell phone companies, after all, is for you to purchase their service plan.

Type of Question: IS   LOD: Easy
Concept tested: Sentence fragment
Correct AC "D"

This is a <u>sentence fragment</u> and <u>slang</u> style of speech. You can simplify the phrase by dropping out "after all" "Their goal is if you buy their contract" you should be able to see the problem here. Their goal is to sell contracts—see AC "D" all the other proposed AC's have poor construction, are wordy, cumbersome or unclear. AC "D" is the most direct and accurate sentence that gets to the point: 'Their goal is to sell contracts'

ACT English Grammar Test

1 section of 75 questions/test

Directions: in the five passages that follow, certain words and phrases are underlined and numbered. In the right-hand column, you will find alternatives for the underlined part. In most cases, you are to choose the one that best expresses the idea, makes the statement appropriate for standard written English, or is worded most consistently with the style and tone of the passage as a whole. If you think the original version is best, choose "NO CHANGE". In some cases, you will find in the right-hand column a question about the underlined part. You are to choose the best answer to the question.
You will also find questions about a section of the passage, or about the passage as a whole. These questions do not refer to an underlined portion of the passage, but rather are identified by a number or numbers in a box.
For each question, choose the alternative you consider best and fill in the corresponding oval on your answer document. Read each passage through once before you begin to answer the questions that accompany it. For many of the questions, you must read several sentences beyond the question to determine the answer. Be sure that you have read far enough ahead each time you choose an alternative.

1 section (usually the first section) Five (5) passages, 75 questions, usually 15 questions per passage

Grandpa's Remote Control

[1]

My grandfather is not known for embracing technological <u>change. He still drives</u> his '59 Chevy
1

Impala. (He <u>says,</u> he can't imagine needing frivolous
2

options like automatic transmission or power steering.) So, when he <u>has went</u> to buy a new color television
3

<u>owing to the knowledge that</u> his old black-and-white
4

model had finally quit—and the salesperson tried to talk him into buying a model with a remote control, he resisted. He said that he had two good legs and was perfectly capable of getting out of his chair ⬚5

[2]

However, the sales person was persistent and, appealing to Grandpa's TV-viewing habits, described the various functions on the remote. <u>However, my grandpa</u>
6

[3]

could punch in the <u>time, and the channel</u> of his favorite
7

daily news program, and the TV would turn on that program at the proper time. In the end, Grandpa did buy the remote, and it has since become something he uses all the time. Grandpa is intrigued by the various uses for that remote. He has confided in me that the volume control is perfect for turning up the sound whenever Grandma asks him to take out the garbage. <u>For example,</u> he says, the
8

button that mutes the sound lets him cut <u>them</u> off in
9

midsentence.

[4]

Grandpa's favorite feature on the remote is the sleep function. This option automatically turns the TV off after a preset amount of time, which is very <u>convenient when</u> he
10

falls asleep while watching a show. <u>For him, Grandpa says</u>
11

<u>what he wants his TV doing, even when he sleeps, is to</u>
11

<u>know a source of both pleasure and power.</u>
11

[5]

[1] As for the programming function, Grandpa not only uses it for the news but also for playing jokes on his youngest grandchildren. [2] Explaining to the unsuspecting child that he has a remote control implanted in his little finger, <u>Grandpa points</u> his finger at the TV and, to the
12

child's amazement, seemingly turns it on. [3] I suppose Grandpa hasn't learned all the possible uses of the remote control, <u>but I don't doubt he will continue to discover new and creative ways of using it.</u>
13

⬚14

1. **A. NO CHANGE**
   B. change he still drives
   C. change still driving
   D. change, and still driving
2. **F. NO CHANGE**
   G. says
   H. says, that
   J. says, that,
3. **A. NO CHANGE**
   B. had went
   C. went
   D. goes
4. **F. NO CHANGE**
   G. due to the understandable fact that
   H. because
   J. so
5. Given that all are true, which of the following additions to the preceding sentence (replacing "chair.") would be most relevant?
   A. chair that was made of black leather.
   B. chair when he wanted to change the channel.
   C. chair by the south window in the family room.
   D. chair where he liked to sit.
6. **F. NO CHANGE**
   G. Additionally, Grandpa
   H. Conversely, my grandpa
   J. Grandpa
7. **A. NO CHANGE**
   B. time and, the channel,
   C. time and the channel
   D. time and the channel,
8. **F. NO CHANGE**
   G. To illustrate,
   H. On the one hand,
   J. On the other hand
9. **A. NO CHANGE**
   B. advertisers
   C. it
   D. its function
10. **F. NO CHANGE**
    G. convenient, when
    H. convenient. When
    J. convenient; when
11. **A. NO CHANGE**
    B. Even when he sleeps, Grandpa says that to know his TV is doing what he wants is a source of both pleasure and power for him.
    C. Doing what he wants, even when he sleeps, is to know his TV is a source of both pleasure and power for him, Grandpa says.
    D. Grandpa says that to know his TV is doing what he wants, even when he sleeps, is a source of both pleasure and power for him.
12. **F. NO CHANGE**
    G. pointing
    H. having pointed
    J. Grandpa has pointed
13. **A. NO CHANGE**
    B. and he probably won't bother learning them either.
    C. so the salesperson should explain how to interpret the 200-page manual.
    D. and Grandma gratefully acknowledges this.
14. Upon reviewing Paragraph 5 and realizing that some information has been left out, the writer composes the following sentence:
    "He programs the TV to turn on at a time when a grandchild will be visiting."
    The most logical placement for this sentence would be:
    F. before Sentence 1
    G. after Sentence 1
    H. after Sentence 2
    J. after Sentence 3.

Grandpa's Remote Control
(Corrected)

My grandfather is not known for embracing technological **change. He still drives** his '59 Chevy Impala. (He **says** he can't imagine needing frivolous options like automatic transmission or power steering.) So, when he **went** to buy a new color television **because** his old black-and-white model had finally quit—and the salesperson tried to talk him into buying a model with a remote control, he resisted. He said that he had two good legs and was perfectly capable of getting out of his **chair when he wanted to change the channel.**

However, the sales person was persistent and, appealing to Grandpa's TV-viewing habits, described the various functions on the remote. **Additionally, grandpa** could punch in the **time and the channel,** of his favorite daily news program, and the TV would turn on that program at the proper time.

In the end, Grandpa did buy the remote, and it has since become something he uses all the time. Grandpa is intrigued by the various uses for that remote. He has confided in me that the volume control is perfect for turning up the sound whenever Grandma asks him to take out the garbage. **On the other hand** he says, the button that mutes the sound lets him cut **advertisers** off in midsentence.

Grandpa's favorite feature on the remote is the sleep function. This option automatically turns the TV off after a preset amount of time, which is very **convenient when** he falls asleep while watching a show. **Grandpa says that to know his TV is doing what he wants, even when he sleeps, is a source of both pleasure and power for him.**

[1] As for the programming function, Grandpa not only uses it for the news but also for playing jokes on his youngest grandchildren. *He programs the TV to turn on at a time when a grandchild will be visiting.* [2] Explaining to the unsuspecting child that he has a remote control implanted in his little finger, **Grandpa points** his finger at the TV and, to the child's amazement, seemingly turns it on. [3] I suppose Grandpa hasn't learned all the possible uses of the remote control, **but I don't doubt he will continue to discover new and creative ways of using it.**

Detailed Explanatory Answer Question 1

Type of Question: Grammar/English **LOD:** Easy **Concepts tested:** Run-on, Connecting word, Complete statement, Main clause, Comma, Grammatically parallel

The Best Answer is A because it provides punctuation (in this case a period) that appropriately separates these two complete thoughts or statements—"My grandfather is not known for embracing technological change." and "He still drives his '59 Chevy Impala."

Given Sentence: My grandfather is not known for embracing technological **change. He still drives** his '59 Chevy Impala.
Corrected: No changes

The following AC's are not correct:
(A) It creates a <u>run-on</u>, or fused, sentence. There is no punctuation or conjunction (<u>connecting word</u>) between the two statements.
(B) The phrase "still driving his '59 Chevy Impala" is not a <u>complete statement</u> because there is no stated subject. It could work in this sentence if it were set off from the <u>main clause</u> with a <u>comma</u>.
(C) It would then modify "My grandfather," the subject of the main clause. But this answer doesn't provide that punctuation.
(D) The conjunction "and" that connects the phrase "still driving his '59 Chevy Impala" to the main clause creates confusion by linking groups of words that are not <u>grammatically parallel</u>.

Detailed Explanatory Answer Question 2

Type of Question: Grammar/English **LOD:** Medium **Concepts tested:** Comma, Direct quotation (not applicable here)

The Best Answer is G because it correctly punctuates this sentence, which is actually a fairly simple subject-verb-direct object sentence except that the direct object is a noun clause. The sentence could also be written with the word "that" introducing the clause.

Given Sentence: (He **says**, he can't imagine needing frivolous options like automatic transmission or power steering.)

Corrected: (He **says** he can't imagine needing frivolous options like automatic transmission or power steering.)

The following AC's are not correct:
(F) Inserts an unnecessary <u>comma</u> between the predicate "says" and the direct object, which is what he says ("he can't imagine needing frivolous options like automatic transmission or power steering"). It's worth pointing out that the comma would be correct if what followed the predicate were a <u>direct quotation</u>, as in speech: He says, "I can't imagine needing frivolous options."
(H) Inserts an unnecessary <u>comma</u> between the predicate and the direct object clause.
(J) Adds the same unnecessary <u>comma</u> as H does, plus it places an unnecessary comma between the pronoun "that" and the clause it introduces.

Detailed Explanatory Answer Question 3

Type of Question: Grammar/English **LOD:** Easy **Concepts tested:** conjugation the verb "to go", Present and past tense

The Best Answer is C because "went" is the past tense of the verb. Also "has went" is the wrong construction—if you wanted to use "has" it would be "has gone". But this construction means the person has gone and has not returned yet. So if the sentence said, "So, when he has gone to buy a new color television…" This would mean grandpa was still at the store…he has gone and has not returned yet.

Given Sentence: So, when he **has went** to buy a new color television <u>owing to the knowledge that</u> his old black-and-white model had finally quit…

Corrected: So, when he **went** to buy a new color television **because** his old black-and-white model had finally quit—and the salesperson tried to talk him into buying a model with a remote control, he resisted.

The following AC's are not correct:

(B) had went—this is a nonstandard construction of the verb "to go". The accepted construction is "had gone".
(D) goes—the sentence is cast in the past tense and "goes" is a present or future tense construction of the verb "to go". When grandpa "goes" to the store he will...the sales person will try and talk him into buying..." But the given sentence says the salesperson "tried (past tense) to talk him into buying..." Therefore, we need a past tense form of the verb "to go" which is "went".

Detailed Explanatory Answer Question 4

Type of Question: Grammar/English **LOD:** Easy **Concepts tested:** Wordiness

The Best Answer is H because we want to know why grandpa went to the store. He went to the store to buy a new TV because his old TV finally broke. The current construction of the sentence is very "wordy". The phrase "...owing to the knowledge that..." can be shortened to simply say "because". He went to the store "because" his TV at home broke. This change reduces 5 words to 1 and does not change the meaning of the sentence. It's a much tighter way to convey the meaning.

Given Sentence: So, when he has went to buy a new color television **owing to the knowledge that** his old black-and-white model had finally quit—and the salesperson tried to talk him into buying a model with a remote control, he resisted.

Corrected: So, when he **went** to buy a new color television **because** his old black-and-white model had finally quit—and the salesperson tried to talk him into buying a model with a remote control, he resisted.

The following AC's are not correct:
(G) due to the understandable fact that—this is an even wordier way of saying "because".
(J) so—this construction does not make sense. Grandpa went to the store so his current TV finally quit. He went to the store to get a new TV "because" his old TV quit working not so his old quit.

Detailed Explanatory Answer Question 5

Type of Question: Logic **LOD:** Medium **Concepts tested:** Paragraph meaning

The Best Answer is B because it most logically finishes the thought. Why does grandpa resists the idea of using a remote control to change channels? Only AC B gives us a logical explanation why grandpa did not want a remote control for his TV. He thinks a remote control is not necessary because he has two good legs and can easily get up from his chair and walk to the TV and change it. The sentence would read: He said that he had two good legs and was perfectly capable of getting out of his chair **when he wanted to change the channel.**

Given Sentence: He said that he had two good legs and was perfectly capable of getting out of his **chair.**

Corrected: He said that he had two good legs and was perfectly capable of getting out of his **chair when he wanted to change the channel.**

The following AC's are not correct:
(A) He said that he had two good legs and was perfectly capable of getting out of his chair that was made of black leather. The fact the chair is made of black leather does not logically follow the clue we get in the sentence that grandpa says he has "two good legs" and that is the reason he does not think a remote control is necessary.
(C) He said that he had two good legs and was perfectly capable of getting out of his chair by the south window in the family room. The fact the chair is by the south window in the family room does not logically follow the clue that grandpa says he has "two good legs" and that is the reason he does not think a remote control is necessary.
(D) He said that he had two good legs and was perfectly capable of getting out of his chair where he liked to sit. The fact the chair is where grandpa likes to sit does not logically follow the clue we get in the sentence that grandpa says he has "two good legs" and that is the reason he does not think a remote control is necessary.

Detailed Explanatory Answer Question 6

Type of Question: Grammar and Logic **LOD:** Medium **Concepts tested:** Paragraph meaning and logically correct introductory word.

The Best Answer is G because it logically completes the meaning of the paragraph. You must look at the prior sentence and paragraph to grasp the full meaning. Grandpa resists the idea of the remote because he thinks it's silly—he's got two good legs why would he want a remote. (does that sound like your grandpa?). But the salesperson was persistent trying to change grandpa's idea that a remote would not be useful. The sales rep explains all the functions on the remote and explains how the remote could be useful. The next sentence is further explanation of the remote functions. **Additionally, Grandpa** could punch in the time, and the channel of his favorite programs... So AC G gives us additional reasons why the remote would be useful and makes the sentence and the paragraph logically flow.

Given Sentence: However, the sales person was persistent and, appealing to Grandpa's TV-viewing habits, described the various functions on the remote. **However, my grandpa** could punch in the time, and the channel of his favorite daily news program, and the TV would turn on that program at the proper time.

Corrected: However, the sales person was persistent and, appealing to Grandpa's TV-viewing habits, described the various functions on the remote. **Additionally, Grandpa** could punch in the time and the channel, of his favorite daily news program, and the TV would turn on that program at the proper time.

The following AC's are not correct:
(F) NO CHANGE However, my grandpa—This AC starts with "However". But the sentence before also begins with "However". It would be logically inconsistent to say something is a certain way, however, ...and then begin the next thought with "however" again. Grandpa resists the idea of a remote, but the sales clerk persists by showing all the benefits...if the next sentence were to remain "however" it would mean grandpa continued to resist the idea of a remote. However, that is not what the content says. The use of "however" in this case is logically inconsistent with the meaning in the sentence.
(H) Conversely, my grandpa—this phrase is very similar to "however" and has the same logical fallacy. We are looking for something like "Furthermore", "Additionally", "Also" etc.
(J) Grandpa—this is the next best answer. However, starting the sentence with "Additionally" gives more meaning than simply starting with "Grandpa". If this AC said "Grandpa also" it would be an equally good AC as G.

Detailed Explanatory Answer Question 7

Type of Question: Grammar/English **LOD:** Difficult **Concepts tested:** Commas in a series, Prepositional phrases

The Best Answer is D because it correctly punctuates the prepositional phrase ",of his favorite daily news programs,".

Given Sentence: However, the sales person was persistent and, appealing to Grandpa's TV-viewing habits, described the various functions on the remote. <u>However, my grandpa</u> could punch in the <u>**time, and the channel**</u> of his favorite daily news program, and the TV would turn on that program at the proper time.

Corrected: Additionally, my grandpa could punch in the <u>**time and the channel,**</u> of his favorite daily news program, and the TV would turn on that program at the proper time…

This is a difficult problem because it requires you to recognize content outside of the underlined content. You are actually punctuating the prepositional phrase that follows the underlined information and you must also recognize this is NOT a list that needs commas between items. This is just two items divided with "and" and this does NOT require a comma.

<u>**Rule: Commas in a Series**</u>—The rule says that we should use commas... AFTER ALL BUT THE LAST ITEM OR ELEMENT IN A SERIES. Be sure that you understand the word "series": A series consists of three or more WORDS...PHRASES...or CLAUSES in a sentence. In our case, we don't have a series. We just have two items: time and the channel. But we also have a prepositional phrase that needs to be offset with commas.

<u>**Rule: Comma and Phrases**</u>— Use a pair of commas in the middle of a sentence to set off clauses, phrases, and words that are not essential to the meaning of the sentence. Use one comma before to indicate the beginning of the pause and one at the end to indicate the end of the pause.

Here are some clues to help you decide whether the sentence element is essential:

- If you leave out the clause, phrase, or word, does the sentence still make sense?
- Does the clause, phrase, or word interrupt the flow of words in the original sentence?
- If you move the element to a different position in the sentence, does the sentence still make sense?

If you answer "yes" to one or more of these questions, then the element in question is nonessential and should be set off with commas. Here are some example sentences with nonessential elements:
Clause: That Tuesday, *which happens to be my birthday,* is the only day when I am available to meet.
Phrase: This restaurant has an exciting atmosphere. The food, *on the other hand,* is rather bland.
Word: I appreciate your hard work. In this case, *however,* you seem to have over-exerted yourself.

The following AC's are not correct:
(A) NO CHANGE (time, and the channel)—the comma rule for items in a series states we should use commas to divide the items when there are three (3) or more items in the series. Here we only have two items joined with "and", therefore, we do not use a comma to divide the items.
(B) time and, the channel, —the comma rule for items in a series states we should use commas to divide the items when there are three (3) or more items in the series. Here we only have two items joined with "and", therefore, we do not use a comma to divide the items. So a comma is not needed after "and,". Also this AC places a comma after "channel,". This part of the answer is correct because this comma is necessary to set off the prepositional phrase that follows. However the first comma after "and," makes this AC incorrect.
(C) time and the channel—this AC correctly follows the rule regarding commas in a series (we don't have a series), however, it fails to include the comma trailing "channel," which is necessary to set off the prepositional phrase *, of his favorite daily news program,*

Detailed Explanatory Answer Question 8

Type of Question: Logic, Grammar/English **LOD:** Medium **Concepts tested:** Paragraph meaning and logically correct introductory word.

The Best Answer is J because "On the other hand" logically completes the idea started in the prior sentence. Grandpa likes the various buttons and functions on the remote. He likes the button that increases the volume because it drowns out grandma. But he also likes the button that mutes the sound. So he likes to raise the volume and mute the volume. These are opposites. Therefore, the introduction "on the other hand" fits logically. He likes to raise the volume to do one things, on the other hand, he likes to mute the volume for another purpose.

Given Sentence: In the end, Grandpa did buy the remote, and it has since become something he uses all the time. Grandpa is intrigued by the various uses for that remote. He has confided in me that the volume control is perfect for turning up the sound whenever Grandma asks him to take out the garbage. <u>**For example**</u>, he says, the button that mutes the sound lets him cut <u>them</u> off in midsentence.

Corrected: In the end, Grandpa did buy the remote, and it has since become something he uses all the time. Grandpa is intrigued by the various uses for that remote. He has confided in me that the volume control is perfect for turning up the sound whenever Grandma asks him to take out the garbage. <u>**On the other hand**</u> he says, the button that mutes the sound lets him cut <u>advertisers</u> off in midsentence.

The following AC's are not correct:
(F) NO CHANGE—The existing start to the sentence "For example" is illogical. It would introduce examples of grandpa increasing the volume to ignore grandma.
(G) To illustrate,—this has the same logical fallacy as AC F. It logically introduces examples or illustrations of grandpa increasing the volume on the TV to avoid hearing grandma.
(H) On the one hand, —this introduces the first of at least two examples. On the one hand....but on the other hand.... In our sentence we don't have such a logical comparison. We want to tie our sentence into the prior sentence and the best option is "On the other hand,"

Detailed Explanatory Answer Question 9

Type of Question: Logic, Vocabulary **LOD:** Easy **Concepts tested:** Sentence meaning -logical vocabulary word.
The Best Answer is B because "advertisers" is the correct noun or subject and can logically replace "them" which is ambiguous. It's always better form to specify the noun rather than use indefinite pronouns--that can become very confusing and can make your reader have to guess. In this case, "them" is the "advertisers" that grandpa likes to mute so he does not have to hear the commercials.

Given Sentence: <u>For example</u>, he says, the button that mutes the sound lets him cut **<u>them</u>** off in midsentence.

Corrected: <u>On the other hand</u> he says, the button that mutes the sound lets him cut **<u>advertisers</u>** off in midsentence.

The following AC's are not correct:

(A) NO CHANGE (them)--this correctly uses the indefinite pronoun that would identify the "advertisers", however, it's ambiguous. It's better to use the actual noun first and then refer to the indefinite pronoun. If the passage had already mentioned that grandpa liked to mute the advertisers then it might have been good form to use the word "them" to refer back.

(C) it--this tests your logical understanding of the passage. Is the sentence referring to an "it" or a "them". The "it" would be the remote control or the buttons on the remote control. However, this sentence is not referring back to the remote control. "Them" refers to the advertisers that grandpa likes to mute.

(D) its function--this tests your logical understanding of the passage. What is "them" referring to--a person/people or a thing. The "its function" would be the remote control. However, this sentence is not referring back to the remote control. "Them" refers to the advertisers that grandpa likes to mute.

Detailed Explanatory Answer Question 10

Type of Question: Logic **LOD:** Medium **Concepts tested**: Comma, Period, Capital, Semi-colon

The Best Answer is F because

Given Sentence: Grandpa's favorite feature on the remote is the sleep function. This option automatically turns the TV off after a preset amount of time, which is very <u>convenient when</u> he falls asleep while watching a show.

Corrected: No changes

The following AC's are not correct:

(G) convenient, when--this creates a phrase "when he falls asleep" but does not complete the thought. It just leaves this notion hanging. The best approach is to leave these two words connected without any punctuation. It's very convenient when he falls asleep.

(H) convenient. When--this would create an incomplete sentence beginning with "When". "When he falls asleep while watching a show" is an incomplete thought. Regardless of the problems created with the logical flow of ideas, this AC creates a grammatically incorrect and incomplete phrase.

(J) convenient; when--separating "convenient" and "when" destroys the logical progression of the idea. It's convenient when he falls asleep. Those ideas need to remain pegged together.

Detailed Explanatory Answer Question 11

Type of Question: Logical flow, Grammar **LOD**: Medium **Concepts tested**: Modifiers (words and phrases), Logical flow

The Best Answer is D because it most correctly arranges the ideas and the modifiers into a logical flow that conveys the information in a way the reader can best understand. This is not to say this AC is the absolute right or best way to phrase this information. However, it is the best from the available AC's. Below is another option that is possibly better than the given correct answer. Logically it flows better to when you place what grandpa actually said as close as possible to the phrase "Grandpa says..." Generally it helps the logic and the flow to place modifiers as close as possible to what they modify.

Given Sentence: <u>For him, Grandpa says what he wants his TV doing, even when he sleeps, is to know a source of both pleasure and power.</u>

Corrected: **<u>Grandpa says that to know his TV is doing what he wants, even when he sleeps, is a source of both pleasure and power for him.</u>** (You could also drop the trailing "for him" and it would not change the sentence and would tighten it further.)

Another Correct Way: <u>Grandpa says it is a source of both pleasure and power to know his TV is doing what he wants, even when he sleeps.</u>

The following AC's are not correct:

(B) <u>**Even when he sleeps, Grandpa says that to know his TV is doing what he wants is a source of both pleasure and power for him.**</u> This AC demonstrates the problem with modifiers. This arrangement makes it seem that Grandpa is talking in his sleep. It says "Even when he sleeps, Grandpa says..." But Grandpa is not saying things in his sleep. So this AC fails for this reason among others.

(C) <u>**Doing what he wants, even when he sleeps, is to know his TV is a source of both pleasure and power for him, Grandpa says**</u>. This AC has the same issues with modifiers. It makes it seem Grandpa is doing things himself in his sleep. "Doing what he wants, even in his sleep..." This AC is unwieldy and has illogical construction.

Detailed Explanatory Answer Question 12

Type of Question: Grammar/English **LOD**: Easy **Concepts tested**: Tense, Subject

The Best Answer is F because it most directly and clearly explains the idea and it maintains the proper present tense for the verb "point". It also uses the active voice, which is always a good idea.

Given Sentence: [1] As for the programming function, Grandpa not only uses it for the news but also for playing jokes on his youngest grandchildren. [2] Explaining to the unsuspecting child that he has a remote control implanted in his little finger, **<u>Grandpa points</u>** his finger at the TV and, to the child's amazement, seemingly turns it on.

Corrected: No changes

The following AC's are not correct:

(G) pointing--this is a present participle but this AC removes the subject from the sentence and creates an incomplete thought (among other things). The subject is "Grandpa" and is necessary to form a complete sentence. If this were a series of actions you could construct the sentence like this: <u>Explaining to the unsuspecting child that he has a remote control implanted in his little finger and pointing his finger at the TV, to the child's amazement, Grandpa seemingly turns it on.</u> This keeps the subject "Grandpa" and arranges the participle "pointing" so it is parallel with "explaining" and a complete thought. But we don't have this option to choose.

(H) having pointed--this is also past tense and it removes the subject "Grandpa" and creates an incomplete thought. It also implies some additional action is going to happen. Having pointed his finger Grandpa does something more. However, the sentence is all present tense. Grandpa is currently explaining something and then Grandpa points his finger at the TV. So "having pointed" won't work in this present tense sentence. You could create a valid sentence with this AC like this: <u>Having pointed his finger at the TV and explaining to the unsuspecting child that he has a remote control</u>

implanted in his little finger, to the child's amazement, Grandpa seeming turns the TV on. This sentence still has some issues with tense, but it would work. However, we don't have this as a given AC.

(J) Grandpa has pointed—the sentence is cast in the present tense and this AC changes to the past tense. But it does keep the subject "Grandpa". Grandpa is explaining and he then points his finger. He did not explain in the past..to use the phrase "Grandpa has pointed" would require a past tense construction of the entire sentence. In the past, Grandpa has pointed his finger. However right now he is explaining and then he points his finger. This is all present tense.

Detailed Explanatory Answer Question 13

Type of Question: Logical flow , Grammar **LOD:** Difficult **Concepts tested:** Logical flow, Understanding the paragraph
The Best Answer is A because the passage says Grandpa is "intrigued by the various uses for that remote." It also explains how Grandpa uses the remote volume and mute controls and the sleep function. So Grandpa has learned many functions already including a use not intended by the manufacturer--using the remote timer function to trick his grand kids into thinking he has a remote control in his finger. So everything in the passage is consistent with the idea that he will continue to discover new and creative ways of using it.

Given Sentence: [3] I suppose Grandpa hasn't learned all the possible uses of the remote control, **but I don't doubt he will continue to discover new and creative ways of using it.**

Corrected: No changes

The following AC's are not correct:
(B) and he probably won't bother learning them either.—Nothing in the passage leads to this conclusion.   The passage says Grandpa is "intrigued by the various uses for that remote." This indicates he will continue learning the remote's functions.
(C) so the salesperson should explain how to interpret the 200-page manual.—there is nothing in the passage that indicates the author of the passage believes the sales person should interpret the 200 page user's manual. Also, this idea would be chronologically out of place. The story relates the interaction between Grandpa and sales person in the first paragraph. By the time we get to the sentence in this question, Grandpa is home and enjoying the TV and the remote for quite some time. He's learned about the mute and volume functions and the auto timer and he's played tricks on the grand kids. It would be awkward at best to refer back to the sales person at this point. Additionally, nothing in the logic leads to this conclusion anyways.
(D) and Grandma gratefully acknowledges this.—there is nothing in the passage that gives us any indication what Grandma thinks (other than the reference to Grandpa remotely turning up the sound to drown out Grandma's voice). This could lend some credibility to the idea that Grandma would be grateful

Detailed Explanatory Answer Question 14

Type of Question: Logical flow **LOD:** Difficult **Concepts tested:** Logical flow, Understanding the paragraph meaning
The Best Answer is G because this information logically fits at this point. We have several pieces of provided information:
1. Grandpa uses the remote to play tricks on grandkids. The introduction
2. A description of the trick in action. The actual trick.
3. A summary by the author that Grandpa will continue to learn more about the remote.

We also have the new piece of information: Grandpa programs the remote so the TV will turn on when a grandchild is likely to visit. So where should this information logically go in the paragraph?

The introduction (Grandpa plays tricks). The setup for the trick (he gets the trick ready). The execution of the trick. A summary.

So the new information fits best between sentence 1 and 2 (after sentence 1).
The paragraph should read: [1] As for the programming function, Grandpa not only uses it for the news but also for playing jokes on his youngest grandchildren. ***He programs the TV to turn on at a time when a grandchild will be visiting.*** [2] Explaining to the unsuspecting child that he has a remote control implanted in his little finger, Grandpa points his finger at the TV and, to the child's amazement, seemingly turns it on. [3] I suppose Grandpa hasn't learned all the possible uses of the remote control, but I don't doubt he will continue to discover new and creative ways of using it.

Grandpa's Remote Control (corrected)

My grandfather is not known for embracing technological **change. He still drives** his '59 Chevy Impala. (He **says** he can't imagine needing frivolous options like automatic transmission or power steering.) So, when he **went** to buy a new color television **because** his old black-and-white model had finally quit—and the salesperson tried to talk him into buying a model with a remote control, he resisted. He said that he had two good legs and was perfectly capable of getting out of his **chair when he wanted to change the channel.**

However, the sales person was persistent and, appealing to Grandpa's TV-viewing habits, described the various functions on the remote. **Additionally, grandpa** could punch in the **time and the channel,** of his favorite daily news program, and the TV would turn on that program at the proper time.

In the end, Grandpa did buy the remote, and it has since become something he uses all the time. Grandpa is intrigued by the various uses for that remote. He has confided in me that the volume control is perfect for turning up the sound whenever Grandma asks him to take out the garbage. **On the other hand** he says, the button that mutes the sound lets him cut **advertisers** off in midsentence.

Grandpa's favorite feature on the remote is the sleep function. This option automatically turns the TV off after a preset amount of time, which is very **convenient when** he falls asleep while watching a show. **Grandpa says that to know his TV is doing what he wants, even when he sleeps, is a source of both pleasure and power for him.**

[1] As for the programming function, Grandpa not only uses it for the news but also for playing jokes on his youngest grandchildren. ***He programs the TV to turn on at a time when a grandchild will be visiting.*** [2] Explaining to the unsuspecting child that he has a remote control implanted in his little finger, **Grandpa points** his finger at the TV and, to the child's amazement, seemingly turns it on. [3] I suppose Grandpa hasn't learned all the possible uses of the remote control, **but I don't doubt he will continue to discover new and creative ways of using it.**

Grammar Study Guide

Part 2: The Approach

<u>**Virtual Classroom>Grammar Study Guide>**</u><u>The Approach "Method of Attack"</u>

This material corresponds to the Virtual Classroom Instructions in the
PowerPrep DVD/Internet/iApp for English Grammar

Virtual Classroom

Important Abbreviations
These abbreviations are used throughout the program

POE:	Process of Elimination
SARR:	Synthesize, Analyze, Reduce, and Restate (has to do with Logical Reasoning)
AC:	Answer Choice
QS:	Question Stem
LOD:	Level of Difficulty

Example Question: What is the least common multiple of 3, 4, and 7? **(This is the call of the question or Question Stem "QS")**

These are Answer Choices "AC" A, B, C, D, E
- (A) 12
- (B) 21
- (C) 28
- (D) 48
- (E) 84

Part 2: Approach

Method of Attack

Tips to Preparation

Understand the difference between standard English and the English that the test will measure.

The importance of oversimplification

Use the process of elimination (POE) to locate the correct answer, and the incorrect choices.

Process of Elimination (POE) 2 of 5 Rule

Creating a good but incorrect AC is much harder than developing the correct answer. For this reason, usually only one attractive wrong answer-choice is presented. This is called the "2 out of 5" rule--only two of the five AC's will have any real merit. Hence, even if you don't fully understand an argument, you probably can still eliminate the three fluff choices, thereby greatly increasing your odds of answering the question correctly.

Example: Carbon-14 dating reveals that the megalithic monuments in Brittany are nearly 2,000 years <u>as old as any of their supposed</u> Mediterranean predecessors.

(A) as old as any of their supposed
(B) older than any of their supposed
(C) as old as their supposed
(D) older than any of their supposedly
(E) as old as their supposedly

Explanation: AC's (A),(C),and(E) do not state a logical comparison. The expression *as old as* indicates equality of age, but the sentence says the Brittany monuments predate the Mediterranean monuments by 2,000 years.

AC (B) *older than* makes a clear comparison. This choice also correctly uses the adjective *supposed*, rather than the adverb *supposedly* used in (D) and (E), to modify the noun phrase *Mediterranean predecessors*.

The "Big Six" of Grammar Tests

- Pronoun Errors
- Subject-Verb Agreement
- Misplaced Modifiers
- Faulty Parallelism
- Faulty Verb Tense
- Faulty Idiom and Usage

THE PARTS OF SPEECH: Great Eight

1. NOUNS (n.)

A noun is a word that names a person, a place, a thing, or an idea.

Persons: police officer, Ms. Stamper, sister
Places: Arizona, lake, Southwest
Things: sock, fish, Of Mice and Men
Ideas: justice, fellowship, indifference

(dates and days of the week are also classified as nouns)

Collective Nouns refers to a group of people, places, things, or ideas. *Examples*: *The committee debated the issue for hours. The flock is flying south.*
Compound Noun consists of words used together to form a single noun. *Examples*: *stagecoach, father-in-law, radio wave, George Washington*

Concrete Nouns refer to material things, to people, or to places. They can also refer to things that you can perceive with your senses: bells, smells and chills. *Examples*: *formaldehyde, hoot, exhaust, chimes, pepper*

Abstract Nouns refer to ideas, qualities, emotions, or attitudes. *Examples*: *optimism, nostalgia, self-control*

2. PRONOUNS (pron.)

A pronoun is a word that replaces a noun. A pronoun identifies persons, places, things, or ideas without renaming them. The **antecedent** is the noun that the pronoun replaces.

Personal Pronouns require different forms to express person, number, and gender.

	Singular	Plural
First Person	I, me (my ,mine)	we, us (our, ours)
Second Person	you (your, yours)	you (your, yours)
Third Person	he, him, (his) She, her (her, hers) It (its)	they, them, (their, theirs)

Demonstrative pronouns (this, that, these, those) specify the individual or the group that is being referred to. **Example**: *This is Jane's sculpture, and that is Eric's painting.*

Reflexive pronouns (myself, ourselves, yourself, yourselves, himself, herself, itself, oneself, themselves) indicate that people or things perform actions to, for or on behalf of themselves. **Example**: *We gave ourselves four days to make the drive.*

Interrogative Pronouns (who, whom, which, what, whose) introduce questions. **Example**: *Who is in the room?*

Relative Pronouns (who, whom, whose, which, that) introduce adjective clauses which modify nouns and pronouns. **Example**: *Have you read "The Tell Tale Heart," **which** was written by Poe?*

Indefinite Pronouns refer to people, places, or things in general. Often used without an antecedent. (all, either, most, somebody, both, few, no one, one, many, each. . .) **Example**: *Somebody won both of the races.*

3. VERBS (v.)

A verb is a word that expresses an action or a state of being. Three kinds of verbs: **action, linking and auxiliary**.

Action Verbs describe the behavior or action of someone or something. Action verbs may represent physical actions or mental activity. **Examples**: *We saw the large satellite. Cal broke the plate.*

Linking Verbs connect a noun or a pronoun with words that identify or describe the noun or pronoun. Many linking verbs are verbs of being (forms of "to be"). **Example**: *That is a painting by Van Gogh. (is links painting to that)*

Auxiliary Verbs: sometimes an action verb or a linking verb needs the help of an auxiliary verb, or helping verb. The verb that it helps is called the main verb. Together, a main verb and an auxiliary verb form a verb phrase. Common auxiliary verbs appear in the following list: (*am, are, be, been, is, was, were, may , might, have, has, had, can, could, did, do, does, will, would, shall, should, must*)

Transitive and **Intransitive Verbs**: all action verbs are either transitive or intransitive. A verb is transitive when its action is directed toward someone or something, which is called *the object of the verb*. A verb is intransitive when its action is not directed toward someone or something. Simply, intransitive verbs do not have objects. Linking verbs are intransitive.

4. ADJECTIVES (adj.)

An adjective is a word that modifies a noun or a pronoun. When we use the word *modify* we mean to change, and an adjective changes the meaning of a noun or pronoun by describing it or making it more specific. **Example**: *Let's not play in the first game.*

Articles are the most frequently used adjectives (a, an, the). *"A"* and *"an"* are indefinite articles because they do not specify a particular person or thing. *"The"* is an definite article because it always points out a particular item.

Proper Adjectives: a name that functions as the modifier of a noun or pronoun. You always capitalize proper adjectives. **Example**: *Let's go to the game on Friday night.*

5. ADVERBS (adv.)

An adverb is a word that modifies a verb, an adjective, or another adverb. An adverb answers one of five questions about the word or phrase that it modifies: How? Where? How often? or To what extent?

To decide whether a modifier is an adjective or an adverb, you need to determine the part of speech that it modifies. If the modified word is a noun or pronoun, the modifier is an adjective. If the modified word is a verb, an adjective or an adverb, the modifier is an adverb.

6. PREPOSITIONS (prep.)

A preposition is a word that expresses a relationship between a noun or a pronoun and another word in a sentence. This will be covered in more depth when prepositional phrases are examined.

Compound Prepositions: a compound preposition is a preposition that consists of more than one word. Here is a list of frequently used compound prepositions.

According to	*in place of*	*in regard to*	*in respect to*	*aside from* *in front of*	*in addition to*
in front of	*prior to*	*out of*			

7. CONJUNCTIONS (conj.)

There are three types of conjunctions: coordinating, correlative, and subordinating.

Coordinating Conjunctions: they connect individual words or groups of words that perform the same function in a sentence. (and, but, for, nor, or, yet) **Example**: *Dorothy stopped, looked **and** crossed the road.*

Correlative Conjunctions: two or more words that function together. (either/or, neither/nor, both/and, whether/or, both/and). **Example**: *Both Janet and Brooke made the swimming team.*

Subordinating Conjunctions introduce a subordinate clause, which is a clause that cannot stand by itself as a complete sentence. A subordinating conjunction connects a subordinate clause to an independent clause, which can stand by itself as a complete sentence. **Example**: *We will go to the roller coaster if we have time.*

INTERJECTIONS (interj.)

An interjection is an exclamatory word or phrase that can stand by itself, although it may also appear in a sentence. **Examples**: *What! How can you say that to me? Good Heavens!*

Determining Parts of Speech

What part of speech a word is depends upon how the word is used.

Exercise 1: Determine what part of speech the word in bold is, and write it in the blank.

    1. Tobby scrambled across the field for the first **down.**   _____
    2. He made a **down** payment on the car.   _____
    3. The child must **down** a spoonful of medicine.   _____

Exercise 2: Determine what part of speech the word in bold is, and write it in the blank.

    1. **Light** the fire now.   _____
    2. A **light** snow began to fall.   _____
    3. A red **light** flashed.   _____

Answers to Exercises 1 and 2

1. **down. Noun** 2. **down** Adjective 3. **down** Verb 1. **Light** (v.) 2. A **light (adj.)** 3. **light (n.)**

THE PARTS OF A SENTENCE

The Three Parts of a Sentence

Subject: the noun or pronoun that names the person place, thing or idea that the sentence is about.
Predicate: a verb or verb phrase that describes the action or states the condition of the subject.
Complement: a word or group of words that completes the meaning of the predicate.

Identifying Subject and Predicate Sentences

Underline the <u>Subject</u> with one line and the <u>predicate</u> with two lines.
    1. Seagulls were flying around the pier.
    2. The members of the club arrived.
    3. The person in the front row   is my sister.

<u>**Answers:**</u> 1. <u>Seagulls</u> <u>were flying around the pier</u>. 2. <u>The members of the club</u> <u>arrived</u>. 3, <u>The person in the front row</u>   <u>is my sister.</u>

Simple and Complete Subjects

The **complete subject** of a sentence includes all the words that tell who or what the sentence is about. **Example**: <u>Everyone on the team</u> scored a goal.

The **simple subject** is the main word or words in the complete subject. **Example**: <u>Everyone</u> on the team scored a goal.

Sometimes the **complete subject** and the **simple subject** are the same. **Example**: <u>Suzie</u> kicked and screamed because the doctored wanted to give her a shot.

A **compound subject** contains two or more subjects that have the same predicate. The simple subjects in a compound subject are usually joined by and or or. **Example**: <u>**The Johnsons and the Sanchez'**</u> attended the 4th of July barbeque together.

The ***complete subject*** consists of all the words that tell *whom* or *what* a sentence is about. **Example**: The huge, green, slimy, alien from Mars waved to us. The simple subject also tells who or what the sentence is about, but it doesn't have all of the descriptive words. The simple subject is usually just a single noun.

Underline the complete subject of each sentence. Then, write the simple subject on the line
1. The furry brown Yak smells like manure. _____
2. The angry ballerina slammed her slippers and tutu on the floor. _____
3. Every teenager in the country wants that phone. _____
4. The little, spotted owl sang because he was happy to see us. _____
5. Cornelius' youngest brother fought in the war. _____
6. The dog guarded the house. _____
7. My neighbor down the street plays the guitar in a band. _____
8. Shaniqua's favorite desert was on sale this week at the grocery store. _____

Complete and Simple Subjects Answer Key
1. <u>The furry brown Yak</u> smells like manure. <u>Yak</u>
2. <u>The angry ballerina</u> slammed her slippers and tutu on the floor. ballerina

3. Every teenager in the country wants that phone. <u>teenager</u>
4. The little, spotted owl sang because he was happy to see us. <u>owl</u>
5. Cornelius' youngest brother fought in the war. <u>brother</u>
6. The dog guarded the house. <u>dog</u>
7. My neighbor down the street plays the guitar in a band. <u>neighbor</u>
8. Shaniqua's favorite desert was on sale this week at the grocery store. <u>desert</u>
9. A bright flash from a camera startled the celebrity. <u>flash</u>
10. The nerve wracking screeches from wild coyotes with captured prey echo down the canyon walls. <u>screeches</u>

Simple Predicate (or Verb) & Complete Predicate

Once you have located the subject, the predicates are easy to find. A predicate shows action. There are different kinds of predicates just like there were for subjects.

<u>Simple Predicate :</u> The simple predicate, or verb, is the main word or word group that tells something about the subject. The simple predicate is the verb inside the complete predicate. **Examples:** The old computer **worked** for only a moment. The fuzzy little poodle **barked** all the way to the veterinarian and all the way back home.

<u>The Complete Predicate :</u> The *complete predicate* consists of a verb and all the words that modify the verb and complete its meaning. Once you know the complete subject, the complete predicate is easy to locate—it's everything else. **Examples:** The old computer **worked for only a moment.** The fuzzy little poodle **barked all the way to the veterinarian and all the way back home.**

<u>Compound Predicate:</u> The compound predicate is two or more verbs joined by a conjunction such as and, or, or but. **Example:** The flowers **bloomed** for only one day and then **wilted** and **died**.

<u>Questions:</u> Underline the complete predicate.

1. During morning recess, the fifth-graders ran around the playground
2. The soccer goalie blocked every shot.
3. Disneyland at night was a spectacular sight for the children.
4. Francisco called Courtney to tell her he could come to her party.
5. Achmed and Jennifer went out to dinner.

<u>Answers</u>:
1. During morning recess, the fifth-graders **ran around the playground**
2. The soccer goalie **blocked every shot.**
3. Disneyland at night **was a spectacular sight for the children.**
4, Francisco **called Courtney to tell her he could come to her party.**
5. Achmed and Jennifer **went out to dinner.**

Sentence Classifications

There are four (4) sentence types: Declarative, Imperative, Interrogative, and Exclamatory

- A **declarative** sentence is used to make a statement.
- An **interrogative** sentence is used to pose a question.
- An **imperative** sentence is used to give a command or to implore or entreat.
- An **exclamatory** sentence is used to express astonishment or extreme emotion.

<u>Declarative sentences</u> . Most of the sentences we speak or write are declarative sentences.
It's lunch time. **Examples**: We are going to the game on Friday. My car is out of gasoline. My parents keep telling me that I should make good grades so I can get a job or go to college.

<u>Interrogative sentences.</u> These sentences ask a question. **Examples**: What time does the movie start?   How many people from your graduating class went to college? Is there a reason why these dirty clothes are in the middle of the floor? What are they serving in the cafeteria today?

How do you know if a sentence is a question? Well, according to comedians Bud Abbot and Lou Costello, it depends on the punctuation mark. "Who's on first**."** If you don't understand it can be both a question and a statement listen to Abbot and Costello "Who's on first" http://www.youtube.com/watch?v=sShMA85pv8M

<u>Imperative sentences</u>. People who have authority use imperative sentences. Sometimes, people who don't have authority use imperative sentences. The results may differ. **Examples**: Wash the car. Clean your room.   Fredrika, report to the principal's office. Please give money to cheerleader's fundraiser. We say that sentences must have a subject and a verb. Note that some of the above sentences do not seem to have a subject. The subject is implied, and the implied subject is **you**. You wash the car. **You** clean your room. **You** is a second person pronoun. It isn't possible to make a command statement in first or third person.

<u>Exclamatory sentences.</u> Exclamatory sentences are rarely used in expository writing. Spoken exclamations are often a single word or an incomplete sentence. Grammarians indicate that formal exclamatory sentences begin with the word <u>what</u> or with the word <u>how</u>. Most of the exclamations we encounter are informal. **Examples**: What a gorgeous little baby! How happy we were when the dawn came and our flag was still there! What did you do to my car! (exclamation formed as a question) I just won a million dollars! (exclamation formed as a declarative sentence)

Questions: Write the classification in identifying the type of sentence—Declarative, Imperative, Interrogative, and Exclamatory

1. Michael Jordan was a multiple winner of the trophy. _____
2. Go to the storm cellar immediately. _____
3. Wasn't her joke funny? _____
4. What hope a rainbow brings after a raging storm! _____

Answers Sentence Classifications

1. Michael Jordan was a multiple winner of the trophy.   Declarative
2. Go to the storm cellar immediately.   Imperative
3. Wasn't her joke funny?   Interrogative
4. What hope a rainbow brings after a raging storm!   Exclamatory

Grammar Study Guide

Part 3: Pronoun Errors

Virtual Classroom>Grammar Study Guide>Pronoun Errors

This material corresponds to the Virtual Classroom Instructions in the
PowerPrep DVD/Internet/iApp for English Grammar

Virtual Classroom

Important Abbreviations
These abbreviations are used throughout the program

POE: Process of Elimination
SARR: Synthesize, Analyze, Reduce, and Restate (has to do with Logical Reasoning)
AC: Answer Choice
QS: Question Stem
LOD: Level of Difficulty

Example Question: What is the least common multiple of 3, 4, and 7? (**This is the call of the question or Question Stem "QS"**)

These are Answer Choices "AC" A, B, C, D, E
   (A)   12
   (B)   21
   (C)   28
   (D)   48
   (E)   84

Part 3: Pronoun Errors

Pronoun Errors

Pronoun: a word that stands for a noun, known as the antecedent of the pronoun.
Key: Pronouns must agree with their antecedents in both number (singular or plural) and person (first, second, or third).
Example: Steve has yet to receive his degree. Here, the pronoun *his* refers to the noun *Steve*.

Singular	Plural	Both Singular and Plural
I, me	we, us	any
she, her	they	none
he, him	them	all
it	these	most
anyone	those	more
either	some	who
each	that	which
many a	both	what
nothing	ourselves	you
one	any	
another	many	
everything	few	
mine	several	
his, hers	others	
this		
that		

Plural pronouns

A pronoun should be plural when it refers to two nouns joined by and. Example: Jane and Katarina believe *they* passed the final exam. The plural pronoun *they* refers to the compound subject *Jane and Katarina*.

Pronoun and or/nor

A pronoun should be singular when it refers to two nouns joined by or or nor. **Faulty Usage:** Neither Jane *nor* Katarina believes *they* passed the final. **Correct:** *Neither Jane nor Katarina believes she passed the final.*

Pronoun agrees with one noun

A pronoun should refer to one and only one noun or compound noun. This is probably the most common error on the exam. When a pronoun follows two nouns, it is often unclear which of the nouns the pronoun refers to. **Faulty Usage:** The breakup of the Soviet Union has left *nuclear weapons* in the hands of unstable, nascent *countries*. It is imperative to world security that *they* be destroyed. Although one is unlikely to take the sentence to mean that the countries must be destroyed, that interpretation is possible from the structure of the sentence. It is easily corrected: **Correct:** *The breakup of the Soviet Union has left nuclear weapons in the hands of unstable, nascent countries. It is imperative to world security that **these weapons** be destroyed.*
Faulty Usage: In Somalia, *they* have become jaded by the constant warfare. This construction is faulty because *they* does not have an antecedent. The sentence can be corrected by replacing *they* with *people*: **Correct:** *In Somalia, people have become jaded by the constant warfare.* **Better:** *The people of Somalia have become jaded by the constant warfare.*

Pronoun must agree with antecedent

In addition to agreeing with its antecedent in number, a pronoun must agree with its antecedent in person. **Faulty Usage:** *One* enters this world with no responsibilities. Then comes school, then work, then marriage and family. No wonder, *you* look longingly to retirement. In this sentence, the subject has changed from *one* (third person) to *you* (second person). To correct the sentence either replace *one* with *you* or vice versa:
Correct: *You enter this world with no responsibilities. Then comes school, then work, then marriage and family. No wonder, you look longingly to retirement. OR One enters this world with no responsibilities. Then comes school, then work, then marriage and family. No wonder, one looks longingly to retirement.*

Sample Question:

In the following, part or all of the sentence is underlined. The answer-choices offer five ways of phrasing the underlined part. If you think the sentence as written is better than the alternatives, choose A, which merely repeats the underlined part; otherwise choose one of the alternatives.

Had the President's Administration not lost the vote on the budget reduction package, his first year in office would have been rated an A.

(A) Had the President's Administration not lost the vote on the budget reduction package, his first year in office would have been rated an A.
(B)   If the Administration had not lost the vote on the budget reduction package, his first year in office would have been rated an A.
(C) Had the President's Administration not lost the vote on the budget reduction package, it would have been rated an A.
(D) Had the President's Administration not lost the vote on its budget reduction package, his first year in office would have been rated an A.
(E) If the President had not lost the vote on the budget reduction package, the Administration's first year in office would have been rated an A.

Explanation:

(A) This is incorrect because *his* appears to refer to *the President*, but the subject of the subordinate clause is *the President's Administration*, not *the President*.
(B) This choice changes the structure of the sentence, but retains the same flawed reference.
(C) In this choice, *it* can refer to either *the President's Administration* or *the budget reduction package*. Thus, the reference is ambiguous.
(D) This choice adds another pronoun, *its*, but still retains the same flawed reference.
(E) **Correct Response.** This choice corrects the flawed reference by removing all pronouns.

Grammar Study Guide
Part 4: Subject Verb Agreement
Virtual Classroom>Grammar Study Guide>Subject Verb Agreement

This material Corresponds to the Virtual Classroom Instructions in the
PowerPrep DVD/Internet/iApp for English Grammar

Virtual Classroom

Important Abbreviations
These abbreviations are used throughout the program

POE: Process of Elimination
SARR: Synthesize, Analyze, Reduce, and Restate (has to do with Logical Reasoning)
AC: Answer Choice
QS: Question Stem
LOD: Level of Difficulty

Example Question: What is the least common multiple of 3, 4, and 7? **(This is the call of the question or Question Stem "QS")**

These are Answer Choices "AC" A, B, C, D, E

  (A)   12
  (B)   21
  (C)   28
  (D)   48
  (E)   84

Part 4: Subject Verb Agreement

SUBJECT VERB AGREEMENT

Because subject verb agreement is heavily tested on the exam we have provided a bonus review of this topic with lots of examples and sample questions. Work hard to understand this subject matter.

Basic Rules

The basic rule: a singular subject takes a singular verb, while a plural subject takes a plural verb. The subject and verb must agree both in number and person. This may seem rather obvious but this area of grammar is one of the most heavily tested and one of the most confusing.

In each of the example sentences the **subject is bolded** and the <u>**verb is bolded and underlined**</u>

A singular subject takes a singular verb:
- My **pencil** <u>**is**</u>/are dull. The subject "pencil' is singular so it takes a singular verb "is".
- My **brother** <u>**is**</u> a computer scientist.

A plural subject takes a plural verb:
- My brain **cells** <u>**is**</u>/are dull. The subject "Cells" is plural and takes a plural verb "are".
- **We** <u>**have**</u> surpassed our sales goal of one million dollars. The first person plural verb *have* agrees with first person plural subject *we*.
- My **sisters** <u>**are**</u> lawyers.

NOTE: *You have to make two decisions: 1. Find the subject and decide if it is singular or plural; 2. recognize the singular and plural form of the verb that goes with your subject.*

Plural and Singular Verbs: Singular verbs go with singular subjects. Use the word "he" or "she" before the verb to decide if the verb is singular. Plural verbs use plural subjects, use the word "they" or "we" before the verb to decide the plural form. **Note**: Third person <u>singular</u> verbs often end in *s* or *es*: **Example:** He *seems* to be fair.

Example: Throws, Throw--Which one is the singular form? Which word would you use with *he or she*? We say, "He throws the ball." Therefore, *throws* is singular. We say, "They or we throw the ball." Therefore, *throw* is plural.

Reversal: When the subject and verb are reversed, they still must agree in both number and person.
- Attached <u>**are**</u> **copies** of the contract. Here, the plural verb <u>**are attached**</u> agrees with its plural subject <u>**copies**</u>. The sentence could be rewritten as: *Copies* of the contract *are attached.*

In present tenses, nouns and verbs form plurals in opposite ways: **nouns** ADD an *s* to the singular form, **BUT verbs** REMOVE an *s* from the singular form. Verbs in the present tense for third-person, singular subjects (*he, she, it* and anything those words can stand for) have *s*-endings. Other verbs do not add *s*-endings. He love<u>s</u> , she love<u>s</u>, they love_

The cat chases the birds.
The cat (singular -s) chases (singular +s) the birds. CAT CHASES
The cats chase the bird.
The cats (plural +s) chase (plural -s) the bird. CATS CHASE

Sometimes modifiers will get between a subject and its verb, but these modifiers must not confuse the agreement between the subject and its verb. **Example:** The **senator**, who has been convicted along with four of his aides on four counts of treason but who also seems, like a rat, to be able to scurry into darkness, **is** finally going to prison.

Technique for Correcting Subject/Verb Agreement Problems

steps to identify and correct any subject/verb problems
1. Isolate the verb. Decide if it is singular or plural.
2. Isolate all prepositional phrases.
3. Determine the subject. Decide if it is singular or plural.
4. Correct any subject-verb agreement problems.

Sample Question

The rise in negative attitudes toward foreigners <u>indicate that the country is becoming less tolerant, and therefore that</u> the opportunities are ripe for extremist groups to exploit the illegal immigration problem.
- (A) indicate that the country is becoming less tolerant, and therefore that
- (B) indicates that the country is becoming less tolerant, and therefore
- (C) indicates that the country is becoming less tolerant, and therefore that
- (D) indicates that the country is being less tolerant, and therefore
- (E) indicates that the country is becoming less tolerant of and therefore that

Explanation:
(A) This AC has two flaws. First, the subject of the sentence *the rise* is singular, and therefore the verb *indicate* should not be plural. Second, the comma indicates that the sentence is made up of two independent clauses, but the relative pronoun *that* immediately following *therefore* forms a subordinate clause.

(B) Correct Response. This corrects the verb's number and removes the subordinating relative pronoun *that*.
(C) This AC corrects the number of the verb, but retains the subordinating relative pronoun *that*.
(D) This AC corrects the number of the verb and eliminates the subordinating relative pronoun *that*. However, the verb *being* is less descriptive than the verb *becoming*: As negative attitudes toward foreigners increase, the country becomes correspondingly less tolerant. *Being* does not capture this notion of change.
(E) This AC corrects the verb's number, and by dropping the comma makes the subordination allowable. However, it introduces the preposition *of* which does not have an object: less tolerant of what?

Subject-Verb Agreement Rules in Detail

*In each of the example sentences the **subject is bolded** and the **<u>verb is bolded and underlined</u>***

1. Phrases/Clause between subject and verb

A phrase or clause between subject and verb does not change the number of the subject.
So intervening phrases and clauses have no effect on subject-verb agreement. **Example:** Only **one** of the President's nominees **<u>was</u>** confirmed. Here, the singular verb **was** agrees with its singular subject **<u>one</u>**. The intervening prepositional phrase "*of the President's nominees*" has no effect on the number of the verb.

- A bucket of baseballs (is, are) waiting for you. **Becomes**: A bucket is...
  <u>A Bucket</u> = subject--singular noun (takes a singular verb)
  <u>of baseballs</u> = prepositional phrase that can be dropped
  <u>is</u> = singular verb agrees with "a bucket" and not with "baseballs" because "baseballs" is part of a prepositional phrase and not the subject of the sentence.
  <u>waiting for you.</u> = unnecessary phrase and can be dropped

- The men who went to the football game (was, were) cheering wildly. *Becomes: The men were...*
  <u>The men</u> = subject--plural noun that takes a plural verb
  <u>who went to the football game</u> = dependent clause (this can be dropped)
  <u>were</u> = plural verb agrees with "the men" and not "the football game" part of clause and not the subject of the sentence.
  <u>cheering wildly</u> = modifies the verb were

2. Indefinite pronouns as subject

Indefinite pronouns reference nonspecific things or people. Most of these pronouns take a singular verb, some are always plural, a few may be either singular or plural. Review the lists below, and notice that most indefinite pronouns are singular.

- *Singular*: another, anybody, anyone, anything, each, either, enough, everybody, everyone, everything, less, little, many a, much, neither, no one, nobody, nothing, one, other, somebody, someone, something
- *Plural*: both, few, fewer, many, others, several, they
- *Singular or Plural*: all, any, more, most, none, some, such

Note: Indefinite pronouns that end in "one" are always singular: anyone, everyone, someone, and one. Indefinite pronouns that end in "body" are always singular. These words include anybody, somebody, nobody.

Singular Indefinite Pronouns

Another twenty minutes **is** enough time to finish.
Anybody under six feet tall **is** excluded.
Anyone with more than two arrests **is** excluded.
Anything blue **is** fine with me.
Each person **is** responsible.
Either option **is** acceptable.
Enough **is** enough.
Everybody **is** waiting for a miracle.
Everyone **is** looking for honesty in government.
Everything the Senate does **is** questionable.
Less **is** more.
Little **is** known about deep space.

Many a boy **is** confused by a girl.
Much more **is** known about our solar system.
Neither answer **is** acceptable.
No one **is** willing to take a risk.
Nobody in congress **is** following the Constitution.
Nothing **is** more necessary.
One vote **is** sometimes very important.
The **other** option **is** even more interesting.
Somebody **is** upstairs.
Someone **is** listening to your phone call.
Something **is** better than nothing.

Note: *Everyone* and *everybody* (listed above) certainly feel like more than one person and, therefore, students are sometimes tempted to use a plural verb with them. But they are always singular. "*Each*" is often followed by a prepositional phrase ending in a plural word (Each of the hats) which can confuse students, but <u>each is always singular regardless of the prepositional phrase that follows--</u>in this case "hats". *Each* of the hats <u>is</u> expensive.

- *Everyone* (*has/have*) finished his or her assignment. "*Everyone*" is always singular even though it feels plural. *Everyone* <u>has</u> finished his or her assignment.

- *Everybody, including the seniors* **is/are** here. Everybody is always singular even though it feels plural. *Everybody, including the seniors* <u>is</u> here.

- *Each of the students* **is/are** responsible for completing his or her assignment. Don't let the word "students" confuse you; the subject is each and each is always singular — *Each* <u>is</u> responsible.

- Each of the PE students **(has, have)** to run a mile. Each is singular, therefore, it takes the singular verb "has"--each of the students has, not each of the students have. This can be tricky because the test-makers love to include a prepositional phrase that sounds plural, but you must stay focused on the actual subject of the sentence. In this example the subject is "each" and the prepositional phrase "of the PE students" can be dropped. Prime testing material on the exam.

- Everyone has done his or her project for history. (Everyone has, not everyone have)
- Somebody in the classroom full of students has left their iPod. (Somebody has left, not somebody have left)

Note: Don't get confused by the prepositional phrase that follows the subject and can make the subject appear plural. However, these are all singular subjects and always take a singular verb.

- *Each* of the dogs **runs/run** fast. "**Each**" is the subject and takes a singular verb "**runs**". *Each* of the dogs **runs** fast.
- **Each and every** of the questions on your final examination has/have the potential to be a trick question. "Each and every" is a singular subject and takes the singular verb "has". **Each and every** of the questions on your final examination **has** the potential to be a trick question.
- **Every one** of the football players is/are hurt. "Every one" is a singular subject and takes a singular verb "is". **Every one** of the football players **is** hurt.

Note: *Everyone* is one word when it means *everybody*. *Every one* is two words when the meaning is *each one*.

Rule 2a. Exception: there is an exception to the "each" rule. When "each" is the subject of the sentence, but followed by a prepositional phrase that has a plural noun (**Each** of the <u>dogs</u> **runs** fast) it remains singular. However, if "each" follows the subjects it can be plural. Like this: (The dogs and the cats each run fast) . The subject is no longer "each" followed by a prepositional phrase "of dogs", the subject is now compounded with "and" (dogs and cats). This compound subject is plural and "each" does not change it. This can be very confusing and tricky. Be sure you spend sufficient time with this to understand it.

Rule 2b. Plural indefinite pronoun subjects take plural verbs. The following are always plural and always require a plural verb: *both, few, fewer, many, others, several*

- **Few** people **run/runs** a four-minute mile. Since "Few" is a plural subject it takes a plural verb "run". **Few** people **run** a four-minute mile.

Rule 2c. Countable vs. Uncountable: Some indefinite pronouns may be either singular or plural. *Uncountable nouns are singular so* use singular verbs; countable nouns are plural so use plural verbs. So the indefinite pronouns like *some, any, none, all, most* can be either singular or plural depending whether the noun is countable or uncountable.

- **Some** milk **is** gone. *Milk is uncountable; therefore, the sentence has a singular verb.*
- **Some** of the marbles **are** missing. *Marbles are countable; therefore, the sentence has a plural verb.*
- **Some** of the beads **are** missing. *Beads are countable, therefore plural.*
- **Some** of the water **is** gone. *Water is uncountable, therefore singular*

Rule 2d. The special case of "none": *The indefinite pronoun "none" can be either singular or plural. Writers generally think of "none" as meaning not any and will choose a plural verb, as in "None of the students are passing" but when something else makes us regard none as singular, we want a singular verb, as in "None of the bread is fresh." For the exam you should look to the context of the sentence to determine its number.* **Example:** *"I invited five friends but* **none have** *(not has) come"*

- *None of you* **has/have** *finished. You cannot tell whether "none" is singular or plural in this sentence. If "none" means "not any", it's plural. However, if "none" means "not one" it's singular.* **Like this:** *None of the students* **have** *finished their homework. Now we know the word "students" and "their" makes "none" plural.*

Examples for Rule 2

- *One of the dancing girls (is/are) missing. The subject is "one" not "girls". "One" is always singular, therefore it takes a singular verb "is". Therefore it becomes:* **"One is** *missing" If you remove the prepositional phrase "of the dancing girls" it makes more sense.*
- *Both of the dancing girls (is/are) missing. The subject is "both", not "girls" and "both" is always plural. Therefore, "both" takes a plural verb "are". Remove the prepositional phrase "of dancing girls" and it becomes:* **Both are** *missing.*
- *All the dirt (was/were) swept from the floor. Here "all" is a singular subject because "dirt" is singular. Therefore,* **"all"** *requires the singular verb was.* **All the dirt was**...
- *All the baseballs (was/were) left out. Now "all" is a plural subject because "baseballs" is a plural. Therefore, "all" requires the plural verb were.* **All the baseballs were**

Questions: Circle the correct verb in each sentence.

1. Mathematics *(depends/depend)* heavily on logic.
2. The light at the end of the tunnel *(are/is)* the headlight of an approaching train.
3. News of a teacher's strike *(causes/cause)* many students to make plans for an extended school vacation.
4. Millions of people around the world watched the Super Bowl but most *(was/were)* tuned in to see the commercials and the half-time show.
5. Some people argue that video games warp your mind; however others, in contrast, *(believes/believe)* video games can improve a student's hand-eye coordination and expand their attention span.
6. Both of those students *(were/was)* on the school's honor roll.
7. The students sit at tables inside the library. A few *(sleep/sleeps)* with their heads resting on their hands.
8. One of our teams *(is/are)* in first place this year.
9. The amount of beta-endorphins in the brain *(is/are)* more difficult to measure during strenuous exercise.
10. Too many cooks in the kitchen *(ruins/ruin)* the soup.

Answers: 1. depends, 2. is, 3. causes, 4. were, 5. believe, 6. were, 7. sleep, 8. is, 9. is, 10. ruin

Rule 2e. Words indicating portions: Words that indicate portions—*percent, fraction, part, majority, some, all, none, remainder*, and so forth —look at the noun in the phrase (object of the preposition) to determine whether to use a singular or plural verb. If the object of the preposition is singular, use a singular verb. If the object of the preposition is plural, use a plural verb.

- *Some* of the jokes *is/are* funny. The noun in the prepositional phrase (jokes) is plural so the subject "Some" becomes plural and takes a plural verb "are". *Some* of the jokes **are** funny.
- *Half* of the cake **has/have** been eaten. *Cake* is the object of the preposition. Since "cake" is singular the subject (Half) is also singular and takes a singular verb "has been...". *Half* of the cake **has** been eaten.
- *Half* of the cakes **has/have** been eaten. "cakes" is the object of the preposition. Since "cakes" is plural the subject (half) is also plural and takes a plural verb "have been...". *Half* of the cakes **have** been eaten.
- *Ten percent* of the nation *is/are* unemployed. The noun in the prepositional phrase (nation) is singular so the subject "Ten percent" is also singular (so singular verb "is"). *Ten percent* of the nation **is** unemployed.
- *Ten percent* of the people *is/are* unemployed. The noun in the prepositional phrase (people) is plural so the subject "Ten percent" is also plural and takes a plural verb "are". *Ten percent* of the people **are** unemployed.

Note: *Hyphenate all spelled-out fractions (one-half, two-thirds, etc.)*
- *All* of the cake *is/are* gone. The noun in the prepositional phrase (cake) is singular so the subject "All" becomes singular and takes a singular verb "is". *All* of the cake **is** gone.
- *All* of the cakes *is/are* gone. The noun in the prepositional phrase (cakes) is plural so the subject "All" becomes plural and takes a plural verb "are". *All* of the pies **are** gone.
- *Some* of the cake *is/are* missing. The noun in the prepositional phrase (cake) is singular so the subject "All" becomes singular and takes a singular verb "is". *Some* of the cake **is** missing.
- *Some* of the cakes *is/are* missing. The noun in the prepositional phrase (cakes) is plural so the subject "Some" becomes plural and takes a plural verb "are". *Some* of the cakes **are** missing.
- *None* of the garbage **was/were** emptied. The noun in the prepositional phrase (garbage) is singular so the subject "None" becomes singular and takes a singular verb "was". *None* of the garbage **was** emptied.
- *None* of the garbage cans **was/were** emptied. The noun in the prepositional phrase (cans) is plural so the subject "None" becomes plural and takes a plural verb "were". *None* of the garbage cans **were** emptied.
- *Of all her books,* **none** *has/have sold as well as the first one.* The noun in the prepositional phrase (books) is plural so the subject "none" becomes plural and takes a plural verb "have". *Of all her books,* **none** *have sold as well as the first one.*

Note: *Also, fractional expressions such as half of, a part of, a percentage of, a majority of are sometimes singular and sometimes plural, depending on the meaning. (The same is true, of course, when all, any, more, most and some act as subjects.) Sums and products of mathematical processes are expressed as singular and require singular verbs. The expression "more than one" (oddly enough) takes a singular verb: "More than one student has tried this."*

Questions

1. Some of the voters *is/are* still angry.
2. A large percentage of the younger demographic *is/are* voting against progressivism.
3. Three-Quarters of the troops *was/were* unwilling to disarm fellow Americans.
4. Two-thirds of the factory *was/were* destroyed by fire.
5. Ninety percent of the students *is/are* in favor of allowing prayer at graduation.
6. Ninety percent of the student body *is/are* in favor of allowing prayer at graduation.
7. Two and two *is/are* four.
8. Six times four divided by two *is/are* twelve.

Answers: 1. are, 2. is, 3. were, 4. was, 5. are, 6. is, 7. is, 8. is

<u>**Rule 2f. money and time:**</u> Use a singular verb with sums of money or periods of time.
- *One thousand dollars* **is** a high price to pay for a flat screen TV.
- *Two minutes* **is** a long time to hold your breath.

3. Compound subjects joined by "and" are always plural

Compound subjects—two or more subjects connected by the word "*and*"—takes a plural verb
- *My* **pencil** *and my* **brain** *is/are* dull. The compound subject "pencil" and "brain" is plural and takes a plural verb "are". Pencil (singular subject) brain (singular subject) but when they are connected with "*and*" together they become a compound plural subject that takes a plural verb—"are". *My* **pencil** *and my* **brain** **are** dull.
- A **cell phone** and a **laptop** *is/are* essential for every student. "Cell phone" is singular, "laptop" is singular, however, when joined with "*and*" the subject becomes compound and plural and requires a plural verb "are".

<u>**Rule 3b. Special case**</u> (WATCH OUT) Sometimes the subject is separated from the verb by words such as *along with, together with, as well as, besides, along with,* or *not*. Ignore these expressions when determining whether to use a singular or plural verb, they are not the same as "and". **For example**, "*as well as*" will modify the earlier word (*senator* in this case), but it does not <u>compound</u> the subjects (as the word "*and*" would do). The **senator** (<u>as well as</u> his **wife** *is/are* going to prison. (singular) The **senator**(<u>as well as</u> his **wife** **is** going to prison. But compare that construction with: The senator <u>and</u> his wife **are** going to jail. Now "and" makes this sentence plural.
- The **teacher**, along with all the students, *is/are* expected shortly. This is very tricky, but the subject is "teacher" ignore the phrase "*along with all the students*". **Along with** is NOT the same as **AND** it does not create a compound subject. The "teacher" is a singular subject and takes a singular verb "is". The **teacher**, along with all the students, **is** expected shortly.
- **Failure to communicate**, as well as distance, *is/are* the cause of the problem. "Failure to communicate" is a singular subject. "As well as" is not the same as "and" and does not create a compound subject. Therefore, the subject/verb agreement is: "**Failure to communicate is**..."

<u>**Rule 3c. Compound subjects joined by 'and' acting as a single unit:**</u> Sometimes there are two subjects joined by 'and', but together they are considered one item.
- Peanut butter <u>and</u> chocolate **is** her favorite. • Macaroni <u>and</u> cheese **is** delicious. • Bacon <u>and</u> eggs **is** my favorite.

It's true they tend to act as a single item, but you can also add the word "dish" or "snack" or similar word. Like this: Peanut butter <u>and</u> chocolate **is** her favorite snack. Macaroni <u>and</u> cheese **is** delicious. **Becomes**: Macaroni <u>and</u> cheese **is** a delicious meal. Bacon <u>and</u> eggs **is** my favorite. **Becomes**: Bacon <u>and</u> eggs **is** my favorite breakfast. You can see that 'snack', 'meal', and 'breakfast' are all singular and are actually functioning as the subject of the sentence.

4. Compound subjects joined by "or/nor"

With **compound subjects** joined by *or/nor*, the verb agrees with the subject nearer to it. Two singular subjects connected by *"or"* or *"nor"* require a singular verb.
- *My math **homework** or my science **project** is/are going to be late.* Since "homework or project" is a singular subject it takes a singular verb "is". *My math **homework** or my science **project** is going to be late.*

<u>**Rule 4b. Singular 'or/nor' plural**</u>: When a singular subject is connected by *"or"* or *"nor"* to a **plural** subject, put the plural subject last and use a plural verb.
- *The **shirt** or the **scarves** <u>go/goes</u> on that shelf. Since the second subject "scarves" is plural it takes a plural verb "go". The **shirt** or the **scarves** <u>go</u> on that shelf.*

5. Compound subjects joined by "either/or" "neither/nor" "not only/but also"

Two singular subjects connected by *either/or* or *neither/nor* require a singular verb.
- *Neither **Juan** nor **Daniel** is/are awake.* Since both subjects (Juan and Daniel) are singular combining them with "neither/nor" they remain singular and take a singular verb "is". *Neither **Juan** nor **Daniel** <u>is</u> awake.*
- *Either **Emily** or **Michaela** is/are studying.* Since these subjects are singular on their own combining them with either/or does not change it and they take a singular verb "is". Either **Emily** or **Michaela** <u>is</u> studying.

<u>**Rule 5b. Singular joined with plural**</u>: However, when one of the compound subjects is plural and one is singular the part of the subject closest to the verb determines the number (whether the verb is singular or plural). In these examples, "father" is singular and "brothers" are plural. So you can see how these affect the verb is/are.
- Neither my **father** nor my **brothers** <u>are</u> hungry.
- Neither my **brothers** nor my **father** <u>is</u> hungry.
- <u>Are</u> either my **brothers** or my **father** hungry?
- <u>Is</u> either my **father** or my **brothers** hungry?

In this next example, the plural verb *"are"* agrees with the nearer subject ***students***.
- Neither the principal (singular) nor the students (plural) is/are willing to attend Saturday school.
  Becomes: Neither the **principal** nor the **students** <u>are</u> willing to attend Saturday school.
In this next example, the singular verb *is* agrees with the nearer subject ***principal***.
- Neither the students (plural) nor the principal (singular) is/are willing to attend Saturday school.
  Becomes: Neither the students nor the principal is willing to attend Saturday school.
Note: *connecting a singular and plural subject by* either/or *or* neither/nor, *put the plural subject last and use a plural verb.*
- *Neither the **actor** nor the **stage-hands** is/are present for the meeting. Since the second subject "stage-hands" is plural it takes a plural verb "are". Neither the **actor** nor the **stage-hands** <u>are</u> present for the meeting.*

<u>**Rule 5b Neither and Either as a subject:**</u> When used as the subject of a sentence, the pronouns *neither* and *either* are singular and ALWAYS take singular verbs although they seem to be referring, in a sense, to two things.
- *Neither of the students is/are passing the class. **The rule is**: neither/either as a subject is always singular. Therefore, the sentence would be: **Neither** of the students <u>is</u> passing the class.*
- *Which teacher do you want for Algebra this year? Either is fine with me. **The rule is**: neither/either is always singular. Therefore, the sentence would be: **Either** <u>is</u> fine with me.*

Note: This is different from the "neither/nor" and "either/or" compound subject rule that says if part of the compound subject is plural and is closest to the verb, then it makes the verb plural. However, Rule 5b speaks to the situation when "either" or "neither" is the subject all by itself. In this case, it's NOT a compound subject --"either" or "neither" stand alone as the subject. In this case, they always take a singular verb.

<u>**Rule 5c. "I" with "either/or" and "neither/nor":**</u> When "I" is one of the two subjects connected by either/or or neither/nor, put it second and follow it with the singular verb "am".
- *Neither he nor **I** am/is going to the ballpark.* Since compound subjects with *"I"* as one of the subjects and connected with neither/nor are considered singular, it takes the singular form of the "to be" verb *"I am"*. Also *"I"* goes last and next to *"am"*. *Neither he nor **I** <u>am</u> going to the ballpark.*

<u>**Review of Compound Subjects: Rules 3,4,and 5**</u>
Compound subjects are nouns that are joined by words like and, or, either/or, not only/but also, and others similar joining words. When you see words like and, or, neither, either, etc. it should alert you that you might have a compound subject. If that happens the verb needs to agree with the subject it's closest to.

Rule: If the subject is compound, the verb agrees with the part of the subject it's closest to.
- <u>Either **Chris** <u>or</u> **Francisco** (<u>has</u>/have) the flu.</u> *Francisco is the noun in the subject that is closest to the verb 'has/has' and 'Francisco' is singular, therefore, the verb is singular-- choose **'has'** not 'have'. **'Francisco** <u>has</u> the flu'*
- A foot long **hotdog** <u>or</u> a bean **burrito** (<u>is</u>/are) your best options at lunch. *"or" joins two nouns together making this a compound subject. The verb is 'is'. The noun 'burrito' is closest to the verb, so it will decide the number of the verb--and, 'burrito' is singular, therefore, we select the singular verb 'is'. 'the **burrito** <u>is</u>...'*

<u>Rule</u>: Next, if one of the compound subjects is singular and one compound subject is plural? We still follow the same rule as above: If the subject is compound, the verb agrees with the part of the subject it's closest to

- Neither the 50' near vertical waterslide nor the annoying **taunts** from the crowd of spectators (was/**were**) enough to keep us from plunging into the abyss. *First find the compound subject created by 'neither/nor'--that would be 'waterslide' and 'taunts'. Now find the verb --that would be 'was/were'. You can drop out the prepositional phrase 'from the crowd of spectators' and your left with 'taunts was/were'. 'taunts' is closest to the verb and 'taunts is plural, therefore the verb must be plural 'were'...'taunts were...'*
- <u>Neither</u> the annoying taunts from the crowd of spectators <u>nor</u> the 50' near vertical **waterslide** (**was**/were) enough to keep us from plunging into the abyss. *First find the compound subject created by 'neither/nor'--that would be '**waterslide**' and '**taunts**'. Now find the verb --that would be '**was/were**'. Looks like '**waterslide**' is closest to the verb and '**waterslide** is singular. Therefore, the verb must be singular 'was'. 'The **waterslide** was'*

<u>Rule</u>: If we join the subjects with words like; <u>and</u> or <u>both</u>, we use the plural form of the verb because and/both indicate there is more than one. Remember these nouns can both be singular or plural, or one singular and one plural...it does not matter what combination they present--the end result will ALWAYS be a PLURAL verb. (except for the exceptions we cover later)

- **Single/Single=> plural verb**: The baseball **bat** <u>and</u> the **glove** (is/**are**) in the locker.
- **Plural/Single => plural verb**: <u>Both</u> the baseball **bats** <u>and</u> the **glove** (was/**were**) left in the car.
- **Single/Plural => plural verb**: The baseball **bat** <u>and</u> the **gloves** (was/**were**) left in the bus.
- **Plural/Plural => plural verb**: The baseball **bats** <u>and</u> the **gloves** (was/**were**) left in the clubhouse.

Exception to the Rule: Sometimes there are two subjects joined by 'and' but the two subjects are considered a single item and therefore not plural. This can be very confusing, spend sufficient time with this concept.
- Peanut butter <u>and</u> jelly **is** my favorite.
- Bread <u>and</u> butter **is** good.
- Bacon <u>and</u> eggs **is** also good.

Usually they'll give you information so you can see the compound subject acting like a collective noun.
- Peanut butter <u>and</u> jelly **is** <u>my favorite **sandwich**</u>
- Bread <u>and</u> butter **is** <u>a good afternoon snack</u>.
- Bacon <u>and</u> eggs **is** also good <u>for supper</u>.

These items are usually thought of together as one item, so we use a singular verb. In the second set of examples you can get a sense of the two items working together as a single item:
- Peanut butter and jelly sandwich (as single thing)
- Bread and butter snack (a single snack)
- Bacon and eggs supper (a single dish for supper)

Exception to the exception to the rule: If a sentence begins with 'each' or 'every' or 'each and every' and contains a compound subject, the verb is singular to agree with a singular subject. Even though you might think these would sound better with the verb **are**, according to the rule we should use **is**.
- <u>Every</u> student and parent (attend/**attends**) the annual conference.
- <u>Each</u> table and chair in the auditorium (**has**/have) the school logo on it.
- <u>Each</u> and <u>every</u> baseball card in the collection (were/**was**) valuable.

Exception to the Exception to the Exception to the Rule: Now one last rule, exception, exception, exception: We just said that "every" or "each" at the start of the compound subject makes the subject singular: Each _____ and _____ **is**. However, when "each" or "every" FOLLOWS the subject, this exception to the rule crumbles
- Each and every student, teacher, and administrator (**is**/are) looking forward to Christmas break.
- **But, when 'each' follows the subject it becomes plural**
- The students, teachers, and administrators each (is/**are**) looking forward to Christmas break.

6. Expletive construction "there/here"

The words *here* and *there* have generally been labeled as adverbs even though they indicate place. In sentences beginning with *here* or *there*, the subject follows the verb.
- *There* **are** many **obstacles** to overcome.
- *There* **is** an **obstacle** to overcome.

Expletive Construction and the special case of "*there*" and "*here*". The words *there* and *here* are never subjects. With these constructions (called expletive constructions), the subject follows the verb but still determines the number of the verb.
- There **are** two foreign exchange **students** (plural subject) in math class.
- There **is** one foreign exchange **student** (singular subject) in language arts class.
- Here **are** the two foreign exchange **students** (plural subject).

In the expletive form of a sentence, the verb comes before the subject, like this:
- Waiter, there **is** a **fly** in my soup.
- Waiter, there **is** a **family** of flies in my soup.
- Waiter, there **are** four **flies** in my soup.

You could change each sentence to the more common "subject" then "verb" form. But it won't change the relationship between the subject and verb.
- Waiter, a **fly is** in my soup.
- Waiter, a **family** of flies **is** in my soup.
- Waiter, four **flies are** in my soup.

7. Inverted subjects

Inverted Subjects must agree with the verb. How are (plural) your classes (plural) this semester? **Becomes**: How **are** your **classes** this semester?

8. Collective nouns as the subject

A **collective noun** is a word used to define a group of objects, people, animals, emotions, inanimate things, concepts, or other things. For example, in the phrase "a pride of lions," *pride* is a collective noun. Collective nouns are always singular when they function as a true collective. However, at times the same noun can be plural when the constituent parts of the noun are acting individually. A pride of lions is a collective singular noun when the "pride" is acting as the collective unit.

- The **pride** of lions **is** hunting. You could also say, "The **pride is** hunting".

However, what would you choose in this example: "The pride of lions (is/are) fighting over the wildebeest carcass." or "The pride (is/are) fighting over the wildebeest carcass." "The pride are fighting" means they are fighting among themselves for a place on the carcass. "The pride is fighting" means the unit as a whole is fighting with another animal or group of animals for the carcass.

Collective Nouns:

army	committee	crowd	group	public	team
audience	company	department	jury	school	troupe
board	corporation	faculty	majority	senate	
cabinet	council	family	minority	society	
class		firm	navy		

Collective nouns may be singular or plural, depending on meaning. When the context of the sentence refers to the unit as a whole then it's a singular subject and it takes singular pronouns and verbs.

- The **jury made** its decision. The jury as a whole acting together made the decision. Therefore it's singular. However, if we say "The jury disagreed..." now it's being used as a plural noun because we are probably talking about the individual members within the jury acting--they are all disagreeing. You can easily add the word "member" to help you see this: "The jury members disagreed" or "The jury disagreed". Either way it's plural when used this way. (unless you meant to say, "the jury disagreed with the other jury". This would be singular. .
- The **class is** going on a fieldtrip. The "class" is acting as one unit; therefore, the verb is singular.
- The **class members are** excited. The individual class members are acting--therefore, it's plural.
- The **crowd is** growing. The "crowd" is a unit and is singular.
- The **crowd members are** talking with each other. The individual members in the crowd are talking.

Example: A people that believes in limited government is more likely to be free. Here "people" is a singular noun referring to the group as a whole. "A **people is** free". The people who lived during the founding believed in limited government and were able to create freedom. Here "the people" are individuals acting independently so the noun is plural. "The **people are** free."

Review of this tricky rule: Collective nouns such as *team* and *staff* and many others, may be either singular or plural depending on their use in the sentence. *Group, public, club, government, union, organization,* and *collection* look plural but are singular.

- *The **group** is/are not interested in hearing about my problems.* "Group" is a singular subject and takes a singular verb "is". *The **group is** not interested in hearing about my problems.*

- *The **collection** of books is/are very rare.* Watch out because this is tricky. The subject is "*collection*" NOT books. "Collection" is a singular subject; ignore the phrase "of books" and focus on the actual subject. It is singular and takes a singular verb "is". *The **collection** of books **is** very rare.*

- *The **jury** is/are in deliberation.* Jury *is acting as a unit here. So "Jury" is a singular subject and takes a singular verb "is".* *The **jury is** in deliberation.*

- *The **jury** is/are in disagreement about the findings.* Now, the ***jury*** are acting as separate individuals in this example. So "jury" is a plural subject and takes a plural verb "are". The sentence would read even better as: *The **jury members are** in disagreement about the findings.*

9. Titles of single entities

The title of *books, names of organizations, countries,* etc. are always **singular**.
- "The Grapes of Wrath" **requires** focused attention to read. (singular subject and verb)
- The United States of America **is** suffering from an economic crisis. (The entire country is suffering)
- The United States of America **are** revolting. (This means civil war--the individual states fighting each other.)
- The United States of America **is** revolting. This means the country as a whole or single unit is revolting. If all the states united to fight against the federal government, you would say --the United States is revolting.
- The Federal Reserve Banking System **is** failing. This would mean the system as a whole is failing.
- Sports Illustrated **is** famous for its coverage of the Super Bowl. (Singular subject and verb)

10. Plural form subjects as singular

10a. Plural form subjects with a singular meaning take singular verbs. (*news, measles, mumps, physics, etc.*) Some words end in "*s*" and appear to be plural but are really singular and require singular verbs.
- The **news** from the Academy Awards **is/are** creating a big buzz among the reporters.

- **Chicken Pox** <u>is/are</u> considered mostly a childhood disease. However, **it/they** <u>cause/causes</u> devastating side effects in adults.

Answer: 1. news is, 2. Chicken Pox is, it causes

<u>**10b. Plural form subjects with a plural meaning.**</u> On the other hand, some words ending in *"s"* refer to a single thing but are nonetheless *plural* and require a plural verb.
- The **assets** of every American family (<u>**was/were**</u>) reduced by fifty percent.
- The average **earnings** for most American families (<u>**has/have**</u>) risen by twenty-five percent.
- The principal said, "Our **thanks** (<u>**go/goes**</u>) out to all the parents who helped booster club."

Answers: assets were, earnings have, thanks go

<u>**10c. Sports teams are plural.**</u> Sports teams that do not end in "s" still take a plural verb:
- The **Miami Heat** <u>have</u> locked up first place and home court advantage throughout the playoffs.
- The **Oklahoma Thunder** <u>are</u> looking to their rookies for help this season.
- The **Utah Jazz** <u>were</u> up by 25 points last night before losing the game by two points.
- The Scottsdale Community College **Fighting Artichoke** <u>want</u> to thank their alumni.
- The **Stanford Cardinal** <u>upset</u> USC last night.

<u>**10d. Plural form subjects with singular or plural meaning.**</u> These take a singular or plural verb, depending on meaning. (e.g. *mumps, politics, economics,* etc.)
- **Politics** (<u>is/are</u>) often discussed at my home. In this example, politics is a single topic; therefore, the sentence should have a singular verb "is". **Becomes**: Politics **is** often discussed at my house.
- The **politics** of war (<u>is/are</u>) always controversial. 'politics' here refers to the many aspects of the situation; therefore, the subject is plural. **Becomes**: 'The politics of war **are** always controversial.'
- **Mumps** (<u>is/are</u>) a disease rarely seen today. In this example, mumps is a single topic; therefore, the sentence should have a singular verb "is". Mumps **is** a disease rarely seen today.

<u>**10e. Special plural form subjects with a plural meaning.**</u> Sometimes it can be very difficult to determine if a noun is singular or plural. Words such as *glasses, pants, pliers, trousers* and *scissors* are regarded as plural (and require plural verbs) unless they are preceded by the phrase *"pair of"* (in which case the word *pair* becomes the singular subject).
- The first graders use **scissors** with plastic handles which <u>are</u> stored in their cubbies.
- My mom has **a pair** of sewing scissors that <u>is</u> incredibly sharp. (be careful, this is tricky because you cannot rely on your ear--it sounds awkward, which is what they will test on the exam)

Note*: In this example, the subject of the sentence is* **pair**; *therefore, the verb must agree with it. (Because scissors is the object of the* <u>preposition</u>, *scissors* <u>does not affect</u> *the number of the verb.)*

More Examples:
- My mom's **glasses** <u>were</u> getting old, so she bought new ones. (plural)
- My mom's **pair** of glasses <u>was</u> getting old, so she bought a new pair. (singular)
- My dad's **pants** <u>are</u> old and torn, so he bought new ones. (plural)
- My new **pair** of pants <u>is</u> torn, just the way I like it. (singular)

11. When subject and subjective complement differ in number

When the subject and subjective complement have different number, the verb always agrees with the <u>subject</u>.
- My favorite **topic** <u>is</u> books by C.S. Lewis. ("topic" is the subject and it's singular--can trick your ear)
- **Books** by C.S. Lewis <u>are</u> my favorite topic. ("Books" is the subject and it's plural)

12. Special case subjects

12a: one of those who, 12b: the only one of those who, 12c: the number of, 12d: a number of, 12e: every _____, _____ and _____, 12f: many a _____,

<u>**Rule 12a**</u>: **"...*one of those* _____ *who*,"** use a plural verb.
- Hannah is **one of those students who** <u>like</u> to play video games. This example implies that others besides Hannah like to play video games. Therefore, use the plural verb "like".

<u>**Rule 12b:**</u> **"...*the only one of those* _____ *who,*"** use a singular verb.
- Hannah is **the only one of those students who** <u>likes</u> to play video games. This implies that no one else except Hannah likes to play video games. Therefore, use the singular verb "likes".

12b variation: Sometimes the pronouns *who, that,* or *which* are the subject of a verb in the middle of the sentence. The pronouns *who, that,* and *which* become singular or plural according to the noun directly in front of them. So, if that noun is singular, use a singular verb. If it is plural, use a plural verb.
- Amy is the **student** *who* (<u>get/gets</u>) straight A's. ("student" is singular, therefore, use the singular verb "gets")
- Jeremy is one of the **students** who (<u>does/do</u>) the work correctly. The word in front of "who" is "students", which is plural. Therefore, use the plural verb "do". **See Rule 12a. above**

<u>**Rule 12c**</u>: **"...*the number of* _____,"** use a singular verb.
- **The number of** students (<u>increase/increases</u>) each year. "The number of..." is considered a singular subject even though "students" make it seem plural. You simply must remember this rule: "the number of_____" will always be singular because it's viewed a singular lump or group and not as many individuals. In this case,

"the number of students" is viewed as a single group called "the number of". So it will always take a singular verb. In this example, the singular verb is "increases"

Rule 12d: "...*a number of* _____," use a plural verb.
- **A number** of students (**study/studies**) for the SAT or ACT exams each year. The only difference between rules 12c and 12d is the word "a" and "the". **The** number of students" is singular. However, "**A** number of students" is plural. "a number of_____" will always be plural because it's viewed as many individuals. In this case, "a number of students" is viewed as a plural group of many individuals. So it will always take a plural verb. Here, the plural verb is "study"

Rule 12e: "...*every* _____, _____, *and* _____" and "...*many a* _____" use a singular verb. This is just a variation of **Rule 2:** indefinite singular pronouns. See Rule 2 for a list of all the singular indefinite pronouns, they include: *each, every one, each and every, every* _____
- **Every man, woman, and child** (**has/have**) to learn humility. The rule says "every, _____, _____, and _____" is a singular subject. The list is viewed as a singular group and not as multiple pieces.
- **Many a** student (**dream/dreams**) about getting straight A's on his or her report card. "Many a" is considered a singular subject, therefore, it takes a singular verb "dreams"

13. Positive and negative compound subjects

If your sentence compounds a positive and a negative subject and one is plural, the other singular, the verb should agree with the positive subject.
- The **students** but not the principal (**have/has**) decided to miss school. (students have)
- The **principal** but not the students (**have/has**) decided to miss school. (principal has)
- It is not the students but the **principal** who (**decides/decide**) who can miss school. (principal decides)
- It is not the principal but the **students** who (**decides/decide**) who can miss school. (students decide)
- It was the **student**, not his ideas, that (**has/have**) caused the questions. (student has)
- It was the **ideas**, not the student, that (**has/have**) caused the questions. (ideas have)

Summary of Subject/Verb Agreement

Technique for Correcting Subject/Verb Agreement Problems

Steps to identify and correct any subject/verb problems
First identify the verb, Then ask the question "Who or what...?"

1. Isolate the verb. Decide if it is singular or plural.
2. Isolate all prepositional phrases.
3. Determine the subject. Decide if it is singular or plural.
4. Correct any subject-verb agreement problems.
5. To find the subject of a question, turn the question into a statement.

The 20 Rules of Subject Verb Agreement in Standard English

Subjects and verbs must agree in number. This is the cornerstone rule. After identifying the subject and verb in a sentence, make certain the two agree. The following rules apply to subject/verb agreement.

1. **Singular Subjects:** If the subject is singular (refers to one person or thing), the verb will have an -s ending. If the subject is plural (refers to more than one person or thing), the verb will not end in s.
Singular Examples: • *The **computer** **runs** MacOS10.* • ***He** **practices** the drums two hours every day.* • *The **lion** **rules** the African wilderness.* • *The **student** **raises** his hand to ask a question.*

Plural Examples: • *The **computers** **run** MacOS10.* • ***They** **practice** the drums two hours every day.* • *The **lions** **rule** the African wilderness.* • *The **students** **raise** their hands to ask a question.*
2. **Words between subject and verb:** Words that come between the subject and verb do not affect agreement.
• *The **student**, who is running late for history class in the new HFAC building **is** ready for the quiz.*
3. **Prepositional Phrases:** Prepositional phrases between the subject and verb usually do not affect agreement.
• *The natural **highlights** in the new hair color products sponsored by the latest 'it' model **are** difficult to apply.*
4. **There and Here:** *There* and *here* are never subjects when they appear at the beginning of a sentence. When sentences start with "there" or "here," the subject will always be placed after the verb, so be careful.
• *There **is** a **problem** with your homework.* • *Here **are** the term **papers** you graded.* • *There **is** the **sandwich** I left in my car last week.*
• *Here **are** the text **books** you left at my house.*
4b. **Delayed Subjects:** Often the subject of a sentence will be delayed. The subject may come after the verb or after a prepositional phrase. Often, the subject of a sentence will come after the verb. A simple way to identify the subject is as follows: These steps may help you select the subject of most sentences. Other points to remember: The subject is never within a prepositional phrase.
• *Over the last hill **appear** William Wallace's **warriors** dressed in full battle gear.*
• *Over the last hill **appears** William Wallace dressed in full battle gear.*
• *In the ocean bay **swim** five large great white **sharks**.*
• *In the ocean bay **swims** a large great white **shark**.*

5. Reverse Subjects: Subjects don't always come before verbs in questions. Identify the subject before selecting the proper verb form.
• Does *your sister* usually ***bother*** you?* • Where ***are*** the ***hamburgers*** we ordered?
*Remember: after auxiliary verbs (like do, does, have, can, etc.) the verb is in the infinitive, without 'to'.
"Does he like swimming?" Not "Does he likes swimming?" or "Do he like swimming?"*

6. Subject 'and' Subject: Two subjects joined by **'and'** typically require a plural verb form-- a verb without an -s.
• *The freshman and the sophomore **are** rooming together this semester.* • *Parents and kids **enjoy** Disneyland.*
• *Hamburgers, pizza, fried chicken, chocolate cake and Rocky Road ice cream have always been my favorite foods.*

7. Compound subjects refer to same thing: Use a singular verb if the two subjects separated by **'and'** refer to the same person or thing.
• *Green eggs and ham is my favorite dish.* (they refer to 'dish', so it's a singular)

8. Singular beginnings: If the words **each, every, or no** come before the subject, the verb is singular.
• *No smoking and drinking is allowed in this restaurant. (a single group or unit 'smoking & drinking'*
• *Every man, woman, and child is required to check in.(a single group--so singular)*
• *The baseball coach and the history teacher is Mr. Daily. (both subjects refer to same person, so singular.)*

9. Both plural subjects: If the subjects are both singular and are connected by the words **or, nor, neither/nor, either/or,** and **not only/but also** the verb is singular.
• *Chris or Devon is assigned the midnight shift.*

10. When to count the object of the Prepositional Phrase: Prepositional phrases are typically ignored when you decide the number of the verb (singular/plural). However, when a noun or pronoun subject like *some, half, any, none, more, most, all,* etc. are followed by a prepositional phrase then the object of the preposition determines the form of the verb.
• *All of the cereal is gone.* • *All of the cereals are gone.* • *Some of the cake was eaten.* • *Some of the cakes were sold.*

11. Singular Verb: The singular verb is usually used for units of measurement.
• *Four gallons of gas is all we need for the go cart to run all day long.*

12. Both plural subjects: If the subjects are both plural and are connected by the words *or, nor, neither/nor, either/or,* and *not only/but also,* the verb is plural.
• *Neither Men nor women are willing to accept responsibility.*

13. One plural and one singular: When one subject is singular and one is plural and the subjects are connected by the words *or, nor, neither/nor, either/or,* and *not only/but also,* choose a verb that agrees with the closest subject.
• *Not only our cat but also our dogs like beef stew. (dogs is plural so uses 'like')*
• *Fudgy Wudgy Peanut Butter Goo ice cream or chocolate brownies with peppermint are my favorite dessert.*
• *Neither Sache nor Max likes to visit the vet.*

Exception (sort of): *Remember: after auxiliary verbs (like do, does, have, can, etc.) the verb is in the infinitive, without 'to'. "Does he like swimming?" Not "Does he likes swimming?" or "Do he like swimming?"*

• *Do your parents or your brother want to go to the game tonight? Even though you have a plural subject (parents) and a singular subject (brothers) joined by 'or', in this case the verb form appears plural 'want', but it is actually the infinitive form without the 'to'. So it mimics the singular and appears to be an exception. See the rule above dealing with questions that have auxiliary verbs like (do, does, have, can, etc)*

14. Indefinite Pronouns: Indefinite pronouns typically take singular verbs. The pronouns **each, either, neither, one, everyone, no one, nobody, anyone, anybody, someone, everybody,** and **much** are singular and will require a verb with an -s ending.
• *Everyone in the building is thankful for the help.* • *Neither student teacher prepares a lesson plan more than a week before class.* • *Someone in Mrs. Thompson's language arts class has a new iPod.* • *Everybody wants pizza for dinner.*

14b. 'Every', 'Many a': When 'every' or 'many a' comes before a subject, the verb should be singular--have an -s ending.
• *Every man, woman and child receives the same ration of food.* • *Many a woman chooses motherhood over a career.*
• *Every dog and cat has been vaccinated.*

15. Plural Pronouns: The pronouns (few, many, several, both) always take the plural form-- without an -s ending.
• *Few were aware of his deep but hidden desire to attend cooking school.* • *Several of the firefighters work 48 hour shifts.*
• *Many in the honor society study long hours.*

16. Infinitives: If two infinitives are separated by **and** they take the plural form of the verb.
• *To sing and to dance well require years of concentrated practice.*

17. Gerunds; When gerunds are the subject of a sentence they take the singular verb, but when they are linked by **'and'** they take the plural form.
• *Jogging every day is a great way to get into shape.*
• *Jogging every day and Swimming in the ocean and lifting weights are even better ways to get into shape.*

18. Collective Nouns: Collective nouns like **herd, senate, class, crowd, team, family, jury, faculty,** and **committee** etc. are singular when considered as a unit and will usually take a singular verb form--an -s ending.

• The **pride** *is* on the hunt. • My **family** <u>visits</u> San Francisco each year. • The **faculty** <u>recommends</u> that students be given less homework.

However, if individual members or parts of a group are considered separate, a plural verb without an s is needed.
• The dance **team** (**members**) <u>buy</u> their own costumes. (think: 'dance team members')
• The Math **Club** (**members**) <u>compete</u> in the individual events. (think 'Math Club members')

19. Titles: Titles of books, movies, novels, etc. are treated as singular and take a singular verb.
• The **Screwtape Letters** <u>is</u> a series of letters written by C.S. Lewis about a senior <u>demon</u>, Screwtape, to his nephew, a junior tempter named Wormwood, so as to advise him on methods of securing the <u>damnation</u> of a British man, known only as "the Patient". This example also shows the word "series" is also a singular noun.

20. Final Rule – Remember, only the subject affects the verb!

PowerPrep Subject Verb Quizzes

Subject--Verb Agreement Quiz 1

1. Either the players throughout the league or the league commissioner *(is/are)* going to have to make a decision about mandatory drug testing.
2. *(Is/Are)* my teacher or the students he sent to detention going to win the appeal?
3. Some of the students *(seem, seems)* to have slept in this morning.
4. The hurricanes that typically hit the gulf states during high season (usually September through December) *(is, are)* becoming easier to detect with ever improving technology.
5. Everyone chosen by the choir director to perform in the Christmas concert *(have, has)* to be willing to practice every weekend between now and the performance.
6. Central High School, together with Washington High School, *(represents, represent)* the biggest challenge to Centennial High School's defense of their state title this year.
7. Molly's mother is concerned that Molly seems to forget that there *(is, are)* things to be done before she can travel to England for a semester abroad.
8. There *(have, has)* to be some people willing to support the principles of the Declaration of Independence.
9. Some of the grain *(seem, seems)* to have leaked from the silo.
10. Two-thirds of the voters *(is, are)* in favor of Constitutional reform.
11. Two-thirds of the electorate *(is, are)* in favor of Constitutional reform.
12. A high percentage of the population *(is, are)* waiting for a leader with values like those of the founding fathers.
13. A high percentage of the people *(was, were)* waiting for a leader with values like those of the founding fathers.

Subject Verb Agreement Quiz 1 Answers

1. Either the players throughout the league or the league **commissioner** (<u>is</u>) going to have to make a decision about mandatory drug testing. *<u>When subjects are connected by or, the subject closer to the verb (which is, in this case, singular) determines the number of the verb (commissioner is). Rule 4 Compound subjects joined by or/nor.</u>*

2. (<u>Is</u>) my **teacher** or the students he sent to detention going to win the appeal? *<u>The subject closer to the verb (my teacher) determines the number of the verb (Is my teacher...). In a question the verb usually comes first (Is my teacher..) however, in a statement the subject would come first (My teacher is...) If you have trouble figuring out what the subject is, change it to a statement. Rule 4 Compound subjects joined by or/nor.</u>*

3. **Some** of the <u>students</u> (<u>seem</u>) to have slept in this morning. *<u>Some is the subject in this sentence; it is plural because the word "students" makes it a countable indefinite pronoun (some students seem).</u>*
*<u>Rule 2c,d Countable/Uncountable:</u> **Some** of the <u>books</u> <u>are</u> missing. **Some** of the <u>milk</u> <u>is</u> spilled.*

4. The **hurricanes** that typically hit the gulf states during high season (usually September through December) (<u>are</u>) becoming easier to detect with ever improving technology. *<u>The subject is "hurricanes" and it's plural (hurricanes are). Don't be confused by the words and phrases that came between the subject and its verb.</u> Rule 1 Phrases and clauses between subject/verb*

5. **Everyone** chosen by the choir director to perform in the Christmas concert (<u>has</u>) to be willing to practice every weekend between now and the performance. *<u>"Everyone" seems to be a plural word, but it is always singular.</u> Rule 2 Indefinite Pronouns*

6. **Central High School**, together with Washington High School, (<u>represents</u>) the biggest challenge to Centennial High School's defense of their state title this year. *<u>Don't be confused by phrases that come between the subject and the verb. The subject is not compounded by phrases such as along with, together with, and as well as. In this case the subject "Central High School" is singular (...school represents...) Rule 3b Compound subjects joined by "and", special cases</u>*

7. Molly's mother is concerned that Molly seems to forget that there (<u>are</u>) **things** to be done before she can travel to England for a semester abroad. *<u>The subject (things) comes after the verb in inverted constructions that begin with "here" or "there" (there are things) and "things" is plural so it takes a plural verb "are". Rules 6 and 7 "there/here" and Inverted subjects.</u>*

8. There (<u>have</u>) to be **some** <u>people</u> willing to support the principles of the Declaration of Independence. *<u>With expletive constructions (which often begin with "here" or "there") the subject comes after the verb. Rule 6&7. The subject is some, which is singular or plural depending on the noun that follows, and this determines the verb (not the word there). In our case, the noun that follows "some" is "people" and people is a plural and countable noun. See Rule 2c,d Countable/Uncountable:</u> **Some** of the <u>books</u> <u>are</u> missing. **Some** of the <u>milk</u> <u>is</u> spilled. In this case it would be "**some** people <u>have</u> to be willing..."*

9. **Some** of the <u>grain</u> **(seems)** to have leaked from the silo. *"Some" is the subject of this sentence and, since it is not countable (you can't count the grain, it's like milk, or flour) it is singular. Rule 2c,d Countable/Uncountable:* **Some** of the <u>books</u> <u>**are**</u> missing. **Some** of the <u>milk</u> <u>**is**</u> spilled. *In this case it would be "some <u>grain</u> <u>**seems**</u>..."*

10. **Two-thirds** of the <u>voters</u> **(are)** in favor of Constitutional reform. *With words that indicate portions—percent, fraction, part, majority, some, all, none, remainder, and so forth —look at the noun in the phrase (object of the preposition) to determine whether to use a singular or plural verb. In our case, the noun is "voters" which is plural and countable, so the subject becomes plural:* **See Rule 2e**. *Words indicating portions and* **Rule 2c** *Countable vs. Uncountable*

11. **Two-thirds** of the <u>electorate</u> **(is)** in favor of Constitutional reform. *With words that indicate portions—percent, fraction, part, majority, some, all, none, remainder, and so forth —look at the noun in the phrase (object of the preposition) to determine whether to use a singular or plural verb. In our case, the noun is "electorate" which is singular because it is non-countable (See Rule 2c), so the subject becomes singular* **See Rule 2e**. *Words indicating portions and* **Rule 2c** *Countable vs. Uncountable*

12. A high **percentage** of the <u>population</u> **(is)** waiting for a leader with values like those of the founding fathers. *<u>**"Percentage" is a mathematical proportion, expressing here a singular lump sum.**</u> See Rule 2e. Words indicating portions and also* **Rule 2c** *Countable vs. Uncountable because "population" is a singular noun so the prepositional phrase that follows the subject, "of the population" does not change "percentage" to a plural. If it said, "A high* **percentage** *of <u>voters</u>..." the subject would be plural because "voters" is countable and plural.*

13. A high **percentage** of the <u>people</u> **(were)** waiting for a leader with values like those of the founding fathers. *<u>**"Percentage" is a mathematical proportion, but here it reflects a countable, therefore plural, quantity because the noun "people" in the prepositional phrase is plural.**</u> See Rule 2e. Words indicating portions and also* **Rule 2c** *Countable vs. Uncountable*

Subject-Verb Agreement Quiz 2

1. Jeremy is the only one of those students who **(has/have)** made the varsity team.
2. The Senate, as well as the Supreme Court and the House of Representatives **(need, needs)** to follow the original intent of the Constitution.
3. One of our cheerleaders **(is/are)** also going to the State Science Fair.
4. Not only five players on the football team but also the coach **(has/have)** been recognized for post-season honors.
5. Most of the student body **(has/have)** registered for next semester. However, several students (is/are) still deciding on electives.
6. Each and every student, teacher, and administrator **(is/are)** looking forward to Christmas break.
7. The students, teachers, and administrators each **(is/are)** looking forward to Christmas break.
8. Ham and eggs **(is/are)** my favorite.
9. A large number of students still **(want/wants)** teachers to eliminate the curve.
10. Ten years **(is/are)** a long time to spend in high school.
11. Politics **(are/is)** the art of lying to accomplish hidden agendas.
12. Most people think the economics of our country **(seems/seem)** to be failing.

Subject-Verb Quiz 2 Answers

1. Jeremy is **the only one** of those students <u>who</u> (**has**) made the varsity team. *The 'who' refers, in this case, to 'the only one,' which is singular.* **See Rule 12b**

2. The **Senate**, <u>as well as</u> the Supreme Court and the House of Representatives (**needs**) to follow the original intent of the Constitution. *Sometimes the subject is separated from the verb by words such as along with, together with, as well as, besides, along with, or not. Ignore these expressions when determining whether to use a singular or plural verb, they are not the same as "and". The subject here is 'The Senate,' which is singular. The modifying phrase that comes after 'as well as' modifies the subject but does not compound it as 'and' would do.* **See Rule 3b.** *Special Case.*

3. **One** of our cheerleaders (**is**) also going to the State Science Fair. *The subject of this sentence is 'one,' which is, of course, singular. Don't let the intervening prepositional phrase (with its plural 'cheerleaders') fool you.* **See Rule 1**

4. <u>Not only</u> five players on the football team <u>but also</u> the **coach** (**has**) been recognized for post-season honors. *With paired conjunctions such as either/or and not only/but also, the subject closer to the verb -- in this case, the singular 'coach' -- determines whether the verb will be singular or plural--"...the coach has..."* **See Rule 5**

5. **Most** of the <u>student body</u> (**has**) registered for next semester. However, **several students** (<u>**are**</u>) still deciding on electives. *'Most' is not a countable noun here* **See Rule 2c**. *('the student body' in the first sentence is a single unit), so the verb must be singular. You can count the students (you know there are several--see **Rule 2b**.) so the subject in the second sentence is plural.*

6. **Each** and every student, teacher, and administrator (<u>**is**</u>) looking forward to Christmas break. *The subject of the verb is 'each and every,' which is singular: the correct verb choice, then, is 'is.'* **See Rule 2**

7. The **students**, **teachers**, and **administrators** each (<u>**are**</u>) looking forward to Christmas break. *When 'each' or 'every' comes after the compound subject, a plural verb -- 'are' -- is appropriate. This is the exception to the exception to the rule.* **See Rule 2a.Exception**

8. **Ham and eggs** (<u>**is**</u>) my favorite. *'Ham and eggs' is one dish, so we need a singular verb to agree with it.* **See Rule 3c.**

9. A large **number** of <u>students</u> still (<u>**want**</u>) teachers to eliminate the curve. *'Number' is a collective noun, but the elements within the collective noun, the students, are acting separately in this case, so the verb should be plural: 'want.'* **See Rule 2c.**

10. **Ten years** (<u>**is**</u>) a long time to spend in high school. *The quantity of 'ten years' here is meant to be taken as a whole, as one quantity, so the verb should be singular.* **See Rule 2f.**

11. **Politics** (<u>**is**</u>) the art of lying to accomplish hidden agendas. *'Politics,' in this case, is one thing, so we need a singular verb.* **See Rule 10d.** *Plural form subjects with singular/plural meanings*

12. Most people think the **economics** of our country (<u>**seem**</u>) to be failing. *'Economics,' in this case, means any number of aspects of or facts about the country's financial health, so we need a plural verb. When the word 'economics' refers to the course or the discipline, it is singular.* **See Rule 10d.** *Plural form subjects with singular/plural meanings*

Subject-Verb Agreement Quiz 3

Instructions: *Select the appropriate verbs to complete each sentence correctly. There are thirty-three "opportunities for error" in these paragraphs. Caution: the singular verb is not always given first.*

Soccer in the US ranks right below synchronized swimming and above the mixed canoe sprints. However in the other 192 countries of the earth Soccer is unknown--to those 5.5 billion folks it's called 'football' or 'foosball' or 'futbol'. Outside the United States, **Soccer or futbol (1)** (<u>**is/are**</u>) surely the most popular sport in the world. Every four years, the world **championship** of soccer called the World Cup, **(2)** (<u>**is/are**</u>) watched by billions of the boisterous, cantankerous, devoted, head-over-heals in love fans from all over the world.

By comparison, the Super Bowl of North American Football beating out the United States professional football's Super Bowl by far. It is estimated that 1.7 billion television viewers watched the World Cup final between France and Brazil in July of 1998. And it is also a genuine world championship, involving teams from 32 countries in the final rounds, unlike the much more parochial and misnamed **World Series** in American baseball (that **(3)** {<u>**don't/doesn't**</u>} even involve Japan or Cuba, two baseball hotbeds). But although soccer has become an important sport in the American sports scene, it will never make inroads into the hearts and markets of American sports the way that **football, basketball, hockey, baseball,** <u>and</u> even **tennis** <u>and</u> **golf (4)** (<u>**has/have**</u>) done. There are many reasons for this.

Recently the New England Revolution beat the Tampa Bay Mutiny in a game played during a horrid rainstorm. Nearly 5000 fans showed up, **which (5)** (<u>**show/shows**</u>) that soccer is, indeed, popular in the United States. However, the **story** of the game **(6)** (<u>**was/were**</u>) buried near the back of the newspaper's sports section, and there **(7)** (<u>**was/were**</u>) certainly no television **coverage**. In fact, the biggest reason for soccer's failure as a mass appeal sport in the United States is that it doesn't conform easily to the demands of television. **Basketball** succeeds enormously in America because **it** regularly **(8)** (<u>**schedule/schedules**</u>) what it calls "television time-outs" as well as the time-outs that the teams themselves call to re-group, not to mention half-times and, on the professional level, quarter breaks. Those **time-outs** in the action **(9)** (<u>**is/are**</u>) ideally made for television commercials. And television coverage is the lifeblood of American sports. College **basketball (10)** (<u>**live/lives**</u>) for a game scheduled on CBS or ESPN (highly recruited high school players are more likely to go to a team that regularly gets national television exposure), and we could even say that television **coverage (11)** (<u>**has/have**</u>) dictated the pace and feel of American football. **Anyone** who **(12)** (<u>**has/have**</u>) attended a live football game knows how commercial **time-outs (13)** (<u>**slow/slows**</u>) the game and sometimes, at its most exciting moments, **(14)** (<u>**disrupt/disrupts**</u>) the flow of events. There is no serious objection, however, because without television, football knows that it simply wouldn't remain in the homes and hearts of Americans. Also, without those advertising dollars, the teams couldn't afford the sky-high salaries of their high-priced superstars.

Soccer, on the other hand, except for its half-time break, has no time-outs; except for half-time, it is constant run, run, run, run, back and forth, back and forth, relentlessly, with only a few seconds of relaxation when a goal is scored, and that can happen seldom, sometimes never. The best that commercial television coverage can hope for is an injury **time-out**, and in soccer **that (15)** (<u>**happen/happens**</u>) only with decapitation or disembowelment.

Second, Americans love their violence, and soccer doesn't deliver on this score the way that American **football** <u>and</u> **hockey (16)** (<u>**do/does**</u>). There are brief moments, spurts of violence, yes, but fans can't expect the full-time menu of bone-crushing carnage that American football and hockey can deliver minute after minute, game after game. In soccer, players are actually singled out and warned — shamed, with embarrassingly silly "yellow cards," for acts of violence and duplicity that would be smiled at in most American sports other than tennis and golf.

Third, it is just too difficult to score in soccer. **America (17)** (<u>**loves/love**</u>) its football games with scores like 49 to 35 and a professional basketball **game** with scores below 100 **(18)** (<u>**is/are**</u>) regarded as a defensive bore. In soccer, on the other hand, **scores** like 2 to 1, even 1 to 0, **(19)** (<u>**is/are**</u>) commonplace and apparently desirable; games scoreless at the end of regulation time happen all the time. (In the 515 games played in the final phase in the history of the World Cup games through 1994, only 1584 **goals (20)** (<u>**was/were**</u>) scored. That's three a game!) And if there **(21)** (<u>**is/are**</u>) no **resolution** at the end of overtime, the teams resort to **a shoot-out** that **(22)** (<u>**has/have**</u>) more to do with luck than with real soccer skills. Worse yet, it is possible for a team to dominate in terms of sheer talent and "shots-on-goal" and still lose the game by virtue of a momentary lapse in defensive attention, a stroke of bad luck, and the opponent's break-away goal. Things like that can happen, too, in baseball, but the **problem** somehow **(23)** (<u>**evens/even**</u>) out over baseball's very long season of daily games. In soccer, it just isn't fair. Soccer authorities should consider making the goal smaller and doing away with the goalie to make scoring easier. And the **business** of starting over after each goal, in the middle of the field, **(24)** (<u>**has/have**</u>) to be reconsidered. It's too much like the center-jump after each goal in the basketball game of yesteryear.

It (25) (<u>**seems/seem**</u>) unlikely that Americans will ever **fully comprehend** or appreciate a sport in which players are not allowed to use their arms and hands. Although the **footwork** of soccer players **(26)** (<u>**is/are**</u>) a magnificent skill to behold, most American fans are perplexed by straitjacketed soccer players' inability and unwillingness to "pick up the darn ball and run with it!" The **inability** to use substitutes (unless the players to be substituted for are lying dead or maimed on the field of play) **(27)** (<u>**is/are**</u>) also bewildering to Americans, who glorify the "sixth man" in basketball and a baseball game in which virtually the entire **roster** (including an otherwise unemployable old man called "the designated hitter") **(28)** (<u>**is/are**</u>) deployed on the field at one time or another.

Finally, the field in soccer is enormous. Considerably larger than the American football field, the soccer field could contain at least a dozen basketball courts. Americans like their action condensed, in a small field of vision — ten enormous sweaty people bouncing off one another and moving rapidly through a space the size of a medium-sized bedroom, twenty-two even larger people in bulky uniforms converging on a small, oddly shaped ball. In soccer, on the other hand, there (29) (**is**/are) a **premium** on "spreading out," not infringing upon the force field occupied by a team-mate, so that fancy foot-passing is possible. **This** spreading out across the vast meadow of the soccer playing field (30) (**does**/do) not lend itself, again, to close get-down-and-dirty television scrutiny. **Soccer** is a great sport and **it** certainly (31) (**deserves**/deserve) the increased attention and popularity it is getting on all levels. But — primarily, again, because it does not lend itself to television — **it** will never make it big in the United States the way **these** other **sports** (32) (has/**have**), not until **it** (33) (**changes**/change) some of its fundamental strategies.

Subject-Verb Quiz 3 Answers

Soccer in the US ranks right below synchronized swimming and above the mixed canoe sprints. However in the other 192 countries of the earth Soccer is unknown--to those 5.5 billion folks it's called 'football' or 'foosball' or 'futbol'. Outside the United States, **Soccer** or **futbol** (1) (**is**/are) surely the most popular sport in the world. Every four years, the world **championship** of soccer called the World Cup, (2) (**is**/are) watched by billions of the boisterous, cantankerous, devoted, head-over-heals in love fans from all over the world. By comparison, the Super Bowl of North American Football beating out the United States professional football's Super Bowl by far. It is estimated that 1.7 billion television viewers watched the World Cup final between France and Brazil in July of 1998. And it is also a genuine world championship, involving teams from 32 countries in the final rounds, unlike the much more parochial and misnamed **World Series** in American baseball (that (3) {don't/**doesn't**} even involve Japan or Cuba, two baseball hotbeds). But although soccer has become an important sport in the American sports scene, it will never make inroads into the hearts and markets of American sports the way that **football**, **basketball**, **hockey**, **baseball**, and even **tennis** and **golf** (4) (has/**have**) done. There are many reasons for this.

Recently the New England Revolution beat the Tampa Bay Mutiny in a game played during a horrid rainstorm. Nearly 5000 fans showed up, **which** (5) (show/**shows**) that soccer is, indeed, popular in the United States. However, the **story** of the game (6) (**was**/were) buried near the back of the newspaper's sports section, and there (7) (**was**/were) certainly no television **coverage**. In fact, the biggest reason for soccer's failure as a mass appeal sport in the United States is that it doesn't conform easily to the demands of television. **Basketball** succeeds enormously in America because **it** regularly (8) (schedule/**schedules**) what it calls "television time-outs" as well as the time-outs that the teams themselves call to re-group, not to mention half-times and, on the professional level, quarter breaks. Those **time-outs** in the action (9) (**is**/are) ideally made for television commercials. And television coverage is the lifeblood of American sports. College **basketball** (10) (live/**lives**) for a game scheduled on CBS or ESPN (highly recruited high school players are more likely to go to a team that regularly gets national television exposure), and we could even say that television **coverage** (11) (**has**/have) dictated the pace and feel of American football. **Anyone** who (12) (**has**/have) attended a live football game knows how commercial **time-outs** (13) (**slow**/slows) the game and sometimes, at its most exciting moments, (14) (**disrupt**/disrupts) the flow of events. There is no serious objection, however, because without television, football knows that it simply wouldn't remain in the homes and hearts of Americans. Also, without those advertising dollars, the teams couldn't afford the sky-high salaries of their high-priced superstars.

Soccer, on the other hand, except for its half-time break, has no time-outs; except for half-time, it is constant run, run, run, run, back and forth, back and forth, relentlessly, with only a few seconds of relaxation when a goal is scored, and that can happen seldom, sometimes never. The best that commercial television coverage can hope for is an injury **time-out**, and in soccer **that** (15) (happen/**happens**) only with decapitation or disembowelment.

Second, Americans love their violence, and soccer doesn't deliver on this score the way that American **football** and **hockey** (16) (**do**/does). There are brief moments, spurts of violence, yes, but fans can't expect the full-time menu of bone-crushing carnage that American football and hockey can deliver minute after minute, game after game. In soccer, players are actually singled out and warned — shamed, with embarrassingly silly "yellow cards," for acts of violence and duplicity that would be smiled at in most American sports other than tennis and golf.

Third, it is just too difficult to score in soccer. **America** (17) (**loves**/love) its football games with scores like 49 to 35 and a professional basketball **game** with scores below 100 (18) (**is**/are) regarded as a defensive bore. In soccer, on the other hand, **scores** like 2 to 1, even 1 to 0, (19) (is/**are**) commonplace and apparently desirable; games scoreless at the end of regulation time happen all the time. (In the 515 games played in the final phase in the history of the World Cup games through 1994, only 1584 **goals** (20) (was/**were**) scored. That's three a game!) And if there (21) (**is**/are) no **resolution** at the end of overtime, the teams resort to **a shoot-out** that (22) (**has**/have) more to do with luck than with real soccer skills. Worse yet, it is possible for a team to dominate in terms of sheer talent and "shots-on-goal" and still lose the game by virtue of a momentary lapse in defensive attention, a stroke of bad luck, and the opponent's break-away goal. Things like that can happen, too, in baseball, but the **problem** somehow (23) (**evens**/even) out over baseball's very long season of daily games. In soccer, it just isn't fair. Soccer authorities should consider making the goal smaller and doing away with the goalie to make scoring easier. And the **business** of starting over after each goal, in the middle of the field, (24) (**has**/have) to be reconsidered. It's too much like the center-jump after each goal in the basketball game of yesteryear.

It (25) (**seems**/seem) unlikely that Americans will ever **fully comprehend** or appreciate a sport in which players are not allowed to use their arms and hands. Although the **footwork** of soccer players (26) (**is**/are) a magnificent skill to behold, most American fans are perplexed by straitjacketed soccer players' inability and unwillingness to "pick up the darn ball and run with it!" The **inability** to use substitutes (unless the players to be substituted for are lying dead or maimed on the field of play) (27) (**is**/are) also bewildering to Americans, who glorify the "sixth man" in basketball and a baseball game in which virtually the entire **roster** (including an otherwise unemployable old man called "the designated hitter") (28) (**is**/are) deployed on the field at one time or another.

Finally, the field in soccer is enormous. Considerably larger than the American football field, the soccer field could contain at least a dozen basketball courts. Americans like their action condensed, in a small field of vision — ten enormous sweaty people bouncing off one another and moving rapidly through a space the size of a medium-sized bedroom, twenty-two even a larger people in bulky uniforms converging on a small, oddly shaped ball. In soccer, on the other hand, there (29) (**is**/are) **a**

premium on "spreading out," not infringing upon the force field occupied by a team-mate, so that fancy foot-passing is possible. **This** spreading out across the vast meadow of the soccer playing field **(30)** (<u>does</u>/do) not lend itself, again, to close get-down-and-dirty television scrutiny. **Soccer** is a great sport and **it** certainly **(31)** (<u>deserves</u>/deserve) the increased attention and popularity it is getting on all levels. But — primarily, again, because it does not lend itself to television — **it** will never make it big in the United States the way **these** other **sports (32)** (has/<u>have</u>), not until **it (33)** (<u>changes</u>/change) some of its fundamental strategies.

Detail answers to Subject-Verb Quiz 3

1. Outside the United States, **Soccer** <u>or</u> **futbol** (<u>is</u>/are) surely the most popular sport in the world. *Soccer and futbol are both singular and joined by 'or'. With **compound subjects** joined by or/nor, the verb agrees with the subject nearer to it--in this case 'futbol (which is singular). Two singular subjects connected by "or" or "nor" require a singular verb. **Becomes**: '...soccer or futbol is the most popular...' **See Rule #4***

2. Every four years, the world **championship** of soccer called the World Cup, (<u>is</u>/are) watched by billions of the boisterous, cantankerous, devoted, head-over-heals in love fans from all over the world. *'Championship' is a singular noun and is the subject of the sentence. 'of soccer called the World Cup' is an intervening prepositional phrase. A phrase or clause between subject and verb does not change the number of the subject. So intervening phrases and clauses have no effect on subject-verb agreement. **Becomes**: 'championship is watched...' **See Rule#1***

3. And it is also a genuine world championship, involving teams from 32 countries in the final rounds, unlike the much more parochial and misnamed **World Series** in American baseball (that {don't/<u>doesn't</u>} even involve Japan or Cuba, two baseball hotbeds). *'World Series' is the subject and even though 'Series' ends in 's' 'Series' is a singular noun so this is a singular subject. **Becomes**: 'World Series doesn't involve...' **See Rule#10***

4. But although soccer has become an important sport in the American sports scene, it will never make inroads into the hearts and markets of American sports the way that **football, basketball, hockey, baseball,** <u>and</u> even **tennis** <u>and</u> **golf** (has/<u>have</u>) done. *Compound subjects---two or more subjects connected by the word "and"---takes a plural verb. In this sentence, the subject is compound 'football, basketball, hockey, baseball, and even tennis and golf'. Therefore the plural subject takes a plural verb 'have'. **Becomes**: '...football...and golf have done.' **See Rule#3***

5. Nearly 5000 fans showed up, **which** (show/<u>shows</u>) that soccer is, indeed, popular in the United States. This sentence is a little tricky. *Indefinite pronouns reference nonspecific things or people. Most of these pronouns take a singular verb, some are always plural, and a few may be either singular or plural. 'which' is a pronoun referring back to the fact that 'nearly 5000 fans showed up' that fact is singular and shows (singular verb) that soccer is popular. **Becomes**: 'it shows' or 'which shows' **See Rule#2.***

6. & 7 However, the **story** of the game (<u>was</u>/were) buried near the back of the newspaper's sports section, and there (<u>was</u>/were) certainly no television **coverage**. *Intervening prepositional phrases do not affect the subject/verb relationship. 'story' is the singular subject. **Becomes**: '...story was buried...' **See Rule#1.** The second question tests your understanding of the inverted sentence--when the subject comes after the verb. Remember that 'there' is not a subject. The words* here *and* there *have generally been labeled as adverbs even though they indicate place. In sentences beginning with* here *or* there, *the subject follows the verb. In this sentence you could reverse the subject verb like this: '...certainly no television **coverage was** there..' That might help you see that 'coverage' is the subject and it's singular. **Becomes**: '...and there <u>was</u> certainly no television **coverage**...' **See Rules#6&7***

8. **Basketball** succeeds enormously in America because **it** regularly (schedule/<u>schedules</u>) what it calls "television time-outs" as well as the time-outs that the teams themselves call to re-group, not to mention half-times and, on the professional level, quarter breaks. *The subject is 'Basketball' and then the pronoun 'it' refers back to 'basketball'. It's also singular so it takes a singular verb 'schedules'. **Becomes**: 'Basketball...regularly schedules...timeouts...' **See Rules# 1&2***

9. Those **time-outs** in the action (is/<u>are</u>) ideally made for television commercials. *'time-outs' is the subject and it's plural so it takes the plural verb 'are'. **Becomes**: '...time-outs are made for television...' **See the general Rule of subject/verb agreement.***

10&11. College **basketball** (live/<u>lives</u>) for a game scheduled on CBS or ESPN (highly recruited high school players are more likely to go to a team that regularly gets national television exposure), and we could even say that television **coverage** (<u>has</u>/have) dictated the pace and feel of American football. *First sentence: the subject is 'College basketball' or just 'basketball' which is singular and takes the singular verb 'lives'. **Becomes**: '...basketball lives for...'. You could consider "College basketball" a collective noun, but either way it's singular. **See the general Rule of subject/verb agreement.** Second Sentence: the subject is 'coverage' which is singular and takes the singular verb 'has'. **Becomes**: '...coverage has dictated...' **See the general Rule of subject/verb agreement.***

12-14. **Anyone** who (<u>has</u>/have) attended a live football game knows how commercial **time-outs** (<u>slow</u>/slows) the game and sometimes, at its most exciting moments, (<u>disrupt</u>/disrupts) the flow of events. *Indefinite pronouns reference nonspecific things or people. Most of these pronouns take a singular verb, some are always plural, and a few may be either singular or plural.* **Note: <u>Indefinite pronouns that end in "one" are always singular. In this case 'Anyone' is the subject and it's singular by rule and takes the singular verb 'has'.</u>** *Becomes:* **<u>'Anyone who has attended...'</u>** *See Rule #2 Second sentence: the subject is 'time-outs' which is plural and so it takes the plural verb 'slow'. Becomes: '...time-outs slow the game...' See the general Rule of subject/verb agreement. Sentence Three: the subject is still "commercial time-outs" which is plural and thus requires a plural verb "disrupt". **Becomes**: '...time-outs disrupt the flow' This one is a little tricky so be careful. If you just rely on your ear and you don't identify the correct subject it can get confusing. **See Rule #1***

15. The best that commercial television coverage can hope for is an injury **time-out**, and in soccer **that** (happen/<u>happens</u>) only with decapitation or disembowelment. *The subject is 'time-out' or 'that" which refers back to 'time-out' which is singular. **Becomes**: '...an injury timeout happens only with...' **See Rule# 1***

16. Second, Americans love their violence, and soccer doesn't deliver on this score the way that American **football** <u>and</u> **hockey** (<u>do</u>/does). *Here we have two nouns joined by 'and' acting as a compound subject. The rule says: **Compound subjects**---two*

*or more subjects connected by the word "and"—take a plural verb. Therefore, it **becomes**: '...football and hockey do deliver...' This one is a little tricky and demonstrates how important it is to systematically follow the rules and not rely exclusively on your ear. **See Rule# 3***

17&18. America (<u>**loves**</u>/love) its football games with scores like 49 to 35 and a professional basketball **game** with scores below 100 (<u>**is**</u>/are) regarded as a defensive bore. *The first sentence: 'America' is the subject and it's a singular noun so it takes a singular verb. **Becomes**: 'America loves its football..." **See the general Rule of subject/verb agreement**, 'America' might also be considered a collective noun, but it's singular. **Second sentence**: This one is a little tricky because you might not immediately recognize the subject is 'game' or 'basketball game' or even 'professional basketball game', but this subject is singular. The tricky part is avoiding the reliance on your ear. If you did that, your ear would want to match the plural word "scores" and "100" which sound like you want to use a plural verb. However, "with scores" and "below 100" are prepositional phrases that can be dropped. The subject is "game". **Becomes**: '...game is regarded as...' **See Rule #1***

19. In soccer, on the other hand, **scores** like 2 to 1, even 1 to 0, (is/<u>**are**</u>) commonplace and apparently desirable; games scoreless at the end of regulation time happen all the time. *Ignore the prepositional phrases at the start of the sentence and focus on the subject 'scores' which is plural and requires a plural verb 'are'. **Becomes**: '...scores are commonplace...' **See Rule# 1***

20. (In the 515 games played in the final phase in the history of the World Cup games through 1994, only 1584 **goals** (was/<u>**were**</u>) scored. *The subject is 'goals' which is plural and requires a plural verb 'was'. **Becomes**: '...goals were scored.' **See Rule #1** and **See the general Rule of subject/verb agreement.***

21&22. And if there (<u>**is**</u>/are) no **resolution** at the end of overtime, the teams resort to **a shoot-out** that (<u>**has**</u>/have) more to do with luck than with real soccer skills. *'there' is not a subject. Sometimes it helps to reword these inverted sentences and put the subject first. They sound a bit odd, but it can be helpful, like this: 'And if no **<u>resolution</u>** is there at the end of overtime...' 'Resolution' is the subject and it's singular so it takes the singular form of 'is'. **Becomes**: '...there is no resolution..." **See Rules 6&7**. **Second sentence**: The subject is 'shoot-out' which is singular. The fact it says 'a' shoot-out helps you know it's singular. **Becomes**: '...a shoot-out has more to do with luck...' **See the general Rule of subject/verb agreement.***

23. Things like that can happen, too, in baseball, but the **problem** somehow (<u>**evens**</u>/even) out over baseball's very long season of daily games. *The subject is 'problem' which is singular. Note it says "the" problem, which also helps you know it's singular. **Becomes**: '...the problem evens out...' **See Rule #1** and **See the general Rule of subject/verb agreement.***

24. And the **business** of starting over after each goal, in the middle of the field, (<u>**has**</u>/have) to be reconsidered. *The subject is 'business' and it's singular and takes the singular verb 'has'. Ignore all the phrases and clauses between the subject and the verb. **Becomes**: '...business has to be reconsidered.' **See Rule #1** and **See the general Rule of subject/verb agreement.***

25. It (<u>**seems**</u>/seem) unlikely that Americans will ever **fully comprehend** or appreciate a sport in which players are not allowed to use their arms and hands. *"It" is the subject and refers to the singular idea that Americans will never fully comprehend..." **Becomes**: 'It seems unlikely..." 'It' is always a singular pronoun. **See Rule #2***

26. Although the **footwork** of soccer players (<u>**is**</u>/are) a magnificent skill to behold, most American fans are perplexed by straitjacketed soccer players' inability and unwillingness to "pick up the darn ball and run with it!" *The subject is 'footwork' which is singular and takes the singular verb 'is'. Ignore the prepositional phrase "of soccer players". **Becomes**: '...footwork is a skill'. **See Rule #1***

27&28. The **inability** to use substitutes (unless the players to be substituted for are lying dead or maimed on the field of play) (<u>**is**</u>/are) also bewildering to Americans, who glorify the "sixth man" in basketball and a baseball game in which virtually the entire **roster** (including an otherwise unemployable old man called "the designated hitter") (<u>**is**</u>/are) deployed on the field at one time or another. *The subject is 'inability' which is a singular noun and therefore takes a singular verb 'is'. **Becomes**: '...inability is bewildering...' You have to ignore all the information between the subject and verb. **See Rule #2**
Second sentence: another example of a bunch of content that does not affect the subject or the verb. The subject is 'roster' which could be considered a collective singular noun...but it's singular no matter what--we say "a roster is" or "the roster is" not "a roster are" or "the roster are". **Becomes**: '...the roster is deployed..." **See Rule #1.***

29. In soccer, on the other hand, there (<u>**is**</u>/are) **a premium** on "spreading out," not infringing upon the force field occupied by a team-mate, so that fancy foot-passing is possible. *Another example of an inverted sentence. You can re-state this sentence like this: 'a premium is there on spreading out...". The subject is 'premium' because 'there' is never a subject. **Becomes**: '...there is a premium...' **See Rule 6&7***

30. **This** spreading out across the vast meadow of the soccer playing field (<u>**does**</u>/do) not lend itself, again, to close get-down-and -dirty television scrutiny. *"This" is a pronoun that refers to the single idea of "spreading out across the vast meadow of the soccer playing field"...you could replace that information with a single word "idea". It's singular. **Becomes**: 'This...idea...does not..." **See Rules #1 and 2***

31. **Soccer** is a great sport and **it** certainly (<u>**deserves**</u>/deserve) the increased attention and popularity it is getting on all levels. *The subject is the pronoun 'it' refers back to 'Soccer'. Everything is singular. **Becomes**:"...it deserves the increased attention..." **See Rules 1&2***

32&33. But — primarily, again, because it does not lend itself to television — **it** will never make it big in the United States the way **these** other **sports** (has/<u>**have**</u>), not until **it** (<u>**changes**</u>/change) some of its fundamental strategies. *This sentence is a good example of following the rules and carefully picking out subjects. First, it's rather obvious that the subject is 'sports' which 'these' refers to. This is a plural subject. **Becomes**: '...sports have...' What comes after 'have' is the unspoken reference back to the first of the sentence--'...sports have made it big'. **Second sentence**: the subject is 'it' which refers back to the sentence before and also back to the 'it' at the start of the sentence. It refers to 'soccer'. Soccer will not make it big until soccer changes some fundamental strategies. Soccer is a singular subject and so is 'it'. **Becomes**: '...it changes..." **See Rule #1***

Subject-Verb Quiz 4

1. The football team as well as the baseball team **(has/have)** to raise funds for their season.
2. The Constitution together with the other founding documents **(is/are)** the foundation of our country.
3. Neither of the students **(is/are)** ready for the final exam.

4. There *(is/are)* a list of students posted in the office.
5. Everybody in the band *(has/have)* practiced for the concert.
6. The jury *(take/takes)* their seats in the jury box.
7. Neither the advisor nor the students *(seem/seems)* concerned about the change of schedule.
8. *(Has/Have)* either the teacher or the students remembered the assignment?
9. Corona, California is one of those cities that *(is/are)* experiencing increases in the housing market.
10. Some of the flour *(has/have)* spilled on the floor.
11. Jackson or his sister (is are) going to the football game.
12. A few of the assignments *(is/are)* graded by the students themselves.
13. Either the Student Resources Committee or the Committee on Extra Curricular events *(decide/decides)* these matters.
14. One of my former employers *(have/has)* written a letter of recommendation.

Subject-Verb Quiz 4 Answers

1. The football **team** <u>as well as</u> the baseball team (<u>has</u>) to raise funds for their season. *Sometimes the subject is separated from the verb by words such as* along with, *together with, as well as, besides, along with, or not. Ignore these expressions when determining whether to use a singular or plural verb, they are not the same as "and". The subject here is 'The football team,' which is singular. The modifying phrase that comes after 'as well as' modifies the subject but does not compound it as the word 'and' would do.* **See Rule 3b.** *Special Case.*

2. The **Constitution** <u>together with</u> the other founding documents (<u>is</u>) the foundation of our country. *Sometimes the subject is separated from the verb by words such as* along with, *together with, as well as, besides, along with, or not. Ignore these expressions when determining whether to use a singular or plural verb, they are not the same as "and". The subject here is 'The Constitution,' which is singular. The modifying phrase that comes after 'together with' modifies the subject but does not compound it as the word 'and' would do.* **See Rule 3b.** *Special Case.*

3. **Neither** of the students (<u>is</u>) ready for the final exam. *When used as the subject of a sentence, the pronouns neither and either are singular and ALWAYS require singular verbs even though they seem to be referring, in a sense, to two things.* **See Rule 5b.**

4. There (<u>is</u>) a **list** of students posted in the office. *The correct response is "IS". Remember that with the constructions "There is" and "There are," the subject ("list," in this case) comes after the verb. You can turn the sentence around and say, "A list <u>is</u> posted in the office".* **See Rules 6 & 7**

5. **Everybody** in the band (<u>has</u>) practiced for the concert. *"HAS" is correct because "everybody" is always singular.* **See Rule 2.**

6. The **jury** (<u>take</u>) their seats in the jury box. *The correct response is the plural form of the verb "TAKE". 'Jury' is a **collective noun** because it is a word used to define a group of objects, people, animals, emotions, inanimate things, concepts, or other things.* **See Rule 8.** *However, in this case the word 'jury' is not used as a single unit or thing. A 'jury' could render a decision as a group, it could disagree with the judge as a group, but it cannot take a seat as a unit. In this case, the individual members of the jury take their seats...so it's plural. You could restate this sentence like this: 'The **members** of the jury <u>take</u> their seats.'*

7. **Neither** the advisor <u>nor</u> the students (<u>seem</u>) concerned about the change of schedule. *The correct response is "SEEM" because the plural noun "students" is closer to the verb and determines the number of the verb.* **See Rule 5**

8. (<u>Has</u>) <u>either</u> the **teacher** <u>or</u> the students remembered the assignment? *The correct response is "HAS" because the singular "teacher" is closer to the verb and determines the number of the verb. See Rule 5*

9. Corona, California is **one of those cities** that (<u>are</u>) experiencing increases in the housing market. **HINT:** *Try re-starting with: 'Of those cities that (is/<u>are</u>) experiencing increases in the housing market, Corona, CA is one.' The correct response is "ARE". The example implies that other cities besides Corona are experiencing increases--so it's plural. Use the plural verb "are".* **See Rule 12a.**

10. **Some** of the flour (<u>has</u>) spilled on the floor. *The correct response is "HAS" because 'flour' is used as single unit and is not countable. Some indefinite pronouns may be either singular or plural. Uncountable nouns are singular so use singular verbs; countable nouns are plural so use plural verbs. So the indefinite pronouns like some, any, none, all, most can be either singular or plural depending whether the noun is countable or uncountable. In this case 'flour' is not countable* **See Rule 2c.**

11. **Jackson** <u>or</u> his **sister** (<u>is</u>) going to the football game. *The correct response is "IS". With **compound subjects** joined by **or/nor**, the verb agrees with the subject nearer to it. Two singular subjects connected by "or" or "nor" require a singular verb. In this case the noun (subject) 'sister' is closest to the verb 'is' and therefore it controls and the verb must be singular.* **See Rule 4**

12. A **few** of the assignments (<u>are</u>) graded by the students themselves. *The correct response is "ARE"; because "few" is always plural. The following are always plural and require a plural verb: both, few, fewer, many, others, several.* **See Rule 2b**

13. Either the Student Resources Committee or the **Committee** on Extra Curricular events (<u>decides</u>) these matters. *The correct response is "DECIDES" because the word "committee" is singular. Two singular subjects connected by either/or, neither/nor, or not only/but also, require a singular verb.* **See Rule 5**

14. **One** of my former employers (<u>has</u>) written a letter of recommendation. *The correct response is "HAS" because the subject is "one." 'One' is always singular.* **See Rule 2**

Subject-Verb Quiz 5

1. Mrs. Sanchez is one of those teachers who *(seem/seems)* to actually love teaching students.
2. *(Have/Has)* either Stephanie or her friends decided what they will wear to the dance?
3. Neither Stephanie nor her friends *(is/are)* ready for the dance.
4. Everybody in the class *(want/wants)* to get an A on the final exam.
5. Because there *(is/are)* so many players on the team, the practice lasted over four hours.
6. Neither team--neither Santiago High School on Center Street nor Centennial High School on Main street--*(was/were)* victorious this week.

7. Ashley, along with her sisters *(have/has)* attended private schools for the last three years.
8. There *(is/are)* no explanations she could give for her unacceptable behavior.
9. Some of the wine *(has/have)* already spoiled.
10. One of these students *(has/have)* won the most outstanding athlete award.
11. Either our school's boys basketball team or our girls basketball team *(is/are)* going to win the league title this year.
12. My dad and his brother Napoleon *(is/are)* working on a new addition to our home.
13. Several of my friends *(have/has)* asked me to hang out this weekend.

Subject-Verb Quiz 5 Answers

1. Mrs. Sanchez is **one** of those teachers who (**seem**) to actually love teaching students. *The correct response is "SEEM." Even though 'one' is always a singular subject, 'one of those who' is always plural. You can also rearrange the sentence to more clear, like this: "Of those teachers who seem to actually love teaching students, Mrs. Sanchez is one." This example implies that others besides Mrs. Sanchez are included in the group of teachers who seem to love teaching. Therefore, use the plural verb "seem".* ***See Rule 12a***

2. (**Has**) either **Stephanie** or her **friends** decided what they will wear to the dance? *The correct response is "HAS". When one of the compound subjects is plural and one is singular the part of the subject that is closest to the verb determines the number (whether the verb is singular or plural). In this example it would be singular: 'either **Stephanie has** decided'. If 'friends' had been closer to the verb, then the plural form 'have' would be correct, 'her **friends have** decided'.* ***See Rule 5b***

3. Neither **Stephanie** nor her **friends** (**are**) ready for the dance. *The correct response is "ARE". The subject closer to the verb determines the number of the verb. When one of the compound subjects is plural and one is singular the part of the subject that is closest to the verb determines the number (whether the verb is singular or plural). In this example it would be plural: 'nor her **friends are** ready'. If 'Stephanie' had been closer to the verb, then the singular form 'is' would be correct, '**Stephanie is** ready'.* ***See Rule 5b***

4. **Everybody** in the class (**wants**) to get an A on the final exam. *The correct response is "WANTS". The subject "Everybody" is always singular.* ***See Rule 2 Indefinite Pronouns***

5. Because there (**are**) so many **players** on the team, the practice lasted over four hours. *The correct response is "ARE". You could also rewrite the sentence like this, "The practice lasted over four hours because so many **players are** on the team." Rearranging it this way puts the subject and verb closer together and should make it easier to see the relationship between subject and verb is plural.* ***Rules 1, 6, & 7***

6. Neither **team**--neither Santiago High School on Center Street nor Centennial High School on Main street--(**was**) victorious this week. *The correct response is "WAS". "Neither," which is always singular, is the subject of this sentence. '**Neither** team **was** victorious'. We can simply drop the part of the sentence between the dashes because it is not relevant to figuring out the subject.* ***See Rule 5b***

7. **Ashley**, along with her sisters (**has**) attended private schools for the last three years. *The correct response is "HAS". "Ashley," the subject, is modified by "along with her sisters," but those sisters are not the subject. When the subject is separated from the verb by words such as along with, together with, as well as, besides, along with, or not, ignore these expressions to decide whether to use a singular or plural verb, they are not the same as "and".* ***See Rule 3b.***

8. There (**are**) no **explanations** she could give for her unacceptable behavior. *The correct response is "ARE"; the subject, "reasons," comes after the verb in this sentence. ' no **explanations are**'* ***See Rules 1, 6, & 7***

9. **Some** of the wine (**has**) already spoiled. *The correct response is "HAS" because "some," in this case, is singular. Some indefinite pronouns may be either singular or plural. Uncountable nouns are singular so use singular verbs; countable nouns are plural so use plural verbs. So the indefinite pronouns like some, any, none, all, most can be either singular or plural depending whether the noun is countable or uncountable.* ***See Rule 2c.***

10. **One** of these students (**has**) won the most outstanding athlete award. *"HAS" is correct. This is the first rule of indefinite pronouns--'one' is always singular, regardless of the plural noun inside the prepositional phrase (in this case 'students'). In this case, the sentence refers to one single individual and not a group...IOW it singles out one particular individual from the group 'of students'. Be careful not to confuse this rule with Rule 12a.'One of those who...' which is always plural because it denotes a group of individuals and the sentence is talking about one of those in that group. But the subject is the group, of which this 'thing' 'person' is a part.* ***See Rules 2 and 12a.***

11. Either our school's boys basketball team or our girls basketball **team** (**is**) going to win the league title this year. *The correct response is "IS" because when "either/or" is the conjunction, you choose the subject closer to the verb to determine the number of the verb and, in any case, the subject would be the singular "team."* ***See Rule 5a***

12. My **dad** and his brother **Napoleon** (**are**) working on a new addition to our home. *The correct response is "ARE". **Compound subjects**—two or more subjects connected by the word "and"—takes a plural verb. In this case, 'dad' and 'Napoleon' are the compound subject and take a plural verb 'are'.* ***See Rule 3***

13. **Several** of my friends (**have**) asked me to hang out this weekend. *The correct response is "HAVE" because "several" is always plural.* ***See Rule 2 and 2b***

Subject-Verb Quiz 6

1. There *(was/were)* several questions on the exam that I did not understand.
2. Marcus and Darrien, who *(love/loves)* playing video games, have decided to upgrade their system.
3. Both of the desks in the front row of Mrs. Lopez' math class *(need/needs)* repairs.
4. The girls soccer team that won fifteen games last year and finished in first place among the six teams in our league *(was/were)* finally beaten yesterday.
5. The President, along with his advisors, *(describes/describe)* the national debt as unsustainable.
6. The issue of inflation and deficits and borrowing *(continue/continues)* to dominate the news.
7. Julian and Bryce *(compete/competes)* for the starting shortstop position on the team.
8. Not one of the players *(was/were)* disrespectful of the coach.
9. The results of tournament *(was/were)* reported on ESPN Sports Center.

10. When there *(is/are)* long reading assignments I like to study with friends.

Subject-Verb Quiz 6 Answers

1. There (**were**) several **questions** on the exam that I did not understand. *The correct response is "WERE". The subject of this verb, "questions," comes after the verb. You can re-write the sentence like this: '...several* **questions** *were'. The following are always plural and always require a plural verb: both, few, fewer, many, others, several.* **Rules 2b, 6, 7**

2. **Marcus** and **Darrien**, who (**love**) playing video games, have decided to upgrade their system. *The correct response is "LOVE".* **Compound subjects**—*two or more subjects connected by the word "and"— always take a plural verb (except* **Rule 3c.**) *"Marcus and Darrien" become 'they' which is plural. 'They love', not 'they loves'.* **See rule 3a.**

3. **Both** of the desks in the front row of Mrs. Lopez' math class (**need**) repairs. *The correct response is "NEED". "Both" is always plural.* **See Rule 2** *Plural indefinite pronouns.*

4. The girls soccer **team** that won fifteen games last year and finished in first place among the six teams in our league (**was**) finally beaten yesterday. *Remember a subject and its verb are not always together. The correct response is "WAS". The phrases and clauses between the subject and verb have no effect on the subject/verb agreement. In this case, 'team was'* **See Rule 1**

5. The **President**, along with his advisors, (**describes**) the national debt as unsustainable. *The correct response is "DESCRIBES". Sometimes the subject is separated from the verb by words such as* along with, *together with, as well as, besides, along with, or* not. *Ignore these expressions when determining whether to use a singular or plural verb, they are not the same as "and". In this example, the subject is 'President' which is a singular noun and the 'along with his advisors' has no effect on the number--it stays singular.* **See Rule 3b.**

6. The **issue** of inflation and deficits and borrowing (**continues**) to dominate the news. *The correct response is "CONTINUES". The subject is 'issue' which is singular. The prepositional phrase 'of inflation and deficits and borrowing' has no effect on the singular subject. Don't get confused with the 'and' inside the prepositional phrase and think they are joining a compound subject like* **Rule 3.** *Anything inside the prepositional phrase does not affect the subject, so you could have a list of a thousand items that make up this 'issue' and it would not convert it to a plural. The subject remains 'issue' and it's singular.* **See Rule 1**

7. **Julian** or **Bryce** (**competes**) for the starting shortstop position on the team. *"COMPETES" is correct.* **Compound subjects** *joined by* **or/nor**, *the verb agrees with the subject nearer to it. Two singular subjects connected by "or" or "nor" require a singular verb.* **See Rule 4**

8. **Not one** of the players (**was**) disrespectful of the coach. *"WAS" is correct. This is a very tricky rule.* **Study it.** *It tests the special rule of 'none'. By definition if "none" means "not any", then it's a plural. However, if "none" means "not one" it's singular. This example does not use the word 'none' but it does use the replacement 'not one' which tells us the subject is singular.* **Rule 2d.** **Special rule of none**

9. The **results** of tournament (**were**) reported on ESPN Sports Center. *The correct response is "WERE". This is a plural form subject that also has a plural meaning. "Results" is a plural noun and it has a plural meaning, so it takes a plural verb.* **See Rule 10b.** *Plural form subjects with a plural meaning*

10. When there (**are**) long reading **assignments** I like to study with friends. *The correct response is "ARE". The subject is 'assignments' which is plural, 'assignments are'. Don't be confused by the inverted construction .* **See Rules 6 and 7**

Subject-Verb Agreement Exercises

Subject-Verb Agreement - Exercise 1

1. Miranda and Jacob *(comes/come)* to practice every Saturday.
2. There *(is/are)* time to lift weights before school.
3. My friends who are in the band *(wants/want)* me to play a musical instrument.
4. My father or my brothers *(is/are)* coming with me to the ball game.
5. Everyone *(needs/need)* time to read the assignment.
6. That bag of potatoes *(looks/look)* rotten.
7. The lacrosse team *(hopes/hope)* to win the tournament next week.
8. Your trousers *(needs/need)* a belt.
9. Some of the homework assignments *(is/are)* really hard.
10. Even though most of the students like the teacher, a few *(thinks/think)* he's too strict.

Subject-Verb Agreement - Exercise 1 Answers

1. The correct answer is **come**. **Miranda** and **Jacob** (comes, **come**) to practice every Saturday. *Rule #3 Compound subjects*
2. The correct answer is **is**. There (**is**, are) **time** to lift weights before school. *Rule #6,7 Inverted subjects must agree with the verb.*
3. The correct answer is **want**. My **friends** who are in the band (wants, **want**) me to play a musical instrument. *Rule #1 A phrase or clause between subject and verb*
4. The correct answer is **are**. My **father** or my **brothers** (is, **are**) coming with me to the ball game. *Rule #4b. Singular 'or/nor' plural*
5. The correct answer is **needs**. **Everyone** (**needs**, need) time to read the assignment. *Rule #2 Indefinite Pronouns*
6. The correct answer is **looks**. That **bag** of potatoes (**looks**, look) rotten. *Rule #1 A phrase or clause between subject and verb*
7. The correct answer is **hopes**. The lacrosse **team** (**hopes**, hope) to win the tournament next week. *Rule #8 Collective nouns*
8. The correct answer is **need**. Your **trousers** (needs, **need**)a belt. *Rule #10e Special plural form subjects with a plural meaning*

9. The correct answer is **are**. **Some** of the homework <u>assignments</u> (is, **are**) really hard. *Rule #2c Indefinite Pronouns (countable vs. uncountable)* and *Rule #1 A phrase or clause between subject and verb.*
10. The correct answer is **think**. Even though most the students like the teacher, a **few** (thinks, **think**) he's too strict. *Rule #2b Plural indefinite pronoun subjects .*

Subject-Verb Agreement - Exercise 2

1. Mumps *(is/are)* not common in the United States.
2. Viruses from south of the boarder *(is/are)* migrating north.
3. Most of the dirt in the infield *(is/are)* raked after every game.
4. Either the lions or the tiger *(wants/want)* fresh meat.
5. A subject of great interest at the symposium *(is/are)* the planets of our solar system.
6. *Hansel and Gretel (is/are)* a famous children's story.
7. The team members *(is/are)* deciding what style of uniforms they want this year.
8. The economics of the budget *(was/were)* disturbing.
9. Why *(is/are)* your friends going to the movies without you?
10. The President and the Senator *(hopes/hope)* their re-election committees don't lose money.

Subject-Verb Agreement - Exercise 2 Answers

1. **"is" is correct**. **Mumps** (<u>is</u>, are) not common in the United States. *Rule #8 Collective nouns Rule #10a. Plural forms subjects with a singular meaning, #10d. Plural form subjects with singular or plural meaning.*
2. **"are" is correct**. **Viruses** from south of the boarder (is, **are**) migrating north. *Rule #10b. Plural form subjects with a plural meaning.*
3. The correct answer is **is**. <u>Most</u> of the **dirt** in the infield (<u>is</u>, are) raked after every game. *Rule #2c Countable vs. Uncountable*
4. The correct answer is **wants**. <u>Either</u> the **lions** <u>or</u> the **tiger** (<u>wants</u>) fresh meat. *Rule #5b. Singular joined with plural*
5. The correct answer is **is**. A **subject** of great interest at the symposium (<u>is</u>, are) the planets of our solar system. *Rule #11 subject and subjective complement of different number and Rule #1 A phrase or clause between subject and verb*
6. The correct answer is **is**. **Hansel and Gretel** (<u>is</u>, are) a famous children's story. *Rule #9 The title of books, names of organizations, countries, etc. are always **singular***
7. **"are" is correct**. The **team members** (is, **are**) deciding what style of uniforms they want this year. *Rule #8 collective noun*
8. The correct answer is **were**. The economics of the budget (was, **were**) disturbing. *Rule #8 collective noun, Rule#10d. Plural form subjects with singular or plural meaning*
9. The correct answer is **are**. Why (is, **are**) your friends going to the movies without you? *Rule #7 Inverted Subjects*
10. The correct answer is **hope**. The **President** <u>and</u> the **Senator** (hopes, **hope**) their re-election committees don't lose money. *Rule #3 Compound subjects*

Subject-Verb Agreement - Exercise 3

1. The books in the special collection section at the school library *(have/has)* to be checked out with special permission from the head librarian.
2. The twins, Jessica and Aimee, *(love, loves)* to watch the Disney Channel together.
3. The family *(has/have)* 2000 minutes they share each month on their cell phone plan.
4. The pair of pliers sitting on the counter in the garage *(has/have)* new shock resistant handles.
5. Either Loren or her friends *(go/goes)* to first lunch every day.
6. Terrel threw the game winning touchdown with two seconds left. The crowd *(was/were)* still cheering as he left the locker room after the game.
7. The politics of this mayor's race *(seem/seems)* more acrimonious than usual.
8. Everyone at the office, including all the workers in section Q *(know/knows)* the login credentials
9. *The Harry Potter series of books (are/is)* my favorite.
10. Mumps *(cause/causes)* painful swelling of the salivary glands.

Subject-Verb Agreement - Answers Exercise 3

1. The correct answer is **have**. The **books** in the special collection section at the school library (**have**) to be checked out with special permission from the head librarian. *Rule #1 A phrase or clause between subject and verb*
2. The correct answer is **love**. The **twins**, Jessica and Aimee, (<u>love</u>, loves) to watch the Disney Channel together. *Rule #3 Compound subjects, Rule# 10b. Plural form subjects with a plural meaning.*
3. The correct answer is **has**. The **family** (<u>has</u>) 2000 minutes they share each month on their cell phone plan. *Rule #1 A phrase or clause between subject and verb*
4. The correct answer is **has**. The **pair** of pliers sitting on the counter in the garage (<u>has</u>) new shock resistant handles. *Rule #10e. Special plural form subjects with a plural meaning*
5. The correct answer is **go**. <u>Either</u> Loren <u>or</u> her **friends** (<u>go</u>) to first lunch every day. *Rule #5b Singular joined with plural*
6. The correct answer is **was**. Terrel threw the game winning touchdown with two seconds left. The **crowd** (<u>was</u>) still cheering as he left the locker room after the game. *Rule #8 collective nouns*
7. The correct answer is **seem**. The **politics** of this mayor's race (<u>seem</u>) more acrimonious than usual. *Rule #1 A phrase or clause between subject and verb and Rule #10d. Plural form subjects with singular or plural meaning.*
8. The correct answer is **knows**. **Everyone** at the office, including all the workers in section Q (<u>knows</u>) the login credentials. *Rule #1 A phrase or clause between subject and verb and Rule #2 Indefinite Pronouns*

9. The correct answer is *is*. The Harry Potter **series** of books (<u>is</u>) my favorite. *Series can be a singular or a plural noun, depending on its meaning. When it is used to refer to a single set of things, it takes a singular verb even if it is followed by the preposition of and a plural noun: A series of medical tests is planned for next week. When series refers to two or more sets of things, it takes a plural verb: Three series of medical tests are planned for next week.* **Rule #8** *collective nouns*

10. The correct answer is **causes**. Mumps (<u>causes</u>) painful swelling of the salivary glands. **Rule #8** *Collective nouns and* **Rule# 10d.** *Plural form subjects with singular or plural meaning.*

Grammar Study Guide

Part 5: Misplaced Modifiers

Virtual Classroom>Grammar Study Guide>Misplaced Modifiers

This material corresponds to the Virtual Classroom Instructions in the
PowerPrep DVD/Internet/iApp for English Grammar

Virtual Classroom

Important Abbreviations
These abbreviations are used throughout the program

POE: Process of Elimination
SARR: Synthesize, Analyze, Reduce, and Restate (has to do with Logical Reasoning)
AC: Answer Choice
QS: Question Stem
LOD: Level of Difficulty

Example Question: What is the least common multiple of 3, 4, and 7? **(This is the call of the question or Question Stem "QS")**

These are Answer Choices "AC" A, B, C, D, E
  (A)   12
  (B)   21
  (C)   28
  (D)   48
  (E)   84

Part 5: Misplaced Modifiers

Misplaced Modifiers

Proximity

As a general rule, a modifier should be placed as close as possible to what it modifies.

- Following are some useful tips for protecting your person and property from the FBI. As written, the sentence implies that the FBI is a threat to your person and property. To correct the sentence put the modifier *from the FBI* next to the word it modifies, *tips:* **Correct:** *Following are some useful tips from the FBI for protecting your person and property.*

Phrases modify subject

When a phrase begins a sentence, make sure that it modifies the subject of the sentence.

- Coming around the corner, a few moments passed before I could recognize my old home. As worded, the sentence implies that the moments were coming around the corner. **Correct:** *As I came around the corner, a few moments passed before I could recognize my old home. Or Coming around the corner, I paused a few moments before I could recognize my old home.*

Sample Question

By focusing on poverty, <u>the other causes of crime--such as the breakup of the nuclear family, changing morals, the loss of community, etc.--have been overlooked by sociologists.</u>

(A) <u>the other causes of crime--such as the breakup of the nuclear family, changing morals, the loss of community, etc.--have been overlooked by sociologists.</u>
(B) <u>the other causes of crime have been overlooked by sociologists--such as the breakup of the nuclear family, changing morals, the loss of community, etc.</u>
(C) <u>there are other causes of crime that have been overlooked by sociologists--such as the breakup of the nuclear family, changing morals, the loss of community, etc.</u>
(D) <u>crimes--such as the breakup of the nuclear family, changing morals, the loss of community, etc.--have been overlooked by sociologists.</u>
(E) <u>sociologists have overlooked the other causes of crime--such as the breakup of the nuclear family, changing morals, and the loss of community, etc.</u>

Explanation

(A) Choice (A) is incorrect since it implies that *the other causes of crime* are doing the focusing.
(B) Choice (B) has the same flaw as AC (A)
(C) This AC is incorrect. The phrase *by focusing on poverty* must modify the subject of the sentence, but *there* cannot be the subject since the construction *there are* is used to introduce a subject.
(D) Choice (D) implies that *crimes* are focusing on poverty, which is incorrect.
(E) **Correct Response.** Choice (E) puts the subject of the sentence *sociologists* immediately next to its modifying phrase *by focusing on poverty*. The answer is (E).

Misplaced Phrases & Clauses

Misplacing phrases can significantly change the meaning of the sentence. Because of the separation, sentences with this error often sound awkward, ridiculous, or confusing. Furthermore, they can be downright illogical.
- <u>On her way home, Jan found a gold man's watch.</u> *This suggests the man was gold. However, if you remember to place the modifier as close as possible to the noun it modifies it will fix most of the confusion. In this case, we can clear up the misunderstanding* **Correct:** <u>On her way home, Jan found a man's gold watch.</u> *We simply moved "gold" next to "watch" because that is what it modifies.*

Misplaced adjectives

Misplaced adjectives incorrectly separated from the nouns they modify almost always distort the intended meaning.

- <u>The child ate a cold dish of cereal for breakfast this morning.</u> *We can correct the error by moving the adjective "cold" next to the noun "cereal" that it modifies. It's not a cold dish, it's cold cereal.* **Correct:** <u>The child ate a dish of cold cereal for breakfast this morning.</u>

Misplaced adverbs

Misplaced adverbs can also create misleading sentences. As we have explained before, place the adverb as close as possible to the verb it modifies.

- <u>We ate the lunch that we had bought slowly.</u> *We did not "buy slowly" we "ate slowly".* **Correct:** <u>We slowly ate the lunch that we had bought.</u>

Watch out for adverbs such as **only, almost, already, even, just, nearly, merely, and always**. They are often misplaced and cause unintended meanings.

- <u>I only contributed $10.00 to the fund for orphaned children.</u> *This sentence, means that I only **contributed** the money--no one else contributed any money, only me. But the author probably wanted to convey that he contributed only $10.00. **Corrected:** <u>I contributed only $10.00 to the fund for orphaned children.</u>*

- They almost worked five years on that system. *Corrected: They worked almost five years on that system.*

Misplaced Modifiers - Exercise 1

Directions: Correct any misplaced words in the sentences below, rewriting the sentence so that the misplaced word is next to the word it modifies.

1. I **nearly made fifty dollars** today.
2. When we opened the **leather woman's purse**, we found the missing keys.
3. The job **scarcely took an hour** to complete.
4. I **only have five minutes** to talk with you.
5. The **striking Honda's paint job** made everyone gasp.

Answers:

1. I made **nearly fifty** dollars today.
2. When we opened the woman's **leather purse**, we found the missing keys.
3. The job took **scarcely an hour** to complete.
4. I have **only five minutes** to talk with you.
5. The Honda's **striking paint job** made everyone gasp.

Misplaced phrases

Misplaced phrases may cause a sentence to sound awkward and may create a meaning that does not make sense. The problem sentences below contain <u>misplaced phrases</u> that modify the wrong nouns. To fix the errors and clarify the meaning, put the phrases **next to** the noun they are supposed to modify.

- <u>The dealer sold the Cadillac to the buyer with leather seats.</u> *Obviously the buyer did not have leather seats, but the Cadillac did have leather seats. So move the phrase "with leather seats" closer to the noun it modifies "the Cadillac".* **Correct:** <u>The dealer sold the Cadillac with leather seats to the buyer</u>
- <u>They saw a fence behind the house made of barbed wire.</u> *Obviously the house was not made of barbed wire. So move the phrase "made of barbed wire" next to what it modifies "fence".* **Correct:** <u>They saw a fence made of barbed wire behind the house.</u> *You could also shorten the sentence* **Correct:** <u>They saw a barbed wire fence behind the house.</u>

Misplaced Modifiers - Exercise 2

Directions: Correct any misplaced phrases in the sentences, rewriting the sentence so that the misplaced phrase is next to the word it modifies.

1. We hiked through the **forest wearing only light shirts and shorts.**
2. The fans stood in line to buy tickets to **the show for twenty minutes.**
3. Marian read a chilling article in *The New York Times* **about the effects of mercury poisoning.**
4. The salesman sold the picture to **the short woman in the silver frame.**
5. Michelle whistled to **the dog on the way to the movies.**
6. My friend uses a pen to write his **essays with a gold cap.**
7. The governor made some remarks about **inflation during her news conference.**
8. Farmers in Ohio were spraying their **crops wearing protective masks.**
9. Joe searched for someone to teach him how **to play the guitar without success.**
10. Ted could see **the airplane using binoculars.**

Answers

1. **Wearing only light shirts and shorts, we** hiked through the forest.
2. The fans **stood in line for twenty minutes** to buy tickets to the show.
3. Marion read a chilling **article about the effects of mercury poisoning** in *The New York Times*.
4. The salesman sold **the picture in the silver frame** to the short woman.
5. **On the way to the movies, Michelle** whistled to the dog.
6. My friend uses **a pen with a gold cap** to write his essays.
7. **During her news conference, the governor made some remarks** about inflation.
8. **Wearing protective masks, farmers** in Ohio were spraying their crops.
9. **Without success, Joe searched** for someone to teach him how to play the guitar.
10. **Using binoculars, Ted** could see the airplane.

Misplaced clauses

Misplaced clauses may cause a sentence to sound awkward and may create a meaning that does not make sense. The problem sentences below contain <u>misplaced clauses</u> that modify the wrong nouns.
To fix the errors and clarify the meaning, put the clauses **next to** the noun they are supposed to modify.

- The waiter served a dinner roll to the woman that was well buttered. *Was the woman well-butter? Move the modifier next to the noun it modifies,* **Correct**: *The waiter served a dinner roll that was well buttered to the woman.* **Another way:** *The waiter severed a well buttered dinner roll to the woman.*

- Fred piled all his clothes in the hamper that he had worn. *Did Fred or the hamper wear the clothes.* **Correct**: *Fred piled all the clothes that he had worn in the hamper.* **Another way:** *Fred piled all his worn clothes in the hamper.*

Ambiguous or Squinting Modifiers

An ambiguous <u>modifier</u> (usually an <u>adverb</u>) appears to qualify the words both before and after it. This will create confusion. Sometimes referred to as a "**squinting modifier, squinting construction**. The term is used of an adverb or phrase that stands between two sentence elements and can be taken to modify either what precedes or what follows.

- What you hear often you will believe. Does *often* modify "hear" or "what u will believe". If you hear something over and over you will believe it, "What you often hear you will believe". Or does it mean, things you hear you will usually believe, "What you here you will often believe. Which one is it? You cannot tell from the placement of "often"

- Instructors who cancel classes rarely are reprimanded. Does "rarely" modify "cancel" or "reprimanded"? You cannot tell. Is it, "Instructors who rarely cancel classes are reprimanded" or is it "Instructors who cancel classes are rarely reprimanded".

- The store that had the big sale recently went bankrupt. Was the big sale recent or was the bankruptcy recent. Is it, "The store that recently had the big sale went bankrupt." or is it, " The store that had the big sale went bankrupt recently." We cannot tell.

- People who use drugs frequently suffer health problems. Is it, " People who frequently use drugs suffer health problems." Or is it, " People who use drugs suffer frequent health problems. We cannot tell.

- Writing an essay clearly will improve your grade. Is it, " Clearly writing an essay will improve your grade. Or is it, " Writing an essay will clearly improve your grade." We cannot tell.

- I told Maxine when the game was over I would drive her to the bingo hall. I is it, "When the game was over I told Maxine I would drive her to the bingo hall. Or is it, "I told Maxine I would drive her to the bingo hall when the game was over." We cannot tell.

Misplaced Modifiers - Exercise 3

1. We gave the old clothes to a local **charity that had been piled up in the basement.**
2. We ate Mexican food after the **movie that was very spicy.**
3. I got a watch for my **graduation that has a solar clock.**
4. My wife found a photograph in **the attic that Smith had given to Jones.**
5. The grass was covered by **the snow that was creating a lush carpet of green.**
6. The terrified patient talked with **the doctor who had a terminal disease.**
7. I used a pen for **the test that contained orange ink.**
8. The student pleaded with **the instructor who cheated on the test.**
9. I returned the tuna to **the fish market that was spoiled.**
10. Marion received a ticket from **the police officer who was speeding.**

Answers

1. We gave the old **clothes that had been piled up in the basement** to a local charity.
2. After the movie, we ate **Mexican food that was very spicy.**
3. I got **a watch that has a solar clock** for my graduation.
4. In the attic, my wife found **a photograph that Smith had given to Jones.**
5. **The grass that was creating a lush carpet of green** was covered by the snow.
6. The terrified **patient who had a terminal disease** talked with the doctor.
7. For the test I used **a pen that contained orange ink.**
8. The **student who cheated on the test** pleaded with the instructor.
9. I returned the **tuna that was spoiled** to the fish market.
10. **Marion, who was speeding,** received a ticket from the police officer.

Misplaced Modifiers - Exercise 4

Identify the phrase or clause that is misplaced, and correctly rearrange the sentence.

1. Plunging more than 1,000 feet into the gorge, we saw Yosemite Falls.

   Corrected Sentence:_____.

2. Please take time to look over the brochure that is enclosed with your family.

   Corrected Sentence:_____.

3. The patient was referred to a psychiatrist with a severe emotional problem.

   Corrected Sentence:_____.

4. Two cars were reported stolen by the Farmingdale police yesterday.

   Corrected Sentence:_____.

Answers

1. **What the writer thinks it says**: The Yosemite Falls plunge 1000 feet. **What the sentence really says**: These people were plunging 1000 feet into the gorge while looking at Yosemite Falls. **Correction**: We saw Yosemite Falls plunging more than 1000 feet into the gorge. **Better Active Voice**: Did you know Yosemite Falls plunges more than 1000 feet into the gorge? or Yosemite Falls plunges more than 1000 feet into a gorge.

2. **What the writer thinks it says**: A request that you and your family review the enclosed brochure. **What the sentence really says**: the family is enclosed with the brochure **Correction**: Please take time with your family to look over the enclosed brochure. **Better Active Voice**: Please review the enclosed brochure with your family.

3. **What the writer thinks it says**: A severely disturbed patient was referred to a psychiatrist. **What the sentence really says**: The psychiatrist is severely disturbed. **Correction** The patient with the severe emotional problem was referred to a psychiatrist. **Better Active Voice**: Dr. Smith referred the severely disturbed patient to a psychiatrist.

4. **What the writer thinks it says**: The Farmingdale police reported two stolen cars. **What the sentence really says**: The police stole the two cars. **Correction**: Yesterday the Farmingdale police reported two cars were stolen.

PowerPrep Practice Questions 1-21

1. One morning I shot an elephant in my pajamas. How he got into my pajamas I'll never know. *Groucho Marx*

_____

2. They just said it's going to rain on the radio. *"Tiger" comic strip*

_____

3. You are welcome to visit the cemetery where famous Russian composers, artists, and writers are buried daily, except on Thursdays. *in a guide to a Russian Orthodox monastery*

_____

4. Hugh Jackman donated a pair of jeans to a charity that sold for over $20,000.

_____

5. The teacher quoted from the news article wearing glasses.

_____

6. As we begin the trial, please banish all information about the case from your mind, if you have heard any.

_____

7. A superb and inexpensive restaurant; fine food expertly served by waitresses in appetizing forms.

_____

8. Many of the trustees congratulated him for his speech at the end of the meeting and promised their support.

_____

9. For sale: An antique desk suitable for a lady with thick legs and large drawers.

_____

10. For sale: Several very old dresses from grandmother in beautiful condition.

_____

11. Wanted: Man to take care of cow that does not smoke or drink.

_____

12. For sale: Mixing bowl set designed to please a cook with a round bottom for efficient beating.

_____

13. We almost made a profit of $10.

_____

14. Her only full-time paid employee is a pleasant young woman with a nose ring named Rebecca, who sits at the front desk. *reprinted in The New Yorker*

_____

15. The President acknowledged the role played by the men who subdued the gunman when he spoke at a dinner on Saturday night.
The New York Times, October 31, 1994

16. Historians have been kept guessing over claims [that] Dr James Barry, Inspector General of Military Hospitals, was in fact a woman for more than 140 years. *The Daily Telegraph, March 5, 2008*

17. Plastic bags are a favorite of grocers because of their price, about 2 cents per bag compared to 5 cents for paper. Used widely since the 1970s, environmentalists now estimate between 500 billion to a trillion bags are produced annually worldwide.
Savannah Morning News, January 30, 2008

18. My parents bought a house from a man with no inside plumbing.

19. The characters find a jewel in the story by Maupassant.

20. My dog was hit by a truck running across the road.

21. I heard my kid outside with the dog yelling and laughing.

PowerPrep Answers 1-21

1. While in my pajamas one morning, I shot an elephant .

2. They just said on the radio it's going to rain. OR I just heard on the radio that it's going to rain.

3. Daily, except Thursday, you are welcome to visit the cemetery where famous Russian and Soviet composers, artists, and writers are buried. **OR** You are welcome to visit daily except on Thursdays, the cemetery where famous Russian composers, artists, and writers are buried. Sometimes it's better to break the information into two sentences, **like this**:
You are welcome to visit the cemetery where famous Russian composers, artists, and writers are buried. The cemetery is open daily except Thursdays.

4. A pair of jeans Hugh Jackman donated to the charity, sold for over $200. The charity sold a pair of Hugh Jackman donated jeans for $200. OR Hugh Jackman donated a pair of jeans to the charity and they sold for $200.

5. Wearing glasses, the teacher quoted from the news article. OR The teacher, wearing glasses, quoted from the news article.

6. As we begin, I must ask you to banish any information about the case from your mind.

7. A superb and inexpensive restaurant; fine food in appetizing forms is served expertly by waitresses.

8. At the end of the meeting, many of the trustees congratulated him for his speech and promised their support.

9. For sale: An antique desk with thick legs and large drawers suitable for a lady.

10. For sale: Several very old dresses in beautiful condition from grandmother.

11. Wanted: Man that does not smoke or drink to take care of cow.

12. For sale: Mixing bowl set with round bottoms for efficient beating designed to please a cook.

13. We made a profit of almost ten dollars.

14. Rebecca who sits at the front desk is her only full-time paid employee. She is a pleasant young woman with a nose ring.   Her only full-time paid employee is a pleasant young woman named Rebecca.   She has a nose and sits at the front desk.

15. When the President spoke at a dinner on Saturday night he acknowledged the role played by the men who subdued the gunman.

16. Historians have been kept guessing for more than 140 years over claims [that] Dr James Barry, Inspector General of Military Hospitals, was in fact a woman.

17. Plastic bags have been used widely since the 1970s and are a favorite of grocers because of their price, about 2 cents per bag compared to 5 cents for paper. Environmentalists now estimate between 500 billion to a trillion bags are produced annually worldwide.

18. My parents bought a house with no inside plumbing from a man. (you could probably drop the phrase "from a man" because it doesn't really had much. The important part of the sentence is the fact the home had no indoor plumbing)

19. In the story by Maupassant, the characters find a jewel.

20. My dog was running across the road when he was hit by a truck.

21. I heard my kid yelling and laughing outside with the dog. It's also possible to say it this way: I heard my kid outside yelling and laughing with the dog

Grammar Study Guide

Part 6: Faulty Parallelism & Shifts

Virtual Classroom>Grammar Study Guide>Faulty Parallelism

This material corresponds to the Virtual Classroom Instructions in the
PowerPrep DVD/Internet/iApp for English Grammar

Virtual Classroom

Important Abbreviations

These abbreviations are used throughout the program

POE: Process of Elimination
SARR: Synthesize, Analyze, Reduce, and Restate (has to do with Logical Reasoning)
AC: Answer Choice
QS: Question Stem
LOD: Level of Difficulty

Example Question: What is the least common multiple of 3, 4, and 7? (**This is the call of the question or Question Stem "QS"**)

These are Answer Choices "AC" A, B, C, D, E
  (A)   12
  (B)   21
  (C)   28
  (D)   48
  (E)   84

Part 6: Faulty Parallelism & Shifts

Adjectives, Lists, Structure

Adjectives

For a sentence to be parallel, similar elements must be expressed in similar form. When two adjectives modify the same noun, they should have similar forms.

- The topology course was both *rigorous* and *a challenge*. *Since both rigorous and a challenge are modifying course, they should have the same form:* **Correct:** *The topology course was both rigorous and challenging.*

Lists or Series

When a series of clauses is listed, the verbs in each clause must have the same form.

- During his trip to Europe, the President will *discuss* ways to stimulate trade, *offer* economic aid, and *trying* to forge a new coalition with moderate forces in Russia. *In this example, the first two verbs, discuss and offer, are active. But the third verb in the series, trying, is passive. The form of the verb should be active.* **Correct:** *During his trip to Europe, the President will discuss ways to stimulate trade, to offer economic aid, and to try and forge a new coalition with moderate forces in Russia.*

- The teacher emphasized collective support, mutual assistance, and being responsible for one another. *In the first example "being responsible" is not parallel with the other two items in the list.* **Correct:** *The teacher emphasized collective support, mutual aid, and responsibility for one another.*

Prepositions in a list: This is fertile ground for testing. Keep the prepositions within a list or series parallel.

- Three of the great Indian nations in the Central Plains are the Cherokee, the Choctaw, and Comanche. **Correct:** *Three of the great Indian nations in the Central Plains are the Cherokee, the Choctaw, and the Comanche. Use the article "the" consistently for each noun.*

- The kitchen has room for a new gas oven but not a new dishwasher. **Correct:** *The kitchen has room for a new gas oven but not for a new dishwasher. Use the preposition "for" consistently.*

Sentence Structure

When the first half of a sentence has a certain structure, the second half should preserve that structure.

- *To acknowledge* that one is an alcoholic is *taking* the first and hardest step to recovery. *The first half of the above sentence has an infinitive structure, to acknowledge, so the second half must have a similar structure:* **Correct:** *To acknowledge that one is an alcoholic is to take the first and hardest step to recovery.*

CONJUNCTIONS [conj.]

There are three types of conjunctions: • coordinating conjunctions • correlative conjunctions, •subordinating conjunctions.

Coordinating Conjunctions

These conjunctions connect individual words or groups of words that perform the same function in a sentence. (and, but, for, nor, or, yet, so). In other words, they connect equals to one another: words to words, phrases to phrases, or clauses to clauses. Coordinating conjunctions go <u>in between</u> items joined, not at the beginning or end. You can remember these with the mnemonic **FANBOYS** (for, and, nor, but, or, yet, so)

- Dorothy *stopped, looked* **and then** she went across the road. **Correct:** *Dorothy stopped, looked* **and crossed** *the road.*

Correlative Conjunctions

These conjunctions consist of two or more words that function together. (either/or, neither/nor, both/and, whether/or, not only/but also). Here is a favorite of the test makers.

- *Neither* Janet *or* Brooke made the swimming team. *Remember these conjunctions always go together. Therefore "neither" always goes with "nor" NOT "or".* **Correct:** *Neither Janet nor Brooke made the swimming team.*

Also don't put any extra words between the two things being compared or contrasted. Another way to say this, don't separate the subject and the verb with the conjunction. We make this mistake all the time in speaking so the "non-standard" form will sound perfectly fine to your ear.

- Markus either likes peanut butter or jelly. *Even though we used the proper combination either/or, it is "non-standard" to separate the subject and verb with "either".* **Correct:** *Markus likes either peanut butter or jelly.*

- Jim Bob will not only pass his math class but also his English class. *Again we have the proper combination of <u>Not only/but also</u>. However, we cannot separate the subject and verb.* **Correct:** *Jim Bob will pass not only his math class but also his English class.* **The test makers love to trick you with this issue.**

Subordinating Conjunctions

These conjunctions introduce a subordinate clause, which is a clause that cannot stand by itself as a complete sentence. A subordinating conjunction connects a subordinate clause to an independent clause, which can stand by itself as a complete sentence. **Example:** We will go to the roller coaster *if* we have time.

Comparisons

Than

When comparing things be sure you watch out for faulty parallelism.
- I like competitive dancing better than to jog around the track. *Correct: I like competitive dancing better than jogging around the track.*

Possessives

The test-makers love this little trick. Remember that you compare like things. When using possessives it can get tricky because the "non-standard" form sounds fine to our ear.

- Evan's motivation to succeed in this program seems to be greater than his sister. *This sentence does not sound too bad because we speak this way all the time. However, the rule says we must compare LIKE things. In this case, we are comparing "motivation"-- Evan's motivation with his sister's motivation. We are not comparing Evan's motivation to his sister, we are comparing Evan's motivation with his sister's motivation. Even though we naturally leave off the word "motivation" at the end of the sentence, it's implied and the word 'sister' needs the possessive. Correct: Evan's motivation to succeed in this program seems to be greater than his sister's.*

Sample Question

This century began with <u>war brewing in Europe, the industrial revolution well-established, and a nascent communication age.</u>
- (A)   war brewing in Europe, the industrial revolution well-established, and a nascent communication age.
- (B)   war brewing in Europe, the industrial revolution surging, and a nascent communication age.
- (C)   war in Europe, the industrial revolution well-established, and a nascent communication age.
- (D)   war brewing in Europe, the industrial revolution surging, and the communication age beginning.
- (E)   war brewing in Europe, the industrial revolution well-established, and saw the birth of the communication age.

Explanation

- **(A)** AC (A) is incorrect. Although the first two phrases, *war brewing in Europe* and *the industrial revolution well-established*, have different structures, the thoughts are parallel. However, the third phrase, *and a nascent communication age*, is not parallel to the first two.
- **(B)** Choice (B) does not make the third phrase parallel to the first two.
- **(C)** Choice (C) changes the meaning of the sentence: the new formulation states that war already existed in Europe while the original sentence states that war was only developing.
- **(D)** **Correct Response.** Choice (D) offers three phrases in parallel form. The answer is (D).
- **(E)** AC (E) is not parallel since the first two phrases in the series are noun phrases, but *saw the birth of the communication age* is a verb phrase. When a word introduces a series, each element of the series must agree with the introductory word. You can test the correctness of a phrase in a series by dropping the other phrases and checking whether the remaining phrase agrees with the introductory word. In this series, each phrase must be the object of the preposition *with*:

  This century began *with* <u>war brewing in Europe</u>
  This century began *with* <u>the industrial revolution well-established</u>
  This century began *with* <u>saw the birth of the communication age</u>

  In this form, it is clear the verb *saw* cannot be the object of the preposition *with*.

PowerPrep Practice Questions

Faulty Parallelism Exercise 1

1. An artist knows how to correctly prepare a canvas and getting all the colors balanced.
2. Explain where you were, what you were doing, and your reasons for doing it.
3. Cody's daily workout includes jogging, sprinting, and a visit to the weight room.
4. To give money to the food bank is helping children who might not have enough to eat.
5. Nicole not only plays the violin in the orchestra but also sings in a band.
6. We followed the path over the river, through the woods, and then we went by Old Man Flanagan's farm.
7. The professor was brilliant but a boaster.
8. After the game, we want to either go to the restaurant or to the mall.
9. Joshua's mom told him to take out the trash, to clean the bathroom, and put his clothes in the washer.
10. Lauren prepared for the final exam by meeting with her study group and she also reviewed her textbook.

Answers Exercise 1
1. An artist knows how to correctly prepare a canvas **and (how to) get** all the colors balanced.
2. Explain where you were, what you were doing, **and why you were doing it**.
3. Cody's daily workout includes jogging, sprinting, **and lifting weights**.
4. To give money to the food bank **is to help** children who might not have enough to eat.
5. Nicole **plays not only** the violin in the orchestra but also sings in a band. Not only does "not only" go with "but also", but also you must remember to NOT split the subject and verb--in this case "Nicole plays..." not " "Nicole not only plays..."
6. We followed the path over the river, through the woods, **and by** Old Man Flanagan's farm.
7. The professor was brilliant but **boastful**. parallel adjective, adjective--not adjective, noun.

8. After the game, we want **to go either** to the restaurant or to the mall. **OR** After the game, we **want to go to either** the restaurant or the mall.

9. Joshua's mom told him to take out the trash, to clean the bathroom, and **to put** his clothes in the washer. **OR** Joshua's mom told him to take out the trash, to clean the bathroom, and **to put the** clothes in the washer

10. Lauren prepared for the final exam by meeting with her study group and **reviewing** her textbook.

Faulty Parallelism Exercise 2

1. It's always safer to tell the truth than weaving elaborate excuses.
2. For Christmas, Hannah received a Visa gift card, some video games, and she got a new iPod.
3. My big brother tried to scare us on Halloween by showing us a horror movie and he told us a ghost story.
4. The child described Santa Clause as big, happy, and with a beard.
5. To have loved and lost is better than never having loved at all.
6. Thomas loved not only listening to classical music but also to play the guitar.
7. The new computer has a four (4) terabyte hard drive, a 32 inch monitor, and the backup system is included.
8. The gold coins are valuable but a problem to convert to cash.
9. I want neither your sympathy nor do I want your pity.
10. Managing your time well is to be prepared for the future.

Answers Exercise 2

1. It's always safer to tell the truth than **to weave elaborate** excuses.

2. For Christmas, Hannah received a Visa gift card, some video games, **and a new iPod**.

3. My big brother tried to scare us on Halloween by showing us a horror movie and **by telling us** a ghost story. **OR** 3. My big brother tried to scare us on Halloween--**he showed us a horror movie** and he told us a ghost story.

4. The child described Santa Clause as big, happy, **and bearded**. (parallel would be a series of 3 adjectives--not a series of two (2) adjectives (big and happy) and one (1) noun (with a beard).

5. To have loved and lost is better than **never to have** loved at all. (maintains the parallel infinitive form of the verb "to have". *To have* _____ is better than *to have* _____

6. Thomas loved not only listening to classical music but also **playing** the guitar. Can you explain why the following example has problems? Thomas loved listening not only to classical music but also playing the guitar. By placing "not only" after listening it implies that Thomas loved listening to two types of music--classical and one other kind. But we don't have a list of the music Thomas likes. We have two things he likes to do. Therefore, the "not only" must be placed before listening so that Thomas loves "not only listening" but also "playing..."

7. The new computer has a four (4) terabyte hard drive, a 32 inch monitor, **and an included backup system**. (parallel requires a series of three (3) nouns with their adjectives: four terabyte hard drive, 32 inch monitor, included backup system. If we say "backup system is included" the series is no longer parallel because we introduce the verb "is" and break the symmetry.

8. The gold coins are valuable but **problematic** to convert to cash. **OR** 8. The gold coins are valuable but **difficult** to convert to cash. **OR** if you don't like the adjective "problematic you could say: The gold coins are **a good value** but **a problem** to convert to cash. Parallelism requires two adjectives or two nouns, but not one of each. It's either two nouns "a value" and "a problem" or it's two adjectives "valuable" and "problematic/difficult"

9. I want neither your sympathy nor **your pity**. This example leaves the subject and verb alone "I want" but it adds "I want at the end of the sentence again. If you split the subject and verb like this, "I neither want..." then it would be correct to duplicate the "I want" a second time. **Like this:** I neither want your sympathy nor do I want your pity. **This can be tricky stuff. Be sure you understand this concept.**

10. Managing your time well **is preparing** for the future. **OR** Managing your time well **is being prepared** for the future. **OR** To manage your time well **is to be prepared** for the future. **OR** To manage your time well **is to prepare** for the future. All of these examples maintain the symmetry required for parallelism. The more parallel examples are the ones that omit "be or to be" because the verb "to be" is not used in the first phrase "Managing your time well..."

Faulty Parallelism Exercise 3

1. Miranda not only needs nine (9) hours of sleep each night but also a nap each day.
2. The players are learning to catch and hitting.
3. Scott taught his children the importance of freedom, truth, and choosing the right.
4. To apologize is demonstrating humility.
5. Learning about freedom is more important than if I get a new video game.
6. David wants neither to study nor does he want to prepare for the exam.
7. The flower store has hundreds of varieties, amazing long-stem roses, and the prices are low.
8. To turn off lights is showing concern about the environment.
9. The computer is brand new but a problem.
10. Exercising stresses your muscles but is invigorating for your body and mind.

Answers Exercise 3

1. Miranda needs not only nine (9) hours of sleep each night but also a nap each day. **OR** Miranda not only needs nine (9) hours of sleep each night but also needs a nap each day. Remember to keep the subject and verb together "Miranda

needs" not "Miranda not only needs". If you simply must separate the subject and verb, then you also must reuse the verb in the second clause.

2. The players are learning to catch and (to) hit. **OR** The players are learning catching and hitting.

3. Scott taught his children the importance of freedom, truth, **and right choices**. OR Scott taught his children the importance **of being free, learning the truth, and choosing the right**.

4. To apologize is **to demonstrate** humility. **OR Apologizing** is demonstrating humility.

5. Learning about freedom is more important than getting a new video game.

6. David wants neither to study **nor to prepare** for the exam. (this example uses the correct combination of neither/nor and it uses the correct parallel form of the infinitive verb "to study" and "to prepare".

7. The flower store has hundreds of varieties, amazing long-stem roses, and low prices. The un-parallel version of this sentence ends with a verbal clause/phrase "... and the prices are low", however, the other items in the list are nouns modified by adjectives, "hundreds of varieties", "amazing long-stem roses". Therefore, we must convert the clause "...and the prices are low" to a noun with an adjective. **It becomes** "low prices".

8. To turn off lights is to show concern about the environment. **OR** Turning off lights is showing concern about the environment.

9. The computer is brand new but problematic. **OR** It is a brand new computer but a problem. The problem here is matching adjectives with adjectives or nouns with nouns but not mixing nouns and adjectives. "Brand new" is an adjective describing the computer. However, "a problem" is a noun. We want adjective, adjective, therefore, the computer is 'brand new" and "problematic". Both are adjectives. You could also convert them to nouns as in the second example.

10. Exercising stresses your muscles but invigorates your body and mind. **OR** Exercising is stressful for your muscles but is invigorating for your body and mind. We want parallel structures. We either employ two verbs "stresses" and "invigorates" or two adjective verbals "is stressful" and "is invigorating"

Faulty Parallelism Exercise 4 (with correlative conjunctions)

1. My brother not only clears the dishes from the table but he also puts them in the dishwasher.
2. Either people buy new technology to improve their lives or just to show off to their friends.
3. An experienced chef can prepare organic foods that are both delicious and full of nutrients.
4. Not only does a pro snowboarder strive for technical perfection in her routine but also amplitude in the tricks.
5. Jessica is either buying a new Toyota or she will lease a Mercedes for a year.
6. The teacher will allow neither iPods nor will she allow phones in her classroom.
7. The store email guaranteed both 100% satisfaction and it guaranteed next-day delivery.
8. Not only are you beautiful, but also talented.
9. In the Super Bowl either the fans are always screaming for their team or watching the big screen.
10. Benjamin's parent's home not only has a fantastic swimming pool but also an amazing batting cage.

Answers Exercise 4

1. My brother **not only clears** the dishes from the table **but also puts** them in the dishwasher. This is a tricky one. It thoroughly tests your understanding of "not only...but also". Remember these go together without any intruding pronouns. You don't need the extra pronoun "he" between "but" and "also". It's **not** "not only" "but **he** also"...it's simply "not only...but also". Be sure you remember this.

2. People buy new technology **either to improve** their lives **or just to show off** to their friends. First, remember that "either always goes with or"...it's "either or" and "neither nor". Next, it's typically best to place "either" as close to phrase it's modifying. In this case we split up the phrase from "Either" with the phrase "people buy new technology". The better approach is given above: People buy new technology for two purposes, either this or that. However, if you simply must start the sentence with "Either", then you must remember to repeat the verb in the second phrase, **like this**: **Either people buy** new technology to improve their lives **or they buy it** to just show off to their friends.

3. An experienced chef can prepare organic foods that are **both delicious and nutritious**. This sentence pairs an adjective "delicious" with a noun "nutrients". We have to choose all nouns or all adjectives to make the sentence parallel. The first fix uses adjectives. You can also fix it with nouns, **like this:** An experienced chef can prepare organic foods that are **both full of delicious flavors and packed with nutrition**.

4. A pro snowboarder strives **not only for technical perfection** in her routine **but also for amplitude** with her tricks. **OR Not only does a pro snowboarder strive** for technical perfection in her routine **but also she strives** for amplitude with her tricks. By now you should be familiar with this construction. Remember to keep the subject and verb together. In this case, "A pro snowboarder strives..." then add "not only". However, if you simply must separate the subject and verb, like they did in the sample question, then you must repeat the verb in the second phrase "Not only **strives** but also **strives**".

5. Jessica is **either buying** a new Toyota **or leasing** a Mercedes for a year. **OR Either Jessica is buying** a new Toyota, **or she is leasing** a Mercedes for a year. In the first example we fixed the sentence by using parallel participle forms "either buying" "or leasing". In the second method we fixed the sentence by keeping things parallel "Either is buying" "or she is leasing". You can make the sentence parallel using either method. In fact there are other ways to make this sentence parallel, but on the exam you will simply have to recognize the mistake and/or select a valid fix from a list. You will not have to write your own suggested fix.

6. The teacher will allow **neither iPods nor phones** in her classroom. **OR** The teacher **neither will allow** iPods **nor will she allow** phones in her classroom. First, we've maintained the proper relationship with neither/nor. Remember it's

NOT neither/or. Next, in the first fix, we placed "neither" close to the first item in the list "iPods"--we also maintained the subject and verb relationship and did not split them apart "the teacher will allow..." However, we split the subject and verb with neither. This means we must repeat the verb in the second phrase, "neither will allow..." and "nor will she allow..."

7. The store email guaranteed **both 100% satisfaction and next-day delivery**. In this situation you do not have to repeat the verb in the second phrase--that would be redundant.   Remember to put "both" next to the first item in the list of two and "and" next to the second item.

8. You are **not only beautiful but also talented**. OR **Not only are you** beautiful, **but also you are** talented. When you start a sentence with "Not only" or if you split the subject and verb (Not only are you ...) or (You not only are...) then you must either repeat the verb in the second phrase or you must move the subject and verb together and place "not only" next to the first item, like this: ...not only beautiful but also talented. **OR** you not only are beautiful, but you are also talented.

9. In the Super Bowl, the fans are always **either screaming** for their team **or watching** the big screen. OR In the Super Bowl, **either the fans are always screaming** for their team **or they are (always) watching** the big screen.

 10. Benjamin's parent's home has **not only a fantastic swimming pool but also an amazing batting cage.** **OR** Benjamin's parent's home **not only has a fantastic swimming pool but also has an amazing batting cage.**

Grammar Study Guide
Part 7: Faulty Verb Tense

Virtual Classroom>Grammar Study Guide>Faulty Verb Tense

This material corresponds to the Virtual Classroom Instructions in the
PowerPrep DVD/Internet/iApp for English Grammar

Virtual Classroom

Important Abbreviations
These abbreviations are used throughout the program

POE: Process of Elimination
SARR: Synthesize, Analyze, Reduce, and Restate (has to do with Logical Reasoning)
AC: Answer Choice
QS: Question Stem
LOD: Level of Difficulty

Example Question: What is the least common multiple of 3, 4, and 7? **(This is the call of the question or Question Stem "QS")**

These are Answer Choices "AC" A, B, C, D, E
    (A)   12
    (B)   21
    (C)   28
    (D)   48
    (E)   84

Part 7: Verb Tense

A verb has four principal parts:

1. Present Tense

It's used to express present tense. *Example*: *He studies hard.*
It's used to express general truths. *Example*: *During a recession, people are cautious about taking on more debt.*
It's used with *will* or *shall* to express future time. *Example*: *He will take the ACT next year.*

2. Past Tense

It's used to express past tense. *Example*: *He took the SAT last year.*

3. Past Participle

It's used to form the *present perfect tense*, which indicates that an action was started in the past and its effects are continuing in the present. It is formed using *have* or *has* and the past participle of the verb. *Example*: *He has prepared thoroughly for the exam.*

It's used to form the *past perfect tense*, which indicates that an action was completed before another past action. It is formed using *had* and the past participle of the verb.
Example: *He had prepared thoroughly before taking the SAT.*

It's used to form the *future perfect tense*, which indicates that an action will be completed before another future action. It is formed using *will have* or *shall have* and the past participle of the verb.
Example: *He will have prepared thoroughly before taking the SAT.*

4. Present Participle (*-ing* form of the verb)

The present participle forms the *present progressive tense*, which indicates that an action is ongoing. It is formed using *is*, *am*, or *are* and the present participle of the verb.
Example: *He is preparing thoroughly for the ACT.*

It's also used to form the *past progressive tense*, which indicates that an action was in progress in the past. It is formed using *was* or *were* and the present participle of the verb.
Example: *He was preparing for the ACT test.*

Also used to form the *future progressive tense*, which indicates that an action will be in progress in the future. It is formed using *will be* or *shall be* and the present participle of the verb.
Example: *He will be preparing thoroughly for the ACT.*

Passive & Active Voice

The passive voice removes the subject from the sentence. It is formed with the verb *to be* and the past participle of the main verb.

<u>Passive</u>: The bill was resubmitted.   <u>Active</u>: The Senator resubmitted the bill.
Unless you want to de-emphasize the doer of an action, you should favor the active voice.

<u>Sample Question</u>

In the past few years and to this day, many teachers of math and science <u>had chosen to return to the private sector.</u>
   (A)   had chosen to return to the private sector.
   (B)   having chosen to return to the private sector.
   (C)   chose to return to the private sector.
   (D)   have chosen to return to the private sector.
   (E)   have chosen returning to the private sector.

<u>Explanation:</u>

(A) Choice (A) is incorrect because it uses the past perfect *had chosen*, which describes an event that has been completed before another event. But the sentence implies that teachers have and are continuing to return to the private sector. Hence, the present perfect tense should be used.
(B) AC (B) is incorrect because it uses the present progressive tense *having chosen*, which describes an ongoing event. Although this is the case, it does not capture the fact that the event began in the past.
(C) Choice (C) is incorrect because it uses the simple past *chose*, which describes a past event. But again, the sentence implies that the teachers are continuing to opt for the private sector.
(D) Correct Response. Choice (D) is the correct answer because it uses the present perfect *have chosen* to describe an event that occurred in the past and is continuing into the present.
(E) Choice (E) is incorrect because it leaves the thought in the sentence uncompleted.

Grammar Study Guide
Part 8: Confusing Words

Virtual Classroom>Grammar Study Guide>Idiom & Usage

This material corresponds to the Virtual Classroom Instructions in the
PowerPrep DVD/Internet/iApp for English Grammar

Virtual Classroom

Important Abbreviations
These abbreviations are used throughout the program

POE: Process of Elimination
SARR: Synthesize, Analyze, Reduce, and Restate (has to do with Logical Reasoning)
AC: Answer Choice
QS: Question Stem
LOD: Level of Difficulty

Example Question: What is the least common multiple of 3, 4, and 7? **(This is the call of the question or Question Stem "QS")**

These are Answer Choices "AC" A, B, C, D, E
    (A)   12
    (B)   21
    (C)   28
    (D)   48
    (E)   84

Part 8: Usage

Arguments over grammar and style are often as fierce as those over IBM versus Mac, and as fruitless as Coke versus Pepsi and boxers versus briefs- Jack Lynch

"I am" is reportedly the shortest sentence in the English language. Could it be that "I do" is the longest sentence? George Carlin

Examples

A, An

'A' and *'an'* are called **indefinite** articles while *'The'* is a **definite** article. *"a"* and *"an"* don't say anything specific about the word that follows. For example, "I smell a rat." You smell the general odor of a rat...not a specific rat named Horace...just a rat. But if you say, "I smell the rat," that refers to a specific rat. That's why *the* is called a definite article—and *'a'* and *'an'* are referred to as indefinite articles. Now we'll look at when to use *'a'* and *'an'*.

Rule: use *'a'* before words that start with a consonant <u>sound</u> and *'an'* before words that start with a vowel <u>sound</u>.

'h and u words' sometimes start with vowel sounds and sometimes they start with consonant sounds. **'h words'**, it is *'a' historic monument** because *historic* starts with an h sound, but it is *'an' honorary degree* because *honorary* starts with an o sound. Also, *'an' hour* is correct, because *hour* starts with a vowel sound. **'u words'**, it is *'a utility'* man, but *'an' unambiguous* statement

'o and m words' usually put *an* before words that start with *o*, but sometimes you use *a*. **'o words'** "This is a one-time offer...," because *one-time* starts with a *w* sound. But you would also say 'This is *an* offer you cannot refuse." **'m words'**, "I wish I had *an* MBA, but it would be *a* monumental task."

Remember it is the sound that governs whether you use *'a'* or *'an'*, not the actual first letter of the word.

"A" goes before all words that begin with consonants.

- **a** pig
- **a** grapefruit
- **a** fried zucchini
- **a** dinosaur
- **a** fat cat

With one exception: Use **"an"** before h words when the 'h' is silent. This part of the rule is demonstrated by the word "herb". In American English we don't pronounce the 'h', so it's spoken as 'erb' which sounds like a vowel which becomes "an herb". But English spoken in Great Brittan pronounces the 'h' and says 'herb' like the man's name. In this case it would become 'a herb'. American English "an erb" in England "a herb".

- **an** honorable judge
- **an** honest mistake (but it's 'a horrible mistake')
- an herb (see above)

"An" goes before all words that begin with vowels:

- **an** apple
- **an** indolent lazy freshman
- **an** icon
- **an** orange blanket
- **an** uproariously good time
- **an** untied shoe
- **an** offer

With two exceptions: When u makes the same sound as the y in you, or o makes the same sound as w in won, then **a** is used.

- **a** used car
- **a** united front
- **a** unicorn
- **a** union of students
- **a** U.S. dollar bill
- **a** once in a lifetime opportunity

Note: Whether you use 'a' or 'an' is based sound of the first letter/syllable in a word. If the first letter makes a vowel-type sound, you use "an"; if the first letter makes a consonant sound, use "a." If you remember this rule, there aren't any exceptions.

Accept vs. Except

accept and *except* get confused because of similar spelling and pronunciation. But their meanings are more or less opposites. In the majority of situations, when you want to use a verb, that verb is *accept*. *Except* is rarely used as a verb.

Accept: means "to agree to" or "to receive." We will *accept* (receive) your manuscript for review.

Accept is a verb that means "to receive, admit, regard as true, say yes." The noun acceptance refers to the "act or process of accepting, approval, or agreement."
- I can't **accept** your explanation.
- He was **accepted** to Stanford.
- Do you **accept** the theory of evolution?
- The students immediately **accepted** a ride to the theaters.

Except: means "to object to" or "to leave out." No parking is allowed, except (leave out) on holidays.
Except is a preposition that means "excluding." The noun exception means "exclusion" or "one that is excepted."
- The new student went to every class **except** math.
- The new student learned all his teacher's names **except** his math teacher.

Except is also a conjunction that means "if not for the fact that" or "other than."
- I would love to go to the dance with you **except** my parents won't let me.
- He never calls me **except** to borrow money.

Except is a fairly uncommon verb that means "to leave out, exclude."
- I hate all lawyers, present company excepted.
- All students must show ID--those who personally know the principle are **excepted**.

Account for

When explaining something, the correct idiom is account for. We had to account for all the missing money. When receiving blame or credit, the correct idiom is account to. You will have to account to the state for your crimes.

Adapted to vs. Adapted for vs. Adapted from

Adapted to means "naturally suited for." The polar bear is adapted to the subzero temperatures.
Adapted for means "created to be suited for." For any "New Order" to be successful, it must be adapted for the continually changing world power structure.
Adapted from means "changed to be suited for." Lucas' latest film is **adapted** from a 1950 B-movie "Attack of the Amazons."

Questions
1. Please (**accept, except**) our invitation to attend the birthday party.
2. Everybody (**accept, except**) all my brothers was paying attention to the pastor.
3. I find it difficult to (**accept, except**) the idea that we are over $65 trillion dollars in debt.
4. My sister just got (**accepted, excepted**) to Stanford University.
5. (**Accept, Except**) for weekends, I study every day.
6. The word "**accept**" is which part of speech?
7. The word "**except**" is which part of speech?
8. The team (**accepted, excepted**) the results of the tournament committee.
9. Every one of my friends (**accept, except**) Joshua has parents that are divorced.
10. Many senators routinely (**accept, except**) bribes from powerful private constituents.

Answers: 1. accept, 2. except, 3. accept, 4. accepted, 5. except 6. verb, 7. preposition, 8. accepted, 9. except, 10. accept

Advice vs. Advise

advice is a noun that means "guidance."
advise is a verb that means to "recommend" or "counsel."
- My coach **advised** me work out more over the summer. I should have followed her **advice**.

Questions
1. (**Advice/Advise**) after injury is like medicine after death.
2. I (**advice/advise**) you to bring an umbrella today because it's going to rain.
3. My (**advice/advise**) to my brother is to study his algebra every night--if you get behind good luck!
4. My friend will always give me (**advice/advise**) even if she has no idea.
5. My math tutor can (**advice/advise**) me whether I should take trigonometry next semester.
6. I would (**advice/advise**) anyone in the honors program to read all the assigned books over the summer.
7. If you take my (**advice/advise**) you will read all the assigned books.

Answers: 1. Advice, 2. advise, 3. advice, 4. advice 5. advise, 6. advise, 7. advice

Adverse vs Averse

Adverse (adj.) means antagonistic, opposing, harmful, hostile or unfavorable. We're most often adverse to actions, events, and things (which we most frequently describe as adverse or designate as adverse forms or adversities).
- During wintertime we typically see **adverse** weather conditions that affect driving.
- We all experience **adverse** situations in our lives and it's typically during those times that we mature.

Averse (adj.) (uh-**vurs**) strongly disinclined, unwilling or loath. having a strong feeling of opposition, antipathy, repugnance, etc.; opposed: He is not averse to having a drink now and then. Most often, it refers to people and it used as someone being '**averse to**' something. We're averse to (rarely from) things and people we dislike, but we almost never speak of an averse thing or person.
- Are you **averse to** studying during the Christmas break?
- Most students are **averse to** anything that might shorten their lunch period.

In summary, *adverse* and *averse* are only synonymous when used of persons and with *to*. *Adverse* is most often used as an attributive adjective and of things; *averse* is extremely rare as an attributive and is regularly used of persons. When used with *to* and of persons a subtle distinction can be drawn, but it is not universally observed, and in negative contexts it is hard to make out whether the distinction is being observed or ignored. Our evidence suggests *averse to* is more frequently used than *adverse to*. *(Merriam-Webster's Concise Dictionary of English Usage,* Merriam-Webster, 2002)

Questions

1. She had an *(adverse/averse)* reaction to the medication.
2. They experienced *(adverse/averse)* weather conditions.
3. He is *(adverse/averse)* to a military draft.
4. Live as brave men; and if fortune is *(adverse/averse)*, front its blows with brave hearts." (Marcus Tullius Cicero)
5. I am very *(adverse/averse)* to bringing myself forward in print." (Mary Wollstonecraft Shelley)
6. I didn't like the play, but then I saw it under *(adverse/averse)* conditions: the curtain was up." (Groucho Marx)
7. Reclusive in recent years, he was not always *(adverse/averse)* to publicity, posing naked for a perfume ad in 1971.

Answers: 1. adverse, 2. adverse, 3. averse, 4. adverse, 5. averse, 6. adverse, 7. averse

Affect vs. Effect

Affect is a verb meaning "to influence."   The rain *affected* their plans for a picnic.
Effect is a noun meaning "a result."   Increased fighting will be the *effect* of the failed peace conference.

That's it, don't overcomplicate it. The majority of the time you use **affect** it's a verb and **effect** is a noun. Here is some more information that might be useful, but don't lose sight of the straightforward and basic rule: Affect is a verb and Effect is the noun. There are some rare exceptions, but keep that rule in mind and you'll get it right 95% of the time.
- It's hard to say how the price of gold will **affect** the economy in the long run.
- It's hard to say what **effect** the rising price of gold will have on the world economy.
- Not doing your home work will **affect** your grade.
- One **effect** of not doing your home work is a failing grade.

Affect (usually a verb)
1. To have an influence on or effect a change in: *Inflation affects (verb) the buying power of the dollar.*
2. To act on the emotions of; touch or move.
3. To attack or infect, as a disease: *Rheumatic fever can affect the heart.*

Effect (usually a noun)
1. It can also be used as a verb, meaning to bring about, as in her actions **effected** a change in the situation. 'The student wanted to **effect** changes in the school'
2. The power to produce an outcome or achieve a result; influence: *The drug had an immediate* **effect** *(noun) on the pain. The government's action had no* **effect** *(noun) on the trade imbalance.*
3. A scientific law, hypothesis, or phenomenon: *the photovoltaic* **effect** *(noun).*
4. Advantage; avail: *used her words to great* **effect** *(noun) in influencing the jury.*
5. The condition of being in full force or execution: *a new regulation that goes into* **effect** *tomorrow.*
6. Something that produces a specific impression or supports a general design or intention: *The lighting* **effects** *(noun) emphasized the harsh atmosphere of the drama.*
7. A particular impression: *large windows that gave an* **effect** *(noun) of spaciousness.*
8. Production of a desired impression: *spent lavishly on dinner just for* **effect**.
9. The basic or general meaning; import: *He said he was greatly worried, or words to that* **effect**.

Remember 'to affect' is a verb and 'effect' is a noun:
Z *impacts* or *affects* **Y**. To affect(v.) is the *action*; but the *end* result is an *effect(n.)*
So if Z *impacts* or *affects(v.)* Y, it has an *impact or effect(n.)* on Y.
So remember: *Affect* is a verb and *Effect* is a noun--I *affect* (v.) you which means I have an *effect(n.)* on you. **affect,** a verb "<u>produces</u> a change," **effect,** a noun, <u>**is**</u> the "change" or "result."

Remember to effect(v.) can be used as a verb: *To effect* means to bring about or to cause or to achieve. 'His last second changes *affected*(v.) the original plan. But the *effect*(n.) was that he *effected*(v.) the plan without a hitch.'

Questions

1. The *(affect, effect)* of studying all weekend and focusing intently on the exam was a high grade.
2. The extra study *(affected, effected)* my grade in a positive direction.
3. My new iPod and the classical music I listen to *(affects, effects)* my mood and makes me feel happier.
4. Classical music has an extreme *(affect, effect)* on my emotions--it touches me deeply.
5. Using marijuana can have severe negative *(affects, effects)* on your level of energy.
6. Scientists continue to study the *(affects/effects)* of loud music on teenagers.
7. But the warnings about loud music have not *(affected/effected)* the sales of iPods and other MP3 players.
8. Interdependence is a natural *(affect, effect)* of trade. Debt *(affects/effects)* interdependent countries.
9. Many people believe that new research and findings might *(affect, effect)* the old theory of macro evolution.
10. How will this quiz *(affect, effect)* my grade?
11. The quiz had a bad *(affect, effect)* on my grade.
12. The decisions had far reaching *(affects/effects)*.
13. The new class president *(affected/effected)* a number of changes.

14. Too many bean burritos had a sudden *(affect, effect)* requiring a trip to the little boys room.
15. His emotional outburst had no *(affect, effect)* on his parents.
16. It takes years of intense preparations to bring such a plan into *(affect, effect)*.
17. She was upset about the changes and sent an email to that *(affect, effect)*.
18. Her tattoos, cornrows, and piercings were only for *(affect, effect)*.
19. New televisions come with the ability to display a three-dimensional *(affect, effect)*.
20. Scientists continue to study the Doppler *(affect, effect)*.
21. Movies continue to expand and improve their ability to create special *(affects, effects)*.
22. The new offensive coordinator finally *(affected/effected)* the changes to the play book.
23. His silence was in *(affect, effect)* a confirmation of the rumor.
24. The exit strategy is now in *(affect, effect)*.
25. The medicine was slow to take *(affect, effect)*.

Answers: *1. effect, 2. affected, 3. affects, 4. affect, 5. effects, 6. effects, 7. affected, 8. effect, affects, 9. affect, 10. affect, 11. effect, 12. effects, 13. effected, 14. effect, 15. effect, 16. effect, 17. effect, 18. effect, 19. effect, 20. effect, 21. effects, 22. effected, 23. effect, 24. effect, 25. effect*

Afterward(s)/ Afterword(s)

Be careful here. The difference is the last part of the word. AfterWARD(s) vs. AfterWORD(s). The difference is "WARD" vs. "WORD". These are two very different words.

Afterward or Afterwards: An adverb that means: at a later time; subsequently. "towards," "forwards," and "homewards,". Adding an 's' to the end of the word "afterwards" does not change the meaning.

Afterword(s) is a completely different word: it's a noun that means 'epilogue'. Adding an 's' just makes it plural. 'Afterwords' are sometimes the explanatory essays at the ends of books or speeches uttered at the end of plays or other works. A short addition or concluding section at the end of a literary work, often dealing with the future of its characters. Also called *epilogue*. They are made up of *words*.
- **Wrong**: Let's go to dinner and then *afterwords* let's go to a movie.
- **Correct**: Let's go to dinner and then *afterwards* let's go to a movie.
- **Wrong**: My favorite spy novel came out last week and the *afterward* hints that Mitch Rapp might die.
- **Correct**: My favorite spy novel came out last week and the *afterword* hints that Mitch Rapp might die.

Aggravate, irritate

Aggravate mean "to make worse." The root is *grave,* meaning "serious." Remember the root when spelling the word.
Irritate means "to exasperate" or "to inflame" or "to annoy."
- I try to be patient with Charles, but his loud laugh *irritates* me. • Since grief only *aggravates* your loss, grieve not for what is past.

Incorrect: His teasing *aggravated* me.
Correct: His teasing *irritated* me.
Incorrect: That meal *irritated* my condition.
Correct: That meal *aggravated* my condition.

Ago vs. Since

Both words speak of the past, and they are often used interchangeably.
Ago - from the present to the past. It is used after the word or phrase it modifies, especially with the simple past tense, not with the perfect tense.
- A few minutes *ago* we were in the cafeteria eating burritos.
Since - from the past to the present. It is used with the present or past perfect tense.
- I haven't eaten *since* I had those burritos for lunch.

Ain't

Ain't is a colloquialism and a contraction originally used for "am not", but also used for "is not", "are not", "has not", or "have not" in the common vernacular. In some dialects it is also used as a contraction of "do not", "does not", and "did not" (e.g. *I ain't know that*). The word is a perennial issue in English usage. It is a word that is widely used by many people, but its use is commonly considered to be improper.
Bottom line: DONOT use Ain't for any reason on the exam. It's considered non-standard.

All ready vs. Already

All ready means "everything is ready or prepared."
Already means "earlier or previously" or by now," "even now," or "by then."
- Penelope and Shawndra are *all ready* (prepared) to study; in fact, they *already* (previously) left for the library.
- We were *all ready* (prepared) for school but we missed our ride because dad *already* (previously) left.
- The order had "*already*" (previously) been shipped.
- The order is "*all ready*" (all prepared) to be shipped.

Questions
1. My friends were *(all ready, already)* to go to the mall when it started to snow and block the roads.
2. I asked my dad if he would take us to the mall, he said he was *(all ready, already)* planning to go.
3. I was *(all ready, already)* to attend a local JC when I was offered a scholarship to Stanford University.
4. For Christmas I had *(all ready, already)* received two sweaters when I opened my grandparent's gift--another sweater.
5. Even though I had *(all ready, already)* finished my Saturday chores, my parents wanted me to wash the car too.

Answers: 1. all ready, 2. already, 3. all ready, 4. already, 5. already

All right vs. alright

"*alright*" (one word) is a misspelling of "**all right**" (two words), which means "adequate," "permissible," or "satisfactory." "His singing was just all right" or "Is it all right if I wait outside?"

For the exam, use "all right" as two words, and stay away from "alright" as one word. There is some further discussion among grammarians, but we are only concerned about the exam.

Alot vs. A lot vs. Allot

Alot is nonstandard. Alot is not a word in the English language and therefore should not to be used.

A lot is the correct form and is an informal phrase meaning a large portion or large quantity of something. "I spend a lot of time studying for the exams."

Allot is a verb that means to distribute or to assign a portion to. "The teacher allotted 20 minutes for the test."

Questions

1. It takes (*allot, a lot*) of humility and strength to admit when you're wrong and ask forgiveness.
2. If you were shipwrecked would you (*allot, a lot*) more food to the teenager or to the grandparent?
3. My grandfather purchased (*allot, a lot*) on the beach 75 years ago--it's now worth over $5,000,000.
4. The casino will usually (*allot, a lot*) several high-end suites for its high-roller guests.
5. It always takes (*allot, a lot*) more time and energy when you cram for an exam.

Answers: 1. a lot, 2. allot, 3. a lot, 4. allot, 5. a lot

Altogether, all together

All together means "collectively"; everyone is doing something all at once or all in one place, as in "We read the Declaration of Independence all together in history class. You can also break up this two-word like this: "We all read the Declaration of Independence together in history class."

Altogether as one word, means "entirely," as in "He ate altogether too many burgers." "He was altogether out of his league." You can't do the separation trick here.

Questions

1. The entire team decided (*all together, altogether*) to elect their captain for the new season.
2. March is (*all together, altogether*) too late in the year to be shoveling snow from your sidewalk.
3. The cheer squad voted (*all together, altogether*) to attend a summer cheer camp.
4. Chocolate fudge ice cream with whipped cream and strawberries is (*all together, altogether*) too delicious.
5. With only 30 seconds left in the state championship football team, Marcus pulled his teammates (*all together, altogether*), and told them they could score on the next play.

Answers: 1. all together, 2. altogether, 3. all together, 4. altogether, 5. all together

Allude vs. Elude

Allude (v.) means 'to refer to indirectly'. The verbs 'to allude' and 'to mention' are close in meaning, but 'to allude' is less direct. It can be translated as 'to hint at' or 'to offer an indication about'.

Elude (v.) means 'to avoid', 'to evade' or 'to escape from'.

• Some passages in the New testament **allude** to incidents and prophecies in the Old Testament, but the meaning of this particular passage **eludes** me.

• This Chinese saying alludes to nature's power: "A spark can start a fire that burns the entire prairie." (The saying does not mention nature's power, but it offers a clue about nature's power. The saying **alludes** to nature's power.)

Questions

1. "Forewarned is forearmed" (*alludes/eludes*) to the importance of being in control.
2. The teacher did not mention the answers specifically, but he (*alluded/eluded*) to them in his review.
3. Butch Cassidy and the Sundance Kid tried to (*allude/elude*) capture.
4. Ice hockey players do their best to (*allude/elude*) the defenders with strong and sometimes tricky skating.
5. In last night's speech, the president (*alluded/eluded*) to his belief that we must cut government spending without ever directly saying it.
6. With the advent of 'instant replay' in professional sports nothing important should ever (*allude/elude*) officials.
7. After escaping from prison, he spent six months on the lamb (*alluding/eluding*) the authorities.
8. The network news anchor (*alluded/eluded*) to her political and ideological beliefs but would never come straight out and disclose them.
9. Her letter (*alludes/eludes*) to terrible wrongdoing but she tries to (*allude/elude*) responsibility for her actions.
10. He used offshore bank accounts and (*alluded/eluded*) discovery of millions of dollars.

Answers: 1.alludes, 2. alluded, 3. elude, 4. elude, 5. alluded, 6. elude, 7. eluding, 8. alluded, 9. alludes, elude, 10. eluded

Allusive vs. Elusive

See "allude and Elude" above because 'allusive and elusive' are just the adjective forms of 'allude' and 'elude'. Something that is *allusive* contains (or is characterized by) indirect references. Someone or something that is *elusive* is hard to describe or skillful at avoiding capture. The logic is the same. *See Allude & Elude.*

• Merdine called attention to the biblically **allusive** title of the White Stripes' CD *Get Behind Me Satan*. The lyrics to some of their songs are fragmented, mysterious, and **elusive**.

Questions
1. Bob Lind sang about "the bright *(allusive/elusive)* butterfly of love."
2. The book's *(allusive/elusive)* title, *Bound Upon a Wheel of Fire*, is from a line in Shakespeare's *King Lear*.

Answers: 1. elusive, 2. allusive

Allusion vs Illusion

Allusion: The noun allusion denotes a subtle or indirect reference to something (i.e., a hint at something). It derives from the verb *to allude*.
Illusion: An illusion is a false impression or deception. Magicians can perform illusions. Getting something for nothing in live is an illusion--it is illusory.

Questions
1. By the end of the long race, we were deceived by an *(allusion, illusion)* that there was a cooler of
2. Chris made a thoughtless *(allusion, illusion)* to the dustiness of their house, and Kay's feelings were hurt.
3. Mark tried to make his point by *(alluding, illuding)* to an empty nest to communicate his wish to leave the relationship.
4. The *(allusion, illusion)* that he would survive alone, without his wife of twenty-five years gave her a few chuckles of relief.
5. The Simpsons is full of *(allusions/illusions)* to well-known films.
6. I am under no *(allusion/illusion)* how much work is required.
7. It's not an oasis - it is an *(allusion/illusion)*.
8. His consistent *(allusions/illusions)* to being poor as a child are not in keeping with his brother's version of their childhood.

Answers: 1. illusion, 2. allusion, 3. alluding, 4. illusion, 5. allusions, 6. illusion, 7. illusion, 8. allusions

Alright vs. All right

Alright **Not Widely Accepted** Many people use 'alright' unaware that it is not widely accepted. It should be written 'all right'. However, the merger of 'all right' to 'alright' has been underway for over a century, and it is becoming more acceptable. Mergers such as 'altogether' and 'already' are fully acceptable. They are far older than 'alright'.
It's Not Right and It's Not Wrong: Interestingly, the Microsoft spellchecker will not highlight 'alright' as an error, but it will also not suggest 'alright' if you spell it incorrectly. Microsoft is sitting on the fence with regard to 'alright' being accepted as standard.
On the exam DON"T use alright--if given the choice, use "ALL RIGHT"

Altar vs. Alter

Altar (n.): It denotes an area (usually a table) where religious worship or sacrifice occurs.
Alter (v.): 'To alter' is a verb meaning to change something.
  • The ancient Britons used to sacrifice animals on elaborate stone *altars*. • Will you *alter* this dress for Saturday's play?

Questions:
1. We were married at the *(altar/alter)* in St Paul's Cathedral.
2. Please *(altar/alter)* your tone of voice.
3. Have you seen the *(altar/alter)* where Princess Di was married?
4. Moses sacrificed animals at the *(altar/alter)* inside the temple.
5. If you don't *(altar/alter)* those ski boots you're going to have massive blisters by the end of the day.
6. After you *(altar/alter)* the dress we will kneel at the *(altar/alter)* and be married.
7. I have a tailor who *(altars/alters)* all my clothes.
8. The *(alterations/altarations)* were perfect!
9. I'll text you if anything comes up and I have to *(altar/alter)* our date this weekend.
10. As they kneeled across from each other at the *(altar/alter)* he reached out and held her hand.
11. The minister stood at the *(altar/alter)* to conduct the wedding ceremony.

Answers: 1. altar, 2. alter, 3. altar, 4. altar, 5. Alter, 6. alter, altar, 7. alters, 8. alterations, 9. alter, 10. altar, 11. altar

Among vs. Between

Between should be used when referring to two things only, and
Among should be used when referring to more than two things.
  • The young lady must choose *between* the two boys who both asked her to the dance.
  • I don't have a favorite *among* all the songs on my iPod.
Note: This is a simply and clear rule but students get it wrong all the time and it's heavily tested. Be sure you memorize this rule and apply it correctly on the exam.

Questions:
1. *(Among/Between)* lunch and PE, I prefer lunch.
2. *(Among/Between)* all of the songs on my iPod, I like 70's rock songs the best.
3. I run my best races when I'm *(among/between)* a group of fast runners.
4. *(Among/Between)* you and me, I know who likes you.
5. Who *(among, between)* all of the athletes at the Olympics would win the gold medals?

Answers: 1. between, 2. among, 3. among, 4. between, 5. among

Amoral vs. Immoral

Amoral (adj.): means lying outside the moral order or **acting without morals** or regard for any particular code of morality. It means 'not related to morality'. It pertains to the noun amorality. Amorality is a state in which the concept of right and wrong is invalid--it does not exist.

Immoral (adj.): means *not* moral--that is, **violating** traditionally held moral principles--'not adhering to moral principles' (i.e., deliberately breaking the rules of right and wrong).

- Robert Greene's book *The 48 Laws of Power* is a coldly ***amoral*** compilation of rules for winning life's wars.
- About morals, I know only that what is moral is what you feel good after and what is ***immoral*** is what you feel bad after." (Ernest Hemingway)

Questions:
1. Her new play examines society's *(amoral/immoral)* fascination with technological progress for its own sake.
2. All the things I really like to do are either *(amoral/immoral)* illegal, or fattening." (Alexander Woollcott)

Answers: 1. amoral, 2. immoral

Amount vs. number

Amount refers to the quantity of something that cannot be counted in individual units (flour, money). **Number** refers to something that can be counted in individual units (boxes of flour, dollars).

This is another heavily tested area that native speakers mess up all the time. So learn the rule and get the points. *Amount* relates to quantities of things that are measured in bulk; *number* to things that can be counted.
Don't over think this issue and wonder if you can count the grains of salt-- we refer to the overall **amount** of salt. We could measure the **number** of cups of water, but we refer to the **amount** of water.

In addition, there are other **amounts** or **numbers** words. If the thing being measured is being considered in countable units, then use *number* words.
- You eat ***fewer*** cookies, but you drink ***less*** milk. ∙ If you eat too ***many*** tacos, you won't have room for ***much*** more food. ∙
  You shouldn't drink too ***much*** milk, but you should also avoid drinking too ***many*** glasses of milk.
The most common mistake of this kind is to refer to an "amount" of people instead of a *"number"* of people.

Just to confuse things, "more" can be used either way: you can eat **more** cookies *and* drink **more** milk.
Exceptions to the less/fewer pattern are references to units of time and money, which are usually treated as amounts: less than an hour, less than five dollars. Only when you are referring to specific coins or bills would you use fewer: "I have fewer than five state quarters to go to make my collection complete."

Amount words: amount, quantity, little, less, much   **Number words**: number, few, fewer, many
- The *amount* of help we received was unprecedented.   • The *number* of people who helped was unprecedented.

As you can see, it's often quite simple to switch between describing things in terms of amounts and numbers, but one form usually sounds better and/or makes more intuitive sense

Questions:
1. The (**amount/number**) of food served in the school cafeteria is staggering.
2. The (amount/**number** of hamburgers severed in the school cafeteria is staggering.
3. I have (few/**little** recourse.
4. I have (**few/less**) alternatives.
5. Every year Americans are able to keep (**less/few**) money after taxes than the year before.
6. Every year Americans are able to keep (lesser/**fewer**) dollars after taxes than the year before
7. Americans waste way too (**much/many**) time preparing their tax returns each year.
8. Americans waste way too (much/**many**) hours preparing their tax returns each year

Answers: 1. amount, 2. number, 3. (amount--little), 4. (number-few), 5. (amount--less), 6. (number--fewer), 7. amount--much, 8. (number--many)

Questions
1. The exam had (an amount, a number) of errors.
2. Even though she had a limited (amount, number) of money, she donated (a number, an amount) of dollars.
3. A huge (amount, number) of politicians lie to the public.
4. Electric cars can save a large (amount, number) of money on gasoline.
5. The (amount, number) of hours we had to read the novel was not enough.

Answers: 1. a number, 2. amount, a number, 3. number, 4. amount, 5. number

Anyone vs. Any one

The compound pronouns **anyone** or **everyone** mean "any person" and "all the people," respectively. The non-compound modified pronoun **any one** or **every one** put a greater emphasis on the word **one** and mean "any single person or thing" and "every single person or thing." They are usually followed by a prepositional phrase beginning with the word **of.**
The indefinite pronoun *anyone* refers to people but not to particular individuals. *Any one* is an adjective phrase that refers to specific but unidentified things or individuals. (A similar distinction applies to anybody and any body, nobody and no body.)

*The enemy is **anyone** who's going to get you killed, no matter which side he's on. **Any one** of your buddies, if he's careless enough, could turn out to be your enemy.* (in the first instance 'anyone' means any person you can think of or imagine, but in the second space, 'any one' means any specific person like maybe your buddy...that specific person could be your enemy.)

Questions:

1. Does (*anyone/any one*) know why we have to read chapter 15 tonight for homework?
2. If (*anyone/any one*) of the 25 barons should die, the remaining barons shall choose a replacement.
3. Did (*anyone/any one*) see the concert last night?
4. Did you visit (*anyone/any one*) of the hotels on the list?
5. Is (*everyone/every one*) ready to begin?
6. I answered (*everyone/every one*) of the algebra and geometry questions correctly.
7. *We can bungee jump off (anyone/any one) of the bridges listed in the "Idiots Guide to Bungee Jumping".*
8. *Has (anyone/any one) seen Ferris Bueller... (anyone/any one)?*
9. (*anyone/any one*) can learn to throw a baseball but few can learn to throw a baseball over 90 mph.
10. Can (*anyone/any one*) of you tell me who the fourth president of the United States was? It was James Madison.
11. (*Everybody/Every body*) requires protein, vitamins, and minerals.
12. (*Everybody/ Every body*) is concerned about the economy and the exploding national debt.
13. I wish I could talk to (*everyone/every one*) of the senators and tell them to STOP spending our children's' money.
14. (*Everyone/Every one*) seated at the senator's table has contributed more than $20,000 to her campaign.
15. I don't want to listen to my iPod (*anymore/any more*).
16. I didn't buy (*anymore/any more*) songs this week.
17. Not (*everyone/every one can*) dance like you--it's not easy.
18. However, (*everyone/every one*) of us can take lessons and become better than we were.
19. She doesn't expect (*anyone/any one*) in the class to help her with the assignment.
20. He seems to like (*everybody/every body*) he meets.
21. (*Anyone/Any one*) of you can have the remainder of the day off if you would like.
22. (*Everybody/Every body*) has a similar skeletal system but unique DNA.

Answers: 1. anyone 2. any one 3.anyone 4. any one 5. everyone 6. every one 7. any one 8. anyone, anyone 9. anyone 10. any one 11. Every body 12. everybody 13. every one 14. everyone 15. anymore 16. any more 17. everyone 18. every one 19. anyone 20. everybody 21. Any one 22. Every body

Appraise vs. Apprise

appraise (v.) to evaluate or set a price or value on something--'to assess' or 'to evaluate'.
apprise (v.) to inform or notify someone.
• When one cannot **appraise** out of one's own experience, the temptation to blunder is minimized, but even when one can, appraisal seems chiefly useful as appraisal of the appraiser. Marianne Moore (1887-1972), U.S. poet.
• Teachers should **apprise** their students about every area that will be tested on the exam. (teachers should notify or inform their students about what's going to be on the exam)

Questions:
1. The ability to locate, access, and (*appraise/apprise*) talent is an important skill for a sports agent
2. The police officer's routine is to first, (*appraise/apprise*) the arrested person of his rights.
3. We buy foreclosed properties, which means we have to (*appraise/apprise*) their value correctly.
4. Parents should (*appraise/apprise*) their kids about the Saturday chores.
5. Parents should also (*appraise/apprise*) their kid's work against a known set standard so the kid knows what a good job looks like .
6. Please (*appraise/apprise*) the contestant of our choice for the next person going to Hollywood.
7. The first part of the new year is the perfect time of year to set goals and (*appraise/apprise*) old goals.
8. Many times people will sign contracts without reading them first and then they will claim they were not (*appraised/apprised*) of the consequences of a breach.
9. The committee met to (*appraise/apprise*) senator about the current massive budget shortfall.
10. The inspector (*appraised/apprised*) the damage to the home after the flood.
11. Before the recession a new home (*appraised/apprised*) at $800,000, but now it's only valued at $425,000.
12. If I had fully (*appraised/apprised*) him of situation, I know he would have been upset.

Answers: 1. appraise, 2. apprise, 3. appraise, 4. apprise, 5. appraise (odd usage) 6. apprise 7. appraise, 8. apprised, 9. apprise, 10. appraised, 11. appraised, 12. apprised

Assure, Ensure, Insure

The verbs *assure, ensure,* and *insure* all mean "to make certain or secure." According to *Merriam-Webster's Collegiate Dictionary,* "*insure* sometimes stresses the taking of necessary measures beforehand, and *assure* distinctively implies the removal of doubt and suspense from a person's mind."
In addition, *insure* means "to protect against financial loss," and *assure,* which is almost always used with reference to people, generally means "to promise."
• "Do not worry about your problems with mathematics. I **assure** you mine are far greater." (Albert Einstein)
• The USDA must act to **ensure** safety in school lunch programs.
• She has not been able to **insure** her Bugatti, a valuable old car.

When to Use Insure: *Insure* relates to the buying and selling of insurance. However, people can also use it to mean "to make sure, certain, or secure,". While you can often substitute *insure* for *ensure,* you cannot use "*ensure*" in relation to the insurance industry.
• *My parents **insured** our home against fire but the insurance policy for earthquake was too expensive.*
• ***Insuring** your home and yourself against disaster, disease, or death is always wise.*
• *I remember when I first got **insured**--it was after I was married.*

When to Use Ensure: Anytime you can properly use *Ensure* you could also substituted *insure* as a synonym.
- *When Max heard the car pull into the driveway he started barking because he was **ensured** dinner was on the way.*
- *My job was to **ensure** that we had sufficient snacks for the road trip.*
- *I like to write all my own lecture notes to **ensure** I know precisely what the teacher said.*

You could also use insure in any of the previous sentences without changing the meaning of the sentence. While either way is technically correct, it is important to note again that insure is most frequently associated with the commercial insurance industry and when use that way you <u>cannot</u> substitute ensure for insure.

When to Use Assure: Just like insure and ensure, assure means "to make certain". However, only assure is used "with reference to a person in the sense of 'to set the mind at rest.'"
- *My mom assured my dad that she loved the vacuum he got her for her birthday.*
- *When Max heard the car doors close he began barking because it assured him dinner was on the way.*
- *Even though I studied all night for this exam, I did not feel assured I passed it until I saw the actual score.*
- *A baby needs the loving arms of her mother to feel assured and safe.*

IMPORTANT TIP Even though insure, ensure, and assure have overlapping definitions, they cannot always be used interchangeably. To help you remember when to use each word, keep the following three hints in mind:
• You assure a person. • You insure your car. • You ensure everything else.

IMPORTANT TIP it is okay to swap ensure for insure unless it relates to insurance policies protecting people or property against risks like floods, death, hurricanes, and the like. Assure cannot be used in place of either insure or ensure, and is the only word which should be used to relate to a person's feelings.

Extra Notes
- "Use *ensure* to mean guarantee: *Steps were taken to ensure accuracy.* "Use *insure* for references to insurance: *The policy insures his life.*" (Norm Goldstein, "ensure, insure," *The Associated Press Stylebook*, 2006)
- "A few commentators . . . suggest *assure* for people, *ensure* for things, and *insure* for money and guarantees (insurance). These are nice distinctions, and you can follow them if you want to. . . .

  "The rest of the recommendation rests on using *ensure* for general senses and reserving *insure* for financial senses. This distinction has been urged at least since Fowler 1926, especially by British commentators. It is in general true that *insure* is used for the financial uses (it must vex the British commentators to find *assure* still occasionally used in this sense by British technical writers). However, both *insure* and *ensure* are used in general senses. . . .
- "A person *assures* (makes promises to, convinces) other people . . .; a person *ensures* (makes certain) that things occur or that events take place . (Bryan A. Garner, *Garner's Modern American Usage*, Oxford University Press, 2003)

Questions:
1. It's wise to insure your car against uninsured motorists because lots of people drive without insurance.
2. "In real life, I assure you, there is no such thing as algebra." (Fran Lebowitz)
3. The Federal government claims it needs more money to ensure our country can respond to any disaster.
4. People should use multilayer encryption technology to ensure their electronic communications are secure.
5. My parents insured my cell phone in case I lose it or break it.
6. When summer finally arrives you can be assured I will be at the beach all the time.
7. Assure your mom that you love her--do the dishes!
8. Ensure you'll be able to go out this weekend--do the dishes!

Answers: 1. insure 2. assure 3. ensure 4. "ensure," because Jimmy needed to make certain that his safe was locked. 5. "insure," because it relates to the commercial industry of money and risk taking. 6. "assure," because it eases your mind to know your ex feels worse. 7. "assure," because you are easing your son's mind regarding his abilities. 8. "ensure," because you are making certain your daughter practices her dance routine.

Award vs Reward

Award (n.)(v.) **noun: 1.** a decision, as by a judge or arbitrator. 2. something that is awarded; prize. An award is an honor (such as a medal or trophy) that is conferred for merit, usually after a decision made by a committee of judges. *transitive* **verb: 1.** to give by the decision of a law court or arbitrator (The jury awarded damages to the aggrieved plaintiff.) 2. to give as the result of judging the relative merits of those in competition; grant to award a prize for the best pie.

Award can be a noun or a verb. As a noun, it generally means something that recognizes some sort of achievement. For example, being called an MVP (Most Valuable Player) is an *award* because it recognizes your achievement of being a good player. Other *awards* are the Oscars, Golden Globes, etc. There is some level of competition involved and the highest achiever gets the *award*. *Award* as a verb is much more generalized. It means to present or give something. It could also mean when something is won. For example, "He was *awarded* a scholarship." That would mean not only was he given the scholarship, he earned it over other students.

Reward (n.)(v.) **noun: 1.** something given in return for good or, sometimes, evil, or for service or merit. 2. money offered, as for the capture of a criminal, the return of something lost, etc. 3. compensation; profit
transitive verb: **1.** to give a reward to 2. to give a reward for 3. to serve as a reward to or for

A reward is something (usually money) given in return for a person's service, merit, hardship, etc. It is an exchange for something good that someone has done. For example, posters for missing pets usually offer a monetary *reward*. If you find the pet, the owner will *reward* you or exchange money for your find. The noun and verb have that same connotation of exchanging.

Questions:
1. A/An *(award/reward)* was offered to anyone who can prove that the speed of light is not an absolute limit.
2. My father was *(awarded/rewarded)* the Medal of Honor because he rescued several Marines from a downed Black Hawk gunship.
3. Some slot machines in Las Vegas pay cash *(awards/rewards)* over a million dollars.
4. He studied all summer for the exam and his efforts were *(awarded/rewarded)* with a 98 percentile mark.
5. The Kid's Choice *(Awards/Rewards)* gives teens and pre-teens a chance to pick TV shows and movies they like.

Answers: 1. reward 2. awarded 3. awards 4. rewarded 5. Awards

Bad vs. Badly

Bad is an adjective that means not good or correct in any way. The degrees of badness are expressed by *bad, worse, and worst*. It describes nouns or pronouns. It is often used with descriptive linking verbs like look, feel, sound, or to be.
- **Wrong**: He felt *badly* because he had to cancel our vacation..
- **Correct**: He felt *bad* about canceling the vacation. (*Bad* describes the pronoun *he*.)
- **Wrong**: Things looked *badly* for the Mudville nine.
- **Correct**: Things looked *bad* for the Mudville nine. (*Bad* describes the noun *Things*.)

Badly is an adverb (like well) used to describe how poorly or unsatisfactorily something is done. It describes verbs and should be used with all verbs other than linking verbs. As many adverbs do, it usually answers the question "How?"
- **Wrong**: Mudville played *bad* last night. • **Correct**: Mudville played *badly* last night. (*Badly* describes the verb *played*.)

Exception: I feel badly. To say, "I feel badly," implies that there's something wrong with your sense of touch. When you say, "I feel badly," it means you have trouble using your hands to feel things--same as "I play golf badly" means I'm not very good at playing. *Badly* is an adverb, it modifies a verb. So when you say, "I feel badly," the adverb *badly* modifies the verb *feel*. Since *feel* means "to touch things," feeling badly means you're not very good at touching stuff.
Keep this in mind: you wouldn't say "I feel madly" or "I feel sadly", so don't say "I feel badly" unless you really do have problems with your sense of touch.

More examples: "I smell bad" and "I smell badly" have completely different meanings! If you say, "I smell badly," *badly* is an adverb that modifies the verb *smell*. This means your nose isn't working (you can't smell stuff), just like when you say you feel badly it means your sense of touch is hampered in some way.

But if you say, "I smell bad," *bad* is an adjective, modifying the noun 'I'. It means you haven't showered in a week and your odor is peeling paint off the walls. It's the same if you say "I feel bad" you're really saying that you are sick or sorry or sad or maybe even cool or mean.

Bear in mind that after most other verbs it's correct to use the adverb (badly).
- I didn't study at all last night and things went badly on the exam
- My little sister throws tantrums--if I acted like that, my parent would tell me to "stop behaving badly".

Questions
1. I overslept and felt so *(bad, badly)* about missing our study group.
2. If she had done *(bad, badly)* on her last math exam, she would have failed the class!
3. He sang that last song so *(bad, badly)* that people were embarrassed for him.
4. My roommate ate so many hotdogs at the barbeque that he felt *(bad, badly)* all night.
5. I want to do well on this next exam so *(bad, badly)* that I've studied every night this week.
6. I feel *(bad, badly)* for my roommates because I really cook *(bad, badly)*.
7. The teacher felt *(bad, badly)* because he gave out the wrong assignment.
8. Her severely burned hands were wrapped with gauze to help them heal. But the gauze eliminated her ability to feel with her hands and feeling *(bad, badly)* made it more difficult to write letters.
9. The surgery on his hands damaged the nerve endings, and now he feels *(bad, badly)*. [He might also feel emotionally bad.]
10. I feel *(bad, badly)* for him because he was cut from the team.

Answers: 1. bad (felt bad exception) 2. badly (describes verb had done) 3. badly (describes verb sang) 4. bad (exception) 5. badly (describes the verb wants) 6. bad (felt bad exception), badly (describes verb cook) 7. bad (felt bad exception) 8. badly (no exception--she really has a bad sense of feel) 9. badly (he actually has a bad sense of touch) 10. bad (feel bad exception)

Bare vs. Bear

Bear
to bear (verb) *third-person singular simple present* **bears**, *present participle* **bearing**, *simple past* **bore**, *past participle* **born, borne**
- To carry something. "imitations that *bear* the same name as the things" *Plato, Sophist. Translation by Lesley Brown. 234b.*
- In the lightness of my heart I sang catches of songs as my horse gaily *bore* me along the well-remembered road. *1852, Mrs. M.A. Thompson, "The Tutor's Daughter", Graham's Am Monthly Magazine of Literature, Art, and Fashion, pg 266*
- To be equipped with something. "the right to *bear* arms"
- To declare as testimony. The jury could see he was *bearing* false witness.
- To put up with something. He *bears* it well.
- To give birth. In Troy she marries Paris', *bearing* him several children, all of whom die in infancy.
- To produce or yield something, such as fruit or crops. (all our hard work began to *bear* results)
- To be - or head - in a specific direction from the observer's position. The harbor *bears* North by Northeast.

bear **adjective (comparative** *more bear*, **superlative** *most bear*) *(*finance, investments) *Characterized by or believing to benefit of declining prices in securities markets.*
- *The great* **bear** *market starting in 1929 scared a whole generation of investors.*

More information about the verb form of "to bear" transitive verb

1 a : to move while holding up and supporting **b** : to be equipped or furnished with **c** : BEHAVE, CONDUCT <bear*ing* himself well> **d** : to have as a feature or characteristic <bears a likeness to her grandmother> **e** : to.give as testimony<bear false witness> **f** : to have as an identification <*bore* the name of John> **g** :to hold in the mind or emotions <bear malice> **h** : DISSEMINATE **i** : LEAD, ESCORT **j** : RENDER, GIVE

2 a : to give birth to **b** : to produce as yield **c** (1) : to permit growth of (2) :CONTAIN <oil-*bearing* shale>

3 a : to support the weight of : SUSTAIN **b** : to accept or allow oneself to be subjected to especially without giving way <couldn't bear the pain> <I can't bear seeing you cry> **c** : to call for as suitable or essential <it bears watching> **d** : to hold above, on top, or aloft **e** : to admit of : ALLOW **f** : ASSUME, ACCEPT

4 : THRUST, PRESS *intransitive verb* **1** : to produce fruit : YIELD

2 a : to force one's way **b** : to extend in a direction indicated or implied **c** : to be situated : LIE **d** : to become directed **e** : to go or incline in an indicated direction

3 : to support a weight or strain —often used with *up*

4 a : to exert influence or force **b** : APPLY, PERTAIN —often used with *on* or *upon* <facts bear*ing* on the question>
— **bear arms 1** : to carry or possess arms **2** : to serve as a soldier
— **bear fruit** : to come to satisfying fruition, production, or development
— **bear in mind** : to think of especially as a warning : REMEMBER
— **bear with** : to be indulgent, patient, or forbearing with

synonyms BEAR, SUFFER, ENDURE, ABIDE, TOLERATE, STAND mean to put up with something trying or painful. BEAR usually implies the power to sustain without flinching or breaking <forced to *bear* a tragic loss>. SUFFER often suggests acceptance or passivity rather than courage or patience in bearing<*suffering* many insults>. ENDURE implies continuing firm or resolute through trials and difficulties <*endured* years of rejection>. ABIDE suggests acceptance without resistance or protest <cannot *abide* their rudeness>. TOLERATE suggests overcoming or successfully controlling an impulse to resist, avoid, or resent something injurious or distasteful <refused to *tolerate* such treatment>. STAND emphasizes even more strongly the ability to bear without discomposure or flinching <unable to *stand* teasing>.

Noun: of large heavy mammals of America and Eurasia that have long shaggy hair, rudimentary tails, and plantigrade feet and feed largely on fruit, plant matter, and insects as well as on flesh
2 : a surly, uncouth, burly, or shambling person <a tall, friendly bear of a man>

Bare
The adjective 'bare' means uncovered, naked or exposed (i.e., without cover, clothing or cladding).

1 a : lacking a natural, usual, or appropriate covering **b** (1) : lacking clothing<bare feet> (2) *obsolete* : BAREHEADED **c** : lacking any tool or weapon <opened the box with his bare hands>

2 : open to view : EXPOSED <laying bare their secrets>

3 a : unfurnished or scantily supplied <a bare room> **b** : DESTITUTE <bare of all safeguards>

4 a : having nothing left over or added <the bare necessities of life> **b** : MERE <a bare two hours away> **c** : devoid of amplification or adornment <the bare facts>

5 *obsolete* : WORTHLESS

Questions:

1. We come *(baring/bearing)* gifts for your Christmas Day party.
2. The scriptures speak of a time when all corruption will be made to lay *(bare/bear)*.
3. Ling Ling the panda was the first Panda to *(bare/bear)* *(bare/bear)* cubs in captivity--they are *(bare/bear)* of any fur at birth.
4. This orchard *(bares/bears)* thousands of tons of oranges every year.
5. When you do something wrong it's important to *(bare/bear)* the responsibility for your actions?
6. If you go out in *(bare/bear)*feet. You'll catch a cold
7. My grandma always *(bared/bore)* a fur coat when it got cold. Without one she would feel *(bare/bear)*.
8. He *(bares/bears)* himself with a certain air of sophistication.
9. You've probably seen streakers run through a sporting event totally *(bare/bear)*. They seem to like *(baring/bearing)* it all for everyone to see.
10. in certain parts of the country *(bare/bear)*pipes will freeze unless they are wrapped.
11. You *(bare/bear)* a slight resemblance to your identical twin brother.
12. Upon further review, the forensic anthropologist determined the letter did *(bare/bear)*Thomas Jefferson's signature.
13. Prior to the industrial age, farmers literally ploughed the fields with their *(bare/bear)*hands--with some help from the horse or ox.
14. I hate to be the *(barer/bearer)* of bad news, but your *(bare/bear)*bottom is showing.
15. The documentary showed the *(bare/bear)*bones of her life and career.
16. *(bare/bear)*left at the next street light and then we'll arrive at my *(bare/bear)*apartment.
17. When you camp out in the wild always *(bare/bear)*a gun--fighting a cougar *(bare/bear)*handed would probably not turn out so good.
18. This road *(bares/bears)* south along the coast for 5 miles and then turns inland and *(bares/bears)* east.
19. Back at the turn of the 20th century boxing was a *(bare/bear)*–knuckle event.

Answers: 1. bearing, 2. bare, 3. bear, bear, bare 4. bears 5. bear 6. bare 7. bore, bare 8. bears 9. bare, baring 10. bare 11. bear 12. bear 13. bare 14. bearer, bare 15. bare 16. Bear, bare 17. bear, bare 18. bears, bears 19. bare

Because vs. Because of

1). Because - is a conjunction, used at the beginning of a clause, before a subject and verb.
- *We were studying* **because** *Mrs. Jacobson assigned homework.*
- *I'm hungry* **because** *we don't have any food.*

2). Because of - is a two - word preposition, used before a noun or a pronoun.
   • *We were studying **because of** the homework assigned by Mrs. Jacobson.* • *I'm hungry **because of** the lack of food.*
Note:: Because and its clause can go after or before the main clause.
   • *I finished early **because** I worked fast.* • ***Because** I worked fast, I finished early.*

Questions:
   1. We stopped playing golf *(because/because of)* the rain
   2. It was all *(because/because of)* her that we got an A on the project.
   3. We had to rush into the cafeteria *(because/because of)* it started raining
   4. I am late *(because/because of)* the traffic jam on the 91.
   5. We didn't arrive until midnight *(because/because of)* the traffic was a nightmare
   6. She thought the exam was easy *(because/because of)* she had worked hard during the semester.
   7. He can't go to school *(because/because of)* his illness.
   8. The restaurant closed down *(because/because of)* the recession.
   9. He found working in India very difficult *(because/because of)* the language barrier.
   10. He's very difficult to understand *(because/because of)* his accent.
   11. They moved to Boston *(because/because of)* her job.
   12. There have been a lot of problems in the US *(because/because of)* the recession.
   13. They came to NY *(because/because of)* he got a job there.
   14. He crashed his car *(because/because of)* he was talking on his cell phone.
   15. He lost his driver's license *(because/because of)* he was convicted of drinking and driving.
   16. She could only eat a salad in the restaurant *(because/because of)* she is a vegetarian.
   17. The newspaper won a Pulitzer *(because/because of)* an article about Government waste.

Answers: 1. because of 2. because of 3. because 4. because of 5. because 6. because 7. because of 8. because of 9. because of 10. because of 11. because of 12. because of 13. because 14. because 15. because 16. because 17. because of

Being that vs. Since
Being that is nonstandard and should be replaced by *since.*
   • Wrong: ***Being that*** we only had half a tank of gas, we had to stop at the next station.
   • Correct: ***Since*** we only had half a tank of gas, we had to stop at the next station.

Beside vs. Besides
Adding an *s* to *beside* completely changes its meaning. *Beside* means "next to."
   • I sat ***beside*** (next to) my girlfriend in Trigonometry class. .
Besides means "in addition."
   • ***Besides*** Youtube (in addition), what other content streaming websites do you like?

Questions:
   1. *(Beside,Besides)* studying for biology, I need to pick up my tickets for the game tonight.
   2. I'm not feeling too well today--I think it was the chicken I ate last night, so I don't think I'll be able to attend Homecoming meeting and,*(beside,besides),* my roommate knows everything about my committee.
   3. A true friend will always stand *(beside,besides)* you, even in difficult times.
   4. My mom asked me, *(beside,besides)* the green coat which scarf to you want?"
   5. In American History I sat *(beside,besides)* the exchange student from England.

Answers: 1. Besides, 2. besides, 3. beside, 4. besides, 5. beside

Brake vs. Break
Brake: (v) the word brake means to stop. (n.) a device for slowing or stopping motion.
Break: (v.) to smash or to shatter as in to break a cup. (n.) to take a recess, as in a coffee break.

Questions
   1. When I first learned to drive a stick shift I confused the *(brake/break)* and the clutch.
   2. To work effectively all day it's important to take a *(brake/break)* now and then.
   3. Has your mother ever told you, "Wear your helmet or you will *(brake/break)* your head on that skateboard!"
   4. It's important to set the emergency *(brake/break),* when you park a car on a hill.
   5. My favorite holiday is the Christmas *(brake/break)* but I also like the Easter holiday.

Answers: 1. brake, 2. break, 3. break, 4. brake, 5. break

Breath vs. Breathe vs. Breadth
Breathe (v): to draw air into the lungs and to exhale it; to inhale and to exhale
   • ***breathe*** with more difficulty when I'm out of shape.
Breath (n.): air filled with a fragrance or odor; the act of breathing; a slight indication or suggestion
   • My ***breath*** always smells in the mornings.
Breadth (n.): the distance abstractly or concretely from one point to another
   • The ***breadth*** of his understanding amazed everyone, he certainly was well read.
Breathe is a verb. ***Breath*** and ***Breadth*** are nouns.

Questions
   1. It's hard to *(breathe/breath/breadth)* inside a smoky casino so I step out periodically for a *(breathe/breath/breadth)* of fresh air.

2. In swimming, during a short race like the 50 yard freestyle most swimmers will hold their *(breathe/breath/breadth)* the entire time.
3. I was so nervous prior to going on stage that I forgot to *(breathe/breath/breadth)*
4. I worked last summer for Parks & Rec cleaning port-a-johns. You can imagine I did not want to *(breathe/breath/breadth)* most of the day.
5. People from San Diego don't know what it's like to see your own *(breathe/breath/breadth)* on a cold day.
6. I have traveled the *(breathe/breath/breadth)* of this country searching for the best Mexican food.
7. I am so busy that I can't even take a *(breathe/breath/breadth)*!
8. People who snore usually *(breathe/breath/breadth)* loudly also.

Answers: 1. breathe, breath 2. breath, 3. breathe, 4. breathe, 5. breath, 6. breadth, 7. breath, 8. breathe

By vs. Bye vs. Buy

By is a preposition that means: near, beside or through.
• Stand **by** your man!
Bye is a greeting of departure.
• "**Bye, Bye**" is a common ending to a phone conversation.
Buy is a verb that means: to purchase.
• I **buy** all my tools from Home Depot.

Questions
1. I *(by, bye, buy)* a lot of music from the apps store.
2. *(By, bye, buy)* studying every day and reading extra books, I feel more prepared for the exam.
3. My mom tries to *(by, bye, buy)* her Christmas gifts by October--I wait until December 24th.
4. *(By, bye, buy)* the way, who won the game last night?
5. "Adios" and "hasta luego" both mean, *"(By, Bye, Buy)"* in English.

Answers: 1. buy, 2. by 3. buy, 4. by, 5. Bye

Compare to vs. Compare with

Compare to - is used to liken two things or to put them in the same category. You should use "compare to" when you intend to simply assert that two things are alike or similar.
• The economy can be **compared** to a stallion charging at the gate. (the two things are alike)
• I **compare** getting comments from students in class to pulling teeth. (they are alike)
• She **compared** her work for women's rights to Susan B. Anthony's campaign for women's suffrage. (they are alike)

Compare with - is used to place two things side by side for the purpose of examining their similarities or differences--often used to illustrate the differences a comparison draws
• The American economy can be **compared** with the European economy to note how military history impacts future economics.
• It would be interesting to **compare** Purdue with Ohio State.
• Ann has a 3.5 GPA, **compared** with Jim's 2.9.

IMPORTANT TIP "He compared me TO Dolly Parton" means he suggested I was comparable to her or put me in the same class; "He compared me WITH Dolly Parton" means he instituted a detailed comparison, or pointed out where and how far I resembled or failed to resemble her. Source: H.W. Fowler.
In writing, "compare with" means examine in order to note similarity or difference, while "compare to" means to suggest similarity. Further, in the sense of being worthy of comparison, only " compare with" is correct: Words do not compare with actions. Source: American Heritage Dictionary
NOTE: this is difficult to understand and that makes it prime testing ground. Do your best to figure this out.

Questions
1. A language may be compared *(with/to)* a living organism.
2. Compared *(with/to)* other Native Americans of the Southwest, the Quechans were singularly uninterested in the accumulation of material wealth or in the crafting of elaborate pottery and basketry.
3. One baby in four is now born to a mother aged thirty or older, compared *(with/to)* just one in six in 1975
4. One noted economist has compared the Federal Reserve *(with/to)* an automobile racing through a tunnel, bouncing first off one wall, then the other; the car may get where it is going, but people may be hurt in the process.
5. Since chromosome damage may be caused by viral infections, medical x-rays, and exposure to sunlight, it is important that the chromosomes of a population to be tested for chemically induced damage be compared *(with/to)* those of a control population.
6. The metabolic rate of sharks is low compared *(with/to)* the rates of most other fishes .
7. In appearance, ripples in ocean water can be compared *(with/to)* frosting spread on a cake.
8. Despite their different capacities, RAM can be compared *(with/to)* ROM in that both involve memory storage.
9. particles are small compared *(with/to)* the wavelength of the light illuminating them,
10. I was asked to compare Sheldon's poetry *(with/to)* Wordsworth's." Placing two things side by side to compare specific resemblances and differences.
11. She compared his home-made wine *(with/to)* toxic waste.
12. The teacher compared Steve's exam *(with/to)* Robert's to see whether they had cheated.
13. He compared her *(with/to)* a summer day.
14. Scientists sometimes compare the human brain *(with/to)* a computer
15. The police compared the forged signature *(with/to)* the original.
16. The committee will have to compare the Senate's version of the bill *(with/to)* the version that was passed by the House.
17. *She compared his handwriting (with/to) knotted string.*

18. *The critic compared the paintings in the exhibit (with/to) magazine photographs.*
19. In order to decide which city to tour, we had to *(compare them with, compare them to)* each other.
20. *(Compared to, Compared with)* running, walking is good for people who have knee problems
21. Andy compared his math teacher *(with, to)* his English teacher and pointed out what they had in common and what they did not.
22. When Geri compares her old boyfriend *(to. with)* her new boyfriend, she points out all the ways in which they are alike.

Answers: 1. to 2. with 3. with 4. to 5. with 6. with 7. to 8. with 9. with 10. with 11. to 12. with 13. to 14. to 15. with 16. with 17. to 18. with 19. with 20. with 21. with 22. to

Detailed answers:

1. A language may be compared to a living organism. *(two things are alike "language is like living organism")*
2. Compared with other Native Americans of the Southwest, the Quechans were singularly uninterested in the accumulation of material wealth or in the crafting of elaborate pottery and basketry. *(side-by-side analysis of Southwest natives and the Quechans)*
3. One baby in four is now born to a mother aged thirty or older, compared with just one in six in 1975. *(It's not saying the age of maternity today is like the age of maternity in 1975...rather it's a side-by-side comparison of the age of maternity today and the age of maternity in 1975.)*
4. One noted economist has compared the Federal Reserve to an automobile racing through a tunnel, bouncing first off one wall, then the other; the car may get where it is going, but people may be hurt in the process. *(two things are alike: the Fed is like an out of control car racing through a dark tunnel--it's not comparing and contrasting and analyzing the Fed with an out-of-control car...it just says they are alike.)*
5. Since chromosome damage may be caused by viral infections, medical x-rays, and exposure to sunlight, it is important that the chromosomes of a population to be tested for chemically induced damage be compared with those of a control population. *(this is an analysis of damaged chromosomes against healthy chromosomes)*
6. The metabolic rate of sharks is low compared with the rates of most other fishes . *(another analysis or side-by-side comparison between sharks and other fish)*
7. In appearance, ripples in ocean water can be compared to frosting spread on a cake. *(it simply says ripples are like frosting--it's not an analysis, but rather a flat statement)*
8. Despite their different capacities, RAM can be compared with ROM in that both involve memory storage. *(this is a side-by-side analysis or comparison it's not saying that RAM is like ROM, it's saying there are similarities and differences)*
9. Particles are small compared with the wavelength of the light illuminating them. *(this shows a difference brought about by a comparison or analysis--it's not saying they are alike)*
10. I was asked to compare Sheldon's poetry with Wordsworth's." *(Placing two things side by side to compare specific resemblances and differences.)*
11. She compared his home-made wine to toxic waste. *(they are alike)*
12. The teacher compared Steve's exam with Robert's to see whether they had cheated. *(a side-by-side analysis or comparison to find out the similarities and differences--it does not say the two things are alike)*
13. He compared her to a summer day. *(two things are alike- 'her' and 'summer day')*
14. Scientists sometimes compare the human brain to a computer. *(two things are alike- 'human brain' and 'computer'.)*
15. The police compared the forged signature with the original. *(side by side analysis)*
16. The committee will have to compare the Senate's version of the bill with the version that was passed by the House. *(side by side analysis)*
17. *She compared his handwriting to knotted string. (two things are alike)*
18. *The critic compared the paintings in the exhibit with magazine photographs. (side-by-side analysis)*
19. In order to decide which city to tour, we had to compare them with each other. *(a side-by-side analysis to find out the similarities and differences...it's not saying one is like the other)*
20. Compared with running, walking is good for people who have knee problems. *(a side-by-side analysis to find out the similarities and differences...it's not saying one is like the other)*
21. Andy compared his math teacher with his English teacher and pointed out what they had in common and what they did not. *(a side-by-side analysis between the two teachers)*
22. When Geri compares her old boyfriend to her new boyfriend, she points out all the ways in which they are alike. *(this is a silly attempt to catch you--but the answer is 'to' because in a very roundabout way she finally says the two are alike)*

Can vs. May

Can means to be physically or mentally able to do something.
May means to have permission to do something.

Can: The word 'can' is used to denote ability.
   • I *can* dance. (I have the ability to dance.)   • *Can* he lift 150 lbs? (Does he have the ability to lift 150 lbs?
May: The word 'may' is used to denote permission.
   • You *may* swim in this pool. (You are allowed to swim in this pool.)
   • *May* I have another can of soda? (Am I permitted to have another can of soda?)

Questions
1. *(can/may)* I get another can of soda?
2. His parents gave him permission this time, "You *(can/may)* stay out until midnight just this once."
3. *(can/may)* I have your attention please?
4. *(can/may))* I get you anything else for dessert tonight?
5. Do you know if you *(can/may)* sign up for biology 201 here?
6. She *(can/may)* sing like an angel. (Alternative: She has the voice of an angel.)

7. Is the Federal Reserve the only one who *(can/may)* create money from thin air? (Alternative: Is the Fed the only entity allowed/permitted to create money from thin air?)
8. Is this seat taken? *(Can/may)* I sit here? (Alternative: Do you mind if I sit down?)
9. I don't think you *(can/may)* lift the sofa. (Alternative: I think the sofa is not too heavy for you.)
10. *(Can/may)* I come to your house to watch the game this weekend?
11. I don't think I *(can/may)* go to the movies this weekend because I have to study for my Spanish final exam.
12. If you *(can/may)* finish your chores on Friday then you can spend the entire day Saturday at the beach.
13. If I get my homework finished on Friday, I *(can/may)* be able to go with you to the beach.
14. My cat, *Sache*, loves to sit on top of the refrigerator so she *(can/may)* see everything that is going.

Answers: 1. May 2. may 3. May 4. may 5. can 6. can 7. can, may 8. May 9. can 10. May 11. can 12. can 13. may 14. can

Canvas vs. Canvass

Canvas (n.): 'canvas' (with one 's' at the end) refers to a heavy woven cloth of hemp, flax or cotton. It is used for sails, tents and paintings. The word 'canvas' is also used figuratively for the floor of a boxing or wrestling ring (i.e., they are often not made of canvas). **Canvas is similar to the denim material used to make jeans.**
Canvass (v.): to solicit votes, opinions, or sales from a group of people. As a noun, *canvass* refers to the act of collecting votes or opinions; it is the close inspection of something. 1. To collect opinions. 2. To electioneer (i.e., to collect votes through persuasion of voters in a political campaign). 3. To examine closely. 4. To ask around.

Questions

1. Politicians typically *(canvas/canvass)* local neighborhoods to calculate the level of support for an issue?
2. Did your *(canvas/canvass)* show any support for increased taxes?
3. The *Dunbar* was a Blackwell frigate that had three masts and full-rigged *(canvas/canvass)* sails. She wrecked in 1857 near the entrance to Sydney Harbor in Sydney, Australia.
4. During the summer, college students who volunteer for various candidates or campaigns *(canvas/canvass)* districts asking questions to gauge the level of support for their candidate or issue.
5. The coach asked the team captain to *(canvas/canvass)* the team members to see who should be awarded the MVP.
6. John is a census taker this year but they altered his *(canvas/canvass)* area after this last election.
7. Jill's *(canvas/canvass)* of students planning to attend college showed 75% of them are worried about our country's debt.
8. Sugar Ray pounded Marvin with a lightning fast combination followed by a devastating uppercut which left Marvin in free fall and his head bouncing off the *(canvas/canvass)*.
9. My mom *(canvased/canvassed)* every clothing store in the mall and she still did not buy anything.
10. The FBI will *(canvas/canvass)* the entire crime scene and speak with all the witnesses.
11. *Leonardo DiVinci* spent days preparing a *(canvas/canvass)* before he would begin a painting.
12. After the election, the political science class was assigned to *(canvas/canvass)* the campus to find out students' opinions about the key issues.
13. The class' *(canvas/canvass)* showed that more students favored the losing candidate and the issues on her slate.
14. My green grocery bag is made of *(canvas/canvass)* and is much stronger than a paper bag.

Answers: 1. canvass 2. canvass 3. canvas 4. canvass 5. canvass 6. canvass 7. canvass 8. canvas 9. canvassed 10. canvass 11. canvas 12. canvass 13. canvass 14. canvas

Capital vs. Capitol

Capital (n.): : (1) a city that serves as the seat of government; (2) wealth in the form of money or property; (3) an asset or advantage; (4) a capital letter (the type of letter used at the beginning of a sentence). 5. the top part of a column. (adj.) As an adjective, *capital* means principal or chief as in "a capital idea." *Capital* also can mean "punishable by death," capital punishment.
Capitol is capitalized if the word is referring to the building in which the U.S. Congress meets. When uncapitalized, the word usually refers to the main government building of a state.

TIP: Remember the o in *capitol* is like the o in the dome of a capitol. Use 'capital' for EVERYTHING EXCEPT the actual building
- The dome of the United States **Capitol** resembles the "o" in the word "capit**Ol**".
- Washington DC is the **capital** of the United States of America.

Questions

1. To contact your Representative or Senator you have to call the United States *(Capital/Capitol)* building because many of them have offices in that building..
2. Just like a person needs food to grow and even live, a company also needs "food" but we call it *(capital, capitol)* which can come from internal cash flow, loans, investments or other sources.
3. Can you name all the state *(capitals, capitols)* in the US?
4. I want to visit every state *(capital/capitol)* city and while there I want to visit the *(capital/capitol)* buildings.
5. When referring to the national *(Capitol/Capital)* building you should begin the word with a *(capital/capitol)* letter.
6. The steps of a state *(capital, capitol)* are prime areas for protestors.
7. The Smithsonian is located in Washington, D.C., the *(capital/capitol)* of the United States.

Answers: 1. Capitol 2. capital 3. capitals 4. capital, capitol 5. Capitol, capital 6. capitol 7. capital

Censor vs. Censure vs. Sensor vs. Censer

censor n. one who decides which cultural products are fit for consumption and which ought to be altered or banned; *v.* to ban cultural products.
censure n. disapproval; an official reprimand. (v.) *censure* means to find fault or condemn someone

sensor n. a device designed to detect a specific stimulus or stimuli.
censer n. a container in which incense is burned.

Pay close attention because these words are very confusing, which makes them prime testing material. First, the word 'censer' is probably too specific to be used on the exam, but we include it for completeness sake. However, 'censor', 'censure', and 'sensor' are all legitimate words that are testable.

Censor
The verb *censor* means to suppress or remove something that is considered objectionable.
The noun *censor* refers to a person who censors things.
- According to the American Library Association, J.D. Salinger's novel *Catcher in the Rye* has been "a favorite of **censors** since its publication."

Censure
The verb *censure* means to find fault or condemn someone.
The noun *censure* refers to a reprimand or a judgment involving condemnation.
- *Censure* is a "formal rebuke" or "official displeasure." It is done by someone, usually some kind of assembly, in authority. The *s* in the word is pronounced like as *sh,* just as in the word **sure.** The U.S. Congress has censured its members a number of times for unbecoming conduct.

Sensor
A **sensor** is something that interprets stimulation: sensor denotes a detector of a stimulus (such as heat, light, motion, pressure).
- The lights are turned on by a movement **sensor**.

To sum up, censoring is regulating or prohibiting types of speech or writing. Censuring is an official rebuke of a person for some offense. While a 'sensor' is an electronic gadget.

Questions
1. The party chose to *(sensor/censure/censor/censer)* the governor rather than call for his resignation.
2. Governments throughout history have tried to *(sensor/censure/censor/censer)* ideas they did not agree with.
3. Soldiers' letters from war zones are frequently read and *(sensored/censured/censored/censered)* to avoid passing on sensitive information.
4. The soldier would have to carefully word his letter so that it would pass the *(sensor/censure/censor/censer)* .
5. Terrorists rig cell phones with an infrared *(sensor/censure/censor/censer)* designed to detect movement which triggers the explosive.
6. The *(sensor/censure/censor/censer)* of Sen. McCarthy effectively ended his career.
7. The Synod voted to *(sensor/censure/censor/censer)* the priest for his unauthorized activities."
8. The principal *(sensored/censured/censored/censered)* all references to smoking in school publications.
9. Kyle Garchar, was severely *(sensored/censured/censored/censered)* for tricking the opposing schools fans to hold up signs that spelled out "WE SUCK".   http://www.youtube.com/watch?v=lemhDgYLbT0&feature=player_embedded
   How many balloons does it take to fill a classroom? http://www.youtube.com/watch?v=a_MzHxY-19E&feature=related
10. A *(sensor/censure/censor/censer)* is a church incense burner.
11. A device which senses any change like changes in light or electrical output is a *(sensor/censure/censor/censer)* .
12. To *(sensor/censure/censor/censer)* somebody's speech or writing is to try to suppress it by preventing it from reaching the public.
13. If found guilty, the player would face a fine or *(sensor/censure/censor/censer)* .
14. When guests on network TV utter obscenities, broadcasters will *(sensor/censure/censor/censer)* them with a bleep.
15. To *(sensor/censure/censor/censer)* someone, however, is to officially denounce an offender.
16. You can be *(sensored/censured/censored/censered)* as much for actions as for words.
17. Your car and your digital camera contain *(sensors/censures/censors/censers)* .
18. The *(sensor/censure/censor/censer)* picked up the sound of the students returning to the common room and the whispered conversation passing between them. "Ack! I forgot my copy of *The Amber Spyglass* in the chapel and brought this *(sensor/censure/censor/censer)* back here by mistake," said Martin. "Uh-oh," Jennifer replied, "that book's been *(sensored/censured/censored/censered)* ! You'd better go make the switch before you're *(sensored/censured/censored/censered)* by the principal."
19. How did that statement end up on the streets? I *(sensored/censured/censored/censered)* the article myself.
20. He has received two letters of *(sensor/censure/censor/censer)* from the unit commander.

Answers: 1. censure 2. censor 3. censored 4. censor 5. sensor 6. censure 7. censure 8. censored 9. censured 10. censer 11. sensor 12. censor 13. censure 14. censor 15. censure 16. censured 17. sensors 18. sensor, censer, censored, censured 19. censored 20. censure.

Center on vs. Center around

Center around is colloquial. It should **not** be used in formal writing.
- **Wrong**: The debate *centers around* the Constitutionality and the cost of government provided healthcare.
- **Correct**: The debate *centers on* the Constitutionality and the cost of government provided healthcare.

Cite vs. Site vs. Sight

Cite is a verb meaning "to quote for purposes of example, authority, or proof." **Example**: "When you **cite** experts it tends to increase credibility."
Site is usually used as a noun meaning "place or scene." **Example**: "Check the **website**," and "We **site** where Thomas Jefferson wrote the Declaration of Independence."

Sight The noun *sight* refers to something that is seen or the power or process of seeing.

Questions

1. The *(cite/site/sight)* for the grand opening will be selected next week.
2. When you include information from an outside source remember to *(cite/site/sight)* the source.
3. When I was 19 years old I could *(cite/site/sight)* a deer a mile away.
4. One of the most famous Revolutionary War *(cites, sites, sights)* is Yorktown where the Americans routed the British and essentially ended the war.
5. When asked why he had withdrawn from the case, the judge *(cited/sited/sighted)* conflicts of interest.
6. Home is always a *(cite/site/sight)* for sore eyes!
7. This style guide explains how to *(cite/site/sight)* sources in a term paper.
8. "The *(cite/site/sight)* of the stars makes me dream." (Vincent Van Gogh)
9. I'll email you my favorite web*(cite/site/sight)*.
10. On this very *(cite/site/sight)* George Washington crossed the Delaware river and led his troops to a critical victory over the Hessian soldiers.
11. When asked how he hit four home runs in the same game, Vinnie *(cited/sited/sighted)* all the help and training his father gave him.
12. "Of all the senses, *(cite/site/sight)* must be the most delightful." (Helen Keller)

Answers: 1. site 2. cite 3. sight 4. sites 5. cited 6. sight 7. cite 8. sight 9. site 10. site 11. cited 12 sight

Clothes vs. Cloths

Clothes (n.) means "clothing."
Cloths (n.) is the plural of cloth (fabric).
• Put your dirty **clothes** in the laundry, and then wipe your face with a damp **cloth**.

Questions

1. The pioneers made their own *(clothes/cloths)* out of home spun *(clothes/cloth)*.
2. Some *(clothes/cloths)* have to be washed and dried before you can wear them.
3. My mom's closet is stuffed full of *(clothes/cloths)*, but she always complains she doesn't have anything to wear.
4. The high end dress boutiques carry expensive *(clothes/cloths)* made from the best quality silk *(clothes/cloths)*.
5. *(Clothes/cloths)* don't make the man, the man makes the *(clothes/cloths)*.
6. The famous "Silk Route" that ran several thousand miles through Europe and the far east was the result of the demand for rich silk *(clothes/cloths)*.
7. My little sister loves to dress up in my mom's *(clothes/cloths)* and pretend she's a mommy.
8. Once upon a time there was an emperor who loved new *(clothes/cloths)* more than anything else.
9. At the end of the story a small child cries out ' But the emperor has no *(clothes/cloths)* on'.
10. They were so poor that they could barely keep the family fed and *(clothesed/clothed)*.
11. Many professions require special *(clothes/cloths)*.
12. At the Oscar Awards we see women in dresses made by famous designers who use the finest *(clothes/cloths)* and other materials from all over the world.
13. I don't think it's wise for parents to *(clothe/cloth)* their children in the latest fashion.
14. Servers in restaurants usually have damp *(clothes/cloths)* to wipe tables and clean spills ?
15. My son's football practice *(clothes/cloths)* smell like something from the bottom of a restaurant garbage can.

Answers: 1. clothes, cloth 2. clothes 3. clothes 4. clothes, cloths 5. clothes, clothes 6. cloths 7. clothes 8. clothes 9. clothes 10. clothed 11. clothes 12. cloths 13. clothe 14. cloths 15. clothes

Coarse vs. Course

Coarse (adj.) means rough, crude, of low quality or not fine in texture.

coarse sand

coarse manners

Perch - a type of coarse fish (not as refined as trout or salmon, which are classified as game fish)

Course The word course has many meanings. It can be an adjective, noun or verb.

• **Education delivered in a series of lessons is an:** 'English **course**'.
• **Also, the students who attend:** You have been an excellent **course**.
• **A direction:** Chart a northerly **course**. After the storm, the captain changed **course**.
• **A series of events:** The government took an unexpected **course**. A **course** of action.
• **To move (of liquids and ships):** The US ships **coursed** the Atlantic. Blood **coursed** through his veins.
• **Part of a meal:** I love six-**course** dining. The first **course** is always my favorite.
• **Naturally:** of **course**
• **Area of land (or water) for sport:** Golf **course**. Skiing course.

Questions:

1. Do you prefer sea or *(coarse/course)* fishing?

2. Of *(coarse/course)*, you have to do your homework tonight.
3. This sand is so *(coarse/course)* it's hurting my bare feet.
4. A shark's skin is extremely *(coarse/course)*.
5. She took an unexpected *(coarse/course)* of action.
6. A bear's fur is extremely *(coarse/course)* so much it can cut your hand.
7. I always try to get my homework finished while I'm at school, of *(coarse/course)*, sometimes I can't do it.
8. The *(coarse/course)* to riches and fame is filled with danger.
9. I took that math *(coarse/course)* and it helped me get college credit--I highly recommend it.
10. Ideas and people shape the *(coarse/course)* of history.
11. It's either salmon or crab for the main *(coarse/course)*.
12. There is a new golf *(coarse/course)* opening up down the road--it's a championship size 36 hole *(coarse/course)*.

Answers: 1. coarse 2. course, 3. coarse 4. coarse 5. course 6. coarse 7. course 8. course 9. course 10. course 11. course 12. course, course

Compare vs. Contrast

Compare - describe the differences and similarities between two things to view one in relation to the other. As a verb it means to examine two or more items for the purpose of noting both similarities and/or differences.
Contrast - describe the differences between two things. Contrast is a verb or a noun that means difference (noun) or to present a difference (verb). compare or appraise in respect to differences

Questions:
1. Even though the identical twins possessed very different personalities, their appearances were often being *(compared, contrasted)*.
2. It doesn't make sense to *(compare, contrast)* apples and bunnies since they are so different.
3. Nights in the desert offer extraordinary *(comparisons, contrasts)* to its days.
4. Always curious about how similar we are, we often *(compare, contrast)* our homes, cars, and the kinds of food we eat.
5. Dark red always *(compares, contrasts)* well with bright yellow.

Answers: 1. compared 2. compare 3. contrasts 4. compare 5. contrasts

Complement vs. Compliment

Complement means "something that completes or brings to perfection."
A *compliment* is an expression of praise.

Complement is a verb, which means to make something seem better or more attractive when combined. Matching or completing things. Complements supplement each other, each adding something the others lack:
• Her brown eyes and her blonde hair *complement* each other.
A complement can also be the full number of something needed to make it complete. If it is preceded by "full" the word you want is almost certainly "complement."
• My new Toyota has a full *complement* of accessories.
When paying someone a compliment like "I can't believe how good you look!" you're being complimentary. A free bonus item is also a complimentary gift. But items or people that go well with each other are complementary.
In geometry, complementary angles add up to 90°
• Cheese and crackers *complement* each other perfectly.
• I received a *complimentary* bottle of wine which was a nice *complement* to the pasta.

Compliment is a noun, which means a remark that expresses approval, admiration or respect.
• The nicest *compliment* anyone had ever paid me was when they mistook me for my daughter.
He said that men and women have strengths that *complement* each other. But she did not take his remark as a *compliment*.

TIP If it complements something it completes it. (With an e.) *I* like compl*i*ments. (With an i.)
• I *complimented* my dad on how much weight he had lost and how much better he looked.
• Soft background music *complements* any good meal.

Questions:
1. Sometimes I give (complements/compliments) but the person does not even realize it.
2. A 32 inch monitor is a perfect (complement/compliment) to a new gaming computer system.
3. His ability to make girls laugh (complements/compliments) his boyish good looks.
4. If you spend more than $50 at the movie theater you get a (complementary/complimentary) bag of popcorn.
5. Vanilla ice cream and hot fudge are perfectly engineered (complementary/complimentary) tastes.

Answers: *1. compliments, 2. complement, 3. complements 4. complimentary, 5. complementary*

Compose vs. Comprise ('comprise of' and 'is comprised of')

Comprise means "have, consist of, or include": Students of several nationalities comprise the class.
Compose means to "make up" and is often used in the passive voice: The class is composed of students of several nationalities.
3 Tips (they all attempt to say the same thing--but this is a difficult concept, so maybe one of these way of saying it will make more sense to you than another.)

Tip 1: the whole comprises its parts, and the parts compose the whole.
Tip 2: If you can replace *comprise* with *include* and your sentence stands, you're safe.
Tip 3: just say, "The rock is made up of three minerals," or "Three minerals make up the rock."

• **Wrong**: The rock is *comprised* of three minerals.   • **Correct**: The rock is *composed* of three minerals.
• **Correct**: The rock *comprises* three minerals.   • **Correct**: Three minerals *compose* the rock.

Comprise means "is made up of" or "consists of." The whole **comprises** the parts.
Compose means "make up" or "make." The parts **compose** the whole.

The Meaning of "Comprise"

To comprise" means "to contain"
• Elvis Presley's mansion comprises 25 room. This mansion is the main subject and it's made up of 25 rooms. When you use "comprise," all the parts make up something.   <u>**The whole comprises the parts**</u>.

Remember with "comprise" **First**: the main subject **Second**: the parts that make up the whole.
• **Correct**: A full baseball team *comprises* nine position players. The team is the whole subject, so it comes first in the sentence, the nine players make up the team.
• **Wrong**: Nine players *comprise* a full team.
• **Correct**: Earth *comprises* seven continents. In this sentence, the Earth is the main item, so it comes first in the sentence and the seven continents make up the whole. <u>**The whole comprises the parts.**</u>
• **Wrong**: Seven continents *comprise* the Earth.

The Meaning of "Compose"

Compose means "to make up,"

• **Correct**: Nine players *compose* a baseball team. Now the parts come before the whole.
• **Wrong**: "A baseball team *comprises* nine players." If you started the sentence with the words "the team," you would use "comprise": <u>**So, the parts compose the whole, but the whole comprises the parts.**</u>

"Is Comprised Of" and "Is Composed Of"

"*is composed of,*" is proper grammar: you could say, "A baseball team is composed of nine players."
"*is comprised of*" NOT accepted. Just as you can't say, "The team includes of nine players," you can't say, "The team is comprised of nine players". You have to say, "The team comprises nine players."

Questions

1. The water molecule *(comprises/composes)* two atoms of hydrogen and one atom of oxygen.
2. The water molecule is composed **of** two atoms of hydrogen and one atom of oxygen.
3. Two atoms of hydrogen and one atom of oxygen *(comprise/compose)* the water molecule.
4. The three wise monkeys *(comprise/compose)* Mizaru (see no evil), Kikazaru (hear no evil) and Iwazaru (speak no evil).
5. The quadriceps femoris *(comprise/compose)* the rectus femoris, the vastus medialis, the vastus intermedius and the vastus lateralis.
6. The water molecule is *(composed of/comprised of)* two atoms of hydrogen and one atom of oxygen.
7. Mercury, Venus, Earth and Mars *(comprise/compose)* the inner planets.
8. The rectus femoris, the vastus medialis, the vastus intermedius and the vastus lateralis *(comprise/compose)* the quadriceps femoris.
9. Two atoms of hydrogen and one atom of oxygen *(comprise/compose)* the water molecule.
10. USA is *(composed of/comprised of)* 50 states.
11. The water molecule is *(composed of/comprised of)* two atoms of hydrogen and one atom of oxygen.
12. A baseball team *(comprises/is comprised of)* five players.
13. A center, two forwards and two guards *(comprise/compose)* a basketball team.
14. The basketball team *(comprises/composes)* a center, two forwards, and two guards.
15. The formula for sulphuric acid is H2SO4. This means that the molecule *(comprises/comprises of)* two hydrogen atoms, one sulphur atom and four oxygen atoms.
16. His website *(is composed of/composes)* more than two dozen award-winning photographs and six videos.
17. His website *(comprises/composes)* more than two dozen award-winning photographs and six videos.
18. It is known as a dibasic acid, because it *(comprises/composes)* two hydrogen atoms. In total, seven atoms *(comprise/compose)* the molecule.
19. The alphabet *(comprises/composes)* 26 letters. The letters A, E, I, O and U *(comprise/compose)* the group of letters known as vowels. The alphabet *(is composed of, is comprised of)* 21 consonants and 5 vowels.

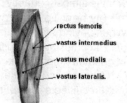
rectus femoris
vastus intermedius
vastus medialis
vastus lateralis.

Answers: **1**. comprises (The whole comprises the smaller parts.) **2**. is composed of **3**. compose (the parts compose the whole) **4**. comprise (the whole comprises the parts) **5**. comprise (the whole comprises the parts) **6**. is composed of (same as comprise) **7**. compose (the parts compose the whole) **8**. compose (the parts compose the whole) **9**. compose (the parts compose the whole) **10**. composed (the parts compose the whole) **11**. is composed of (same as comprise) **12**. comprises (the whole comprises the parts) **13**. compose (the parts compose the whole) **14**. comprises (the whole comprises the parts) **15**. comprises (the whole comprises the parts) **16**. is composed of (same as comprise) **17**. comprises (the whole comprises the parts) **18**. comprises (the whole comprises the parts) **19**. comprises (but the whole comprises the parts), compose (the parts compose the whole), is composed of (same as comprise)

Conscience vs. Conscious

The noun <u>***conscience***</u> means "the sense of what is right and wrong."
The adjective <u>***conscious***</u> means "being aware" or "deliberate" or "awake".
Your conscience helps you choose the right and makes you feel guilty when you do bad things. But 'conscious' is an adjective that describes the state of being alert, awake, aware, or coherent.   If you are awake, you are ***conscious***.

Questions
1. Happiness is a (*conscious/conscience*) choice, not an automatic response. My (*conscious/conscience*) tells me so.
2. No pillow is as soft as a clear (*conscious/conscience*) .
3. I am always (*conscious/conscience*) of my faults.
4. Your (*conscious/conscience*) is your guide and helps you choose the right.

Answers: 1. conscious, conscience 2. conscience 3. conscious 4. conscience

Conform to (not *with*)
Conform with is colloquial. It should **not** be used in formal writing.
   • **Wrong**: Parents teach their children correct moral principles and hope their kids *conform with* the truth.
   • **Correct**: Parents teach their children correct moral principles and hope their kids *conform to* the truth.

Consensus of opinion
Consensus of opinion is redundant: *consensus* means "general agreement."
   • **Wrong**: Many politicians claim there is a *consensus of opinion* in anthropogenic global climate change.
   • **Correct**: Many politicians claim there is a *consensus about* anthropogenic global climate change.
   • *Correct: Among political women . . . there is a **clear consensus** about the problems women candidates have traditionally faced" (Wendy Kaminer).*
   • *Correct: A democracy is often described as government **by consensus**.*

Continually vs. continuously
Continually means repeated again and again, with breaks in between--like a pattern, off and on--periodic.
Continuously means without interruption, in an unbroken stream.
   • Heidi has to wind the cuckoo clock *continually* to keep it running *continuously*.
   • I was *continually* interrupted by the crying baby.
   • The baby has been crying *continuously* for three hours.

Note: If it's important to emphasize the distinction, it's probably better to use *periodically* or *intermittently* instead of *continually* to describe something that starts and stops. The same distinction, by the way, applies to *continual* and *continuous*, the adjective forms" (O'Conner, *Woe Is I* 95-96).

Questions:
1. The snow fall (**continually/continuously**) in Barrow, Alaska.
2. You have a problem with your (**continual/continuous**) checking of your Facebook and email.
3. The robbers tripped the silent alarm but in the monitoring station it sounded (**continually/continuously**) until the employee turned it off.
4. Sometimes my little brother's (**continual/continuous**) questions can make me crazy.
5. When you look out an airplane window, it seems there is a (**continual/continuous**) skyline that goes on forever.
6. My alarm has a 10 minute doze feature that buzzes (**continually/continuously**) every 10 minutes.
7. My mom used to own a bird and I had to listen to its (**continual/continuous**) squawking and complaining.
8. At the tomb of the unknown soldier the honor guard maintain a (**continual/continuous**) vigil 24/7/365.
9. The planets move (**continually/continuously**) in their orbits around the sun.
10. I hate watching TV because of the (**continual/continuous**) commercials.

Answers
1. The snow fall **continually** in Barrow, Alaska. (Even though it snows a lot in Barrow, AK it does not snow without ceasing forever. It snows off and on, therefore, we choose 'continually'.
2. You have a problem with your **continual** checking of your Facebook and email. (off and on checking)
3. The robbers tripped the silent alarm but in the monitoring station it sounded **continuously** until the employee turned it off. (it sounded in one long unbroken stream until it was turned off)
4. Sometimes my little brother's **continual** questions can make me crazy. (a broken stream of questions...off and on)
5. When you look out an airplane window, it seems there is a **continuous** skyline that goes on forever. (an unbroken vista that goes on forever)
6. My alarm has a 10 minute doze feature that buzzes **continually** every 10 minutes. (this one is a little tricky--but you need to look at the subject--it's the 10 min doze feature. The doze feature buzzes then goes off for 10 minutes and then buzzes again.)
7. My mom used to own a bird and I had to listen to its **continual** squawking and complaining. (the bird squawks for awhile and then stops, then starts, then stops...)
8. At the tomb of the unknown soldier the honor guard maintain a **continuous** vigil 24/7/365. (unbroken)
9. The planets move **continuously** in their orbits around the sun. (unbroken)
10. I hate watching TV because of the **continual** commercials.(off and on)

Questions:
1. We are (**continually/continuously**) interrupted at dinner by phone calls.
2. About 22 days after conception our hearts begin to beat and they will beat (**continually/continuously**) until the day we die.
3. If you have to (**continually/continuously**) remind your grandparent about things, it could be a sign of dementia.
4. (**Continual/Continuous**) visits to the doughnut shop have increased his waistline.
5. I have to (**continually/continuously**) restart my computer--I'm going to get an Apple.
6. From News Chopper 11 you could see the traffic jam stretched out in a (**continual/continuous**) line of cars as far as the eye could see.

7. Many people **(continually/continuously)** listen to the same radio stations.
8. A spyware application must keep **(continual/continuous)** watch for any sign of malware.
9. **(Continually/Continuously)** making late payments (even 3 in a year) can hurt your credit rating.
10. The father penguin **(continually/continuously)** holds the baby egg on the tops of his feet all through the Antarctic winter.

Answers

1. We are **continually** interrupted at dinner by phone calls. (off and on, periodic)
2. About 22 days after conception our hearts begin to beat and they will beat **continuously** until the day we die. (one unbroken stream of heartbeats)
3. If you have to **continually** remind your grandparent about things, it could be a sign of dementia. (off and on)
4. **Continual** visits to the doughnut shop have increased his waistline. (off and on visits)
5. I have to **continually** restart my computer--I'm going to get an Apple. (off and on--even though it seems like an unbroken stream.)
6. From News Chopper 11 you could see the traffic jam stretched out in a **continuous** line of cars as far as the eye could see. (a long unbroken line of cars)
7. Many people **continually** listen to the same radio stations. (listen, stop, listen, stop...etc)
8. A spyware application must keep **continuous** watch for any sign of malware. (it never stops guarding)
9. **Continually** making late payments (even 3 in a year) can hurt your credit rating. (late, not late, late, not late, etc)
10. The father penguin **continuously** holds the baby egg on the tops of his feet all through the Antarctic winter. (he never lets the egg drop)

Correspond to/with

Correspond to means "in agreement with":
 • The punishment does not ***correspond*** to the severity of the crime.
Correspond with means "to exchange letters":
 • Benjamin Franklin ***corresponded*** with Thomas Jefferson during the Revolutionary war.

Could of

Could of does **not** exist. Neither do **should of, will of,** or **would of**. Write **could have, should have, will have,** or **would have.** If you want to emphasize the pronunciation, write it as a verb contraction: **could've, should've, will've,** or **would've.**

Council vs. Counsel

Consul (n.) is "an official appointed by a foreign government to reside in a foreign country to represent the commercial interests of citizens of the appointed country"
Council (n.) is a legislative body or an assembly of people who serve in an administrative capacity. A government body or an assembly of officials or a committee elected to lead or govern could be described as a council (e.g., a church council, a town council and student council).
 • The emergency session was convened due to the failure of the United Nations Security **Council** to resolve the instability at the Suez Canal.
 • In December 1046, Holy Roman Emperor Henry III established a church **council** to reform the papacy.

Counsel (n.,v.) is a legal adviser or a supervisor. The noun *counsel* means advice, guidance, or consultation. As a verb, *counsel* means to advise. The word 'counsel' is most commonly a verb meaning 'to give advice'. It is also a noun meaning advice (usually legal assistance) or opinion. Counsel can also refer to a body of people set up to offer advice (usually legal advice); e.g., the Queen's Counsel, the General Counsel of the Army.
 • Religious leaders seek to **counsel** their membership.   (Counsel is a verb in this example.)
 • The litigation team offers excellent **counsel** on a wide range of subjects. (Counsel is a noun in this example.)
 • After bereavement, who **counsels** the **counselor**?

Questions:

1. Peace is not made at the **(council/counsel)** table or by treaties, but in the hearts of men." (Herbert Hoover)
2. Go not to the elves for **(council/counsel)** , for they will say both yes and no." (J. R. R. Tolkien)
3. Evil **(council/counsel)** travels fast. (Sophocles)
4. All wars are planned by old men in **(council/counsel)** rooms.
5. To date, no one has claimed responsibility for the bombing of the American **(consul's/council's/counsel's)** official residence.
6. Anyone suspected of committing a crime may request that **(consul/council/counsel)** be present during an interrogation.
7. It came as no surprise when city **(consul members/council members/counsel members)** voted down the plan to ban all cell phone use by drivers, given that cell companies made such sizable contributions to various members' campaigns.
8. The administration received over 200 applications for camp **(consulor/councilor/counselor)** this year.
9. Among the items on the agenda at next week's **(consul/council/counsel)** meeting will be earthquake preparedness.
10. Superior Court Judge John Pitman denied a request by Paul Denbigh for post-conviction relief that named ineffective **(council / counsel)** as a reason to have his case re-examined
11. In my experience, most young people have no understanding of the right to **(council / counsel)**.
12. The General **(Council / Counsel)** is the Army's chief lawyer, who is ultimately responsible for determining the Army's position on any legal question. It serves as legal **(council / counsel)** to the Secretary, Under Secretary, five Assistant Secretaries and other members of the Army Secretariat.
13. I think you stand an excellent chance of winning your case. You see, the town **(council / counsel)** under the leadership of the mayor is responsible for setting policy. I have appointed you our top man, Mr Williams. He is a first-class attorney who provides excellent **(council / counsel)** to executive teams and boards of directors.

Answers: 1. council, 2. counsel, 3. counsel, 4. council, 5. consul's, 6. counsel, 7. council members, 8. counselor, 9. council, 10. counsel, 11. counsel, 12. Counsel, counsel, 13. council, counsel

Decent vs. Descent vs. Dissent

Decent (adj.) (dee-suh nt) it means fitting, appropriate or in good taste. conforming to the recognized standard of propriety, good taste, modesty, seemly, proper, decorous, apt, fit, becoming., as in behavior or speech.
2.respectable; worthy: *a decent family.***3.**adequate; fair; passable: *a decent wage.* **4.**kind; obliging; generous: *It was very decent of him to lend me his watch.***5.**suitable; appropriate: *She did not have a decent coat for the cold winter.*

Descent (n.) [dih-**sent**] means a decline or the act of moving downward. a downward inclination or slope. a passage or stairway leading down.**4.**derivation from an ancestor; lineage; extraction. any passing from higher to lower in degree or state; decline.

1. The act or an instance of descending. A way down. A downward incline or passage; a slope.
2.
    a. Hereditary derivation; lineage: *a person of African descent.*
    b. One generation of a specific lineage.
    c. The fact or process of coming down or being derived from a source: *a paper tracing the descent of the novel from old picaresque tales.*
    d. Development in form or structure during transmission from an original source.
3.
    a. The fact or process of coming down or being derived from a source: *a paper tracing the descent of the novel from old picaresque tales.*
    b. Development in form or structure during transmission from an original source.
4. *Law* Transference of property by inheritance.
5. A lowering or decline, as in status or level: *Her career went into a rapid descent after the charges of misconduct.*

Dissent (v.) [dih-**sent**] to disagree or to differ in opinion. to differ in sentiment or opinion, esp. from the majority; withhold assent; disagree (often fol. by *from*): *Two of the justices dissented from the majority decision.* to disagree with the methods, goals, etc., of a political party or government; take an opposing view. to disagree with or reject the doctrines or authority of an established church.

–noun difference of sentiment or opinion. dissenting opinion. disagreement with the philosophy, methods, goals, etc., of a political party or government. separation from an established church, esp. the Church of England; nonconformity.

Questions
1. When the evidence revealed the actual events of the case, the defendant, a public servant who once had earned great respect from his constituents, experienced a fast *(decent/descent/dissent)* into painful notoriety.
2. Our right to *(decent/descent/dissent))* from a majority opinion enables us to examine issues carefully and to discover new perspectives and new ways of solving problems.
3. Now it is time to offer *(decent/descent/dissent)* to the argument that chocolate ice cream is better than vanilla.
4. The father made a *(decent/descent/dissent)* attempt to talk his children into going to the zoo on the rainy day.
5. The plane's *(decent/descent/dissent)* at such a rapid rate caused my stomach to quiver.
6. Students manifest *(decent/descent/dissent)* during rally today at UCLA.
7. The arrest marked the halfway point of her *(decent/descent/dissent)* from successful business owner to a woman accused of multiple crimes
8. Yay for seemingly *(decent/descent/dissent)* unemployment news!
9. The current draft has "almost been gutted" because of *(decent/descent/dissent)*, Hatoyama told an Upper House budget committee meeting broadcast on NHK television yesterday.
10. Home prices slow dizzying *(decent/descent/dissent)*.
11. Left wing ideology, the pursuit of government grants and the stifling of scientific *(decent/descent/dissent)* work together to hobble progress, reduce freedom and raise costs.
12. Along with the electronic traction-stability control systems and anti-lock brakes come hill start and hill *(decent/descent/dissent)* control systems
13. The Rochester area economy continued its *(decent/descent/dissent)* in January, with an increase in the unemployment rate and a drop in private-sector
14. Good Columbia River chinook returns should create *(decent/descent/dissent)* opportunities off the coast this summer.
15. Vijai Nathan, a rising local stand-up comic of Indian *(decent/descent/dissent)* who regaled the crowd with slightly ribald tales of her dating woes
16. Is the Southern Poverty Law Center terrorizing *(decent/descent/dissent)* American patriots?
17. The plan focuses on creating *(decent/descent/dissent)* work and avoiding deindustrialisation through growth in infrastructure spending and public works programs.
18. EPA chief to testify on hill as *(decent/descent/dissent)* over carbon rules grows.

Answers: 1. descent 2. dissent 3. dissent 4. decent 5. descent 6. dissent 7. descent 8. decent 9. dissent 10. descent 11. dissent 12. descent 13. descent 14. decent 15. descent 16. decent 17. decent 18. dissent

Delusion vs. Illusion vs. Allusion

Allusion (n.) means a casual or subtle reference. An **allusion** is a subtle reference or hint: Rita Book made an allusion to the most recent novel she read in our conversation yesterday. **An allusion is an indirect reference to something.** The noun allusion denotes a subtle or indirect reference to something (i.e., a hint at something). It derives from the verb to allude.

Delusion (n.) means a mistaken conviction about reality that has resulted from impaired or misleading judgment. A **delusion**, in everyday language, is a fixed belief that is either false, fanciful, or derived from deception-- a belief based on false or incomplete information, incorrect" dogma, stupidity, apperception, illusion, or other effects of perception.

Illusion (n.) means fanciful or unreal occurrence. An **illusion** is a deception, mirage, or a wild idea: The teacher said she had no illusions about how much work teaching demands. An illusion is a false impression or deception. **An illusion is deception.**

Questions

1. The Simpsons is full of *(illusions/delusions/allusions)* to well-known films.
2. His consistent *(illusions/delusions/allusions)* to being so poor as a child are not in keeping with his brother's version of their childhood.
3. Teenage cannabis smokers who carry on using the drug in adulthood are more likely to suffer from hallucinations or paranoid *(illusions/delusions/allusions)*, research suggests.
4. It's not an oasis - it is an *(illusion/delusion/allusion)*.
5. I am under no *(illusion/delusion/allusion)* how much work is required.
6. A psychosis can cause a person to experience *(illusions/delusions/allusions)*.
7. His comment about the cross he has to bear was an obvious *(illusion/delusion/allusion)* to the Bible.
8. Wearing special 3D glasses, the movie presents the *(illusion/delusion/allusion)* of being three dimensional.
9. It's an optical *(illusion/delusion/allusion)* a person close to the camera uses their fingers and appears to squish another person far away.
10. Marcus suffers from the *(illusion/delusion/allusion)* that he's actually Spiderman.
11. Does examination of points, passes, data and standings produce reality or *(illusion/delusion/allusion)*
12. Everyone can identify with making the transition from the comforting realm of childhood into the structured and confusing world of adults. Or perhaps it's the less-that-innocent *(illusions/delusions/allusions)* to mind-altering substances that speak to a certain segment of the audience. (speaking about Alice in Wonderland)
13. It's a great opportunity to see live grand-scale magic and *(illusion/delusion/allusion)* that is appropriate for the whole family
14. Certainly, the ideas and reversals of logic in the books, as well as many of the *(illusions/delusions/allusions)* , sail right over children's heads.
15. It is an *(illusion/delusion/allusion)* to believe that the central bank could engineer the money supply without endangering the country.
16. But how likely is it that people who live under economic and political philosophies and programs that are contradictory to one another can both be free? Not very likely at all! In fact, the likelihood is that one of them is suffering a very serious case of self-deception and self-*(illusion/delusion/allusion)* bordering on what psychiatrists might call psychosis.
17. The film was packed with literary *(illusions/delusions/allusions)*, either overtly or covertly referencing Charles Dickens.

Answers: 1. allusions 2. allusions 3. delusions 4. illusion 5. illusion 6. delusions 7. allusion 8. illusion 9. illusion 10. delusion 11. illusion 12. allusions 13. illusion 14. allusions 15. illusion 16. delusion 17. allusions

Dependant vs. Dependent

Dependant: A dependant is person who is dependent on someone else. (For example, a child is dependent on its parents. Therefore, a child is a dependant of its parents.)
Dependent: The word "dependent" is an adjective meaning 'contingent on', 'relying on', 'supported by' or 'addicted to'. The word 'dependant' refers to a person and is a noun.

Questions:

1. Thus, flowering plant species *(dependant/dependent)* on insect pollination, as opposed to self-pollination or wind pollination, could be endangered when the population of insect-pollinators is depleted by the use of pesticides.
2. This need based scholarship is awarded to a single applicant who is the sole bread earner of his/her family and has *(dependant/dependent)* parent/sibling
3. This species is highly *(dependant/dependent)* on the insect-pollinators most vulnerable to Matacil.
4. "If the *(dependant/dependent)* child has no income, or very low income, he is considered a *(dependant/dependent)* and it essentially allows the amount to be tax-free," says Golombek
5. Millions of Somalis are *(dependant/dependent)* on humanitarian aid for their survival
6. Plant species *(dependant/dependent)* solely on seeds for survival or dispersal are obviously more vulnerable to any decrease in plant fecundity that occurs, whatever its cause.
7. All embassy staff and their *(dependants/dependents)* must be at the airport by 6 o'clock.
8. People who cross the oceans in ships are entirely *(dependant/dependent)* on the weather for a safe crossing.
9. The 4th of July celebration is *(dependant/dependent)* on the weather. We hope all the police officers and all their *(dependants/dependents)* won't have to stand in the rain like last year. The *(dependants/dependents)* are younger and are more susceptible to catching cold and getting sick.
10. Freedom is *(dependant/dependent)* on every generation having the same beliefs and convictions as the founders.
11. if we want to be noticed, we need everyone and their *(dependants/dependents)* in attendance tonight.
12. Getting a good paying job is *(dependant/dependent)* on working hard in school.
13. I intend for my *(dependants/dependents)* to live with me in the British Consulate grounds. However, this is *(dependant/dependent)* on the security situation improving to last year's level. Two of my *(dependants/dependents)* are young children.

Answers: 1. dependent 2. dependant 3. dependent 4. dependent, dependant 5. dependent 6. dependent 7. dependants 8. dependent 9. dependent, dependants, dependants 10. dependent 11. dependants 12. dependent 13. dependants, dependent, dependants

Desert vs. Dessert

desert (n.) a dry, sandy region or wasteland, arid/dry region that supports only sparse vegetation.
deserts (n.) plural of desert...the Sahara and the Sonora are deserts.

deserts (n.) just deserts...if you cheat, you'll get what's coming to you-- your just deserts (not just desserts).
To desert (v.) means "to abandon."
dessert (n.) a sweet dish served at the end of a meal.

TIP Dessert has two "s" letters so think how great it would be to get two desserts.

Usage Notes
There are two nouns and a verb spelled desert. The first of these is the barren desert, (dez-ert)
The second desert is 'just desserts' [di-**zurt**] (which one gets). but it's not spelled desserts, as if chocolate cake or cherries jubilee were being substituted for what one deserves--
Third is the verb "to desert" [di-**zurt**] to abandon.
But a dessert is something you eat, like cake and it's pronounced [di-**zurt**] or [da-**zurt**]

Questions
1. Many plants and animals possess special features which allow them to cope with the **(dessert/desert)** conditions.
2. An ice **(dessert/desert)** is defined as a polar area that supports little or no vegetation and that is permanently covered by snow and ice.
3. If disturbed too often, the adult birds will **(dessert/desert)** the fledglings.
4. **(dessert/desert)** includes the scrumptious pies, cakes, and ice cream we get to eat if we finish dinner.
5. If you **(dessert/desert)** the army, you will be shot when you're caught.
6. As soon as the bell rang, the kids **deserted** the building.
7. Would you like to see the **(dessert/desert)** menu?
8. If you put the federal government in charge of the Sahara **(Dessert/Desert)**, in five years there would be a shortage of sand. (Milton Friedman)
9. Work is the meat of life, pleasure the **(dessert/desert)**. (B. C. Forbes)
10. A correction in this space on Wednesday misspelled the name of the city where the Fords' church was located. It is Palm **(Dessert/Desert)**, not Palm **(Dessert/Desert)**.
11. *It may appear that they're getting ahead by cheating, but they'll get their* just **(dessert/desert)** *in the end.*
12. The luxurious resort features a rich, regional flair complete with luscious views of the unique topography of the Arizona **(dessert/desert)**.
13. Marriage is like a dull meal with the **(dessert/desert)** at the beginning.
14. "Man is a complex being who makes **(desserts/deserts)** bloom and lakes die." (G. B. Stern)
15. My daughter's first question after every meal is, "What's for **(dessert/desert)**?"
16. Some drug addictions can cause their victims to **(dessert/desert)** everything they love.
17. California is fortunate to have beaches, ski resorts and **(deserts/desserts)** all within a couple hours drive.
18. Skeletal remains found in the **(dessert/desert)** this week near Boron have triggered a forensic investigation to determine the victim's identity and cause of death
19. Gilligan was cast away on a **(desserted/deserted)** **(dessert/desert)** island?
20. After the game, the reporter asked him "Do you feel like you **(desserted/deserted)** your team?"

Answers: 1. desert 2. desert 3. desert 4. dessert 5. desert 6. deserted 7. dessert 8. desert 9. dessert 10. Desert, Dessert 11. deserts 12. desert 13. dessert 14. deserts 15. dessert 16. desert 17. deserts 18. desert 19. deserted, desert 20. deserted

Device vs. Devise

Device (n.) means apparatus or machinery.
Devise (v.) to develop, create, or construct an idea, system, plan or product of some kind.

The noun device means "a gadget." The verb to devise means "to plan."
• Video games are a great **device devised** for wasting time.

Questions
1. The company announced Friday that it will ship the Wi-Fi-only version of its new tablet **(device/devise)**.
2. We must **(device/devise)** a way to rescue Lassie from the well.
3. there are always unscrupulous individuals who **(device/devise)** scams to take advantage of people in need
4. Industry analysts at Gartner expect touchscreen mobile **(device/devise)** sales to grow by 96.8% this yea
5. The company has created a low-power **(device/devise)** that can transfer information at high speeds using light
6. We are challenging our nation's best and brightest to use their expertise and creativity to **(device/devise)** new ways to generate green energy.
7. Jacques Polak also **(deviced/devised)** a winning approach to Scrabble.
8. A new portable **(device/devise)** that delivers a magnetic pulse to the back of the head could prevent or treat migraines in people susceptible to them
9. The administration moved quickly to **(device/devise)** an alternative plan for border security.
10. The new **(device/devise)**, which is under patent processing, uses embedded software technology.

Answers: 1. device 2. devise 3. devise 4. device 5. device 6. devise 7. devised 8. device 9. devise 10. device

Different from vs. Different than

If you want to follow traditional guidelines, use **'from'** when the comparison is between two persons or things:
• The new Cadillac's are very **'different from'** the imported luxury cars.
*Use **different than** where the second object of comparison is expressed by a full clause (subject and a verb):*

- The campus is *different than* it was twenty years ago. ('...it was twenty years ago...' is a complete clause with a subject and verb)

How to remember: 'Different' comes from 'to differ'. You would say (x differs from y) and **not** (x differs *than* y)
Exception: Use *different from* with a clause if the clause starts with a *conjunction and so functions as a noun:
- The campus is *different from* how it was twenty years ago. ('...how it was twenty years ago...' is a complete clause with a subject and verb, but it starts with the conjunction 'how' which makes 'different from' more acceptable.) * A conjunction is a word that links words, phrases, or clauses together

Here is the progression of the rule:
1. Use *'different from'* always, never use *'different than'*--you'll get it right most of the time.
2. Use *'different from'* always unless the second object of comparison is part of a clause (in which case you use *'different than'*)--you'll get it right 95% of the time.
3. Use "*different from'* always, unless the second object is part of a clause (in which case you use *'different than'*) unless the clause begins with a preposition (in which case you use *'different from'*)--you'll get it right 100% of the time.

When to Use 'Different from'
Use 'different from' for simple comparisons, as in comparing two persons or things.
- My textbook is *different from* (not than) her textbook.
- The iPod I bought is *'different from'* the one her brother got for Christmas.

It is important to remember that when using 'different from', the two things being compared (my textbook and her textbook) should have the same grammatical structure. This is called parallel construction.
- Students at Washington high school reacted differently from students at Jefferson high school.
- Students who major in literature write differently from those who major in business.

When 'Different than' is Acceptable
According to the American Heritage Dictionary's usage panel (1992), different than is acceptable only if the words following 'different than' make up a clause (have a subject and a verb). Here's an example:
- It seems so different than the way things were in Paris.
- It seems so different than Paris was.
- It seems so different than what happened in Paris.

Review:
'Different from' means not the same.
- Jennifer's study habits are different from mine.
'Different than' -- is an alternative to be used only before a clause.
- Jennifer's study habits were very different than I'd expected. ('I'd expected' is a clause)
Bottom line: On the exam different than is generally always wrong when comparing two nouns. Different than is only correct when a sentence compares a noun and a clause.
- Baseball is *different from* softball. • Your notes from biology look *different than* they used to since your dog ate them.
- Classical music is very *different* from rap. • Things are *different* than they were when you were here last year.
One way to remember 'different from' is preferred over 'different than': *different* has two *f*'s and only one *'t'*, so the best choice between *than* and *from* is the one that starts with an *f*' and not the one that starts with *'t'* (Fogarty, *Grammar Girl's Quick and Dirty Tips* 22).

Discrete vs. Discreet

Discreet (adj.) means tactful, prudent, self-restraint, judicious, or circumspect. Tends to be applied to people;
Discrete (adj.) means distinct or separate. discrete usually applies to ideas, categories, etc. and is found in more technical or impersonal contexts
- "Be *discreet* in all things, and so render it unnecessary to be mysterious about any." (Arthur Wellesley)
Discrete means individually distinct. **Discreet** means inconspicuous.

Questions
1. Because of the writers' strike and the economic crisis, the opulent parties have been a little more *(discrete/discreet)* over the last two years
2. Electricity is composed of *(discrete/discreet)* particles of equal size.
3. Many young socialites are not known to be *(discrete/discreet)* about their love lives and they even about it.
4. Most congressional works don't know how to be *(discrete/discreet)* and information constantly leaks to the press.
5. Congress should have put together five or six *(discrete/discreet)* and digestible pieces of legislation that people could review separately.
6. You can trust my aide, Monica - she's is very *(discrete/discreet)* .
7. Defense and diplomacy are no longer *(discrete/discreet)* choices, one to be applied when the other fails, but must complement one another throughout the messy process
8. Oftentimes bidders at auctions want privacy and demand a *(discrete/discreet)* process.
9. The charges are driven primarily by *(discrete/discreet)* events that management does not consider to be directly related to the company's core operating performance.
10. There is a rack on the bench that contains all the *(discrete/discreet)* electronic components.
11. The cops busted through the dining room and none were *(discrete/discreet)* . It was like they just assumed we were already guilty.
12. Our country club has several *(discrete/discreet)* membership levels.

13. Don't worry though, the display is *(discrete/discreet)* so a nosy eye will not know what they are looking at.

Answers: 1. discreet 2. discrete 3. discreet 4. discreet 5. discrete 6. discrete 7. discrete 8. discrete 9. discrete 10. discrete 11. discreet 12. discrete 13. discreet

Disinterested vs. uninterested

Disinterested means "impartial" and "without bias."
Uninterested means "indifferent" or "unconcerned."
 • "Disinterested intellectual curiosity is the life blood of real civilization." (G. M. Trevelyan)
A person is *uninterested* in a thing if it holds no interest for them; if they prefer to give their attention to other things.
 • I am interested in golf and American history, but I am uninterested in modern interpretive dance.

In traditional usage, *disinterested* can only mean 'having no stake in an outcome. To be *disinterested*, is to have no stake in the subject matter.
 • Judges should be interested in cases they decide, but they must be disinterested in them. (impartial)
 • *Since the judge stands to profit from the sale of the company, she cannot be considered a disinterested party in the dispute.*

Questions

1. Since she discovered skiing, she is *(uninterested/disinterested)* in her schoolwork.
2. His unwillingness to give five minutes of his time proves that he is **(uninterested/***disinterested***)** in finding a solution to the problem.
3. Without an unbiased, *(uninterested/disinterested)* witness there is no way to know if the patient was of sound mind.
4. A lively, *(uninterested/disinterested)*, persistent looking for truth is extraordinarily rare. (Henri Amiel)
5. A cable operator surveyed its subscribers several years ago and found that 75% were either *(uninterested/disinterested)* or only mildly interested in sports and didn't want to pay more if ESPN increased its fees.
6. The narrative of the *(uninterested/disinterested)* scientist is a myth. Scientists get their money from government, and in return, they dance to the music of big government.
7. The Panthers are quarterback-challenged, with Jake Delhomme and Matt Moore, but they were *(uninterested/disinterested)* in Vick last summer.
8. The leadership wants to pass a resolution of the *(uninterested/disinterested)* shareholders authorizing the Corporation to issue, subordinate voting shares.
9. The newly appointed United States Olympic Committee (USOC) leadership is apparently *(uninterested/disinterested)* in submitting a 2020 candidate.
10. But both parties are suitably middle-of-the-road at the moment that a *(uninterested/disinterested)* observer can hardly tell one from the other.
11. Iraq remains a mess from which the US military seems increasingly *(uninterested/disinterested)* in withdrawing fully and Afghanistan a disaster area.

Answers: 1. uninterested 2. uninterested 3. disinterested 4. disinterested 5. uninterested 6. disinterested 7. uninterested 8. disinterested 9. uninterested 10. disinterested 11. uninterested

Double negatives

This list has words that are regarded as negative. If you use them in your sentences, your statements will be negative.

no	nowhere	hardly
not	neither	scarcely
none	nobody	barely
nothing	no one	

A double negative is the nonstandard usage of two negatives used in the same sentence so that they cancel each other and create a positive. In Shakespeare's day, double negatives were considered emphatic, but today, they are considered mistakes. Remembering that two negatives form a positive will help you to avoid the "double negative" grammar problem:

	Sentence	Meaning
Positive Construction	I <u>hardly</u> have <u>none</u>.	I have some.
negative + negative	I <u>don't</u> want <u>nothing</u>.	I want something.
Negative Construction	I <u>hardly</u> have <u>any</u>.	I have few.
negative + positive	I <u>don't</u> want <u>anything</u>.	I want nothing.

Questions

1. I think the new homeroom teacher will not last barely a month.
2. Since the student failed the last exam, the teacher has not had no time to help him.
3. The cafeteria did not have none of my favorite dishes.
4. The coach couldn't find nowhere to practice.
5. The students hardly took no warm clothes to the game.
6. It hardly never rains in southern California.
7. The players couldn't barely do nothing after practice.
8. There is hardly nothing worse than going to track practice after eating a big lunch.

Answers:

1. I think the new homeroom teacher will barely last a month. OR I think the new homeroom teacher will not last a month.
2. Since the student failed the last exam, the teacher has not had any time to help him. OR Since the student failed the last exam, the teacher has had no time to help him.
3. The cafeteria did not have any of my favorite dishes. OR The cafeteria had none of my favorite dishes.
4. The coach couldn't find anywhere to practice. OR The coach found nowhere to practice.

5. The students hardly took any warm clothes to the game. OR The students hardly took any warm clothes to the game.
6. It hardly ever rains in southern California. Or It never rains in southern California.
7. (This is a triple negative) The players couldn't do anything after practice. OR The players could barely do anything after practice. OR The players could do nothing after practice.
8. There is hardly anything worse than going to track practice after eating a big lunch. OR There is nothing worse than going to track practice after eating a big lunch.

Questions

1. I couldn't do (nothing, anything)
2. You (can, can't) scarcely breathe after playing that song.
3. I hardly had (no, any) time to do my homework.
4. The Olympic track star (was, wasn't) hardly sweating after the race.
5. Of all the songs on his iPod, I did not like (none, any).
6. After the accident she (could, couldn't) hardly walk.
7. He put on the headset but didn't hear (anything, nothing).
8. You (can, can't) scarcely tell them apart.
9. I didn't talk with (anybody, nobody) I knew.
10. She didn't have (nothing, anything) to help her.
11. I don't like (none, any) of those dinner choices.
12. I didn't have (no, any) money.
13. I (was, wasn't) hardly allowed to go (anywhere, nowhere).
14. Stephanie won't study with (either, neither) Jake or Joshua.

Answers

1. I couldn't do **anything**.
2. You **can** scarcely breathe after playing that song.
3. I hardly had **any** time to do my homework.
4. The Olympic track star **was** hardly sweating after the race.
5. Of all the songs on his iPod, I did not like **any**.
6. After the accident she **could** hardly walk.
7. He put on the headset but didn't hear **anything**.
8. You **can** scarcely tell them apart.
9. I didn't talk with **anybody** I knew.
10. She didn't have **anything** to help her.
11. I don't like **any** of those dinner choices.
12. I didn't have **any** money.
13. I **was** hardly allowed to go **anywhere**.
14. Stephanie won't study with **either** Jake or Joshua.

Doubt that vs. Doubt whether

Doubt whether is nonstandard.
- **Wrong**: I *doubt whether* his new business will succeed. • **Correct**: I *doubt that* his new business will succeed.

Dual vs. Duel

Dual (adj.) means double or twofold.
Duel (v./n.) referring to a fight or struggle.
- In 1954 the U.S. Supreme Court ordered that the system of *dual* schools for whites and blacks be dismantled.
- In an 1804 *duel* in New Jersey, Aaron Burr shot and killed former Treasury Secretary Alexander Hamilton.

Questions

1. An undeclared and mostly bloodless *(dual/duel)* was fought for the control of Indonesia's 3,000 islands.
2. They said a *(dual/duel)* buy would spur competition between the two companies and result in a better deal for the Air Force
3. The story will unfold now of how these two great pitchers tangled in what is one of the greatest *(duals/duels)* in the history of baseball
4. Sidney Poitier has *(dual/duel)* American-Bahamian citizenship.
5. Based on Intel® latest CPU with *(dual/duel)* core capability delivers performance and flexibility for embedded applications
6. Interested students in Carnegie Mellon University's mechanical engineering program are being selected to participate in a new *(dual/duel)* doctoral program
7. Defending world heavyweight champions will resume their *(dual/duel)* for supremacy in this next bout.
8. Boise State University's women's golf team will host instate-rival Idaho State University this Friday in a *(dual/duel)* match.
9. The *(dual/duel)* between #1 ranked Michigan State and #2 Penn will determine the national champs.
10. This is the second in a four-part series focusing in on *(dual/duel)* language learning in early childhood.
11. After a grueling *(dual/duel)* with US lawmakers, Akio Toyoda visits China.

Answers: **1.** duel 2. dual 3. duels 4. dual 5. dual 6. dual 7. duel 8. dual 9. duel **10.** duel 11. dual

Due to

Due to means "caused by." Use it only if it can be substituted with "caused by." 'Due to' does not mean "because of."
Incorrect: The game was postponed *due to* rain. **Correct**: The game was postponed *because of* rain.

Correct: The game's postponement was *due to* rain.

Remember to use 'due to' when you can replace it with 'caused by'; this usually occurs when a form of the verb 'to be' (is, am, was, were, are) is used by itself. Like this:
- The newspaper article claimed the exploding debt <u>is</u> **due to** congress' lack of fiscal restraint.

In this example, you can substitute 'caused by' and it will still make sense (the exploding debt is caused by congress'...) But if we change the sentence a little watch what happens.
- The newspaper article claimed the debt <u>exploded </u>**due to** congress' lack of fiscal restraint.

Now if we substitute "*caused by*' for *'due to'* it makes the sentence awkward. Because in this case we used *'due to'* to actually mean *'because of'* or *'on account of'* or *'owing to'* which is not acceptable. So we would have to change it to:
- The newspaper article claimed the debt exploded **because of** congress' lack of fiscal restraint.

We are using 'because of' or 'owing to' or 'on account of' because the sentence does not have a form of '*to be*' by itself (it uses the verb 'exploded'). So when we substitute '*on account of*' or '*because of*', the sentence does, indeed, make sense, Becomes: '*...the debt exploded on account of (because of) congress'.*'
Here are another couple of examples:
- *The football team won the state championship last night (due to/because of) a last second field goal.*
- *The victory in the state football championship game was (due to/because of) a last second field goal.*

In the first sentence we don't have a 'to be' verb directly before 'due to' (we have the verb won--to win) so we should use 'because of'. Also we can use the other test, try using 'caused by' in place of 'due to' **test it**; 'the team won **caused by** a last second field goal' That is awkward construction. Both tests lead us to choose 'because of'. **Becomes**: 'The team won because of a last second field goal' (you could test it using 'owing to')

In the second sentence notice we do have a 'to be' verb (was) which tells us to use 'due to'. But we can also use the second test, plug in 'caused by'. **Test it**: 'The victory was *caused by* a last second field goal.' That makes total sense and is a proper construction. So we choose 'due to'.

Note: The wordy expression **due to the fact that** should be replaced by **because** or **since**.

TIP 1. Substitute 'caused by' if it works use 'Due to" if not use 'Because of'. Converse test: 2. Substitute 'owing to' or 'because of', if it works don't use "Due to"

Questions
1. The company delayed filing its annual report to the US Securities and Exchange Commission (**because of/due to)** the company's continued accounting investigation.
2. Zilker Kite Festival postponed until March 14th **(because of/due to)** rain
3. Ubaldo Jimenez' failure to attend his spring debut Friday was **(because of/due to)** his involvement in a major traffic jam on a Phoenix highway.
4. This announcement is primarily used to inform the public about road closures that typically occur during the winter months **(because of/due to)** ice or snow on the road.
5. An autopsy revealed that the infant elephant's death was **(because of/due to)** long-term malnutrition.
6. The Yankees DH Nick Johnson was scratched from Thursday's game **(because of/due to)** a stiff low back
7. The flight from Rochester to Chicago with 127 people on board was forced to land in Buffalo **(because of/due to)** a fire that broke out in the bathroom of the plane, filling the cabin with smoke.
8. Shipping delays in the first batch of Apple's latest Wi-Fi iPad were **(due not to/not because of)** hardware production issues but to Apple putting the final touches on the software for the device.
9. The removal of Fire Chief Yasmine Yurt by the district's board of trustees was **(because of/due to)** a misunderstanding.
10. Library cuts last year were **(because of/due to)** decreased public use of the library.

Answers: 1. because of 2. because of 3. due to 4. because of 5. due to 6. because of 7. because of 8. due not to 9. due to 10. due to

Eminent vs. Imminent vs. Immanent vs Emanant

Eminent (adj.) [**em**-*uh*-nuh nt] means prominent or outstanding, famous. (used of persons) standing above others in character or attainment or reputation. When a government exercises its power over private property it is drawing on its eminent status in society, so the proper legal phrase is "eminent domain." means "of high rank, outstanding, or prestigious": An eminent author came to read at the university. conspicuous, signal, or noteworthy: *eminent fairness*. lofty; high: *eminent peaks*. prominent; projecting; protruding: *an eminent nose*.
Imminent (adj.) [**im**-*uh*-nuh nt] means impending, about to occur, threatening. near at hand. means "close to happening or near": Everyone waited anxiously for an imminent storm predicted to arrive shortly. facing imminent disaster
Immanent (adj.) [**im**-*uh*-nuh nt] means remaining within; indwelling; inherent. used by philosophers to mean "inherent" and by theologians to mean "present throughout the universe" when referring to God. Existing or remaining within; inherent: *believed in a God immanent in humans.*
Emanant (adj.) [**em**-*uh*-nuh nt] means "sending or issuing forth": Emanant thoughts like those should be kept to yourself. Flowing forth; emanating or issuing from or as if from a source.

Questions
1. Charles Dodgson was an **(eminent/imminent/immanent/emanant)** mathematician.
2. "Personal disintegration remains always an **(eminent/imminent/immanent/emanant)** danger." (Christopher Lasch)
3. A long term deal would at this point seem **(eminent/imminent/immanent/emanant)**, as it would benefit both sides
4. Novelist Naguib Mahfouz was considered the **(eminent/imminent/immanent/emanant)** literary voice of the Arab world.

5. The death of conventional newspapers appears to be *(eminent/imminent/immanent/emanant)* .
6. City council members will decide Monday whether to use *(eminent/imminent/immanent/emanant)* domain to get property needed for two road.
7. Just a year ago, some experts were predicting the *(eminent/imminent/immanent/emanant)* demise of General Motors and Chrysler.
8. However, what one can say without absolute certainty is that Russia is not facing an *(eminent/imminent/immanent/emanant)* and bloody internal revolution.
9. The Chicago Sun Times reports that a deal between the Bears and their highest paid free agent "is *(eminent/imminent/immanent/emanant)* ."
10. The central bank said it would conduct monetary policy strictly using technical criteria and saw no threat of an *(eminent/imminent/immanent/emanant)* interest rate hike in the next week.
11. Mr. Ganga Prasad Birla, the *(eminent/imminent/immanent/emanant)* industrialist and philanthropist, died here on late Friday night.
12. In the week that Hollywood's *(eminent/imminent/immanent/emanant)* eccentric releases his big-budget, 3D extravaganza, the first-ever film of Alice in Wonderland.
13. The council is discussing the current state of the water problem in the city and the ongoing water rationing did not convince the members of the council in declaring the city under the state of the *(eminent/imminent/immanent/emanant)* danger of a calamity.

Answers: 1. eminent 2. imminent 3. immanent 4. eminent 5. imminent 6. eminent 7. imminent 8. immanent (this could also be imminent--meaning about to happen, however, emanant means issuing forth--a revolution issuing forth from Russia) 9. imminent 10. imminent 11. eminent 12. eminent 13, imminent

Enthuse (verb)

To cause to be enthusiastic: The emotion of the play *enthused* the audience.
To show or express enthusiasm: "Princess Anne...*enthused* over Sarah Ferguson..." (Georgia Howell)

Usage Note: The verb *enthuse* is not well accepted. Its use in the sentence "*The majority leader enthused over his party's gains*" was rejected by 76 percent of the Usage Panel in the late 1960s, and its status remains unfavorable: the same sentence was rejected by 65 percent of the Usage Panel in 1997. This lack of enthusiasm for *enthuse* is often attributed to its status as a back-formation; such words often meet with disapproval on their first appearance and only gradually become accepted over time. But other back-formations such as *diagnose* (a back-formation from *diagnosis* that was first recorded in 1861) and *donate* (first cited in 1785 as a back-formation from *donation*) are considered unimpeachable English words. Since *enthuse* dates from 1827, something more significant may be overriding the erosion of popular resistance. Unlike *enthusiasm,* which denotes an internal emotional state, *enthuse* denotes either the external expression of emotion, as in *She enthused over attending the awards ceremony,* or the inducement of enthusiasm by an external source, as in *He was so enthused about the diet pills that he agreed to provide a testimonial.* Possibly, some people's distaste for this emphasis on external emotional display and manipulation is the source of unease that is manifested by a distaste for the word itself. **See** **www.thefreedictionary.com**

Bottom line: you can use 'enthuse' as a verb in almost every other setting, but not on the exam. Because there is lingering debate among grammarians about the correctness of 'enthuse' it probably will NOT show up on the exam.

Envelop vs. Envelope

Envelop (v.) [in **vel** up] meaning "cover" or "enclose." Fog enveloped the house. (envelop with social, intellectual, or moral darkness), wrap, wrap in or as if in a cocoon, as for protection, engulf. enclose or enfold completely with or as if with a covering
Envelope (n.) [**en** vuh-lohp] meaning "container used for mailing." Take the envelope to the post office.
 • If you place a folded paper inside an **envelope**, the **envelope** will snuggly **envelop** the paper.

Questions

1. A smoky haze from the steel mills used to *(envelop/envelope)* the city.
2. "Letters are expectation packaged in an *(envelop/envelope)* ." (Shana Alexander)
3. For most men, life is a search for the proper manila *(envelop/envelope)* in which to get themselves filed." (Clifton Fadiman)
4. Military leaders fear the dreaded 'fog of war' that can *(envelop/envelope)* troops in chaos and calamity in the blink of an eye.
5. The man handed her an *(envelop/envelope)* for her son, Alex, and said he wanted to see "George,".
6. Still, judging by the perfectly clipped hedges that *(envelop/envelope)* the manicured mansions, residents may be doing with less, but not much less.
7. Cirrhosis can *(envelop/envelope)* the liver if chronic hepatitis advances to end-stage liver disease.
8. Sean Devlin, who lives at 20 Tudor Lane, said his dog, Layla, jumped on his bed and woke him up as the fire began to *(envelop/envelope)* his neighbor's shed.
9. Simply answer 10 short and simple questions and mail the form back in the provided postage-paid *(envelop/envelope)* .
10. Analysts warn a new political struggle could *(envelop/envelope)* Africa's most populous country that for weeks had no clear leader but now has a stricken president.

Answers: 1. envelop 2. envelope 3. envelope 4. envelop 5. envelope 6. envelop 7. envelop 8. envelope 9. envelope 10. envelop

Even though, even so, even if

Even though means **despite the fact that** and is a more emphatic version of though and although.

Even if means **whether or not** and has to do with the conditions that may apply. Compare the following:
- **Even if** we studied all night, we still wouldn't be ready for the exam tomorrow.
- **Even though** we studied all night, we didn't pass the exam.

The **first example** describes an **unreal situation** where we could substitute 'just supposing' for **even if** and say: **just supposing** we studied all night, we still wouldn't pass the exam.

The **second example** describes a **real situation** where the student (we) studied all night long, but we still did not pass the exam. When we attach **even** to **though** in this way, we are in effect saying: **you may find this surprising but...!**

- **Even though** he was convicted of fraud, he continued to serve in the US congress.
- **Even if** he is convicted of fraud, I think he'll continue to serve in the US congress.
- **Even though** the jury convicted him of fraud, he decided to continue serving in the US congress.
- I know he'll want to continue serving in the US congress, **even if** he is convicted.
- **Even though** we've studied and prepared for the exam, I still don't think we're ready.
- **Even if** we washed and waxed the truck, I still don't think it will look new.

even : cannot be used as a **conjunction** like **even if** and **even though** when it stands alone. **We cannot say**: Even we washed and waxed the truck, it still doesn't look new.
When **even** stands alone, it functions as an **adverb** and means **this is more than or less than expected**. Again, you are registering something that may be **surprising** when you use it.
- I can't dance. I can't **even** walk very well!
- She got A's in every class, Math, English, History, Biology. She **even** got an A in Music Theory!

Even can also go at the **beginning** of a phrase when it refers to words or expressions that we wish to emphasize, again because this is **surprising** information for the listener:
- He has to work every day--**even** Christmas and New Year! • I know the class can be difficult but **even** I can get a good grade!

even so: prepositional phrase that can be used in a similar fashion to introduce **a fact that is surprising** in the context of what has been said before. It connects ideas between clauses or sentences:
- I know the class can be difficult, but **even so** I can get a good grade.

Eventually vs. Ultimately

Eventually (adv.) refers to an unspecified time in the future.
Ultimately (adv.) means "in the end.", at last, after all is said and done.
- Rulers who are loved and praised are *eventually* feared and *ultimately* despised. (Lao Tzu)

Questions
1. "If it's going to come out (*eventually/ultimately*), better have it come out immediately." (Henry Kissinger)
2. "(*Eventually/Ultimately*), we're all dead men. Sadly we cannot choose how." (Proximo in Galdiator)
3. Sometime in the next year China will (*eventually/ultimately*) move away from its current exchange-rate policies.
4. (*Eventually/Ultimately*), every team in baseball is scheduled to play 81 games at home and 81 games on the road, so things tend to even out over the course of the season.
5. Patricia began violin lessons at 3 1/2, (*eventually/ultimately*) studying with the violinists Jacques Gordon and Hans Letz. At 6. Over the course of several weeks, her charm, beauty, kindness, and humor (*eventually/ultimately*) won him over and he agreed to go out on a date.
7. (E*ventually/Ultimately*), this competition is more about the fans' enjoyment, with one group gaining the edge for a day or two.
8. Basic economics tells us that when Americans, over all, spend more on housing, they must (*eventually/ultimately*) spend less on something else.
9. Kohl's has closed a deal to buy a large distribution center in San Bernardino and will (*eventually/ultimately*) hire 500 employees to man it
10. It was the street life, however, that called loudest to Chatfield, and (*eventually/ultimately*) it claimed him. He was shot dead in October at age 31.

Answers: *1. eventually 2. Ultimately* 3. eventually 4. Ultimately 5. eventually 6. eventually 7. Ultimately 8. ultimately 9. eventually 10. ultimately

Every day vs. Everyday

Everyday (adj.) (written as one word) means routine, ordinary, or commonplace. *These are my everyday clothes.* t means 'casual' or 'informal' with an implied contrast to formality, as well as the meaning of 'familiar, ordinary', accepted, chronic, common, conventional, customary, established, everyday, expected, general, habitual, ordinary, orthodox, regular, routine, set, traditional, typical
Every day (adv.) (two words) means each day. *I learn something new every day.* day after day, continually, daily, day by day, day in day out, every day, regularly, steadily,

Questions
1. "Do something for somebody (*everyday/every day*) for which you do not get paid." (Albert Schweitzer)
2. "There is nothing in philosophy which could not be said in (*everyday/every day*) language." (Henri Bergson)
3. Try doing something (*everyday/every day*) for no other reason than you would rather not do it.
4. "Music is supposed to wash away the dust of (*everyday/every day*) life." (Art Blakey)
5. When asked if the player had re-established himself as an (*everyday/every day*) player, a guy who would start five or six days a week, Manager said, "I think so.

6. *(Everyday/Every day)* that I can train is a good day.
7. He's out to prove he still can be an *(everyday/every day)* first baseman.
8. Consumers are overpaying for many *(everyday/every day)* products and services.
9. We feel we have depth and guys that want to play *(everyday/every day)*.
10. My goal is to break into the Big Leagues and be an *(everyday/every day)* player.
11. The gallery shows 130 ethnographic items, *(everyday/every day)* or ritual objects from indigenous societies in Africa, the Americas, and Southeast Asia.
12. In addition to sun exposure, smoking and drinking, there are small things that we do *(everyday/every day)* that could affect how we look.
13. Demand for reliable energy grows *(everyday/every day)* as our reliance on technology builds and the need for power grows.

Answers: 1. every day 2. everyday 3. every day 4. everyday 5. everyday 6. Every day 7. everyday 8. everyday 9. every day 10. everyday 11. everyday 12. every day 13. every day

Faint vs. Feint

Faint (v.) to lose consciousness temporarily. (adj.) lacking brightness, vividness, clearness, loudness, strength, etc.: *a faint light; a faint color; a faint sound.* **2.** feeble or slight: *faint resistance; faint praise; a faint resemblance.* **3.** feeling weak, dizzy, or exhausted; about to lose consciousness: *faint with hunger.* **4.** lacking courage; cowardly; timorous: *Faint heart never won fair maid.*
Feint is a noun or a verb that has to do with deception, especially in an attack. A feint is an attack aimed at one place or point as a distraction from the intended spot of attack. **–noun 1.** a movement made in order to deceive an adversary; an attack aimed at one place or point merely as a distraction from the real place or point of attack: *military feints; the feints of a skilled fencer.* **2.** a feigned or assumed appearance: *His air of approval was a feint to conceal his real motives.* **–verb** (used without object) **3.** to make a feint. **–verb** (used with object) **4.** to make a feint at; deceive with a feint. **5.** to make a false show of; simulate.

Questions

1. When Fred saw the needle the nurse was using to give him a shot, he *(fainted/feinted)*.
2. The boxer *(fainted/feinted)* with a jab at his opponent's jaw before he landed a hit square into the opponent's stomach.
3. The fumes from the paint caused several of the employees **to** *(faint/feint)* .
4. The patient's mother has *(fainted/feinted)*.
5. All of the talk of reconciliation is just another head *(faint/feint)*. Once the House passes the Senate bill we've got Obamacare.
6. ROUND TWO: They both *(faint/feint)* punches early.
7. Unemployment rates for New York City and the state dipped in January, providing a *(faint/feint)* signal that the waves of layoffs have subsided.
8. That's only because its brightest stars are fourth magnitude which is on the *(faint/feint)* side for those of us living in cities and suburbs.
9. The Fed move was another *(faint/feint)* designed to trick consumers. But there is no economic recovery, and the Fed cannot stop its extraordinary accommodation.
10. The "Ron Paul for President" crowd got a *(faint/feint)* glimmer of hope the straw polls showed a victory in the first primary.
11. This life is not for the *(faint/feint)* of heart.
12. This is, in other words, just a rhetorical *(faint/feint)*, in the attempt of selling his memoir.

Answers: 1. fainted 2. feinted 3. faint 4. fainted 5. feint 6. feint 7. faint 8. faint 9. feint 10. faint 11. faint 12. feint

Farther vs. Further

Farther shows a relation to physical distance. If you can replace the word farther with "a distance" then you have done it correctly. **Farther** refers to **length** or **distance**. It is the comparative form of the word **far** when referring to distance.

- Yesterday I rode my bike *farther* than ever before. • I wanted to ride even *farther*, but I became too exhausted.
  •Eventually I want to ride even *farther*, but I think the *farthest* I'll ever ride in a day is 100 miles.

Further relates to metaphorical distance or depth. It is a time, degree, or quantity. It is also another way of saying "additional".
Further means 'more' "to a greater degree," "additional," or "additionally." It refers to **time** or amount. It is the comparative form of the word far when meaning "much."
The *'farther'* we travel in space the closer we will get to that 'galaxy FAR, FAR AWAY. The *farther* we travel the *further* our technology advances

- I think we need further discussion before deciding how to spend our budge this year.
- We should analyze the data further before we declare our new club can hit golf balls farther than any other club.
- It's doubtful that the price of gold will drop further below $1000 per ounce

IMPORTANT TIP remember that 'farther' deals with distance and has the word 'FAR'.
IMPORTANT TIP remember if you can substitute the word *'more'* or *'additionally'* it's probably 'further'.
IMPORTANT TIP farther relates to physical distance and *further* relates to figurative distance. If you can't decide which one to use, you're safer using *further* because *farther* has some restrictions, also consider using *furthermore* instead of *further*.

Exercise

1. My dad said we'd talk *(farther/further)* tomorrow.
2. Usually a taller person can hit a golf ball *(farther/further)* than anyone else.
3. If you reduce the amount of black ink coverage in your printer the cartridge will go *(farther/further)*
4. Sometimes the *(farther/further)* a teachers 'explains' the less I understand
5. The *(farther/further)* the forensic artist examined the painting, the more convinced he became it was a fake.

6. Who on the baseball team can throw the *(farthest/furthest)*?
7. Most baseball players prefer metal or composite bats because they hit the ball *(farther/further)*.
8. It would not have taken six (6) hours to put the table together if IKEA had provided *(farther/further)* details.
9. Sometimes a strong headwind can stop a well hit baseball from going any *(farther/further)*
10. We'll pick this up tomorrow and debate it *(farther/further)*.

Answers

1. My dad said we'd talk *further* tomorrow.
2. Usually a taller person can hit a golf ball *farther* than anyone else.
3. If you reduce the amount of black ink coverage in your printer the cartridge will go *farther*.
4. Sometimes the *further a teachers 'explains' the less I understand*
5. The *further* the forensic artist examined the painting, the more convinced he became it was a fake.
6. Who on the baseball team can throw the *farthest*?
7. Most baseball players prefer metal or composite bats because they hit the ball *farther*.
8. It would not have taken six (6) hours to put the table together if IKEA had provided *further* details.
9. Sometimes a strong headwind can stop a well hit baseball from going any *farther*.
10. We'll pick this up tomorrow and debate it *further*.

Exercise

1. The more you argue your opinion you can push people *(farther/further)* away.
2. Reno Nevada is *(farther/further)* west than both Los Angeles and San Diego California
3. Working hard in school will *(farther/further)* your education.
4. The bald eagle flies *(farther/further)* north than all other eagles.
5. The *(farther/further)* we stray from the principles in the Declaration of Independence the more freedom we will lose.
6. To *(farther/further)* my baseball career I'm going to play in the Cape Cod league this summer.
7. Who hit the *(farthest/furthest)* homerun in the history of baseball?
8. In the dictionary, *(farther/further)* refers to a physical distance and *(farther/further)* refers to figurative space.
9. The *(farther/further)* an Olympic athlete advances towards a gold medal, the *(farther/further)* their wallet will expand after the Olympics.
10. Yesterday I ran *(farther/further) than anyone else on the team.*

Answers

1. The more you argue your opinion you can push people *further* away. It's further because it's not referring to a physical distance, but rather an ideological distance or emotional distance.
2. Reno Nevada is *farther* west than both Los Angeles and San Diego California
3. Working hard in school will *further* your education.
4. The bald eagle flies *farther* north than all other eagles.
5. The *further* our country strays from the principles set forth in the Declaration of Independence the more freedom we will lose. (this is a metaphysical distance or an ideological distance, not a physical distance)
6. To *further* my baseball career I'm going to play in the Cape Cod league this summer.
7. Who hit the *farthest* homerun in the history of baseball?
8. In the dictionary, *farther* refers to a physical distance and *further* refers to figurative space.
9. The *further* an Olympic athlete advances towards a gold medal, the *farther* their wallet will expand after the Olympics.
10. Yesterday I ran *farther than anyone else on the team.*

Fewer vs. Less

1). Less is the comparative of little (used especially before uncountable nouns).
  • I earn *less* money than you.
Fewer is the comparative of few (used before plural nouns)
  • I've got *fewer* problems than I used to have.
2). Less of and fewer of - used before determiners such as the,, my, this and before pronouns.
  • At the college reunions, there are *fewer* of us each year. • I'd like to spend *less* of my time answering mails.
Before nouns without determiners, of is not used.
  • If you want to lose weight, eat *less* food. (NOT less of food)

3). Nouns can be dropped after less and fewer if the meaning is clear.
  • Some people go to church, but *less/fewer* than 20 years ago
Less can be used as an adverb (the opposite of adverb more)
  • I worry *less* than I used to.
4). Lesser - used to mean "smaller" or "not so much"
  • the *lesser* of two evils.
5) Use less when referring to statistical or numerical expressions.
  • Sara is *less* than five feet tall • Your essay should be a thousand words or *less*

TipUse *'less'* when referring to a single item.
TipUse *'fewer'* when referring to more than one item.

Use fewer when referring to a number of items. In the past, we had fewer options.
Use less when referring to a continuous quantity.   The impact was less than what was expected.
Few and fewer refer to people or objects that can be counted. Little and less refer to a small quantity.

- "I'm a woman of *few* words," Mae West said. I have even *less* to say than Mae.
- *Fewer* than 12,000 pupils were learning Latin in the year 2010.

Use less with nouns that can't be counted: less sugar, less paper, less money; and we are supposed to **Use fewer with nouns that can be counted:** fewer students, fewer cars, fewer minutes.

- I have *less* money than I thought. A *few* bills are missing from my wallet.

Questions

1. Now that I'm broke, I have *(less/fewer)* friends than before
2. The salad has *(less/fewer)* calories than that piece of pie.
3. But because of budget cuts at the university, *(less/fewer)* money is available for some departments.
4. That school had to cancel several classes because there were *(less/fewer)* students enrolling for the fall semester than anticipated.
5. He owns *(less/fewer)* stock in that company than his stockbroker told him.
6. The participation of women as judges in India's higher judiciary is *(less/fewer)* than 10 per cent.
7. During the bus strike, we found there were *(less/fewer)* people using some bus lines than was generally thought.
8. Because residents of the area conserved water so diligently, there is *(less/fewer)* chance of a water shortage this year.
9. The dollar posted its biggest five- day gain versus the yen in two weeks as *(less/fewer)* Americans lost jobs last month.
10. Google is planning a more affordable version of its popular phone, one with *(less/fewer)* features to attract users from emerging economies.
11. This tells us that *(less/fewer)* than two thirds of the population is in the labor force- employed or unemployed.
12. WALL Street stocks jumped on Friday after the government reported US companies shed *(less/fewer)* jobs than expected.
13. The city has made changes to earthen levees, which will mean *(less/fewer)* sandbags will need to be filled.
14. The governor's defiant statement came on the same day that a new poll found that *(less/fewer)* than half of New Yorkers believe he should remain in office.

Answers: 1. fewer 2. fewer 3. less 4. fewer 5. less 6. less 7. fewer 8. less 9. fewer 10. fewer 11. less 12. fewer 13. fewer 14. less (less than half...not less than New Yorkers--so one-half is singular)

Formally vs. Formerly

Formally means properly or officially (adv.) With official authorization "in a formal way." according to protocol, befittingly, ceremoniously, conventionally, correctly, customarily, fittingly, formally, orderly, precisely, properly, regularly, suitably
Formerly means earlier (adv.) At a previous time. a while back, aforetime, already, anciently, at one time, away back, back, back when, before, before now, before this, down memory lane, earlier, eons ago, erewhile, erstwhile, heretofore, in former times, in the olden days, in the past, lately, long ago, of old, of yore, olden days, once, once upon a time, radically, some time ago, time was, used to be, water under the bridge

- *Formerly* an art movement, surrealism is no longer distinguishable from everyday life.   • I have never studied art *formally*.

Look at the two words with the suffix removed--*formal*, *former*. Think of formal invitations, formal dress, formality. In each of these is the idea of proper manner, politeness, doing things according to form.

Former has to do with time, or order of sequence. Thus we say On a former occasion he talked about Italian lakes. We mean that he talked about Italian lakes on a previous occasion. In a similar manner we say *Formerly* he worked for Sage & Allen. You would never think of writing *formerlity* for *formality*; then why is it that sometimes you substitute formally for formerly?   (Alfred M. Hitchcock, Junior English Book, Henry Holt and Company, 1920)

Questions:

1. This cafe was *(formerly/formally)* a swank restaurant.
2. Guests were greeted *(formerly/formally)* at the door
3. I recognize her name, but I don't remember ever being *(formerly/formally)* introduced.
4. Having *(formerly/formally)* served as a deck-hand onboard an Alaskan crabbing vessel, I can manage working at Wal-Mart.
5. *(Formerly/Formally)* envied the world over, the National Aeronautics Space Administration, also known as NASA, has suffered a series of recent setbacks, not the least of which has been waning public interest.
6. Tenants were so outraged when they learned that the city was planning to build a landfill less than one mile away from their apartment that they *(formerly/formally)* lodged a complaint in court.
7. The Yankees' Babe Ruth faces the team he *(formerly/formally)* captained for the first time.
8. The Miami Dolphins have signed free agent linebacker Karlos Dansby, *(formerly/formally)* of the Arizona Cardinals, to a five-year contract.
9. The man accused of shooting and killing a Chattahoochee Hills Police Lt. has been *(formerly/formally)* charged.
10. Roethlisberger has not yet been *(formerly/formally)* interviewed by the Georgia Bureau of Investigations regarding the incident that occurred on Thursday night.
11. *(Formerly/Formally)* known as the Mystery of the Blue Planet, Avatar is based on a popular book.
12. The recreation center was *(formerly/formally)* under the supervision of Lee County but the town of Fort Myers Beach took over full control of the facility last year.
13. Scott Brown is expected to *(formerly/formally)* announce Tuesday that he's running for the Republican Party's nomination for Senator of Massachusetts.
14. The Food and Drug Administration on Friday *(formerly/formally)* approved a new drug called velaglucerase alfa for injection (tradenamed VPRIV) for treatment of the rare genetic disorder Gaucher disease.
15. On Tuesday night in Hollywood the *(formerly/formally)* abandoned Big Lots on Vine was packed with Angelenos uniting in the name of art.

Answers: 1. formerly 2. formally 3. formally 4. formerly 5. Formerly 6. formally 7. formerly 8. formerly 9. formally 10. formally 11. Formerly 12. formerly 13. formally 14. formally 15. formerly

Forth vs. Fourth

Forth (adv.) is "out into notice or view" or forward, 'onward'. from this day forth, bring forth, go forth). It can also mean 'come out into view' (e.g., Come forth from the crowd).

Fourth (adv.) is one more than third in order. Fourth relates to the number four (e.g., fourth place). The word 'fourth' (with a u) relates to the number four. It can be a noun (e.g., one fourth, i.e., a quarter), an adjective (e.g., the fourth car) or an adverb (e.g., the new driver came fourth).

Questions

1. Elise was hardly *(forthright/fourthright)* about the dissolution of her marriage. In fact, she refused to disclose any of the details of the break up.
2. According to legend: famine, pestilence, and death are three of the plagues suffered by mankind. The *(forth/fourth)* is war.
3. The *(Forth/Fourth)* Amendment guards against unreasonable searches and seizures.
4. If you want to be successful, put *(forth/fourth)*) all your efforts and don't hold back.
5. In the Olympic Games, there are no medals for athletes who finish in *(forth/fourth)* place.
6. After the Blue Devils fought a back-and-*(forth/fourth)* battle with Tech for nearly 34 minutes, they came alive to pull away for the double-digits win.
7. I rocked myself back and *(forth/fourth)* against the midnight blue loneliness
8. Ott recorded his fifth save and preserved the 3-2 win giving LSU its *(forth/fourth)* one-run victory of the year.
9. The victory was the Spurs' *(forth/fourth)* straight and extended the Grizzlies' skid at home to eight losses in a row.
10. Louisiana's Ragin' Cajuns put *(forth/fourth)* a valiant effort and appeared to have a come-from-behind victory over UL Monroe in the first round of the Sun Belt Conference Championships.
11. The ballots are separated into 10 groups: those with "Yankees" No. 1 in one group, those with "Red Sox" as the top pick in another, and so *(forth/fourth)* .
12. Sandra Richard, in her *(forth/fourth)* try at state, won the girls title Saturday at Super Bowl in Canton, defeating Lindsey Strongbottom.
13. St. Louis University wrapped up *(forth/fourth)* place in the Atlantic 10 Conference without lifting a finger Saturday.
14. If charter operators opt out, the teachers will have no incentive to put *(forth/fourth)* their plans, and the entire initiative fails.
15. Winchester won its *(forth/fourth)* consecutive IHSAA Class 2A boys basketball sectional title with a 56-43 victory over Lapel at Alexandria High School.

Answers: 1. forthright 2. fourth 3. Fourth 4. forth 5. fourth 6. forth 7. forth 8. fourth 9. fourth 10. forth 11. forth 12. fourth 13. fourth 14. forth 15. fourth

Good vs. Well

Good means having the proper qualities. Good is an adjective.
Well means in an excellent or proper manner.
The general rule with good and well is that well is an adverb and good is an adjective. This means *well* modifies verbs, adjectives and other adverbs and *good* modifies nouns. Unfortunately, there are exceptions to this rule. "Well" may be used to describe when something is proper, healthy or suitable. As in, "I am well (healthy) today."

Examples

1. That is a good song. (Good is modifying the noun, song.)
2. You sang the song very well. (Well is modifying the verb, sang.)
3. The bike is pedaling well. (Well is modifying the verb, pedaling.
4. The car is in good shape. (Good is modifying the noun, car.)

Exceptions: With verbs of sensation like touch, feel, looks, hears, and smells it would be proper to say, "The cake smells good." To say that the cake smells well would imply that the cake has a nose that can smell appropriately. But, it is also correct to say, "I feel good today." Good refers to how you are physically and spiritually feeling.
How are you feeling? I feel good. How are you? I am well, thank you.

Questions

1. Because I studied very hard for the exam, I did *(good/well)* and my dad gave me $100.
2. After eating two hamburgers, a hotdog, a milkshake, French fries, fired cheese, 44 oz. Coke, and a salad, Jeremiah did not feel very *(good/well)*.
3. Last quarter's investments had been so *(good/well)* for both companies.
4. We should learn how to be *(good/well)* losers and gracious winners--but it's always more fun to win.
5. We all turned out at the dock and wished Swenson Thatcher *(good/well)* on his round the world adventure in a 24 foot sailing vessel.
6. "I still feel we have a very *(good/well)* shot," Hewitt said, after his team lost the fifth time in seven games.
7. He was in *(good/well)* spirits. We had a *(good/well)* conversation, and he was very alert.
8. The doctor told me that he is doing *(good/well)* .
9. For a change, they were *(good/well)* omens.
10. He rebounded *(good/well)* . He defended *(good/well)* .
11. I'm throwing *(good/well)* and feeling *(good/well)* .
12. I feel pretty *(good/well)* , it's a *(good/well)* place to start," Lackey told reporters following the game.
13. The Wisconsin Lottery said Mega Millions sales are going pretty *(good/well)* .

14. Chelsea captain John Terry has hit back at criticism over his current form and insisted he is playing *(good/well)* for both club and country.
15. It's all for a *(good/well)* cause.

Answers: 1. well 2. good 3. good 4. good 5. well 6. good 7. good, good 8. well 9. good 10. well, well 11. well, good 12. good, good 13. well 14. well 15. good

Hanged vs. Hung

For centuries, hanged and hung were used interchangeably as the past participle of hang. But now, most contemporary usage guides insist that hanged, not hung, should be used when referring to executions.
• convicted killers are **hanged**; posters are hung. • "A room hung with pictures is a room **hung** with thoughts." (Joshua Reynolds)

Notes: "Hanged, as a past tense and a past participle of hang, is used in the sense of "to put to death by hanging," as in Frontier courts hanged many a prisoner after a summary trial. A majority of the Usage Panel objects to hung used in this sense. In all other senses of the word, hung is the preferred form as past tense and past participle, as in I hung my child's picture above my desk. (The American Heritage Dictionary of the English Language, Fourth Edition, 2000)

Bottom line: use 'hanged' for executions and 'hung' for everything else. A person is hanged, everything else is hung.

Questions:
1. "One should forgive one's enemies, but not before they are *(hung/hanged)*." (Heinrich Heine)
2. All the stockings were *(hung/hanged)* by the chimney with care..."
3. AN INQUEST into the death of a Zimbabwean man found *(hung/hanged)* in the woods near Oxford, England, has recorded an "open verdict"
4. The hangman *(hung/hanged)* the noose that would be used to *(hung/hang)* to convicted horse thief.
5. Tensions boiled over, deliberations broke down and the judge was forced to declare a mistrial because of the *(hung/hanged)* jury.
6. I *(hung/hanged)* around Richmond through Sunday's CAA Tournament Semifinals.

Answers: 1. hanged 2. hung 3. hanged 4. hung, hang 5. hung 6. hung

Hear vs. Here

Hear (v.) means to perceive sound or to gain knowledge or information.
Here (adv.) means a close-by location

TIP remember that with the word "hear" had the word "ear" at the end.

Questions:
1. The Supreme Court agreed to *(here/hear)* an appeal from Snyder's father.
2. Thousand of aerospace workers are eager to *(here/hear)* what the President will say about the future of the space industry.
3. If you missed it, you can watch it right *(here/hear)* !
4. You can read more about it *(here/hear)* on our blog, leave a comment and *(here/hear)* the song and see a larger photo in our gallery linked below.
5. Did you know that you not only *(here/hear)* sounds with your ears but also with your skin?

Answers: 1. hear 2. hear 3. here 4. here, hear 5. hear

Hole v. Whole

Hole (n.) means a gap or opening; or (v.) meaning to climb into an opening.
Whole (n.) means the entire thing; or (adj.)means full or entire.
• *Science shall get lost in a big black* **hole** • *Art would die to make man a* **whole**

Questions
1. The coach explained, "We dug ourselves a little *(whole/hole)*."
2. But, for many, eating more fruits, vegetables, *(whole/hole)* grains and foods lower in fat and calories is easier said than done.
3. There seems to be a black *(whole/hole)* of bookstores where I live.
4. All four will tee-off on the first *(whole/hole)* during the third round at the Honda Classic golf tournament
5. I ate my *(whole/hole)* lunch in under five minutes so I could get back to work.
6. My favorite pastry are doughnut *(wholes/holes),* they also cost less.
7. The dentist told my mom I have a *(whole/hole)* or cavity that must be filled.
8. I studied the *(whole/hole)* weekend preparing for the exam today.
9. On the *(whole/hole)*, I'd rather play video games than study.
10. He's stronger, leaner and he's got a look that is a *(whole/hole)* lot more serious.
11. "The *(whole/hole)* campus is kind of buzzing about it," says a sophomore at UCLA. "We need school spirit.

Answers: 1. hole 2. whole 3. hole 4. hole 5. whole 6. holes 7. hole 8. whole 9. whole 10. whole 11. whole

Identical with (not *to*)

This bid is *identical with* the one submitted by you.

Implicit vs. Explicit

Explicit means clearly expressed or readily observable.

Implicit means implied or expressed indirectly.
- "Go home now!" was the principal's *explicit* command.
- With poetry you must read carefully and critically to understand the author's *implicit* message.

Question
1. Several critics discerned a hidden (*implicit/explicit*) political statement in the bishop's remarks.
2. Cigarette packs carry (*implicit/explicit*) health warnings.
3. Citigroup can still operate under an unstated but (*implicit/explicit*) guarantee of investor support.
4. The government should not use taxpayer money to support private business. If a business fails there is no stated (*implicit/explicit*) guarantee, in fact there is no wink-and-nod (*implicit/explicit*) guarantee of government support.
5. Think back to your childhood and all the words you soaked up automatically, children learn most of their language (*implicitly/explicitly*).
6. Pornography is defined as "sexually (*implicit/explicit*) " content that has no redeeming value.
7. After an uproar from concerned parents, Apple purged thousands of sexually (*implicit/explicit*) applications from iTunes this week.
8. In a televised event, the Chinese officially stated the yuan's current de facto peg to the dollar may not be maintained--his comments were the most (*implicit/explicit*) statements to date.
9. At various points the White House either remained silent or gave (*implicit/explicit*) support to Democrats.
10. It's called "Dante's Inferno" and the (*implicit/explicit*) nature of this game is stirring up some controversy.
11. Good Internet etiquette includes: Be civil and avoid name calling; stay on-topic; and don't post profanity or sexually (*implicit/explicit*) comments.

Answers: *1. implicit 2 explicit* 3 implicit 4. explicit, implicit 5. implicitly 6. explicit 7. explicit 8. explicit 9. implicit 10. explicit 11. explicit

Imply vs. infer

"If you *imply* something, you hint or suggest it.
If you *infer* something, you reach a conclusion on the basis of evidence.
- Her email *implied* that her sales-team was going to miss the projected goals this month.
- The team leader *inferred* from the email that they were not going to reach the monthly goals"
 (Alred, Brusaw, and Oliu, *The Technical Writer's Companion* 294).

Note: Typically you can think of communication this way, "I (the sender) imply" and "You (the receiver) infer". Another, more accurate way to look at it: The sender *implies* while the receiver *infers*.
- *To imply is for the **giver** of information to suggest indirectly*
- *To infer is for the **receiver** of information to make a guess using specific evidence*

Here's another way to think about it:
- **Imply** means "to state indirectly."
- **Infer** means "to draw a conclusion."

You may infer something from an implication, but you would not imply something from an inference.
1. The candidate implied from the research that he was going to **Incorrect**
2. The candidate inferred from the research that he was going to lose. **Correct**
3. The Constitution infers that intrastate commerce is a matter for the states. **Incorrect**
4. The Constitution implies that intrastate commerce is a matter for the states. **Correct**
5. He inferred from the Constitution that intrastate commerce is a matter for the states. **Correct**

Explanations:
1. The candidate looked at some information and then drew a conclusion--he was going to lose. When you draw a conclusion you 'infer' from the information--which is what our loser of a candidate did. If he wanted to 'imply' he would have to state something like: 'The candidate spoke to the news media and implied the polls were not looking good.' Now our candidate is directly saying something. The news media could then 'infer' from the speech that the candidate was going to lose.
2. The candidate correctly 'inferred' from the given information (the lack of support) that he was going to lose. If he wanted to 'imply' he'd have to saying something like: "In the candidates speech, he implied he was going to lose."
3. An inanimate object cannot 'infer'. "Inferring" requires a sentient being. Someone has to absorb the information and then make a conclusion...the act of making the conclusion is 'inferring'. In the given sentence we'd have to say something like: 'The student inferred from the Constitution that intrastate commerce is a matter for the states.'
4. Inanimate objects can 'imply' all day long. So the Constitution can imply things, but people will infer from the Constitution. Look at sentence 5.
5. Our guy (a sentient being) looked at the document and then drew a conclusion--which means he 'inferred'. He drew a conclusion from reading the Constitution that intrastate commerce is a matter for the states.

Note: this is a very fertile testing area. Make sure you understand the difference between "imply vs. infer"

Here is some more detailed information about "imply vs. infer" but don't lose sight of the rule.
Infer: (inferable, inferably, inferrer)
1. To conclude from evidence or premises.
2. To reason from circumstance; surmise: We can infer that his reason for publishing the article was less than honorable.
3. To lead to as a consequence or conclusion:
4. To hint; imply

Imply: (implied, implying, implies)

1. To involve by logical necessity; entail: Life implies growth and death.
2. To express or indicate indirectly: His tone implied anger.
3. Obsolete To entangle.

Infer and *imply* are often confused, but there is a distinction between the two. When something is *implied*, it is suggested without being stated outright. When something is *inferred*, the **reader** is in control of drawing a conclusion that is not explicitly said. In other words, a writer *implies* and a reader *infers*. Another way to explain: information is categorized as a message, a sender and a receiver. The person sending the message *implies*, while the person receiving the message *infers*.

Here are some examples for further clarification:

1. The student's behavior during class *implied* she was not feeling well. The teacher *inferred* from the student's behavior that she was not feeling well.
2. The players *inferred* that they were going to have a hard practice because the coach seemed angry at the way they played the day before. The coach's demeanor *implied* they were going to have a long and difficult practice.
3. When I gave you a Valentine, I was *implying* I like you. When I received your Valentine, I *inferred* you liked me.

Communication consists of a **message**, a **sender**, and a **receiver**. The **sender** can *imply*, but the **receiver** can only *infer*. The error that usually occurs is that the word *infer* is mistakenly used for *imply*.

If someone gets the idea from your behavior that you are in love, then he is *inferring* from your behavior that you are in love. But if he is subtly doing and saying things to let you know that he loves you, then he is *implying* that he loves you. You, of course, can then *infer* from his *implication* (actions) that he loves you.

IMPLY = to put the suggestion *into* the message (sender *implies*)
INFER = to take the suggestion *out of* the message (receiver *infers*)
IMPLICATION = what the *sender* has *implied*
INFERENCE = what the *receiver* has *inferred*

Questions

1. This latest information seems to *(imply/infer)* that the old boom-and-bust cycles will continue.
2. An Oscar Award is an honor which *(implies/infers)* a distinction and support from the industry.
3. Did the rhetoric *(imply/infer)* perhaps he managed to avoid the biggest of bombs?
4. Certain types of evidence can present special problems associated with a jury's tendency to *(imply/infer)* guilt .
5. The defendant did not produce evidence sufficient to permit the court to draw an *(implication/inference)* of discrimination.
6. There is evidence from which a jury could *(imply/infer)* that the company acted knowingly and willingly.
7. What the lawsuit seems to *(imply/infer)* is that representatives were granted power of attorney.
8. These findings *(imply/infer)* that resistance might be reversible, provided antibiotic use is reduced.
9. When asked if one could *(imply/infer)* that if no Republican votes in favor of the bill , then Rep. Matheson would vote no, Heyrend replied: "I would not *(imply/infer)* anything. I'd wait to see what develops.
10. The intimidation element of § 2113(a) is satisfied if an ordinary person in the teller's position reasonably could *(imply/infer)* a threat of bodily harm.

Answers: 1. imply 2. implies 3. imply 4. infer 5. inference 6. infer 7. imply 8. imply 9. infer, infer 10. infer

In contrast to (not *of*)

In *contrast to* the conservative attitudes of her time, Mae West was quite provocative.

Incidence vs. Incident(s)

Incidence (n.) a measure of the **risk** of developing some new condition within a specified period of time. Although sometimes loosely expressed simply as the number of new cases during some time period. It usually relates to a disease but the broader definition is "the rate of occurrence" of anything.

Incidents (n.) the plural of incident, which means an occurrence or an event. "occurrences of actions or situations that are separate units of experience"

• The chart *'Incidence* of Flu by Area' shows the number of people with flu and flu-like illnesses.
• There is no evidence to link the two *incidents* at this time.

Questions

1. The newspaper published an article to generate awareness of the high *(incidence/incident)* of multiple sclerosis.
2. They suffer a higher *(incidence/incident)* of measles as they did not invest in health-care systems to deliver vaccinations effectively.
3. The police are investigating two *(incidence/incidents)* of graffiti tagging that occurred last night .
4. The *(incidence/incident)* was part of a series of foolish acts last Friday that included riding a tiger statue and hoisting a pirate flag at the ROTC building, the statement said.
5. The high school has taken new steps to curb the high *(incidence/incidents)* of cheating on exams.
6. But he ruled out an inquiry into the *(incidence/incident)* saying the people concerned had apologized.
7. No injuries or damage was reported during the *(incidence/incident)* . The $1,000 reward is for information leading to the arrest and conviction of the suspect. No further information about the *(incidence/incident)* is being made available at this time. However, the police said they didn't have statistics on the *(incidence/incident)* of home invasion robberies in the area, but that the crime is relatively rare.
8. The article title read: "Full Body Scanners at Airport Cause International *(incidence/incident)* ".
9. University of California researchers found that the *(incidence/incident)* rate for all causes of dementia in people age 90 and older is 18.2% annually.

Answers: 1. incidence 2. incidence 3. incidents 4. incident 5. incidence 6. incident 7. incident, incident, incidence 8. Incident 9. incidence

Incite vs. Insight

Insight (n.) means 'an understanding of something'. It often carries the connotation of 'a clear understanding with an insider's perspective'. looking within and gaining understanding. The principal gained useful insight into students' behavior.
Incite (v.) means 'to stimulate action', 'to rouse' or 'to stir up'. He was arrested for trying to incite a riot.
   • *She has a good **insight** into the company's strategy.*   • *The event is seeking to **incite** enthusiasm in young people.*

Questions
1. It is normal for certain things to *(insight/incite)* anger in the human brain, but anger is a fleeting emotion.
2. I was left with a fair *(insight/incite)* into the possibilities ahead.
3. This is a very readable book that gives a good *(insight/incite)* into the frontiers of mathematics.
4. The media must guard against *(insighting/inciting)* a war.
5. The trip to visit the college campus provided excellent *(insight/incite)* into life as a freshman.
6. The interactive models gave us good *(insight/incite)* into basic scientific concepts.
7. In Arizona the freeway cameras and constant monitoring have *(insighted/incited)* a mini revolt.
8. A power pitcher who can throw close to 100mph can *(insight/incite)* fear in opposing batters simply by moving the ball on the inside part of the plate.
9. During the Revolution our founding fathers used the power of the press to *(insight/incite)* anger against Britain for abusing the natural freedoms of the colonists.
10. We'll update breaking news as it occurs, as well as offer *(insight/incite)* and commentary not available in the print edition.

Answers: *1. incite 2. insight 3. insight 4. inciting 5. insight 6. insight 7. incited 8. incite 9. incite 10. insight*

Independent of (not *from*)

The judiciary is *independent of* the other branches of government.

Ingenious vs. Ingenuous

ingenious (adj.) means extremely clever--marked by inventive skill and imagination.
Ingenuous (adj.) means straightforward, candid, without guile, frank, Lacking in cunning, guile, or worldliness;
   • "To read of a detective's daring finesse or **ingenious** stratagem is a rare joy." (Rex Stout)
   • She was enchanted by his **ingenuous** expression and frank blue eyes.

NOTE: Be careful to distinguish "ingenuous" from "disingenuous" they are opposites. But many times in our language the prefix 'in' means not and that could cause you to think that 'in genuous' would mean 'not genuous', but 'genuous' is not a word. This is prime testable content because it's counterintuitive to native speakers.
1. Her plan was *(ingenious/ingenuous)*, but she lacked the courage to carry it out.
2. She flashed a wide, *(ingenious/ingenuous)* smile.
3. The proto-Web camera had an *(ingenious/ingenuous)* technology for ensuring that users would be safe from visual snooping: a lens cap.
4. The design is *(ingenious/ingenuous)* and simple.
5. Their pure delight and love of each other's company melted a cynic's cold heart, and reflected the disconnect between the self-important, stuffed shirts from the IOC who award the medals, and the *(ingenious/ingenuous)* athletes who joyously receive them.
6. Disney is known for *(ingenious/ingenuous)* viral marketing campaigns.
7. It would be unfair to reveal much more of Fish Tank's plot, which tracks Mia as she moves from (perhaps) *(ingenious/ingenuous)* flirtation to friendship.
8. He was criticized for his hairstyle and appearance, but girls loved his *(ingenious/ingenuous)* charisma.
9. It sounds complicated but it is *(ingenious/ingenuous)*
10. The Chairman is *(ingenious/ingenuous)* about his firm's motivation, saying: "I want us to be seen as a friend to the public."

Answers: *1. ingenious 2. ingenuous 3. ingenious 4. ingenious 5. ingenuous 6. ingenious 7. ingenuous 8. ingenuous 9. ingenious 10. ingenuous*

Instance vs. Instants

Instance (n.) means a case or example of something. to cite as an instance or example. An example that is cited to prove or invalidate a contention or illustrate a point, exemplify.
Instants (n. adj.) a plural form of instant, which means a moment of time. A particular or precise time. *instant coffee; instant powdered milk.*

—Idioms
at the instance of, at the urging or suggestion of: *He applied for a scholarship at the instance of his advisor.*
for instance, as an example; for example: *If you were 75 years old, for instance, you would get a perspective.*

Questions
1. Two surfers were *(instants/instance)* from getting enveloped by this wall of water when a photographer captured the moment a large wave battered the harbor.
2. Pumpkin, the cocker spaniel loves sweets--for *(instants/instance)* marshmallows and cake.
3. Since the matter was in the Supreme Court, then previous *(instants/instance)* of allowing discussion on similar issues would be cited

4. An *(instants/instance)* of incorrect usage of grammar is: between he and I.
5. At any given *(instant/instance)*, a sonata or sonnet is meaningless, and only by a juxtaposition of *(instants/instance)* in time can form or meaning be built up".
6. Those *(instants/instance)* are burned into my memory by the powerful flash of young-love.
7. The Internet is a perfect *(instance/instant)* of technology in the classroom.
8. However, you can expect one of the great comic artists drawing little *(instants/instance)* from the film.
9. For *(instant/instance)* , 75 percent of African Americans reported watching television routinely in the hour before going to bed, compared with 64 percent of whites.
10. For *(instant/instance)* , who knows how much the Space Shuttle and the International Space Station programs cost?
11. After several *(instances/instants)* of silence, the instructor resumed the lecture he had suddenly stopped.
12. The quick (instance, **instants**) of pleasure were well worth the price of consuming too many calories.

Answers: 1. *instants* 2. *instance* 3. *instants* 4. *instance* 5. *instant, instants* 6. *instants* 7. *instance* 8. *instants* 9. *instance* 10. *instance* 11. *instants* 12. *instants*

Into vs. in to

Into: *'Into'* is a preposition which often answers the question, "where?"
   • The divers swam deeper and deeper *into* the ocean as they searched for the sunken ship.
The "where" can also be metaphorical, like,
   • He was drafted against his will *into* the military. • He ran *into* a double play. • They decided to go *into* business together.   • When it started to rain, they ran *into* the cafeteria. • As the cold wind blew, he dug his hands deeper *into* coat pockets. • After talking for a few a minutes in the foyer, they walked into the conference room.

It can also refer by analogy to time
   • The storm continued well *into* the night.

Definition of "*into*":
   1. from the outside to the inside of; to the midst or depths of (we walked *into* the mall, we jumped *into* the pool)
   2. advancing or continuing to the midst of (a period of time) studying far *into* the night
   3. to the form, substance, or condition of (she changed *into* a swan, it divided *into* parts)
   4. so as to strike; against (to bump *into* a dresser)
   5. to the work or activity of (to go *into* computing)
   6. in the direction of (heading *into* a mess, heading *into* turmoil, heading *into* trouble, heading *into* a blizzard)

In to: *'In to'* consists of two separate particles. In some cases, "to" is part of an infinitive ("to see," "to learn," etc.); in other cases, it is a preposition.
   • *I went in to help my mom with dinner.* • *I went in, to the cheers of everyone in the stadium.*

Another way to think of it is that "in to" combines the meanings of two separate words — someone goes "in," *in order* "to" do something. Sometimes the "in" is idiomatic, such as the case of "turning oneself in" to police.
   • *He turned himself in … to the police.* Great.
   • *She went in … to the cave.* That's a little strange — it should be "into." She went into the cave.
   • He dived back *into* second base. (he dived back) Where did he dive? He dove 'into' second base.
   • He dived back *in to* avoid being tagged out. (he dived back in) Why? ...in order to avoid being tagged)
   • The firefighter dived *into* the lake to rescue the drowning boy. (where did the ff dive? into the lake)
   • The firefighter dived *in to* rescue the drowning boy. (the firefighter 'dived-in'...why? in order to rescue the boy...the firefighter did not "dive *into* rescue" you cannot dive *into* a rescue because rescue is a verb. "to" belongs with "rescue" and means "in order to," not "where." Try speaking the sentence aloud, pausing distinctly between "in" and "to." If the result sounds wrong, you probably need "into."
   • When it started to rain, they ran *in to* find someplace dry. (they ran-in to-find)
   • As the cold wind blew, he pulled his hands *in to* keep them warm. (pulled his hands-in   to-keep)
   • After talking for a few a minutes in the foyer, they walked *in to* start the meeting. (they walked-in to-start)
   • He handed his badge *in to* the police chief. (he handed in his badge to the police chief)
   • The demands of training for a marathon made him want to give *in to* the grueling schedule. (give-in   to the schedule)

Questions:
   1. When I was a child, I loved to go *(into/in to)* the ocean while we were on vacation.
   2. After he won the $300,000,000 lotto he turned the winning ticket *(into/in to)* the proper authorities.
   3. I'm going to get a new cell phone because I constantly have to plug it *(into/in to)* the wall.
   4. In the 6th inning last night, Frankie Patino went *(into/in to)* replace the starting pitcher--he struck out the side.
   5. No one could have predicted, though, that NASCAR's first true test would come a mere four races *(into/in to)* the season
   6. The companies announced that they had entered *(into/in to)* an agreement in a $635 million transaction.
   7. Tune *(into/in to)* the season-opening games this weekend.
   8. Colleges and universities have to do something about verifying the identification off individuals coming *(into/in to)* take entrance exams and classes at those institutions.
   9. There's no doubt that one wrestling company is going *(into/in to)* tonight's official launch of the new Monday Night War with momentum in the ratings
   10. Now, customers will gain greater visibility *(into/in to)* their assets
   11. Biotechnology industries, announces that it has incorporated a new technology platform *(into/in to)* its growing suite of data management applications.

12. Paterson has already given up his bid for a full term but refused **to** give **(into/in to)** critics who want him **to** resign altogether.
13. Talks continue for Europe and America jointly step **(into/in to)** shore up global financial regulation--this would be a huge mistake.
14. A little more than a year **(into/in to)** its ascendancy at the White House, behavioral economics as a key policy-making tool may be on the wane.
15. A 10-month-old boy was taken **(into/in to)** protective custody Sunday night

Answers: *1. into, 2. in to, 3. into 4. in to 5. into 6. into 7. in to 8. in to 9. into 10. into 11. into 12. in to 13. in to 14. into 15. into*

Irregardless (see regardless)

'irregardless' is always non-standard. The rule is simple: NEVER use it EVER, EVER, EVER. Regardless of what you have heard, "irregardless" is a redundancy. The suffix "-less" on the end of the word already makes the word negative. It doesn't need the negative prefix "ir-" added to make it even more negative.

Its vs. it's

This one is simple if you remember that **it's** is a contraction of **it is** or **it has**.
  • *It's great to be home for Christmas in California because it's been freezing at school.*
'Its' is the possessive form of **it**.
  • *It's beautiful today at the beach so don't forget your camera and **its** memory card.*
Never confuse It with It's
Its - is a possessive. • *Turn the camera on its side.*
It's - short form for either 'it is' or 'it has'. (Contraction) • *It's my fault.* • *It's been a hot day.*

If you have trouble keeping them straight, try remembering this phrase: Use its like his ; use it's like he's.
  • *His tact impressed us. --- He's tactful.* • *Its beauty pleased us. --- It's beautiful.*

Questions

1. Toyota has highlighted **(its/it's)** technicians in several television ads aimed at assuring customers that it is fixing the problems.
2. A year after the stock market hit bottom and began a spectacular comeback, **(its/it's)** getting harder to dazzle investors.
3. The newspaper was cutting from **(its/it's)** staff two of **(its/it's)** most prominent writers.
4. The Coca-Cola Company and **(its/it's)** bottlers share a legacy of supporting education through programs like the Coca-Cola Scholars Foundation.
5. At the Oscars last night, **(its/it's)** doubtful anyone other than the songwriters much minded having their work reduced to a few fast clips.
6. During the Winter Olympics we saw the US downhill skiers bridge from **(its/it's)** past to **(its/it's)** future.
7. The company's conservative pricing and reserving practices have contributed to **(its/it's)** improved overall profitability.
8. That's more fans than the NCAA will draw for **(its/it's)** March Madness and **(its/it's)** twice as many as last year.
9. **(Its/it's)** a campaign the leading companies will devote to providing free resources and information to better inform consumers.
10. However **(its/it's)** true -- in spite of our very best efforts, this deal did not work out.
11. **(Its/it's)** been a tough policy to implement and encourage, because finding conventional oil is not easy in North America.

Answers: *1. its 2. it's 3. its, its 4. its 5. it's 6. its, its 7. its 8. its, it's 9. It's 10. it's 11. It's*

Later vs. Latter

Later (adv.) means "at an advanced point of time" After the expected, usual, or proper time: a train that arrived later; woke later than expected and had to skip breakfast. At or until an advanced hour: talked later into the evening than I planned. At or into an advanced period or stage: she had children later in life.
Latter (adj.) means "more recent", being the second mentioned of two (distinguished from former): *I prefer the latter offer to the former one.* 2. more advanced in time; later: *in these latter days of human progress.* 3. near or comparatively near to the end: *the latter part of the century.*
  • *Though Amy said that she would join me **later**, I never saw her again.*
  • "There are two kinds of worries: those you can do something about and those you can't. Don't spend any time on the **latter**." (Duke Ellington)

TIP Use later when referring to time. Use latter when referring to the second of two persons or things mentioned previously.

Questions

1. "Were it left to me to decide whether we should have a government without newspapers, or newspapers without a government, I should not hesitate a moment to prefer the **(later/latter)** . (Thomas Jefferson)
2. Merdine told Gus a joke, and two minutes **(later/latter)** he began laughing
3. Given a choice between rocky road and vanilla ice cream, I choose the former over the **(later/latter)**.
4. The **(later/latter)** you wait to get healthy, the more difficult it can be.
5. The results from last night's game were reported **(later/latter)** than expected.
6. The lot of townswomen eyed me with suspicion; it was as if I had transmogrified into a **(later-day/latter-day)** Hester Prynne.
7. During the **(later/latter)** part of the concert, people started to get bored.
8. Seven years **(later/latter)**, Newsome got a chance to correct his draft day error, trading third and fourth-round picks to the Cardinals.
9. He **(later/latter)** attended Reedley College and received a bachelor's degree from Fresno State.
10. The extended Osmond family gathered Monday at the Church of Jesus Christ of **(Later/Latter)**-day Saints Chapel in Provo, Utah, to honor the life and memory of Marie Osmond's 18-year-old son.
11. At last night's Academy Awards, Miley Cyrus made bigger news than Sandra Bullock. The **(later/latter)** won Best Actress, but the former admitted she was dating Liam Hemsworth.

12. I actually live in Houston in the offseason, so I always thought about in the *(later/latter)* part of my career playing down there.
13. One year and a 70% stock market rally *(later/latter)*, investors' confidence--and appetite for risk--has returned.
14. Some diseases have the ability to hide in bone marrow and wake up at a *(later/latter)* date to cause illness to the body.
15. Researchers at the University of California, Berkeley have found that naps may help your brain work better *(later/latter)*.
16. Girardi said Rivera will make the first of his eight or nine game appearances either March 16 or 17. The *(later/latter)* date would be a rare road game for the pitcher.

Answers: *1. latter 2. later 3. latter 4. later 5. later 6. latter-day 7. latter 8. later 9. later 10. Latter-day 11. latter 12. latter 13. later 14. later 15. later 16. latter*

Lay vs. lie

Lie and lay have different meanings and different forms of conjugation.
The question becomes: Who is Lying down – the Subject or the Object?

LIE: **intransitive**: An intransitive verb does not take an object; 'Lie' or 'lie down' is something a person or animal does by him or herself. something just lies there. If you're tired of holding something, you should *lay it down*; if you're not feeling well, you should *lie down*.
LAY: **transitive** – A transitive verb requires an object; 'Lay' or 'lay down' is something a person does to something or someone. something just lies there. If you're tired of holding something, you should *lay it down*; if you're not feeling well, you should *lie down*.

But it gets worse: because the past tense of *lay* is *laid*, and the past tense of *lie* is *lay*.

Present Tense	Past	Past Participle	Present Participle
Lie: to recline or rest on a surface	Lay	Lain	Lying
Lay: to put or place something or someone	Laid	Laid	Laying

Lie => **lay** => lain => lying
Lay => laid => laid => laying

Lie: To lie down is an act that can be attributed to the subject. There is no object of this verb, as the subject is doing the action without a receiver. **Conjugation of LIE:**
• Present tense: I *lie* down today. • Past tense: I *lay* down yesterday. • Future tense: I will *lie* down tomorrow.
• Perfect tense: I have *lain* down before. (use perfect tense with have, had, has)

Lay: To lay is to put or place something or someone. It must have a direct object. One lays *something or someone* down. The something or someone is the direct object. **Conjugation of LAY:**
• I lay the video game down. (present tense) • I *laid* it down yesterday. (past tense) • I will *lay* it down again tomorrow. (future tense) • I have *laid* it here many times before. (use perfect tense with have, had, has)

IMPORTANT TIP* substitute "put". If "put" works, then "lay" is also correct.

This can be very confusing unless you use the tip above. Notice that the past tense of lie is lay which is also the present tense of lay. Also, the Past and Past Participle of Lay are both laid.
Lie is an **intransitive verb**; it does not take a direct object.
Lie	Stefan *lies* down for a nap every day.
Lay	Yesterday, Stefan *lay* down for a nap.
Lain	Stefan has *lain* down for a nap every day.
Lying	Stefan is *lying* down for a nap.

Lay is **transitive**; it takes a direct object.
Lay	Jacob is ready to *lay* the carpet.
Laid	Jacob *laid* the carpet yesterday.
Laid	Jacob has *laid* carpet in several homes.
Laying	*Laying* carpet in new homes is Jacob's best job.

Lie
• **The baby** is **lying** in the crib. • **She lies down** for a nap in the crib every day. • Yesterday **I lay down** for a nap. *(past tense)* • **I have lain** here for an hour trying to go to sleep. • **You should lie down** a little while longer.

Lay (use the TIP!!! Replace the 'lay' verb with 'put')
• I am **laying the baby in the crib** for a nap. (I am putting the baby in the crib--the tip works)
• I **lay the baby in the crib** for her nap every day. (I put the baby in the crib--the tip works)
• I **laid the newspaper on** the table before I **lay** down for a nap. (I put the newspaper on the table...I lay (past tense of lie down.)
• I **have** just **laid her down** for a nap. (I have put her down for a nap--the tip works)
• I will **lay your suit out** for you. (I will put your suit out for you--the tip works)

Lie (Additional Uses)
• The new stadium *lies to* the east of town. (present tense)
• The old stadium *lay to* the west of town. (past tense)
• After attacking the British clipper ship the HMS Stonebreaker, the US frigate *lay in anchor* in Boston Harbor. (past tense)
• If we *lie in* anchor in this protected harbor, we can wait for the storm to pass. (present tense)
• The city *lay between* the two rivers. (past tense)
• The city *lies between* the two rivers. (present tense)
• If you don't get sufficient rest, you'll be tempted to just *lie down* on the job (present tense)

- He was so tired he just *lay down* on the job. (past tense)
- Bonnie told Clyde, "We better *lie low* for a few days until the heat blows over." (present tense)
- Bonnie and Clyde *lay low* while the heat was on. (past tense)
- We will never take such an insult *lying down*. (present tense)
- We used to take such insults just *laying down*. (past tense)

Lay (Additional Uses) ***Remember** to use the TIP and replace with "put"
- After the accident, he was *laid up* at home watching TV and playing videos. *(passive voice)*
- Someday Israel and the Arab countries will *lay aside* **their differences**. *(past tense)*
- He *lays away* part of **his allowance** each month.
- In the bad economy, people have started to put things on *lay-away*.
- The Storm Troopers *laid down* their weapons. (past tense)
- Over 10% of the entire work-force has been *laid off*. (passive voice, past tense)
- We *laid out* over $1000 for our new flat screen TV.
- Jimmy the gold fish was *laid to rest*. (past tense)
- After studying all weekend, I think we have *laid to rest* any fears of not passing the exam. (past tense)
- The Declaration of Independence *laid the foundation* for the Constitution.
- The Federal Reserve *laid the blame* for the recession on high interest rates. (past tense)
- Until I get the *lay of the land* I'm not going to feel at home.
- When I came home after curfew my dad *laid down the law*. (past tense)
- The witness said, "I have never *laid eyes* on him before."
- We were stuck in LAX and had to *lay over* for the night.
- Columbus *laid claim* to the land he discovered.

Wrong: Laid-off workers lay the blame on the government. "We're not going to take this *laying* down!"
   Correct: Laid-off workers lay the blame on the government. "We're not going to take this *lying* down!"
Wrong: I *laid down* for bed.
   Correct: I *lay down* for bed. *(lie – past tense)*   Correct: I *laid the baby down* for bed. *(lay – past tense)*
Wrong*: Lay down*!
   Correct: **Lie down**. *(lie – past tense)*   Correct: **Lay down** your gun! (lay-present tense)
Wrong: She *has laid* in her bed all day.
   Correct: She *has lain* in her bed all day. *(lie – past perfect)*
   Correct: She *has laid* her clothes out on the bed. *(lay – past perfect)*

Questions (Remember to use the TIP--replace "lay" with "put"!)
*1. I babysit four year old Stefan all the time. Most of the time he will (**lay** , **lie**) down when I ask him to.*
*2. Most of the time Stefan has lots of energy and runs around, but sometimes he likes to (**lay, lie**) around playing video games.*
*3. If he gets too wild and crazy I have to ask him to go (**lay, lie**) down.*
*4. If he refuses then I have to (**lie, lay**) him down and close his door.*
*5. Sometimes he sneaks out, but if I speak in a stern voice he'll usually go back upstairs and (**lay low, lie low**) for awhile.*
*6. When I check on Stefan I've found him (**lying, laying**) down in his closet, under the bed, on top of stuffed animals and other crazy places.*
*7. One time he (**laid, lay**) out all his stuffed animals and then (**laid, lay**) down on them like a bed.*
*8. Stefan's parents (**laid out, lay out**) over $500 for his new bed.*
*9. But Stefan seems to prefer using his bed to (**lay out, lie out**) his toy soldiers and stuffed animals.*
*10. He (**lays, lies**) them down one-by-one on opposing sides as if he's getting the (**lay of, lie of**) the land.*
*11. Then the war between the two sides begins--Stefan will even (**lay to rest, lie to rest**) fallen victims.*
*12. He enjoys being the general and (**laying down, lying down**) the law to his troops.*
*13. One time he even (**laid, lay**) the blame on the stuffed iguana.*
*14. Whichever side ultimately wins gets to (**lay, lie**) claim to the entire bed.*
*15. After an hour or so the tired general (**lays, lies**) down (sometimes using the stuffed iguana as a pillow).*
*16. It's the cutest thing I've ever (**laid, lay**) eyes on.*

Answers: *1. lie, 2. lie, 3. lie, 4. lay, 5. lie low, 6. lying, 7. laid, laid, 8. laid out, 9. lay out, 10. lays, lay of, 11. lay to rest, 12. laying down, 13. laid, 14. lay, 15. lies, 16. laid*

Questions
Choose the lie or lay for each of the blanks below. Be sure to use the correct tense.
1. He _____ on the hard pavement this morning, gasping for breath.
2. How long did he _____ there?
3. I don't know how long he had _____ there.
4. He picked up the wounded bird and _____ it gently on the table.
5. She _____ her sewing aside and went to the door.
6. Are you going to _____ there all day?
7. The three puppies _____ in the basket.
8. Linda _____ her coat on the couch.
9. Not feeling well, he _____ in his bed all day.
10 He decided to just _____ around the house all summer.
11 Someone _____ the dictionary on my glasses.
12 The money _____ there all day in plain sight.
13 She had _____ the book on the ground under the tree.

14 Ginny _____ down on a beach towel.
15 I saw the hat that you _____ on the hall table.
16 She had just _____ down for a nap when the phone rang.
17 The two teenagers _____ in the sun all day.
18 Have they _____ the cornerstone of the building yet?
19 She had _____ the blanket over the child.
20 He should not _____ the blame for the accident on the other driver.

Answers: 1. lay, 2. lie, 3. lain, 4. laid, 5. laid, 6. lie, 7. lay, 8. laid, 9. lay, 10 lie, 11 laid, 12 lay, 13 laid, 14 lay, 15 laid, 16 lain, 17 lay, 18 laid, 19 laid, 20 lay

Paragraph Questions:

Ann ___1___ the baby on the bed and then ___2___ his stuffed bear beside him. I wondered how long the baby would ___3___ there without crying. Aunt Marge said that she remembered one day when he had ___4___ in the same position for an hour. She said another time when she was there, the puppy had ___5___ next to the baby on the bed. She remembered picking up the puppy while it was still asleep. Then she ___6___ the puppy on the rug. When Aunt Marge left, the puppy was still there. It had ___7___ there for nearly two hours sound asleep! Meanwhile, the baby woke up and ___8___ quietly for fully half an hour just watching the puppy snore. Finally, neither the puppy nor the baby could ___9___ there any longer, so the baby ___10___ on the old sympathy play and started whining pitifully until Ann was forced to ___11___ aside the sweater that she had hoped to finish knitting while the baby ___12___ down.

Answers for Paragraph: 1. *laid, 2. laid, 3. lie, 4. lain, 5. lain, 6. laid, 7. lain, 8. lay, 9. lie, 10 laid, 11 lay, 12 lay*

Lead vs. Led

Lead (v.) to guide or to begin (n.)"a thin stick of marking substance in or for a pencil"
Led is the past tense of (v.) to lead. Led is both the past and past participle form of the verb to lead (which rhymes with bead).
• We *led* the game until the eighth inning. Now the Cubs lead the game.   • Your advice will *lead* me into trouble.
• Your advice has *led* me into trouble many times before.

Questions
1. The band, (*lead/led*) by its star (*led/lead*) guitarist, received a standing ovation for its performance.
2. I couldn't find my pen so I completed the form with a (*lead/led*) pencil.
3. Last night's news broadcast (lead/**led**) with a story a woman who had eight babies at once.
4. The (*lead/led*) story last night on the news was about a woman who had eight babies at once.
5. Any child who receives a steady diet of graphic sex and violence via the media, eventually will be (*lead/led*) astray.
6. The dog walker used the (*lead/led*) to maintain control of his pack.
7. Miguel Olivo had three hits and three RBIs to (*led/lead*) the Colorado Rockies to a 5-4 exhibition win.
8. The NY Stock Exchange's top share index hit an 18-month closing high on Monday, (*led/lead*) by oil stocks.
9. Monterey County sheriff deputies arrested a man who they say (*led/lead*) them on a high-speed pursuit from Salinas to Soledad.
10. Sandra Bullock humbly accepted the Oscar for Best Actress in a (*led/lead*) performance.
11. Supplies of (*led/lead*) from China, the world's largest producer of the refined metal, will decline as the government raises environmental concerns.
12. Three more US-(*led/lead*) NATO soldiers were killed in Afghanistan in separate incidents on Sunday.
13. The team's second-leading scorer, tweeted that it was comments he made on Twitter that (*led/lead*) to his benching for his last game.
14. Canadian Sebastian Schnuelle has regained the early (*led/lead*) in the Iditarod Trail Sled Dog Race.
15. The (*led/lead*) singer of our band got sick and we had to cancel the event.

Answers: *1. led, lead 2. lead 3. led 4. lead 5. led 6. lead 7. lead 8. led 9. led 10. lead 11. lead 12. led 13. led 14. lead 15. lead*

Leave vs. Let

Leave as a verb means to depart or to go away from or to cause to remain behind. As a noun, leave refers to a departure.
Let as a verb means to allow or to permit. Let also can mean to rent or to lease. As a noun, let can mean a hindrance or an obstacle.

Questions
1. What time should we (**leave**, let) to go to the movie tonight?
2. Will you please (**leave**, let) me alone so that I can finish my homework?
3. "Please (leave, **let**) us have more time to finish our essays," pleaded the students.
4. Spending three of our four-week vacation away will (**leave**, let) us one week to relax at home.
5. If we (leave, **let**) our apartment for the summer, we can use the money to travel for a month.
6. Spending three of our four weeks away (leaves, **lets**) us unwind before we return to our old routine.

Answers: *1. leave 2. leave 3. let 4. leave 5. let 6. lets*

Lessen vs. Lesson

Lessen (v.) means to decrease or reduce. lessen your calorie intake to lose weight.
Lesson (n.) means an instructive example, a piece of practical wisdom, or a unit of instruction.
• "Lying increases the creative faculties, expands the ego, and *lessens* the frictions of social contacts." (Clare Boothe Luce)
• "The chief *lesson* I have learned in a long life is that the only way to make a man trustworthy is to trust him; and the surest way to make him untrustworthy is to distrust him and show your distrust." (Henry L. Stimson)

Questions

1. "And how many hours a day did you do *(lessens/lessons)*?" said Alice, in a hurry to change the subject.
   "Ten hours the first day," said the Mock Turtle: "nine the next, and so on."
   "What a curious plan!" exclaimed Alice.
   "That's the reason they're called *(lessens/lessons)*," the Gryphon remarked: "because they *(lesson/lessen)* from day to day."
   (Lewis Carroll, Alice's Adventures in Wonderland, 1865)
2. To lengthen your life, *(lesson/lessen)* your meals.
3. "Life is a long *(lesson/lessen)* in humility." (James M. Barrie)
4. Scientists have claimed that electromagnetic pulses significantly *(lesson/lessen)* soreness and swelling linked with osteoarthritis of the knee.
5. Summer thunderstorms will be likely with wind gust to help *(lesson/lessen)* the amount of haze.
6. It's a life *(lesson/lessen)* that has allowed him to speak wisdom into his son's situation.
7. There are plenty of *(lessons/lessens)* to learn here.
8. The company is actively seeking ways to strengthen its capital base and **lessen** its debt burden.
9. A bill introduced to the Colorado legislature could *(lesson/lessen)* jail time for substance abuse offenses.
10. So it's back to the *(lesson/lessen)* plan for the teacher and back to the desks for the students.
11. The boys have been working hard and the loss was a good *(lesson/lessen)* – they need to work hard all the time.

Answers: *1. lessons, lessons, lessen 2. lessen 3. lesson 4. lessen 5. lessen 6. lesson 7. lessons 8. lessen 9. lessen 10. lesson 11. lesson*

Liable v. libel

Liable (adj.) [**lahy**-*uh*-b*uh* l] (a three-syllable word) means Legally obligated, subject to, obligated to, or responsible for something. legally responsible: *You are liable for the damage caused by your action.*
2. subject or susceptible: *to be liable to heart disease.* **3.** likely or apt: *He's liable to get angry.*
Libel (n., v.) [**lahy**-b*uh* l] (a two-syllable word) refers to a false publication that damages a person's reputation. *(n.)* **a.** defamation by written or printed words, pictures, or in any form other than by spoken words or gestures. **b.** the act or crime of publishing it. **c.** a formal written declaration or statement, as one containing the allegations of a plaintiff or the grounds of a charge. **2.** anything that is defamatory or that maliciously or damagingly misrepresents. (v.) **3.** to publish a libel against. **4.** to misrepresent damagingly. **5.** to institute suit against by a libel, as in an admiralty court.
   • The court ruled that school officials cannot be held financially **liable** for the improper search.
   • Because of rising legal costs, regional newspapers may not be able to defend themselves in **libel** actions.

—Usage note

LIABLE is often interchangeable with LIKELY in constructions with a following infinitive where the sense is that of probability: *The Sox are liable* (or *likely*) *to sweep the Series.* Some usage guides, however, say that LIABLE can be used only in contexts in which the outcome is undesirable: *The picnic is liable to be spoiled by rain.* This use occurs often in formal writing but not to the exclusion of use in contexts in which the outcome is desirable: *The drop in unemployment is liable to stimulate the economy.* APT may also be used in place of LIABLE or LIKELY

Questions

1. He denied the charge of *(liable/libel)*, slander and wrongful termination.
2. The speaker is discussing the effects of *(liable/libel)* laws on science publishing.
3. Do not *(liable/libel)* anyone. *(Liable/Libel)* is writing something false about someone that damages that person's reputation.
4. The terms would make vendors *(liable/libel)* for software defects that lead to security breaches.
5. The law also provides that owners/operators of hotels, resort, or amusement parks are generally *(liable/libel)* for the acts of their employees and respective agents.
6. Too many people with no connection to the US are suing for *(liable/libel)* in American courts.
7. An Australian court Friday held Merck & Co. *(liable/libel)* in the heart attack of a patient using the painkiller Vioxx.
8. Overall, the Dollar is *(liable/libel)* to drift weaker as the Federal debt expands past $15,000,000,000,000,000 and the amount of unfunded, but actual liabilities, approaches $100 Trillion dollars.
9. Senator Goldwater successfully sued Fact's publisher, Mr. Ralph Ginzburg, for *(liable/libel)*.
10. Attorneys warn owners of those Toyota vehicles who don't heed the recall could be held *(liable/libel)* in an accident.
11. While *(liable/libel)* and slander are regulated by law in the real world, in the cyberworld almost anything goes.
12. An employer can be held *(liable/libel)* even for unintentional discrimination.

Answers: *1. libel 2. libel 3. libel, Libel 4. liable 5. liable 6. libel 7. liable 8. liable 9. libel 10. liable 11. libel 12. liable*

Lightening vs. Lightning

Lightening (n.) [**lahyt**-n-ing] means making lighter in weight or changing to a lighter or brighter color.
Lightning (n.) [**lahyt**-ning] is the flash of light that accompanies thunder.
   • The sun, not bleach, was responsible for **lightening** my hair.
   • A church steeple with a **lightning** rod on top seems to show a lack of confidence.
NOTE: Be very careful here. Native speakers mix this up all the time. The electrical discharge in the sky is LIGHT--NING it's NOT 'Light en ning'

Questions

1. She considered *(lightning/lightening)* her load by donating her winter clothes to charity.
2. Electricity is really just organized *(lightning/lightening)*.
3. While the Tampa Bay *(Lightning/Lightening)* can still advance to the postseason for the first time in three seasons, they don't have much time to get back on track.

4. Cisco Systems today unveiled its new "*(lightning/lightening)* -bolt" fast CRS-3 Internet core router.
5. And the Pentagon agency wants to give those warriors an underground navigation system that works on *(lightning/lightening)* bolts.
6. Faust provided some fairly radical changes to Notre Dame's basic uniforms by *(lightning/lightening)* the color of blue and adding sleeve stripes.
7. Swedish power-metal band HammerFall is equally adept at *(lightning/lightening)* the mood.
8. The skin *(lightning/lightening)* , the hair and heavy makeup assist in making it worse.
9. Long-term, he has aspirations of continuing his domination with *(lightning/lightening)* -quick times.
10. A downpour after sundown, and the growing storm could bring "frequent and dangerous cloud-to-ground *(lightning/lightening)* " to the areas.
11. Friday's US employment report provided enough reason to start *(lightning/lightening)* the safe-haven payload of government debt.

Answers: *1. lightening 2. lightning 3. Lightning 4. lightening 5. lightening 6. lightening 7. lightening 8. lightening 9. lightning 10. lightning 11. lightening*

Like vs. as

General Rule: In formal writing, avoid using like as a conjunction. In other words, something can be like something else (there it's a preposition), but avoid "It tastes good **like** a cigarette should" — it should be "**as a** cigarette should." ***There should be no verb in the phrase right after like.*** Even in phrases such as "It looks **like** it's going to rain" or "It sounds **like** the motor's broken," **as if** is usually more appropriate than like — again, at least in formal writing.

Like is used to compare two nouns. e.g
   • *Romeo and Juliet, like all couple who are too young got themselves into trouble.*
As - used to compare two clauses. (A clause is a phrase that includes a verb).
   Incorrect - Just like swimming is good exercise, running is also a good way to burn calories.
   Correct - Just as swimming is good exercise, running is also a good way to burn calories.
   Note: Do not use '*Like*' when you mean '*for example.*'

More detailed information about 'Like vs. As'
Like means "same form, appearance, kind, character" and is followed by a noun or noun phrase.
   • My sister is *like* my mother.   My sister acts *like* a dragon. • He's crazy *like* a fox. *He's crazy as a fox is crazy.*
   • *Her eyes sparkled like diamonds.* • *His teeth shone like pearls. He teeth shone as pearls shone.* • *He lives like a king. He lives as a king lives.*
As means "in the manner" and is followed by a clause (subj + verb).
   • My brother thinks *as* I do.   *My brother thinks like I.* • He is *as* smart *as* a fox . *He is smart like a fox*
   • He writes *as* a man in his forties writes. *He writes like an older man.*
Characteristic (prep.) It would be *like* her to bring a sack lunch to school.
Similar or comparable (prep.) There is nothing *like* a five mile run on the beach.
Example (adv.) You could watch any show you want, *like* the news, football, or the History Channel.
Inclined (idiom–prep.) Do you *feel like* going out to dinner? (it's an idiom and breaks the rule)
Promise / indicative (idiom- prep.) It *looks like* rain today. (another idiom that breaks the rules) You could also say, "It looks as if it might rain today"
Example (adv.) Some flowers, *as* the rose, require a lot of care
Considered to be (adv.) We view the church and state *as* two separate entities.
In the manner (adv.) He paid for the room and dinner *as* agreed. *(as we had agreed.)*
That (pronoun) I have had the same problem *as* you have.
   • He looks *as if* he needs a place to rest. (not like) • He looks *like* a tired dog. • You need to act *as if* you know the answers (not like) • She talks to her friends *as if* they were her slaves. (not like) • She types *as* she was taught in business school. (not like)   • He saves money *like* a squirrel.

Questions
1. But numerous sources describe the situation *(like/as)* very fluid.
2. The ball player said he felt *(like/as)* a prisoner in his own home when he played for the Cubs last year.
3. *(Like/As)* Elisabeth Bumiller reports, that would be a more ambitious date than one set by the President.
4. He said many tablet-*(like/as)* devices will be launched in China.
5. The movie star said that he sometime has to live *(like/as)* a vampire--only coming out at night to avoid fans.
6. Nomar Garciaparra has retired *(like/as)* a member of the Boston Red Sox.
7. If I were in charge, I'd leave the things *(like/as)* they are.
8. A Mill Valley woman accused of using her 13-year-old son *(like/as)* a designated driver last year .
9. It was slippery, slightly crunchy and tasted *(like/as)* pickles.
10. "When he throws the ball, it's *(like/as)* an explosion." The Tigers' manager explained.
11. She ordered a three-tiered strawberry vanilla cake for her mom *(like/as)* a Mother's Day gift.

Answers: *1. as 2. like 3. As 4. like 5. like 6. as 7. as 8. as 9. like 10. like 11. as*

Loath vs. Loathe

Loath (adj.) meaning unwilling or reluctant, and it's usually followed by to.
Loathe (v.) means to dislike intensely.
   • "I would be *loath* to speak ill of any person who I do not know deserves it." (Samuel Johnson)

- "We should be eternally vigilant against attempts to check the expression of opinions that we *loathe*." (Oliver Wendell Holmes, Jr.)

Note: if you make a mistake here, it will be adding the "e" to loath and saying something like "I am loathe to study all weekend". Remember it's "I am loath to do something" (no 'e') but I "loathe doing it" (with the 'e'). It's only an "e" but it makes a difference.

Questions

1. I *(loathe/loath)* people who dress their pets.
2. Samantha was *(loathe/loath)* to get out of bed.
3. Oh Howard Stern... how some love you and a great many *(loathe/loath)* you!
4. China is *(loathe/loath)* to sign onto some treaty that would limit their emissions
5. These cuts are on top of a proposed income tax increase, which lawmakers are *(loathe/loath)* to touch in an election year
6. *(Loathe/Loath)* them or love them, humans stand in awe of the skillful activities of the spider's impressive web work.
7. Whether you laud or *(loathe/loath)* her politics, she undeniably has an effect on people.
8. But the feds don't know if they have the authority to protect consumers, and local governments have often been *(loathe/loath)* to do anything about cable companies.
9. The Governor was *(loathe/loath)* to substitute his judgment as a governor for that of the legal system.
10. And, while some choose to *(loathe/loath)* birthdays and any reminder of old age, the American Cancer Society is trying to ensure you'll have them.
11. The Internet is a rogue technological behemoth that seems to *(loathe/loath)* its own creator — government.
12. Internet service providers will be *(loathe/loath)* to reduce pricing to accommodate those who want broadband access but can't afford it.

Answers: *1. loathe 2. loath 3. loathe 4. loath 5. loath 6. Loathe 7. loathe 8. loath 9. loath 10. loathe 11. loathe 12. loath*

Loose (loos,) vs. Lose (Looz)

Lose means to lack the possession of, to come to be without.
Loose means not tight.
Loosen means to unfasten something or make it less constraining.
Loose is a common misspelling of *lose*. Your shoelace can become *loose*. But if you don't win, you *lose*.
Loose rhymes with goose.
Lose: While, your shoelace can become *loose*, if you don't stop and tie it, you may *lose* your shoe altogether! *Lose* rhymes with booze
Lose your appetite or loose your appetite? They mean two very different things. If you lose your appetite, then you're no longer hungry--your appetite is gone. But if you loose your appetite, you set it free to eat whatever it wants.
Lose (Looz)
Lose is a verb that can be transitive (taking an object) or intransitive (making meaning by itself, with no object).

- **Transitive verb**: *If I were to **lose** my marbles, I'd be friends with Toodles.*
- **Intransitive verb**: *If we don't stop them from scoring, we will **lose**.*

The meanings of lose range from failing to win to failing to keep possession of something to getting rid of something to having something taken away against one's will. Lose also forms part of the phrasal verb lose out:

- *You will **lose** out on the worms unless you get up early!*

Loose (loos,)
Loose can also be both a transitive and intransitive verb.

- **Transitive verb**: *When he felt safe, he let **loose** a verbal barrage.*
  It's rare to find the form loose used in the intransitive sense.

Loose is also the positive form of an adjective, the form used for simple description. The comparative form is looser, while the superlative form is loosest. The meanings of loose range from untightened to relaxed to lacking restraint to in exact.

- *You wore my jeans and now they are too loose for me*

Examples: • We've worked way to hard to lose this game.   • During Spring Break I got too much sun, now I'm so sunburned I can only wear loose clothes.   • If we live in fear, we'll never set loose our dreams.   • No matter how many times we play, I always lose.   • Stretching out before you begin exercising will loosen your muscles.

Questions

1. The 3x shirt hung *(lose/loose)* on the teenager.
2. On the final lap of the 1500 meter race, Tyrell began to *(lose/loose)* the other runners.
3. Even though we will probably *(lose/loose)* most of our games this year, we are building for the future.
4. After rehabilitating the sea lions, they were set *(lose/loose)* in the bay.
5. If you don't *(lose/loosen)* that top button, I think you're going to turn blue.
6. Those pants are much too *(lose/loose)*! We don't allow sagging in this school.
7. If you *(lose/loosen)* up your muscles you'll have less stress.
8. Relax your hands on the bat. You should have a nice *(lose/loose)* grip.
9. Even if we were to *(lose/loose)* this game, it's not the end of the world.
10. You will *(lose/loose)* out if you don't study this weekend.

Answers: *1. loose, 2. lose, 3. lose, 4. loose, 5. loosen, 6. loose, 7. loosen, 8. loose, 9. lose, 10. lose*

Many vs. Much

Many refers to people or objects that can be counted.
Much refers to a large quantity.

- Because so ***much*** of the food had spoiled, ***many*** of the picnickers went home either hungry or sick.

How much ....? = uncountable nouns   • How ***much*** milk do you drink?
How many ....? = countable nouns   • How ***many*** cups of milk do you drink?

Many reviewers praised Emma's first novel.   Emma's first novel received *much* praise from the reviewers.

Questions

1. *(Many/Much)* of them have worked their way into comfortable management or administrative posts that are long on privileges and short on stress.
2. If you have that *(many/much)* star power at your command, why not show it off?
3. More than 10 million Americans experience chest pain each year and *(many/much)* have not been diagnosed with heart disease.
4. If it's perceived value of the drug is off by so *(many/much)* , will there be problems in deciding how *(many/much)* to invest in the development of the drugs?
5. Fans and *(many/much)* of us in the media expect teams to do what it takes to get contracts done.
6. The Federal Reserve Bank of New York and the insurer agreed to shoulder as *(many/much)* as $450 million in losses.
7. Some 17 companies, *(many/much)* based in South Florida, have been subpoenaed because of complaints about deceptive business practices.
8. You might have to lay off two people who are young and productive to save as *(many/much)* money as one older worker.
9. You might have to lay off two people who are young and productive to save as *(many/much)* dollars as one older worker.
10. Making a human character move perfectly costs *(many/much)* more than several hundred automobiles.
11. But my concern here is that he doesn't have the prodigious power that *(many/much)* scouts feel he has.
12. The severe winter weather that hit *(many/much)* of the United States in February cost Southwest Airlines an estimated $15 million in lost passenger revenue.

Answers: *1. Many 2. much 3. many 4. much, much 5. many 6. much 7. many 8. much 9. many 10. much 11. many 12. much*

Marital vs. Martial

Marital (adj.) [**mar**-i-tl] refers to marriage. *marital status; marital problems; marital relations*
Martial (adj.) [**mahr**-sh*uh* l]refers to battle, war, or military life. **1.** Of, relating to, or suggestive of war. **2.** Relating to or connected with the armed forces or the profession of arms. **3.** Characteristic of or befitting a warrior.
   • Her husband flew to Argentina for an extra-*marital* fling with a female friend.
   • Tony had his arm broken by a *martial* arts instructor.
Note: these two words differ because of the placement of the letter 'i'. In the word "*marital*" the letter 'i' comes after the letter 'r' "Mar i tal', however, in the word 'Martial' the letter 'i' comes after the letter 't' "Mart i al'

Questions

1. The couple tried to resolve their *marital* difficulties.
2. The king declared *martial* law.
3. The building is a **marital** asset and therefore subject to the community property laws of California.
4. Multiple allegations of **marital** infidelity surfaced.
5. Hand injuries aren't the most common in mixed **martial** arts.
6. The Army said it has referred charges including burglary to a general court-**martial** in the case of 24-year-old .
7. How would you like to re-ignite that **marital** spark?
8. Homer's Iliad is the most renowned and lasting **martial** epic of all.
9. He argued for **martial** law in cases brought to the Supreme Court.
10. Six young **martial** arts superstars are getting ready for the toughest fight of their lives.
11. His new book is all about **marital** skirmishes in the kitchen.
12. It is hard, cognitively, to get out of **marital** ruts.

Answers: *1. marital 2. martial 3. marital 4. marital 5. martial 6. martial 7. marital 8. martial 9. martial 10. martial 11. marital 12. marital*

May be vs. Maybe

Maybe (adv.) meaning "perhaps or possibly" An uncertainty: *There are so many **maybes** involved in playing the stock market.* An uncertain reply: *It's better to receive a fast and honest no than a drawn-out **maybe**.*
May be (v.) verb phrase showing possibility.
   • I heard that our instructor *may be* absent today. *Maybe* class will be canceled.

Questions

1. I'm not sure, but I think Tyrell *(maybe/may be)* hiding in the shed.
2. *(Maybe/May be)* Tyrell is hiding with him.
3. *(Maybe/May be)* I will go to the pool later today.
4. I *(maybe/may be)* the first person to do the tango underwater.
5. It *(maybe/may be)* possible to touch your kneecaps
6. That's a definite *(maybe/may be)* .
7. *(Maybe/May be)* one day I will visit Paris.
8. You *(maybe/may be)* the only person I like more than Alf.
9. I *(maybe/may be)* able to fix your radiator with chewing gum.
10. *(Maybe/May be)* if you ask nice I will touch it.

Answers: *1. may be 2. Maybe 3. Maybe 4. may be 5. may be 6. maybe 7. Maybe 8. may be 9. may be 10. Maybe*

Questions

1. That *(maybe/may be)* the largest rash in Rodchester
2. *(Maybe/May be)* if drink enough silver you will turn blue.

3. It *(maybe/may be)* on the roof or in the bushes.
4. When I told you "*(maybe/may be)* " I really meant "no" but I was afraid to tell you.
5. I *(may not be/maybe not)* able to continue without splitting my infinitives.
6. I think that *(maybe/may be)* if you ask your mother she will tell you to have removed.
7. *(Maybe/May be)* you will, maybe you won't, but either way I'm not going to clean it.
8. She *(maybe/may be)* able to fix you supper without salt.
9. There *(maybe/may be)* craters filled with spaghetti sauce.
10. *(Maybe/May be)* you can help me tell the difference between red and green.

Answers: *1. may be 2. Maybe 3. may be 4. maybe 5. may not be 6. maybe 7. Maybe 8. may be 9. may be 10. Maybe*

Questions

1. *(Maybe/May be)* when the moth comes back it won't be so angry.
2. I *(maybe/may be)* going to Tanzania to visit my uncle.
3. When you at my rooster, that *(may have been/maybe have)* the saddest moment of my childhood.
4. I *(maybe/may be)* related to the guy who invented sushi.
5. *(Maybe/May be)* this will start to get tiresome.
6. I *(may not be/maybe not)* able to stop wiggling my elbow.
7. *(Maybe/May be)* one day we can all live in Kentucky.
8. *(Maybe/May be)* nobody will notice your scar.
9. This *(may be/maybe)* what you expected to find, but *(maybe/may be)* not.
10. *(Maybe/May be)* I will send you a t-shirt when I get back from Tanzania.

Answers: *1. Maybe 2. may be* 3. may have been *4. may be 5. Maybe* 6. may not be *7. Maybe 8. Maybe 9. maybe,* may be *10. Maybe*

The contents of this page *(maybe/may be)* reproduced only with correct attribution. See http://www.maybe.com/

Me, Myself, and I

There is a rather straight forward way to determine when to use "me," "myself," and "I." So don't overcomplicate this. Each one has a proper place but sometimes people talk as if we avoid the word "me". For example, you will hear things like:
• Please turn in your homework to Mr. Stevenson or *I.*
As she was dancing her shoelace came undone and she tripped and fell into the director and myself.
Both are incorrect: The word "I" or it's substitute "myself" are only used when you are speaking of yourself as the subject of the sentence. In other words, you are the one taking action.
• I turned in my homework. I hit the ball. I went to the mall. I ran after the ice cream truck.

When to use "I". We would never say: Me turned in my homework. Me hit the ball. Me went to the mall. Me ran after the ice cream truck. Nevertheless lots of us get confused when we add another person to the mix. Is it "Mia and me" or "Mia and I" or "Mia and myself"? The easiest way to figure out which pronoun to use for yourself is to remove the other person from the sentence. For example, which of these is correct? Remove the other person to see which sounds best.
• Mia and I went to the mall. Remove Mia and it becomes: "...I went to the mall."
• Mia and myself went to the mall. Remove Mia and it becomes, "...myself went to the mall."
• Mia and me went to the mall. Remove Mia and it becomes, "...me went to the mall."
That should make it much easier to decide. Your ear should tell you the correct answer is "...I went to the mall."
When is it correct to use "me"? Use it when someone else will perform the action to, or for, you. For example, which of these is correct? Remember you still remove the other person from the sentence and let your ear tell you which one sounds right.
• When you're ready to go just text Penelope or myself. Remove Penelope and it becomes, "..just text myself."
• When you're ready to go just text Penelope or I. Remove Penelope and it becomes, ".. just text I."
• When you're ready to go just text Penelope or me. Remove Penelope and it becomes, ".. just text me."
Removing the 'other person' from the sentence should make it much easier for your ear to tell you the correct pronoun to use. It's obviously, "...just text me."

When is it correct to use "myself"? Us 'myself' only when you are referring back to yourself in a sentence in which you already used I or me. So, it is never used in conjunction with another person like "John and myself" but rather to refer back,
• I love working on computers myself.   • I can finish the homework myself, I don't need your help.   • I'll send out the emails myself.
Remember that 'myself' is never used in tandem with another person as a substitute for "me" or "I". It is NEVER correct to say, "Mia and myself went..." or "...text Penelope or myself"

The rule is this: • Use "John and I" when you are doing the action. (subject)   • Use "John and me" when you are receiving the action (object)   • Use "John and myself" NEVER

Tip: Remove the other person from the sentence and then let your ear tell you which way sounds right.

Questions:

1. On behalf of my wife and *(me/myself/I),* we would like to thank you for attending our daughter's wedding.
2. My wife and *(me/myself/I)* would like to thank you for attending our daughter's wedding.
3. The teacher asked Shantel and *(me/myself/I)* to stay after class.
4. The issue is between you and *(me/myself/I).*
5. You and *(me/myself/I)* have an issue between us.

Answers:

1. **Becomes**: "..my wife and me..." because it's an object receiving the action. The subject is 'we' and the action is 'thanking'. We thank (the subject and verb)...on behalf of us (the object) and (my wife and me) are just a restatement of 'us'. **You could also use the tip** (remove the other person) it's not quite as clear in this case, but it does work. If you remove the other person (my wife) it **becomes**, "On behalf of ....me, I would like to thank..." Even though that sounds a bit silly, it's still grammatically correct. **Test the other options**, "On behalf of I, I would like to thank..." this is clearly wrong. The final option "myself" probably sounds the best to your ear, however, you MUST remember that "myself" is NEVER used in conjunction with another and is only used to refer back to "I". So don't fall into that trap, "On behalf of myself, I would like to thank..." The reason this sounds the best is because it's correct. But it's correct if we were just testing that exact sentence. But we are using the TIP where we drop the other person (the wife). So, 'myself' would be correct if it were actually alone, but that's not the case here. Make sure you understand this issue so you don't make silly mistakes on the exam.

2. **Becomes**: "**My wife and I** would like to thank you..." Because they are the subject of the sentence and doing the action (thanking). Also you could drop the other person and test it. Is it "...I would like to thank you..." or "Myself would like to thank you..." or "Me would like to thank you..." Pretty clearly it should be "I would like to thank you..."

3. **Becomes**: 'Shantel and me' because it's an object receiving the action. The teacher is the subject doing the action (asking). You can also use the tip: drop 'Shantel' from the sentence. **It becomes**, "The teacher ask...(me/myself/I) to stay after class." Clearly your ear tells you it's "me". The teacher asked Shantel and me to stay after class.

4. **Becomes**: "The issue is between you and me (us)" The subject is 'issue' and the verb is 'is' and the object is 'us' (you and me).

5. **Becomes**: "You and I have an issue..." Now, 'you and I" is the subject and the verb is 'have', and what do we have? 'an issue between us' which is the object.

More Details: but don't lose sight of the simple rules stated above.

Short Rule: The first person singular pronoun is 'I' when it's a subject and 'me' when it's an object,"
Each of the forms *me, myself, and I* refers to the same person (you), but they work in different contexts. They are all first person singular pronouns. This means that you use them when speaking about yourself.
- Subject Pronoun (Used for subject and nominatives): I
- Object Pronoun (Used for direct or indirect object and informal nominatives): me
- Possessive Pronoun: my, mine
- Reflexive Pronoun: myself

Subject: in all these cases, the subject is "I"
Linking verb: "I am hungry." "I went to bed late last night." "I'm ready to start playing video games."
Action verb: "I got an A in math." "I found my iPod." "I love Mexican food."
Passive verb: "I was helped by a fellow student" "I was pushed down by my little brother"

Predicate Nominative (subject is still "I")
A predicate nominative is the noun or pronoun that follows a linking verb and restates the subject. When you refer to yourself in the predicate nominative, it is proper to use *I*.
Predicate nominative: "It was I who sent you the text message."

Direct and Indirect Object (now we use 'me')
Simply put, the direct object is generally said to be what "receives" the action of a transitive verb. In this situation, *me* is the proper form to use:
Direct object: "The ball hit me in the face." "My big brother gave me a backpack for my birthday."
Indirect object: The indirect object is what receives the direct object. It can either follow the verb directly or also appear in a prepositional phrase.
- The teacher gave me an "A". The teacher gave the "A" to me.
- The waiter handed me an extra dessert. The waiter handed the extra dessert to me.
- The violin teacher paid me a compliment. The violin teacher paid a compliment to me.

Reflexive Pronouns
Reflexive pronouns are used as objects (direct or indirect), but not as subjects and refer back to a noun already mentioned. They can also be appositives, renaming another noun for emphasis. In either case, the correct reflexive pronoun to use is *myself* when you are referring back to yourself in a sentence in which you already used *I* or *me*.
- Reflexive pronoun • direct object: "I slapped myself on the leg." "I kicked myself."
- Reflexive pronoun • indirect object: "I bought myself a nice gift." "I gave myself a pep talk."
- Reflexive pronoun • appositive: "I, myself, programmed that application." "Who made the salad? It was I, myself."

All Three at Once
- *I* can't believe that *I, myself*, was picked for the talent show.   • If you text *me, I, myself*, will respond immediately.

Miner vs. Minor

Miner (n.) refers to a person who works in a mine.
Minor (n.) refers to someone who is under legal age or to a secondary area of academic study. As an adjective, minor means lesser or smaller.
- "It is only because *miners* sweat their guts out that superior persons can remain superior." (George Orwell, The Road to Wigan Pier)
- In many states, it is illegal for a *minor* to rent a car.

Questions
1. The earth is a *(miner/minor)* planet of a very average star.
2. MLB.com is reporting that 50 game suspensions were handed down to four *(miner/minor)* league players on Wednesday.
3. *(Miner/Minor)* burns, unlike more serious ones, usually heal without leaving a scar.

4. *(Miner/Minor)* flooding is being reported along rivers and streams around Ohio as warm weather melts what's left of the recent heavy snows.
5. Mr. Castle is the grandson of a *(miner/minor)* from the Kentish coalfields.
6. At the time he got his first job, when he was 16, Pablo was still a *(miner/minor)* .
7. In line with the initial unbundling agreement, one department was separated into a steel entity, and another department was separated into an iron-ore *(miner/minor)* .
8. Sharper revealed that he had *(miner/minor)* arthroscopic surgery on his left knee.
9. Minex, the world's biggest contract *(miner/minor)* , began work today on the new South Bendix mine operation.
10. Two of America's largest coal *(miner/minor)* are in merger talks.
11. Three children suffered *(miner/minor)* injuries today in an accident.

Answers: *1. minor 2. minor 3. Minor 4. Minor 5. miner 6. minor 7. miner 8. minor 9. miner 10. miners 11. minor*

Moot vs. Mute

Moot (adj.) [moot] refers to something that is debatable or of no practical importance. 1. open to discussion or debate; debatable; doubtful: *a moot point.* **2.** of little or no practical value or meaning; purely academic. **3.** *Chiefly Law.* not actual; theoretical; hypothetical.
Mute (adj.) [myoot] means unspoken or unable to speak. silent; refraining from speech or utterance.
2. not emitting or having sound of any kind. **3.** incapable of speech; dumb. Expressed without speech; unspoken: *a mute appeal. Music* Any of various devices used to muffle or soften the tone of an instrument.
   • The court ruled on Thursday that the appeal was *moot* because the last offer had been withdrawn.
   • Several factors help to make sense of Russia's *mute* response to the crisis.

Usage Notes: "A moot point was classically seen as one that is arguable. A moot case was a hypothetical case proposed for discussion in a 'moot' of law students (i.e., the word was once a noun). In U.S. law schools, students practice arguing hypothetical cases before appellate courts in moot court.

"From that sense of moot derived the extended sense 'of no practical importance; hypothetical; academic.' This shift in meaning occurred about 1900 <because the question has already become moot, we need not decide it.> Today, in American English, that is the predominant sense of moot, especially in the set phrase moot point. (Bryan A. Garner, Garner's Modern American Usage, Oxford University Press, 2003)

Questions
1. Because medical bills ate up his estate, the inheritance issue became a *(mute/moot)* point.
2. She has been *(mute/moot)* since suffering the trauma of losing her parents.
3. Kathryn Bigelow is the first woman to win the best director Oscar - but she longs for the day when gender becomes a "*(mute/moot)* point" in Hollywood.
4. I like to play games on *(mute/moot)* , while listening to music.
5. It is worth noting that the course included 15 citizens of *(mute/moot)* and deaf from the local community.
6. One parent's decision not to appeal does not necessarily render the other parent's appeal *(mute/moot)* .
7. Plenty of BlackBerry users have noticed with 5.0 the *(mute/moot)* key standby mode function doesn't work.
8. The Senate parliamentarian's ruling that the President must sign a bill into law before the Senate can change it through reconciliation largely renders *(mute/moot)* the attempt to shield members from a direct vote.
9. But since they say that such disorders in children are frequently misdiagnosed, the distinction often is *(mute/moot)* .
10. All lines have been placed on *(mute/moot)* to prevent any background noise.
11. But when he had cast out the demon, the *(mute/moot)* man spoke.
12. That might sound like a *(mute/moot)* point, since the tax will be passed on to consumers in higher prices.

Answers: *1. moot 2. mute 3. moot 4. moot 5. moot 6. moot 7. moot 8. mute 9. mute 10. mute 11. mute 12. mute*

Moral vs. Morale

Moral (adj.) [mor -*uh* l] (with the accent on the first syllable) means "ethical" or "virtuous." As a noun moral refers to the lesson or principle taught by a story or event. of, pertaining to, or concerned with the principles or rules of right conduct or the distinction between right and wrong; ethical: *moral attitudes.* **2.** expressing or conveying truths or counsel as to right conduct, as a speaker or a literary work; moralizing: *a moral novel.* **3.** founded on the fundamental principles of right conduct rather than on legalities, enactment, or custom: *moral obligations.* **4.** capable of conforming to the rules of right conduct: *a moral being.*
Morale (n.) [m*uh*-ral] (second syllable accented) means "spirit" or "attitude." emotional or mental condition with respect to cheerfulness, confidence, zeal, etc., esp. in the face of opposition, hardship, etc.: *the morale of the troops.*
   • "Will springs from the two elements of *moral* sense and self interest." (Abraham Lincoln)
   • " *Morale* is the greatest single factor in successful wars." (Dwight Eisenhower)

Usage Notes: if you look up these two nouns in a good dictionary, you will see that they are intimately intertwined. The chief problem seems to be the sense 'espirit de corps.' In present-day English morale is the usual spelling for this sense "We recommend, however, that you use morale for the 'espirit de corps' sense--most people do. Few, if any, use morale instead of moral for the lesson in a story." (Merriam-Webster's Concise Dictionary of English Usage, 2002)

Questions
   1. "A nation as a society forms a *(moral/morale)* person." (Thomas Jefferson)
   2. *(moral/morale)* is self-esteem in action.
   3. Low *(moral/morale)* and poor leadership is affecting performance.
   4. The plot mostly focuses on the *(moral/morale)* struggle of Wei as he has to stay true to his mission.

5. It makes sense that there might be low (***moral/morale***) in VDOT offices around the state.
6. They appeared to be expressions of the same traditionalist (***moral/morale***) framework, destined to succeed or fail together as twin pillars of the culture war.
7. He became a (***moral/morale***) compass on making decisions.
8. Long before the financial crisis, Fannie Mae and Freddie Mac were synonymous with (***moral/morale***) hazard in the minds of most informed observers.
9. From an outsider's point of view, (***moral/morale***) within the armed forces seems extremely high.
10. I would say (***moral/morale***) is very good in our company.

Answers: *1. moral 2. Morale 3. morale 4 moral 5. morale 6. moral 7. moral 8. moral 9. morale 10. morale*

Not only . . . but also:

Be sure you learn the rules of parallelism because "not only...but also" is heavily tested regarding parallelism. If you start with "not only" you MUST continue with "but also". These two always, always, always go together. You CANNOT say "Not only...and also".

• Wrong: Vinnie is ***not only*** the best centerfielder ***and also*** the best hitter on the team.
• Correct: Vinnie is ***not only*** the best centerfielder ***but also*** the best hitter on the team.

Notable vs. Noticeable

Notable (adj.) worthy of distinction" a person of note" 'worthy of comment', 'obvious' 'worthy of distinction', 'celebrated', 'widely known' or 'esteemed'. As a noun, it can mean 'a person of note'.
Noticeable (adj.) "attracting attention" detectable (i.e. sufficient to be noticed).
• I would like to discuss some ***notable*** omissions from the text I gave you.   • Be respectful. He is a very ***notable*** fellow.
• The blue sheen in your hair is hardly ***noticeable***.   • The difference in processing speed is very ***noticeable***.
Tip Notable means worthy of comment. Noticeable means detectable.

Questions
1. While the Nasdaq and the S&P 500 posted large and (***notable/noticeable***) gains.
2. Exxon Mobil Corp. said it would expand its oil and natural gas production this year, (***notable/noticeable***) feat for any large Western oil company.
3. Tonight's' episode will be (***notable/noticeable***) for a number of reasons.
4. It predicts a "(***notable/noticeable***) " first-quarter contraction but doesn't give a precise figure.
5. There was a (***notable/noticeable***) absence at the Palace on Sunday afternoon before the Pistons faced the Rockets.
6. Increase in salaries of Supreme Court judges was made due to (***notable/noticeable***) difference in salaries of private sector lawyers.
7. It sends out a powerful acoustic signal audible to almost all young people under the age of 20 years but barely (***notable/noticeable***) to anyone over the age of 25.
8. I realize that with the (***notable/noticeable***) exceptions of the myopic and hyperopic, hindsight always is 20/20.
9. With foaling season now well underway, Seelster Farms today announced a number of (***notable/noticeable***) births.
10. The only way to finance Social Security, Medicare and Medicaid is through a (***notable/noticeable***) increase in the tax burden or a (***notable/noticeable***) reduction in services.

Answers: *1. notable 2.notable 3.notable 4. noticeable 5. noticeable 6. noticeable 7. noticeable 8. notable 9. notable 10. noticeable, noticeable*

Obsolescent vs. Obsolete

Obsolescent (adj.) refers to the process of passing out of use or usefulness--becoming **obsolete**.
Obsolete (adj.) means no longer in use--outmoded in design, style, or construction.
• A computer tends to ***obsolesce*** during the one or two year period as it is becoming ***obsolescent*** until finally it is completely ***obsolete***.
• "About the time President Abraham Lincoln issued his initial Emancipation Proclamation in 1862, the New York State Legislature declared the Erie Canal Enlargement Project complete. Then, another major engineering triumph, the New York Central Railroad, consolidated in 1853, was hauling more freight and passengers quicker and cheaper. That brought about the bigger but already ***obsolescent*** New York State Barge Canal." (M.D. Morris, "Erie Canal Exemplifies Engineering," *Ithaca Journal*, February 17, 2003)

Questions
1. "Adults are just (***obsolete/obsolescent***) children and the hell with them." (Dr. Seuss)
2. Senate and House conferees are considering a bill to close (***obsolete/obsolescent***) military bases.
3. Although CD writers are (***obsolete/obsolescent***) , writable CD discs continue to sell by the billions.
4. The goal of this initiative is to promote the recycling of (***obsolete/obsolescent***) electronic equipment and components.
5. Google's App Marketplace has gone live in yet another step forward for cloud computing which Google predicts will make desktops (***obsolete/obsolescent***) .
6. Libya's arsenal is composed of (***obsolete/obsolescent***) Soviet-sourced equipment that is in urgent need of modernization.
7. The plan is to then either reverse-engineer the new weapons or produce them under license to force-march its (***obsolete/obsolescent***) military to the 21st century.
8. We need to think forward or we will be stuck with an (***obsolete/obsolescent***) and decaying structure of no architectural significance .
9. In Anderson County, 25 bridges are classified by engineers as being structurally deficient and 25 are structurally (***obsolete/obsolescent***).

Answers: *1. obsolete 2. obsolete 3. obsolescent 4. obsolete 5. obsolete 6. obsolescent 7. obsolescent 8. obsolescent 9. obsolete*

On account of vs. Because

Because is always better than the circumlocution *on account of*.   The best approach is to simply remove "*on account of*" from your vocabulary.
   • **Wrong**: *On account of* his study habits he got straight A's on his report card.
   • **Correct**: *Because* he studies all the time, he got straight A's on his report card.   .

One another vs. Each other

Each other should be used when referring to two things.
One another should be used when referring to more than two things.
   • The business partners (two) congratulated ***each other*** on their successful first year.
   • The members of the basketball team (more than two) congratulated ***one another*** on their victory.
   • The squadron planes never got within five to seven miles of ***one another***, officials said.
   • The two planes never got within five to seven miles of ***each other***, officials said.

Questions
   1. The couple always says they love *(each other/one another)* dearly.
   2. Researchers say over 10,000 stars in HM Cancri are so near to *(each other/one another)* that they could not get much closer without smushing together.
   3. This week, two Shinwari subtribes took up arms to fight *(each other/one another)* over an ancient land dispute.
   4. In a bizarre ritual, Karnataka villagers threw fireballs at *(each other/one another)* .
   5. The panelists examined the ways that jazz and modern art fed *(each other/one another)* throughout their development.
   6. The two freshmen lean on *(each other/one another)* for support.
   7. It's what makes us proud, when great horses go out and run against *(each other/one another)* .
   8. After a pitcher hit a batter during a game in Cuba, players started to chase *(each other/one another)* around the field with bats.
   9. To a degree, the two agendas are at odds with *(each other/one another)* .
   10. I love how this team gets excited for *(each other/one another)* when one of them hits a big shot.

Answers: *1. each other 2. one another 3. each other 4. one another 5. each other 6. each other 7. one another 8. one another 9. each other 10. one another*

Pair, Pare, Pear

Pare (v.) means to remove, reduce, or cut back.
Pair (n.) means a couple.
Pear (n.) refers to the fruit.
   • Universities are trying to ***pare*** their budgets as funds from donors and the state shrivel.
   • Originality is simply a ***pair*** of fresh eyes.
   • ***Pear*** trees are more tolerant of the cold than apples.

Questions:
   1. On cold days I wear an extra *(pare/pair/pear)* of socks.
   2. When you travel, try to *(pare/pair/pear)* down your belongings to the essentials.
   3. A fresh, ripe *(pare/pair/pear)* is intensely sweet.
   4. Property prices jumped the most in almost two years, adding pressure on policy makers to *(pare/pair/pear)* stimulus measures adopted during the global recession.
   5. She scored a *(pare/pair/pear)* of goals and added three assists in the match.
   6. School officials continued to *(pare/pair/pear)* a budget for next school year, losing 16 teaching positions through attrition.
   7. Arrange the slices of *(pares/pairs/pears)* on the bottom of the baking pan and top with cake batter.
   8. The state is giving permits to kill does during special seasons set to *(pare/pair/pear)* the herd in some regions.
   9. Bloomsburg University men's tennis team split a *(pare/pair/pear)* of matches on its final two days in Hawaii.
   10. Here are some wines that *(pare/pair/pear)* nicely with corned beef and cabbage.
   11. Northwest *(pare/pair/pear)* shippers are finished with the Brazil market for this crop season.

Answers: *1. pair 2. pare 3. pear 4. pare 5. pair 6. pare 7. pears 8. pare 9. pair 10. pair 11. pear*

Passed vs. Past

Past: refers to a period of time before now or a distance
   • In the ***past*** I've done well on these exams.   • Tyron drove ***past*** his girl friend's home.

Passed: refers to the action of *passing*
   • He passed the written exam papers to the student seated behind him.   • I studied all night, I know I have ***passed*** this test.
Note: you have "passed the time" but you have never "*past* the time," but a hobby is called a 'past time' not a 'passed time'

More details about 'passed and past'
Pass
Passed and past are both forms of the verb 'to pass', which can be transitive (take an object) or intransitive (make meaning without an object).
   • **Transitive**: *During rush hour traffic it is difficult to* ***pass*** *other vehicles.*
   • **Intransitive**: *If you study all of chapter four and read over all your notes, you may* ***pass*** *the exam.*

Passed

Since pass is a regular verb, it forms the past tense and the passed participle both by adding 'ed', resulting in the form *'passed'*. *Passed* is used by itself as the past tense, and with the helping verbs *have* or *has* for the present perfect and the helping verb *had* for the past perfect for both the transitive and the intransitive form.

Transitive:
- **Past tense**: *Congress **passed** the law, but the President vetoed it.*
- **Present Perfect tense**: *Congress has **passed** the law, but the President has vetoed it.*
- **Past Perfect tense**: *Congress had **passed** the law, but the President had vetoed it.*

Intransitive:
- **Past tense**: *The elections **passed**, and things settled down again.*
- **Present Perfect tense**: *The elections have **passed**, and things have settled down again.*
- **Past Perfect tense**: *The elections had **passed**, and things had settled down again.*

Notice that the form of the helping verb have in the present perfect tense is altered only to match the number of the subject (have for a plural subject; has for a singular subject).

Past

Past is the adjective, adverb, prepositional, and noun form of pass.
- **Adjective**: *The teacher always includes questions on the exam from the **past** year.*
- **Adverb**: *After receiving a perfect score on the last exam, I moved **past**. everyone in the class.*
- **Preposition**: *At half **past** two the bells tolled once.*
- **Noun**: *If we fail to learn from the **past** we are doomed to repeat it.*

Differentiating Passed and Past

Remember to use **passed** for the regular, standard, and past tense verb form (with the simple past or past participle), and use **past** for all other parts of speech.

Questions

1. Would you change anything from your *(past/passed)* ?
2. The Congressman proposed legislation that, if *(past/passed)* , would reduce federal spending.
3. Lawmakers *(past/passed)* a nearly $1 billion bonding bill today.
4. Armon Bassett scored 38 points to lead Ohio *(past/passed)* top-seeded Kent State.
5. The fourth-seeded Hokies (23-7) eliminated Miami (19-12) the *(past/passed)* two years.
6. He *(past/passed)* up the chance to attend Stanford University on a full ride scholarship.
7. It's sad to see the list of famous people who have *(past/passed)* away each year.
8. Iditarod leader John Baker of Kotzebue with Seward's Dallas Seavey right behind him *(past/passed)* through the Cripple checkpoint and kept right on going.
9. His criminal *(past/passed)* could impact his pending burglary case.
10. "All the negative things you better be leaving in the *(past/passed)* ", was his sage advice.

Answers: *1. past 2. passed 3. passed 4. past 5. past 6. passed 7. passed 8. passed 9. past 10. past*

Peace vs. Piece

Peace (n.) [pees] is a state of calm, contentment or the absence of war. "hold your peace." a state of mutual harmony between people or groups, esp. in personal relations: *Try to live in peace with your neighbors.* Inner contentment; serenity: *peace of mind.*

Piece (n.) [pees] is a part of a whole or the joining of two or more parts to form a whole, a unit or a portion. a separate or limited portion or quantity of something: *a piece of land; a piece of chocolate.* You also *'say your piece'* (not peace) but this is more idiomatic.

Questions

1. "When the power of love overcomes the love of power, the world will know *(piece/peace)* ." (Jimi Hendrix)
2. "Always give people a *(piece/peace)* of your heart, not a piece of your mind."
3. "*(Piece/Peace)* is not merely a distant goal that we seek, but a means by which we arrive at that goal." (Martin Luther King, Jr.)
4. I never met a *(piece/peace)* of chocolate I didn't like.
5. The Nobel *(Piece/Peace)* Prize is awarded each year.
6. It provided the people of Bethlehem more *(piece/peace)* of mind.
7. Derivatives reform doesn't get the kind of news play as other *(pieces/peaces)* of the financial-reform debate.
8. Imagine a jigsaw puzzle *(piece/peace)* dropped from a 20-foot height falling miraculously and perfectly into the last space in a 1000-*(piece/peace)* puzzle.
9. This might not be the most beautiful beach in the world, but the people and the *(piece/peace)* here are like no other.
10. The Americans, the French, the British, the Russians and the Chinese all support the Middle East *(piece/peace)* process.
11. Meteorites, *(pieces/peaces)* of asteroids that break away and plunge to Earth, are "toasted on their way through Earth's atmosphere.
12. The war parties among the nations of the Middle East are holding hostage the possibility of *(piece/peace)* .
13. If they want *(piece/peace)* ... this is the only way to move forward.
14. The singer has created a 17-*(piece/peace)* women's wear line for the company.
15. We're having serious conversations about the *(piece/peace)* with a private collector.

Answers: *1. peace 2. piece 3. Peace 4. piece 5. Peace 6. peace 7. pieces 8. piece, piece 9. peace 10. peace 11. pieces 12. peace 13. peace 14. piece 15. piece*

Perquisite vs. Prerequisite

Perquisite (n.) [**pur**-kw*uh*-zit] (sometimes informally shortened to perk) is a benefit (beyond pay) that is associated with a particular job. an incidental payment, benefit, privilege, or advantage over and above regular income, salary, or wages: *Among the president's perquisites were free use of a company car and paid membership in a country club.* **2.** a gratuity or tip. **3.** something demanded or due as a particular privilege: *homage that was once the perquisite of royalty.*

Prerequisite (adj., n.) [pri-**rek**-w*uh*-zit, pree-] something required as a prior condition of something else. required beforehand: *a prerequisite fund of knowledge.* –*noun* **2.** something prerequisite: *A visa is still a prerequisite for travel in many countries.* Required or necessary as a prior condition: *Competence is prerequisite to promotion.* Something that is prerequisite, as a course that is required prior to taking an advanced course.

- "Personal **perquisites** can include a cook, a steward, a garden boy and a night watchman. Because ministers enjoy such **perks**, the senior civil servants who work with the ministers also demand, and often get, **perks** that are only of a marginally lower quality." (Cameron Duodu, "Water and Waste," The Guardian, March 23, 2006)
- Proper insulation is the first **prerequisite** for the effective use of any energy-saving device.

TIP remember the word 'perquisite' has first syllable sound of 'pur' or 'per' which sounds like 'Per' in "perk"

Questions
1. The *(perquisite/prerequisite)* of her job almost made up for the low salary.
2. The cops saw it as an unwritten *(perquisite/prerequisite)* in their benefits package.
3. A high degree of emotional intelligence may be a *(perquisite/prerequisite)* for outstanding achievement.
4. They're fundamental skills that kids need to master and acquire and *(perquisite/prerequisite)* for success in most other learning.
5. Tomlinson said a *(perquisite/prerequisite)* for any team before he will consider joining will be that it can contend for a championship.
6. We can save $19 million a year but would mean taking away a *(perquisite/prerequisite)* for the bosses.
7. Management wouldn't hire women to work in the tire bay, a job that is a *(perquisite/prerequisite)* for advancement.
8. Cash to spend and save, jump-starting the financial rehabilitation, or "deleveraging," that economists see as a crucial *(perquisite/prerequisite)* to robust growth.
9. Now here's a *(perquisite/prerequisite)* you won't find many places: a company that starts garden seeds for its workers.
10. More than a *(perquisite/prerequisite)* , what company car you drive says whether you've arrived and how far you've moved up the corporate ladder.

Answers: *1. perquisite 2. perquisite 3. prerequisite 4. prerequisite 5. prerequisite 6. perquisite 7. prerequisite 8. prerequisite 9. perquisite 10. perquisite*

Persecute vs. Prosecute

To persecute (v.) [**pur**-si-kyoot] is to oppress, harass, or bother. to pursue with harassing or oppressive treatment, esp. because of religion, race, or beliefs; harass persistently. **2.** to annoy or trouble persistently.

To prosecute (v.) [**pros**-i-kyoot] is to enforce by legal action. *Law.* **a.** to institute legal proceedings against (a person). **b.** to seek to enforce or obtain by legal process. **c.** to conduct criminal proceedings in court against. **2.** to follow up or carry forward something undertaken or begun, usually to its completion: *to prosecute a war.*
- A prosecutor should *prosecute*, not *persecute*.
- "To announce truths is an infallible recipe for being *persecuted*." (Voltaire)
- "If you violate Nature's laws you are your own *prosecuting* attorney, judge, jury, and hangman." (Luther Burbank)

Questions
1. Governments have always chosen which groups and practices to tolerate and which to *(prosecute/persecute)*.
2. Even assuming that Najmabadi is a member of a disfavored group, she points to no evidence of an individualized threat to *(prosecute/persecute)* her.
3. Federal courts can also *(prosecute/persecute)* offenses against the laws of war under federal legislation.
4. The police didn't want to *(prosecute/persecute)* since the student has behavioral issues.
5. Jiang Feng, Mei Xuan's husband, became destitute because of the unrelenting *(prosecution/persecution)* of Falun Gong.
6. Northern Ireland prosecutors have confirmed they will review a decision not to *(prosecute/persecute)* a police officer accused of protecting a suspect.
7. Blessed are ye when men shall revile you, and *(prosecute/persecute)* you, and shall say all manner of evil against you falsely, for my sake.
8. Governments typically use the army, police, media, and security sector to unfairly *(prosecute/persecute)* its opponents.
9. The U.S. Attorney's office should send a message that the government will *(prosecute/persecute)* the wrongdoers.
10. The DA's office is threatening to *(prosecute/persecute)* the witness for perjury if she denies her sworn affidavit.

Answers: *1. persecute 2. persecute 3. prosecute 4. prosecute 5. persecution 6. prosecute 7. persecute 8. persecute 9. prosecute 10. prosecute*

Personal vs. Personnel

Personal (adj.) [**pur**-s*uh*-nl] (accent on the first syllable) means "private" or "individual." of, pertaining to, or coming as from a particular person; individual; private: *a personal opinion.* **2.** relating to, directed to, or intended for a particular person: *a personal favor; one's personal life; a letter marked "Personal."*
Personnel (n.) [pur-s*uh*-**nel**] (accent on the last syllable) refers to the people employed in an organization, business, or service. *All personnel are being given the day off.*
- "The true teacher defends his pupils against his own *personal* influence." (Amos Bronson)

• "Outstanding leaders go out of their way to boost the self-esteem of their *personnel*." (Sam Walton)

Usage Notes:

"A surprisingly large number of books warn against confusing these two words. It is possible that they both may be misspelled sometimes as **personel**." ("personal, personnel," Merriam-Webster's Concise Dictionary of English Usage, 2002)

"*Personal* is often criticized as being redundant: That's my personal opinion is wordier but not otherwise different from That's my opinion. But some other applications of this very high frequency word seem to impart useful information: *She has an entourage of some size, including her personal maid, her personal secretary, and her personal trainer.* We understand these people to be dedicated, like *personal* computers, to the requirements of this one woman; the idea of exclusivity adds to our sense of her importance, even if the use of personal doesn't add much other information.

"*Personal* and *personnel* come from the same root, but they are spelled and pronounced differently (**PUHR**-suhn-uhl and PUHR-suhn-**NEL**) and have only person in common: *personnel* as noun means 'people, especially employees,' and 'the field of employee matters itself' and as adjective refers to 'departments responsible for hiring and keeping records about the employees of an enterprise.'" (Kenneth G. Wilson, The Columbia Guide to Standard American English, Columbia University Press, 1993)

Questions

1. "Most people in big companies are administered, not led. They are treated as *(personal/personnel)*, not people." (Robert Townsend)
2. Education officials outlined a host of potential *(personal/personnel)* changes in a 250-page booklet.
3. The US Census was never intended as a vehicle for gathering *(personal/personnel)* information on citizens.
4. Senator Smith chairs the Senate panel that oversees military *(personal/personnel)* policy.
5. Consumers can be deceived by the misuse of the 'organic' label on *(personal/personnel)* care products.
6. When it comes to getting a low income unsecured *(personal/personnel)* loan are low interest rates possible?
7. During the relief effort, 1400 medical *(personal/personnel)*from the US military treated those affected.
8. In January, *(personal/personnel)* trainer Brian Cole set out to climb the world's tallest free-standing peak.
9. Why has it become so taboo for us to talk openly about our *(personal/personnel)* finance questions?
10. *(Personal/Personnel)* matters were addressed during the School Board meeting on Monday evening.

Answers: *1. personnel 2. personnel 3. personal 4. personnel 5. personal 6. personal 7. personnel 8. personal 9. personal 10. Personnel*

Perspective vs. Prospective

Perspective (n.) refers to a view or outlook. A view or vista. A mental view or outlook: *"It is useful occasionally to look at the past to gain a perspective on the present"(Fabian Linden).* The relationship of aspects of a subject to each other and to a whole*: a perspective of history; a need to view the problem in the proper perspective.* Subjective evaluation of relative significance; a point of view: *the perspective of the displaced homemaker.* The ability to perceive things in their actual interrelations or comparative importance: *tried to keep my perspective throughout the crisis.* The appearance of objects in depth as perceived by normal binocular vision. The technique of representing three-dimensional objects and depth relationships on a two-dimensional surface. adj. Of, relating to, seen, or represented in perspective

Prospective (adj.) means likely or expected to happen or become. of or in the future: *prospective earnings.* potential, likely, or expected: *a prospective partner.* **1** : relating to or effective in the future *prospective* effect> **2** : likely to come about : expected to happen <*prospective* inability to perform the contract> **3** : likely to be or become *prospective* buyer>
   • The movie retells the Frankenstein myth from the *perspective* of the creature.
   • Stricter requirements for *prospective* parents have made international adoptions more difficult.

Questions

1. The lawyers from both sides questioned the *(perspective/prospective)* jurors.
2. The no-contract policy will help assuage fears from *(perspective/prospective)* iPad buyers who've heard the horror stories.
3. Studying history can help put the problems of our own time in *(perspective/prospective)* .
4. This helps gain some *(perspective/prospective)* on how evenly matched so many teams in Des Moines are.
5. How do we put proper *(perspective/prospective)* on this stunning defeat?
6. The coach explained the rules to *(perspective/prospective)* football players and parents at the meeting.
7. When a *(perspective/prospective)* buyer is just getting "warmed up" to the marketplace, he/she will frequently begin by bopping into some open houses on a Sunday afternoon.
8. We will start with a recap of the quarter to provide a *(perspective/prospective)* on our outlook for next year.
9. From an airline *(perspective/prospective)* , the past 10 years have been wrenching to put it mildly.
10. Alex had a very different *(perspective/prospective)* .
11. The university rolled out the red carpet to welcome *(perspective/prospective)* students and their families.

Answers: *1. prospective 2. prospective 3. perspective 4. perspective 5. perspective 6. prospective 7. prospective 8. perspective 9. perspective 10. perspective 11. prospective*

Plain vs. Plane

Plain (n.) The word plain has several meanings: Simple (i.e., not elaborate). a plain girl, a plain cake, a plain color, Also simple as in apparent. It is plain to see. It seems quite plain to me.
   • An expanse of level and low land. The Russian Plain.
   • I joined the Chinese farmers as they attempted to drive the yaks across the plain in western China.

Plane (n.) The word plane has several meanings: An airplane. What time is your plane? A flat surface especially in mathematics . In a 3D space, a plane can be defined by specifying a point and a normal vector to the plane.

Also means a level (usually figurative). I was hoping for a conversion on a higher plane. A tool for smoothing or shaping wood (a carpenter's plane).

Also the verb 'to plane' (i.e., to shape wood). • Can you plane a few inches off the top of the door? To travel on the surface of water. • The car hit the puddle and **planed** straight into the back of the lorry. (also known as 'to aquaplane')

Questions
1. In Mexico, prairie dogs are primarily found at the southern end of the great *(plains/planes)*.
2. I need to take an inch off this plank. Pass the *(plain/plane)*.
3. I'm not a fancy cook. It will be a *(plain/plane)* meal.
4. Catch the morning *(plain/plane)* to Los Angeles.
5. I was such a *(plain/plane)* girl when I was younger.
6. He's an experienced, *(plain/plane)* -talking guy.
7. Where all that water goes is a big concern of FEMA's, as the agency re-draws flood *(plain/plane)* lines.
8. Specify a point and normal vector to define a *(plain/plane)* .
9. Flex your mind and reach a higher *(plain/plane)* .
10. Some stuff is just *(plain/plane)* vanilla, leaving us entertained but not really intellectually challenged.
11. House Speaker Nancy Pelosi and Senate Leader Harry Reid just *(plain/plane)* do not get it.
12. A pilot is dead after a World War II-era *(plain/plane)* crashed during landing at a Chandler airport.
13. Plus, as purists point out, Irish soda bread is, by definition, *(plain/plane)*, *(plain/plane)*, *(plain/plane)*: It includes flour, salt, baking soda, and sour milk or buttermilk.
14. In geometry, I had learned three points make a *(plain/plane)*.
15. Our company takes network transformation to a higher *(plain/plane)*.
16. This is a class of movie that operates on a higher *(plain/plane)* than its peers.

Answers: *1. plains 2. plane 3. plain 4. plane 5. plain 6. plain 7. plain 8. plane 9. plane 10. plain 11. plain 12. plane 13. plain, plain, plain 14. plane 15. plane 16. higher*

Pore vs. Pour

Pore (v.) means to study or examine something carefully. (n.) pore means an opening as in the skin or in the leaves of plants.
Pour (v.) means to flow freely or to empty a fluid from one source to another. to dispense a drink or other substance
• The lawyer **pored** over the rules, searching for a loophole.
• Happiness is a perfume which you cannot **pour** on someone without getting some on yourself. Ralph Waldo Emerson

Questions
1. "*(Pore/Pour)* down your warmth, great sun!" (Walt Whitman)
2. She *(pored/poured)* over the small print on the medicine label.
3. If our loquacious president has more thoughts that do not *(pore/pour)* forth in the torrential course of his relentless rhetoric during the State of the Union, he can mail those thoughts to Congress. The Postal Service needs the business.
4. Inspectors will *(pore/pour)* through the site's rubble when demolition starts.
5. Rep. Heinz, D-Tucson, noting that lawmakers had less than 24 hours to *(pore/pour)* over 15 budget bills.
6. Threats against IRS workers and facilities continue to *(pore/pour)* in after last month's plane crash.
7. To warm the glass, *(pore/pour)* hot water into a coffee glass, swirl around and empty.
8. High Performance Sintered Porous Plastic Materials are available in *(pore/pour)* sizes from 5 to 100 micron.
9. Investors and media will *(pore/pour)* over every word to find out how the firm makes its substantial returns.
10. The beauty brand famous for the *(pore/pour)* -purging blackhead strips, has launched Makeup Removing Towelettes.
11. *(Pore/Pour)* coffee into the glass and add brown sugar.

Answers: *1. Pour 2. pored 3. pour 4. pore 5. pore 6. pour 7. pour 8. pore 9. pore 10. pore 11. Pour*

Precede vs. Proceed

Precede (v.) [pri-**seed**] means "to come before." to go before, as in place, order, rank, importance, or time. **2.** to introduce by something preliminary; preface: *The teacher* **preceded** *her lecture with a funny anecdote.*

Proceed (v.) [proh-**seed**] means "to go forward." to move or go forward or onward, esp. after stopping.
2. to carry on or continue any action or process. **3.** to go on to do something. **4.** to continue one's discourse.
• George W. Bush **preceded** Barak Hussein Obama in the White House. Obama **proceeded** with plans to increase spending.

Questions
1. After keeping us for an hour, the guard let us *(precede/proceed)* without him.
2. The storms of April *(precede/proceed)* the gentle rains of May.
3. A judge ruled that Chevron can *(precede/proceed)* with an international arbitration claim against Ecuador.
4. The team is took batting practice and all the other workouts that *(precede/proceed)* a spring training game.
5. Walton County will *(precede/proceed)* with a feasibility study for a sports and arts complex.
6. The parade will begin at 10 am at the down town bus station and will *(precede/proceed)* down Grant Street.
7. The *(precedes/proceeds)* of the offering will be used for the Company's ongoing exploration programs.
8. Gait changes *(precede/proceed)* overt arthritis and strongly correlate with symptoms and histopathological events in pristane-induced arthritis.
9. A moment of silence will *(precede/proceed)* the game.
10. He needs a few days to decide whether he will *(precede/proceed)* with the plan.
11. The annual Brian P. Kelly Memorial Run will *(precede/proceed)* Saturday's 49th St. Patrick's Parade.

12. Three-quarters of the *(precedes/proceeds)* will be donated to local charities.
13. During the *(precedings/proceedings)* the district attorney objected only once to the line of questioning.
14. *(Precede/Proceed)* with caution or you might better understand the saying that "Fools rush in where angels fear to tread."
15. His reputation *(preceded/proceeded)* him.

Answers: *1. proceed 2. precede 3. proceed 4. precede 5. proceed m 6. proceed 7. proceeds 8. precede 9. precede 10. proceed 11. precede 12. proceeds 13. proceedings 14. Proceed 15. preceded*

Prescribe vs. Proscribe

Prescribe (v.) means to establish, direct, or lay down as a rule.
Proscribe (v.) means to ban, forbid, or condemn.
• "Doctors are men who **prescribe** medicines of which they know little, to cure diseases of which they know less, in human beings of whom they know nothing." (Voltaire)
• "When a legislature undertakes to **proscribe** the exercise of a citizen's constitutional rights it acts lawlessly and the citizen can take matters into his own hands and proceed on the basis that such a law is no law at all." (William Orville Douglas)

Questions

1. In no state are psychologists permitted to *(proscribe/prescribe)* medication.
2. China's laws tightly *(proscribe/prescribe)* public demonstrations.
3. The probation conditions *(proscribe/prescribe)* the minor from associating with gang members.
4. It's an act of violence, and the law should *(proscribe/prescribe)* it.
5. He treated Rodriguez and *(proscribed/prescribed)* anti-inflammatories but did not *(proscribe/prescribe)* human growth hormone.
6. The new law will *(proscribe/prescribe)* interest rate hikes within 12 months a consumer has a new card.
7. For example, a radiation oncologist is more likely to *(proscribe/prescribe)* radiation therapy.
8. The state legislature passed legislation extending the authority to *(proscribe/prescribe)* medical marijuana.
9. The rules governing a single currency *(proscribe/prescribe)* a bailout for a country on the brink of insolvency.
10. Municipalities possess the power to *(proscribe/prescribe)* lower speed limits on highways.
11. It is not right to *(proscribe/prescribe)* how people should dress as long as they are not dressed in an indecent manner.

Answers: *1. prescribe 2. proscribe 3. proscribe 4. proscribe 5. prescribed, prescribe 6. proscribe 7. prescribe 8. prescribe 9. proscribe 10. prescribe 11. prescribe*

Presence vs. Presents

Presence (n.) [**prez**-*uh* ns] is essence or actuality. the state or fact of being present, as with others or in a place. **2.** attendance or company: *Your presence is requested.* **3.** immediate vicinity; proximity: *in the presence of witnesses.* **4.** the military or economic power of a country as reflected abroad by the stationing of its troops, sale of its goods, etc.: *the American military presence in Europe; the Japanese presence in the U.S. consumer market.*
Presents (v.) (prĭ-zĕnts') is to show or to bring forth formally, To bring before the public: *present a play.* To make a gift or award of. To afford or furnish: **The situation presented us with a chance to improve our knowledge.** To turn or position in the direction of another: *presented his face to the camera.* To hold, carry, or point (a weapon) in a particular manner as a salutation or sign of honor, usually along the center axis of the body.
• "He continues to possess the **presence**, mental as well as physical, of the young man"(Brendan Gill).
• Clifton High School **presents** "The Wizard of Oz" March 19, 20 and 21.

Questions

1. We are, as it were, swimming in God's *(presents/presence)*.
2. Because she *(presents/presence)* herself as the quintessence of tranquility, Grace is the person whom family and friends turn to most often in times of crisis.
3. At the site if the riot, observers reported a heavy police *(presents/presence)* Friday.
4. Pakistan is concerned about an Indian *(presents/presence)* in Afghanistan.
5. If James *(presents/presence)* the new budget now, the board of directors will reject it out-of-hand.
6. The company says it will increase its *(presents/presence)* in the global market for wireless network testing.
7. "The American diplomatic *(presents/presence)* in London began in 1785 when John Adams became our first minister"
8. Thankfully, Lloyd had the *(presents/presence)* of mind to warn the tenants to get out before the building it burned down.
9. This is the weekend that the film company *(presents/presence)* its latest feature.
10. While boyfriend has a certain *(presents/presence)* that makes me feel safe.

Answers: *1. presence 2. presents 3. presence 4. presence 5. presents 6. presence 7. presence 8. presence 9. presents 10. presence*

Plus vs. And

Do not use *plus* as a conjunction meaning *and*.
• **Wrong**: His contributions to this community are considerable, **plus** his character is beyond reproach.
• **Correct**: His contributions to this community are considerable, **and** his character is beyond reproach.
Note: *Plus* can be used to mean *and* so long as it is not being used as a conjunction.
• His generous financial contribution **plus** his donated time has made this project a success.
In this sentence, *plus* is being stued as a preposition. Note, the verb *has* is singular because an intervening prepositional phrase (*plus* his donated time) does not affect subject verb agreement.

Principal vs. Principle

Principal (n.) commonly means "administrator" or "sum of money." As an **_adjective_**, principal means "most important."

Principle (n.) means "basic truth" or "rule."
- According to the Peter *Principle*, a worker will rise to his or her level of incompetence.
- Ms. Benson said that boredom was her *principal* reason for retiring.

Usage Notes: "principal, principle' only principal is an adjective. *Principal* is also a noun, signifying either a person or money. *Principle* is only a noun, usually designating a law or rule.

"Ah, but even if you know the difference, it is still easy to **goof** by writing 'the basic *principal'* or 'their *principle* occupation.' These **errors** seem to be the ones that are most common. And bear in mind that if you have a word processor, it will not help you here.

"One thing to remember is that **principle** is always a noun, never an adjective. It means 'a standard of conduct,' 'an essential element,' or 'a general truth.'

"**Principal** is an adjective meaning 'first in authority or importance.' When used as a noun, as in principals of a lay, principal of a school, or the principal of a loan, it is the shortened form of a phrase ('principal players,' principal teacher,' and 'principal sum').
TIP" if you can substitute 'main' (which contains an 'a'), use principal (which also contains an 'a'). If you can substitute 'rule' (which ends in 'le'), use principle (which also ends in 'le')." (Wm & Mary Morris, Harper Dict of Contemp Usage, Harper & Row, 1975)

Questions

1. The *(principles/principals)* underpinning the American system are in the Declaration of Independence.
2. Mr. Bill retired as school *(principle/principal)* .
3. His *(principle/principal)* ambition now is to tend to his garden.
4. The *(principle/principal)* of gardening is the same as the principle of teaching: to provide nourishment.
5. Walpole High Assistant *(Principle/Principal)* Snard Harshbreather has been named the new *(principle/principal)*.
6. A corporation's "*(principle/principal)* place of business" is deemed to be its "nerve center".
7. The parties agreed in *(principle/principal)* to a one-year contract.
8. The Company also granted the initial purchasers of the notes an option to purchase up to an additional $60 million aggregate *(principle/principal)* amount of notes.
9. The state will recover from these violators following the well-established *(principle/principal)* of polluter pays.
10. This is causing problems for many lenders, but it also hurts the credit score of homeowners, so there are plans in the works for *(principle/principal)* reductions.
11. The two *(principle/principal)* characters are Snow and Lightning.
12. A new rule in hockey states: "A lateral, back pressure or blindside hit to an opponent where the head is targeted and/or the *(principle/principal)* point of contact is not permitted.
13. In America we have a legal *(principle/principal)* that even unpopular defendants deserve a lawyer.
14. Hopkins asserted the *(principle/principal)* that the Constitution protects all persons, even foreigners, within US jurisdiction.
15. We guarantee that you will see a twelve percent return on the *(principle/principal)* within the first year.
16. Critics had nothing but flowers for the playwright; but for the *(principle/principal)* , they had only stones.
17. The science of economics is based on the *(principle/principal)* of supply and demand.
18. The *(principle/principal)* of courtesy seems to be lost in modern society.
19. According to the *(principle/principal)* spokesperson for the president, spending trillions of debt based money will somehow save the country from further financial disaster.

Answers: *1. principles 2. principal 3. principal 4. principle 5. Principal, principal 6. principal 7. principle 8. principal 9. principle 10. principal 11. principal 12. principal 13. principle 14. principle 15. principal 16. principal 17. principles 18. principle 19. principal*

Quiet vs. Quit vs. Quite

Quiet (n.) [kwahy-it] means "silence." or it means to silence (v.) *to quiet a crying baby.* 1. making no noise or sound, esp. no disturbing sound: *quiet neighbors.* **2.** free, or comparatively free, from noise: *a quiet street.* **3.** silent: *Be quiet!* **4.** restrained in speech, manner, etc.; saying little: *a quiet person.* **5.** free from disturbance or tumult ; tranquil; peaceful: *a quiet life.*
Quit (v.) [kwit] means "to leave." 1. to stop, cease, or discontinue: *She quit what she was doing to help me paint the house.* 2. to depart from; leave (a place or person): *They quit the city for the seashore every summer.* 3. to give up or resign; let go; relinquish: *He quit his claim to the throne. She quit her job.* to stop trying, struggling, or the like; accept or acknowledge defeat.
Quite (adv.) [kwahyt] means "very" or "actually." truly or considerably 1. completely, wholly, or entirely: *quite the reverse; not quite finished.* 2. actually, really, or truly: *quite a sudden change.* 3. to a considerable extent or degree: *quite small; quite objectionable.*
- I was *quite* tired and wanted a *quiet* place to nap. I asked the boys to *quit* playing games.
- Henry needed peace and *quiet* so he *quit* his job and moved to the woods. Now he is *quite* content.

Questions

1. After Sunday, the Cup schedule has *(quit/quiet/quite)* weekends April 4, July 17 and Aug. 29.
2. Garn is Utah States Majority Leader admitted to paying a woman over $150000 to keep *(quit/quiet/quite)* over an incident that occurred 25 years ago.
3. The American Lung Association reports 75 percent of smokers report wanting to *(quit/quiet/quite)* ..
4. (I) putted *(quit/quiet/quite)* nicely and managed my game *(quit/quiet/quite)* well.
5. As the opus number reveals, Chopin's "Là ci darem" Variations almost (though not *(quit/quiet/quite)*) marked the beginning of his career as a published composer.
6. Researchers called The Acreage's pediatric brain cancer cluster a "*(quit/quiet/quite)* hurricane".
7. In the meantime, dolphin shows at the aquarium have been canceled to allow "*(quit/quiet/quite)* time" for the mother and calf to bond.

8. Despite some intriguing visual aspects, the film proves to be *(quit/quiet/quite)* dull, unable to overcome an internal battle with the film's overall tone.

9. Employees worried about losing their benefits in the company's upcoming bankruptcy sale are taking vacation days or *(quitting/quietting/quiteing)* altogether.

10. Democrats in Washington are going through one of those "It's *(quit/quiet/quite)* out there... too *(quit/quiet/quite)* ..." cliché moments, as everyone holds their breath in anticipation .

11. I'm not going to *(quit/quiet/quite)* the fight.

12. *(Quit/Quiet/Quite)* talking about repealing the 16th amendment. Bring a bill to do it.

13. Gemma Arterton almost *(quit/quiet/quite)* her role as a Bond girl in Quantum Of Solace when a movie executive disparaged her "common" accent.

14. Looking for change, but not *(quit/quiet/quite)* ready for a revolution?

15. It has been a source of speculation and debate for *(quit/quiet/quite)* some time that the cafeteria is serving week-old leftovers.

16. The rowdier members of the crowd began to *(quiet/quit/quite)* down once they saw the police.

17. I found her patronizing attitude towards my ideas *(quiet/quit/quite)* insulting.

18. Eager to flee the hustle and the bustle of San Francisco, Kelly sought the *(quiet/quit/quite)* of Morro Bay.

19. One rarely sees a performer *(quiet/quit/quite)* show business after scoring only one hit.

20. *(Quiet/Quit/Quite)* a few of his clients left him after he was implicated in an embezzlement scheme.

Answers: *1. quiet 2. quiet 3. quit 4. quite, quite 5. quite 6. quiet 7. quiet 8. quite 9. quitting 10. quiet, quiet 11. quit 12. Quit 13. quit 14. quite 15. quite 16. quiet 17. quite 18. quiet 19. quit 20. Quite*

Quotation vs. Quote

Quotation (n.) something that is quoted; a passage quoted from a book, speech, etc.: *a speech full of quotations from Lincoln's letters.* **2.** the act or practice of quoting. **3.** *Commerce.* **a.** the statement of the current or market price of a commodity or security. **b.** the price so stated.

Quote (v.) to repeat (a passage, phrase, etc.) from a book, speech, or the like, as by way of authority, illustration, etc. **2.** to repeat words from (a book, author, etc.). **3.** to use a brief excerpt from: *The composer quotes Beethoven's Fifth in his latest work.*

 • I hate *quotations*. Tell me what you know." (Ralph Waldo Emerson)
 • She defended her case by *quoting* passages from the Bible.

TIP in formal writing use "quotation" for the noun form, even though you'll be tempted to use the more common form "quote(s)". In formal writing 'quote' is a verb only. In informal speech feel free to mix and match.

Usage Notes: The problem with quotation is that, to the writer who hopes to deliver goods quickly, the three syllables sound and read as if they were slowing the sentence down. The single syllable of quote, meanwhile, sounds apt to such a writer. And it sounds more and more natural all the time, as it seems to predominate in spoken English. So although it remains informal for now, it's likely to gain ground in formal prose. (" Bryan A. Garner, Garner's Modern American Usage, Oxford University Press, 2003)

Questions

1. The old saying, and I *(quote/quotation)*, "The problem with socialism is that you eventually run out of other people's money."

2. Shannon began each of her essays with a familiar *(quote/quotation)* .

3. When I can't think of an answer, I *(quote/quotation)* from a song lyric.

4. Investors should be aware that not all market *(quotes/quotations)* are shown at all websites.

5. I recall a *(quote/quotation)* that well applies to Ed Jones: "Every job is a self-portrait of the person who did it.

6. He recently told CBS News he hopes his critics on that front, *(quote/quotation)*, "die screaming of rectal cancer."

7. Washington Post policy says that "[w]hen we put a source's words inside *(quote/quotation)* marks, those exact words should have been uttered in precisely that form.

8. Pop diva Mariah Carey has professed to being a big fan of Woody Allen's work, and claims she can "*(quote/quotation)* every word" of his 1994 movie *Bullets Over Broadway*.

9. First, Leach's (somewhat rough) *(quote/quotation)* is from Revelation 3:16, which reads "So, because you are lukewarm--neither hot nor cold--I am about to spit you out."

10. Common Stock will be quoted on the OTC Bulletin Board® ("OTCBB"), a centralized electronic *(quote/quotation)* service for over-the-counter securities.

11. To *(quote/quotation)* Albert Einstein: "The most powerful force in the universe is compound interest."

12. I'll *(quote/quotation)* three paragraphs from my favorite poem.

Answers: *1. quote 2. quotation 3. quote 4. quotations 5. quotation 6. quote 7. quotation 8. quote 9. quotation 10. quotation 11. quote   12. quote*

Rain vs. Reign vs. Rein

All three of these words can be used as both nouns and verbs.
Rain refers to precipitation (falling water). ***It's been raining for 40 days and nights.***
Reign refers to a period or demonstration of sovereign power. ***A king reigns over his subjects.***
Rein refers to restraint or the means by which power is exercised. ***Rein in the horses.***
 • "My face looks like a wedding cake left out in the (rein/reign/*rain*) ." (W. H. Auden)
 • "Let freedom *reign*. The sun never set on so glorious a human achievement." (Nelson Mandela)

Questions

1. The world is run with far too tight a *(rain/rein/reign)* for luck to interfere.

2. In the epic poem "Paradise Lost" Satan rises up to claim Hell as his own domain and delivers a rousing speech to his followers "Better to *(rain/rein/reign)* in Hell than serve in Heaven." (John Milton)

3. Banks will have to *(rain/rein/reign)* in bonuses for a second year.

4. He enjoys running through the *(rain/rein/reign)* .

5. The teacher encouraged me to give free *(rain/rein/reign)* to my imagination.

6. In our adoration of pop stars we have produced a new *(rain/rein/reign)* of idolatry.

7. There is a 40 percent chance of *(rain/rein/reign)* in the form of showers and thunderstorms.

8. Oswalt finished just as *(rain/rein/reign)* began pounding Kissimmee.

9. The president's stuttering bid to *(rain/rein/reign)* in the largest US banks got a shot in the arm Monday.

10. The festival continues as normal, *(rain/rein/reign)* or shine.

11. The most profitable movie in history continued its *(rain/rein/reign)* over the box office this weekend.

12. Bikinis might always *(rain/rein/reign)* supreme, as most women find them more flattering.

13. Palm Beach got soaked with more than 7 inches of *(rain/rein/reign)* Thursday night.

14. China could raise bank reserve ratios in a bid to *(rain/rein/reign)* in inflation and avoid an asset bubble.

15. The nonprofit is trying to improve its accounting practices and *(rain/rein/reign)* in wasteful spending.

16. As *(rains/reins/reigns)* fell from the heavens in epic proportions, dozens of commuters worked their iPhones.

17. During iPod's *(rain/rein/reign)* , Apple's stock climbed about 170 percent.

18. Queen Elizabeth I *(rained, reigned, reined)* over England between 1558 to 1603.

19. It has *(rained, reigned, reined)* for the past six weekends.

Answers: *1. rein 2. reign 3. rein 4. rain 5. rein 6. reign 7. rain 8. rain 9. rein 10. rain 11. reign 12. reign 13. rain 14. rein 15. rein 16. rains 17. reign 18. reigned 19. rained*

Rational vs. Rationale

Rational (adj.) [**rash**-*uh*-nl] means having or exercising the ability to reason. agreeable to reason; reasonable; sensible: *a rational plan for economic development.* **2.** having or exercising reason, sound judgment, or good sense: *a calm and rational negotiator.*
Rationale (n.) [rash-*uh*-**nal**] refers to an explanation or basic reason. the fundamental reason or reasons serving to account for something.
  • "No *rational* argument will have a *rational* effect on a man who does not want to adopt a *rational* attitude." (Karl Popper)
  • The senator challenged the government's *rationale* for the financial bailout.

Questions

1. Whether that *(rational/rationale)* is *(rational/rationale)* we won't know for at least another year.
2. What is the mayor's *(rational/rationale)* for trying to sell three of the city's public hospitals?
3. "It is not to be forgotten that what we call *(rational/rationale)* grounds for our beliefs are often extremely irrational attempts to justify our instincts." (Thomas Huxley)
4. When you can't give a *(rational/rationale)* explanation for the latest random fluctuation of the stock market, you produce some pseudo-scientific garbage.
5. It is, therefore, necessary to see whether there is any *(rational/rationale)* behind the demand.
6. If fans are unhappy, whether *(rational/rationale)* or irrational, the fans are less likely to buy tickets and merchandise.
7. If that sounds like a paper-thin *(rational/rationale)* for locking up content that comes on the disc you paid for at retail, you may not find yourself alone.
8. Then take an honest look at yourself and see if your expectations are *(rational/rationale)* .
9. Letting broadcasters sell airwaves they don't fully need is such a *(rational/rationale)* , sensible approach.
10. The district court's lack of findings or *(rational/rationale)* makes review difficult.

Answers: *1. rationale, rational 2. rationale 3. rational 4. rational 5. rationale 6. rational 7. rationale 8. rational 9. rational 10. rationale*

Regard vs. Regards

Use "in regard to," "with regard to," "regarding," or "as regards." Never use "in regard**s** to" or "with regard**s** to." Only use 'regards' if you are giving best wishes to someone.
  • **Wrong:** *The school counselor spoke* **in regards to [with regards to]** *college applications.*
  • **Correct:** *The school counselor spoke* **regarding [as regards, in regard to, with regard to]** *college applications.*
'With regards to' is nonstandard and frequently functions as a shibboleth. It never appears in Edited English.
  • **Wrong:** **In regard**s** to** your application, we would like to offer you a full-ride academic scholarship.
  • **Correct:** **In regard to** your application, we would like to offer you a full-ride academic scholarship.

Regardless vs. Irregardless

Regardless means "not withstanding." Hence, the "ir" in *irregardless* is redundant. *Regardless* is the correct form. **Rule:** NEVER, ever, ever, ever use *irregardless. (easy rule to remember)*

Regretful vs. Regrettable

Regretful (adj.) refers to people and means full of regret. full of regret; sorrowful because of what is lost, gone, or done.
Regrettable (adj.) applies to incidents or situations and means causing or deserving regret. Eliciting or deserving regret: *a regrettable lack of funds; regrettable remarks.*
  • She told her parents that she was profoundly *regretful*.
  • She apologized for the *regrettable* mistakes and bad choices she made.

Note: 'regretful' applies to people and 'regrettable' refers to situations (not people). Politicians use the word "regrettable" because it is in the passive voice...no one is to blame for anything...it's just 'regrettable' that things happened that way.

Questions
1. The principal described the incident as *(regretful/regrettable)* .
2. When he heard the concert had been canceled, he felt both *(regretful/regrettable)* and relieved he would get his money back.
3. He sounded *(regretful/regrettable)* that this situation has come to a lawsuit.
4. It was *(regretful/regrettable)* that this situation has come to a lawsuit.
5. Now residents of this normally neighborly Southern city say they feel *(regretful/regrettable)*, and slightly guilty, for allowing one of its most revered figures to disappear into a sleepy ranch house with little company.
6. "We are deeply *(regretful/regrettable)* of the incident and any distress caused," a spokesman said.
7. It is *(regretful/regrettable)* that in most recent times, a lot of things have gone terribly wrong.
8. There was a *(regretful/regrettable)* incident that was done in all innocence and was hurtful, and which certainly should not have occurred.
9. Jacobellis has never publicly seemed overly *(regretful/regrettable)* about the blunder.
10. It is therefore most *(regretful/regrettable)* that this noble project was aborted by the same people for whom it was designed to elevate.

Answers: 1. *regrettable* 2. *regretful* 3. *regretful* 4. *regrettable* 5. *regretful* 6. *regretful* 7. *regrettable* 8. *regrettable* 9. *regretful* 10. *regrettable*

Respectfully vs. respectively

Respectively (adv.) [ri-**spek**-tiv-lee] means "one by one in the order designated or mentioned." in precisely the order given; sequentially. **2.** (of two or more things, with reference to two or more things previously mentioned) referring or applying to in a parallel or sequential way: *Joe and Bob escorted Betty and Alice, respectively.*

Respectfully (adj.) [ri-**spekt**-*fuh* l] "with respect." full of, characterized by, or showing politeness or deference: *a respectful reply.*
• The central roles of ghost and detective are played **respectively** by comedians Vic Reeves and Bob Mortimer.
• "My cat does not talk as **respectfully** to me as I do to her." *(Sidonie-Gabrielle Colette)*

Questions
1. Mike and Ike Johnson, a sixth grader and a fourth grader *(respectfully/respectively)* , begin every day with one hour of schoolwork.
2. "I *(respectfully/respectively)* decline the invitation to join your hallucination." (Scott Adams)
3. Loan originations were $119.4 million and $169.0 million during the years ended December 31, 2010 and 2011, *(respectfully/respectively)* .
4. I *(respectfully/respectively)* disagreed then, and I *(respectfully/respectively)* disagree now. T
5. Compared to last year, these sales were 3.3 and 2.1 per cent lower *(respectfully/respectively)* , primarily due to continuing weakness in the Eastern European markets and Russia.
6. Instead of shouting, jumping, and bullying people into hearing their message, the demonstrators stood *(respectfully/respectively)* with their signs and greeted people on the street.
7. Nor was it shocking when the Big East and Big 12 earned eight and seven bids, *(respectfully/respectively)* .
8. We *(respectfully/respectively)* ask that you bring for a vote before the full Senate.
9. MERCEDES GP PETRONAS' Nico Rosberg and Michael Schumacher take fifth and sixth place *(respectfully/respectively)* in the opening race of the Formula One season.
10. And if you come, we will treat you *(respectfully/respectively)*.

Answers: 1. *respectively* 2. *respectfully* 3. *respectively* 4. *respectfully, respectfully* 5. *respectively* 6. *respectfully* 7. *respectively* 8. *respectfully* 9. *respectively* 10. *respectfully*

Retroactive to (not *from*)
The correct idiom is *'retroactive to'* not *'retroactive from'*. The retroactivity goes from the current time backwards to an older point in time. Retroactive does not start at an older point in time and then move forward. In other words, we start now and move back TO an older date, we do not start at an older date and move FROM that date forward.
• **Wrong**: The tax increase is **retroactive from** last year. • **Correct**: The tax increase is **retroactive to** last year.

Rise vs. Raise vs. Raze
Raise means to lift or elevate.
Rise means to move from a lower position to a higher position. It has the same meaning as 'to ascend'. The past tense of rise is rose. There is no such word as 'rised'.
Raze is a less common word. It means to demolish completely or to delete. (It can also be written 'rase'. This is not a UK convention. It is simply an alternative spelling.)

He is *raising* the ball in his hand.
With "raise", there is usually something lifting something else.

The ball on the floor is *rising*.
With "rise", the object ascends itself.

raise   rise

Remember, *raise* is not always about lifting - you can *raise* a question and *raise* children.
• The construction guys need to *raise* the platform.
• Wearing a tee shirt with "Ron Paul Brings the Ruckus" will *raise* a few eyebrows.

- The tee shirt made his eyebrows *rise*.
- Exercising with *raise* your heart rate.
  - It would be too expensive *raise* the remnants of the Titanic.
  - The fire *razed* the forest to the ground.
  - A bulldozer can *raze* a house in a few minutes.
  - Properly placed explosives will *raze* even the biggest structure.

More Information

Rise: INTRANSITIVE – An intransitive verb does not take an object; Get up or ascend • Please rise from the chair. • The sun rises in the morning. • The bread dough rose quickly. *(past)* • He rises at 6:00 a.m. every morning

Raise: TRANSITIVE – A transitive verb requires an object lift, increase, elevate • The Boy Scouts **are raising** the flag. • Please **raise** your hand if you want to speak. • The farmer **raises** wheat and barley. • My employer **raised** my salary •

Raise, raises, raised, No version (araise)

RISE – Additional Meanings

• He **rises** at 6:00 a.m. every morning. • The towers of the bridge **rise** up 1,000 ft. • A storm in **rising** in the North. • A quarrel **arose** among the two lovers. • The plane **rose** as it approached the mountains. • The **rise** of the middle class was easy to predict. • They tried **to get a rise out of** him by insulting him. • The Industrial Revolution gave rise to Urbanization. (**rise, rises rose, have risen, arise, arises, arose, arisen**) **1** : to get up : RISE **2 a** : to originate from a source **b** : to come into being or to attention **3** : ASCEND)

RAISE – Additional Meanings

• My grandparents **raised** me. • Mrs. Green **raises** roses. • The engineer **raised** over four million dollars for his battery-operated engine. • The landlord **raised** my rent. • **Raise** the window shades and let some light in. • The good news **raised** his spirits. • The king had to **raise** an army before he could go to war. • He was **raising Cain** in the back of the bus.

Questions

What about recent temperature *(1.) (raises/rises)* in the last century? 65% of the warming this century occurred in the first three decades, and then, while CO_2 levels continued to *(2). (raise/rise)* , temperatures fell for four decades in a row.

Since the last ice age 18,000 years ago the global sea level has *(3.) (risen/raised)* by 130 meters, and is still doing so at a current rate of around 20cm per century, which is dwarfed by local tectonic movements. The Cheney 3C rule states that if the CO2 level in the air is doubled from pre-industrial, the temperature will *(4.) (raise/rise)* 3C.

Dr James Hansen of NASA adds it will *(5.) (raise/rise)* another 3C in the long run due to feedbacks.

To explain the warming now observed, Mr. Towne would have to postulate a "factor X," when instead the current warming can be adequately explained by the *(6.) (raise/rise)* in CO2 (and CH4) levels in the air, caused by mankind's emissions. That is why the IPCC states with over 90% certainty that warming is occurring, and it is caused by mankind's emissions.

As long as they have no personal vested interests that may be damaged by their policies, the global warming hysteria is a windfall for the simple reason that it is a cause that virtually everyone supports and is thus a guaranteed way of being able to *(7.) (raise/rise)* tax revenue with no political backlashes.

And to that I would say "really?". If under 'natural' conditions Nature decided to *(8.) (raise/rise)* the global conditions another 10deg, would that be acceptable, because its 'natural'? Or is their theory that Nature would never do this sans Mankind?

No, most scientists believe that the CO2 increase will *(9.) (raise/rise)* the average temperature a few degrees F in the next several decades.

Answers: *1. rises 2. rise 3. risen 4. rise 5. rise 6. rise 7. raise 8. raise 9. raise*

Role vs. Roll

Role (n.) a character or part played by a performer. proper or customary function: *the teacher's role in society.*

Roll usually a verb, but as a noun it has many senses, including a portion of bread and a list of names belonging to a group.

  - "The *role* of a writer is not to say what we all can say, but what we are unable to say." (Anais Nin)
  - "When they call the *roll* in the Senate, the Senators do not know whether to answer 'Present' or 'Not Guilty.'" (Theodore Roosevelt)

Questions

1. Bart Simpson is not the best *(roll/role)* model for youngsters.
2. The teacher nibbled on a cinnamon *(roll/role)* while reading the class *(roll/role)* .
3. I need to purchase a *(roll/role)* of wire.
4. Every year I find more *(rolls/roles)* of fat, by the time I die I'll weigh 500 lbs.
5. Favre took an active *(roll/role)* in the recruitment of Tomlinson, according to veteran NFL the Newsday writer.
6. Nirvana is found in the deep *(roll/role)* of a breaking wave.
7. As the nation's premier law enforcement agency, the FBI has played a prominent *(roll/role)* in American history and popular culture for more than 100 years.
8. Everybody understands their *(roll/role)* .
9. He took out an impressive *(roll/role)* and paid the check with a $100 bill.
10. People were encouraged to shoot their *(rolls/roles)* on mining speculation.
11. They would *(roll/role)* in later and later every night.
12. He's been on a *(roll/role)* since taking that course on sales techniques.
13. Her new manager has managed to hook her up with a cameo *(roll/role)* in the film.
14. Many stars have been considered for the lead *(roll/role)* of Captain America in the upcoming film.

Answers: *1. role 2. roll, roll 3. roll 4. rolls 5. role 6. roll 7. role 8. role 9. roll 10. rolls 11. roll 12. roll 13. role 14. role*

Sensual vs. Sensuous

Sensual (adj.) means affecting or gratifying the physical senses. typically sexual connotations.
Sensuous means pleasing to the senses, especially those involved in aesthetic pleasure, as of art or music. (not sexual) But as explained in the usage notes below, this fine distinction is often overlooked.

- "If one wants another only for some self-satisfaction, usually in the form of *sensual* pleasure, that wrong desire takes the form of lust rather than love." (Mortimer Adler)
- "The web, then, or the pattern, a web at once *sensuous* and logical, an elegant and pregnant texture: that is style, that is the foundation of the art of literature." (Robert Louis Stevenson)

Usage Notes:

"*Sensuous* is an interesting word. The OED says it was apparently invented by Milton, because he wanted to avoid the sexual connotations of the word sensual (1641). "The OED cannot find any evidence of the use of the word by any other writer for 173 years, not until [Samuel Taylor] Coleridge: Thus, to express in one word what belongs to the senses, or the recipient and more passive faculty of the soul, I have reintroduced the word *sensuous*, used, among many others of our elder writers, by Milton. (Coleridge, "Principles of General Criticism," in Farley's Bristol Journal, August 1814) "Coleridge put the word into ordinary circulation--and almost immediately it began to pick up those old sexual connotations that Milton and Coleridge wanted to avoid." (Jim Quinn, American Tongue and Cheek, Pantheon Books, 1980)

"The consensus of the commentators, from Vizetelly 1906 to the present, is that *sensuous* emphasizes aesthetic pleasure while *sensual* emphasizes gratification or indulgence of the physical appetites.

"The distinction is true enough within one range of meanings, and it is worth remembering. The difficulty is that both words have more than one sense, and they tend often to occur in contexts where the distinction between them is not as clear cut as the commentators would like it to be." (Merriam-Webster's Dictionary of English Usage, 1994)

Questions

1. Glide into the *(sensual/sensuous)* world of ballroom dancing!
2. The taste of a barbecued steak off the grill held a special, almost *(sensual/sensuous)* hold on him, "that amazing, awesome flavor that fills your mouth.
3. From the "*(Sensual/Sensuous)* Seafood" menu dishes, I selected the combination spicy seafood, which included shrimp, calamari, mussels and clams.
4. The photographer asked her to take the very *(sensual/sensuous)* pose on the bed.
5. This is one of the softest, most delicate and *(sensual/sensuous)* love songs I've heard.
6. The soulful Chicago septet Lubriphonic fuses roots music with explosive rock 'n' roll and *(sensual/sensuous)* old-school dance music.
7. In the past 30 years TV programming has drastically changed. Now you can watch all that sexual and *(sensual/sensuous)* tension going on in living color.

Answers: *1. sensuous 2. sensuous 3. Sensuous 4. sensual 5. sensuous 6. sensuous 7. sensual*

Speak to vs. Speak with

To *speak* **to** someone is to tell them something: The counselor *spoke to* Jennifer about her grades.
To *speak* **with** someone is to discuss something with them: Jennifer *spoke* **with** her friend Ashley for hours.

Sit vs. Set

Sit means to rest on one's buttocks.
Set means to put in a place or to adjust.
The transitive verb set means "to put" or "to place"; it takes a direct object, and its principal forms are set, set, and set.
The intransitive verb sit means "to be seated"; it does not take a direct object, and its principal forms are sit, sat, and sat.

- Last night I <u>*set*</u> the table for dinner. When I <u>*sat*</u> down for dinner last night, only my cat joined me.

Questions

1. His injury will cause him to *(set/sit)* out at least one game.
2. I got so tired of thinking that I just wanted to *(set/sit)* down somewhere and think about the strange dichotomies of life
3. The Civil Liability for Nuclear Damage Bill seeks to *(set/sit)* **down** mechanisms and rules for liability claims.
4. The centre of Bangkok has been flooded with more than 100000 protestors, who have threatened to *(set/sit)* there for a week unless there is a new election.
5. "Invariably," he said, "the flight attendant will come by and say, 'Do you realize what it means to *(set/sit)* in this row?'
6. The San Francisco Police Department is proposing an ordinance that would make it against the law for anyone to *(set/sit)* or lie on a public sidewalk.
7. "Irish dancing is as much a lifestyle as it is an art," said Gately, as she *(set/sit)* **her** students back in motion to practice another number.
8. I *(sit/set)* the Teriyaki chicken on the table and when I got back, it was gone.
9. My parents *(sit/set)* their alarm for 5 a.m.
10. Have you *(set/sit)* any goals for the new year?

Answers: *1. sit 2. sit 3. set 4. sit 5. sit 6. sit 7. set 8. set 9. set 10. set*

Shall vs. Will

In America, will has replaced shall in all but a few cases

The Legal Shall

Shall in a legal sense often indicates explicit obligation. Lawyers distinguish between "may" and "shall". the word 'may' means you have the option, however, the word "shall" means 'must'--no option ("the lessee shall repair all damage caused by day-to-day wear and tear" means the lessee has this obligation.   However, if it said, "the lessee may..." it would mean they can but they don't have to make the repairs.

The Lofty Shall
You will encounter shall in the Bible, and you've probably heard it in famous songs or speeches. "We shall overcome" and the end of the Gettysburg Address: "...that we here highly resolve that these dead shall not have died in vain -- that this nation, under God, shall have a new birth of freedom -- and that government of the people, by the people, for the people, shall not perish from the earth" (4).

The Polite Shall
Shall does have a couple of other legitimate uses in American English. You might hear it in a first-person question in which the speaker is being polite or offering an invitation: "Shall I take your coat, ma'am?" or using playful formality, as in "Shall we dance?"

Questions
1. He *(will/shall)* probably be discharged on Wednesday.
2. Every bill which *(will/shall)* have passed the House of Representatives and the Senate, *(will/shall)* , before it become a law, be presented to the President of the United.
3. Exporting Countries *(will/shall)* keep output levels unchanged.
4. Notice of attendance *(will/shall)* contain name and personal or corporate identification number.
5. The actual enumeration *(will/shall)* be made within three years after the first meeting of the Congress of the United States.
6. The trial court *(will/shall)* conduct a hearing to determine whether appellant desires to prosecute this appeal.
7. This press release *(will/shall)* not constitute an offer to sell or the solicitation of an offer to buy.
8. Season 2 *(will/shall)* be much bigger and much longer.

Answers: *1. will 2. shall, shall 3. will 4. shall 5. shall 6. shall 7. shall 8. will*

More information about Shall and Will if you really want to know
In British English, *shall* and *will* are often used interchangeably with no difference of meaning in most circumstances. Internationally, *will* is now the standard choice for expressing future plans and expectations. However, in first-person questions *shall* is often used to express politeness, and in legal statements, *shall* is used with a third-person subject for stating requirements.

According to R.L. Trask (see below), traditional rules regarding *shall* and *will* are "little more than a fantastic invention." The editors of Merriam-Webster's Dictionary of English Usage conclude that such rules "do not appear to have described real usage of these words very precisely at any time, although there is no question that they do describe the usage of some people some of the time and that they are more applicable in England than elsewhere." Bryan A. Garner observes that "there's simply no reason to hold on to shall. The word is peripheral in American English" (Garner's Modern American Usage).

- "Change will not come if we wait for some other person or some other time." (Barack Obama)
- "The British Constitution has always been puzzling and always will be." (Queen Elizabeth II)
- I will call you later.
- "Here is my principle: Taxes shall be levied according to ability to pay. That is the only American principle." (Franklin D. Roosevelt) (It also happens to be a plank in the *Communist Manifesto* and expressed by *Karl Marx*: To each according to his needs, from each according to his ability)
- "Down the stairs? Well, don't stop when you get to the basement. Keep straight on. Give my regards to the earth's core! And if you give us any more trouble, I shall visit you in the small hours and put a bat up your nightdress." (Basil Fawlty in Fawlty Towers)
- Shall we dance?

Usage Notes:
"There is a traditional textbook ruling that runs as follows. For simple futurity, you use shall after I or we but will after everything else, while, to express determination or command, you use will after I or we but shall after everything else. By these rules, the required forms are We shall finish tonight **(simple statement)** versus We will finish tonight**(expressing determination)**, but They will finish tonight **(simple statement)** versus They shall finish tonight **(an order)**.

"As grammarians never tire of pointing out, these bizarre rules do not accurately describe the real usage of careful speakers at any time or in any place in the history of English, and they are little more than a fantastic invention. If you are one of the handful of speakers for whom these rules now seem completely natural, then by all means go ahead and follow them. But, if you are not, just forget about them, and use your natural forms.

"However, in Britain, the very formal written English used in drafting laws and regulations requires the use of shall with a third-person subject for stating requirements. Example: An average of 40 percent shall be deemed a pass at Honors level. Britons engaged in doing such writing must fall into line here.

"Do not try to use shall if the word does not feel entirely natural, and especially don't try to use it merely in the hope of sounding more elegant. Doing so will probably produce something that is acceptable to no one."
(R.L. Trask, Say What You Mean! A Troubleshooter's Guide to English Style & Usage, David R. Godine, 2005)

"[T]he distinction between intention and futurity can be hazy, and grammarians of C17 and C18 devised an odd compromise whereby both shall and will could express one or the other, depending on the grammatical person involved. . . . Research by Fries (1925) into the language of English drama from C17 on showed that this division of labor was artificial even in its own time. These paradigms were however enshrined in textbooks of later centuries and still taught a few decades ago. Their neglect is one of the better consequences of abandoning the teaching of grammar in schools." (Pam Peters, The Cambridge Guide to English Usage, Cambridge University Press, 2004)

"British people use I shall/I will and we shall/we will with no difference of meaning in most situations. However, shall is becoming very much less common than will. Shall is not normally used in American English. . . .

"Shall and will are not only used for giving information about the future. They are also common in offers, promises, orders and similar kinds of 'interpersonal' language use. In these cases, will (or 'll) generally expresses willingness, wishes or strong intentions (this is connected with an older use of will to mean 'wish' or 'want'). Shall expresses obligation (like a more direct form of should)." (Michael Swan, Practical English Usage, Oxford University Press, 1995)

"In colloquial and indeed all spoken English . . . will is fast displacing shall in all cases in which shall was formerly used and in which we are recommended to use it. . . . It survives chiefly in first person questions, where it usefully distinguishes 'Shall I open the window?' (as an offer or proposal) from 'Will I need a towel?' (= will it be necessary). It is useful that the construction 'll stands for both shall and will." (Eric Partridge, Usage and Abusage, edited by Janet Whitcut, W.W. Norton, 1995)

"Use shall to express determination: We shall overcome. You and he shall stay. "Either shall or will may be used in first-person constructions that do not emphasize determination: We shall hold a meeting. We will hold a meeting. "For second- and third-person constructions, use will unless determination is stressed: You will like it. She will not be pleased." (The Associated Press 2009 Stylebook and Briefing on Media Law, Basic Books, 2009)

Shear vs. Sheer

Shear (v.) means to cut or clip. As a noun, shear refers to the act, process, or fact of cutting or clipping.
Sheer (adj.) means fine, transparent, or complete. As an adverb, sheer means completely or altogether.
  • Few people these days know the proper way to *shear* a sheep.
  • "English usage is sometimes more than mere taste, judgment and education--sometimes it's *sheer* luck, like getting across the street." (E.B. White)

Questions
1. "From the first day to this, *(shear/sheer)* greed has been the driving spirit of civilization." (Friedrich Engels)
2. Giving children vitamin D supplements may *(shear/sheer)* their risk of developing diabetes later in life.
3. Across the nation, people this week will begin watching the NCAA Tournament for its dramatic moments, Cinderella stories and *(shear/sheer)* excitement.
4. The *(shear/sheer)* volume of different PC models can be confusing.
5. Durandet acknowledges that adhesives provide excellent *(shear/sheer)* strength but believes self-piercing rivets are required for making adhesive joints stronger.
6. The win in the final girls basketball game came from *(shear/sheer)* determination, not from any playbook.
7. It's that moment of *(shear/sheer)* panic, when you dig deep into your purse and can't find your smartphone.
8. The hiker was discovered Saturday at the base of a *(shear/sheer)* cliff.
9. When you *(shear/sheer)* the bushes heavily in the spring, it makes them branch out and become more dense.

10. Foundations most commonly come in matte or *(shear/sheer)*. *(Shear/Sheer)* foundations are light and have translucent pigments, so they don't cover the skin color but even out any differences in it.
11. You can *(shear/sheer)* a sheep many times, but you can only lead them to slaughter once.
12. I praised Fumihiko Maki for daring to insert a *(shear/sheer)* glass building amid the red brick of the University of Pennsylvania campus
13. Ului is expected to turn west in two days, and steer toward the east coast of Australia, while gradually weakening from increased wind *(shear/sheer)* .

Answers: *1. sheer 2. shear 3. sheer 4. sheer 5. shear 6. sheer 7. sheer 8. sheer 9. shear 10. sheer, Sheer 11. shear 12. sheer 13. shear*

Simple vs. Simplistic

Simple (adj.) means plain, ordinary, uncomplicated.
Simplistic (adj.) is a pejorative word meaning overly simplified--characterized by extreme and often misleading simplicity.
  • "Everything should be made as **simple** as possible, but not **simpler**." (Albert Einstein)
  • "Pupils are being set **simplistic** science exam questions when they have been taught to a much higher level, scientists claimed today." (The Guardian, June 30, 2008)

Usage Note:

Simple is an uncomplicated word which means 'straightforward, easy,' as in a *simple* solution. Compare a *simplistic* solution, which is too easy, i.e. it oversimplifies and fails to deal with the complexities of the situation. So *simplistic* is negatively charged, whereas *simple* is neutral or has positive connotations. Because *simplistic* is the longer and more academic-looking word, it's sometimes misguidedly chosen by those who want to make their words more impressive. The results can be disastrous, as in:
  • This software represents the state-of-the art in information-retrieval systems, and comes with *simplistic* instructions on how to operate it. Heaven help the operator! (The Cambridge Guide to English Usage, Cambridge University Press, 2004)

Questions
1. Senator Stevens was lampooned for his *(simple/simplistic)* description of the internet as a series of "tubes."
2. "The truth is rarely pure and never *(simple/simplistic)* ." (Oscar Wilde)
3. It is too *(simple/simplistic)* to explain the wave of concern about the euro in terms of Greece's problems.
4. Every time I travel through Brooklyn I realize how many *(simple/simplistic)* things I love about it.
5. Now that is a *(simple/simplistic)* and ill-informed opinion. I'm 60 years old and I never learned that in school.
6. The check sheet is another *(simple/simplistic)* and effective tool useful in Lean Six Sigma projects.
7. They both use *(simple/simplistic)* slogans which obscure important truths about the political process.

8. Before recording her latest CD, she knew she wanted a *(simple/simplistic)* and clean sound.
9. Climate change rhetoric is chalked full of **simplistic** fear mongering and moralizing.
10. Their solution was *(simple/simplistic)* and elegant.
11. The traditional Irish kitchen didn't boast a wide choice of ingredients, rather it was stocked with *(simple/simplistic)* , mostly inexpensive fare: bacon, potatoes, and fish.
12. I don't think 'Avatar' lost because it was too radical, I think it lost because its story is so derivative and overly *(simple/simplistic)* .

Answers: *1. simplistic 2. simple 3. simplistic 4. simple 5. simplistic 6. simple 7. simplistic 8. simple 9. simplistic 10. simple 11. simple 12. simplistic*

So as to

Often the word "to" alone will do the trick.
  • *Mail your package early so as to ensure its timely arrival.* **BECOMES**: *Mail your package early to ensure its timely arrival.* **OR** *Mail your package early so it arrives on time.*
Bottom Line: Eliminate the wordy expression "So as to"

Sometime vs. Some time vs. Sometimes

Sometime (adv.) means "at an indefinite or unstated time in the future." at some indefinite or indeterminate point of time: *He will arrive **sometime** next week.* 2. at an indefinite future time: *Come to see me **sometime**.* 3. A**r**chaic sometimes; on some occasions. 4. Archaic. at one time; formerly. –*adjective* 5. having been formerly; former: *The diplomat was a **sometime** professor of history at Oxford.* 6. being so only at times or to some extent: *Traveling so much, he could never be more than a **sometime** husband.* 7. that cannot be depended upon regarding affections or loyalties: *He was well rid of his **sometime** girlfriend.*

Some time means "a period of time." The two-word form SOME TIME means "an unspecified interval or period of time": *It will take **some time** for the wounds to heal.*
Sometimes (adv.) means "occasionally, now and then." on some occasions; at times; now and then.
  • *"Why don't you come up **sometime** and see me?"* (Mae West in She Done Him Wrong, 1933)
  • *"You must give **some time** to your fellow men. Even if it's a little thing, do something for others--something for which you get no pay but the privilege of doing it."* (Albert Schweitzer)
  • *"I am so clever that **sometimes** I don't understand a single word of what I am saying."* (Oscar Wilde)

Questions
1. "*(Sometimes/Sometime/Some times)* a scream is better than a thesis." (Ralph Waldo Emerson)
2. "I've been trying for *(sometime/sometimes/some time)* to develop a lifestyle that doesn't require my presence." (Garry Trudeau)
3. "If you want an interesting party *(sometime/sometimes/some time)*, combine cocktails and a fresh box of crayons for everyone." (Robert Fulghum)
4. We all guessed that Tiger Woods would be away from golf for *(sometime/sometimes/some time)*.
5. *(Sometime/Sometimes/Some time)* soon, Google will announce that it's shutting down its China operations.
6. *(Sometime/Sometimes/Some time)* silence really is golden.
7. It'll take *(sometime/sometimes/some time)* to pore through the 3,000 page bill.
8. The space shuttle Discovery's next launch is scheduled for *(sometime/sometimes/some time)* in April.
9. I think we're on track for a vote *(sometime/sometimes/some time)* this weekend.
10. The Big 12's coaches spent an entire season, even *(sometime/sometimes/some time)* before it, telling anyone who'd listen this was the conference's strongest year ever.
11. Quote from former Memphis Tigers guard Derrick Rose when asked if he enjoys playing in the NBA, " "You just don't know, man," he said with a smile. "*(sometime/sometimes/some time)* it's so hard on the next level where you just want to be a kid *(sometime/sometimes/some time)* . I'm only 21. It's hard, man. "*(sometime/sometimes/some time)* I wish I want to be back here *(sometime/sometimes/some time)* .
12. It disturbed me that such an important issue had been on hold for *(sometime/sometimes/some time)* now.
13. The bold robbery took place *(sometime/sometimes/some time)* early Sunday morning.
14. *(Sometime/Sometimes/Some time)* this spring a small jet that looks like a torpedo will be attached to the wing of a B-52 bomber and lifted to 50000 feet over Edwards Air Force.
15. *(Sometime/Sometimes/Some time)* you have to break backwards compatibility for the betterment of the product itself.
16. The coach's commanding presence will be the main discussion topic for *(sometime/sometimes/some time)*.
17. Singer and *(sometime/sometimes/some time)* actress Jessica Simpson has paid the price of beauty, and now she's examining people's obsession with looking good.
18. While the Nintendo Wii has had this segment of the market cornered for *(sometime/sometimes/some time)* , Microsoft is developing a camera-only motion control system for the Xbox that will be released *(sometime/sometimes/some time)* next year.
19. When electrical power went out, the poor *(sometime/sometimes/some time)* survive better than others.
20. *(Sometime/Sometimes/Some time)* live throws you a lemon and you've got to make lemonade out of it.

Answers: *1. Sometimes 2. some time 3. sometime 4. some time 5. Sometime 6. Sometimes 7. some time 8. sometime 9. sometime 10. some time 11. Sometimes, sometimes, Sometimes, sometimes 12. some time 13. sometime 14. Sometime 15. Sometimes 16. some time 17. sometimes 18. some time, sometime 19. sometimes 20. Sometimes*

Stationary vs. Stationery

Stationary (adj.) means not moving, still. (n.) refers to an individual who is unmoving or stays in one place.
Stationery (n.) refers to the paper on which one writes or to other related items.

Tip The adjective stationary means "remaining in one place." The noun stationery means "writing materials."

Associate the er in stationery with the er in letter and paper.
- "The law is *stationary*. The law is fixed. The law is a chariot wheel which binds us all regardless of conditions or place or time." (Emma Goldman)
- In his suitcase I found a hodgepodge of hotel *stationery*, postcards, and transit maps.

Questions

1. Swoozie's Inc, a maker of luxury gifts and *(stationery/stationary)* filed for bankruptcy just weeks ago.
2. The hurricane remains near *(stationery/stationary)* for the past hours about 360 miles southwest of Houston.
3. Other activities included things such as ballroom dancing, *(stationery/stationary)* cycling and swimming.
4. Just 10 years ago a person could purchase nice *(stationery/stationary)* . I can't even find a store that stocks *(stationery/stationary)* today.
5. A Los Angeles design studio was chosen to create the *(stationery/stationary)* for the wedding.
6. A bus carrying a baseball team rammed into a *(stationery/stationary)* vehicle on a bridge.
7. NASA said it was resigned to leaving the rover in place and making adjustments to help it survive as a remote but *(stationery/stationary)* science robot.
8. Two-thirds of the *(stationery/stationary)* source emissions emmit more than 100000 tons per year.
9. Aid agencies provide school kits containing teaching materials, *(stationery/stationary)*, and games.
10. The Post-it Note has become standard *(stationery/stationary)* in offices and homes around the world.

Answers: *1. stationery 2. stationary 3. stationary 4. stationery, stationary 5. stationery 6. stationary 7. stationary 8. stationary 9. stationery 10. stationery*

Statue vs. Stature vs. Statute

Statue (n.) [**stach**-oo] refers to a model of a person or animal carved in stone or modeled in clay or plaster.
Stature (n.) [**stach**-er] refers to the standing height of a body, literally or figuratively.
Statute (n.) [**stach**-oot] refers to a law or rule.
- A *statue* is a carved or molded figure.   • Our *minister is of great stature in the community*.   • A *statute* is a rule or law.

Questions

1. The Jefferson Memorial exhibit in Washington, D.C. presents a giant *(statue/stature/statute)* of the second U.S. President and on panel three it quotes Jefferson: "God who gave us life gave us liberty. Can the liberties of a nation be secure when we have removed a conviction that these liberties are the gift of God?
2. Accordingly, the absence of a writing violates the *(statue/stature/statute)* of frauds, rendering the alleged oral promise as to stock redemption unenforceable.
3. Duffey sees a rise in *(statue/stature/statute)* as a result of the new legislation.
4. "Every block of stone has a *(statue/stature/statute)* inside it, and it is the task of the sculptor to discover it." (Michelangelo)
5. A judge may sentence under a newly enacted *(statue/stature/statute)* if it results in a reduction in punishment.
6. "No *(statue/stature/statute)* has ever been put up to a critic." (Jean Sibelius)
7. Lawyers challenge the constitutionality Federal *(statues/statures/statutse)* in every court.
8. The New York Jets are once again playing up to their long-assumed *(statue/stature/statute)* as the neglected "little brother" who, in their collective minds, always seems to get the short end of the stick.
9. We saw a terrified-looking Homo floresiensis, nicknamed the "Hobbit" for her tiny *(statue/stature/statute)*.
10. Parish members of a Catholic church in Salt Lake City are overjoyed as a priceless *(statue/stature/statute)* makes its way back home.
11. The base of a *(statue/stature/statute)* memorializing the World War I doughboy has been relocated as restoration efforts continue.
12. A striking nine-and-a-half-foot bronze *(statue/stature/statute)*of Sacagawea will soon be moved.
13. They cannot prosecute because the *(statue/stature/statute)* of limitations expired three years after the assault.
14. They contend on appeal California's DUI *(statue/stature/statute)* is not substantially similar to Virginia law.
15. Pursuant to General *(Statues/Statures/Statutes)* § 52-212 (a), a trial court may set aside a default judgment within four months of the date it was rendered.
16. Sculptor Lawrence Noble, commissioned by Hampton to commemorate its 400th anniversary, is best known for creating *(statues/statures/statutes)* of Yoda, Obi-Wan Kenobi and other Star Wars characters.
17. Women of short or petite *(statue/stature/statute)* have a hard time shopping for clothes at the mall.
18. When construing a *(statue/stature/statute)* , [o]ur fundamental objective is to ascertain and give effect to the apparent intent of the legislature.
19. The eight-time major winner said that Tiger "has not carried the same *(statue/stature/statute)* as the other great players that have come along like Jack [Nicklaus] or Arnold Palmer.
20. The iconic *(statue/stature/statute)* of Christ with outstretched arms that overlooks Rio de Janeiro is getting a $4 million renovation.

Answers: *1. statue 2. statute 3. stature 4. statue 5. statute 6. statue 7. statutes 8. stature 9. stature 10. statue 11. statue 12. statue 13. statute 14. statute 15. Statutes 16. statues 17. stature 18. statute 19. stature 20. statue*

Temerity vs. Timidity

Temerity (n.) [t*uh*-**mer**-i-tee] means daring or recklessness, boldness; rashness.
Timidity (n.) [tim-**id**-i-tee] means the opposite of 'temerity' it means fearful. lacking in self-assurance, courage, or bravery; easily alarmed; timorous; shy.
- "A great deal of talent is lost to the world for want of a little courage. Every day sends to their graves obscure men whose *timidity* prevented them from making a first effort." (Sydney Smith)
- Harry Truman had the *temerity* to tell General MacArthur to shut up.

Questions

1. The students lacked the *(timidity/temerity)* to correct their teacher's mistake.
2. The first symptom of love in a young man is *(timidity/temerity)* ; in a girl, boldness." (Victor Hugo)
3. His *(timidity/temerity)* was displayed when he flinched from the fight for freedom the nation needs.
4. The film looks back at the movers and shakers who had the *(timidity/temerity)* and gall to break all the rules.
5. Justice Alito had the *(timidity/temerity)* to speak out against the President at the State of the Union.
6. The word "chutzpah" long ago moved beyond its Hebrew roots generally to mean pushy acts characterized by a show of blatant nerve, unwarranted gall, even *(timidity/temerity)* .
7. Symptoms of mercury poisoning include excessive *(timidity/temerity)* , diffidence, increasing shyness, loss of self-confidence, anxiety, and a desire to remain unobserved and unobtrusive.
8. Where does the City Council get the *(timidity/temerity)* to spend $6.2 million of Santa Clarita residents' money buying up a 2-acre block in Newhall last November?
9. It might have been the lack of confidence going into the tournament that caused their *(timidity/temerity)* .
10. Kohl's independent wealth scares off would-be challengers and his *(timidity/temerity)* and unwillingness stick his neck out in Washington haven't helped his reputation.
11. The *(timidity/temerity)* of some politicians exposes their cowardice and lack of a moral compass.
12. In 1776 the Americans had the raw *(timidity/temerity)* to declare to the world they were FREE and separate from England.

Answers: *1. temerity 2. timidity 3. timidity 4. temerity 5. temerity 6. temerity 7. timidity 8. temerity 9. timidity 10. timidity 11. timidity 12. temerity*

Then vs. Than

Than is used to indicate difference (conj.)
Then means next or consequently (adv.)
Use than to make a comparison. Use then when referring to time.
        • The quiz was harder *than* I had expected.   • I answered two questions and *then* got stuck.

Usage Notes:

"Look here, Jimmy. You misspelled culpable. And you're confusing then and than. T-h-e-n is an adverb used to divide and measure time. 'Detective McNulty makes a mess, and then he has to clean it up.' Not to be confused with t-h-a-n, which is most commonly used after a comparative adjective or adverb, as in: 'Rhonda is smarter than Jimmy.'" (Judge Daniel Phelan to Detective Jimmy McNulty in the episode "The Wire," The Wire, 2002)

"then for than is an error much commoner than highbrows seem to think: it is not merely the illiterate who fall into it. The reason is not that, several centuries ago, than and then were spellings and pronunciations frequently interchanged, but that, where than bears no stress and is spoken very rapidly and lightly, it tends to approximate to then." (Eric Patridge, The Wordsworth Book of Usage and Abusage, rev. 1995)

In some parts of the United States, we are told, then and than not only look alike, they sound alike. Like a teacher with twins in her classroom, you need to be able to distinguish between these two words; otherwise, they'll become mischievous. They are often used and they should be used for the right purposes.

Than is used to make comparisons. In the sentence "Piggy would rather be rescued than stay on the island," a comparison is being made between Piggy's two choices. In the sentence, "Other than Pincher Martin, Golding did not write another popular novel," the adverbial construction "other than" helps us make an implied comparison; (Burchfield).

Generally, the only question about than arises when we have to decide whether the word is being used as a conjunction or as a preposition. If it's a preposition (and Merriam-Webster's dictionary provides for this usage), then the word that follows it should be in the object form.   • He's taller and somewhat more handsome than me.   • Just because you look like him doesn't mean you can play better than him.

Most careful writers, will insist that than be used as a conjunction; it's as if part of the clause introduced by than has been left out: • He's taller and somewhat more handsome than I [am handsome].   • You can play better than he [can play].

In formal, academic text, you should probably use than as a conjunction and follow it with the subject form of a pronoun (where a pronoun is appropriate). Then is a conjunction. We can use the FANBOYS conjunctions to connect two independent clauses; usually, they will be accompanied (preceded) by a comma. Too many students think that then works the same way:
        • "Caesar invaded Gaul, then he turned his attention to England."

You can tell the difference between then and a coordinating conjunction by trying to move the word around in the sentence. We can write "he then turned his attention to England"; "he turned his attention, then, to England"; he turned his attention to England then." The word can move around within the clause.

Try that with a conjunction, and you will quickly see that the conjunction cannot move around. "Caesar invaded Gaul, and then he turned his attention to England." The word 'and' is stuck exactly there and cannot move like then, which is more like an adverbial conjunction (or conjunctive adverb — see below) than a coordinating conjunction. Our original sentence in this paragraph — "Caesar invaded Gaul, then he turned his attention to England" — is a comma splice, a faulty sentence construction in which a comma tries to hold together two independent clauses all by itself: the comma needs a coordinating conjunction to help out, and the word then simply doesn't work that way.

Questions

1. I took a couple years off, but *(than/then)* I got the itch again and decided to return to painting.

2. First their together, *(than/then)* they're friends, *(than/then)* they're making out in the kitchen at the golden globes, *(than/then)* they're friends again in Cabo.
3. US crude inventories were up by 1 million barrels, less *(than/then)* some analysts expected.
4. A lot of the most famous coaches hate one-and-done players -- guys who star as freshmen, *(than/then)* bolt.
5. India, the world's biggest potash importer, will offer a higher price *(than/then)* China.
6. Baseball's Irish connections run deeper *(than/then)* green hats and jerseys.
7. Since *(than/then)* , all eyes have been fixed on the Senate.
8. If it does increase debt balances and operating results do not rebound, *(than/then)* ratios could remain high.
9. More Americans are unhappy with the job the President is doing *(than/then)* are happy with it.
10. Wholesale prices in the US fell in February more *(than/then)* anticipated.

Answers: *1. then   2. then   3. then, then, than   4. then   5. than   6. than   7. then   8. then   9. than   10. than*

The reason is because

This structure is redundant. Equally common and doubly redundant is the structure *the reason why is because.* Erase both of them from your vocabulary and never use them in written English.
  • **Wrong**: The *reason why* I could not attend the party *is because* I had to work.
  • **Correct**: I could not attend the party *because* I had to work.

There, their, they're (heavily tested area)

They're: is the contracted form of **They are**. This form is used in sentences using "they" as the subject of the sentence with the verb "to be"
  • **They're** *interested in buying a company that has positive cash flow.*
  • *If they want the club owners to support this initiative* **they're** *in for a surprise.*
There: is used as an introductory subject is sentences with "There is" and "There are". It is also used as an adverb of place meaning "in that place".
  • **There** *are several items in the contract that remain unresolved.*   • *That office over* **there** *is where we negotiated the contract.*
Their: is the possessive pronoun form. This form is used to express that "they" have a specific quality, or that something belongs to "them".
  • *The people of Los Angeles think of the Lakers as their team.*
  • *Their homes were in danger from the wildfires and then the mud slides.*
Note: *don't use the contraction "there are" "there're" so don't confuse it with "they're", it's not that same.*

More Information:
Their: is the third person plural dependent possessive pronoun, and fits into this group of possessive pronouns:

First Person Singular: **my**	Third Person Singular: **his, her, its**
First Person Plural: **our**	Third Person Plural: **their**
Second Person Singular and Plural: **your**	

Dependent means that it is a modifier and cannot stand alone. One can say: *Let's meet after school and I'll have my notes your friends can bring their notes.* **But we can't say**: *I'll have my notes and they will* **their.**

For that construction, the independent third person plural possessive pronoun *theirs* is needed.
It can also be viewed in the context of the other third personal plural pronouns:

Personal Subjective: **they**	Possessive Independent: **theirs**
Personal Objective: **them**	Reflexive: **themselves**
Possessive Dependent: **their**	

There: is half of the set of adverbs *here* and *there. Here* refers to the place in which one is, while *there*, in contrast, refers to another, previously established and more distant place.
  • *I understand you like that red car over there in the second row, however, it's too expensive.*
They're: is a contraction of the personal third personal plural subjective pronoun *they* and the plural present indicative verb *are*. The apostrophe replaces the letter *a*. All of the personal subjective pronouns are customarily contracted with the appropriate verb form, like this:

First Person Singular + am: **I'm**	
First Person Plural + are: **we're**	Third Person Singular + is: **he's, she's, it's**
Second Person Singular and Plural + are: **you're**	Third Person Plural + are: **they're**

You can see from this chart that *you're* and *they're* create similar issues: in each case, the word resulting from the contraction looks similar to and sounds exactly the same as the possessive dependent form *'your'* in the first case and *'their'* in the second.
  • *All my friends met last night to plan* **their** *spring vacation.* **They're** *planning a trip to Southern California!*

Questions

1. *(They're/their/there)* is no time to waste!
2. I went to *(they're/their/there)* school for over a year before deciding to return.
3. I think *(they're/their/there)* in Washington DC for a conference.
4. When was the last time we used *(they're/their/there)* office for a meeting?
5. *(they're/their/there)* seems to be people who want to force us to be good.
6. Unless we gain control over the exploding national debt the people will lose *(they're/their/there)* freedom!
7. Over here, over *(they're/their/there)*, we have hit the dusty trail.

8. All men are endowed by *(they're/their/there)* creator with certain unalienable rights!
9. *(They're/their/there)* aware of *(they're/their/there)* rights and are willing to fight over *(they're/their/there)*.
10. Unless the people protect *(they're/their/there)* freedoms, they will lose them.

Answers: *1. there, 2. their, 3. they're, 4. there, 5. There 6. their, 7. there, 8. their, 9. They're, their, there 10. their*

Threw vs. Through

Threw (v.) the past tense of throw which means to toss or to fling
Through (adv.) means from one point to its end; or (prep.) meaning because of
• He **threw** nine curveballs, five of them for strikes. • He's obviously going **through** an extremely tough situation.

Questions
1. The fact that Democrats are going to try and push legislation on Health Care Reform *(threw/through)* the House without a direct vote is appalling to me. "Sen. Mitch McConnell, Ky"
2. Pitching for the first time since he clinched the Yankees' 27th world title, Mariano Rivera *(threw/through)* 27 pitches in a scoreless inning.
3. The weather service advises that river flooding will continue *(threw/through)* late in the week.
4. Surfside voters *(threw/through)* out the incumbents Tuesday in races for mayor and the Town Commission.
5. They were thrust into stardom together and were the only people who knew what the other was going *(threw/through)*.
6. I almost *(threw/through)* up when I read the report.
7. Microsoft's Valhalla redesign of the Xbox 360 was seen for the first time *(threw/through)* a new security leak.
8. A believer in the Jedi religion won an apology from a job center that *(threw/through)* him out for refusing to remove his hood.
9. The coach *(threw/through)* the player off of the team after the player questioned the coach's ability.
10. Thieves cut down trees before driving *(threw/through)* a security fence to steal $50,000 worth of metal.

Answers: *1. through 2. threw 3. through 4. threw 5. through 6. threw 7. through 8. threw 9. threw 10. through*

To, too, two

"**To** generally shows direction. **Too** means 'also.' **Two** is the number.
• I, *too*, want *to* go *to* the concert in *two* hours.

"**To**" is one of the more widely used words in the English language. In its most common contexts, it is used as part of infinitive verb phrases, such as: • *to* run • *to* help, **and as a preposition with widespread connotations, such as** • Get ready, it's time to go *to* the game • Give it *to* me • The USA Olympic team has 20 gold medals *to* 10 for the next highest country •*To* those who study economic history, today's debt is a warning sign.

"**Too**," can mean "in addition, like this: • I want to go, *too*! • The two students went to the library too. **or can refer to excess or degree, as in:** • I'm *too* hungry to care what we have for dinner! •I drank *too* much soda and now I can't sleep. • My parents weren't *too* pleased with me last night.

"**Two**" is simply the number 2, exclusively. **Note: in formal writing, numbers between 0-10 should be written out, as in** • I have *two* hotdogs, • but I have *zero* hotdog buns, • I was *three* years old and my brother was *five* when we went to Disneyland. **while larger numbers are typically written in numerical format, as in** • I have eaten over *9,347* hotdogs in my lifetime. • Last week at our party we served more than *250* hotdogs.

Summary: When in doubt, use "*to*," but remember that if you're meaning to say "in addition" or "*to* an excessive degree," use "*too*." If you're referring to a numerical amount, use "*two*."

More details about "to, too, and two"
Too: is an adverb, and two different meanings give it two different distinct placements. **Too meaning excessively, to an excessive degree.** In these cases, the *adverb too* precedes an adjective.
• You worry *too* much.   Isn't it just *too* obvious?
***Too* meaning also, in addition**
• If you get to go to the concert then I want to go *too*.
• When you go online to buy your ticket don't forget to buy one for me *too*.
To: The confusion about *to* and *too* comes from two obvious facts: the words look very much alike, the only difference being that *too* has one more **o** than *to*, and they sound exactly alike.

***To* is a particle.** The infinitive in English consists of two parts: the particle *to* and the verb.
to eat   *to chew*   *to scarf to gorge to ingest*   *to feast*   *to swallow*

If you see *to* before a verb, as above, it's acting as part of the infinitive verb. "*Too*" *is* never used that way.
• I sat down at the Thanksgiving meal ready *to gorge* on the food. But as I prepared *to eat* and I started *to chew* I realized it was impossible *to swallow*.
'*To*' used as a particle and '*too*' used to modify a following adjective can look deceptively similar:
• I'm going *to* run an errand. If I get back *too* late you can start dinner without me.

You may have to actually stop and think:
• *to* before a verb or a prepositional phrase • *too* before an adjective to keep them separate in your mind.
***To* is a preposition.** Definitions of preposition are not very clear, which might be one reason why it's hard to distinguish *to* and *too*. The definitions of prepositions say things like "connects a substantive with a verb, adjective or other substantive."

Usually people just learn a group of standard prepositions, like

above	about	after	around	at	before
behind	beside	beyond	for	from	in
near	of	off	on	over	past
through	under	until	upon	with	without

and remember that they introduce prepositional phrases. Prepositional phrases can be either adjectival or adverbial phrase. (they can either modify nouns or verbs)

- the student *with the iPod* ('with the iPod' is the adjective phrase tells *which* student--the noun)
- the student was putting his iPod *into his old torn up back pack.* ("into his old torn up back pack" tells *where* the putting was taking place).

It's fairly easy to identify '*to*' as a preposition in sentences that have prepositional phrases.

- Ashley drove *to* the restaurant while we waited.
- The contestant was nervous to sing *to* the audience. ('to the audience' is the prepositional phrase)

***To* is an anaphora.** it's an important use of *to* and one that's often confused with *too*, because it can come at the end of a sentence. An anaphora is simply a word that stands for or replaces another word or group of words.

There is one type of anaphor that you've probably heard of: pronoun. A pronoun stands in for a noun or noun phrase. **Here's how it works:**

First look at a phrase beginning with an infinitive:

- *to go out every weekend to the mall* (this is an infinitive verb phrase)

Then, there's a reference back to the phrase in which '*to*' stands for or replaces the entire phrase (so we don't have to be repeat the entire phrase). In these cases, '*to*' usually ends the sentence.

- Melissa wants to go out every weekend to the mall, but I don't want *to*.

THIS IS NOT A DANGLING PREPOSITION! It can't be, because it's not a prepositional use of '*to*'! But, because the *to* comes at the end of the sentence, where we are used to seeing *too* meaning "in addition," we may unthinkingly substitute '*too*' for '*to*'. In our example, ending the sentence with '*to*' is a short hand way of saying 'to go to the mall'. The 'to' refers back to the phrase 'to go out every weekend to the mall' so this sentence is actually ending this way, " Melissa wants to go out every weekend to the mall, but I don't want *to go out every weekend to the mall.*' But this is very long and cumbersome, so we can substitute '*but I don't want to*".

Questions:
1. I have wanted **(to/too/two)** visit New York for years.
2. But **(to/too/two)** travel **(to/too/two)** New York could take many days if I drive.
3. That's why I want **(to/too/two)** fly because **(to/too/two)** drive would take **(to/too/two)** long.
4. If I have **(to/too/two)** choose between Southwest Airlines and American Airlines, I would have **(to/too/two)** choose Delta Airlines.
5. The first flight is a Red Eye and leaves at **(to/too/two)** a.m.
6. If I think about it **(to/too/two)** much I might become **(to/too/two)** nervous **(to/too/two)** go.
7. Next month I'm going **(to/too/two)** clear my schedule and I'm going **(to/too/two)** make my reservations.
8. Would you like **(to/too/two)** go **(to/too/two)**?

Answers: 1. *to,* 2. *to, to,* 3. *to, to, too,* 4. *to, to,* 5. *two,* 6. *too, too, to,* 7. *to, to,* 8. *to, too*

More Questions:
1. I gave my textbook **(to/too/two)** Bryce.
2. I hope you can come **(to/too/two)** the game, **(to/too/two)**
3. We bought **(to/too/two)** tickets **(to/too/two)** the game
4. **(to/too/two)** many politicians believe there is no alternative to war.
5. My **(to/too/two)** sisters share a room.
6. His desire **(to/too/two) get good grades is (to/too/two)** strong.
7. I planned **(to/too/two)** study all weekend **(to/too/two)** be prepared for the exam on Monday.
8. How much is **(to/too/two)** much?
9. I'd love **(to/too/two)** see your YouTube video!
10. Can a person be **(to/too/two)** wealthy?
11. It's such a beautiful day and it's not **(to/too/two)** far, so I'm going to walk to the bus stop today

Answers: *1. to, 2. to, too, 3. two, to, 4. Too, 5. two 6. to, too, 7. to, to, 8. too, 9. to, 10. too, 11. too*

Until vs. as long as

Until is both a preposition and a conjunction. *Until* is used to express a point of time in the future--**Until (preposition) -**
1. *Up to the time of: We walked on the beach **until** we got cold.*
2. *Before (a specified time): We can't go to Disneyland **until** next month.*

Until (conjunction) -
1. *Up to the time that: We ate **until** our stomachs hurt.*
2. *Before: You cannot go out **until** your room is clean.*
3. *To the point or extent that: I worked out **until** I could barely move anymore.*

As long as means that one thing will occur while another thing is still true...**As long as (conjunction) -**
1. *During the time that: We'll keep researching **as long as** your sister is gone.*
2. *Since: **As long as** we've been studying every week our grades have gone up.*

3. *On the condition that: We'll keep studying* **as long as** *you have sodas.*

Idioms
1. **For the period of time**: 'You may eat at the Buffet **as long as** you want'
2. as long as, since, **because**: "*As long as* you're up, would you get me a sandwich."
3. long as; just so, **provided that**: "*So long as* you're home on time, you can go out tonight." or "*As long as* you can keep a secret, I'll tell you." or "*So long as* you meet your quota, you'll get the bonus." or "You may have all the spicy chicken wings, *as long as* you wash your hands first."
1. In order to express a future idea. after as long as, we use a present tense. "*As long as* I live, I will never forget."
2. Before a number, *as long as* can be used to suggest great length. "The lecture can last *as long as* a three hours."

Questions
1. They need to give themselves 72 hours from the release of the bill *(as long as/until)* the vote.
2. I think that people do have a right to smoke *(as long as/until)* it doesn't affect other people.
3. I'm going to continue coaching *(as long as/until)* I feel good enough and have the passion.
4. However, the most anticipated version of the film will not come out *(as long as/until)* next year.
5. He's waiting for the Bill to arrive on his desk and won't vote yes *(as long as/until)* he's seen it.
6. We can beat any team out there *(as long as/until)* we stay focused.
7. *(as long as/until)* guys get held accountable for their head shots and for deliberate attempts to injure, there's not going to be respect in this league.
8. Six days a week, he swims, runs or bikes for *(as long as/until)* two hours in the morning.
9. But *(as long as/until)* Manning is the quarterback, this is a playoff team.
10. Despite his gruff upbringing, Tyson was allegedly not violent *(as long as/until)* a bully messed with one of his beloved pigeons.

Answers: *1. until 2. as long as 3. as long as 4. until 5. until 6. as long as 7. Until 8. as long as 9. as long as 10. until*

Vain vs. Vane vs. Vein

Vain (adj.) means without much value or significance; excessively proud or concerned about one's own appearance, personal qualities or achievements, conceited or fruitless. The expression "in vain" as in "I argued in vain" means without achieving one's purpose.

Vane (n.) most frequently refers to a device used to determine the direction of wind.

Vein (n.) refers to blood vessels that carry blood from various body parts to the heart. Similarly, veins also are tissues that form the principal framework of a leaf or line-markings in marble or rocks-- a streak, or a crack. Also, vein means a condition or manner (as in "in a serious vein.") As a verb vein means to supply with veins.
   • Fame often makes a writer *vain*.   • The *vane* on top of Faneuil Hall in Boston is in the shape of a grasshopper.
   • "It is in men as in soils, where sometimes there is a *vein* of gold which the owner knows not of." (Jonathan Swift)

Questions
1. Varicose *(vains/vanes/veins)* tend to worsen over time.
2. "How *(vain/vane/veins)* it is to sit down to write when you have not stood up to live." (Henry David Thoreau)
3. Sitting on top of the copper ball was a huge weather *(vain/vane/veins)* .
4. Carly Simon sings, "You're so *(vain/vane/vein).* You probably think this song is about you."
   http://popup.lala.com/popup/360569470942675140
5. This second bulk sample demonstrates a continuance of the mine's rich *(vain/vane/veins)* structure beyond the previous production zones
6. But it's impossible, because Greg is so arrogant, so *(vain/vane/veins)* , so self-centered and selfish.
7. Mr Rudd slammed Mr Abbott's response, claiming he had a weather *(vain/vane/veins)* as a moral compass.
8. The jobs being created are too few, are temporary (with *(vain/vane/veins)* hopes attached to eventual full time conversion), and fall mostly into the public domain.
9. He needed surgery to remove the clot, angioplasty to repair the damaged *(vain/vane/veins)* and then had a rib removed to prevent the pinching of the *(vain/vane/veins)* .
10. The Democrats, on the other hand, will be extremely busy "backing and filling" in a *(vain/vane/veins)* attempt to repair all the damage they will have done to their party.
11. A practice offering *(vain/vane/veins)* treatment and cosmetic plastic surgery in Tampa Bay, Florida is embracing what is being touted as the latest breakthrough laser.
12. Politicians who constantly watch polls become little more than weather-*(vain/vane/veins)* politicians.
13. The sculpture used wind to power a wind *(vain/vane/veins)*, laser and tuning forks inside the building.
14. PUPILS and staff have appealed to the person who bought their school's weather *(vain/vane/veins)* after it was mistakenly put up for sale.
15. The boy falls in love with the rose until the very *(vain/vane/veins)* , very beautiful flower tells a fib one day.
16. The plane has a mechanism with a *(vain/vane/veins)* that pokes out of the fuselage and senses the angle of the airflow and can trigger the plane's stall protection system.
17. His new book discloses details of conversations with US officials who pushed for a war in Iraq that he fought in *(vain/vane/veins)* to prevent.
18. South American Silver Corp. has discovered a potentially significant new high-grade silver-gold-indium *(vain/vane/veins)* system at Malku Khota.

Answers: *1. veins 2. vain 3. vane 4. vain 5. vein 6. vain 7. vane 8. vain 9. vein, vein 10. vain 11. vein 12. vane 13. vane 14. vane 15. vain 16. vane 17. vain 18. vein*

Vary vs. Very

Vary (v.) means to differ, change, or to give variety to something.

Very (adv.) means truly, absolutely, or extremely.
- Prices may *vary* in different markets.   • A friend is *very* different from an acquaintance.

Questions
1. The depth, range and integration of programs and services widely **vary**.
2. Our approach was **very** different from that.
3. Paterson said that he's "**very** disappointed" that he pulled out of the race for governor last month.
4. The insect mortality rate can also **vary** from one part of the horse's body to another.
5. Hong Kong air pollution reached "**very** high" levels today, prompting a government warning.
6. The NCAA basketball tournament predictions are bound to **vary** from one sportscaster to another.
7. Officials still cautioned that despite the slight uptick, homeowners' tax bills will **vary** wildly.
8. Sleep problems and sleep habits **vary** among different ethnic groups, according to a new national survey.
9. If interest rates are below their normal levels it's because the economy is operating at a **very** low level.
10. We all have a responsibility to all of God's children, including the poor and sick, the old and the **very** young.

Answers: *1. vary 2. very 3. very 4. vary 5. very 6. vary 7. vary 8. vary 9. very 10. very*

Veracious vs. Voracious

Veracious (adj.) [vuh-**rey**-shuhs] means honest or truthful. habitually speaking the truth; truthful; honest: *a veracious witness*.
Voracious (adj.) [voh-**rey**-shuhs] means greedy, insatiable, or extremely hungry. craving or consuming large quantities of food: *a voracious appetite*. **2.** exceedingly eager or avid: *voracious readers; a voracious collector*.
- President Kennedy was a *voracious* reader.   • By all accounts, Mr. Soprano's testimony was candid and *veracious*.
Tip A truthful person has "veracity." but "Voracity," means "extreme appetite"

Questions
1. There are, it seems to me, few more responsible callings for a human being armed with a pen than that of being a *(voracious/veracious)* witness to great and grave events.
2. Farmers have been complaining about damage to their crops by *(voracious/veracious)* deer.
3. *Most politicians fail to be (voracious/veracious) if they feel being so would negatively impact their support.*
4. There appears to be only a very small number of *(voracious/veracious)* news consumers who have to have their news from a particular site.
5. He has a reputation for being *(voracious/veracious)* , so people generally take his word for things.
6. A *(voracious/veracious)* moth has prompted an aggressive quarantine across Napa Valley wine country.
7. The drumbeat of gossip is only going to get worse for him -- and better for *(voracious/veracious)* consumers of rumor, innuendo or harmless hot stove banter.
8. This movie must be the most *(voracious/veracious)* portrayal of daily politics ever put on a cinema screen.
9. After a four-month hiatus investors showed a *(voracious/veracious)* appetite for the high yielding bonds.
10. The consumption of beans was prohibited by Pythagoras and Plato to those who desired *(voracious/veracious)* dreams, as they tended to inflate; and for the purpose of truthful dreaming, the animal nature must be made to lie quiet.

Answers: *1. veracious 2. voracious 3. veracious 4. voracious 5. veracious 6. voracious 7. voracious 8. veracious 9. voracious 10. veracious*

Waist vs. Waste

Waist (n.) refers to the middle section of a person's body--below the rib cage and above the hips.
Waste (n.) refers to uncultivated or uninhabited land or to discarded material or barren land. (v.) waste means to devastate or to ruin; to wear away. to use or spend thoughtlessly
- "I may be paralyzed from the *waist* down, but unlike Gray Davis, I'm not paralyzed from the neck up." (Larry Flynt)
- "We cannot *waste* time. We can only *waste* ourselves." (George Matthew Adams)

Questions
1. "Humanity is the rich effluvium, it is the *(waist/waste)* and the manure and the soil, and from it grows the tree of the arts." (Ezra Pound)
2. He told deputies it was possible the man had a gun because he kept reaching toward his *(waist/waste)* .
3. "I believe that all government is evil, and that trying to improve it is largely a *(waist/waste)* of time." (H. L. Mencken)
4. He tied a rope around his *(waist/waste)* and shinnied up the tree.
5. What you're doing is a *(waist/waste)* of time.
6. A new Government report is calling on companies to rethink their attitude to *(waist/waste)* management.
7. Red wine is now not only heart-healthy, it seems to be *(waist/waste)* -healthy as well.
8. Anger and disgust at fraud and government *(waist/waste)* continue to motivate the opposition.
9. Vivien Leigh, the star in the original "Gone with the Wind" film, was famous for her 18-inch *(waist/waste)*.
10. After losing 200 lbs. he had to have the *(waistband/wasteband)* of his pants altered.
11. After the movie I felt so *(waisted/wasted)* maybe it was the 55 gallon bucket of buttered popcorn laced with Milk Duds and the 200 oz. Coke...nah...I probably just need more than twelve hours of sleep.

Answers: *1. waste 2. waist 3. waste 4. waist 5. waste 6. waste 7. waist 8. waste 9. waist 10. waistband 11. wasted*

Weak vs. Week

Weak (adj.) means fragile or not strong.
Week (n.) refers to seven days, Sunday through Saturday.
- Fewer Americans filed first-time claims for jobless benefits last *week*.   • We want a *weak* dollar and we want exports.

Questions

1. Consumer prices likely ticked up slightly last month as the *(week/weak)* economy limits the ability of companies to charge more for goods and services.
2. The Kansas City housing market continued its *(week/weak)* performance in February.
3. The Census Bureau mailed out its forms this *(week/weak)* .
4. The Dodger's managers said they would announce this *(week/weak)* who's going to pitch opening day.
5. The Treasury announced plans to sell $175 billion next *(week/weak)* in short-term and longer-term securities.
6. Tiger Woods will return to the PGA TOUR at the Masters in the second *(week/weak)* of April.
7. Though The Tonight Show won the late night wars in Leno's second *(week/weak)* back, compared to the same *(week/weak)* last year the victory was much narrower.
8. Eastern European states are particularly *(week/weak)* links in a not very strong chain.
9. American Idol helped Fox win an extremely *(week/weak)* Wednesday night permeated with reruns.
10. *(Week/Weak)* interactions are responsible for the decay of massive quarks and leptons into lighter quarks and leptons.

Answers: *1. weak 2. weak 3. week 4. week 5. week 6. week 7. week, week 8. weak 9. weak 10. Weak*

Were vs. We're vs. Where vs. Wear

Were (v.) the past plural of the verb 'to be'.
We're (v.) a contraction of "we are"
Where (adv.) means "at what place"
Wear (v.) to grate or to clothe

TIP the key to these words is focus. If you take your time and focus, you won't miss these because they are not difficult, but it's also very easy to make a dumb mistake simply by going too fast and not focusing.

 • We *were* lost in the middle of Timbuktu.   • Next time we travel, *we're* going to bring along a map.
 • No one knew *where* we were.   • Whenever we travel to Timbuktu, I never know what to *wear*.

Questions

1. *(We're/Were/Where/Ware)* going to New York to see a Broadway play.
2. We don't know *(where/ware/were/we're)* the theater is located.
3. Last year we *(where/ware/were/we're)* planning a trip to Southern California, but I got sick and could not go.
4. When I travel I like to pack light which means I *(where/ware/were/we're)* the same clothes multiple times.
5. *(We're/Were/Where/Ware)* grateful *(where/ware/were/we're)* here and *(where/ware/were/we're)* going to do our best because we *(where/ware/were/we're)* not hear last year.
6. There *(where/ware/were/we're)* about 30 people sitting on pew-like benches, facing the middle, *(where/ware/were/we're)* there was a table.
7. Senate Bill 2535 requires anyone younger than 18 who rides a motorcycle to *(where/ware/were/we're)* a helmet.
8. If we *(where/ware/were/we're)* to come down here and think *(where/ware/were/we're)* going to play hard or come and think *(where/ware/were/we're)* going to lose, I would rather not come at all.
9. I think it's in a perfect place for us to recruit *(where/ware/were/we're)* *(where/ware/were/we're)* located.
10. While we *(where/ware/were/we're)* on vacation I forgot *(where/ware/were/we're)* I parked the car at the airport.
11. In Rhode Island, at a failing high school *(where/ware/were/we're)* all of the teachers *(where/ware/were/we're)* fired, the students got extra vacation.
12. Investigation of runaway Prius vehicle found a particular pattern of *(where/ware/were/we're)* on the car's brakes that raises questions about the driver's version of the event.
13. Now *(where/ware/were/we're)* healthy.
14. As far as she knew, she and her hubby of nearly five years *(where/ware/were/we're)* madly in love.
15. The coach urged students to *(where/ware/were/we're)* red and black to the SDSU Aztecs football game.
16. *(We're/Were/Where/Ware)* excited about *(where/ware/were/we're)* we're going.
17. US blue-chip stocks *(where/ware/were/we're)* poised to extend recent gains to an eighth straight day.
18. You looked like you *(where/ware/were/we're)* at peace with the decision. Is that what you *(where/ware/were/we're)* feeling?
19. Market-research firm Hitwise recently decided to see *(where/ware/were/we're)* all those Twitter users go when they leave Twitter.com.
20. The models *(where/ware/were/we're)* asked to pick off one item of clothing from a mannequin, and they *(where/ware/were/we're)* only allowed to *(where/ware/were/we're)* that one item for the shoot.

Answers: *1. We're 2. where 3. were 4. wear 5. We're, we're, we're, were 6. were, where 7. wear 8. were, we're, we're 9. where, we're 10. were, where 11. where, were 12. wear 13. we're 14. were 15. wear 16. We're, where 17. were 18. were, were 19. where 20. were, were, wear*

Weather vs. whether vs. rather

Weather (v.) [we**th**-er] means to endure or resist exposure to the weather: *a coat of paint that weathers well.* To expose to the action of the elements, as for drying, seasoning, or coloring. (n.) the state of the atmosphere with respect to wind, temperature, cloudiness, moisture, pressure, etc.
Whether (conj.) [we**th**-er] means 'if'. used to introduce the first of two or more alternatives, and sometimes repeated before the second or later alternative, usually with the correlative *or*: *It matters little whether we go or stay. Whether we go or whether we stay, the result is the same.*
Rather (adv.) [**rath**-er]means on the contrary or preferably. **1.** in a measure; to a certain extent; somewhat: *rather good.* **2.** in some degree: *I rather thought you would regret it.* **3.** more properly or justly; with better reason: *The contrary is rather to be*

supposed. **4.** sooner; more readily or willingly: *to die rather than yield.* **5.** more properly or correctly speaking; more truly: *He is a painter or, rather, a watercolorist.* **6.** on the contrary: *It's not generosity, rather self-interest.*
 • Today we had quiet **weather** activity over most of the West.   • **Whether** it's today, **whether** it's next week or next month is hard to say.   • Gold is actually acting **rather** impressively today.

Questions

1. *(Rather/Weather/Whether)* than look for blame, let's work together to create a strategy that works.
2. Thanks to thermal data from a network of telescopes in Chile and Hawaii, Orton can rattle off the kind of stats you might hear in a morning *(weather/whether/rather)* report.
3. Canings and church fire bombings have some wondering *(weather/whether/rather)* the nation's Muslims are becoming less tolerant of Christians and other minority groups.
4. The National *(Rather/Weather/Whether)* Service forecasts the river to crest at 20 feet above flood stage.
5. I'd *(weather/whether/rather)* die than lose my freedom--the creed the founders followed.
6. More Americans would *(weather/whether/rather)* focus on economic growth than healthcare.
7. What is not known is *(weather/whether/rather)* the throttle was wide open because the driver had the gas pedal mashed to the floor or *(weather/whether/rather)* it stuck wide open on its own.
8. *(Rather/Weather/Whether)* the bill passes or fails, both GOP and Dem strategists say, members have already taken votes that will mark them come November.
9. I have felt for some time that we have auctions **rather** than elections.
10. I would *(weather/whether/rather)* do my computer business on a computer while having the TV for shows.
11. The question addressed here is *(weather/whether/rather)* conditions over and around the Antarctic affect daily weather in the Northern Hemisphere.
12. Of course, in a place like that, the *(weather/whether/rather)* is always on one's mind.
13. Severe *(weather/whether/rather)* preparedness week is under way in Indiana.

Answers: *1. Rather 2. weather 3. whether 4. Weather 5. rather 6. rather 7. whether, whether 8. Whether 9. rather 10. rather 11. whether 12. weather 13. weather*

Whether vs. As to whether

The circumlocution **as to whether** should be replaced by **whether**. This is another construction you should erase from your vocabulary and never use **'as to whether'** in written English.
 • **Wrong**: The Congress has not decided **as to whether** to authorize the multi-billion dollar bailout.
 • **Correct**: The Congress has not decided **whether** to authorize the multi-billion dollar bailout.

Whether vs. If

"It's good practice to distinguish between these words. Use **if** for a conditional idea, **whether** for an alternative or possibility. Thus, *Let me know if you'll be coming* means that I want to hear from you only if you're coming. But *Let me know whether you'll be coming* means that I want to hear from you about your plans one way or the other" (Garner, *The Oxford Dictionary of American Usage and Style*)

Whether introduces a choice; *if* introduces a condition. This rule causes many mistakes.
Incorrect: The student asked *if* he had passed the exam.
Correct: The student asked **whether** he had passed the exam.

Note: This is very fertile ground for the exam because native speakers typically make this mistake so you cannot depend on your ear. You have to learn the rule and then apply it on the exam.

Detailed Explanation:

1). Use 'whether' not 'if' after prepositions
 • *The teacher couldn't make the decision of **whether** to include an essay on the exam.*
 • *The two lawyers were at odds **about** whether the judge should allow the evidence.*

2). Use 'Whether' not' if before infinitives.
 • *The band can't decide **whether to travel** to Japan or Europe next year*
3). Use 'whether' not 'if' with question-words and where a clause is a subject or complement
 • ***Whether the sun will come out tomorrow** is still being debated. (Subject)*
 • *The question is **whether** the sun will come out tomorrow. (Complement)*
 • *The question is **if** the sun will come out tomorrow. (Correct but less preferred.)*
4). Use 'whether' not 'if' if an indirect question is fronted.
 • ***Whether I'll have time to study** tonight I'm not sure at the moment.*
 fronting (framflytting): moving a clause element that is usually placed after the verb to the first position in the clause (i.e. before the subject and the verb). The effect of fronting is usually that the fronted element receives special emphasis, often because it contrasts with something mentioned earlier. E.g.That programme I always watch. (fronting of direct object). In a few cases fronting causes inversion (fronting of negative or restrictive element, fronting of obligatory adverbial or adverbial particle, fronting of so + adjective/adverb, fronting of -ing or past participle clause)

5). Whether is generally preferred in a two - part question with or.
 • *The teacher has not told the students **whether** they will have to read chapter 4 **or** chapter 5.*
6). Use 'whether' not 'if' after verbs that are more common in a formal style.
 • *The students **discussed** whether they would go to the game tonight.*

7). 'Whether' and 'if' can both introduce indirect questions.
  • *I'm not sure **whether/if** I'll have time.*
8). 'Whether' and 'if' can both be used with Yes/No questions.
  • *I'm not sure **if/whether** the class started at 8:00 or 9:00 a.m.*

Note: - The word IF does not always signal a conditional sentence. In such cases, the Exam prefers "whether" instead of "if"
• *I don't know if I will go to the dance. (Incorrect)*   • *I don't know whether I will go to the dance. (Correct)*

Who, that, which

Rule 1: 'who' refers to people. 'That' and 'which' refer to groups or things.
  • Elizabeth is the one ***who*** takes care of all her friends.
  • Stefan is a member of the Science club ***that*** competed at Nationals.
  • My family belongs to a church ***that*** meets once a week.
Rule 2: 'that' introduces essential clauses while 'which' introduces nonessential clauses.
  • I only buy cars that have four wheel drive because they are safer and more fun. We would not know which products were
    being discussed without the *that* clause. Now we know it's the cars with "four-wheel drive"
  • I trust Four-wheel drive vehicles that have manual wheel locks
  • The four-wheel drive trucks with manual wheel locks, which arrived at the Toyota dealership last week, are on sale.
The trucks are already identified. Therefore, "which" begins a nonessential clause.
Note: Nonessential clauses beginning with 'which' have commas at the start and end while essentials clauses do not have commas.

Rule 3: If 'this', 'that', 'these', or 'those' has already introduced an essential clause, you may then use 'which' to introduce the next clause, whether it's essential or nonessential.
  • That is a decision which you will need to explain to the supervisor.
  • Those rules, which we reviewed last night, must be included in the updates to the manual.
Note: Many times you can also leave out the word 'which' and it won't affect the meaning.
  • That is a decision which you will need to explain to the supervisor.
  • That is a decision you will need to explain to the supervisor.

More Details about: That, Which, Who
That, among other things, **is a restrictive relative pronoun**: it tells you a necessary piece of information about its
antecedent.   In other words, the information continues to drill down and identify the subject.
  • The teacher *that* likes his or her students will always do a better job.
The phrase answers the question: which teachers? **answer:** the ones that like the students.
Another way to say the same things is ***that*** introduces a restricted clause referring to a thing, like this:
  • *The pizza **that** is sold at Graziano's is my favorite.*
Think about it as categories and you want to drill down and identify your original subject ever more precisely. When you begin
with a subject and then you add information that drills down and actually identifies that subject more precisely, you use 'that' to
introduce the more precise description. In this example, we begin with 'Pizza' then we drill down (narrow down) the category
of all pizza and add the qualifier "that is sold at Graziano's" this information narrows the subject more precisely.

All pizza => just Graziano's pizza

Note: that sometimes people omit the *that* at the beginning of such clauses and say:
  • *The pizza sold at Graziano's is my favorite.*
Which, **among other things, is non-restrictive relative pronoun**: it does not limit the word it refers to.
  • *The pizza sold at Graziano's, which is rather expensive compared to national chains, is my* favorite.
The *which clause* provides an extra piece of information about the topic we're already discussing. It does not drill down further
or more precisely identify the subject. It simply gives you an interesting side piece of information about the category but it
does not narrow the category any further.   **We started with a category:** "The pizza sold at Graziano's"   The next piece of
information provides a little side note about the existing category of "Graziano's pizza" it's also expensive...but it's "my favorite"
because it's Graziano's pizza, NOT because it's also relatively expensive.

So, the information introduced by the clause, "which is rather expensive compared to national chains" is extra. It does not continue to "drill
down" and identify the subject--the information goes laterally and gives you an "oh by the way, it's also more expensive".

Now let's add the 'white sauce' to our particular pizza: like this
  • The pizza sold at Graziano's that is made with white sauce is my favorite.

Now we have a new category with more detail that more precisely identifies the subject.
Pizza=>sold at Graziano's=>made with white sauce. Because we are drilling down more and more to identify this particular
pizza we use 'that' to introduce the clause.

Now let's go one more step.
  • The pizza with the white sauce sold at Graziano's, which is rather expensive compared to national chains, is my favorite.

We could keep this up and drill more and more and each time we more precisely identify the subject we would introduce the
clause with 'that' and each time we give lateral information (stuff that is more 'by the way') we would introduce that information
with 'which'. One more time:
  • The pizza with the white sauce sold at Graziano's that is really expensive, is my favorite.

Now we are drilling down and identifying with ever more precision the category of pizza that "is my favorite"

Pizza=>at Graziano's=> with white sauce=>the really expensive ones (as opposed to the cheap white sauce pizzas at Graziano's) **THOSE** are my favorites.

Take the time to understand these concepts.

One more example of 'that' and 'which'. If the clause introduces information that moves laterally and does NOT drill down and more precisely identify the subject, use 'which'. If the clause drills and specifies, use 'that'.
  • The olives have pits   • The olives that are in my salad have pits   • The olives in my salad, which is delicious by the way, have pits.   • The delicious olives in my salad that are green have pits.   • The delicious green olives in my salad, which cost over $8.00 by the way, have pits.
And on and on...

It boils down to this: if you can tell which thing is being discussed without the *which* or *that* clause, use *which*; if you can't, use *that*.

Tip 1 (commas): if the phrase needs a comma, you probably mean *which*. "The delicious green olives in my salad, which cost over $8.00 by the way, have pits." or "The pizza with the white sauce sold at Graziano's, which is rather expensive compared to national chains, is my favorite."

Tip 2 (which or that): Another way to keep them straight is to imagine '*by the way*' following every *which* "The delicious green olives in my salad, which cost over $8.00 __by the way__, have pits.   The *which* adds a useful, but not grammatically necessary, piece of information. On the other hand, we wouldn't say " The pizza **that** is sold at Graziano's __by the way__ is my favorite." because *the pizza* on its own isn't enough information — *which* pizza?
Note: A paradoxical mnemonic--use *that* to tell which, and *which* to tell that.

'Who' is a pronoun that can be used as both an interrogative pronoun and a relative pronoun. As a relative pronoun, it introduces a clause in cases in which the antecedent (what is modified by the clause) is one or more persons, or something to which personality is ascribed, like a character in a book, film, or television show; a pet; or something else that is personified. Some experts feel that the use of *who* should be restricted to references to people.
  • Person: *Frankie is the pitcher **who** has the best record.*
  • Character: *The droids, **who** helped Luke Skywalker, were named R2-D2 and C-3PO*
  • Pet: *My dog Sache is the one **who** always seems to get into trouble.*
  • Other: *In the story about the contest between the Sun and the Wind, the Sun, **who** took a gentler approach than the Wind, was much more effective in getting the man to take off his coat.*

Questions:
1. Samantha is the student **(that, whom, who, which)** received 100% on the exam.
2. That is a video game **(who, which, that, whom)** takes over 40 hours to play.
3. That is a car **(that, who, whom, which)** can accelerate to 60 mph in under 4 seconds.
4. Newton's First Law of Motion, **(who, that, which, whom)** states that an object at rest tends to stay at rest and an object in motion tends to stay in motion, is taught in every high school physics class.
5. The subject **(which, whom, who, that)** gives me the most difficulty is Spanish.
6. Michael Phelps, **(whom, who, that, which)** has the most Olympic medals, is a role model to many young swimmers.
7. The Redwood trees **(that, which, who, whom)** grow in N. California are a tourist attraction and can live over 2000 years.
8. The Redwood trees in Northern California, **(that, which, who, whom)** live over 2000 years, are some of the oldest plants on the earth.
9. The student **(which, whom, that, who)** studied the most should receive the highest grade.

Answers
1. **Correct Answer: who** Samantha is the student **(who)** received 100% on the exam. **Explanation**: Use "who" or "whom" when referring to people. Remember the formula: "he = who" "him = whom." You could say, " Samantha is the student. She received 100% on the exam."
2. **Correct Answer: which** That is a video game **(which)** takes over 40 hours to play. **Explanation**: Use "which" to introduce an essential clause if you have already used "that" to introduce a previous clause.
3. **Correct Answer: which** That is a car **(which)** can accelerate to 60 mph in under 4 seconds. **Explanation**: Use "which" to introduce an essential clause if you have already used "that" to introduce a previous clause.
4. **Correct Answer: which** Newton's First Law of Motion, **(which)** states that an object at rest tends to stay at rest and an object in motion tends to stay in motion, is taught in every high school physics class. **Explanation**: Use "which" to introduce a nonessential clause; i.e., one that follows a noun previously identified sufficiently. " Newton's First Law of Motion " is already sufficiently identified. Introduce "which" with a comma and follow a "which" clause with a comma if the sentence continues.
5. **Correct Answer: that** The subject **(that)** gives me the most difficulty is Spanish. **Explanation**: Use "that" to introduce an essential clause; i.e., one that is necessary to identify a previous word. You don't know which subject is being referred to so the information that follows is essential.
6. **Correct Answer: who** Michael Phelps, **(who)** has the most Olympic medals, is a role model to many young swimmers. **Explanation**: Use "who" or "whom" when referring to people. Remember the formula: "he = who" "him = whom." You could say, "Phelps has the most medals. He is a role model." Note that the main clause was interrupted by another clause.
7. **Correct Answer: that** The Redwood trees **(that)** grow in Northern California are a tourist attraction. can live over 2000 years. **Explanation**: Use "that" to introduce an essential clause; i.e., one that is necessary to identify a previous word. You wouldn't know which redwood trees were being referred to so the clause that follows is essential for identification.
8. **Correct Answer: which** The Redwood trees in Northern California, **(which)** live over 2000 years, are some of the oldest plants on the earth. **Explanation**: Use "which" to introduce a nonessential clause; i.e., one that follows a noun previously identified sufficiently.

Introduce "which" with a comma and follow a "which" clause with a comma if the sentence continues. Because of the phrase "in Northern California," you already know which redwood trees are some of the oldest plans on the earth.

9. **Correct Answer: who** The student **(who)** studied the most should receive the highest grade. **Explanation:** Use "who" or "whom" when referring to people. Remember the formula: "he = who" "him = whom." You could say, "the student should receive the highest grade. He/she studied the most." Note that the main clause was interrupted by another clause.

Who vs. Whom

Who: Use who when a sentence requires a subject pronoun (equivalent to he or she).
Whom: In formal English, use whom when a sentence requires an object pronoun (equivalent to him or her).

Note: Contemporary usage increasingly favors the use of who in both cases. But strictly speaking, it is correct to use **who as the subject of a verb** and **whom as the object**,
   • 'Who saw you?' but 'Whom did you see?'
It is also strictly right to use whom after a preposition, as in 'To whom were you talking just now?' In practice, few people follow this rule; most use who all the time, and a sentence like 'To whom were you talking?' can sound too formal." ("Who or Whom?" AskOxford.com, 2008)
   • "A circus is like a mother in **whom** one can confide and who rewards and punishes." (Burt Lancaster)
   • The academic--**who** authorities have long believed was connected to the group--was seized on Wednesday.

Usage Notes: It is . . . not surprising that writers from Shakespeare onward should often have interchanged who and whom. And though the distinction shows no signs of disappearing in formal style, strict adherence to the rules in informal discourse might be taken as evidence that the speaker or writer is paying undue attention to the form of what is said, possibly at the expense of its substance. *In speech and informal writing who tends to predominate over whom;* a sentence such as
• Who did John say he was going to support? will be regarded as quite natural, if strictly incorrect. By contrast, the use of whom where who would be required, as in Whom shall I say is calling? may be thought to betray a certain linguistic insecurity. When the relative pronoun stands for the object of a preposition that ends a sentence, whom is technically the correct form: the strict grammarian will insist on Whom (not who) did you give it to? But grammarians since Noah Webster have argued that the excessive formality of whom in these cases is at odds with the relative informality associated with the practice of placing the preposition in final position and that the use of who in these cases should be regarded as entirely acceptable." ("who," The American Heritage Dictionary of the English Language, 3rd edition, 1992)

"Whom is a word invented to make everyone sound like a butler. Nobody who is not a butler has ever said it out loud without feeling just a little bit weird." (Calvin Trillin)

"Use of whom has all but disappeared from spoken English, and seems to be going the same way in most forms of written English too. If you are not sure, it is much better to use who when whom would traditionally have been required than to use whom incorrectly for who, which will make you look not just wrong but wrong and pompous."
(David Marsh, Guardian Style, Guardian Books, 2007)

"Our evidence shows that present-day uses of who and whom are in kind just about the same as they were in Shakespeare's day. What sets us apart from Shakespeare is greater self-consciousness; the 18th-century grammarians have intervened and given a reason to watch our whos and whoms. . . . All that remains to be said is that objective who and nominative whom are much less commonly met in print than nominative who and objective whom. In speech you rarely need to worry about either one. In writing, however, you may choose to be a bit more punctilious, unless you are writing loose and easy, speech like prose. Our files show that objective whom is in no danger of extinction, at least in writing." ("who, whom," Merriam-Webster's Concise Dictionary of English Usage, 2002)

Questions
1. Any person *(who/whom)* hates dogs must have other problems.
2. It's human nature to want to protect the speech of people with *(who/whom)* we agree.
3. Neil Young is one of those musicians *(who/whom)* people either love or hate.
4. Heidi Montag fired Aiden Chase, a Malibu-based psychic *(who/whom)* she hired last week.
5. A man *(who/whom)* struck a match on a flight to Boston's Logan International Airport is facing prosecution.
6. The producer *(who/whom)* discovered Lady Gaga is suing her company, claiming he got cut out of millions after turning her from a "guidette" into a mega-star.
7. Michael Mann is still scheduled to direct "For (Who/Whom) the Bell Tolls".
8. About 60% of those *(who/whom)* are diagnosed with the tuberculosis are cured.
9. There wasn't a great deal of information available on Miguel Celestino, the minor league pitcher *(who/whom)* the Red Sox acquired as the player-to-be-named-later.
10. I talked to a Texas A&M fan *(who/whom)* made the trip from Texas. But really, *(who/whom)* cares?

Answers: *1. who   2. whom   3. who   4. whom   5. who   6. who   7. Whom   8. who   9. whom   10. who, who*

Whoever vs. Whomever

Whoever: just like who and whom, use whoever when a sentence requires a subject pronoun--equivalent to he or she.
Whomever: In formal English use whomever when a sentence requires an object pronoun-equivalent to him or her.
   • "*Whoever* is winning at the moment will always seem to be invincible." (George Orwell)
   • She wanted to be fair to *whomever* or whatever she was writing about.

Usage Notes: "If you're unsure of the correct word, choose whoever; even when the objective whomever would be strictly correct, the whoever is at worst a casualism (in other words, not bad except in formal concepts).

"Like who and whom, this pair is subject to more than occasional hypercorrection." (Bryan A. Garner, Garner's Modern American Usage, Oxford University Press, 2009)

"Whoever baits a slightly different trap: If the front door swings open for Mr. Wilson it opens too for whomever else can hang on to those charismatic coat-tails. The writer has been misled by the preposition for, which is normally followed by the objective case ('It opens for them'). But here for introduces a clause, and the subject of that clause should be whoever, not whomever. There is no doubt that whomever else is wrong here. It is equivalent to anyone else who, and whoever is necessary." (Sir Ernest Gowers, revised by Sidney Greenbaum, The Complete Plain Words, David R. Godine, 2002)

From: "Money," The Office, 2007

Ryan: What I really want, honestly Michael, is for you to know it, so that you can communicate it to the people here, to your clients, to **whomever**. _(correct)_
Michael Scott: [chuckles] Okay.
Ryan: What?
Michael Scott: It's "**whoever**," not "**whomever**." _(wrong)_
Ryan: No, it's "**whomever**." _(correct)_
Michael Scott: No, "**whomever**" is never actually right. _(wrong)_
Jim: Sometimes it's right.
Creed: Michael is right. It's a made-up word used to trick students.
Andy: No. Actually, "**whomever**" is the formal version of the word. _(sort of)_
Oscar: Obviously it's a real word, but I don't know when to use it correctly.
Michael Scott: [to camera] Not a native speaker. . . .
Pam: It's "**whom**" when it's the object of the sentence and "**who**" when it's the subject. _(correct)_
Phyllis: That sounds right.
Michael: Well, it sounds right, but is it?
Stanley: How did Ryan use it, as an object?
Ryan: As an object.
Kelly: Ryan used me as an object.
Stanley: Is he right about that . . .?
Pam: How did he use it again?
Toby: It was . . . Ryan wanted Michael, the subject, to explain the computer system, the object . . .
Michael Scott: Thank you!
Toby: . . . to **whomever**, meaning us, the indirect object--which is the correct usage of the word. _(correct)_
Michael Scott: No one asked you anything ever, so **whomever's** name is Toby, why don't you take a letter opener and stick it into your skull. _(wrong)_

Questions

1. Delegates can vote for _(whoever/whomever)_ they want.
2. _(Whoever/Whomever)_ gossips to you will gossip about you.
3. _(Whoever/Whomever)_ emerges victorious can affirm his place among the upper echelon of UFC's fighters.
4. She's behind Jennifer 100 percent in _(whoever/whomever)_ she wants to date.
5. I think that _(whoever/whomever)_ wrote this letter is simply trying to make some point just for the sake of it.
6. I think people are just attracted to _(whoever/whomever)_ they find attractive.
7. _(Whoever/Whomever)_ came up with the saying "The devil is in the details," must have been thinking about socialized medicine.
8. _(Whoever/Whomever)_ wins, it isn't likely to be terribly aesthetic, probably something like New Yorkers jostling their way onto a crowded subway line.
9. He can do whatever He wants whenever He wants with _(whoever/whomever)_ He wants. He doesn't need our opinion. He doesn't need us to vote on it. He just does it.
10. We try to focus on _(whoever/whomever)_ we're playing, make them the most important thing and then move on.

Answers: 1. whomever 2. Whoever 3. Whoever 4. whomever 5. whoever 6. whomever 7. Whoever 8. Whoever 9. whomever 10. whomever

Who's vs. Whose

When should you use **who's** vs. **whose** in a sentence?
Who's (contraction--who is)
Who's is a contraction of who is or, less commonly, who has. Use **who's** in your writing only when you can substitute the words "who is" or "who has". Example: "Who's going to the mall?" This means: "Who is going to the mall?"
   • Who's playing video games? • Do you know who's eating dinner with us tonight? • Who's going to the dance? • Who's in the biology lab? • Who's that new student? • Who's ready for lunch?
Whose (possessive)
Whose is the possessive of who or, somewhat controversially, which. Whose is a possessive pronoun just like _my, his, her, their_, and _our._ It means "belonging to whom." Use **whose** in your writing only when you mean to show ownership. For example, "Whose bike is this?" is the same as, "To whom does this bike belong?"
   •Whose iPod is this? • Do you know whose textbook this is? • Mr. Tomkinson, whose class scored highest of all, will receive an award as Best Math Teacher. • Whose side are you on? • An idea whose time has come.
The Bottom Line
The trouble here is due to the apostrophe, which on 99% of English words indicates possession, but on this one simply indicates a contraction. If you can replace the word with _who is_ or _who has_, use _who's._ If not, use _whose._

IMPORTANT TIPAlways mentally replace *who's* with the words *who is* or *who has* to see if you've used the correct form.

Incorrect: *Who's* physics class are you in?
Correct: *Whose* physics class are you in?
Correct: *Who's* the new physics teacher?
Correct: *Who's* the student *whose* backpack was left at my desk in Biology class?

More details about "who's vs. whose)

Who's: (contraction of 'who is' or 'who has' *Who's* is pronounced /HOOZ/) *Who's* is a contraction formed of the nominative form *who* (the interrogative and relative pronoun that refers to people, as opposed to *that*, which refers to animals and inanimate objects) and one of the verbs *is* or *has*. When *who* is combined with *is*, the apostrophe replaces the *i*. When *who* is combined with *has*, two letters '*h*' and '*a*' are replaced by the apostrophe.

Contraction of interrogative *who* and *has*:
  • *Who's* studied for the American History final exam scheduled for next week? (Who has studied . . .)
Contraction of interrogative *who* and *is*:
  • *Who's* going to introduce me to the new student in Mrs. Sanchez' Spanish class? (Who is going to introduce...)
Contraction of relative *who* and *has*:
  • *Mr. Flagwell is, of all the school counselors, the one **who's** always took the time to talk with me.* (. . . the one who has always taken the time . . .)
Contraction of relative *who* and *is*:
  • *Babe Ruth is the baseball player **who's** credited with popularizing professional baseball in America!* (. . . the one who is credited . . .)
Whose (possessive pronounced /HOOZ)
Whose is the possessive form of *who* and, like *who*, can perform an interrogative or relative function. Here are some

Interrogative pronoun:
  • *This is my iPod, **whose** is this one?*
  • *I wonder **whose** iPod was left at my desk?*
Relative pronoun
  • *Chelsea is the student whose personality and looks got her elected Home Coming Queen.*

Differentiating Who's and Whose

In English, most possessives are formed by adding apostrophe '*s*'. So the pronoun contraction *who's* looks like the kind of construction that fits the meaning situation in which it is grammatically correct to use *whose*, the possessive form. Knowing that there is a special reason that *who's* in place of *whose* may not, at a glance, appear to be wrong, may help you to stay alert so that you catch it.

In addition, because *who's* and *whose* are both correct spellings, it is necessary to use the grammar check in your word processor in addition to the spell check in order to catch this error. If you are impatient when the grammar checker, for example, flags all the passive constructions that, given your context, are perfectly fine, one idea is to do a Find on *who's* and check each spot.

Questions
  1. *(Who's/Whose)* reality show is more popular?
  2. *(Who's/Whose)* coming to game tonight?
  3. The textbook was found in *(who's/whose)* backpack?
  4. We haven't found out yet *(who's/whose)* the new class president.
  5. Do you know *(who's/whose)* the runner on third base?
  6. Brandon is the one *(who's/whose)* mp3 player has been lost.
  7. Brandon is the one *(who's/whose)* lost his mp3 player.
  8. *(Who's/Whose)* dogs got out?
  9. Yesterday at lunch you gave me *(who's/whose)* burrito?
  10. It is Tamara *(who's/whose)* leading the polls for prom queen.

Answers: *1. Whose 2. Who's 3. whose 4. who's 5. who's 6. whose 7. who's 8. Whose 9. whose 10. who's*

Would of

Basic Rule: '*Of*' is a preposition. Do **not** use *of* in the place of '*have*' after verbs such as *could, should, would, might* and *must*. It is WRONG to say: *could of, should of, would of, might of,* and *must of*. These should be: *could have, should have, would have, might have,* and *must have*.
  • **Wrong**: You **would** *of* cleaned your room if you could of opened the door.
  • **Correct**: You **would have** cleaned your room if you could have opened the door.
Note: while it's acceptable to use the contraction 'would've' 'could've" in informal speech and informal writing, you typically don't use contractions like this in formal writing--so avoid these contractions on the exam.

Your vs. You're

This is not a difficult rule, however, students routinely miss questions related to "*your vs. you're*" not because they don't understand the rule, but rather because *(your/you're)* in a hurry and *(your/you're)* more worried about getting finished and *(your/you're)* concentration lags and *(your/you're)* mind can skip over these 'easy' issues. But keep in mind that on *(your/you're)* exam the 'easy' questions are worth 1 point and the difficult questions are worth 1 point, so keep *(your/you're)* mind focused and *(your/you're)* more likely to pick up all the 'easy' points and more of the 'difficult' points.

You're is the contracted form of You are. It's used in sentences where "you" is the subject of the sentence and the verb "to be" is either the helping verb or the principal verb of the sentence.

• **You're** *going to have trouble on the exam unless you study every day this month!*
• *Because **you're** studying several hours every day **you're** much better prepared than most students.*

"Your" is the possessive pronoun form. This form is used to express that something belongs to "you".

• **Your** *notebook is falling apart because of all **your** studying.*
• **Your** *effort and **your** preparation are superior compared with most students, so I know you're going to be happy with **your** results.*

Rule Summary: "**You're**" is always a contraction of "*you are.*" If you've written "**you're**," try substituting "*you are.*" If it doesn't work, the word you want is "**your.**" **Your** writing will improve if **you're** careful about this.

Why Mistakes Happen

Substituting *your* or *you're* for the other word happens because the words sound the same, are spelled very similarly, and have related meanings. Also, because they are pronouns we pay less attention to them when we are proofreading. Because both spellings are accurate, spell check alone will not catch them

Questions (Alaska Flight 438)

Before takeoff...

Hello, and welcome to Alaska Flight 438 to Portland. If **(1.)** *(your/you're)* going to Portland, **(2.)** *(your/you're)* in the right place. If **(3.)** *(your/you're)* not going to Portland, **(4.)** *(your/you're)* about to have a really long evening."

We'd like to tell you now about some important safety features of this aircraft. The most important safety feature we have aboard this plane is...The Flight Attendants. Please look at one now.

There are 5 exits aboard this plane: 2 at the front, 2 over the wings, and one out the plane's rear end. If **(5.)** *(your/you're)* seated in one of the exit rows, please do not store **(6.)** *(your/you're)* bags by **(7.)** *(your/you're)* feet. That would be a really bad idea. Please take a moment and look around and find the nearest exit. Count the rows of seats between you and the exit. In the event that the need arises to find one, trust me, you'll be glad you did.

We have pretty blinking lights on the floor that will blink in the direction of the exits. White ones along the normal rows, and pretty red ones at the exit rows.

In the event of a loss of cabin pressure these baggy things will drop down over **(8.)** *(your/you're)* head. You stick it over **(9.)** *(your/you're)* nose and mouth like the flight attendant is doing now. The bag won't inflate, but there's oxygen there, promise. If **(10.)** *(your/you're)* sitting next to a small child, or someone who is acting like a small child, please do us all a favor and put on **(11.)** *(your/you're)* mask first. If **(12.)** *(your/you're)* traveling with two or more children, please take a moment now to decide which one is **(13.)** *(your/you're)* favorite. Help that one first, and then work **(14.)** *(your/you're)* way down.

In **(15.)** *(your/you're)* seat pocket in front of you is a pamphlet about the safety features of this plane. I usually use it as a fan when I'm having my own personal summer. It makes a very good fan. It also has pretty pictures. Please take it out and play with it now.

Please take a moment now to make sure **(16.)** *(your/you're)* seat belts are fastened low and tight about **(17.)** *(your/you're)* waist. To fasten the belt, insert the metal tab into the buckle. To release, it's a pulley thing -- not a pushy thing like **(18.)** *(your/you're)* car because **(19.)** *(your/you're)* in an airplane -- HELLOOO!!

There is no smoking in the cabin on this flight. There is also no smoking in the lavatories. If we see smoke coming from the lavatories, we will assume **(20.)** *(your/you're)* on fire and put you out. This is a free service we provide. There are two smoking sections on this flight, one outside each wing exit.

In a moment we will be turning off the cabin lights, and it's going to get really dark, really fast. If **(21.)** *(your/you're)* afraid of the dark, now would be a good time to reach up and press the yellow button. The yellow button turns on **(22.)** *(your/you're)* reading light. Please don't press the orange button unless you absolutely have to. The orange button is **(23.)** *(your/you're)* seat ejection button.

We're glad to have you with us on board this flight. Thank you for choosing Alaska Air, and giving us **(24.)** *(your/you're)* business and **(25.)***(your/you're)* *(your/you're)* money. If there's anything we can do to make **(26.)** *(your/you're)* flight more comfortable, please don't hesitate to ask.

If you all weren't strapped down you would have given me a standing ovation, wouldn't you?

Answers: *1. you're 2. you're 3. you're 4. you're 5. you're 6. your 7. your 8. your 9. your 10. you're 11. your 12. you're 13. your 14. your 15. your 16. your 17. your 18. your 19. you're 20. you're 21. you're 22. your 23. your 24. your 25. your 26. your*

Sample Question

The studio's retrospective art exhibit refers back to a simpler time in American history.
(A)   The studio's retrospective art exhibit refers back to
(B)   The studio's retrospective art exhibit harkens back to
(C)   The studio's retrospective art exhibit refers to
(D)   The studio's retrospective art exhibit refers from
(E)   The studio's retrospective art exhibit looks back to

Explanation

(A) Choice (A) is incorrect. *Retrospective* means looking back on the past. Hence, in the phrase *refers back*, the word *back* is redundant.
(B) This AC is incorrect because *harkens back* is also redundant.
(C) **Correct Response**. Dropping the word *back* eliminates the redundancy.
(D) Choice (D) is incorrect because the preposition *from* is non-idiomatic.
(E) This AC is incorrect because *looks back* is also redundant.

Note: One could argue that the phrase *American history* also makes the sentence redundant. However, it is not underlined in the sentence. It is not at all uncommon to find questionable structures in parts of the sentence that are not underlined. In fact, you may even find questionable structures in the underlined part of the sentence that are not corrected by any of the answer choices because the writers are testing a different mistake. Concern yourself with correcting only the underlined part of the sentence.

USAGE PHRASES & CLAUSES

Phrases

A phrase is a group of related words that is used as a simple part of speech and does not contain a verb and its subject.

Prepositional Phrases
A **prepositional phrase** starts with a preposition and ends with a noun or pronoun.

Along	Among	Around	At	Before	Behind	Beneath	Beside
Between	Beyond	By	Despite	Down	During	Except	From
In	Near	Off	On	Onto	Outside	Over	Past
Through	Till	To	Toward	Under	Underneath	Until	Up
Upon	With	Within	Without				

Questions: Identify the prepositional phrase by underlining the entire phrase.
   1. In front of our apartment building was a water tower.
   2. Scientists have discovered interferon in their fight against cancer.
Answers: 1. <u>In front of our apartment building</u> was a water tower.
   2. Scientists have discovered interferon <u>in their fight against cancer</u>.

Verbals and Verbal Phrases
Participles: Present with an –ing or Past ending with an –ed.
Questions: Identify the prepositional verbal phrase by underlining the entire phrase.
   1. Outwitting the hounds, the raccoon easily escaped.   2. I saw her fishing contentedly.
Answers: 1. <u>Outwitting the hounds</u>, the raccoon easily escaped.   2. I saw her <u>fishing contentedly</u>.

Gerund Phrases
Gerund: A verb form ending in -ing that is used as a noun.

Questions: Identify the gerund phrase by underlining the entire phrase.

   1. Walking around the block is good exercise.   2. Lauren enjoys reading romance novels.
Answers: 1. <u>Walking</u> around the block is good exercise.   2. Lauren enjoys <u>reading</u> romance novels.

Infinitive Phrases
An **infinitive verb phrase** usually follows "to". It can be a noun, adjective or adverb. "To" with a noun or pronoun becomes a prepositional phrase
Questions: Identify the infinitive phrase by underlining the entire phrase.
   1. To forgive is to forget.   2. The player to watch is the quarterback.
Answers: 1. <u>To forgive</u> is to forget.   2. The player <u>to watch</u> is the quarterback.

Appositive Phrases
An **appositive phrase** is a noun or pronoun that follows another noun or pronoun to identify or explain it.

Within the sentence will usually be broken off with a comma before and after the phrase.

Questions: Identify the appositive phrase by underlining it.
   1. Danny, a star cornerback, was awarded a college football scholarship.
   2. A man of integrity, Mr. Loomis never cheats anybody.
Answers: 1. Danny, <u>a star cornerback</u>, was awarded a college football scholarship.
   2. <u>A man of integrity</u>, Mr. Loomis never cheats anybody.

Clauses

Independent Clause
Independent clauses are also referred to as the main clause. It expresses a complete thought and can stand alone as a complete sentence

Questions: Identify the independent clause by underlining **it.**
   1. Mr. Torres cut pieces of stained glass with a diamond wheel and his partner put the pieces together with wax and lead.
      (Gender consistency)
Answer: 1. Mr. Torres cut pieces of stained glass with a diamond wheel and <u>his partner put the pieces together with wax and lead</u>.

Subordinate Clause

The subordinate clause is also referred to as the dependant clause and it does not express a complete thought and it cannot stand alone as a sentence, it is a sentence fragment

Questions: Identify the subordinate clause by underlining **it.**
1. Before you know it, the arrow had hit the target. 2. Prather won the race, yet still looked fresh.
Answers: 1. <u>Before you know it</u>, the arrow had hit the target. 2. Prather won the race, <u>yet still looked fresh</u>.

Adjective Clause

The adjective clause functions as an adjective and modifies the noun or pronoun. It is also a subordinate clause

Questions: Identify the adjective clause by underlining it.
1. In the case at school is the trophy that Katie won.
Answer: 1. In the case at school is the trophy <u>that Katie won</u>.

Adverb Clause

An adverb clause modifies a verb, adverb, or adjective and is called a subordinate clause

Questions: Identify the adverb clause by underlining it.
1.   Before the game started, Meagan and I ate lunch in the stadium.
Answer__1.   Before the game started, Meagan and I ate lunch <u>in the stadium</u>.

Sentence Structure

Simple Sentence (SS) contains: One independent clause
Compound Sentence (CS) contains: Two or more independent clauses that are joined.
Complex Sentence (CXS) contains: One independent clause and one or more subordinate clauses.
Compound-Complex Sentence (CCS) contains: Two or more independent clauses and one or more subordinate clauses.

Question

Identify the type of sentence structure for each example below by placing the abbreviation in the blank. SS, CS, CCS, or CXS

1. George Vancouver was exploring the northwest territory. _____
2. Since it was not a harbor, Vancouver had been deceived, and Deception Pass became its name._____
3. Vancouver originally thought the channel was a harbor. _____
4. In 1792 Vancouver discovered a channel, and he gave it an unusual name. _____
5. The play Les Miserables, which we are producing ourselves, had better be a success, or we cannot afford another one. _____

Answers:

1. George Vancouver was exploring the northwest territory. **SS**
2. Since it was not a harbor, Vancouver had been deceived, and Deception Pass became its name. **CCS**
3. Vancouver originally thought the channel was a harbor. **SS**
4. In 1792 Vancouver discovered a channel, and he gave it an unusual name. **CS**
5. The play Les Miserables, which we are producing ourselves, had better be a success, or we cannot afford another one. **CXS**

Ism's Causing Errors

1. **SPOONERISMS**-unintentionally changing sounds in a sentence. *"Is it kistomary to cuss the bride?"*

2. **GOLDWYNISM-**a humorous phrase or sentence that is contradictory.
    "A verbal contract isn't worth the paper it's printed on."
    "Please, include me out."
    "Anybody that goes to a psychiatrist should have his head xamined."

3. **BERRAISMS**- a humorous phrase or sentence that is contradictory.
    "Sometimes you can observe a lot by watching."
    "No wonder no one comes out here, it's too crowded."
    "If people don't want to come out to the park, nobody's going to stop them."

4. **COLLOQUIALISMS-**everyday language not appropriate for formal speech and writing.
    "I'll catch you at noon when we hook up at the Arches.
     Colloquial Jargon:
    "Burn the pup."
    "On wheels"
    "Steak on the hoof"
    "Cream Cheese with warts."
    "Black bottom."

5. **MALAPROPISMS-**the use of words in an illiterate but humorous manner.
    "The first thing that they do when a baby is born is cut the <u>biblical</u> cord."
    "The referee penalized the team for unnecessary <u>roughage.</u>"
    "They decided to raise my benefits, and they made them <u>radioactive</u>.

6. **EUPHEMISMS**- a "mild" word or phrase used in place of a more direct word or phrase.
   Disadvantage or Underprivileged (poor people)
   Visually Impaired (blind, or poor vision)
   Vertically Challenged (short)

The Non-Ism Errors

1. **IRISH BULL**- a statement fueled by a delightful absurdity that sparks forth a memorable truth.
   "An Irish bull is always pregnant."
   "May you never live to see you wife a widow."
   "I marvel at the strength of human weakness"

2. **IDIOMS**-any English phrase that is natural and normal, and clearly understandable to a native speaker. ***RAN ACROSS"*:**
   *"The quarterback **ran across** the field."*
   *"The fire truck **ran across** a hose."*
   *"I **ran across** an old friend."*

3. **SPLIT INFINITIVES**-infinitive phrases with a word between "to" and the infinitive.
   *Wrong: I plan **to** hurriedly **complete** the work and leave.*
   *Right: I plan **to complete** the work hurriedly and leave.*
   *Wrong: Mr. Jasper always likes **to** closely **examine** every report.*
   *Right: Mr. Jasper always likes **to examine** closely every report.*

4. **DOUBLE NEGATIVES**- two or more negative words in a single sentence (no, not, never. . .)
   "I don't never go swimming in September."
    "She never sees none of her old friends any more."

5. **WORDINESS**- the use of more words than necessary to convey the point of the sentence. (Superfluous wording)
   *"When Pete and the guard were finally alone they spoke **to each other** in a relaxed manner."*
   *"The smoke from the camp fire rose softly **through the air**. Superfluous Phrases:*
   "half of an hour" (half hour)
   "neighbor of mine" (my neighbor)
   "in an appropriate manner (appropriately)

6. **OVERSTATEMENT-**careless choice of words—exaggeration. Absolutism)
   "Every fan was thrilled with Sosa's homer!."
   "Like all Irishmen, he thrilled to music!"

7. **PARALLELISM**- similar elements in a sentence should be phrased in a similar structure or grammatical form.
   *"Mr. Saffer planned on hunting, fishing, and **sleep**.*
   *"On her desk were her books, papers and **the** old math book".*
   *"I like to swim, **playing** tennis, and **riding**.*

8. **NONSEQUITORS**- a conclusion that does not follow the premise of the sentence.
   "My car sustained no damage whatsoever, and the other car somewhat less."
   "In an attempt to kill a fly, I drove into a telephone poll."
   "A pedestrian hit me and went under my car."

9. **THE USE OF –ISH**- not to be used in formal writing.
   "offish"(should be aloof)
   "fortyish" (should be forties)

10. **DOUBLE TITLING-** crediting the person referenced twice with the same title.
    Dr. Marcus Welby, M.D.
    Mr. Greg Wenneborg, Esq.

11. **MIXED METAPHORS**- a metaphor is a comparison between two things. A mixed metaphor is a comparison of two or more figurative ideas that creates a contradiction or impossibility.
    "That's a horse of a different feather."
    "A bird in hand is worth a diamond in the rough."

12. **WORD USAGE CLARITY**- precise language to convey the information and not confuse the reader.
    "Local high school dropouts cut in half."
    "A man was found dead in the cemetery."
    "Utah girl was successful in state dog show."
    "City police begin campaign to run down jaywalkers."
    "Poll shows that death causes loneliness and feelings of isolation."

Grammar Study Guide
Part 9: Mechanics & Meaning

Virtual Classroom>Grammar Study Guide>Mechanics & Meaning
This material corresponds to the Virtual Classroom Instructions in the
PowerPrep DVD/Internet/iApp for English Grammar

Virtual Classroom

Important Abbreviations
These abbreviations are used throughout the program

POE: Process of Elimination
SARR: Synthesize, Analyze, Reduce, and Restate (has to do with Logical Reasoning)
AC: Answer Choice
QS: Question Stem
LOD: Level of Difficulty

Example Question: What is the least common multiple of 3, 4, and 7? **(This is the call of the question or Question Stem "QS")**

These are Answer Choices "AC" A, B, C, D, E
  (A)   12
  (B)   21
  (C)   28
  (D)   48
  (E)   84

Part 9: Mechanics

Punctuation & Marks

Capital Letters Rules

- First word in every sentence
- March v. march, May v. may
- "I","O'" and interjections (*O'Captain, My Captain*)
- The title or position of respect (*President Clinton*)
- Family relationships (*mother v. Aunt Mabel*)
- "First and last word in titles of works of Art"
- References to the Deity (*God, and His universe*)
- Proper Nouns and Adjectives
- Geographical Names
- Persons

- Organizations
- Business Firms
- Government Bodies
- Historical Events and Periods
- Special Events
- Calendar Items
- Nationalities, Races and Religions
- Business Products
- Ships, Planets, Monuments, Awards
- The first letter in a Quote

Common noun	Proper Noun	Proper Adjective
A poet	Homer	Homeric simile
A goddess	Athena	Athenian wisdom

End Marks

1. **Period--** Sentences that are statements end in a period. (Also used for abbreviations, adv.) *It is snowing.*
2. **Question Mark** – used after all interrogative sentences. *Is it snowing?*
3. **Exclamation Mark** – used following all exclamations. *Oh my gosh, it is snowing!*

Commas

- Separate items in a series (*pencil, pen, and paper*)
- Two or more adjectives preceding a noun (*A vain, talkative DJ annoys me.*)
- Before and, but ,or, nor, for, yet when they join an independent phrase.
- Setting off non-essential clauses and phrases (*appositive phrases as an example*)
- Use after Well, Yes, No, Why when they are introductory elements.
- To set off elements that interrupt the sentence (*He , of course, won't be attending tonight.*)
- Parenthetical Phrases (*consequently, however, moreover, nevertheless, therefore, as a matter of fact*)
- Separate dates and addresses
- After Salutations and Closings
- After a name with Jr., Sr., Dr, etc

Semicolons

- Between independent clauses if not joined by a conjunction
- Between independent clauses joined by such words as however, therefore, consequently, instead, hence, otherwise
- May be used to separate independent clauses of a compound sentence if comma's are used in the clause
- Items in a series if the items contain commas

Colons

- Use a colon to mean- "Note what follows"
- Use a colon for time, Bible reference of verse, business letter salutations

Italics

- Titles of books, plays, movies, periodicals, works of art, and musical compositions. (*The Screwtape Letters, Star Wars, Flight of the Bumblebee*)
- When the sentence refers to the word.
- For foreign words. (*Dónde esta el baño?*)

Quotation Marks

- Direct quote—a person's exact words. *"I believe,"* Dan said, *"that she is ill."*   Rodney whispered under his breath, *"Does she really love me?"*
- Punctuation rules: commas and periods inside the quote—colons and semicolons outside the quote.
- Paragraph quotes not at the end of a paragraph where the quote continues into the next paragraph.
- Quote within a quote is a ('). *Jill exclaimed, "My mom always says, 'Put the cap back on the toothpaste.'"*
- Enclosing titles of short stories, articles, poems, songs, chapters, or other parts of books/periodicals. *"Screwtape Letters", "Star Wars", "Of Mice and Men"*

Apostrophes

- Possessive case of singular nouns, add apostrophe and "s" to the end of the word

Mom's car   a hard day's work   a dollar's worth

- Possessive case of a plural noun ending in s, add only the apostrophe to the end of the word

Both girls' behavior   Two weeks' vacation   Knives' edges

Singular	Singular Possessive	Plural	Plural Possessive
Friend	friend's home	friends	friends' home
Month	month's work	months	two months' work
Dollar	dollar's worth	dollars	three dollars' worth
Box	box's lid	boxes	boxes' lid

- Possessive personal pronouns do not need an apostrophe.

Our, ours   Their, theirs   Your, yours   Their, their

- Indefinite pronouns in the possessive case require an apostrophe and an "s."

Everyone's idea   Somebody's pencil

- Compound words, organizations, names, joint possessions—only the last word is possessive in form.

School board's decision
Nobody else's business
American Medical Association's endorsement

- When two or more persons possess something individually, each of their names are in possessive form.

Mrs. Wheeler's and Mrs. Stuart's children were in the same class.

- To show where letters and numbers have been omitted.

let, let's   they're, they are   don't, do not

- Use an apostrophe and "s" to form plurals of letters, signs, numbers, and of words referred to as words.

The word grammar has two r's, two a's and two m's.
The weather today calls for lows in the 40's.

Other Punctuation Marks

Hyphen Rules
- Used to divide a word at the end of a line • Used with numbers twenty-one to ninety-nine • Used with ex-, self-, all-, -elect

ex-champ, self-esteem, all-star, pre-revolution, President-elect

Dash Rules
- Use a dash to indicate an abrupt break in thought

"I hope—" Audrey began and then stopped.   Stephans—Ms. Stephans, I mean--was waiting for me in her office.

Parentheses Rules
- To enclose matter which is added to a sentence, but is not considered of major importance

During the middle ages (from about A.D. 500 to A.D. 1500) Moslems and Vikings invaded Europe.

Ellipsis Rules
- Shows that one or more words has been omitted in a quote

We the people. . .in order to establish a more perfect Union . . . establish this constitution of the United States of America.

- May be used to show a pause

I brought my trembling hand to my focused eyes. It was red, it was. . .it was. . .a tomato.

Brackets Rules
- Used before and after material that has been added when quoting another writer.
- Used when adding a word to a quote

*Sometimes I think <**my writing**> sounds like I walked out of the room and left the typewriter running.*

- Material that was added by someone else

"Congratulations to the astronomy clubs softball team which put in a 'stellar' performance. <groans>"

- Use around an editorial correction

Brooklyn alone has eight percent of lead poisoning <victims> in the county.

- Use around the letters "*sic*" to indicate that an error appearing in the quoted material was made by the original speaker/writer.

No parent can dessert <sic> his child without damaging a human life.

Construction Problems

Wordiness

Wordiness means using more words than necessary to convey the point of the sentence. (also called Superfluous wording). You should work to eliminate words that don't add meaning or add redundancy

Examples: "*When Pete and the guard were finally alone they spoke **to each other** in a relaxed manner.*" If Pete and the guard are alone and they speak, of course it will be to each other...no one else is present. "*The smoke from the camp fire rose softly **through the air**.* The smoke must rise "through the air" it's not rising through the water or any other substance...so that phrase is redundant.

Superfluous Phrases
"half of an hour" better said (half hour).   "neighbor of mine" better said (my neighbor).   "in an appropriate manner better said (appropriately)

Sentence Fragments

- Identify sentences that are dependent/subordinate clauses

Immediately after the fall of the Roman Empire in the 5th century. (more is needed to complete the thought)

Sentence Run-Ons

- The sentence appears, or sounds, bulky and cumbersome in communicating its message clearly.
- The sentence contains more than two or more independent clauses without a conjunction. (not an absolute, but a clue)

I will give you directions for the shortest way here, the traffic is heavy along that route. (a comma alone can't connect two independent clauses)

Comparative vs. Superlative Use

A modifier in the **comparative** degree would compare a person, a thing, an action, or an idea with another one. A modifier in the **superlative** degree would be used to compare a person, a thing, an action, or an idea with at least two others.

Comparative: *That line is longer than the one for the other movie.*
Superlative: *That line is the longest one that I have ever seen.*

Incorrect Example: *Jim is more funnier than anyone else in the group.*
Correct: *Jim is funnier than anyone else in the group.*
Confusing Example: *Richard plays the oboe better than anyone in the class.*

This sentence says either that Richard plays the oboe better than anyone in the class, including himself, or that Richard plays the oboe better than anyone in a class of which he is not a part.
Less Confusing Example: *Richard can play the oboe better than anyone else in the class.*
OR… *Richard is the best oboe player in his class.*

Idiomatic Words and Phrases

What is an idiom? An **idiom** is any English phrase that is natural and normal, and clearly understandable to a native speaker.

"Did you hear that Madison got a scholarship?" *"Yes, I heard it through the grapevine."*

Of course, the second speaker does not mean he heard the news about Madison by putting his ear to a grapevine! He is conveying the idea of information spreading around a widespread network, usually similar to a grapevine.
We use idioms to express something that other words do not express as clearly or as cleverly. Idioms tend to be informal and are best used in spoken rather than written English.

Idioms: The Good News--Sometimes idioms are very easy for learners to understand because there are similar expressions in the speakers' mother tongue. For example: He always goes at things like a bull in a china shop! Unfortunately, the test does not favor the use of idiomatic language, and recognizing an idiomatic phrase will help you find mistakes.
Here "B" some Idioms:

bad-mouth (verb)	beat around the bush	break someone's heart
be a piece of cake	beat one's brains out	broke
be all ears	Beats me.	bug (verb)
be broke	bent out of shape	bull-headed
be fed up with	before long	buck(s)
be in and out	bite off more than one can chew	a bundle
be on the go	blabbermouth	burn the midnight oil
be on the road	blow one's top	bushed
be over	boom box	by one's self
be up and running	the bottom line	by the skin of one's teeth
be used to	blow one's top	
beat (adj.)	Break a leg!	

Paired Words of Confusion

*****Important Note***** See the extensive list of words in section 8

1. accept	vs.	except	11. leave	vs.	let	21. delusion	vs.	illusion
2 affect	vs.	effect	12. rise	vs.	raise	22. disinterested	vs.	uninterested
3. and	vs.	etc.	13. shall	vs.	will	23. farther	vs.	further
4. beside	vs.	besides	14. sit	vs.	set	24. hanged	vs.	hung
5. between	vs.	among	15. than	vs.	then	25. loose	vs.	lose
6. bring	vs.	take	16. way	vs.	ways	26. maybe	vs.	may be
7. discover	vs.	invent	17. cite	vs.	site	27. moral	vs.	morale
8. fewer	vs.	less	18. complement	vs.	compliment	28. passed	vs.	past
9. good	vs.	well	19. conscience	vs.	conscious	29. quiet	vs.	quite
10. learn	vs.	teach	20. council	vs.	counsel	30. principal	vs.	principle

Single Words and Phrases Of Confusion

*****Important Note***** See the extensive list of words in the Big Book of Grammar Drills

- **sick** should not be used for displeased, bored, disgusted
- **party** should only be used for legal references
- **alibi** again legal term, a formal defense descriptive term
- **dilemma** two unsatisfactory choices
- **average** computation needs to be made
- **essential** necessary for the existence of

- **per** only in standard business expressions (per diem)
- **plus** does not mean "and"
- **sadistic** form of sexual perversion
- **irregardless** nonstandard
- **could of / would of** nonstandard
- **unique** only one of a kind
- **vital** that which is necessary for existence
- **want in / want out** nonstandard
- **a lot** nonstandard

- **get** informal; use arrive, recover, receive
- **thing** too broad, should be avoided
- **finalize** nonstandard, "fad word"
- **firm up** nonstandard, "fad word"
- **if and when** impossible phrase
- **ought** nonstandard, should not

Misplaced Phrases & Clauses

Misplacement of phrases can significantly change the meaning of the sentence.

Exercise: Identify the phrase or clause that is misplaced, and correctly rearrange the sentence.

1. *Plunging more than 1,000 feet into the gorge, we saw Yosemite Falls.*
Corrected Sentence: We saw Yosemite Falls plunging more than 1,000 feet into the gorge.

2. *Please take time to look over the brochure that is enclosed with your family.*
Corrected Sentence: Please take some time with your family to look over the enclosed brochure.

3. *The patient was referred to a psychiatrist with a severe emotional problem.*
Corrected Sentence: The patient with a severe emotional problem was referred to a psychiatrist.

Comma Splices & Run-On Sentences

The comma-splice and run-on sentence (and the fused sentence, as a variant is called) are all examples of the problem in which two or more sentences are improperly joined. In the typical ***comma-splice*** sentence, two sentences are joined by a comma without an intervening coordinating conjunction (*and, or, nor, but, yet*). Technically, the ***run-on*** sentence is a sentence that goes on and on and needs to be broken up; it's likely to be a comma splice as well. A ***fused*** sentence is two complete sentence just jammed together without any punctuation and without a conjunction.

Example: *Sometimes, books do not have the most complete information, it is a good idea then to look for articles in specialized periodicals.*
Correct: *Sometimes, books do not have the most complete information; it is a good idea then to look for articles in specialized periodicals.*

Example: *Most of the hours I've earned toward my associate's degree do not transfer, however, I do have at least some hours the University will accept.*
Correct: *Most of the hours I've earned toward my associate's degree do not transfer. However, I do have at least some hours the University will accept.*

Example: *Some people were highly educated professionals, others were from small villages in underdeveloped countries.*
Correct: *Some people were highly educated professionals, while others were from small villages in underdeveloped countries.*

Example: *This report presents the data we found concerning the cost of the water treatment project, then it presents comparative data from other similar projects.*
Correct: *This report first presents the data we found concerning the cost of the water treatment project and then comparative data from other similar projects.*

Modifiers

Modifier problems occur when the word or phrase that a modifier is supposed to modify is unclear or absent, or when the modifier is located in the wrong place within the sentence. A **modifier** is any element--a word, phrase, or clause--that adds information to a noun or pronoun in a sentence. Modifier problems are usually divided into two groups: misplaced modifiers and dangling modifiers.

Misplaced modifier
They found out that the walkways had collapsed on the late evening news. (Was that before or after the sports news?)
The committee nearly spent a hundred hours investigating the accident. (Did they spend even a minute?)
The supervisor said after the initial planning the in-depth study would begin. (Just when did she say that, and when will the study begin?)

Dangling modifier
Having damaged the previous one, a new fuse was installed in the car. (Who damaged that fuse?)

After receiving the new dumb waiter, household chores became so much easier in the old mansion. (Who received the dumb waiter?)
Using a grant from the Urban Mass Transportation Administration, a contraflow lane was designed for I-45 North. (Who used that money?)

To correct misplaced modifier problems, you can usually relocate the misplaced modifier (the word or phrase). To correct dangling modifiers, you can rephrase the dangling modifier, or rephrase the rest of the sentence that it modifies.

On the late evening news, we heard that the walkways had collapsed. **OR...** *The committee spent nearly a hundred hours investigating the accident.* **OR...** *The supervisor said that the in-depth study would begin after the initial planning.*

Because the previous fuse had been damaged, a new one had to be installed. **OR...** *Having damaged the previous one, I had to install a new fuse in my car.*

After we received the dumb waiter, it was immediately installed. **OR...** *After receiving the dumb waiter, we immediately installed it.*

When the Urban Mass Transportation Administration granted funds to the city, planners began designing a contraflow lane for I-45 North.
OR...*Using a grant from the Urban Mass Transportation Administration, city planners designed a contraflow lane for I-45 North.*

Fragments

Fragments are simply incomplete sentences—grammatically incomplete.

Example: Mary appeared at the committee meeting last week. And made a convincing presentation of her ideas about the new product. **Revision**: Mary appeared at the committee meeting last week and made a convincing presentation of her ideas about the new product.

Example: *The committee considered her ideas for a new marketing strategy quite powerful. The best ideas that they had heard in years.* **Revision**: *The committee considered her ideas for a new marketing strategy quite powerful, the best ideas that they had heard in years.*

Example: *In a proposal, you must include a number of sections. For example, a discussion of your personnel and their qualifications, your expectations concerning the schedule of the project, and a cost breakdown.* **Revision**: In a proposal, you must include a number of sections: for example, a discussion of your personnel and their qualifications, your expectations concerning the schedule of the project, and a cost breakdown.

Example: *The research team has completely reorganized the workload. Making sure that members work in areas of their own expertise and that no member is assigned proportionately too much work.* **Revision**: The research team has completely reorganized the workload. They made sure that members work in areas of their own expertise and that no member is assigned proportionately too much work.

Example: *She spent a full month evaluating his computer-based instructional materials. Which she eventually sent to her supervisor with the strongest of recommendations.* **Revision**: She spent a full month evaluating his computer-based instructional materials. Eventually, she sent the evaluation to her supervisor with the strongest of recommendations.

Shifts in Construction

A **shift in construction** is a change in the structure of style midway through a sentence. One example of this covered earlier is Subject/Verb agreement. On the test, you will be expected to identify shifts in the construction of the sentence. The test will offer you selections, and you will need to pick the best possible solution to correct the shift that occurs in the sentence. There is more than one way to correct these problems. Each suggested change offered below is probably not the only correct one for the sentence.

Sample Questions: Shift in verb construction

1. If the club limited its membership, it will have to raise its dues.
2. As Barbara puts in her contact lenses, the telephone rang.
3. Thousands of people will see the art exhibit by the time it closes.
4. By the time negotiations began, many pessimists have expressed doubt about them.
5. After Capt. James Cook visited Alaska on his third voyage, he is killed by Hawaiian islanders in 1779.
6. I was terribly disappointed with my grade because I studied very hard.
7. The moderator asks for questions as soon as the speaker has finished.
8. Everyone hopes the plan would work.
9. Harry wants to show his friends the photos he took last summer.
10. Scientists predict that the sun will die in the distant future.
11. The boy insisted that he has paid for the candy bars.
12. The doctor suggested bed rest for the patient, who suffers from a bad cold.

Answers: *1. (change will to would), 2. (change puts to put), 3. No change, 4. (change have to had), 5. (change is to was), 6. (change studied to had studied), 7. (asks as habitual action; will ask is also possible), 8. (change hopes to hoped), 9. NO Change, 10. No Change, 11. (change has to had), 12. (change suffers to was suffering)*

Grammar Study Guide

Part 10: Review

<u>**Virtual Classroom>Grammar Study Guide>**</u>Review
This material Corresponds to the Virtual Classroom Instructions in the
PowerPrep DVD/Internet/iApp for English Grammar

<u>Virtual Classroom</u>

Part 10: Review

FINAL REVIEW

☑ Understanding the direction ahead of time will prove a to be a valuable time saver on the test.
☑ Once you can identify ways to "fix the sentence", you will have the upper hand on the test.
☑ Those that construct the test stick to the basic rules, and don't implement controversial grammar rules.
☑ The "best" answer may not sound correct to you.
☑ The test relies on your understanding of English grammar and not solely on your ear.
☑ Understand the difference between standard English and the English that the test will measure.
☑ The importance of oversimplification
☑ Use the process of elimination (POE) to locate the correct answer, and the incorrect choices.
☑ "2 OUT OF 5" RULE Process of Elimination (POE)
☑ The "Big Six" of Sentence Completion Tests
    1. Pronoun Errors
    2. Subject-Verb Agreement
    3. Misplaced Modifiers
    4. Faulty Parallelism
    5. Faulty Verb Tense
    6. Faulty Idiom and Usage

Parts of Speech

• Noun (person, place, thing, idea)

• Pronoun (a word used in place of a noun)

• Verb (a word or group of words that express action or being)

• Adjective (a word that modifies a noun or pronoun)

• Adverb (a word that modifies the meaning of a verb, adjective, or another adverb)

• Preposition (a word that connects a noun or pronoun to another word in the sentence)

• Conjunction (a word that joins words, phrases, or clauses)

• Interjection (a word or group of words that express surprise, anger, pleasure or another emotion)

<u>**Note**</u>: **A word can belong to more than one part of speech**

Clauses and Phrases

Clauses   Main and subordinate   Phrases

Part of a Sentence

Definition: a group of words with a subject and a verb
Declarative, interrogative, or exclamatory
Simple, compound, complex, compound-complex
Parts of a sentence (subject, verb, complement)
Subject (a word or group of words) that tells who or what is being talked about)
Subject can be a noun, pronoun, verbal, phrase, or clause
Verb (tells what the subject does)
3 kinds of verbs (transitive, intransitive, and linking)

Verbs

Five characteristics of every verb are number, person, tense, mood, voice, and complement.
Four ways a complement maybe used in a sentence (direct object, indirect object, predicate noun, predicate adjective)

Nouns and Pronouns

Nouns (proper, common, collective, concrete, and abstract)
Proper Nouns: Common (names a general sort of person, place or thing)
Collective (names a group of individuals)
Concrete (names any material object that is inanimate)
Abstract (names a quality, state, or idea)
Personal pronoun stands for the speaker, the person spoke to or the person or thing spoken about.
Relative Pronouns (whom, which, what, that)
Interrogative pronoun (asks a question)
Indefinite pronoun (refers to a number of persons, places, or things in general)
Demonstrative pronoun (points out a specific person or thing)
Reflexive pronoun (refers back to the noun it stands for)

Three characteristics of nouns and pronouns (gender, number, case)
Gender (indicates sex—masculine, feminine, or neuter)
Number (indicates whether one or more)
Case (shows how the noun or pronoun is used in the sentence): Subjective case, Objective case
Nominative case, Possessive case
Appositive (a noun or pronoun usually placed next to another noun or pronoun to rename it)

Subject-Verb Relationship

A verb must agree with its subject in number and in person
Collective nouns are followed by a singular or plural verbs according to the sense of the sentence.
Some indefinite pronouns are always singular in meaning
Some indefinite pronouns are always plural in meaning
A verb should be singular if its subject has "every" or Many a" just before it.
Some indefinite pronouns maybe singular or plural.
When singular subjects are joined by "or" or "nor" the subject is considered singular
When a singular and one plural subject are joined by 'or" or 'nor" the subject closer to the verb determines the number of the verb
When the subjects joined by "or" or "nor" are of different persons, the subject nearer the verb determines the person.
Even if the verb comes before the subject, the verb agrees with the true subject in number and person

Tense

Tense specifies the moment of an action or condition
Six tenses (present, past, future, present perfect, past perfect, and future perfect)
All six tenses may be expressed in a progressive form by adding a present participle of a verb to the appropriate form of "to be" Principal parts of irregular verbs

Present Tense	Past Tense	Past Participle	Present Participle
Eat	ate	eaten	eating
Begin	began	begun	beginning
Blow	blew	blown	blowing

Verbals

A verbal is a word formed from a verb. 3 kinds of verbals (gerunds, participles, and infinitives). Gerund acts like a noun, ends in "ing". Participle acts like an adjective (present participle ends in "ing", past participle usually ends in "d", "ed", "t", "n", or "en"
Infinitive is used as a noun or adjective or an adverb. Gerunds can be present or perfect. Participles may be present, past, or perfect. Infinitives may be present or perfect

Mood and Voice

Mood (indicative, imperative, subjunctive), Indicative, Imperative, Subjunctive (a wish or condition that is not real)
Voice (active or passive), Active (indicates the subject performs the action), Passive (indicates that something is being done to the subject), Transitive verbs can be used as passive or active

Modifiers (Adjectives, adjective phrases and clauses)

Modifiers (adds information to another word in the sentence), Modifiers can be a word, phrase, or a clause
Adjectives modify nouns, Articles, Single adjectives and compound adjectives, Multiple modifiers
Three degrees of comparison (positive, comparative, and superlative)

Positive	Comparative	Superlative
good	better	best
bad	worse	worst
little	less, lesser	least

Dangling modifiers (account for both items in the comparison)
Infinitives, infinitive phrases, participles, and participial phrases as adjectives
Infinitive and participial phrases must refer logically and grammatically to the subject
Infinitive and participial phrases as dangling modifiers
Prepositional phrases as adjectives
Subordinate clauses as adjectives
Restrictive and nonrestrictive clauses
"whose" is the possessive form for the pronoun "who" "which" and "that"
> The big yellow canary whose feathers were falling out could no longer fly
> The twin boy whose hair is the same color as his twin reads advanced novels.
> The president, whose wife is a libranrian, will miss the next election.
> the DVD whose packaging is damaged is not listed on the inventory.

A word, phrase, or clause should be placed as close as possible to the word it modifies
Misplaced modifiers
Wrong: The injured player went to the doctor with crutches.
Correct: The injured player with crutches went to the doctor.
Squinting modifiers (misplaced so you cannot tell if the word, phrase, or clause modifies the words before or after the modifier.
Wrong: Billy said today he would wash the windows.
Either of the following is correct: Today Billy said he would wash the windows. **OR** Billy said he would wash the windows today.

Modifiers (adverbs, adverbial phrases and clauses)

Above	fast	only	better	first
slow	cheap	hard	well	deep
long	early	much		

Adverbs modify verbs, adjectives, and adverbs. The five kinds of adverbs are signified by the question they answer (How, When, Where, How much, Why).
Words that can be adjectives or adverbs depending on use:
Bad or badly, sweet or sweetly (adverb or predicate adjective)

Adverbs hardly, scarcely, only, barely, should not be used with a negative
Correct: Frank has hardly begun working. **Incorrect**: Frank has not hardly begun working.
Correct: Rafael and I have scarcely see each other in the last year. **Incorrect**: Rafael and I have not scarcely seen each other in the last year.
Adverbs may show greater or lesser degrees of its characteristic quality.
> Doug arrived late
> Diane arrived later than David
> Oscar arrived latest of all.

The positive, comparative, and superlative degree, An infinitive or infinitive phrase can be used as an adverb.
A prepositional phrase may be used as an adverb. A subordinate clause may be used as an adverb. An adverb or adverbial phrase should be placed as close as possible to the word it modifies. An adverbial clause may be placed anywhere in the sentence, but they should be placed so that only one meaning is possible.

Connectives

A connective joins one part of the sentence to another. A connective may be a preposition, a conjunction, an adverb or a pronoun.
Prepositions as connectives
A preposition joins a noun or pronoun to the rest of the sentence. **Common prepositional idioms:** Absolve from liability, abstain from rowdy behavior, accede to a demand, accommodate to a request, accompanied by an escort (a person),

accompanied with laughter (a thing), account for one's actions, account to one's boss, acquit of an allegation, adapted to the surroundings, Wait at the gym (a place), wait for your brother (a person), worthy of praise

Prepositions can be overused (don't end a sentence with a preposition) **correct**: Where is your sister? **Incorrect**: Where is your sister at? **Correct**: Where are you going? **Incorrect**: Where are you going to? **Correct**: David started to swim. **Incorrect**: David started in swimming.

Conjunctions as connectives, Conjunctions are coordinate, correlative, or subordinate, Coordinate conjunctions Correlative conjunctions (neither, nor....not neither, or) either…or, neither…nor, not only…but also, both…and, if…then, since…therefore, Conjunctive adverbs, Parallelism, Connection elements of unequal rank

PAMS PAL TIM

<u>P</u>ronoun, <u>A</u>greement, <u>M</u>odifier<u>S</u>, Par<u>AL</u>lelism, <u>T</u>ense, <u>I</u>diom, <u>M</u>echanics

1. **PRONOUN Errors are located**
   A. Antecedent problems
   B. Singular and plural agreement
   C. 1st, 2nd, and 3rd person consistent

2. **Subject-Verb AGREEMENT is checked**
   A. Agreement in both number and person
   B. Eliminate phrases and clauses

3. **Misplaced MODIFIERS correctly identified**
   A. Modifiers placed close to noun and verb
   B. If modifier begins a sentence, modifies noun

4. **Observe Faulty PARALLELISM**
   A. Similar elements must be in similar form
   B. Two adjectives modifying same noun need to be in same form

5. **Locate Faulty Verb TENSE**
   A. Present, Past, Past Participle, Present Participle are consistent
   B. Active and Passive Voice

6. **Faulty IDIOM and Usage**
   A. Analysis of usage
   B. Know the key phrases and words

7. **MECHANICS and Meaning need to repair**
   A. Syntax errors
   B. Wordiness
   C. Run-on sentences
   D. Fragments
   E. Sentence logic

CONGRATULATIONS!!

You Have Completed The Grammar Study Guide.

Take A Break Before Moving On To The Drills.

Big Book of Grammar Index

Vocabulary Study Guide
Table of Contents

This material corresponds to the Vocabulary Workshop Section in the
PowerPrep DVD/Internet/iApp

Vocabulary Workshop

Vocabulary Study Guide

Part 1: Introduction

Vocabulary Workshop>Introduction
This material corresponds to the Vocabulary Workshop in the
PowerPrep DVD/Internet/iApp

Vocabulary Workshop

Important Abbreviations
These abbreviations are used throughout the program

POE: Process of Elimination
SARR: Synthesize, Analyze, Reduce, and Restate (has to do with Logical Reasoning)
AC: Answer Choice
QS: Question Stem
LOD: Level of Difficulty

Example Question: What is the least common multiple of 3, 4, and 7? **(This is the call of the question or Question Stem "QS")**

These are Answer Choices "AC" A, B, C, D, E

   (A)   12
   (B)   21
   (C)   28
   (D)   48
   (E)   84

Part 1: Introduction

OVERVIEW

Having a strong grasp of vocabulary is an essential factor in performing well in any written or verbal task you may have. Whether it's a test you must take, a speech you must give, an assignment you wish to perform well on, or to improve your reading, understanding words and increasing your vocabulary will help you feel more confident and help you to be more successful.

First, you must realize that you *already* know more than you may think you do, and that you *can* learn what you need! This workshop is designed to help you do just that by studying vocabulary through word "cells". Most words in the English language can be broken down into parts, and those various parts have their own meanings. You probably learned these in elementary school as prefixes, roots and suffixes, but we are going to refer to all of them here as simply word "cells." You will discover not only the meaning of these individual cells, but also how knowing just one part of a word can help you come to understand its general meaning.

You will be given some overall suggestions of things you can do throughout your day to improve your personal vocabulary, and then we will practice some specific strategies together as we tackle some vocabulary drills.

Your **Student Study Guide** follows the video, so it will be most helpful to you if you have it open in front of you as you view the video. This guide will be used in various ways.
1. It has the outline of everything in the video.
2. It has places for you to take notes during the video.
3. It has activities and check tests for you to complete. When you reach a check test, pause the video and complete the check test. When you return, we will review the correct answers together.
4. It contains a Word Cell Builder at the end. Since it is not possible for us to cover every word cell during this video (well, it is possible but you would not want to sit here for that long!) additional cells and words are listed in the Word Cell Builder.

You may pause this video at any time if you need a break.

GENERAL SUGGESTIONS

In addition to studying words as we are doing here, there *are* some overall suggestions for you to help increase your vocabulary. These are things that you can be doing at any time, and really could be doing all the time.

In order for a word to be "yours", you must use it repeatedly. Only then will you feel that you know it well enough to recognize it and understand its general meaning. The suggestions I am about to give you will help you in this task.

Read

One of the most important things you can do to improve your vocabulary is to READ as much as you possibly can. You should especially try to read those things that are a bit of a challenge for you and which force you to think, and specifically publications which use the type of vocabulary you are likely to encounter tests or wish to use in your speech and writing.

For example, publications such as the Wall Street Journal and the New York Times contain high level reading, and you can even read them online! Since much of what we do now, from taking tests to conducting research and doing our own writing, is done online, it is good practice to read longer, more difficult articles *online*. You can access both the Wall Street Journal and the New York Times from the URLs listed in your study guide.

Of course these aren't the only publications you should read, and a computer screen does not compare with curling up on the couch or reading in the bathtub, but they are just a couple which consistently use a higher level vocabulary. **The MOST important thing is to READ.**

Use a Dictionary

As you are reading (*any* material, not just the New York Times or Wall Street Journal) and you come across a word that is unfamiliar to you, do NOT skip it; instead, *write it down*. Or, when you are listening to a lecture and the speaker uses a word you don't know, *write it down!*

Take the time to stop and look these words up in the dictionary. And, don't stop with the first definition in the list. A good dictionary will list several meanings, give the etymology or the history of the word, and list synonyms and antonyms. Pay special attention to the synonyms or antonyms. Write them down. Keep your own personal vocabulary list. At some point in your education, you probably had a teacher who told you to do this, and you may or may not have followed that advice. It was good advice then and it is good advice now! **Try it—you just might like it.**

This may sound like a lot of work, but it will pay off. There seems to be this interesting phenomenon about a new word: once you start to recognize a word, and especially when you look it up, it seems as if you begin to see it frequently.

For example, I often come across words that are new to me as I do crossword puzzles. Once I get the clue, and I must admit I sometimes cheat a bit by using a Crossword Puzzle dictionary or even looking up the answer, then it seems to me I suddenly see that or hear that word repeated several times in the next week. It makes me much more cognizant, or conscious, of the words I see and hear.

Think about Words!

Once we begin to study the way words are put together and you become familiar with the meanings of different cells, make a conscious effort to *think* about words as you come across them. You can do this when you are reading, when you hear them in conversation, or when you hear them over the radio or on television.   Playing a trivia game or doing a crossword puzzle is also a great way to practice your knowledge of word meanings.   The key is to make a conscious effort to think about "new" words you see or hear.   A few seconds ago, I used the word cognizant. If you don't recognize that word, by the end of this video you should be able to figure out it means.

Ask yourself: Can I explain what that word means? If not,   What "cells" can I identify in that word?

Make Flash Cards

Another useful tool is to make flash cards. You have probably not used flash cards since elementary school, but they are a really good way for you to practice new word cells. Put cells you want to practice on flash cards and carry them with you. (A perfect time to pull them out and use them is when you are waiting in lines!)

Do it this way: Put one word cell and one definition on opposite sides of a card. Make the definition simple and concise and something you will remember. In addition, put several words that use that cell on the card. There is an example in your study guide, so let's refer to that now.

AQUA **AQU**	**WATER** Aqueduct, Aqua-lung Aquarium, Aquatic

Make as many cards as you need; just the process of making the cards alone is a useful study technique since you are writing down the cells, their definitions and words which use them.

Carry only 5 or 6 cards with you at a time. Never go through the whole stack at one time—you will become overwhelmed. It is much better to break it into small chunks.

Once you have learned a word cell (or word cells) replace it with another. That way you will constantly have a small, new group of cards to work with.

Use your knowledge of other languages

Many of our words come to us from other languages. If you speak French you may recognize the word *bibliotheque,* or if you speak Spanish the word *biblioteca;* this is the word in both languages for a library, the place of books.   In English, the words that have to do with books, such as bibliography and bibliophile, begin the same way: biblio.

 Don't be afraid to use your knowledge of other languages to help you understand words in English since so many of our words are derived from those languages. Some other examples: dormir (Spanish for *to sleep)* and dormitory (English for *a place to sleep);* amor (Spanish for *to love)* and amorous (English for *full of love).*

This works, of course, because so much of the English language comes to us from other languages. It comes to us from what are called the Romance languages: French, Spanish and Italian…so called because they all have roots in Latin which is of course Roman. Also, much of our language comes to us from Greek. However, where a word comes from is NOT really important. What is important is to try to find a part or parts of a new word that you already recognize.

The point of this is to use everything you know about words and their origins to help you with vocabulary. It's a very fair way to play the language game!

REVIEW OF GENERAL SUGGESTIONS

✐ **Read**
  ☐ Read as much as you can.
  ☐ Read material that will challenge your vocabulary.
  ☐ Read lengthy material online:
  ☐ Wall Street Journal: http://interactive.wsj.com/ushome.html
  ☐ New York Times: http://www.nytimes.com/

✐ **Use a Dictionary**
  ☐ Look up words you don't know.
  ☐ Write down the definition.
  ☐ Note synonyms and antonyms.
  ☐ Make your own personal word list.

✐ **Think about Words!**
  ☐ Pay attention to the words around you. Make a conscious effort to try to dissect words into their parts and then see if you can define those word parts.
  ☐ Ask yourself:
  ☐ Can I explain what that word means?
  ☐ Can I identify the "cells" in the word?

✎ **Make Flash Cards**
  ☐ Put one word cell and one definition on opposite sides of a card.
  ☐ Put several words that use that cell on the card.
  ☐ Make as many cards as you need.
  ☐ Carry only 5 or 6 cards with you at a time.
  ☐ Once you have learned a word cell (or word cells) replace the card or cards with new ones.
  ☐ Sample card:

AQUA **AQU**	**WATER** Aqueduct, Aqua-lung Aquarium, Aquatic

✎ **Use your knowledge of other languages**
  ☐ If you know another language such as French or Spanish, use what you know about words in that language to help build your vocabulary in English!

SPECIFIC SUGGESTIONS

Now that you have some general suggestions for studying and remembering words, we are going to discuss some specific strategies you can use to help learn those words. The most important one is to learn the basic parts of words, that is: prefixes, roots, and suffixes. We will refer to all three of these as word cells.

As we study these cells, you will realize that you already know many of them and just may not have put them into quite this framework. We will study cells and their definitions and we will group them together in clusters so you can learn to recognize the general meaning of a word by thinking about other, similar words.

Word Cells

Let's use the AQUA example that we used on the sample flash card and put it together with the other cells in those sample words:

An aquarium is a place with water: Aqua means *water*, -arium means *a place*. "He keeps a huge aquarium in his living room."
An **aqua duct (**aqueduct**)** is a conduit for flowing water: Aqua, of course, means *water*, and -duct *means to carry*.
"The aqua duct (aqueduct) carried water from the Colorado River to Phoenix, Arizona."
Aquatic--having to do with water: Aqua, *water*, and –ic means *having to do with*. "Sea lions and dolphins are aquatic animals."

So, you see, it really is all very logical. Of course, not all words break down this easily, but if you can learn some basic cells, you can usually figure out the general meaning of most words.

Let's try another one:
A **bibliography** is a *written* list of sources (and originally all the sources in a bibliography were books—now we list many, many other types of sources in our bibliographies!). **Biblio** means *books*; **graphy** means *writing*. The Christian Bible is also known as The Book.
A **bibliophile** is someone who loves books. **Biblio**, of course, is *book*; **phile** means *to love*.
As you see, if you can recognize at least one part, or cell, of a word, you will have a very good chance at being able to figure out a meaning for the word. It may not be the exact meaning, but it will be enough for you to successfully answer a test question.

For example: If you know the words *synchronize* (to set the same time) and *chronological* (to put in time order), then you can figure out that *chronometer* is also going to have something to do with time (in this case, the measurement of time).

Clusters

This brings us to our next strategy which is to learn words in clusters. As we study the cells, we will do so in clusters because it will help you remember them more easily. We will study, for example, number cells, such as uni, bi, di, tri, quad, pent, penta, sexta, septa, oct, octa, non, nona, deca, cent and words which use them. Then we will move on to Body Parts, Measurements, Actions, Emotions and Qualities, and Things.

Vocabulary Lessons

As we begin the lessons to help you learn the word cells, you need to realize that it is not as important to know whether a cell is a prefix, a root, or a suffix as it is to be able to affix a meaning to that cell.

Each of the lessons corresponds with your Study Guide. We will discuss the word cells in each lesson, do some practice activities together, and then you will pause the video and do some check tests on your own. Once you have completed a section, we will discuss the correct answers. We will repeat this for all of the lesson activities.

Many word cells have more than one *spelling* (remember the AQUA and AQU example?), but they are close enough that you should have no problem recognizing them.

Your study guide also includes a Word Cell Builder with over 800 words and cells and their definitions.

Let's get started.

Vocabulary Study Guide

Lesson 1: Numbers

Vocabulary Workshop>Numbers

This material corresponds to the Vocabulary Workshop in the
PowerPrep DVD/Internet/iApp

Vocabulary Workshop

Important Abbreviations
These abbreviations are used throughout the program

POE: Process of Elimination
SARR: Synthesize, Analyze, Reduce, and Restate (has to do with Logical Reasoning)
AC: Answer Choice
QS: Question Stem
LOD: Level of Difficulty

Example Question: What is the least common multiple of 3, 4, and 7? **(This is the call of the question or Question Stem "QS")**

These are Answer Choices "AC" A, B, C, D, E

   (A)   12
   (B)   21
   (C)   28
   (D)   48
   (E)   84

Lesson 1: Numbers

WORD CELL BUILDER FOR: NUMBERS

One
Unicycle
Unicorn
Unilateral
Unilingual
Unipod

Write the correct number for each cell as you hear it read on the video or find the definition for each word in the information provided below in the section called **"Number Cells Vocabulary and Definitions"**

Uni means one. You know that all of these mean "one" of something: A **unicycle** has one-wheel, a **unicorn** has one horn, **Unify** means to "make as one"; **unilateral** is one-sided, **unilingual** means one language, and **unipod** means one leg.

Now, use what you know about those words to help you understand some other cells: If you know that to UniFY is to get people to come together as one, and uni means one, then –fy must mean *to make*! Hold onto that, even write it down…fy is to make, because you will see it on other words and it will help you figure out what they mean as well.

Let's look at a couple more: *Bi is Two, and Tri is three.* We can add these number cells to some of the same cells as we did with Uni.

Two	Three
Bicycle	Tricycle
Bicorn	Tricorn (remember the hats worn by men during Colonial days? With the three corners? They are called tricorn hats.)
Bilateral	Trilateral (usually used to refer to the number of "sides" or parties in an agreement)
Bilingual	Trilingual
Bipod	Tripod (as in a chair or a camera stand)

We will now learn various cells using numbers as the main cluster. This cluster covers a broad range of words.

Cells You Should Know:

Write the correct meaning for each cell as you hear it on the video or find the definition for each cell in the information provided below in the section called: *Number Cells Vocabulary and Definitions*

Important Number Cells

Cells	Meaning
1. Uni, mono	
2. Bi, di, dich	
3. Tri, ter	
4. Quad, quadr, quadru, quart, tetr	
5. Pent, penta, quint, quintu	
6. Sex, sexta	
7. Sept, septa	
8. Oct, Octo	
9. Non, Novem	
10. Dec, deca	
11. Cent, centa	

Answers: Important "Number" Cells

Cells	Meaning
1. Uni, mono	one
2. Bi, di, dich	two
3. Tri, ter	three
4. Quad, quadr, quadru, quart, tetr	four
5. Pent, penta, quint, quintu	five
6. Sex, sexta	six
7. Sept, septa	seven
8. Oct, Octo	eight
9. Non, Novem	nine
10. Dec, deca	ten
11. Cent, centa	hundred

That one should have been pretty simple. Let's go over the answers and see how you did:
Of course these are not the only cells which indicate Numbers. However, these are among the most common.

Now let's look at *words* with these cells to determine the meaning of the words as well as the meaning of other cells in the words. As we go through these words, you might want to use the chart to jot down the meaning of the different cells.

Knowledge
Freedom to Learn

NUMBER CELLS VOCABULARY AND DEFINITIONS

Now let's look at *words* with those cells to determine the meaning of the words as well as the meaning of other cells in the words. As we go through these words, you might want to use the to jot down the meaning of the different cells. There is a chart for this called Additional Cells added to Number Words.

You are probably familiar with people who compete in various events such as the **Biathlon, triathlon, pentathlon, decathlon:** these are competitions with 2 (bi), 3 (tri), 5 (penta) and 10 (deca) athletic events. If we take off the number, then we can deduce that **Athlon** means athletic event. You will see in the chart where Athletic Event is written in for you. Continue filling in the chart for the other cells as we go over them.

Monogamy means married to one person, **bigamy** means married to two people, polygamy means married to many people. *Gamy*, then, means marriage

Quadrant, quarantine, quaternary: all of these words have to do with "four."

Quadrant: one part of four (as in Look in Quadrant 3).

Quarantine: to isolate (originally, period of quarantine was 40 days)

Quaternary: pertaining to the number four

If **quaternary** is "pertaining to" the number four, then *ary* is pertaining to (or having to do with).

Therefore, **binary** is….pertaining to the number 2 (binary code is made of two numbers, a Zero and a One)

Tertiary is…pertaining to the number three. (Brown is a tertiary color—it is made by mixing two other colors).

Di-chothomy is to have been cut into two parts. *Tom* is to cut.

Bi-sect is to cut into two parts. *Sect* is to cut.
You will find that sometimes two cells share the same meaning, as tom and sect do here. Although that can be a little confusing at first, don't let it throw you—it's just an opportunity to know more words!

Decimate is to, literally, cut 1 of every 10. It has now come to mean to totally destroy…as in, The army was decimated.

Triplets, quintuplets, septuplets…you have a part of three, a part of five, a part of seven. *Plet*, then, is "a part of"

Quintessence is the pure essence of something or the perfect example of something. Originally, however, it meant the *fifth* essence. (air, fire, earth and water were the first four, and the fifth, or quintessence, was ether) which is why it has Quint in it. Essence itself means basic or simple.

Additional Cells added to "Numbers"

Fill in the meaning for each cell as you hear it in the video or read it in the text.

Additional Cells for "Number" Words

Cells	Meaning
athlon	
gamy	
ary	
tom	
sect	
plet	
essence	

Additional Cells Added to "Number" Words. Lets' review the list of Additional Cells added to "Number" Words

Answers

Cells	Meaning
athlon	athletic event
gamy	marriage
ary	of or pertaining to
tom	to cut
sect	to cut
plet	a part of
essence	Basic or simple

CHECK TESTS #1 AND #2

Check Test #1

Match the cells with the correct definitions. You can then check your answers using the answer key below and then return to the video when you are finished and we will review the answers.

Question	Answer Choices
_____ 1. Bi, Di	A. One
_____ 2. Quad	B. Two
_____ 3. Non	C. Three
_____ 4. Septa	D. Four
_____ 5. Dich	E. Five
_____ 6. Pent	F. Six
_____ 7. Ter	G. Seven
_____ 8. Mono	H. Eight
_____ 9. Centa	I. Nine
_____ 10. Deca	J. Ten
_____ 11. Uni	K. Hundred
_____ 12. Oct	
_____ 13. Tri	
_____ 14. Sexta	
_____ 15. Quint	

Answer Key Check Test 1:

1.B 2.D 3.H 4.G 5.B 6.E 7.C 8.A 9.K 10.J 11.A 12.H 13.C 14.F 15.E

Check Test #2

Match the cells with the correct definitions. You can then check your answers using the answer key below and then return to the video when you are finished and we will review the answers.

Question	Answer Choices
_____ 1. athlon	A. pertaining to the number two
_____ 2. bilingual	B. three cornered hat
_____ 3. decimate	C. marriage
_____ 4. tertiary	D. three sided (as in an agreement)
_____ 5. tripod	E. athletic event
_____ 6. tricorn	F. two languages
_____ 7. bilateral	G. of or pertaining to
_____ 8. decathlon	H. a split or cut into two
_____ 9. septuplet	I. to isolate (as for 40 days)
_____ 10. dichotomy	J. pure essence of something
_____ 11. binary	K. married to one person
_____ 12. quarantine	L. a part of
_____ 13. quaternary	M. to destroy (cut 1 of every 10)
_____ 14. monogamy	N. pertaining to the number three
_____ 15. quintessence	O. three legged
_____ 16. plet	P. to cut
_____ 17. tom, sect	Q. pertaining to the number four
_____ 18. ary	R. one (or a part of) of seven
_____ 19. gamy	S. 10 event athletic competition
_____ 20. trilateral	T. two sided (as in an agreement)

Answer Key Check Test #2

1.E 2.F 3.M 4.N 5.O 6.B 7.T 8.S 9.R 10.H 11.A 12.I 13.Q 14.K 15.J 16.L 17.P 18.G 19.C 20.D

Vocabulary Study Guide
Lesson 2: The Body

Vocabulary Workshop>The Body
This material corresponds to the Vocabulary Workshop in the
PowerPrep DVD/Internet/iApp

Vocabulary Workshop

Important Abbreviations
These abbreviations are used throughout the program

POE: Process of Elimination
SARR: Synthesize, Analyze, Reduce, and Restate (has to do with Logical Reasoning)
AC: Answer Choice
QS: Question Stem
LOD: Level of Difficulty

Example Question: What is the least common multiple of 3, 4, and 7? **(This is the call of the question or Question Stem "QS")**

These are Answer Choices "AC" A, B, C, D, E

(A) 12
(B) 21
(C) 28
(D) 48
(E) 84

Lesson 2: The Body

WORD CELL BUILDER FOR: BODY PARTS

We will now learn various cells using the parts of the body as the main cluster. This cluster covers a broad range of words, some you may recognize as more scientific or medical in nature. **Cells You Should Know:** Write the correct meaning for each cell as you hear it on the video or find the definition for each cell in the information provided below in the section called: *Body Part Cells Vocabulary and Definitions*

Important Cells about "The Body"

Cells	Meaning	Words to Know
1. Anthrop		anthropology, misanthrope
2. Bio		biology, bioluminescence, biography
3. Brac		bracelet, brace, embrace
4. Capit, cephal, cap		captain, decapitate, capitulate, encephalitis
5. Card		cardiac, cardio-pulminary, cardiogram
6. Carn		carnivorous, carnal, incarnate
7. carp		carpal, metacarpal
8. Caud		caudal
9. Cerebr		cerebral
10. Corp		corpse, corps, corporeal, incorporate
11. Dent, odont		dentist, dentifrice, orthodontist, periodontist
12. Ling, lang		language, linguistic, bilingual, lingo
13. Lipo		liposuction, lipid, lipoma
14. Man, manu		manual, emancipate, manuscript
15. Nasus		nasal, nostril
16. Oss		ossify
17. Ped, pod		pedestrian, biped, tripod
18. Pulm, pneum		pulmonary, pneumonia
19. Stom		stomach, colostomy

Answers: Important "Body Parts" Cells

Cells	Meaning	Words to Know
1. Anthrop	Human	anthropology, misanthrope
2. Bio	Life	biology, bioluminescence, biography
3. Brac	Arm	bracelet, brace, embrace
4. Capit, cephal, cap	Head	captain, decapitate, capitulate, encephalitis
5. Card	Heart	cardiac, cardio-pulminary, cardiogram
6. Carn	Flesh	carnivorous, carnal, incarnate
7. carp	Wrist	carpal, metacarpal
8. Caud	Tail	caudal
9. Cerebr	Brain	cerebral
10. Corp	Body	corpse, corps, corporeal, incorporate
11. Dent, odont	Teeth	dentist, dentifrice, orthodontist, periodontist
12. Ling, lang	Tongue	language, linguistic, bilingual, lingo
13. Lipo	Fat	liposuction, lipid, lipoma
14. Man, manu	Hand	manual, emancipate, manuscript
15. Nasus	Nose	nasal, nostril
16. Oss	Bone	ossify
17. Ped, pod	Foot, leg	pedestrian, biped, tripod
18. Pulm, pneum	Lung	pulmonary, pneumonia
19. Stom	Mouth	stomach, colostomy

Of course these are not the only cells which indicate Body Parts. However, these are among the most common.
Now let's look at *words* with these cells to determine the meaning of the words as well as the meaning of other cells in the words. As we go through these words, you might want to use the chart to jot down the meaning of the different cells.

BODY PART CELLS VOCABULARY AND DEFINITIONS

Anthropology is the study of the human race. Anthrop is human, and ology is study of. On your Additional Cells added to Body Parts, you should have "study of" as the definition for ology.

Anthropomorphic means in human form. Therefore, if Anthrop is human, then Morph means form. Other words with Morph: **morhpology** (study of how things are formed); **amorphous** (without—A—form or shape).

A **Misanthrope** is someone who hates mankind. "Mis" is to hate. It can also mean bad or badly. Another example of a cell with two meanings. Mis it to hate AND it means bad or badly. Other words with Mis: **misogyny** (hating women); **misinform** (badly informed).

Biology is the study or science of life. Logy, then, is science or study of. **Bioluminescence** is the production of light (lum) by living organisms. A **Biography** is the writing or story of someone's life. **Graphy** is the writing of.

Embrace means to put your arms around or to accept, but literally it means to "put into" (em) arms.

A **Captain** is the one who (an) is the "head" or person in charge. To **Decapitate** means to cut off (de) or take away the head. To **Capitulate** is to give in to someone else (literally, the head).

Any time the word **Cardiac** (ic—of or pertaining to) is used it is referring to the heart such as in cardiac arrest and cardiac unit. **Cardiopulmonary** is that which pertains to (ary—as we had in lesson one) the heart and lungs together.

Another cell for lungs is **pneu** as in **Pneumonia**, which is an inflammation of the lungs. However, **pneu** literally means "air" and is used for words such as **Pneumatic**, which means pertaining to (ic) air. A **pneumatic** drill for example, works by the force of air.

Carnivorous means one who (ous) eats (vor) meat or "flesh". **Carnal** means having to do with the body or the flesh; **Incarnate** means "in" or "into" the flesh as in "the devil incarnate"—which means the devil has taken on a human form.

Anything **Carpal** means having to with, or pertaining to (al), the wrist as in "carpal tunnel syndrome" which is a wrist injury; **Metacarpal** means beyond (meta) the wrist, as in the metacarpal part of the hand. This is the part of the hand "beyond" the wrist and before the fingers.

A **Corpse** is a dead body and a Corps is a body of people as in the **Marine Corps**. **Corporeal** means having to do with or pertaining to (that al again) the human body; and **Incorporate** means to make (ate) into (in) one body (corp). When you incorporate a town, for example, you take various neighborhoods and communities and make them one.

A **Dentist** is one who (ist) works with teeth, an *Orthodontist* is one who (ist) makes teeth straight (ortho), and a **Periodontist** is one who (ist) works with the area around (peri) the teeth—usually referred to as the gums. All of these will suggest you regularly use a **Dentifrice** which literally means to rub (fric) the teeth, but which we commonly refer to as toothpaste.

The words related to language come from the cells **langu** or **lingu**: **Linguistic** means of or pertaining to (ic) **language** and **Bilingual** means having two languages. **Lingo** refers to the words of a particular language, such as a foreign language or a specialized language. For example, there is a whole "language" unique to computer users or to certain sports.

While **lipo** (which means fat) is not technically a body term, it is certainly associated with the body. **Liposuction**, for example, means literally to suction fat out of the body. A **Lipid** is something related to (id) fat (lipo) such as an organism that is soluble in a fat solvent. A **Lipoma** is a fatty growth or tumor (oma).

Manual means pertaining to (al) the hand. **Emancipate**, which is to free, can be broken down into take away (e) from that which is holding or seizing (cip) the hand (man). A **Manuscript** means written (script) by hand.

To **Ossify** means to make (fy) like a bone.

A **Pedestrian** is one who (ian) uses the feet. It is commonly used, of course, to refer to the people who are walking, but it also means people who are simple or behind. A **biped** is a two footed creature and a tripod is something with three legs.

The last body part is **stom**, which literally means mouth or *opening*. A **Colostomy** is an opening (stom) to the colon. We are most familiar with the term **Stomach**, which is actually called that because it is an *opening* in the alimentary canal!

Additional Cells added to "Body Parts"

Fill in the meaning for each cell as you hear it in the video or read it in the text.

Cells	Meaning
ology	
morph	
a	
mis	
mis	
bio	
logy	
graphy	
lum	
em	
an	
de	
ic	
pulm	
pneu	
ous	
vor	
in	
al	
meta	
ate	
ist	
ortho	
peri	
fric	
id	
oma	
e	

cip	
script	
fy	
ian	

Let's review the list of Additional Cells added to the "Body Parts"   Answers: Additional Cells "The Body Parts"

Cells	Meaning
ology	study of
morph	form
a	without
mis	hate
mis	bad, badly
bio	life
logy	study or science of
graphy	Writing of
lum	Light
em	Put into
an	One who
de	Cut off or take away
ic	Of or pertaining to
Lungs	Air
ous	One who

Cells (2)	Meaning (2)
vor	Eats
in	In, into
meta	Of or pertaining to
al	Beyond
ate	To make
ist	One who
ortho	Straight
peri	Around
fric	Rub
id	Related to
oma	Tumor
e	Take away from
cip	Seize or hold
script	Written
fy	To make
ian	One who

CHECK TESTS #3 AND #4

Match the cells with the correct definitions. check your answers using the answer key below then return to the video and we will review the answers.

Test 3 Questions	Answer Choices
_____ 1. dent, odont	A. form
_____ 2. ling, lang	B. written or writing
_____ 3. capit, cephal, cap	C. study, science of
_____ 4. anthrop	D. take away from
_____ 5. lum	E. one who
_____ 6. logy	F. air
_____ 7. lipo	G. of or pertaining to
_____ 8. morph	H. around
_____ 9. ic, al	I. beyond
_____ 10. ortho	J. light
_____ 11. oma	K. language
_____ 12. peri	L. seize or hold
_____ 13. meta	M. teeth
_____ 14. ian, ist, an, ous	N. human
_____ 15. em	O. head
_____ 16. mis	P. straight
_____ 17. cip	Q. tumor
_____ 18. script, graphy	R. put into
_____ 19. e, de	S. hate or bad, badly
_____ 20. pneu	T. fat

Test 4 Questions	Answer Choices
_____ 1. Anthropology	A. in the flesh
_____ 2. Anthropomorphic	B. pertaining to human form
_____ 3. Misanthrope	C. one who straightens teeth
_____ 4. Embrace	D. put your arms around, accept
_____ 5. Decapitate	E. fatty tumor
_____ 6. Cardiopulmonary	F. break away from that which is seizing
_____ 7. Lipoma	G. someone who hates human race
_____ 8. Incarnate	H. study of human race
_____ 9. Metacarpal	I. to rub the teeth (toothpaste)
_____ 10. Corporeal	J. opening in the colon
_____ 11. Dentifrice	K. cut the head off
_____ 12. Orthodontist	L. one who uses the feet; simple
_____ 13. Emancipate	M. pertaining to the human body
_____ 14. Pedestrian	N. beyond the wrist
_____ 15. Colostomy	O. related to heart and lungs together

Answer Key Check Test #3

1.M **2.**K **3.**O **4.**N **5.**J **6.**C **7.**T **8.**A **9.**G **10.**P **11.**Q **12.**H **13.**I **14.**E **15.**R **16.**S **17.**L **18.**B **19.**D **20.**F

Answer Key Check Test #4

1 H **2** B **3** G **4** D **5** K **6** O **7** E **8** A **9** N **10** M **11** I **12** C **13** F **14** L **15** J

Vocabulary Study Guide
Lesson 3: Measurements, Time, and Locations

Vocabulary Workshop>Measurements, Time, Locations

This material corresponds to the Vocabulary Workshop in the
PowerPrep DVD/Internet/iApp

Vocabulary Workshop

Important Abbreviations
These abbreviations are used throughout the program

POE:	Process of Elimination
SARR:	Synthesize, Analyze, Reduce, and Restate (has to do with Logical Reasoning)
AC:	Answer Choice
QS:	Question Stem
LOD:	Level of Difficulty

Example Question: What is the least common multiple of 3, 4, and 7? (**This is the call of the question or Question Stem "QS"**)

These are Answer Choices "AC" A, B, C, D, E

  (A)   12
  (B)   21
  (C)   28
  (D)   48
  (E)   84

Lesson 3: Measurements, Time, Locations

WORD CELL BUILDER FOR: MEASUREMENTS, TIME AND LOCATIONS

We will now learn various cells using measurement, time and location as the main cluster

Cells You Should Know: Write the correct meaning for each cell as you hear it on the video or find the definition for each cell in the information provided below in the section called: *Measurement, Time and Locations, Cells Vocabulary and Definitions*

Important Cells about "Measurement, Time and Locations"

Cells	Meaning	Words to Know
Ab, a		Abnormal, abrogate, abscond
Ann, enn		Annual, annuity, biennial, perennial
Ante, pre		Anticipate, antebellum, precede, presage, prescient
Anti, ant, ob		Antithesis, antipathy, antonym, obstruct
Chron		Chronology, chronic, anachronism
Circum		Circumference, circumnavigate, circumscribe, circumspect
Di, diurn		Diary, diurnal
Intra, intr		Intravenous, intrastate, intrinsic
Medi, meri		Mediate, intermediary, antemeridian
Meter, mens		Perimeter, commensurate, immense
Omni, Pan		Omnipresent, omnipotent, omnivorous, panoramic, panacea
Peri		Perimeter, periscope, peripatetic
Trans		Transport, translucent, transient

Answers: Important "Measurement, Time, and Location" Cells

Cells	Meaning	Words to Know
Ab, a	From, away, apart	Abnormal, abrogate, abscond
Ann, enn	Year	Annual, annuity, biennial, perennial
Ante, pre	Before	Anticipate, antebellum, precede, presage, prescient
Anti, ant, ob	against	Antithesis, antipathy, antonym, obstruct
Chron	Time	Chronology, chronic, anachronism
Circum	Around	Circumference, circumnavigate, circumscribe, circumspect
Di, diurn	Day	Diary, diurnal
Intra, intr	Within	Intravenous, intrastate, intrinsic
Medi, meri	Middle	Mediate, intermediary, antemeridian
Meter, mens	Measure	Perimeter, commensurate, immense
Omni, Pan	All	Omnipresent, omnipotent, omnivorous, panoramic, panacea
Peri	Around	Perimeter, periscope, peripatetic
Trans	Across, through, over, beyond	Transport, translucent, transient

These are not the only cells which indicate Measurement, Time, and Location. However, these are among the most common.

Now let's look at *words* with these cells to determine the meaning of the words as well as the meaning of other cells in the words. As we go through these words, you might want to use the chart to jot down the meaning of the different cells.

MEASUREMENT, TIME AND LOCATIONS CELLS – VOCABULARY & DEFINITIONS

If something is **Abnormal** it is apart (ab) away from normal. To **Abrogate** is to do away with (again, ab) a law (rogate). When you **Abscond** with something you take off with it; (scond) actually means to stow or hide.

Annuals and **perennials** are both types of flowers, which helps remember the meaning of the words. Annuals flower once in a year, and perennials flower year round. This especially makes sense as **peri** means around, so the word is literally "around the year." If something is **biennial**, it occurs every two years.
Cip, as mentioned in Lesson 1, means to seize. **Anticipate**, then, means to seize or get something before it occurs.

Bellum, as we will see in Lesson 6, means war. Anything that is **Antebellum** is before (ante) the war (bellum). This is generally used to refer to the Civil War.

To **cede** means "to go", so **Precede** means to go before (pre). If you can presage something, you know about it ahead of time—sage, therefore, meaning to know. **Prescient** is similar in meaning, that is "knowing before," but in a more scientific way: (**scient**) means knowledge, so it is having knowledge ahead of time.

Let's look at the cells meaning: against—**anti**, ant, **ob**. The **Antithesis** of something is the exact opposite.

To have **Antipathy** toward something means to have feelings (**pathy**) against it. For example: the student felt *antipathy* toward the test he had to take.

The cell **onym** means word. An **Antonym** is a word that is the opposite of another word; a **synonym** means the same (**syn**).

To **Obstruct** something means to go against it happening; literally it means to be against the structure, which is "to build" so it is to go against the building of something.

If a person is **chronically** late, or you have a **Chronic** pain, that means it happens all the time. **Chronology** is the science or study (ology) of time, and an **Anachronism** is something out of or apart from its own time. (A) is apart; chron time. For example, the people who put on medieval fairs, put on period costumes and hold jousting matches, are often part of the Society for Creative **Anachronism**.

When we measure the distance around a circle, that is the **Circumference**. To travel (nav) around the globe is to **Circumnavigate**. Scribe means to write and **Circumscribe** means to "draw a line around." To be **Circumspect** means to look around, look at all sides, and be cautious. "**Spect**" means to look.

The idea behind a **Diary** is that you write in it every day. It truly means: of or pertaining to (**ary**) the day (**di**). **Diurnal** also means of or pertaining to (al) the day, but it is referring to animals that come out during the day.

Nocturnal (noct being night) animals come out at night.

If you have ever had an IV, you probably know that it stands for **Intravenous**—in your veins. **Intra** (within) and venous (vein). An **Intrastate** highway is an highway that is only within that state. And, of course, every teacher would like students whose motivation is all **Intrinsic**, or coming from within.

When you **Mediate** a problem, you get in the middle. An **Intermediary** is one who (ary) gets within (intr) the middle (medi).

The **Medieval** period is also known as the Middle Ages. And, **AM** and **PM** are abbreviations for **Antemeridian**: that which is (an) ante (before) the meri (middle) of the day (di) AM, and for **Postmeridian**: that which is (an) post (after) the meri (middle) of the day (di) PM.

When you measure around an item, it is the **Perimeter**: peri being *around* and meter being *measure.*

If two things are **Commensurate** with each other, it is because they are within (com) the same measurement. As in: Your findings are *commensurate* with mine.   If what you try to measure is **Immense**, it means it is huge, or it is without (im) measure.

A being that is **Immense** may also be **Omnipresent**…Always (omni) present and even **Omnipotent**…all powerful (potent). This same being may also be **Omnivorous**…one that eats (vor) all things.

When you stand on top of a mountain you can get the **Panoramic** view and see everything: Pan, of course, is All and **orama** is View. You could also get a **Panoramic** view from a **Periscope** because it allows you to look or to (scope) around. Another word with **Peri** is **Peripatetic**. This word refers to Aristotle and his style of teaching because he walked *around* while he taught.

The last set of cells in this cluster is from **Trans**. When you transport an item you carry (port) it across an area. If that item were translucent, it would mean the light (luc) would shine through. And perhaps the one carrying it were a **transient**…that quite literally **translates** to one who is going across.

Additional Cells added to "Measurement, Time and Locations"

Fill in the meaning for each cell as you hear it in the video or read it in the text.

Additional Cells for "Measurement, Time, and Locations" Words

Cells	Meaning
Rogate	
Scond	
Cip	
Bellum	
Cede	
Scient	
Pathy	
Struct	
Onym	
Nav	
Spect	
Venous	
Im	
Com	
Pot	
Orama	
Acea	
Scope	
Luc	

Lets' review the list of Additional Cells added to "Measurement, Time, and Location" Words
Answers: Additional Cells Added to "Measurement, Time, and Location" Words

Cells	Meaning
Rogate	law
Scond	Stow, hide
Cip	Seize
Bellum	War
Cede	To go
Scient	Knowledge
Pathy	Feeling
Struct	Build
Onym	Word
Nav	Travel
Spect	Look
Venous	vein
Im	Without
Com	Within
Pot	Power
Orama	View
Acea	Cure
Scope	Look
luc	light

CHECK TESTS #5 AND #6

Check Test #5

Match the cells with the correct definitions. check your answers using the answer key below then return to the video and we will review the answers.

Test 5 Questions	Answer Choices		Test 6 Questions	Answer Choices
1. ab, a	A. time		1. Abscond	A. coming from within
2. Chron	B. written or writing		2. Annual	B. to draw a line around
3. Anti, ant, ob	C. within		3. Anticipate	C. without measure
4. Ann, enn	D. take away from		4. Antebellum	D. having knowledge ahead of time
5. Circum	E. look		5. Antithesis	E. take off with something
6. Di, diurn	F. light		6. Prescient	F. Aristotle's style of teaching (walking around)
7. Intra, intr	G. view		7. Anachronism	G. into the vein
8. Omni, pan	H. from, away, apart		8. Circumnavigate	H. to seize or get something before it occurs
9. Meter, metr, mens	I. day		9. Circumscribe	I. exact opposite
10. Scond	J. stow, hide		10. Diary	J. something out of its own time
11. Cede	K. all		11. Intravenous	K. to travel around the globe
12. Onym	L. against		12. Intermediary	L. one who gets in the middle of
13. Spect, scope	M. travel		13. Antemeridian	M. to see an entire view
14. Pot	N. to go		14. Precede	N. that which is before the middle of the day
15. Orama	O. power		15. Omnipotent	O. before the war
16. Luc	P. word		16. Immense	P. all powerful
17. Peri	Q. measure		17. Panoramic	Q. once a year
18. Script, graphy	R. middle		18. Peripatetic	R. pertaining to the day
19. Medi, meri	S. around		19. Intrinsic	S. one who is going across
20. Nav	T. year		20. Transient	T. to go before

Answer Key Check Test #5

1.H **2.**A **3.**L **4.**T **5.**S **6.**I **7.**C **8.**K **9.**Q **10.**J **11.**N **12.**P **13.**E **14.**O **15.**G **16.**F **17.**S **18.**B **19.**R **20.**M

Answer Key Check Test #6

1.E **2.**Q **3.**H **4.**O **5.**I **6.**D **7.**J **8.**K **9.**B **10.**R **11.**G **12.**L **13.**N **14.**T **15.**P **16.**C **17.**M **18.**F **19.**A **20.**S

Vocabulary Study Guide

Lesson 4: Actions

Vocabulary Workshop>Actions

This material corresponds to the Vocabulary Workshop in the
PowerPrep DVD/Internet/iApp

Vocabulary Workshop

Important Abbreviations
These abbreviations are used throughout the program

POE: Process of Elimination
SARR: Synthesize, Analyze, Reduce, and Restate (has to do with Logical Reasoning)
AC: Answer Choice
QS: Question Stem
LOD: Level of Difficulty

Example Question: What is the least common multiple of 3, 4, and 7? **(This is the call of the question or Question Stem "QS")**

These are Answer Choices "AC" A, B, C, D, E

  (A) 12
  (B) 21
  (C) 28
  (D) 48
  (E) 84

Lesson 4: Actions

WORD CELL BUILDER FOR: ACTIONS

We will now learn various cells with "actions" as the main cluster.

Cells You Should Know: Write the correct meaning for each cell as you hear it on the video or find the definition for each cell in the information provided below in the section called:
Action Cells – Vocabulary and Definitions

Important Cells about "Action"

Cells	Meaning	Words to Know
Aud		Audio, audience, auditorium, audible
Cide		Suicide, homicide, genocide, herbicide
Cogn, gno		Recognize, ignorant, cognition, incognito
Crac, crat		Democracy, anarchy, theocracy
Cred		Incredible, credit, credulous
Dic, dict		Diction, predict, dictum
Port		Portable, transport, rapport
Rid, ris		Ridiculous, deride, derision
Somn		Insomnia, somnolent, somnambulist
Trem, trep, turb		Tremble, tremor, trepidation, intrepid, turbulent
Vict, vinc		Victory, evict, invincible
Vor		Devour, omnivorous

Answers: Important "Actions" Cells

Cells	Meaning	Words to Know
Aud	Hear	Audio, audience, auditorium, audible
Cide	Kill	Suicide, homicide, genocide, herbicide
Cogn, gno	Know	Recognize, ignorant, cognition, incognito
Crac, crat	Rule, power	Democracy, anarchy, theocracy
Cred	Trust, believe	Incredible, credit, credulous
Dic, dict	Speak	Diction, predict, dictum
Port	Carry	Portable, transport, rapport
Rid, ris	Laugh	Ridiculous, deride, derision
Somn	Sleep	Insomnia, somnolent, somnambulist
Trem, trep, turb	Shake	Tremble, tremor, trepidation, intrepid, turbulent
Vict, vinc	Conquer	Victory, evict, invincible
Vor	Eat	Devour, omnivorous

Of course these are not the only cells which indicate action. However, these are among the most common.

Now let's look at *words* with these cells to determine the meaning of the words as well as the meaning of other cells in the words. As we go through these words, you might want to use the chart to jot down the meaning of the different cells.

ACTION CELLS – VOCABULARY AND DEFINITIONS

A good deal of our language centers on our ability to hear. The cell for hearing is **Aud**. We use the **Audio** button on our stereo and our phone and our television so we can hear. An **Audience** listens to us in an **Auditorium** (a place—orium—for hearing. And if we're lucky, our voice is **Audible**, or able (ible) to be heard when we get up to speak!

Unfortunately there are also many words which use the cell for **Kill**. Suicide means to kill your self (**sui** means self). **Homicide** means to kill a person. Hitler committed **Genocide** because he was trying to kill an entire race (gen). And, if you're trying to get rid of the weeds in your garden, you may have used an **Herbicide**.

When we Recognize an **acquaintance**, it literally means we "know"—cogn—them again (re). If we are Ignorant it means we do not (I) know much. On the other hand, **Cognition** is the state of (tion) knowing. And if we don't want to be recognized, we can travel **Incognito** (in) not, cogn (known).

In the United States we live in a **Democracy**. That means rule or power (crac) by the people (dem). Some people believe in **Anarchy** which is no (A) rule. And yet others believe in a **theocracy**—rule by god (the or theo).
It is Incredible to some people (In—not, ible—able to, and cred—believe) that their credit is no good!

Dic, Dict means to speak; it comes from Word (which is why we have a **dictionary**—a place for words). When we **Predict**, we anticipate what will be said before it is said. A **Dictum** is a final command (um) or final word—an ultimatum.

When something is **Portable** we are able to carry (port) it; it is easier to **Transport** or carry (trans) across (port).

If you find a person or action **Ridiculous**, you may laugh with **Derision**. **Rid**, and **Ris** are to laugh.

Knowledge
Freedom to Learn

Insomnia (In) Not being able to sleep (somn) is no laughing matter, but someone who is a somnambulist just may be! A **Somnambulist** is one who (ist) walks (amb) in their sleep (somn)!

However, the sleepwalker may find it a cause to shake or **Tremble** with **Tremors**, unless she is quite **Intrepid**—that is, without (in) fear or **trembling**.

A **Victory** may go to someone who is quite **invincible** or not (in) able (ible) to be **conquered** (vinc).

Additional Cells added to "Actions"

Fill in the meaning for each cell as you hear it in the video or read it in the text.

Additional Cells for "Action" Words

Cells	Meaning
Able, ible	
Orium	
Sui	
Geno	
Re	
Tion	
In	
Demo	
A	
Theo, the	
Um	
Amb	

Lets' review the list of Additional Cells added to "Action" Words

Answers: Additional Cells Added to "Action" Words

Cells	Meaning
Able, ible	Able to
Orium	Place
Sui	Self
Geno	People or race
Re	Again
Tion	State of
In	Not
Demo	People
A	No, not
Theo, the	God
Um	Command
Amb	walk

CHECK TEST #7

Match the cells with the correct definitions. check your answers using the answer key below then return to the video and we will review the answers.

Question	Answer Choice
_____ 1. Aud	A. a place to hear someone
_____ 2. Cide	B. laughter
_____ 3. Cogn, cog	C. rule by no one
_____ 4. Port	D. without fear
_____ 5. Somn	E. hear
_____ 6. Orium, arium	F. kill
_____ 7. The, theo	G. carry
_____ 8. Vict, vic	H. not able to believe
_____ 9. Cred	I. eat
_____ 10. Auditorium	J. to rule
_____ 11. Homicide	K. one who walks in his sleep
_____ 12. Ignorant	L. sleep
_____ 13. Anarchy	M. to know
_____ 14. Cognition	N. god
_____ 15. Somnambulist	O. place
_____ 16. Intrepid	P. to kill a person
_____ 17. Incredible	Q. conquer
_____ 18. Crac, crat	R. not knowing, not known
_____ 19. Rid, ris	S. the state of knowing
_____ 20. Vor	T. believe, trust

Answer Key Check Test #7

1.E 2.F 3.M 4.G 5.L 6.O 7.N 8.Q 9.T 10.A 11.P 12.R 13.C 14.S 15.K 16.D 17.H 18.J 19.B 20.I

Vocabulary Study Guide

Lesson 5: Emotions or Qualities

Vocabulary Workshop>Emotions or Qualities

This material corresponds to the Vocabulary Workshop in the
PowerPrep DVD/Internet/iApp

Vocabulary Workshop

Lesson 5: Emotions or Qualities

WORD CELL BUILDER FOR: EMOTIONS OR QUALITIES

We will now learn various cells with "emotions" or "qualities" as the main cluster.
Cells You Should Know: Write the correct meaning for each cell as you hear it on the video or find the definition for each cell in
the information provided below in the section called: *Emotion or Quality Cells – Vocabulary and Definitions*

Important Cells about "Emotions or Qualities"

Cells	Meaning	Words to Know
Am, ami		Amorous, amicable, amiable, amity
Bene, ben		Benevolent, benefit, benefactor, beneficent, benign
Grat		Grateful, gratitude, congratulate, gratis, ingrate, gratuity
Mal, male		Malfunction, malice, malevolent, malodorous
Mis		Misunderstand, mishap, misanthrope, misconstrue
Phob		Phobia, claustrophobia, xenophobia
Plac		Complacent, placate, implacable, placid

Answers: Important "Emotion or Quality" Cells

Cells	Meaning	Words to Know
Am, ami	Love, friendship	Amorous, amicable, amiable, amity
Bene, ben	Good	Benevolent, benefit, benefactor, beneficent, benign
Grat	Pleasing, free, thankful	Grateful, gratitude, congratulate, gratis, ingrate, gratuity
Mal, male	Bad	Malfunction, malice, malevolent, malodorous
Mis	Wrong, bad, hate	Misunderstand, mishap, misanthrope, misconstrue
Phob	Fear	Phobia, claustrophobia, xenophobia
Plac	Calm, please	Complacent, placate, implacable, placid

Of course these are not the only cells which indicate Emotion or Quality. However, these are among the most common.
Now let's look at *words* with these cells to determine the meaning of the words as well as the meaning of other cells in the words. As we go
through these words, you might want to use the chart to jot down the meaning of the different cells.

EMOTION OR QUALITY CELLS – VOCABULARY AND DEFINITIONS

If someone is **Amorous**, **Amicable**, **Amiable** or showing **Amity**, they are showing some shade of Love or friendship. If
someone is **amorous** they have the quality of (ous) love. If they are **amicable** or **amiable**, they are *able* to be loved. And,
since –ty is the quality of, then **Amity** is having the qualities of friendship.

A **Benefactor** is one who (or) makes (fact) good. Usually this is someone who does good things, such as providing money or
opportunities, for someone else. To **Benefit** is to make (fit) good. **Benevolent** is related to (ent) good will (vol). The person
who received good things from a **Benefactor** would be **Grateful**, that is full of (ful) **Grat** (which is to thank). If you got
something **Gratis**, you got it for free, and a **Gratuity** is a tip, and literally means the quality of (ty) giving thanks.

The opposite of **Good** of course if **Bad**, and that is **MAL**. If a *good* person is **benevolent**, then a *bad* person is **MALevolent**: or having bad will. Something that is **Malodorous** has a bad odor, or smell.

Another cell for bad is mis. This means wrong, bad and hate. To **Misunderstand** means to get the wrong understanding of something. A **Misanthrope** is someone who hates humans (anthro).

A **Phobia** is a fear. **Claustrophobia** is a fear of closed (claus) places. **Xeno phobia** is a fear of people (xeno). **Triskaidekaphobia** is fear of the number 13!

Once you overcome your **phobia**, you may be calm or **Placid**. **Placid** literally means that which is (id) calm. A placid lake, for example, is perfectly calm. To **Placate** is to make (ate) calm. An Implacable person is not (im) able (able) to be calm.

Additional Cells added to "Emotion or Quality"

Fill in the meaning for each cell as you hear it in the video or read it in the text: **Additional Cells for "Emotion or Quality" Words**

Cells	Meaning
Ous	
Ty	
Fact	
Or	
Ent	
Vol	
Claus	
Xeno	
Im	
Id	

Lets' review the list of Additional Cells added to "Emotion or Quality" Words: **Answers:** Additional Cells Added to "Emotion or Quality" Words

Cells	Meaning
Ous	Quality of
Ty	Quality of
Fact	To make
Or	One who
Ent	Related to
vol	To will
Claus	Closed
Xeno	People
Im	Not
id	That which is

CHECK TEST #8

Match the cells with the correct definitions. check your answers using the answer key below then return to the video and we will review the answers.

Question	Answer Choices
1. Bene, ben	A. having a bad smell
2. Grat	B. able to be liked
3. Mal, male	C. to make calm
4. Phob, phobia	D. not
5. Plac	E. pleasing, free, thankful
6. Ous, ty	F. good
7. Vol	G. not able to be calmed
8. Xeno	H. fear
9. Im	I. bad
10. Claus	J. fear of people and crowds
11. Amorous	K. someone who hates people
12. Amicable	L. having the quality of love
13. Benefactor	M. having bad will
14. Gratuity	N. quality of
15. Malevolent	O. calm
16. Malodorous	P. one who makes good (helps others)
17. Misanthrope	Q. closed
18. Xenophobia	R. to will
19. Placate	S. quality of giving thanks
20. Implacable	T. people

Answer Key Check Test #8

1.F **2.**E **3.**I **4.**H **5.**O **6.**N **7.**R **8.**T **9.**D **10.**Q **11.**L **12.**B **13.**P **14.**S **15.**M **16.**A **17.**K **18.**J **19.**C **20.**G

Vocabulary Study Guide
Lesson 6: Things
Vocabulary Workshop>Things
This material corresponds to the Vocabulary Workshop in the
PowerPrep DVD/Internet/iApp

Vocabulary Workshop

Lesson 6: Things

WORD CELL BUILDER FOR: THINGS

We will now learn various cells with "things" as the main cluster. **Cells You Should Know:** Write the correct meaning for each cell as you hear it on the video or find the definition for each cell in the information provided below in the section called: *Things Cells – Vocabulary and Definitions*

Important Cells about "Things"

Cells	Meaning	Words to Know
Belli, bell		Rebellion, belligerent, bellicose, ante-bellum
Chrom		Chromatic, monochrome
Cosmo, cosm		Cosmopolitan, cosmos, microcosm
Demo, dem		Democrat, epidemic, demographics, pandemic
Hydr		Hydrant, hydrate, dehydrate
Lith		Monolith, lithograph, megalith
Phon		Phonograph, phonics, cacophony, telephone
Pyr		Pyromaniac, pyre, pyrotechnics
The, theo		Atheist, theology theocracy
Therm		Thermometer, thermal, hypothermia

Answers: Important "Things" Cells

Cells	Meaning	Words to Know
Belli, bell	war	Rebellion, belligerent, bellicose, ante-bellum
Chrom	Color	Chromatic, monochrome
Cosmo, cosm	World	Cosmopolitan, cosmos, microcosm
Demo, dem	People	Democrat, epidemic, demographics, pandemic
Hydr	Water	Hydrant, hydrate, dehydrate
Lith	Stone	Monolith, lithograph, megalith
Phon	Sound	Phonograph, phonics, cacophony, telephone
Pyr	Fire	Pyromaniac, pyre, pyrotechnics
The, theo	God	Atheist, theology theocracy
Therm	Heat	Thermometer, thermal, hypothermia

Of course these are not the only cells which indicate Things. However, these are among the most common.
Now let's look at *words* with these cells to determine the meaning of the words as well as the meaning of other cells in the words. As we go through these words, you might want to use the chart to jot down the meaning of the different cells.

"THINGS" CELLS – VOCABULARY AND DEFINITIONS

Now that we are at our last cluster, you should be seeing some repetition and should be able to recognize some of the cells!

Let's starts with **War**, which is **Belli** or **Bell**. Earlier we had the cell ante used with **bellum** to mean before a war, or antebellum. A few other warlike words are **Rebellion**, **Belligerent**, and **Bellicose**.

If something is **Monochromatic**, that means it has only one (mono) color. **Polychromatic** would be many (poly) colors. **Chromatic**, of course, means of or pertaining to (ic) color.

Cosmos means world, and **Cosmopolitan** means that which is (an) is a city (polit) of the world. A **Microcosm** is a very small (micro) part of the world

The United States is a **Democratic** society, meaning we have rule (crat) by the people. If something is **Pandemic**, it is spread over all (pan) the people, and an **Epidemic** is a disease which can spread to all people.

Before you participate in anything physical, you should **hydrate** your system, it is the act of (ate) giving it water. If you don't, you could get **Dehydrated**, meaning without (de) water.

A **Monolith** is a single (mono) structure out of stone (lith). A **Lithograph** is a writing (graph) or print in stone. A **Megalith** is a huge (mega) stone.

A **Cacophony** is a bad (cac) sound. If you learned to read using **Phonics**, you learned from combining the sound of the letters.

A **Pyromaniac** is someone who is crazy (mania) about fire and would probably enjoy **Pyrotechnics**, which are fireworks, but which means literally the show (tech) fire.

If **democracy** is rule by the people, then a **Theocracy** is rule by a god. **Theology** is the study of god or religion.

The last "thing" we will discuss is heat. If the **Thermometer** (which measures heat) drops you might suffer from **Hypothermia**. Hypo (under) therm (heat), meaning you're very cold!

ADDITIONAL CELLS ADDED TO "THINGS"

Fill in the meaning for each cell as you hear it in the video or read it in the text: **Additional Cells for "Things" Words**

Cells	Meaning
Poly	
Polit	
Micro	
Crat	
Pan	

Lets' review the list of Additional Cells added to "Things" Words: **Answers:** Additional Cells Added to "Things" Words

Cells	Meaning
Poly	many
Polit	City
Micro	Small
crat	rule
pan	all

CHECK TEST #9

Match the cells with the correct definitions. You can then check your answers using the answer key below and then return to the video when you are finished and we will review the answers.

Question	Answer Choices
1. Belli, bell	A. without water
2. Chrom	B. that which is war like
3. Cosmo, cosm	C. someone who is crazy about fire
4. Demo, dem	D. city
5. Lith	E. color
6. Hydr	F. war
7. Phon	G. rule by god
8. Pyr	H. people
9. Polit	I. world
10. Therm	J. a bad sound
11. Micro	K. single stone
12. Belligerent	L. small
13. Monochromatic	M. spread over all people
14. Cosmopolitan	N. water
15. Pandemic	O. stone
16. Dehydrated	P. one color
17. Monolith	Q. heat
18. Cacophony	R. sound
19. Pyromaniac	S. a city of the world
20. Theocracy	T. fire

Answer Key Check Test #9

1.F 2.E 3.I 4.H 5.O 6.N 7.R 8.T 9.D 10.Q 11.L 12.B 13.P 14.S 15.M 16.A 17.K 18.J 19.C 20.G

Vocabulary Study Guide
Lesson 7: Conclusion

Vocabulary Workshop>Conclusion

This material corresponds to the Vocabulary Workshop in the
PowerPrep DVD/Internet/iApp

Vocabulary Workshop

Lesson 7: Conclusion

We have covered many word cells, and along the way have discussed many words. To make these words your "own" and to become even more comfortable with them, you should do the following:

☐ **Review** your Student Study Guide, the charts, and the check tests.

☐ **Study** the Word Cell Builder at the end of your study guide.

☐ **Remember** the suggestions given at the beginning of this session:
   • **Read**
   • **Use a Dictionary**
   • **Think about Words!**
   • **Make Flash Cards**
   • **Use Your Knowledge of other languages**
   • And, use the video session again!

Good luck!

CONGRATULATIONS!!

You Have Completed the Vocabulary Review!!

Take a Break Before Moving on to the Next Section.

Short Dictionary:

the main eDictionary in the DVD program has many more words and more detailed definitions with words used in sample sentences, part of speech, pronunciation etc.

Word	Short Definition
Abate	to diminish, to lessen
Abet	to assist, to promote
Abhor	to hate, to despise
Abjure	to retract, to take back
Abolish	to put an end to
Abridge	to shorten
Abstemious	having self-restraint in behavior or appetite
Abstract	difficult or unusual (adj), to remove (vb), a summary (n)
Accede	to agree to, to consent
Accolade	praise, acknowledgement
Acquiesce	to agree, to comply
Acrimony	bitter or harsh in speech or behavior
Adamant	stubborn, insistent
Adroit	Skillful
Adulation	extreme praise
Advocate	to defend, to promote
Aesthetic	concerning beauty
Affiliation	association
Affinity	fondness for, affection for
Affirmation	statement of truth or confirmation
Affront	an insult, an offensive statement
Aggrandize	to amplify, to expand
Alacrity	liveliness, alertness
Alleviate	to ease, to lessen
Altruistic	kind, unselfish
Amass	to gather, to accumulate
Ambiguous	vague, unclear
Ambivalence	inconsistent or opposing feelings toward an object or person
Ambulatory	moving about, able to walk
Ameliorate	to improve
Amenity	courtesy, pleasantry
Amiable	pleasant, likeable
Amity	friendly relations
Anatomize	break down to parts, scrutinize
Anchor	to secure
Anecdote	a short, amusing story
Animated	lively
Annul	cancel, invalidate
Anomaly	an abnormality, an irregularity
Anonymity	state of being unknown or unrecognized
Antagonize	to oppose
Antediluvian	ancient, primitive, old-fashioned
Antipathy	dislike, repulsion
Antithetical	opposed, contrary
Apathy	indifference
Apocryphal	not authentic, fake

Apprentice	beginner, a learner of a trade
Arable	fertile, farmable
Ardor	fervor, zeal
Aristocratic	noble
Articulate	well-spoken
Artificer	designer, contriver
Ascendancy	authority, power
Asinine	stupid, foolish
Assiduous	diligent
Astute	discerning, intelligent
Atrophy	to waste, to decay
Audacious	courageous, bold
Augment	to increase, to enlarge
Austere	harsh, severe, stern
Autocrat	despot, tyrant
Avaricious	greedy
Balk	to refuse to proceed
Banal	common, dull
Baneful	corrupt, fatal
Beguile	to deceive, to trick
Belies	to mislead, to disguise
Bequeath	to hand down, to pass on
Berate	to scold, to reprimand
Bereft	deprived
Bilk	to cheat, to deceive
Bizarre	unusual, weird
Blunder	mistake, error
Brevity	shortness, briefness
Brittle	fragile, breakable
Bungle	to fail, to fumble
Burgeon	to flourish, to grow
Cacophony	dissonant or harsh sound
Cajole	to persuade
Callous	heartless, insensitive
Candor	honesty, sincerity
Canvass	to survey, to poll
Capitulate	to submit, to surrender
Capricious	inconstant, impulsive
Castigate	to punish, to scold
Caviler	faultfinder, quibbler
Censorious	critical, faultfinding
Circuitous	roundabout, indirect
Circumlocution	talking in a roundabout way
Clairvoyant	having keen perception
Clamor	noise, racket
Clarity	clearness, precision
Clemency	compassion, mercy
Cloy	satiate, overdo
Coalesce	to blend, to combine
Cogent	persuasive
Cohere	to bind, to cling
Colloquial	informal, casual

Conciliatory	agreeable, harmonious
Confide	to trust, to disclose
Conform	to agree, to correspond
Confound	to confuse
Congeal	to solidify, to harden
Congenial	agreeable, pleasant
Congruous	appropriate, corresponding
Consonant	compatible, harmonious
Construe	to interpret, to understand
Consummate	to perfect, to complete
Contaminant	something that pollutes
Contentious	argumentative, hostile
Converge	to meet, to intersect
Convivial	friendly
Copious	abundant
Corroborate	to confirm, to prove
Corrosive	acidic, sarcastic
Corrugated	wrinkled
Credulity	willingness to believe
Cryptic	mysterious, obscure
Cursory	superficial, insincere
Cynic	a skeptic, a doubter
Daunt	to frighten, to frustrate
Debacle	failure, disaster
Debilitate	to hurt, to weaken
Debunk	to discredit, to expose as false
Decorous	correct, demure
Decry	to condemn, to censure
Defer	to delay, to postpone
Delegate	a representative (n), to appoint (vb)
Deleterious	harmful, destructive
Delineate	to describe
Delude	to deceive, to betray
Deplete	to use up, to consume
Deplorable	unfortunate, tragic
Deprecate	to censure, to object
Derelict	abandoned (adj), an outcast (n)
Desiccate	to dry out
Deter	to discourage, to prevent
Deviate	to vary, to digress
Devotee	a follower, a believer
Discrepancy	difference, incongruity
Disillusion	to deceive, to disappoint
Disparity	difference, dissimilarity
Disputatious	argumentative
Dissipate	to misuse, to scatter
Dissonance	harshness, without harmony
Distend	to expand, to enlarge
Docile	submissive, compliant
Dogmatic	opinionated, authoritative
Dominant	controlling
Droll	amusing, ridiculous

Dynamic	energetic, active
Ebb	to decrease, to retreat
Ebullience	enthusiasm, vitality
Eccentric	strange, odd
Efface	to cancel, to erase
Effervesce	to bubble
Efficacy	effectiveness, capability
Elocution	effective speech
Emaciated	thin, starved
Embitter	to anger, to irritate
Emend	to improve, to correct
eminent	famous, celebrated
Empyreal	heavenly, not earthly
Emulate	to imitate, to copy
Encumbrance	burden, hindrance
Enervate	to weaken
Engender	to promote, to excite
Enhance	to improve, to make better
Enigmatic	mysterious, secretive
Enmity	hostility, malice
Entity	separate or independent item
Ephemeral	brief, momentary
Equilibrium	balance, steadiness
Eradicate	to remove, to destroy
Erratic	random, irregular
Erroneous	inaccurate, wrong
Erudition	learnedness, scholarship
Eschew	to avoid, to shun
Esoteric	understood by select few
Ethereal	heavenly, airy
Euphemism	a pleasant word or phrase substituted for an unpleasant one
Euphonious	melodious, enjoyable sound
Euphoric	happy, exalted
Evacuate	to void, to empty
Evanescent	fleeting, momentary
Exacerbate	to aggravate, to worsen
Exasperate	to annoy, to disturb
Exclude	to bar, to eliminate
Exonerate	to clear from blame
Exorbitant	excessive, wasteful
Expeditious	prompt, quick
Expendable	nonessential, insignificant
Exposition	a display, a commentary
Extol	to commend, to praise
Exuberant	enthusiastic
Facetious	humorous, sarcastic
Facilitate	to simplify, to ease
Fallacious	false, deceptive
Fallow	idle, inactive
Fastidious	demanding, hard to please
Feasible	achievable, likely
Fertile	fruitful, plentiful

Fickle	inconstant, changeable
Figurative	representative
Flagrant	scandalous
Flourish	to prosper, to increase
Fluent	flowing, capable of clear speech
Forlorn	abandoned, desolate
Fortitude	courage, strength
Fractious	irritable
fraudulent	false, dishonest
Frivolous	foolish, unimportant
Frugal	thrifty, economical
Garish	showy, gaudy
Garner	to accumulate, to collect
Garrulous	talkative, wordy
Gregarious	sociable
Grievance	a complaint, an objection
Guile	deceit, fraud
Hackneyed	worn-out, commonplace
Haughty	arrogant, proud
Haven	shelter, refuge
Hedonist	one who seeks pleasure
Hefty	strong, sturdy, heavy
Heresy	religious nonconformity, rejection of religion
Heritage	legacy, tradition
Hierarchy	structure of power, ranking
Hilarity	fun, excitement
Hindrance	an obstacle, an interference
Hospitable	generous, friendly
Hostile	aggressive, vicious
Humane	kind, compassionate
Hypercritical	severe, faultfinding
Hypocrisy	pretending to do or believe one way when acting in another
Icon	a symbol, an idol
Idyllic	simple, pleasant
Ignoble	inferior, dishonorable
Impecunious	poor, penniless
Imperturbable	calm, even-tempered
Impetuous	impulsive, abrupt
Impinge	to disturb, to intrude, to strike
Implicit	understood, but not stated outright
Impugn	to attack, to challenge
Inaccessible	unattainable, unapproachable
Inane	foolish, shallow, without meaning
Incessant	constant, continuous
Incite	to induce, to stimulate
Incorrigible	unruly, without hope of correction
Indecorous	vulgar, distasteful
Indefatigable	inexhaustible, tireless
Indelible	permanent, cannot be erased
Indolent	inactive, lazy
Indomitable	invincible, unconquerable
Infamy	a bad reputation, dishonor

Innocuous	harmless, innocent
Inscrutable	incomprehensible, mysterious
Insipid	uninteresting, dull
Instigate	to provoke, to urge to act
Insuperable	unbeatable, unattainable
Inundated	flooded, swamped
Invariable	constant, unchanging
Invincible	cannot be conquered
Inviolable	sacred, holy
Irascible	irritable, easily upset
Iridescent	colorful, rainbow-colored
Ironic	using words that convey the opposite of what a person means
Irreparable	ruined, destroyed
Jettison	throw overboard, discard
Jocular	funny, humorous
Jovial	happy, jolly
Jubilation	celebration, happiness
Kindle	to ignite a flame, to animate
Laconic	brief, concise
Latent	inactive, concealed
Laud	to praise, to honor
Lenient	mild, gentle
Leonine	authoritative, commanding
Lethargic	sluggish, heavy movement
Levity	flightiness, without seriousness
Listless	indifferent, unconcerned
Lithe	flexible
Litigate	dispute, to contest in court
Livid	discolored from emotional upset, furious
Longevity	long life
Lucid	clear, understandable
Magnanimous	generous, unselfish
Maladroit	clumsy, awkward
Malice	hostility, hatred
Malinger	to pretend illness to escape work
Mandate	a command
Mediate	to negotiate for two parties
Medicament	a remedy, a medication
Mediocrity	commonness, ordinariness
Menial	common, low
Mercurial	inconstant, changeable
Meticulous	painstakingly careful
Mirage	an illusion
Miscreant	a criminal, a scoundrel
Mitigate	to lessen or ease
Mobile	moveable
Modicum	a bit, a little amount
Modulate	to restrain, to temper
Monomaniacal	extreme, fanatical
Morose	gloomy, depressed
Mottle	blotch, smudge
Mundane	worldly

Munificent	charitable, generous
Myriad	infinite, great in number
Nabob	a rich or powerful person
Nefarious	wicked
Negate	to cancel out, to annul
Nonchalant	unconcerned
Nostalgia	homesickness, sentiment for the past
Notorious	disreputable, known for evil
Novelty	newness, originality
Novice	a beginner, a learner
Objective	fair, impartial
Obscure	unclear, vague
Obsolete	extinct, outmoded
Opaque	nontransparent, cloudy
Opulent	rich
Ostracize	to expel
Pallid	pale, colorless
Panegyrize	to glorify, to praise
Paradigm	an example
Paramount	supreme, principal
Pariah	a social outcast
Pariah	an outcast
Parsimony	selfishness, frugality
Partisan	a strong supporter of a cause
Pathetic	inciting sympathy
Paucity	scarcity
Pedagogue	a teacher, an educator
Penury	poverty, extreme need
Perfidious	deceitful, dishonest
Perfunctory	indifferent, apathetic
Peripheral	outer boundary
Perturb	to annoy, to disturb
Philanthropic	offering charitable service
Phlegmatic	indifferent, apathetic
Pinion	to hold in place
Placate	to calm, to satisfy
Pragmatic	practical, sensible
Premature	early, unanticipated
Premeditated	planned ahead of time, intentional
Presumptuous	arrogant, assuming
Pretense	a false appearance, dishonesty
Prevalent	commonly occurring
Proclivity	inclination, disposition
Prodigal	wasteful
Profuse	extravagant, abundant
Prophetic	predictive, foretelling
Proselyte	a convert, a new believer
Proximity	nearness
Pulverize	crush
Punitive	imposing punishment
Quandary	a dilemma, a predicament
Querulous	discontented, complaining

Query	to inquire, to question
Rant	yell, shout
Ratify	to approve, to endorse
Raucous	harsh or loud sound
Recalcitrant	disobedient, rebellious
Recant	to withdraw, to retract
Recapitulate	to summarize, to review
Reclusive	antisocial, shut out from society
Recriminate	counter an accusation with another accusation
Rectify	to correct, to remedy
Refurbish	to renew
Relegate	to banish, to eliminate
Relic	an artifact from an ancient time
Remedial	corrective, healing
Remiss	negligent, careless
Remuneration	payment for a service
Renunciation	denial, rejection
Replete	abundant, full
Repudiate	to reject, to disclaim
Rescind	to revoke, to cancel
Reserve	self-restraint
Resilient	flexible, easily recovered
Resplendent	radiant, bright
Rhapsody	delight, ecstasy
Rupture	to break, to split
Saccharine	sweet
Sagacious	intelligent, wise
Salubrious	healthy
Salvage	to save, to rescue
Sanctimonious	hypocritical in religious belief
Scrupulous	honest, exact
Semaphore	a visual signaling system
Serene	calm, peaceful
Servile	slave-like, submissive
Shrewd	sharp, perceptive
Sinister	threatening
Solace	comfort, relief
Somber	drab, gloomy
Sonorous	resonant, harmonious
Spurious	false, deceitful
Spurn	to shun, to reject
Squander	waste, misuse
Stagnant	motionless, stale
Staid	quiet, solemn
Stentorian	loud, thundering
Stoic	indifferent, showing no emotion
Stygian	gloomy, evil
Stymie	to confuse, to delay
Submissive	compliant, obedient
Subsidiary	supplementary, assistant
Subtle	difficult to detect
Sully	to shame, to stain

Sumptuous	extravagant, costly
Surfeit	an excess, an overabundance
Surreptitious	secretive, sneaky
Tantamount	equivalent
Temporal	temporary, worldly
Tenacious	persistent
Terminate	to end, to complete
Thwart	to prevent
Tirade	an angry speech
Torpor	idleness, apathy
Tranquil	calm, peaceful
Transient	temporary, fleeting
Treacherous	dangerous, untrustworthy
Trite	commonplace, stale
Truculent	brutal, mean
Truncate	to condense, to shorten
Turbulence	confusion, agitation
Tyrant	dictator, oppressive ruler
Unequivocal	definite, absolute
Unfetter	to free, to release
Unprecedented	unparalleled, uncommon
Unscrupulous	corrupt, unethical
Unstinting	generous, unselfish
Untenable	indefensible
Utopian	idealistic, perfect
Vacillate	to waver, to fluctuate
Vanquish	conquer, defeat
Venerate	respect, admire
Venturesome	risky, adventurous
Verbose	wordy, repetitive
Verify	confirm, prove
Viable	conceivable, workable
Vibrant	active, lively
Vicarious	substituted, taking the place of something else
Vigorous	energetic, enthusiastic
Vilify	to defame
Vindicate	to clear, to excuse from blame
Virile	masculine, strong
Virtuoso	an expert or master in a certain skill
Virulent	deadly, toxic
Vivacious	lively, active
Volatile	unstable, short-lived
Whet	to stimulate, to spur
Whimsical	changeable
Wizened	withered, decayed
Zany	funny, crazy
Zealot	a fanatic, a devotee

Science Reasoning Workbook

ACT ONLY

Table of Contents

This material corresponds to the ACT Virtual Classroom instructions in the
PowerPrep DVD/Internet/iApp for Science Reasoning

Virtual Classroom

Science Reasoning
Part 1: Overview & Directions

<u>Classroom>Science Reasoning>Overview & Directions</u>

This material Corresponds to the ACT Virtual Classroom Instructions in the
PowerPrep DVD/Internet/iApp for Science Reasoning

Virtual Classroom

Important Abbreviations
These abbreviations are used throughout the program

POE: Process of Elimination
SARR: Synthesize, Analyze, Reduce, and Restate (has to do with Logical Reasoning)
AC: Answer Choice
QS: Question Stem
LOD: Level of Difficulty

Example Question: What is the least common multiple of 3, 4, and 7? (**This is the call of the question or Question Stem "QS"**)

These are Answer Choices "AC" A, B, C, D, E

   (A)   12
   (B)   21
   (C)   28
   (D)   48
   (E)   84

Part 1: Overview & Directions

Overview

There's one specific section of the ACT exam called **Science Reasoning**. The **questions measure interpretation, analysis, evaluation, reasoning, and problem-solving skills within a science context.** The questions measure your ability to interpret given information, analyze it, and evaluate it.

The science reasoning section does not test your knowledge of science. You don't have to know scientific facts or figures or even have any background in science. For example, you won't be tested on the atomic weight of a certain element or a specific physics formula. But they will test whether you can interpret data they give you? Can you analyze information that's already in front of you? The majority of the information you need will be provided in the tables or other data they give you. You will then be asked to extract conclusions from the data.

The ACT does not test Science principles per se. The exam tests your understanding of the data they supply.

<u>Summary:</u> 40 Multiple Choice Questions • Based on 7 passages • 5 – 7 questions per passage • 35 Minutes • Average of 5 minutes per passage

<u>What the questions measure</u>: Interpretation Skills • Analysis Skills • Evaluation Skills • Reasoning Skills • Problem-Solving Skills

<u>The two main objectives</u>: Find data WITHIN the passage • Use logic and reason to EXTRAPOLATE assumptions, conclusions, etc.

<u>Science categories</u>: Biology • Earth/Space Science • Chemistry • Physics

Passage Types

There are seven passages you will see on the exam. Those seven (7) passages are divided among three(3) different types of passages. So let's look at the three different types of passages

Data Representation (DR)

<u>DR Passages</u>: The first passage is called Data Representation (DR). There will be three (3) DR passages and each will have five (5) questions. This is the most basic, straightforward type of passage. It is based on tables, graphs, or diagrams with a little bit of accompanying text. You will work with numbers or graphs–information provided that you're asked to interpret.

• 3 passages • 5 questions per passage • DR questions are based on tables/graphs/diagrams and text.

DR Strategies
1. **Get a feel for what's being tested.** Figure out the kind of data they have given you. Don't get hung up on unfamiliar terms. If they're testing an enzyme of something you don't recognize, don't worry about it. If you get numbers that have units you don't understand or recognize, don't worry about it. **Just get an overall view of what is being tested**.
   • Read the text to get an overview of the passage, and • Don't get hung up on unfamiliar terms.
2. **Review the Table--**not just the numbers in the table, but make sure you read all the titles and understand what is being tested. Take a look at the axis labels, any footnotes, and any other general information that goes with the table. Many times the test makers place specific information in the titles or the axis that they're going to come back and test. **Make sure you notice all the information around the table**, and get a feel for the type of quantitative information you've been given.
   • Look at the table. • Read all titles, axis labels and any footnotes or other information. • Get a feel for the type of quantitative information you are given.
3. **Determine how the rows and columns are related to each other.** On a graph the **independent/controlled variable** is what the experimenter controls (how hot the stove is, the length of time the grass is watered, etc.) The **dependent variable** is what reacts to the independent variable (how quickly the chicken cooks, how tall the grass grows).

   If you have a table with something being tested over time, or over a certain distance, get a feel for how the rows and columns relate to each other. On a graph you actually have data.

   Independent or Controlled Variable: On a graph the independent or controlled variable is what the experimenter controls. It's what the person doing the experiment had control over. It might be how hot the stove is, because we can control the temperature of a stove. Or it might be the length of time we water the grass, because that's within our control. **So, the independent or controlled variable is what the experimenter has control over.**

   The dependent variable is what reacts to the independent variable. If our independent variable is how hot the stove gets, then the dependent variable might be how quickly the chicken cooks. Obviously as we change the temperature we vary how quickly the chicken cooks.

   Controlled variable: the temperature; **Dependent variable:** the time it takes to cook the chicken.
   Our second example was 'watering the grass'. The controlled variable would be how long we water the grass. Then the dependent variable, what would be affected by what we control, would be how tall the grass grows. If I control how much I water the grass it affects how tall the grass grows. So again, just keep in mind on graphs you have independent and dependent variables.

   Controlled variable: watering time **Dependent variable:** grass length

- Determine how the rows and columns are related to each other.
- On a graph, the experimenter controls the independent/controlled variable.
- How hot we make the stove or the length of time the grass is watered
- The <u>dependent</u> variable is what reacts to the <u>independent</u> variable.
- How quickly the chicken cooks or how tall the grass grows

4. **Observe the units of measurement.** Even if the units are unusual and you don't recognize them, you must try to understand them, you will get a question about a reference to the units of measurement.
- Observe the units of measurement.
- Even if they are unusual and you do not recognize them, make a note of what they are.

5. **Look for obvious trends in the data.** Notice any significant changes. If something increases by 10 units for 3 or 4 years and then suddenly changes by 50 units--that's a sudden increase. Chances are pretty good you're going to see a question about that. So, notice any increasing or decreasing trends in data, time periods, and then notice any significant variations from that. **Notice any sudden increase or decrease in value, is there any other unusual information in the data.**
- Look for obvious <u>trends</u> in the data and note any <u>significant changes</u>.
- Is there a sudden increase/decrease in values?
- Is there any other unusual information?

Review of Strategies for data representation:

1. **Read the text** to get an overview of the passage. Don't get hung up on unfamiliar terms.
2. **Look at the table.** Read all titles, axis labels, and any footnotes or other information. Get a feel for what type of quantitative information you are given.
3. **Determine how the rows** and columns are related to each other.
4. **You might also have to extrapolate data.** This means you must come up with a value beyond the range you are given. If the scale goes from 1 to 10 and you are asked about data at point 11, you can predict what that value might be based on the previous information. (Usually this means simply extending the line graph.) However, you cannot determine what data would be at point 25.
5. **Finally, be ready to make predictions** from data presented and determine if new information is consistent with presented data.

DR Questions

The most common questions for data representation require you to read a table or graph and extract information. This means reading points on a graph or finding the difference between values in a table, etc. Can you extract data out of the numbers you're given.
- Read the <u>table/graph</u> and extract information.
- This is the most common type of question for Data Representation.
- These questions require that you read points on a graph, find the difference between values on a table, etc.

Interpolate: In addition, you might have to interpolate data. This means determining or estimating data between points. For example, if your scale goes from 1 to 2 and you're asked for a value at 1.5, then you're obviously trying to find the midpoint between the two given data points, or some kind of an average between data point 1 and data point 2. Interpolating data means making estimations from the given numbers or data. If your scale goes from 1 to 2 and you are asked for a value at 1.5, simply find the average of the data at 1 and at 2.

Extrapolate: You might also have to extrapolate data. This means you have to come up with a value beyond the given range. Take a look at the trends, and estimate what would happen if the table or the trend continued.
For example, if you had a table with a scale that goes from 1 to 10 you would be asked about data point 11, then you would predict what that value might be based on the given information for data points 1 through 10.
Usually this just means extending the line on a graph, or increasing some value by the same amount.
There are limitation to extrapolating data. You would not be able to make assumptions about data point 25 if you only know about data points 1 though 10. So realize these limitations.

- You might also have to *extrapolate* data.
- This means you must come up with a value beyond the range you are given.
- For example, if data goes from 1 to 10 and you are asked about data point 11, you can predict what that value might be based on the previous information. (Usually, this means simply extending the line graph.)
- However, you cannot determine what data would be at point 25.

Predictions: Be ready to make predictions from the given data. You will be asked to determine whether the new information is consistent with the information that you've already been given. Be ready to make predictions from data presented and determined if new information is consistent with presented data.

Research Summaries (RS)

RS Passages
The second type of passage you will see is called a Research Summary (RS) passage. **RS also usually include several tables or graphs.** However, you will be given additional information that will require you to understand what is being tested and how the studies are performed. Specifically, you can expect to see

- 3 passages – 6 questions each • Purpose of the study •Design of the experiment • Results (this is usually the table/graph) •Experiment 1, 2, 3

A research summary is similar to data representation--you usually get a table or graph with numbers involved.

However, Research Summaries give you some additional information that will require you to understand what is being tested and how the studies were set up and performed. So in addition to the data tables you can also expect to see the purpose of the study and some general background information—why do we want to know how tall the grass grows, or how quickly the chicken cooks. The research summary is an expansion of the data passages. It gives you the design of the experiment, how it was actually set up, and then finally the results in a table or a graph, some information on multiple experiments, etc.

Research Summary questions include several tables or graphs and additional information that will require that you note what is being tested and the studies performed.

Expect to be given: • The purpose of the study • The design of the experiment • The results, usually in the form of tables/graphs

RS Purpose

The purpose of an experiment is usually to determine what effect "a" (**an independent variable**) has on "b" (**dependent variable**)—**cause and effect**. Once you recognize the purpose, you will need to evaluate how the experiments were set up to test these relationships.

More Details: The purpose of the experiment is usually to determine what effect "a", some independent variable, has on "b", the dependent variable, or what we call **cause and effect.** How does "how hot the stove is" affect "how quickly the chicken cooks". So there's some kind of cause and effect. Once you recognize the purpose you will need to evaluate how the experiments were set up to test these relationships.

The purpose of an experiment is usually to determine what affect *a* had on *b*.
  a = independent variable   and   *b* = dependent variable

This is sometimes called the cause and effect.

Once you recognize the purpose, evaluate how the experiments were set up to test these relationships.

RS Design of Experiment

An effective experiment usually tests one variable that is a possible cause and keeps all other factors constant. If more than one factor is allowed to vary, it becomes impossible to determine which factor caused the observed result. Watch out for defective designs like this. Also, realize that some experiments, by their very nature, cannot always be ideal. When an experiment lacks controls its usefulness is limited. You could be asked to create a good control. If they ask for conclusions, be careful! It's hard to make concrete conclusions when there is a lack of experimental control.

More Details: The design of the experiment, the actual physical setup itself of an effective experiment, usually tests one variable that might be a possible cause while keeping all of the other factors constant.

So if there are five things that could affect how quickly our chicken cooks, we're going to vary only one at a time while keeping all the other factors constant.   If more than one factor is allowed to vary, it becomes impossible to determine, which factor caused the result we see.   If you change three variables and the chicken cooked in five minutes, You can't be sure whether it was variable a, variable b, or variable c that caused the chicken to cook in that amount of time. So, when a passage asks you to draw conclusions, make sure you understand exactly what was controlled before you start drawing conclusions about the results.

Keep your eyes open for passages where you can tell that more than one thing was tested at a time or some other design problem, because that means our outcome can't be tied back to what we were actually testing.
  • A good design usually tests one variable and keeps the other factors constant.
  • If more than one factor varies, it's impossible to determine which factor was the cause of the observed result.
  • Watch out for defective designs.
  • Realize that some experiments cannot always be ideal.
  • When an experiment lacks controls, the experiment is limited.
  • You could be asked to create a good control.
  • Be careful when asked to make conclusions for an experiment that lacks good control.

RS Results

Make sure you notice trends in data and observe titles and units. For the results of the passages, make sure you're looking at the titles of the tables or graphs, how the axes are labeled and the specific units that you're given.
  • Same as Data Representation, and • Note trends in data and observe the titles and units.

Strategy

1. **Expect to start with straightforward questions about the results.** These will mirror the data representation questions, asking you to pull data out of a table.
2. **You will also be asked about the experimental design**, about how the whole process was set up. This tests your ability to follow the logic of the design itself. Why was one variable chosen over another variable, how are things set up, what assumptions were made, what was the experimenter's hypothesis, what was he actually trying to test, what were the controls and variables, what was held constant, and what was allowed to change. Note as you read the passage how things were actually set up.
3. **Be careful with questions that ask you to draw conclusions.** Make sure you pay close attention to the actual question stems. If you're asked about experiment 2, make sure you only use information from experiment 2 to find the correct answer. This is a very, very common trick on the ACT. An answer choice might have correct information in it, but it might be from a different experiment. So make sure you understand exactly what you're referencing and only pull data from that table or that graph or that section of the design. Make sure you're pulling your information from the correct place.
4. **Finally you could be asked to find additional results.** This asks you to determine how new results affect what you have already learned about a specific experiment. Do the results confirm previous ones or do they conflict? New results make you decide if you must alter your conclusions. After setting up a whole new experiment and getting results, what happens if a new test gives different results? How does that affect what we've already seen?

How the research summary questions are set up: General passage, data, additional information about the setup and what was being tested.

RS Questions

The research summary questions will usually ask you about the following:
  1. **Straightforward questions about the results.** These will mirror the Data Representation questions.

2. **Experimental design**. This tests your ability to follow the logic of the design itself. Why was one control variable chosen over another? How were things set up? What assumptions were made? What was the experimenter's hypothesis? What were the controls and variables?

3. **Conclusions**. Make sure you pay attention to the actual question stem. If you are asked about experiment 2, make sure you only use information from experiment 2 to determine the correct answer.

4. **Additional results**. This is where you must determine how new results affect what you have already learned about a specific experiment. Do these results confirm previous ones, or do they conflict? New results make you decide if you must alter your conclusions.

Conflicting Viewpoints (CV)

CV Passages

The third type of passage you'll see is called Conflicting Viewpoint (CV). You will have only one CV passage, and it will have seven (7) questions. That means you will have three (3) data representation passages, three (3) research summary passages, and one (1) conflicting viewpoint passage.

Conflicting viewpoints contain two major bodies of text with separate titles. These two bodies of text explain the same occurrence or situation, but from two different viewpoints. You will analyze historical data and results of a test, where person A agrees with the research but person B disagrees with it.

For example, you could have data relating to global warming where scientist A thinks it is caused by man-made pollution but person B thinks it's caused by natural cycles of increased solar activity because evidence shows similar warming on Venus and Earth and ice cores show prior warming and cooling patterns on earth.

Conflicting Viewpoints--two different viewpoints explaining the same results.
- 1 passage - 7 questions
- Conflicting Viewpoints contain two major bodies of text with separate titles. The two bodies of text explain the same occurrence or situation – but from two different points of view.

CV Strategies

1. **Read the introduction** to determine what occurrence or situation is being debated. Make sure you understand what result is in controversy.
2. **Read the first viewpoint and note the author's stance**. It's important to take a look at the first passage independently before reading the second point of view and note whether this person is pro or con, yes or no, are they disputing something or actually trying to substantiate it.
3. **Identify the evidence the first author uses to support his or her views**. Look at the first passage and figure out what the author believes and what evidence they use to support that belief. Note whether the evidence actually supports their conclusions or are they just making assumptions.
4. **Read the second viewpoint**. This will predictably dispute or oppose the conclusions of the first viewpoint.
5. **Identify the evidence the author uses to support that view**. Look at the second passage independently and determine what evidence or assumptions that author is using to support their viewpoint. Realize the evidence used might be exactly the same as the first viewpoint, just interpreted differently.
6. **Figure out the logic behind each viewpoint**. This is not to determine whether you agree or disagree with the authors or what is correct and incorrect. You're simply following along with what the author is stating.

Strategy Review

1. **Read the introduction** to determine what occurrence or situation is being debated.
2. **Read the first viewpoint** and note the author's stance. Are they pro or con? Yes or No?
3. **Identify the evidence** the first author uses to support her views. Is there evidence or just assumptions?
4. **Read the second viewpoint**. This should be a bit predictable because it will be opposite the first.
5. **Identify the evidence** the second author uses. The evidence might be the same–just interpreted differently.
6. **Realize your job is simply to follow the logic** behind each viewpoint–not to determine who is correct.

CV Questions

First: Conflicting viewpoint questions ask you to support or weaken a given viewpoint. Given author A, how would you support or how would you refute the view point? The best way to do this is by determining what assumptions were made, then come up with evidence that shows the assumptions are valid or not valid. **Evidence is evidence**, but when people make assumptions, it weakens. So find the assumptions and then decide if there's evidence that agrees or disagrees with the assumptions. **Assumptions are always the weak link.**

Also realize that strengthening the second viewpoint does not necessarily weaken the first viewpoint. This is another very common way to get tripped up on these types of questions. If author B disagrees with something, and you make his argument stronger, you do not necessarily make author A's argument weaker. **Remember that strengthening the second viewpoint does not necessarily weaken the first.**

Second: Be very careful to keep the evidence and assumptions of each viewpoint separate. You will see if a question asks about author B but they pull in information from author A, even if the information from author A is correct, it's not properly referring to author B. Make sure you keep the assumptions and evidences from each viewpoint separate. Some of the incorrect answers will try to mix in details from one of the other authors or one of the incorrect viewpoints.

Review

1. **Some questions ask you to support or weaken a given viewpoint.** The best way to do this is to determine what assumptions were made, then come up with evidence that shows the assumptions are valid. Assumptions are always the weak link. Also, realize that strengthening the second viewpoint does not weaken the first!

2. **Be very careful to keep the evidence and assumptions of each viewpoint separate.** Some of the incorrect answers will be mixed in with the details of the wrong viewpoint.

Science Reasoning

Part 2: Practice Questions

Classroom>Science Reasoning>Practice Questions
This material corresponds to the ACT Virtual Classroom instructions in the
PowerPrep **DVD/Internet/iApp** for Science Reasoning

Virtual Classroom

Part 2: Practice Questions

Passage "Greenhouse" Conflicting Viewpoints

Greenhouse Effect: The Greenhouse effect is a warming of the lower atmosphere and surface of a planet by a complex process involving sunlight, gases, and particles in the atmosphere. The greenhouse effect is so named because the atmosphere acts much like the glass roof and walls of a greenhouse, trapping heat from the sun.

Human Theory: Recent human activity has added to the natural greenhouse effect, causing global warming. The amounts of heat-trapping atmospheric gases, called greenhouse gases, have greatly increased since the mid-1800s, when modern industry became widespread. Since the late 1800s, the temperature of the earth's surface has also risen. Scientists say that the increase in atmospheric carbon dioxide due to human pollution and rainforest removal has contributed to global warming.

Cyclical Theory: Scientists have examined evidence from the distant past to study the changes in carbon dioxide concentration and temperature. They conclude that the earth goes through cycles in temperature that directly correlate with carbon dioxide concentration. Cores of ice drilled from great depths provide a record for the past 160,000 years. During those years, the climate warmed and cooled several times. During the cooler periods, the atmosphere contained about 30 percent less carbon dioxide than during the warmer periods. The scientists conclude that the recent increase of carbon dioxide levels and warming of the globe is due to the earth's normal cyclical behavior.

Questions 1-6

1. **Which of the following assumptions is implicit in the Human Theory?**

   (A) Carbon Dioxide gas is bad for the environment.
   (B) Humans are the cause for the rise in atmospheric carbon dioxide levels.
   (C) Humans produced less carbon dioxide gas in the 1800s than they did in the 1900s.
   (D) Humans have no part in the recent warming of the earth.

2. **Which of the following would supporters of the Human Theory and the Cyclical Theory agree on?**

   (A) Carbon dioxide levels have risen due to human activity.
   (B) Temperatures have not changed dramatically over the past 100 years.
   (C) There is a relation between carbon dioxide and temperature levels.
   (D) Global warming is a natural phenomenon.

3. **According to the Human Theory, the rising temperature levels are a result of:**

   (A) Increased carbon dioxide levels from human activity.
   (B) Abnormal cyclical behavior in the earth's atmosphere.
   (C) Normal cyclical behavior in the earth's atmosphere.
   (D) Widespread industrial activity and factory pollutants in the mid-1800s.

4. **Which statement or fact would supporters of the Human Theory use to explain the facts cited by the Cyclical Theory?**

   (A) Historically, temperatures have been lower when carbon dioxide levels have been low.
   (B) The earth has never before experienced temperatures of the current magnitude.
   (C) Carbon dioxide levels have been steadily increasing for over 100 years.
   (D) Humans exude more carbon dioxide than any other gas.

5. **Which of the following is a criticism that supporters of the Cyclical Theory would make of the conclusions made in the Human Theory?**

   (A) There is no relation between increased temperatures and increased levels of carbon dioxide.
   (B) There is no proof that the earth's temperature levels are on the rise.
   (C) There is no proof that human activity is the cause for increased carbon dioxide levels.
   (D) There is no proof that carbon dioxide levels are on the rise.

6. **According to the Cyclical Theory, carbon dioxide levels have been much lower**

   (A) When temperatures have been higher.
   (B) When pollution levels have been low.
   (C) When industry was nonexistent.
   (D) During cool periods.

Answers 1-6

General Overview of Passage

We're told the greenhouse effect is a warming of the lower atmosphere and surface of a planet by a complex process involving sunlight, gases, and particles in the atmosphere. It's called the greenhouse effect because the atmosphere acts much like the glass roof and walls of a green house, trapping heat from the sun. Warming temperatures happen because it traps heat from the sun. Looks like the issue will be what causes global warming.

Human Theory. This theory states that recent human activity has added to the natural greenhouse effect, causing global warming. The amount of heat trapping atmospheric gases, called greenhouse gases, have greatly increased since the mid 1800s when modern industry became widespread.

There's our first fact, that the heat-trapping atmospheric gases (greenhouse gases) have increased since the 1800s when modern industry became widespread. Actually, we're not sure it's a fact, but that could be an assumption or a link between the two. Possible cause and effect.

Next we're told since the late 1800s, the temperature of the earth's surface has also risen. There's a fact. That's something that we can actually measure. Since the late 1800s, the temperature of the earth has gone up. We're told that scientists say the increase in atmospheric carbon dioxide due to human pollution and rainforest removal has contributed to global warming. So we have a working definition of global warming.

To summarize: we're giving three pieces of information.
1. Since the mid 1800s there's been an increase in these greenhouse gases because of industry.
2. The temperature of the earth has gone up since the late 1800s.
3. An increase in carbon dioxide from pollution and rainforest removal has contributed to overall global warming.

Okay, we understand the theory that it's human activity. We see two places where we have human activity:
1. in industry, creating greenhouse gases,
2. in pollution and rainforest removal, creating carbon dioxide gases.

And then we have this overall trend that temperature is increasing.

Cyclical Theory. Scientists examined evidence from the distant past to see changes in carbon dioxide concentration and temperature. They conclude—the earth goes through cycles in temperature that directly correlate with carbon dioxide concentration.

So this theory says:
1. Temperature is related to carbon dioxide concentration.
2. Cores of ice drilled from great depths provide a record for the past 160,000 years.
3. During those years the climate warmed and cooled several times.

Now we have proof. We have ice they tested for carbon dioxide. They found the concentration of carbon dioxide varies with the temperature of the earth. During the cooler periods, the atmosphere contained about 30% less carbon dioxide than during the warmer period.

The scientists conclude the recent increase of carbon dioxide levels and warming of the globe is due to the earth's normal, cyclical behavior.

Compare the two theories: Human: the humans are causing global warming through the greenhouse effect.
Cyclical: it's a normal cycle that the earth is going through.

Answer to Question 1

Human Theory—Causes of Global Warming: 1. Human activity.   2. Heat trapping gases have increased since late 1800s (modern industry).   3. Earth temperature has risen since late 1800s.   4. CO_2 has increased due to human pollution and rainforest removal.

Reasoning: Which of the following assumptions is implicit in the human theory?
(A) Human theory: carbon dioxide gas is bad for the environment. That was never stated. Only that there's an increase in carbon dioxide because of pollution and rainforest removal. **Answer choice A is not correct.**
(B) Humans are the cause for the rise in atmospheric carbon dioxide levels. Well it says it right there – carbon dioxide due to human pollution. So humans are the cause for the rise in atmospheric carbon dioxide levels – absolutely. It's stated right in the passage. **Answer choice B looks like a very strong, convincing statement.**
(C) Humans produced less carbon dioxide gas in the 1800s than they did in the 1900s. This is an example how the test makers try to trip you up, because they assume you will bring in "real life" or "outside" information. **You should use ONLY the information specifically PROVIDED. DO NOT assume anything else.**   The only thing we're told about the 1800s is that the greenhouse gases increased. We don't have any information on the carbon dioxide gases in the 1900s, based on passage 1. So statement C is not correct because it's not information that we're given in the passage.
(D) Humans have no part in the recent warming of the earth. Obviously the whole theory of statement 1 is based on the effects of humans. So answer choice D is not correct. Again, that leads us back to our strong feelings about answer choice B.

POE: We can eliminate answer choice A because we are only told about the source of carbon dioxide and its effect on global warming. We are not given any information on how it affects the environment. We can eliminate answer choice C because we have no information on carbon dioxide production in the 1900s vs. the 1800s. We are only told the source of the carbon dioxide. We can eliminate answer choice D because the first sentence in the Human Theory states that human activity caused global warming.

We know answer choice B is correct because the carbon dioxide levels come from human pollution.

Answer: (B)

Answer to Question 2

Cyclical Theory: 1. Earth cycles through levels of corresponding temperature and carbon dioxide levels. 2. Cores of ice prove this cycle.   3. During cooler periods the earth contained lower levels of carbon dioxide. 4. Recent increase in carbon dioxide levels and overall warming is normal cyclical behavior.

Reasoning: Which of the following would supporters of the human theory and the cyclical theory agree on?
(A) Carbon dioxide levels have risen due to human activity. That's not what the cyclical theory says. They think it's just normal. **So answer choice A is not correct.**
(B) Temperatures have not changed dramatically over the last hundred years. But, in the human theory it tells us, "Since the late 1800s the temperatures of the earth's surface have also risen." **So it can't be answer B.**
(C) There is a relation between carbon dioxide and temperature levels. The cyclical theory states, during the cooler periods the carbon dioxide is less, so we know it's a part of cyclical theory. Let's look at human activity, we also see an increase in atmospheric carbon dioxide contributes to global warming. In both theories there is an agreement on the relationship between carbon dioxide and temperature levels. **Answer C seems good.**
(D) This choice restates the Cyclical Theory, but is directly opposed to the man caused theory. Obviously both sides would **not** agree on this statement. In comparing these two theories, the only point of agreement is the current increased level of carbon dioxide and earth's temperature. When one increases, so does the other.

Answer: (C)

Answer to Question 3

Human Theory—Causes of Global Warming
1. Human activity.
2. Heat trapping gases have increased since late 1800s (modern industry).
3. Earth temperature has risen since late 1800s.
4. CO_2 has increased due to human pollution and rainforest removal.

Reasoning: According to the human theory, the rising temperature levels are a result of which of the following?

(A) Increased carbon dioxide level from increased human activity. There you go–exactly what the passage was saying. Recent human activity has added to the natural greenhouse effect, causing global warming.
Human activity caused the increased carbon dioxide levels. Here they say human activities cause global warming, and then again in the last statement, "Carbon dioxide from human pollution has contributed to global warming." So we link humans to the pollution to the global warming. **So answer choice A seems correct**
(B) Abnormal cyclical behavior in the earth's atmosphere. That is information from the second passage on Cyclical Theory, not the first. **So it's incorrect.**
(C) Normal cyclical behavior in the earth's atmosphere. Again, that's information from the second theory, not the first human theory. **So it's incorrect.**
(D) Widespread industrial activity and factory pollutants in the mid 1800s. This is a tricky one, because you might be tempted to assume information from outside sources. The first part of the statement is true: widespread industrial activity. The passage says, "The greenhouse gases have increased when modern industry became widespread."

But the problem with statement number 4 is the second half where it says "factory pollutants." We don't have any information on factory pollutants in the 1800s. The only information on pollution we have is the general statement below that says, "The increase in carbon dioxide from human pollution and rainforest removal has contributed to global warming." But no dates are associated with that. **So answer choice D is incorrect because the second half of the statement is not correct.**

<u>POE</u>: Answer choice B and C can be eliminated because there is no information on cyclical behavior in the Human Theory. Answer choice D can be eliminated because no information is given on factory pollutants in the mid 1800s.

Answer: (A)

Answer to Question 4

<u>Human Theory</u>—Causes of Global Warming: 1. Human activity. 2. Heat trapping gases have increased since late 1800s (modern industry). 3. Earth temperature has risen since late 1800s. 4. CO_2 has increased due to human pollution and rainforest removal.

<u>Cyclical Theory:</u> 1. Earth cycles through levels of corresponding temperature and carbon dioxide levels. 2. Cores of ice prove this cycle. 3. During cooler periods the earth contained lower levels of carbon dioxide. 4. Recent increase in carbon dioxide levels and overall warming is normal cyclical behavior.

<u>Reasoning</u>: Which statement or fact would supporters of the human theory use to explain the facts cited by the cyclical theory? IOW, what facts do they agree on? Remember the cyclical theory says that as temperatures increase, carbon dioxide increases. So, what fact of the cyclical theory corresponds with the human theory.

(A) Historically, temperatures have been lower when carbon dioxide levels have been low. Human theory doesn't have anything to do with that. **Incorrect.**
(B) The earth has never before experienced temperatures of the current magnitude. Do the human theory people believe that? The middle of the paragraph tells us since the late 1800s the temperature of the earth's surface has also risen. So our temperature has been increasing. We haven't experienced temperatures this hot before. That agrees with the human theory information. What about the cyclical theory? Do hot temperatures correspond with increased carbon dioxide? **Absolutely. So answer choice B** would be a good statement that the human theory's people would use to explain why there's more carbon dioxide level now for the increasing heat.
(C) Carbon dioxide levels have been steadily increasing for over a hundred years. **That doesn't explain the cyclical theory.**
(D) Humans exude more carbon dioxide than any other gas. There's no information on humans creating gases of any kind in either of these passages. **So that's obviously incorrect.**

<u>POE:</u> The only place where these two theories agree is the increase in recent temperature and levels of carbon dioxide. We can eliminate answer choice A because the Human Theory does not give any information on low temperatures and carbon dioxide levels. We can eliminate answer choice C because the Cyclical theory does not give time periods related to temperature and carbon dioxide levels. We can eliminate answer choice D because we don't have any information on human carbon dioxide production.

Answer: (B)

Answer to Question 5

<u>Reasoning</u>: Which of the following is a criticism that supporters of the cyclical theory would make of the conclusions made in the human theory? Which of the following would the cyclical theory people not like? What is the criticism they would have?

(A) There is no relation between increased temperatures and increased level of carbon dioxide. Well that was information in the cyclical theory in the first place, so they wouldn't argue that point, because that's what they believe. Also it's not information in the human theory. **So answer choice A is incorrect.**
(B) There is no proof that the earth's temperature levels are on the rise. Both theories support the idea that temperature levels are currently on the rise **so B is incorrect**.
(C) There is no proof that human activity is the cause for increased carbon dioxide levels. That's the part of the human theory that the Cyclical folks would say is unsupported, because there's no proof that human activity is the cause for increased carbon dioxide levels—they do not provide any statistical or numerical data…it's only an assumption.

  A Cyclical Theory person might turn to someone who was a believer in the human theory and say, "Hey, there's no link between human activity and increasing carbon dioxide. How do you prove that?
(D) There is no proof that carbon dioxide levels are on the rise. Both theories support the idea that there is an increase in temperature and an increase in carbon dioxide, **so answer choice D is not correct.**

<u>POE</u>: Answer choices A, B, and D can all be proven with data cited in the Human Theory. We can prove that as temperature increases, so do carbon dioxide levels. We can prove that the earth's temperature is increasing. We can also prove that carbon dioxide levels are increasing. But the FACTS do not prove these things were CAUSED by people--that's what the Cyclical folks would argue.

Answer: (C)

Answer to Question 6

Reasoning

<u>Cyclical Theory:</u> 1. Earth cycles through levels of corresponding temperature and carbon dioxide levels. 2. Cores of ice prove this cycle. 3. During cooler periods the earth contained lower levels of carbon dioxide. 4. Recent increase in carbon dioxide levels and overall warming is normal cyclical behavior.

#3 states specifically that as temperatures decrease, so do carbon dioxide levels.

Answer: (D)